COMPUTER DATA STRUCTURES

JOHN L. PFALTZ

Department of Applied Mathematics and Computer Science
University of Virginia

McGRAW-HILL BOOK COMPANY

New York   St. Louis   San Francisco   Auckland   Bogotá   Düsseldorf
Johannesburg   London   Madrid   Mexico   Montreal
New Delhi   Panama   Paris   São Paulo   Singapore   Sydney   Tokyo   Toronto

Library of Congress Cataloging in Publication Data

Pfaltz, John L
    Computer data structures.

    Bibliography: p.
    Includes index.
    1. Data structures (Computer science) I. Title.
QA76.9.D35P42   001.6'42   76-26041
ISBN 0-07-049743-5

COMPUTER DATA STRUCTURES

1 2 3 4 5 6 7 8 9 0 KPKP 7 8 3 2 1 0 9 8 7

This book was set in Times Roman by Textbook Services, Inc.
The editors were Peter D. Nalle and Douglas J. Marshall;
the cover was designed by Anne Canevari Green;
the production supervisor was Leroy A. Young.
The drawings were done by Danmark & Michaels, Inc.
Kingsport Press, Inc., was printer and binder.

CONTENTS

PREFACE

Donald Knuth (1968) has described programming, and possibly computer science as well, as an art. This appears to be unquestionably true. And as with any art, it can be learned only through experience. Reading about what others have done is no substitute. Neither the calculus nor any other scientific discipline can be mastered by just secondary observation of previous results. Beginning mathematicians reprove theorems long-since established; chemists repeat well-known reactions. It seems to be the only way to make the discipline a part of the individual learning it. Consequently the primary thrust of this text is to "lead" the reader to actually implement the data structures that are described, and to program various procedures that can use them. A semester course based on this text should require seven or eight programming assignments *as a minimum*. A full-year course (in which longer assignments might be expected) should include at least ten to twelve.

Probably the major reason that many students, particularly undergraduates, have never written programs to manipulate data structures (for example, to thread a tree structure) is that they are seldom stand alone programs. The procedure is normally only one routine in a system of processes. Some of the procedures allocate and deallocate the blocks of storage that are used to build the data structure, others build the structure itself, while still more must be invoked to display it. To write and code all of these becomes an unrealistic assignment. But they can be developed piecemeal—and used in subsequent assignments. One of the first programming problems (Sec. 3-2) will be to write three dynamic allocation routines. Virtually every subsequent problem then makes use of these procedures. Gradually more and more pieces are added to the collection of operators and representational techniques, so that by Chap. 6 the reader should be able to assemble a reasonably powerful system of structure-manipulating software.

Although the procedures of this text are expressed in a concise Algol-like notation, all are designed to be (and have been) implemented using Fortran. Fortran is certainly not an ideal structure-manipulation language (and if another language with special data handling-capability is available, it should be used). But it is widely known and widely implemented, and a process that can be implemented in this idiom can be implemented in virtually any language. Furthermore, there is a strong tendency to regard data structures as primarily academic playthings. Many practical applications programmers do not regard the use of linked lists, tree structures, or hash-coded access as useful tools of the trade. But they should be. Since many programming shops support only Fortran, the development of concepts which are realizable in this language can lead to immediate practical application. As a further aid to instructors developing a course, complete listings of most programming exercises are provided in the supplementary instructor's manual. These have been tested on several different computing systems. With these as a nucleus, a wide variety of individualized problems can be devised. By selectively providing certain modules, while leaving others to be coded, a "laboratory" course can be created in which students learn the art by performing "experiments" of varying difficulty. Tape files of all these source programs are available from the author for the cost of reproduction.

While the primary goal of this text is to develop the practical use of a variety of data structures, those calling themselves computer scientists or systems analysts should be attempting to develop those theoretical results which form the basis of their practice. They should be constantly asking: *Why* does this procedure work (or fail to work)? We will establish a theoretical model based on the concept of a directed graph. We will use the terminology of graph theory. To illustrate this more formal aspect of the study of data structures, we will—whenever possible—state results precisely in the form of mathematical theorems. But no proofs will be given in the text (they are given in full in the instructor's manual), since the author feels that the precise rigorous *statement* of a result, assertion, or conjecture is often more important than its proof. Many important results cannot be rigorously proven in a mathematical sense, but they can often be convincingly justified by observable evidence. (The precise formulation of conjectured results becomes especially critical when one seeks to affirm or deny them by means of empirical evidence.) Such empirical results and understanding will be gained largely by simulations presented as exercises for the reader.

In each section a number of exercises have been marked with an asterisk. This is not meant to indicate difficulty, since some are nearly trivial, while others may be quite involved. Instead it is an effort by the author to call attention to those exercises which he feels likely to be the most rewarding, and which he would most likely assign to a class.

Unfortunately, given the current state of the art, there are a great many "holes" in our understanding of data structures and of the processes that operate on them. There will undoubtedly occur situations where the reader's experience is contrary to some assertion made within this text. (This will most likely occur in conjunction with statements pertaining to the efficiency of some procedure or the appropriateness of some data construct, which have themselves been based on the author's experience.) In these cases we hope that the reader will have gained the ability, and particularly the inclination, to try to explain the discrepancy, and thus fill the "hole."

One area of both practical and theoretical weakness concerns that of large data structures. Representations and associated procedures that are most appropriate for small data structures may be totally inadequate in situations involving, say 50,000 elements. As Dijkstra (1972) points out, "identical" problems whose only difference is data sets that vary by one or two orders of magnitude are really completely different problems. Experience with small data structures cannot be safely extrapolated to large data structures. We have attempted to minimize the shock of transition from small to large applications by (1) avoiding the use of array representations (which must of necessity be in-core), (2) referencing elements of data structures in terms of storage location, (3) presenting a variety of techniques that have been found to be appropriate for larger structures, and (4) simulating the behavior of certain classes of large systems. Still, no classroom-oriented presentation can completely prepare a programmer to cope with applications of reasonably large magnitude; this can be achieved only by special projects or an advanced laboratory approach.

The body of the text really begins with Chap. 3. Chapters 1 and 2 are primarily designed to provide the terminology and conceptual framework from which following techniques are to be viewed. They provide a reference to which the reader can turn when questions as to the author's meaning arise. When presented in a classroom context, the author normally tries to skim the high points in a week or less, and begins Chap. 3 by the start of the second week. Casual readers are advised to do the same, lest they become bogged down in preliminaries. They will be there when necessary. In a one-semester course, Chaps. 3 and 4 (Linear Structures), 5 (Trees), 9 (Data Access), and 10 (Dynamic Storage Allocation) should be covered fairly thoroughly. Portions of other chapters would be included according to interest. (The author normally includes portions of Chaps. 6 and 8.)

By and large, an introductory text is not the place for extensive references to the literature. We have tried to select from articles in *Computing Surveys,* which are normally well written and authoritative, and contain extensive bibliographies; from published books; and from articles in the *Journal,* and *Communications of the ACM,* which are the most likely to be available in local libraries. Where several references are appropriate we have often picked only one (usually quite arbitrarily) with the idea that the interested reader will use it as an entry into the literature.

Computer data structures represent a rich field in computer science with many different aspects and approaches. It is hoped that this text will provide the reader with some measure of proficiency in the area, and even more, with an interest and desire to further explore the many "nooks and crannies" of this fascinating subject.

John L. Pfaltz

COMPUTER DATA STRUCTURES

MATHEMATICAL MODELS AND COMPUTER REPRESENTATIONS

1-1 WHAT IS A DATA STRUCTURE?

What is a data structure? Since this is a surprisingly difficult question to answer, we might break the question down and try to answer the subquestion "What is data?" Intuitively, data is a collection of facts, of numbers, or of symbols. It is the raw "stuff" that computer programs use and manipulate. Thus we set up a dichotomy between programs (or procedures) that use data and the data itself. Familiar terms from mathematics are *operator* and *operand*.

Similarly one might consider the term *information* to mean "useful data." Here we introduce a kind of outside criterion of utility, or meaningfulness. In the formal study of information theory, the information content (value) of a message is its degree of unexpectedness or of surprise. In consequence it is a current vogue to speak of *information structures* with the implied assumption that these are more meaningful than more mundane data structures.

If we accept these intuitive concepts of data and information, we may then attempt to define the concept of structure. Very often, individual facts in a collection of data are related. For example, a collection of data about a corporation may contain the names of all its employees and the titles of all its job positions. Each name is related to some job title—the job performed by that employee. Further, we may consider a relation between the job titles—that is, which job position is superior to (can give orders to) which other job positions, regardless of the current individual filling that position. The result is often called an *organizational* structure, which can be visually diagrammed as in Fig. 1-1.

1

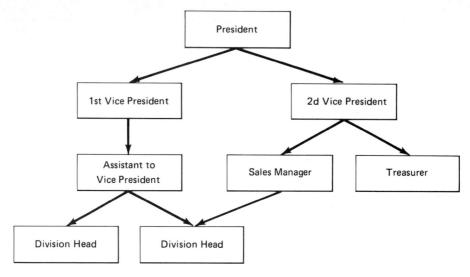

Figure 1-1 A portion of a corporate organizational structure.

Let us then accept as a tentative interpretation of the term *data structure* that *data* denotes a collection of facts that can serve as operands to a computer program and that *structure* denotes relations (if any) between individual items within that collection. We now want to take a hard look at this interpretation.

An important distinction has been made between the program (or procedure) as the operator and the data as operand. But does this distinction hold up under close scrutiny? When the source code, as written by a programmer, is being translated by a compiler or assembler into an object deck, it is certainly being treated itself as data. Both the source deck and the object deck that is generated are regarded as data files. They can be manipulated just like any other data files.

While sometimes a program may be indistinguishable from data, say at compilation and load time, it would seem clear that during execution itself there is a well-defined separation between the program and the data structure on which it operates. Or is there? Consider a program which modifies itself. During execution a program may operate on itself, changing both the sequence or nature of its own instructions. In some programming languages, there is little, if any, distinction between the program and its data; LISP (Weissman, 1967) is a notable example. A LISP program can modify itself at will. One can conceive of the lovely image of an executing LISP program which gradually eats itself up until, perhaps like the Cheshire cat, nothing is left but a smile!

There have been several attempts to differentiate between operators and operands in the computing context. None has been notably successful. Thus, in spite of its intuitive appeal, this distinction is a poor foundation on which to build a formal theory of data structures.

In a similar vein, consider a *program structure*—that is, the relation between individual instructions or modules of instructions in a procedure. Such a program structure can be diagrammed as a familiar flowchart, as in Fig. 1-2. This flowchart looks very similar to the data structure of Fig. 1-1, with the exception that the "facts" are descriptions of dynamic operations instead of static job titles. One often wants to consider a procedure such as this as a data structure. Appropriate questions would then be: Can we characterize its structure? Will the procedure halt? Does subprocedure A depend on the completion of subprocedure B? and Can we transform it into an equivalent structure? These are precisely the kinds of questions we will be asking about a variety of data structures.

The statement of an intuitive concept of a data structure, followed by its critical rejection, has not been merely an academic exercise. First of all, intuition is a valuable asset, whether or not it can be made precise enough to rigorously develop a formal theory. It can carry us far in the practical world of computing. And theory that runs contrary to intuition should, at least, be viewed with a jaundiced eye. Second, it has demonstrated that data structures cannot be viewed in a narrow frame. We are all prepared to regard real numbers and arrays as examples of data and data structures, but how many of us think of programs themselves as data structures? Our study of data structures will overlap many other areas of computer science; boundaries of knowledge are always fuzzy. You should be prepared to encounter results that are also applicable to theories of operating systems, of computation, and of programming languages, as well as our central concern with data structures themselves.

Figure 1-2 An imaginary procedure to calculate income taxes.

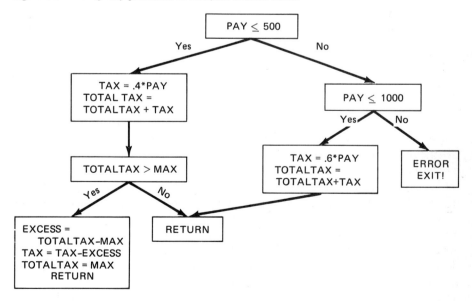

1-2 MATHEMATICAL MODELS

Many of the phenomena of our daily lives have strong intuitive existence, a real immediacy, and yet we find it difficult or impossible to precisely define the phenomena. The force of gravity comes to mind. Generally imprecise metaphor, specific examples, or vague analogy are used to convey a feeling for the concept. Perhaps the most powerful tool of the scientific approach is *the substitution of a model* (usually mathematical) *for the phenomenon itself.* It is the model that scientists discuss, that they validate, and whose implications they derive. So "gravity" becomes a mathematical equation, and the earth's gravitational field becomes a complex mathematical surface. The behavior of gases—or of human populations—similarly become "collections" of mathematical equations.

We shall adopt the same course. In reality a data structure (or information structure, since we will use these terms interchangeably) can probably mean whatever the speaker intends it to mean. Therefore we will replace the intuitive concept of a data structure with a precise mathematical model. From now on we will assume that *a data structure is a directed graph with assignment functions.* (These terms will be clarified in following paragraphs.) Perhaps we should call this an *abstract data structure,* since we will see examples in which a corporate organization structure, the directory of a computer operating system, and the parse of a statement in a programming language can all be modeled by the same directed graph. All three can be regarded as identical abstract structures, even though they have very different significance to the user "outside" the computer. The techniques we will develop for describing, for storing, and for manipulating the graph that is their model will be appropriate in all three practical situations.

Few scientists ever believe that their models exactly mirror a real-world phenomenon. The models are admittedly approximations. A major task is one of *validation*—that is, of demonstrating a high degree of correspondence to the real world—and of pointing out where the correspondence falls down. We will attempt to validate our graph-theoretic model by frequent examples, pointing out how the model coincides with our intuitive understanding of data structures. However, there do exist sophisticated data structures for which simple directed graphs are inadequate models. One refinement of this simple model is established in Chap. 8. A variation is given in Chap. 9. Nevertheless, our simple model will be adequate for most of the computer data structures now in common use.

A second task of scientists is to demonstrate the *utility* of their model. They must show that by employing it they can gain useful insights and results about the phenomena they are investigating. We let the rest of this text speak for itself on this issue.

Finally, there may be completely *different models of the same phenomena.* In spite of their incompatibility, each may have validity and utility. The wave- and particle-motion models of light are classic examples. For an alternative model of data structures, the reader might consider "Another Look at Data" by G. H. Mealy (1967), in which data structures are regarded as collections of functions, transformations, or operations.

Let us now see what we mean by a "directed graph with assignment functions." Let X be any set of elements, points, numbers, or whatever. By a *relation R on* X we mean any set of ordered pairs of elements from X. Thus

$$R = \{(x, y)|x, y \in X\}$$

As an example of a relation, let $X = \{a, b, c, d\}$ and let

$$R = \{(a, a), (a, b), (b, a), (b, d), (c, a), (d, a), (d, b), (d, c)\}$$

We can graphically represent this relation as in Fig. 1-3. Arrows are used to indicate the elements (ordered pairs) of the relation. This graphic representation is commonly called a *graph of the relation.*

By a *directed graph,* denoted $G = (P, R)$, we mean simply a relation R on a set of *points* P. There is no real distinction between a graph and a relation. In certain contexts it is more natural to use the term *graph,* and in others the term *relation* is more customary. We will use both. An individual ordered pair (x, y) in the relation, which is represented by an arrow, line, or arc in the Fig. 1-3, is normally called an *edge* of the graph.

In applications we normally associate data, in the form of one or more values or data items, with each of the points of the graph and possibly with each of its edges. Such graphs we will call graphs with *point assignments* (and/or with *edge assignments*) over a set of (possibly several) values. The symbols a, b, c, and d in Fig. 1-3 are *not* assigned data values; they are identifiers. An *identifier* (many authors call it a *label*) is a symbolic string by which individual elements of the structure can be referenced. Points can be arbitrarily identified, as can edges or entire data structures.

1-3 REPRESENTATIONS

We are going to let graphs with assignments serve as the mathematical model of a data structure. This abstract model serves as an admirable vehicle to derive theoretical results about the nature and use of data structures. But if the models

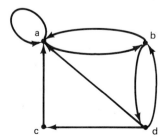

Figure 1-3 A graphic representation of a relation.

are to be of practical use we must have a way of constructing a *representation,* or concrete version, of the data structure within a computing system. Furthermore, we must be able to demonstrate a correspondence between the computer representation and the abstract data structure it represents. To emphasize this distinction we will use the notation S_M to denote the abstract structure (or model) and S_R to denote its computer representation. For any given abstract structure S_M a variety of techniques normally exist by which the structure can be represented within a computer; that is, there exist several representational structures S_R. The actual technique chosen depends on the nature of the data structure itself, its intended use and size, and various constrictions imposed by the computing system, its hardware, and its software.

The text will explore many (but far from all) of these possible representational techniques. Initially our attention will be largely confined to the representations themselves. But after a while our focus will begin to shift. Gradually the reader will find that more and more of the processes and operations are defined in terms of the model S_M, with correspondingly less emphasis on any particular representation S_R.

First we must establish some common terminology. By a *cell* we mean the smallest addressable unit of a data structure *in a given application*. The most common implementation of a cell is a block of one or more consecutive words, or bytes, in which case we will adopt the convention that the *address of a cell* is the address of the first word, or byte, of the cell.

By a *field* we mean a portion of a cell. Fields are not individually addressable. Thus to access them we must qualify the field identifier by a specific cell identifier (its address). For instance, suppose FIELD1 denotes a certain portion of a class of cells. The expression FIELD1 by itself is meaningless, but the qualified expression FIELD1 (CELL) denotes the value contained in that field of the cell whose address is the value of CELL. As written, the expression FIELD1 (CELL) would be naturally implemented in Fortran or Algol as a function.† A typical cell within a computer data structure might look like Fig. 1-4, where the symbols A, B, LINKF, Z, DATA, R, LINK3, and C denote fields within the cell. Two visualizations are presented. The former seems more natural in a word oriented machine; the latter seems more natural in a byte- or character-oriented machine. In the latter case it is more customary to refer to the cell as a *record.*‡

---

†The relationship between fields and cells may be expressed differently in other languages. For example, we would expect to use FIELD1 OF CELL in Cobol, CELL.FIELD1 in PL/1, and CELL:FIELD1 in Pascal. Of particular interest is the assembly-level language L⁶ (Knowlton, 1966), in which characters of the symbolic identifier denote actual accessing procedures involving fields of the structure.

‡The terminology "record" is standard in business-oriented languages, e.g., Cobol, as well as several other high-level languages such as PL/1 and Pascal. It is also used with reference to input and output where it has a similar meaning as "an indivisible unit of transferable data." Simply because it is so widely used we prefer to use the word *cell* in the data structure context and reserve the usage of *record* for cases involving actual data transfer.

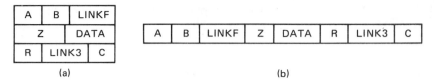

Figure 1-4 Formats of a "typical" computer cell: (*a*) as viewed in a word-oriented machine, (*b*) as viewed in a byte-oriented machine (and most likely called a *record*).

Both *cell* and *record* may be regarded as synonyms denoting a block of consecutive storage that may be subdivided into individual fields or *data items*. For consistency we will use the term *cell* and assume a word-oriented machine for illustrative purposes, but the reader should feel free to visualize the format of cells in the manner most closely analogous to the implementing computer and programming language. By the *size* of a cell we will mean the number of consecutive words constituting the cell; in a byte-oriented context one might refer to the number of consecutive bytes (or characters) and call this the *length* of the record.

The terms *link* and *pointer* may, or may not, be used synonymously in the literature. A link or pointer is any value which denotes the storage location, commonly its core address, of a cell. Thus a link "points" to a cell, while the pointer provides a "link" to a cell. A field in a cell whose value is always a cell address is typically called a *link field*. Although we will really treat these terms as synonyms, we will generally follow the convention of using the term *link* when referring to a field of a cell that points to another cell, and using the term *pointer* when referring to an ordinary variable within a program that points to a particular cell of a structure.

Most of our computer representations will be constructed using cells, fields, links, and pointers as their components. We establish the correspondence between the abstract data structure (directed graph) and its computer realization as follows: Cells will usually correspond to points of the graph. Link fields will be used to represent edges, while all other fields, which we may call *data fields*, represent assigned values associated with the point. Finally, pointers will be used as identifiers to "point to," or identify, individual elements, cells, or points of the structure. This "standard correspondence" may be summarized in tabular form:

Components of S_M		Components of S_R
point	↔	cell
edge	↔	link field
assignment	↔	data field
identifier	↔	pointer

1-4 IMPLEMENTING PROCEDURES IN A PROGRAMMING LANGUAGE

We must now consider how we will manipulate the cells, fields, links, and pointers using some existing programming language. Regardless of the host language in which our procedures are to be coded—it may be assembly language, PL/1, Algol, Fortran, or any other—it is unlikely to have all the features we would wish for operating on data structures. Some coding conventions will have to be established and followed. Depending on the language, it may be easier or harder to program certain constructs, but this is solely a coding matter. The theory and general techniques will remain invariant. In the following sections we will generally assume that the existing programming language is Fortran. It is certainly widespread and reasonably well known. But the coding conventions that will be suggested are equally appropriate for other host languages.

In the higher-level languages, such as Fortran, Cobol, PL/1, and Algol, symbols and expressions always denote values—that is, the contents of computer registers. Thus, in the statement

$$X = Y + Z - TEMP$$

each of the symbols Y, Z, and TEMP denote values (which have been previously assigned), as does the expression, $Y + Z - TEMP$. The value of that expression is to be assigned to the symbol X. At no time in such languages is the programmer concerned with the actual address or location within the computer where these values are physically stored. Any operand symbol (variable, constant, etc.) and any expression can be replaced by a literal data value, and the program will still be syntactically and logically correct.†

In assembly languages, on the other hand, all symbols and expressions denote addresses or known registers within the computer.‡ For example, in the assembly-code equivalent to the preceding statement

LD	Y	load contents of location Y
FAD	Z	floating add contents of location Z
FSB	TEMP	floating subtract contents of location TEMP
STO	X	store in location X

all the operand symbols can be replaced by register names or core addresses.

It is extremely important that we agree on a uniform convention. Since all the procedures in this text are designed to be coded in a high-level language we will adopt the convention that *all symbols denote actual data values.*§ Of

---

†Except when they occur to the left of a replacement operator. In this context only variable symbols can appear.

‡There are limited exceptions in the case of "immediate" symbols, whose values are used in conditional decisions at assembly time, and literal symbols.

§If all our implementing code were to be in an assembly language, then it would have been more reasonable to adopt the convention that symbols denote computer registers as does Knuth (vol. 1, 1968).

course, we may interpret the value assigned to a particular variable symbol, say L, as denoting an address and use it as such within the program. We will frequently do this. But such interpretation is purely a matter of program logic. It is equivalent to asserting that the value of a symbol (or variable) denotes a "velocity" and should not be used as a value denoting a "dollar cost."

Given this convention, we need a way of referencing storage registers and the contents of these registers. By the expression

$$LOC(V)$$

we mean the integer value that is the storage *location,* or address, in which V is stored. By either of the expressions

$$CONT(L) \text{ or } \uparrow L$$

we mean the value that is the *contents* of the storage location designated by the value of L if it is interpreted to be an address. With this understanding, $\uparrow L$ and $CONT(L + 1)$ denote the contents of the first and second words of the cell, respectively.

In coding a procedure, programmers are free to organize the fields within a cell in any manner they choose. A field may be of any desired size (number of bits or characters). It may cross word or byte boundaries (although this is usually poor practice and will not occur in this text). Because the design of a data structure that is most appropriate to any given application is dependent on the implementing computer system, the implementing language, and the kinds and size of values expected in each field, the choice of final cell format will normally be left to the programmer or analyst who is most familiar with these application variables.

Although fields may be of any size, there are three standard-sized fields of prime importance. These are a *tag field* of at least two bits, a *link field* of sufficient size to contain any cell address, and a *whole-word field*. The *name* of a field, for instance LINKF, is presumed to describe the field; that is, it describes the relative location of the word of the cell containing it, the field's position within that word, and its length in bits.†

Now in an "ideal" programming language one would like to be able to describe procedures that operate on cell fields by statements such as

$$LINKF(X) \leftarrow LINK3(Y) + DATA(Y) - 1 \qquad (1\text{-}1)$$

where this might naturally be interpreted to mean "Fetch the contents of the LINK3 and DATA fields in the cell Y, add them, decrement by one, and store in the LINKF field of cell X." But two serious problems arise. One is a question of logical ambiguity, and the other is a problem of implementation.

---

†If a byte-oriented machine is employed, then we would agree that the name of a field describes the field by (1) designating the relative position (within the record) of the first byte of the field and (2) specifying its length. But how the field is described is really unimportant. In all our procedures we merely assume that the name describes the field and that appropriate accessing mechanisms will use that description.

If the symbol Y is an ordinary variable, the expression DATA(Y) can mean either of two things. Several values may be packed into the variable Y itself, one of which, in the field DATA is wanted; or the value of Y may be the address of a cell whose DATA field is to be fetched. The first interpretation is known as *direct access*†, and the second is called *indirect accessing*. In the formal description of procedures in the text we will use an Algol-like language with expressions similar to (1-1). To resolve the direct-indirect accessing ambiguity we will always assume that when the identifiers LINKF, LINK3, and DATA are declared to be fields, then the expression (1-1) will be taken to mean "Fetch the LINK3 and DATA fields *indirectly* from the cell whose address is the value of Y, add them, subtract one, and store this value *indirectly* in the LINKF field of the cell whose address is the value of X." Hence the identifiers X and Y must be declared to be pointers, that is, variables whose values are to be interpreted as a storage location.

The distinction between direct and indirect reference is a crucial one in the concept of programming languages. Yet many programmers are unfamiliar with it because most high-level languages simply don't permit indirect accessing. You will undoubtedly stumble over the concept in the first few programs you write; virtually everyone does, even experienced programmers. But careful study of the procedures described in the text, together with a few sample implementations, should see you over the hump.

The second problem with using statements such as (1-1) is implementational. Indirect references to fields such as DATA(Y) which occur to the right of the replacement operator are easily implemented by function calls. But such a functional form cannot be used to the left of the replacement symbol (at least in Fortran-like languages). It must be implemented by a subroutine call. The subroutine must be passed as arguments: (1) a pointer to the cell of which the field is a part, (2) the name of the field (e.g., a description of its size and location within the cell), and (3) the value to be stored in the field.

With this discussion as background, we can now describe six primitive functions and subroutines that must be handcoded in assembly language and appended to the Fortran language to give it a full capability for processing data structures. They are:

Functions:	FIELD(WORD, RBIT, SIZE)
	FETCH(CELLADDR, FIELD)
	CONT(ADDRESS)
	LOC(VARIABLE)
Subroutines:	STORE (CELLADDR, FIELD, VALUE)
	STOREW (ADDRESS, VALUE)

---

†The subdivision of a variable or word into several fields or values, and their subsequent *direct* access, is frequently called *packing* and *unpacking*. The partial word operators, implemented in several languages, provide examples of such direct field access.

The function FIELD creates a field descriptor consisting of the triple (word, rbit, size) and returns it packed in a single word. WORD denotes the relative location of the word containing the field within the cell—first word, second word, etc. RBIT denotes the position of the rightmost bit of the field within the word. (A right-justified field will normally have RBIT = 0.) SIZE denotes the number of bits comprising the field. Used in the following manner

$$\text{LINKF} = \text{FIELD}(1, 0, 12)$$

the variable LINKF becomes the descriptor, or name, of a right-justified field of 12 bits in the first word of a cell. The variable LINKF may now be used whenever the description of this field is needed.

The function FETCH retrieves (or gets) the value contained in the field specified by the second argument, the field descriptor FIELD, indirectly from the cell whose address is given as the first argument.

The subroutine STORE sets (or packs) the value specified by its third parameter indirectly into the field of the cell whose address is given.

The function LOC returns as its value the storage location, (or address) of its argument.

These four subprocedures are completely sufficient in themselves to implement any data structure using Fortran; however, the routines CONT and STOREW are added for efficiency's sake. These are whole-word indirect accessing routines. CONT delivers the contents of the entire word whose address is given. STOREW stores the value in the word. Since the primitive field-accessing routines create masks and shifting sequences to pack or unpack the field in the word, these operations take an appreciable amount of time. CONT and STOREW can ignore these preliminaries, since they are known to be whole-word accesses. But since there is no field descriptor passed, if the word to be retrieved (or set) is offset from the cell address, the programmer must provide for this in the code. For example, to access the second word of a cell, one would code

$$\text{VALUE} = \text{CONT}(\text{CELL} + 1)$$

Consequently, while the use of CONT and STOREW results in slightly more efficient code, it also increases the probability of programmer error, and more importantly, makes the process dependent on the particular cell format of the representation.† Although we will occasionally make use of the routines CONT and STOREW in some of our examples, their use is not especially recommended.

---

†If all instructions are given with respect to the field primitives alone, then the entire layout of constituent cells can be modified with no change to the coded processes, save for the redefinition of the field descriptors.

With these primitive routines available, the statement (1-1) would be coded in Fortran as

```
LINKF  = FIELD(1, 0, 12)     assumes a cell format as in Fig. 1-4, with the
DATA   = FIELD(2, 0, 15)     rightmost bit called bit zero
LINK3  = FIELD(3, 12, 12)
         :
         :
RESULT = FETCH(Y, LINK3) + FETCH(Y, DATA) − 1
CALL STORE (X, LINKF, RESULT)
```

or equivalently,

```
CALL STORE (X, LINKF, FETCH(Y, LINK3) + FETCH(Y, DATA) − 1)
```

If the inability to designate field assignment by functional expressions to the left of the replacement symbol and the consequent need for subroutines to handle indirection are considered the most irritating feature of an algebraic language such as Fortran, one must rank its real-integer mode conventions close behind. Most of the values one encounters in data structures are either integer (e.g., addresses), typeless strings of bits (packed data), or alphanumeric characters. But under implicit typing conventions, most variable symbols are presumed to denote real values. In consequence one must be constantly wary of unwanted, and unannounced, mode conversions based on this implicit convention. Unless one has a compiler that permits the redefinition of these implicit type conventions, one is inevitably forced to explicitly declare every variable and function symbol in the manner of Algol. While this enforced discipline on the programmer may, in fact, be beneficial, it is certainly bothersome.

To help avoid these unwanted integer-real mode conversions, two additional primitive functions may be implemented: REALV and INTV. They do nothing. But writing

$$I = INTV(FETCH(X, LINKF))$$

ensures that the compiler won't "fix" the value of the LINKF field of cell X before assigning it to I.

Coding data manipulation algorithms in a work-a-day programming language such as Fortran, with constant attention to direct-indirect accessing and to implicit mode-conversion conventions, will seem extremely awkward at first, as indeed it is. But several years of experience have shown that facility with the primitive routines is quickly acquired. We have also found unintentionally beneficial side effects. Many programming languages deliberately hide the important distinction between direct and indirect access of data. The necessity of writing actual code to manipulate data structures serves to emphasize the difference. Moreover, one develops a very real appreciation for the problems involved in the design of more advanced languages and the linguistic constructs they must employ. It is hoped that readers will frequently ask themselves: What would be the kind of language in which I would want to express the computational concepts that are of importance in my data structure applications?

EXERCISES FOR SECTION 1-4

1-1 Compose an intuitive English definition of the meaning of *data structure*. Critique it.

1-2 Describe the following physical phenomena by a mathematical model:

    (*a*) the gravitational attraction between two bodies

    (*b*) the behavior of gas under pressure

    (*c*) the world of classical mechanics (e.g., laws of conservation of mass, energy, and momentum)

    (*d*) the behavior of electricity in a resistive network

*1-3 (*a*) Show that in all cases

$$CONT(LOC(V)) = V$$

where V is any scalar variable or expression. (This shows that the operator CONT is a left inverse of the operator LOC, since their composition CONT ∘ LOC is the identity operator for all such V. Mathematically we would like it to be a two-sided inverse, but it is not.)

    (*b*) Show that, even if the value of V is a valid machine address, in general,

$$LOC(CONT(V)) \neq V$$

(In fact, given the way most compilers handle actual parameters that are functional references, equality virtually never holds.)

*1-4 The numbers 10 and −5 are astract mathematical concepts S_M with several different computer representations S_R. Describe their representation as

    (*a*) binary integers

    (*b*) octal or hexadecimal integers

    (*c*) real numbers in

        (*1*) sign magnitude representation

        (*2*) 1's complement representation

        (*3*) 2's complement representation

    (*d*) double precision

    (*e*) decimal "display" numbers (e.g., Cobol DISPLAY)

    (*f*) computational numbers (Cobol mode as implemented on your machine)

1-5 Why are expressions or functional references not allowed to appear to the left of the replacement symbol? (Note that this is not strictly true. It is permitted in the declaration of "in-line function statements"—an optional feature of many Fortran compilers. How is the "replacement" different in these kinds of nonexecutable statements?)

1-6 Let X, Y, and Z be variables that identify (point to) words in a computer with values as shown in the accompanying figure. Let LHALF and RHALF denote functions which unpack the corre-

X: | Y | 112 |

Y: | 10 | X |

Z: | | X |

        Ex. 1-6

sponding field of the word whose address is given as argument. What will be the functional values associated with these expressions:

CONT(Z)
RHALF(CONT(Z))
LHALF(X)
LHALF(LHALF(RHALF(Y)))

Discuss the problems (if any) involved in designing a compiler for a language which explicitly declares field identifiers and pointer variables, as in:

field   lhalf, rhalf;
pointer   x, y, z;
variable   a, b, c;

$\vdots$

a ← lhalf(x);
b ← lhalf(lhalf(rhalf(y)));
c ← rhalf(z);

What would be the most natural interpretation of the expression

rhalf(x) ← lhalf(lhalf(x));

How might it be implemented?

1-5 FUNDAMENTAL DEFINITIONS AND CONCEPTS OF GRAPH THEORY

In this section we introduce a number of definitions, notational conventions, and results from graph theory that we will be using repeatedly in our discussions of data structures as abstract models S_M. For some readers this section will serve largely as a review of a preceding course in discrete mathematics and graph theory; for others it must serve as an introduction, and more careful attention will be required. In either case it will be most important that the notation (which may be slightly different from other texts) and the concepts they denote be thoroughly understood. Graph theoretic results will be stated in the form of formal theorems, but their proofs will be omitted. For the most part they are standard results whose proofs can be found in texts such as Berge (1962), Harary (1969), or Ore (1962); mathematically inclined readers may wish to develop their own skills by proving the theorems as exercises.

Let S and T be any sets. A *relation* R *from* S *to* T is any subset of the cartesian product S × T, or equivalently any set of ordered pairs of the form

$$R \subseteq \{(x, y)|x \in S, y \in T\}$$

By its *inverse* R^{-1} we mean the relation

$$R^{-1} = \{(y, x)|(x, y) \in R\}$$

S is customarily called the *domain* of R, and T is called its *range*. If the domain S and range T are identical sets, as will usually be the case in our work, we simply speak of the *relation* R *on* S.

A relation R may have many different kinds of properties that lead to interesting mathematical theory. If, for example, R has the property that for all $x \in S$, there exists exactly one ordered pair of the form $(x, y) \in R$, then we call R a *function*. Thus all the mathematical study of functions can be regarded as no more than the study of a highly restricted class of relations. But even though it has a common root in the concept of relations, classical functional mathematics generally assumes that the sets involved are infinite, while graph theory is characterized by the fact that S, T, and R are essentially finite.

In all subsequent work we will implicitly assume that *all sets are finite sets*. Sometimes we will explicitly state this finiteness assumption for emphasis; most often we will not.

Other desirable properties (normally asserting the existence of certain elements in R) lead to a study of algebraic structures such as lattices and boolean algebras. Here the characteristic distinction seems to be that even the weakest algebraic structure seems to be far more "regular" and "well-behaved" than do those we encounter in graph theory.

The following properties, which a relation may or may not possess, will be frequently referenced. Let R be a relation on S. R is said to be *reflexive,* if for all $x \in S$, $(x, x) \in R$; *antireflexive,* if for all $x \in S$, $(x, x) \notin R$; *symmetric,* if $(x, y) \in R$ implies $(y, x) \in R$; *antisymmetric,* if $(x, y) \in R$ implies $(y, x) \notin R$; *weakly antisymmetric,* if (x, y) and $(y, x) \in R$ implies $x = y$; and *transitive,* if (x, y) and $(y, z) \in R$ implies $(x, z) \in R$.

We can now define two very important properties in terms of these more basic properties. A relation R is said to be an *equivalence relation* if R is reflexive, symmetric, and transitive. An *equivalence class* of R is a set R_x of the form

$$R_x = \{y_i | (x, y_i) \in R\} \quad \text{same } x, \text{ multiple } y's$$

The concept of equivalence provides the foundation for all subsequent definitions of *equality* and of *similarity,* which become crucial when we seek to apply these concepts to data structures. Further equivalence relations are intimately tied to the concept of a partition of a set by the following theorem. Recall that a *partition* of a set S is a covering of S by a collection $\mathscr{P} = \{S_1, S_2, \ldots, S_n\}$ of disjoint subsets of S (that is, $S = S_1 \cup S_2 \cup \ldots \cup S_n$, $S_i \subseteq S$, and $S_i \cap S_j = \emptyset$ for all $i \neq j$).

Theorem 1-1 Every partition $\mathscr{P}$ of a set S induces an equivalence relation R on S such that $(x, y) \in R$ if and only if $x, y \in S_i$. Conversely every equivalence relation R implicitly defines a partition $\mathscr{P}$ with the same property.

If a relation R on S is reflexive, weakly antisymmetric, and transitive, it is called a *partial order* relation (or simply a *partial ordering* of S). If further R satisfies the property that for all $x, y \in S$, either $(x, y) \in R$ or $(y, x) \in R$, then it is said to be a *total ordering*. (Relations which satisfy this last property, called the *law of dichotomy*, but not necessarily any of the other properties, are known as *tournaments*.) A set S which is partially ordered by a relation R is frequently known in the literature as a *poset*.

If we let S be the set of real numbers, or set of integers, then the familiar "equal" relation, denoted by the symbol $=$, and "less than or equal" relation, denoted by the symbol $\leq$, provide examples of equivalence and total order relations respectively. In fact, it is common to use $\leq$ (instead of R) as a standard relational symbol for all order relations, both partial and total. An example of a partial order can be constructed as follows: Let $\mathscr{C} = \{S_1, S_2, \ldots, S_n\}$ be any collection of subsets of some given set S. It is easy to verify that the "subset inclusion" relation, denoted by $\subseteq$, is a partial order relation on $\mathscr{C}$, not on S. This example is of importance, since there will occur several instances in the following discussions when we will have a collection $\mathscr{C}$ of subsets, and we will want to induce a partial order on that collection. In these cases we will simply say, "We partially order $\mathscr{C}$ by inclusion."

Let R be any relation on a set S and let $Y \subseteq S$ be any subset. By the *restriction of R to Y*, denoted $R|_Y$, we mean the set of all ordered pairs

$$R|_Y = \{(x, y) \in R | x, y \in Y\}$$

Theorem 1-2 The restriction of any partial order is itself a partial order.

Now let R be any relation on a set S, and again let $Y \subseteq S$ be any subset. An element y will be called *minimal in Y with respect to R* if $y \in Y$, and $x \in Y$, $(x, y) \in R$ implies $x = y$ (or alternatively, if there exists no distinct $x \in Y$ such that $(x, y) \in R$). Similarly y is said to be *maximal in Y with respect to R* if $y \in Y$, and $z \in Y$, $(y, z) \in R$ implies $y = z$. In general a subset Y may have several (or possibly none) minimal and maximal elements. These sets of elements we denote by $min(Y)$ and $max(Y)$ respectively. If $Y = S$, then we commonly call these the minimal elements of R, or just the minimal elements. [Technically, minimality or maximality must always be expressed with respect to a specific subset and a specific relation. Normally these will be clear from the context. In those cases where a discussion involves several relations and several possible subsets, one can resort to subscripted notation, as in $x \in min_R(Y)$.]

It is not hard to create relations R which have neither minimal nor maximal elements. Therefore it is of interest to give properties of R which are sufficient to insure the existence of such elements.

Theorem 1-3 Let S be any finite nonvoid set that is partially ordered by R. The set of minimal elements with respect to R, $min(S) = \{x_1, x_2, \ldots, x_n\}$ is not empty; and further, for all $y \in S$ there exists $x_i \in min(S)$ such that $(x_i, y) \in R$.

Given these preliminary results about relations in general, we can now turn to the notion of a graph. A *directed graph* (which we will henceforth simply call a graph), denoted G = (P, E), is just a relation E on a set P. Elements of P are commonly called *points* (or nodes or vertices). Elements of the relation are commonly called *edges* (or arcs or lines). Note that P or S or any other symbol may be used to denote the set of points, just as E, R, or some other symbol may be used to denote the relation on P; but the notational choice of P to denote the point set and E to denote the edge set seems natural. Edges of the form (x, x) are traditionally called *loops*. By and large, the existence of loops in either a graph or a data structure is a nuisance, and most authors consider only loop-free graphs. The construction of our definitions will be such that the presence, or absence, of loops is largely irrelevant.

The sets P and E that constitute a graph may be described in several ways. In mathematics one traditionally describes sets either by enumeration or by a rule (formula) that makes it possible to determine whether any particular element is in the set or not. Both methods are commonly used to define relations occurring in practice, and their resulting graphs. There is an important third technique for defining set membership that has been developed largely by linguists and computer scientists, not mathematicians; that is, by means of a grammar. In effect one presents a well-defined computational process that can generate all the elements of a set (generation with respect to the grammar) or, given an element, can determine whether or not it belongs to the set (parsing with respect to the grammar). While the use of grammars has generally been confined only to sets whose elements are strings, called *languages,* there has been some exploration toward the description of other mathematical objects, including graphs and data structures, by such computational processes.

A graph may be defined by enumeration in the following manner. Let G = (P, E), whose point set P = {a, b, c, d, e, f, g} and whose edge set E = {(a, b), (a, c), (b, b), (b, d), (c, d), (c, f), (e, c), (f, e), (f, g)}. Unfortunately such a description gives little, if any, intuitive feeling for the "structure" of the graph. It is far more common to illustrate the graph by means of a "drawing" such as Fig. 1-5. This figure, which is what is usually meant by the term *graph,* is simply a graphic representation of the graph G defined above, in which points of P are denoted by literal points in the drawing, and edges of E are denoted by arrows connecting the points.

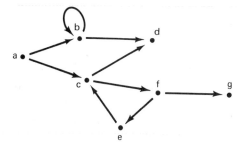

Figure 1-5 A directed graph G = (P, E).

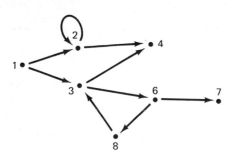

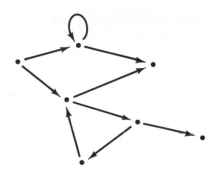

Figure 1-6 The graph of Fig. 1-5 with numeric point identifiers.

Figure 1-7 The graph of Fig. 1-5 without any identifiers.

Because of their intuitive clarity, we will frequently use such "drawn" graphs to define a graph, particularly in examples. (However, it is important to note that such graphic representations should not be included in arguments or proofs about graphs, save possibly to provide clarification by means of an example. The rigor of a proof which includes a drawing as an integral part of the argument is at best suspect.) Further we should note that the letters a through g have no particular significance. They are merely a convenient choice of *labels,* or *identifiers,* by which individual points in the set P can be referenced. Any set of unique identifiers may be used to label the points of a graph, or they may be left unlabeled. Figures 1-6 and 1-7 both represent identically the same graph as Fig. 1-5. Individual edges may, or may not, be labeled in the same fashion.

Another commonly used method of representing a graph is by means of matrix notation. A boolean matrix A_G is said to be the *adjacency matrix* of the graph G if, for all points i, j $\in$ P, $a_{ij} = 1$, provided (i, j) $\in$ E, and $a_{ij} = 0$ otherwise. Figure 1-8 illustrates the adjacency matrix of the graph G given above. Since the use of matrix notation is straightforward in most computer languages, it is a very common practice to represent graphs by means of their associated adjacency matrix. The advantages and disadvantages of such representation are explored in Chap. 7.

A graph G = (P, E) is said to have *point assignments over* a set V if there exists a function f:P → V. We say it has *edge assignments over* V' if there exists a function g:E → V'. (By the abbreviated expression *graph with assign-*

	a	b	c	d	e	f	g
a	0	1	1	0	0	0	0
b	0	1	0	1	0	0	0
c	0	0	0	1	0	1	0
d	0	0	0	0	0	0	0
e	0	0	1	0	0	0	0
f	0	0	0	0	1	0	1
g	0	0	0	0	0	0	0

Figure 1-8 The adjacency matrix A_G of the graph G of Fig. 1-5.

ments we will implicitly mean point assignments.) Note that there may be several assignment functions into different sets, such as $f_1:P \to V_1$, $f_2:P \to V_2$, and $f_3:P \to V_3$, in which case we say the graph has assignments over V_1, V_2, and V_3.

To graphically illustrate a graph with assignments we will, by convention, represent a point by an n-tuple of its assigned values enclosed in parentheses, e.g., $(f_1(x), f_2(x), \ldots, f_n(x))$. Labels identifying the point, if any, will precede the point separated by a colon. Similar notation, written along the arrow, will be used for edge assignments and labels. Figure 1-9 shows our running graph G with two assignment functions over the sets $V_1 = \{reals\}$ and $V_2 = \{integers\}$. Notice that only three of the points have been identified with labels a, d, and e.

The graph $H = (P', E')$ is said to be a *subgraph* of $G = (P, E)$ if $P' \subseteq P$ and $E' = E|_{P'}$. If the second condition is relaxed to read $E' \subseteq E$, then H is called a *partial subgraph*. The distinction between a subgraph and a partial subgraph is important, especially since many authors use the term *subgraph* to mean the latter concept, and *full* or *complete subgraph* to refer to the former. The reader who supplements this text with outside references must make special note of the intended usage of this critical term. If $G = (P, E)$ is any graph and $P' \subseteq P$ is any subset, then the subgraph over P' is unique. Consequently we will often treat the subset and its associated subgraph synonymously; for example, we may simply say "x is minimal in H" rather than the more precise "x is minimal in P' with respect to $E|_{P'}$."

As a review of previously defined concepts we consider various elements of the graph illustrated in Fig. 1-5. The point a is minimal in G, while d and g are maximal points. The point d is *both* minimal *and* maximal in the subgraph $H_1 = \{d, f, g\}$, while f and g are minimal and maximal, respectively. The subgraph $H_2 = \{c, e, f\}$ has neither minimal nor maximal points.

A *path* in a graph (or subgraph) G from x to z, denoted $\rho_G(x, z)$, is a sequence of points $\langle y_0, y_1, \ldots, y_n \rangle$ with $n \geq 0$, such that

1. $x = y_0$, $z = y_n$,
2. $y_{i-1} \neq y_i$, and
3. $(y_{i-1}, y_i) \in E|_G$ for $1 \leq i \leq n$.

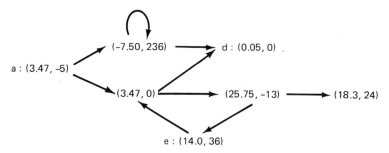

Figure 1-9 The graph G of Fig. 1-5, with two assignment functions over $V_1 = \{reals\}$ and $V_2 = \{in-tegers\}$.

A path is said to be *simple* if all y_i are distinct, save that possibly $y_0 = y_n$. Its *length*, denoted by $|\rho_G(x, z)|$, is n, the number of edges "in the path." A *cycle* is a simple path $\rho_G(x, x)$ of length ≥ 1. A graph without cycles is said to be *acyclic*.

Intuitively one regards a path as a sequence of directed edges by which one may progress from one point of the graph to another. We have chosen, however, to define paths in terms of a sequence of points. Note that with this definition, for every point $x \in P$ there exists a path $\rho(x, x)$ of length zero, and that a loop, if present in the graph, is not regarded as a cycle. (Consequently all cycles must, in fact, have length ≥ 2.) The points $\langle c, f, e, c \rangle$ constitute a cycle in the graph of Fig. 1-5. When the expression *path* is used, one invariably thinks of a simple path. The following result shows that this is legitimate.

Theorem 1-4 If $\rho_G(x, z) = \langle \ldots, y_i, \ldots \rangle$ is a path then there exists a simple path $\rho^*_G(x, z) = \langle \ldots, y^*_j, \ldots \rangle$ such that $y^*_j \in \rho_G(x, z)$ for all j.

The notation $\rho_G(x, z)$ may be used to denote either a specific path (sequence of points) from x to z or the existence of at least one path between these points that is contained in G. Used in this latter sense, we are really introducing a new relation on the point set P which we may call the *path relation*. More formally, if $H = (P, E)$ is any graph (or subgraph), then the relation ρ_H, defined by $(x, z) \in \rho_H$ if and only if $\rho_H(x, z)$, is called the path relation induced by $E|_P$. (Note that we will drop the subscript in ρ_H when it is evident which graph or subgraph is meant.)

Early in this section we listed a number of "nice" properties that a relation might have. A quick glance at the graph of Fig. 1-5 shows that the edge relation E possesses none of these "nice" properties, save for antisymmetry. It is neither reflexive, because $(a, a) \notin E$, nor antireflexive, because $(b, b) \in E$. More importantly it is not transitive because (a, c) and $(c, f) \in E$, but $(a, f) \notin E$. The path relation ρ, on the other hand, is both reflexive (by definition) and transitive. [It is trivial to verify that $\rho(x, y)$ and $\rho(y, z)$ imply $\rho(x, z)$.] Consequently we are often primarily concerned with the path relation ρ that is induced by some given edge relation E. The induced graph $G^T = (P, \rho)$ is called the *transitive closure* of G. Readily, two distinct graphs G_1 and G_2 may have the same transitive closure. (Verify that the graph of Fig. 1-10 has the same transi-

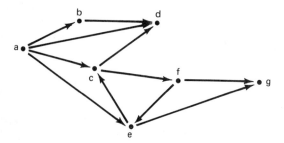

Figure 1-10 A graph with the same transitive closure G^T as that of Fig. 1-5.

tive closure as does that of Fig. 1-5.) Further, it is clear that $G = G^T$ if and only if E itself is transitive; and that, regarded solely as relations on P, $E \subseteq \rho$.

Since the transitive closure (P, ρ) is both reflexive and transitive—and these represent two of the three properties necessary for a relation to be either an equivalence relation or a partial order relation—it is natural to consider graphs for which ρ is one of these two special relations.

A graph (or subgraph) G will be called *strongly connected* if its induced path relation ρ is an equivalence relation consisting of a single equivalence class. Strongly connected graphs (or subgraphs) are characterized by the fact that given *any* pair of points x and z there exists a path $\rho_G(x, z)$. The subgraph {c, e, f} of Figs. 1-5 and 1-10 is strongly connected. On the other hand, if ρ is a partial order on P, one can show that:

Theorem 1-5 A graph $G = (P, E)$ is acyclic if and only if its induced path relation ρ is a partial order relation.

Let y be any point of a graph $G = (P, E)$. By its *left neighbors,* denoted L(y), we will mean the set

$$L(y) = \{x | (x, y) \in E\}$$

Similarly its set of *right neighbors* R(y) will be the set

$$R(y) = \{z | (y, z) \in E\}$$

The cardinality of the two sets $|L(y)|$ and $|R(y)|$ is called the *in degree* and *out degree* at y, respectively. In many texts it is denoted by id(y) and od(y). If $A \subseteq P$ is a subset of points, then the preceding definition can be extended to sets in the natural manner; that is,

$$L(A) = \{x | (x, a) \in E \text{ for some } a \in A\}$$
$$R(A) = \{z | (a, z) \in E \text{ for some } a \in A\}$$

The terminology "left" and "right" is purely a matter of convention arising from the habit of drawing graphs in a "left to right" fashion. This "left to right" graphic representation is in turn a result of our preoccupation with linear and acyclic data structures that are most often encountered in computer applications. Since one usually represents number lines in this fashion, it is often intuitively helpful to do the same with ordered and partially ordered data structures. The convention seems far less natural if one is primarily concerned with cyclic or strongly connected structures. The reader will find a variety of notation and of graphic representations in the literature, each reflecting the preference of the individual author. For example, another widely used notation for these neighborhood operators is that of E(y) to denote those elements $\{z_i\}$ that are related to y under E, and $E^{-1}(y)$ to denote those elements $\{x_j\}$ that are associated with y under the inverse relation E^{-1}. Either notation is perfectly acceptable. We prefer to use L and R simply because of their pictorial suggestiveness.

In ordered algebraic structures the set of all elements that are "less than" (or greater than) some given element or set of elements (for example, $\{x|x \leq y\}$) is customarily called an *ideal*. If the ideal is generated by a single element it is called a principal ideal. By analogy, if $G = (P, E)$ is a graph and $A \subseteq P$ is any subset, we will call the sets

$$\bar{L}(A) = \{x|\rho(x, a_i) \qquad \text{for some } a_i \in A\}$$

and

$$\bar{R}(A) = \{z|\rho(a_j, z) \qquad \text{for some } a_j \in A\}$$

the *left* and *right ideals* generated by A, respectively. If A is a singleton point $\{y\}$, then $\bar{L}(y) = \{x|\rho(x, y)\}$ and $\bar{R}(y) = \{z|\rho(y, z)\}$ are said to be left and right *principal ideals*.

The set $\bar{R}(y)$ (verbally called "R-bar") may be regarded as the set of all points that are "reachable" or "accessible" from y by following paths, or edges, in E. It is evident that for all $y \in P$ we have $y \in \bar{L}(y)$ and $y \in \bar{R}(y)$, and that $\bar{R}(y)$ in G is simply the set R(y) in $G^T = (P, \rho)$. To review this terminology the reader should verify that in the graph of Fig. 1-5, $R(f) = \{e, g\}$ while $\bar{R}(f) = \{c, d, e, f, g\}$, that $L(b) = \{a, b\}$, and that $\bar{L}(A) = \{a, b, c, e, f\}$ where $A = \{b, e\}$.

The intuitive meaning of a least element is an element which is "less than all other elements." Least points assume importance in data structures as those elements from which all other elements can be accessed, that is, elements which can serve as "entry points" to the structure. We can make this concept more precise in the case of graphs by saying that a point x is a *least* point of a graph (or subgraph) $G = (P, E)$ if for all $y \in P$, $\rho_G(x, y)$. Similarly, the point z is called a *greatest* point of G if $\rho_G(y, z)$ for all $y \in P$. Note that a minimal point need not be a least point, and conversely, a least point need not be minimal. For instance, every point of a strongly connected graph is a least point, but none are minimal. However, it is not hard to show the following:

> **Theorem 1-6** Let G be an acyclic graph or subgraph. x is a least (greatest) point of G if and only if it is the unique minimal (maximal) point of G.

When graphically representing or drawing a partial order relation on a set, it is customary to omit many of the actual edges in the drawing itself. Those edges (x, y) whose presence can be inferred by the existence of a path $\rho(x, y)$ are normally omitted for the sake of clarity. Consider, for example, the two graphs of Fig. 1-11. Both are representations of the same partial order relation (which in this case happens to be a distributive lattice). The reader should verify that G_1 is just the transitive closure of G_2. Clearly the "structure" of the relation is much more apparent in the second graph G_2, in which all "extraneous" edges such as (0, d), (0, e), (0, f), and (0, 1) have been omitted. G_2 is called a *basic graph*. The economies achieved by using a basic graph to graphically represent a relation can also be exploited (by eliminating redundant edges) in designing computer representations. For this reason we seek a rigorous definition that will be applicable for all graphs, not just acyclic ones. To do this we

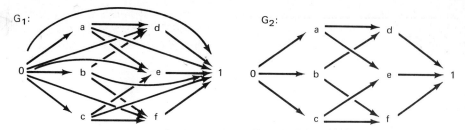

Figure 1-11 Two representations of the same partial order relation.

consider the set $\mathscr{G}$ of *all* graphs $\{G_1, G_2, \ldots, G_n\}$ with the same transitive closure G^T. Then we partially order the elements (each an entire graph) of this collection by edge inclusion. That is, we consider $G_i \le G_j$ in $\mathscr{G}$ (where $G_i = (P, E_i)$ and $G_j = (P, E_j)$) if and only if $E_i \subseteq E_j$. Now a graph G_i that is minimal in $\mathscr{G}$ will be called a *basic graph*. G' will be called a *basic representation* of G if $G' \le G$ in $\mathscr{G}$ and G' is basic.

If G is any finite graph, then by the fact that $\mathscr{G}$ is finite and by Theorem 1-3 we know that there exists at least one basic representation of G. But it need not be unique; it may have several basic representations, as illustrated in Fig. 1-12. Furthermore, this definition provides no effective guide for determining whether any given graph G is basic or not. To construct all the graphs of $\mathscr{G}$ and then find its minimal elements is clearly impractical. We want to be able to characterize "basicness" in terms of properties of only the graph G itself. For acyclic graphs we can do this.

Theorem 1-7 An acyclic graph $G = (P, E)$ is basic if and only if it is loop-free, and for all $x, z \in P$, $|\rho(x, z)| \ge 2$ implies that $(x, z) \notin E$.

Theorem 1-8 If G is acyclic, then there exists a unique basic representation G^b of G.

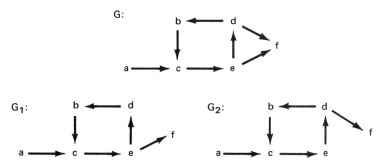

Figure 1-12 G_1 and G_2 are distinct basic representations of G.

As a result of this theorem we are justified in referring to *the* basic representation of any acyclic structure or partial order relation. Virtually all the computer representations considered in this text will be basic.

A path is a sequence of points traversed by following edges of G in the direction indicated by the relation E. There are situations where one wants to be able to "walk" from point to point along edges, but ignoring their direction. In precisely the same manner as one defines paths, one lets a *walk from* x *to* z in G, denoted $\omega_G(x, z)$, be a sequence of points $\langle y_0, y_1, \ldots, y_n \rangle$ but allows (y_{i-1}, y_i) or (y_i, y_{i-1}) to be an edge in E. It is said to have *length* n. The walk is *simple* if all points y_i are distinct, except possibly that $y_0 = y_n$. (It is easy to prove the analogue of Theorem 1-4 about walks.) A walk $\omega(x, z)$ of length ≥ 1 is called a *circuit* if $x = z$.

In the graph of Fig. 1-13, the sequences $\langle e, f, d, b \rangle$ and $\langle a, c, e, f, d, a \rangle$ are simple walks; the latter is a *simple circuit*. Neither the circuit $\langle a, c, e, f, j, i, f, d, a \rangle$ nor the walk $\langle f, i, i, j \rangle$ is simple. There is no walk from g to d. Considering only the subgraph H, there is no walk $\omega_H(c, d)$.

As in the case with paths, we can define a "walk relation" based on the existence of individual walks. By the *walk relation* ω in a graph (or subgraph) $G = (P, E)$ we mean that subset of $P \times P$ defined by $(x, z) \in \omega$ if and only if a walk $\omega_G(x, z)$ exists. It is evident that the walk relation will be both reflexive and transitive, as was the path relation. But the walk relation is also symmetric; that is, $(x, z) \in \omega$ if and only if $(z, x) \in \omega$. Consequently:

Theorem 1-9 The walk relation ω is an equivalence relation.

The equivalence relation ω induces a partition on the point set P (Theorem 1-1) whose sets, or equivalence classes, are called the *connected components* of G. Connectivity is an important concept, and one frequently encounters the following definition: A graph (or subgraph) G is said to be *connected* if for any pair of points $x, z \in P$, a walk $\omega_G(x, z)$ exists.

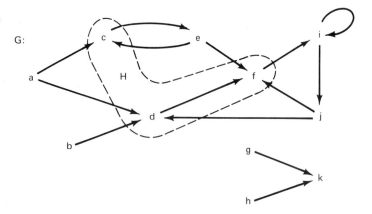

Figure 1-13 A disconnected graph G and a disconnected subgraph H = {c, d, f}.

The graph G of Fig. 1-13 is not itself connected, since there exists no walk $\omega_G(g, d)$. Neither is the subgraph H = {c, d, f} connected, since there is no walk $\omega_H(c, d)$. The subgraphs H_1 = {a, b, c, d, e, f, i, j} and H_2 = {g, h, k} are connected; they are its connected components. Obviously, if a subgraph H is not wholly contained within a connected component, it cannot itself be connected; but as shown by the subgraph H in this example, such containment by itself is not sufficient to ensure connectivity of the subgraph.† Readily, if a graph has too few edges, it cannot possibly be connected, and if it has too many, it cannot possibly be disconnected. One can find bounds on |E| that establish the number of edges that constitute too few and too many. Of considerable importance will be the following theorem:

Theorem 1-10 If G = (P, E) consists of exactly k ≥ 1 connected components, then |E| ≥ |P| − k. In particular, G connected implies that |E| ≥ |P| − 1.

We have previously said that a graph would be called *strongly connected* if the path relation ρ is an equivalence relation. This is indeed a "stronger" concept of connectivity because it says, in effect, that there are connecting walks $\omega(x, z)$ and $\omega(z, x)$ that are in fact directed paths. Unfortunately, many graphs of interest in computer applications are not strongly connected, but they may have nontrivial strongly connected subgraphs that we can exploit in representations considered in Chap. 8.

Finally we must make rigorous what we mean by the expression "these two graphs are the 'same,' or 'equal.'" Two graphs $G_1 = (P_1, E_1)$ and $G_2 = (P_2, E_2)$ could be called "equal" only if one has $P_1 = P_2$ and $E_1 = E_2$; that is, the symbols G_1 and G_2 were literally only different identifiers for the "same" graph.‡ The problem with such a definition of equality is that we may have two "different" graphs on different point sets, which nevertheless "look alike" (for instance, G_1 and G_2 of Fig. 1-14). We would like to call these graphs equal. Consequently, in

---

†The practical importance of connectivity concepts arises when one designs search procedures which "walk" through a data structure searching for certain elements. Normally it is sufficient merely to have the entire structure G be connected. Although of theoretical interest, the fine distinction of whether a subset of elements (or subgraph H) is connected in itself is of practical importance only if the search procedure is in some way constrained to look only at certain elements.

‡In many respects such a definition would be analogous to saying that two variables X and Y in a procedure are "equal" only if they denote the same storage location (and hence must have a common value).

Figure 1-14 Two "obviously" isomorphic graphs.

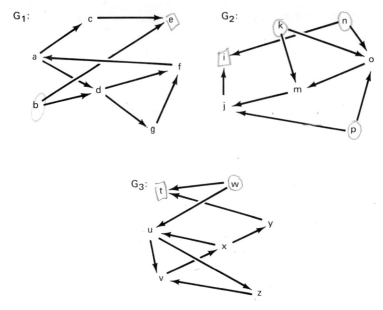

Figure 1-15 Two of these graphs are isomorphic to each other; the other is distinct.

graph theory, it is customary to express equality in terms of an isomorphism concept. Two graphs $G_1 = (P_1, E_1)$ and $G_2 = (P_2, E_2)$ are said to be *isomorphic*, denoted $G_1 \cong G_2$, if there exists a 1-1, onto function $\varphi : P_1 \to P_2$ (called an *isomorphism*) with the property that for all $x, y \in P_1$, $(x, y) \in E_1$ if and only if $(\varphi(x), \varphi(y)) \in E_2$.

Two of the three graphs in Fig. 1-15 are isomorphic; one is not. (Note that the drawings of isomorphic graphs need not look alike, but they can always be redrawn so that they do.) The reader should test each pair for isomorphism and supply a proof for the following theorem.

Theorem 1-11 The isomorphism relation $\cong$ defined on a set $\mathscr{G} = \{G_i\}$ of graphs (that is, $(G_i, G_j) \in \cong$, if $G_i \cong G_j$) is an equivalence relation.

It should be apparent that isomorphism really indicates that the relations E_1 and E_2 behave in the same way on their respective point sets. It asserts, in effect, "structural" equality. If the graphs involved are graphs with assignments over some set V, there is no commonly accepted standard of equality. One would naturally expect them to be structurally equivalent under some isomorphic mapping φ. It also seems reasonable to expect that their assignment functions map into the same sets V_i. Whether equality also demands that $f_i(x) = f_i(\varphi(x))$ for all x seems to be largely dependent on the application context.

EXERCISES FOR SECTION 1-5

1-7 Since relations are simply sets (of ordered pairs), we may define the standard set operations on them. For example, if R and Q are both relations on P, then we can form new relations $R \cup Q$ and $R \cap Q$, or we can ask questions such as "Is $R \subseteq Q$?" (Note that in this latter case, containment denoted by $\subseteq$ is itself a relation between two relations.) Let $P = \{a, b, c, d, e\}$ and let $R = \{(a, b), (a, c), (a, d), (b, d)\}$, $Q = \{(c, e), (d, a), (e, d)\}$, and $S = \{(a, b), (a, d), (c, e), (e, d)\}$.

    (*a*) Draw a single graph representing all three relations (i.e., a single point set with three different kinds of edges).

    (*b*) Describe $R \cup Q$, $R \cap S$. Is $S \subseteq R \cup Q$?

1-8 The basic properties of relations may be presented using a more obviously set-theoretic notation as follows: Let I_P denote the identity relation on P defined by $I_P = \{(x, x)$ all $x \in P\}$, and let $\emptyset_P$ denote the empty relation on P consisting of no elements. We can then say that R is:

    (*a*) reflexive if $I_P \subseteq R$

    (*b*) antireflexive if $I_P \cap R = \emptyset_P$

    (*c*) symmetric if $R = R^{-1}$

    (*d*) antisymmetric if $R \cap R^{-1} = \emptyset_P$

    (*e*) weakly antisymmetric if $R \cap R^{-1} \subseteq I_P$

    (*f*) transitive if $R^2 \subseteq R$ (where R^2 denotes the *composition* $R \circ R$ of R, defined $R \circ R = \{(x, z) | (x, y)$ and $(y, z) \in R$ for some $y \in S)$.

Show the equivalence of the alternative definitions.

1-9 Using either the definitions above or those in the text, prove that:

    (*a*) R antisymmetric implies R is antireflexive.

    (*b*) R transitive and reflexive implies $R^2 = R$.

    (*c*) If R is a partial order, then R^{-1} and R^2 are partial orders.

    (*d*) If R is a partial order, then $R \cap R^{-1} = I_S$.

*1-10 Prove that if $\mathscr{P} = \{S_1, S_2, \ldots, S_n\}$ is a partition of S into disjoint subsets S_i, then the "naturally" induced relation $R = \{(x, y) | x, y \in S_i$ for some $i\}$ is an equivalence relation; and conversely, any equivalence relation R on S induces a partition of S in this "natural" way (Theorem 1-1).

*1-11 Show that if $\mathscr{C} = \{S_i | S_i \subseteq S\}$ is any collection of subsets of some set S, then the *subset inclusion* (or containment) relation, denoted by $\subseteq$, is a partial order relation on $\mathscr{C}$.

1-12 Let $P = \{t, u, v, w, x, y, z\}$ and let $E = \{(t, u), (t, v), (u, u), (u, w), (v, w), (v, y), (x, v), (y, x), (y, z)\}$. Let $A = \{t, u, w, x, y\}$ and $B = \{v, x, y\}$.

    (*a*) Enumerate $E|_A$ and $E|_B$.

    (*b*) List the minimal elements of each. Are both connected relations?

    (*c*) Graphically represent (P, E). Compare this with Fig. 1-5.

1-13 Prove Theorem 1-2, and show the analogous result that any restriction of an equivalence relation is itself an equivalence relation.

1-14 Show that:

    (*a*) the point i is maximal (minimal) in G if and only if the i*th* row (column) of the adjacency matrix A_G is all zeros.

    (*b*) G is loop-free if and only if the main diagonal of A_G is all zeros.

    (*c*) It is possible to relabel the points of G in such a way that A_G is upper (or lower) triangular if and only if G is acyclic.

1-15 (*a*) Give an example of a relation R on a set S for which there are no minimal elements.

    (*b*) Prove Theorem 1-3. (*Hint:* use induction, together with Theorem 1-2 and the property of transitivity.)

1-16 Draw the transitive closures of the graphs G_1 and G_2 in Fig. 1-12.

1-17 Draw a few graphs without circuits. (These will be important.)

*1-18 Prove Theorem 1-5—that a graph is acyclic if and only if ρ is a partial order.

*1-19 Since functions are merely special kinds of relations, it is reasonable to expect that at least some of the results that can be proven in the case of functions will also be true for arbitrary relations. Let E be any relation on a set P, and let A, B, T, V be subsets of P. Now *if* E *is a function,* it is known that the following assertions are true:

(*a*) A ⊆ B implies R(A) ⊆ R(B)
(*b*) R(A ∪ B) = R(A) ∪ R(B)
(*c*) R(A ∩ B) ⊆ R(A) ∩ R(B)
(*d*) L(T ∪ V) = L(T) ∪ L(V)
(*e*) L(T ∩ V) = L(T) ∩ L(V)
(*f*) R(L(T)) = T ∩ R(P)
(*g*) L(R(A)) ⊇ A

(Note that we are using the neighborhood notation R(A) and L(T), whereas standard functional notation would use E(A) and E^{-1}(T) to signify the image of A under E and preimage of T under E, respectively.) If E is an arbitrary relation, some of these assertions remain true; in some, equality must be replaced by containment; and some are false. Prove at least one true assertion. Give counterexamples to each false, or partially false, assertion.

1-20 L̄ and R̄ may be regarded as *operators* on the power set of P (set of all subsets of P). Such operators are called *closure operators* if they satisfy the Kuratowski closure axioms listed below.

(*a*) L̄(∅) = ∅ = R̄(∅)

for all subsets A, B ⊆ P

(*b*) A ⊆ L̄(A) and A ⊆ R̄(A)
(*c*) L̄(L̄(A)) = L̄(A) and R̄(R̄(A)) = R̄(A)
(*d*) L̄(A ∪ B) = L̄(A) ∪ L̄(B) and R̄(A ∪ B) = R̄(A) ∪ R̄(B)

Show that L̄ and R̄ satisfy these four properties and are hence closure operators.

*1-21 Consider the graph G in the accompanying figure, and the three subgraphs consisting of G itself, H_1 = {h, i}, and H_2 = {c, d, e, f, i}.

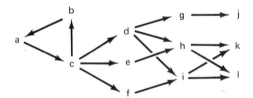

Ex. 1-21

(*a*) For each of these subgraphs (subsets), enumerate the sets of minimal and maximal points, and least and greatest points.

(*b*) Enumerate the sets L(H_1), R(H_1), L̄(H_1), R̄(H_1) and R̄(H_2).

*1-22 Consider the following graph, where P is the set of positive integers ≤ 12; that is, P = {1, 2, 3, . . . , 11, 12} and E is the relation {(x, y)|x evenly divides y}.

(*a*) Draw, as clearly as possible, the basic representation of this graph. What "extra" edges would have to be drawn to illustrate the complete transitive relation?

(*b*) Give its adjacency matrix A_G.

1-23 Prove Theorem 1-10. (*Hint:* Begin an induction on |P| with |P| = k, and observe that the result follows immediately, since each component is a singleton point; hence |E| = 0.)

1-24 Although these bounds are so high as to be of little practical use, it is of interest to prove (in contrast to Theorem 1-10) that G *must* be connected

(*a*) if |E| ≥ (|P| − 1)² + 1
(*b*) if |E| ≥ (|P| − 1)(|P| − 2)/2 + 1, and G is acyclic

Can you conjecture, and prove, an upper bound if G is both acyclic and basic?

*1-25 Two graphs can be shown to be isomorphic by actually presenting the isomorphic correspondence φ. For instance, in Fig. 1-14 the (obvious) correspondence is φ(a) = v, φ(b) = w, etc. One then simply verifies that the correspondence is "edge-preserving." Enumerate the correspondence under which the two isomorphic graphs of Fig. 1-15 are isomorphic.

It may be much more difficult to prove that two graphs are not isomorphic. Just because one has tried several different correspondences and none were edge-preserving does not show that none exist. Of course, one can try all possible correspondences $\varphi : P \to P'$ but this is often a bit tedious, since there are $|P|!$ possible 1-1 onto maps. (In the case of the small graphs of Fig. 1-15 there would be $7! = 5040$ different possible correspondences to test.) Nevertheless in the case of the nonisomorphic singleton in Fig. 1-15, one may make a simple observation that *proves* that isomorphism is impossible. Find it. For an interesting discussion of this problem see Unger (1964) and Corneil and Gotlieb (1970).

TWO

A SIMPLE EXAMPLE OF LINKED AND SEQUENTIAL REPRESENTATIONS

In this chapter we model a familiar real-life situation, games involving a standard deck of playing cards, and illustrate two different kinds of representations. The purposes are (1) to provide familiarity with basic terminology, (2) to give practice with the primitive field manipulation operations of Sec. 1-4, (3) to lay groundwork for the fundamental distinction between linked and sequential representation, and (4) to illustrate the effect that a particular choice of data structure may have on further usage (in this case, simulations).

A standard deck of playing cards consists of 52 individual cards or elements. When organized as a deck there is a definite relation between individual cards. Beginning with the top card, the cards follow one another in a definite sequence. They are *totally* (or linearly) *ordered*. This configuration is easily modeled as a directed graph $G = (P, E)$. We can let each card (object in the situation being modeled) be represented by a single point in P. If x and y are elements of P (cards in the deck), we will let $(x, y) \in E$ if and only if card y immediately follows card x in the deck. Consequently the resulting graph looks like that of Fig. 2-1. If we were to *name* (or identify) this graph, the string DECK would seem to be an admirable identifier.

But the abstract model S_M of Fig. 2-1 is rather uninformative. It only indicates that there are 52 individual elements in the model that are organized to follow one after another. Each of the cards has associated properties, its rank and its suit, which must certainly be available if we are going to make any prac-

DECK: •⟶•⟶•⟶•⟶ ⋯ ⟶•⟶•⟶•⟶•

Figure 2-1 An abstract graph DECK = (P, E), with |P| = 52, that models an ordinary deck of playing cards.

tical use of this model, say in the simulation of an actual card game. We therefore define the *assignment functions*

$$f_1: P \to V_1 \qquad \text{where } V_1 = \{\text{club, diamond, heart, spade}\}$$
$$f_2: P \to V_2 \qquad \text{where } V_2 = \{\text{ace, 2, ..., 10, jack, queen, king}\}$$

to represent these important point properties.

In the model S_M of Fig. 2-1 we used the suggestive identifier DECK to name the entire graph. By the same token we can replace many of the formal identifiers used in formulating this model with suggestive identifiers that are far more appropriate to this particular application. For example, we can denote the set of points of the graph by CARDS rather than P, and the relation between them by NEXT rather than E. Similarly, f_1 is a rather sterile name for the first assignment function; surely SUIT is more apt, as would be RANK instead of f_2. Finally we may choose to identify a few individual points of the graph—the TOP and BOTTOM cards of DECK are natural candidates.

With these modifications, the abstract model S_M now looks like that of Fig. 2-2.

Let us suppose that we are simulating a card game in which initially three

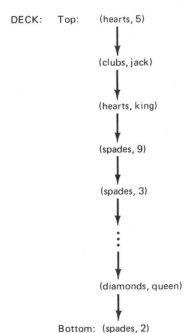

DECK: Top: (hearts, 5)

(clubs, jack)

(hearts, king)

(spades, 9)

(spades, 3)

⋮

(diamonds, queen)

Bottom: (spades, 2)

Figure 2-2 An abstract graph DECK = (CARDS, NEXT) with assignment function SUIT and RANK, that models an ordinary deck of playing cards.

DECK:

top: (diamonds, 6) ——▶ (clubs, ace) ——▶ • • • ——▶ (diamonds, queen) ——▶ bottom: (spades, 2)

hand$_1$: (clubs, 9) ——▶ (spades, 3) ——▶ (hearts, 5)

hand$_2$: (hearts, 4) ——▶ (diamonds, 8) ——▶ (clubs, jack)

hand$_3$: (spades, 10) ——▶ (hearts, jack) ——▶ (hearts, king)

hand$_4$: (hearts, 8) ——▶ (clubs, 6) ——▶ (spades, 9)

Figure 2-3 State of a card deck after three cards have been dealt to each of four hands.

cards are dealt to each of four players. After the deal we would expect the model of the situation to look like that of Fig. 2-3.

Comparison of these two figures reveals a great deal about this model-building process, and particularly about the use of identifiers. We note first that the use of DECK to name the entire graph was a mistake. This new graph consists of five separate pieces, each of which is a connected component. DECK merely names one of the components, while the strings HAND$_1$, HAND$_2$, HAND$_3$, and HAND$_4$ simultaneously identify both the other components and the top card of each. We see from this example that a name may serve to identify an entire graph by identifying a single point within it. (We will encounter this phenomenon frequently in our study of data structures, and the question "When can we be assured that the identification of a single element of a data structure is sufficient to identify, or *access*, the entire structure?" will be an important one.)

Next we note that TOP no longer identifies the same element (or card) that it did in Fig. 2-2. In the same manner we may expect that BOTTOM, HAND$_1$, ..., HAND$_4$ will identify various elements from time to time. For this reason we can call these strings *variable identifiers,* in that the object being identified may vary in the course of an application.†

Finally we observe that our graphs are really modeling the *states* s_i of some system at a given point in the time of the simulation process. The entire process might be represented as in Fig. 2-4. Moreover, subprocesses, such as dealing, should be regarded as *operators* (or transformations) that transform one data structure (or abstract graph such as Fig. 2-2) into another (such as Fig. 2-3). While the major emphasis of this text is on the data structures themselves and their representations, there is constant reference to intended processes that will

---

†This terminology should be completely familiar. In standard programming languages a variable, say the string X, denotes or identifies some value, say the number 5.0, stored somewhere within the computer. Of course, the value it denotes may be changed by means of an assignment statement.

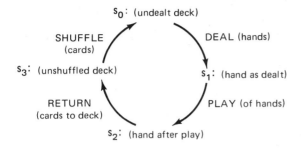

Figure 2-4 Simplified model of a total simulation, with points denoting states and edges denoting subprocesses.

operate on them, with respect both to feasibility and to efficiency. These operations are presented in the form of specific processes; as yet there is no formal "theory of data structure transformations." But it is not unreasonable to expect that some day this subject will become a fundamental area of computer science, in the same manner that numerical analysis is concerned primarily with operations on real and complex numbers, not the computer representations of these numbers themselves.†

Having discussed the model in considerable detail, let us now consider various computer representations of it. Corresponding to each point x of the graph is a computer cell, $cell_x$, of one or more consecutive words. The format and contents of the cell must still be determined, but we can be relatively sure that we will want to store the function values SUIT(X) and RANK(X) in the cell. Thus we might begin with a cell format in which the first two words contain these functional values, as in Fig. 2-5. But a moment's reflection should convince us that such a layout is unnecessarily wasteful of computer storage. It would be much more efficient to *code* the assignment values with some integer code, such as:

$$\{1, 2, 3, 4\} \Longleftrightarrow \{\text{club, diamond, heart, spade}\}$$

$$\{1, 2, \ldots, 11, 12, 13\} \Longleftrightarrow \{\text{ace, } 2, \ldots, \text{jack, queen, king}\}‡$$

---

†Of course a thorough understanding of the representation of the object being transformed is a necessary prerequisite to the study of the operations themselves. Much of the error analysis of numerical processes is rooted in the finitary representation of real numbers in the computer.

‡This code may be chosen differently so as to optimize some particular process. If, for example, we will be comparing face values where the ace is considered to be the high card, it would be better to code the ace as 14, rather than 1. Similarly, in many card games rank is more important than suit in determining value. By packing rank in a field to the left of the field containing suit, a single whole-word comparison can replace two separate field comparisons.

Figure 2-5 Preliminary cell layout, showing the first two words of a cell corresponding to the card, the queen of diamonds.

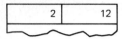

Figure 2-6 A compacted cell layout, showing the first word of a cell corresponding to the card, the queen of diamonds.

Since these integer values are small, they can be safely *packed* into smaller link or tag-sized fields of a single computer word. Figure 2-6 illustrates the resulting compactification. This is a fairly standard way of representing assignment values, but alternative methods exist. See, for example, Exercise 2-5.

Choosing the computer representation of the relation NEXT, the edges of the graph S_M, is typically more difficult. In this case there exist three very different alternative choices, each with its own assets and drawbacks. The first alternative is a *sequential* representation in which we use the total order A imposed on the computer storage registers by its *addressing* convention, to *implicitly* represent the NEXT relation. In terms of computer storage used, this will be the most efficient; each point can be represented by just a one-word cell. Consequently the DECK and hands HAND$_1$, ..., HAND$_4$ may be just singly subscripted arrays of dimensions 52 and 3, respectively. Using a sequential representation, the computer representation S_R of the model S_M would look like Fig. 2-7.

A significant disadvantage of the representation of Fig. 2-7 occurs in the DEAL subprocess [which the reader should have no trouble coding (Exercise 2-4)]. Each time a card is "dealt" from the "top" of the deck it is "moved" from the array DECK to the appropriate location in the array HAND$_i$ and all the remaining "cards" in DECK are shifted one location. Such shifting is quite time-

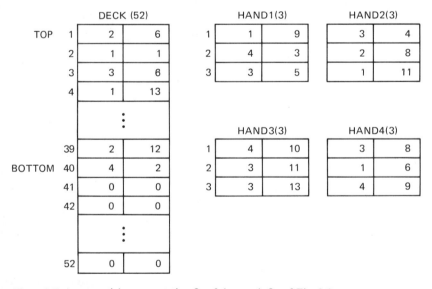

Figure 2-7 A sequential representation S_R of the graph S_M of Fig. 2-3.

consuming, so that one must balance the relative efficiency in terms of storage against the relative inefficiency in terms of time. This trade-off between storage and computation time is a recurring theme in the study of data structures, and one is tempted to advance the following general law: *Any storage efficiency obtained by compacting the computer representation of a given data structure is compensated by a corresponding increase in the computation time of processes operating on it.* There are an abundance of counterexamples to this principle; for instance, a simple modification to the structure of Fig. 2-7 (see Exercise 2-4) eliminates most of the shifting, at least in the dealing operation, while still retaining its compact storage. Consequently it is at best a "pseudo" principle. But it describes such a common phenomenon that most computer scientists bear it in mind as a working rule of thumb. For example, even though the modification described in Exercise 2-4 eliminates most shifting in the dealing subprocess, virtually any process that emulates the play of the hand will still require additional steps, either to shift cards or to examine cards that have been already played.

In a *linked* representation the NEXT relation is *explicitly* represented by storing in each point cell a link to the cell corresponding to the next point in the relation. That is, if $(x, y) \in E$, then a field of cell_x will contain the address of cell_y. Let's call this field the NEXT field. Since we are now using an extra field, we must increase the size of the point cells to two consecutive words† with format as illustrated in Fig. 2-8. Notice that one field is unused and is, in a sense, wasted.

By using a linked, instead of a sequential, representation we induce several significant changes in S_R. First of all, we shall see that we will never have to "move" or "shift" a card. By simply changing the address in the link field NEXT of cell_x we can effectively alter the relation of cell_x to all the other cells of the data structure. Consequently there is no need to designate separate arrays HAND1 , . . . , HAND4. But we must include some other method of denoting which card (cell) is the top card of the deck and which cards belong to which hands. For this we use *reference pointers,* which are variables in the processes operating on the data structure that "point" to certain specified cells of interest. In Fig. 2-9 the two scalar variables TOP and BOTTOM and the array of four variables HAND[4] serve as reference pointers.

Figure 2-9 is not at all clear, since we have inserted actual register

---

†There are many situations where one can pack several items of information into a single word, either because the computer word is long or the information is short (as in this case, where SUIT needs no more than 2 bits). But for purposes of this example we will assume no more than two fields per word, so that the extra word is necessary.

2	12
	loc(cell$_y$)

Figure 2-8 A cell layout of cell_x, corresponding to the queen of diamonds. $(x, y) \in$ NEXT.

ADDRESS
(decimal)   DECK(104)

1001	3	5
		0000
1003	1	11
		0000
1005	3	13
		0000
1007	4	9
		0000
1009	4	3
		1001
1011	2	8
		1003
1013	3	11
		1005
1015	1	6
		1007
1017	1	9
		1009
1019	3	4
		1011
1021	4	10
		1013
1023	3	8
		1015
1025	2	6
		1027
1027	1	1
		1029
	⋮	
1101	2	12
		1103
1103	4	2
		0000

TOP

1025

BOTTOM

1103

HAND(4)

1017
1019
1021
1023

Figure 2-9 A linked representation S_R of the graph of Fig. 2-3, using actual core addresses.

addresses in appropriate link fields and pointers. But it should be apparent that the particular numbers used are really irrelevant. The 52 cells of the structure might just as well have been stored in the 104 locations, 3154 through 3258, or any other such block. Consequently it seems reasonable to replace all the actual addresses with arrows which point to the cell whose address would have been found in the field. Doing this we get Fig. 2-10, which is quite a bit easier to interpret. Note also that in Fig. 2-9 we used the value 0000 to indicate that there was no NEXT cell. (See cells 1001, 1003, 1005, 1007, and 1103.) Such a value is called the *nullvalue* and should be any distinctive nonnegative value, preferably one that would normally be an illegal address. In Fig. 2-10 we use a capital lambda (Λ) as the *nullsymbol* to denote such a nullvalue.

Figure 2-10 is a considerable improvement over Fig. 2-9. But there is still a mess of crisscrossing arrows, which are a bit confusing. However if we realize that there is no real significance to the order in which pairs of words in the 104 words of DECK were assigned to particular cells, then we can draw the cell anywhere on the page, provided we do not alter the relational structure indicated by the arrows. Figure 2-11 is the result.

One is immediately struck by the degree to which the illustration of S_R in Fig. 2-11 coincides with the illustration of S_M in Fig. 2-3. In both, the display of the data structure is stripped to its bare essentials. For this reason we will illustrate all further linked representations S_R in the manner of Fig. 2-11. While it has been a bit tedious to work through these three different figures in detail, it is important to realize that, *provided the sequential location of a cell within computer storage has no significance with respect to the representation, then the three figures* (Figs. 2-9, 2-10, and 2-11) *are totally equivalent illustrations of the same data structure* S_R. Comparison of these three methods of display is important because, while the latter may be the way we, as designers, mentally visualize the data structure, the former will be the way the computer, in a typical core dump, will display it. In order to debug actual computer implementations one must be able to easily transform a display such as Fig. 2-9 into Fig. 2-11 and back again.

Since a linked computer representation such as Fig. 2-11 may be unfamiliar to many readers, it will be worthwhile to illustrate how a typical process might operate on it. We give below an algorithm to implement the DEAL subprocess. It is written in an Algol-like language, which will be used to describe all the processes of this book. It is usually a straightforward task to translate a process given in this language into some more standard language. Note in particular that NEXT is declared to be a field; hence, the expressions NEXT(TOP) and NEXT(CARD) are indirect references to the NEXT field of the cell whose address is the current value of TOP or CARD, respectively.

```
procedure deal   (top, hand, m, n);
integer array    hand [1:m];
integer          top, m, n;
```

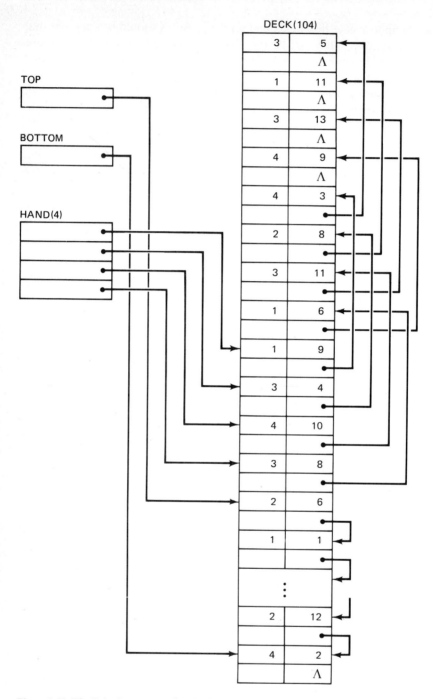

Figure 2-10 The linked representation S_R shown in Fig. 2-9, except that core addresses have been replaced by arrows in the drawing.

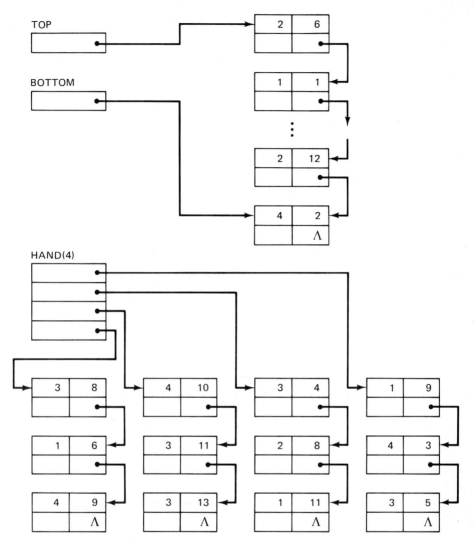

Figure 2-11 The linked representation S_R of Fig. 2-10, but drawn without regard to the sequential position of cells within DECK(104).

This procedure deals m separate hands of n cards each in the normal cyclic order, beginning with the top card.

```
begin
      integer   card;
      field      next;
      Initialize the hand pointers to the nullvalue;
      for j = 1 thru m do hand [j] ← nullvalue;
      Deal n rounds of cards;
      for i = 1 thru n do
            for j = 1 thru m do
```

Peel off the top card of the deck, if any, and place it on top of hand$_j$.

```
            if top = nullvalue then execute "deck exhausted";
α:          card ← top;
β:          top ← next(top);
γ:          next(card) ← hand[j];
δ:          hand[j] ← card;
      end
```

In this process, TOP and HAND are *global* reference pointers. TOP is passed as a parameter by the calling procedure so that this subprocess has a way of referencing (or finding or identifying) the first cell of the data structure. The process itself alters the data structure by subdividing the initially connected linear structure, the deck, into several separate connected components, the deck and the individual hands. It sets the pointers HAND[J] to reflect this new configuration and "passes" them back to the calling routine. Note that one additional *local* pointer (or variable) CARD is used to identify specific cells within the procedure as a temporary variable.

It is important that the reader perceive clearly that this process acting on the computer representation S_R, as illustrated in any of the preceding figures, really modifies the structure as expected—and how it does it. The sequence of four statements labeled α, β, γ, and δ are so typical that we will work through them in some detail. Figure 2-12(a) illustrates the configuration of the data structure after pointers HAND[J] have been initially set to the nullvalue. (This step is necessary. Why?) In step α the variable CARD is made to point to the same element as the variable TOP. The right side of statement β "follows" the NEXT link to find the next cell (card in the deck) and sets the variable TOP to point to this cell. Figure 2-12(b) illustrates the configuration after just these two statements have been executed. Note that by changing the value of a pointer, or link, as in step β, one effectively "erases" the existing link as illustrated by the dashed line of the figure. Statement γ sets the link in the NEXT field to the current value in HAND[J], thereby "erasing" that link and "removing" that card from the deck and placing it on top of the other cards in HAND[J], if any. Finally step δ resets the pointer HAND[J] to identify this new top card of the hand. Figure 2-12(c) shows this intermediate configuration after one card has

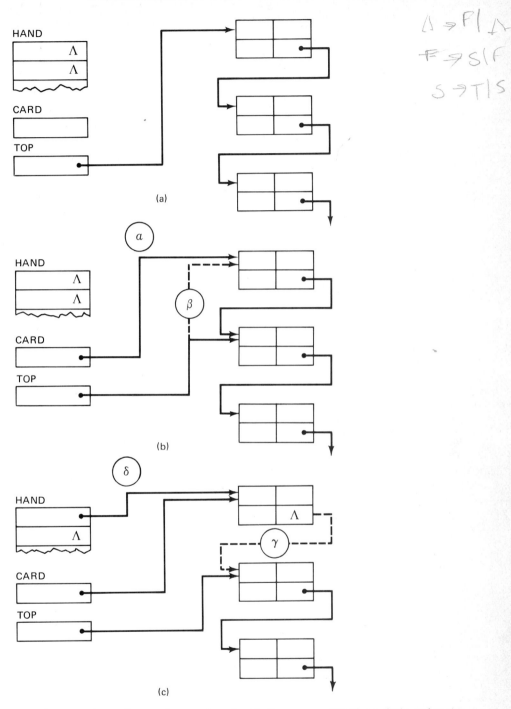

Figure 2-12(a), (b), (c) Intermediate configurations in the process of dealing a single card to one hand.

been dealt to the first hand. The reader should continue this operation until at least two or three cards have been dealt to each hand.

The linked representation we have just been examining is distinguished by the fact that actual storage addresses have been used to link the various cells of the data structure. Figure 2-9 emphasized this point. In consequence, indirect subprocedures must be used in coding the process to both fetch and store information associated with the NEXT field. There is an alternative.

The words from which the cells of the data structure are constructed existed originally as 104 consecutive words, perhaps in an array DECK[1:104]. Although we made no use of this sequential structure, it was there nevertheless and it could have been used in the following sense. Instead of referring to a cell by giving the address of its first word, we could have referenced it by giving the index (or subscript) of its first word in the singly subscripted array DECK. If we had followed this convention, the actual link and pointer values illustrated in Fig. 2-9 would have been different. For example, the value of the variable reference pointer TOP would have been the integer subscript 25 instead of the storage address 1025, because the first word of the cell being referenced is the twenty-fifth element of DECK. All other links and pointers would be similarly changed.

Although this alternative linked representation would mean that the drawing of the data structure as shown in Fig. 2-9 must be changed, Figs. 2-10 and 2-11 both remain valid. Both illustrate linked data structures, regardless of the convention used to link individual cells. But while the linked data structure remains "conceptually invariant," the processes operating on it must be changed. To reference a cell, the process must now know not only the index of the cell within the array, but the name of the array as well. Consequently, in coding the process DEAL we would have to pass as an additional parameter the name of the array DECK. Further, in every reference to a cell, this array name must be included. For instance, statement β would now be coded as

$$\beta': \text{top} \leftarrow \text{next}(\text{deck}[\text{top}])$$

where this is now regarded as a direct unpacking of the referenced field.

If we employ the convention of referencing cells by means of array subscripts instead of machine addresses, we are in effect "readdressing" that sequence of locations relative to an array name, and using this set of new addresses to denote explicit links. The array name functions as a kind of *base register*.

Is one convention superior to the other? The use of indices as cell addresses eliminates, for the most part, any need for indirect data referencing. This is of value, particularly if one is using a language such as Fortran to code processes. For this reason all Fortran texts which include introductory chapters on list processing follow this convention. On the other hand, it requires that at least one extra parameter be passed (possibly through COMMON) to every subprocess that operates on the data structure, and makes the representation very in-core–oriented. While superiority may be largely a matter of personal choice, we pedagogically prefer to use actual machine addresses for three reasons. First, it gives the impression of being closer to the implementing hardware. Second, the concept of indirect addressing (or reference) is an important one and is well worth mastering. Finally, using machine addresses when working with in-core data structures makes the transition somewhat easier when one begins to consider larger data structures, part of which must be resident on peripheral storage devices. For consistency, this text will always follow this convention: *The address of a word (or cell) will always mean its actual machine address (or virtual address), and a link or pointer field must always be large enough to hold any such legal address.*

EXERCISES FOR CHAPTER 2

* **2-1** Write a Fortran main program that creates a deck of cards, represented as a linked data structure, and routines to both DEAL m hands of n cards each and DISPLAY the resulting configuration. The main program should also call two other subroutines REPLAC and SHUFFL (which replace hands in the deck and shuffle it, respectively) to complete the simulation cycle. Code these routines and generate a series of bridge, poker, or go-fish hands. (An efficient shuffling routine is a bit of a challenge. Several seemingly reasonable approaches yield, in special cases, ill-formed data structures. Be careful.)

2-2 Show that the shuffling procedure of the preceding problem actually generates random decks with a uniform distribution (that is, any given sequence of cards is equally likely to occur). This difficult problem may be approached in either of two ways:

(*a*) a formal mathematical proof of randomness (assuming a uniform random number generator), or

(*b*) empirical evidence of uniform randomness, based on statistics collected from a series of shuffled decks.

2-3 There are almost limitless ways to modify the simulation of various card games based on Fig. 2-4 and the basic operators DEAL, REPLAC, and SHUFFL described in Exercise 2-1. The play of hands for games such as blackjack, go-fish, etc., is relatively straightforward and fun. The play of poker hands, including their evaluation, betting, and drawing new cards (in draw poker) demands considerably more thought and sophistication. The decision processes involved should rely heavily on statistical inference and artificial intelligence. The play of bridge hands is equally challenging, and the aspect of bidding adds even more. A successful bidding procedure demands considerable research into information theory, since one is faced with the problem of devising a code that will convey maximum information about the hand over a noisy channel (opponents also introduce signals) of limited bandwidth (only a finite number of bids are possible). Such research is probably of thesis level.

* **2-4** Almost all the shifting of information inherent in a DEAL process operating on the sequential representation can be eliminated by simply letting the "top" card be the "last" card in the array, not the "first." Redraw Fig. 2-7 using this convention, and write a simple procedure to deal n cards to each of m hands.

* **2-5** The drawings of Figs. 2-2 and 2-3 subtly induced us to store the actual functional values of the assignments $f_1(x)$ and $f_2(x)$ within a field of the cell corresponding to x. But a drawing, as shown in the accompanying figure, suggests an alternative method of representing these assignment functions in which information sufficient to retrieve the function value (e.g., a storage location) or to generate the function value (e.g., a process entry point and one or more arguments) is stored in the fields. Design such an alternative computer representation S_R in more detail, and give statements that would determine the rank and suit of any cell for a process operating on your data structure.

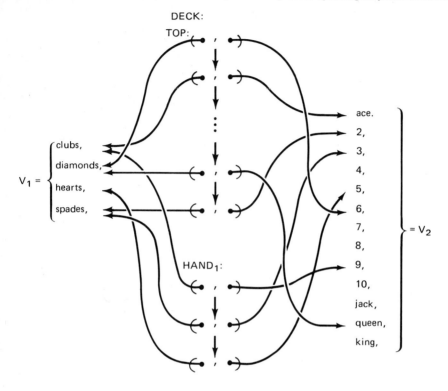

THREE

LINEAR DATA STRUCTURES

Linear, or totally ordered, data structures are probably the nicest of all computer data structures. They are without question the most commonly used data structure. They appear under a wide variety of names. Mathematicians would typically call them *sequences,* or if they contain a fixed number of elements, *vectors.* Linked representations of linear structures are normally called *lists* by computer scientists, while sequential representations are called *singly subscripted arrays.* In formal languages they appear under the guise of *strings,* while automata theory refers to *stacks.* In the design and analysis of operating systems one often speaks of *chains* and *queues.*

3-1 LINEAR RELATIONS AND LISTS

These constitute a bewildering collection of names, and before using them it might be wise to get a firm grasp on just what we are talking about. Total order relations—that is, partial orders which satisfy the additional law of dichotomy—are familiar kinds of relations. Intuitively, given a totally ordered set, one can pick any two elements x and y and ask the question: Is x "less than" y or is y "less than" x? The real numbers and the integers are two totally ordered sets.

Graphs for which the path relation ρ is a total order relation are also quite familiar. Because they are linelike, as illustrated in Fig. 3-1, they are frequently

Figure 3-1 A linear graph.

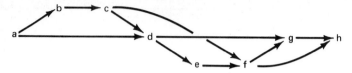

Figure 3-2 A totally ordered graph.

called *linear* graphs. But we should note that the path relation on the graph of Fig. 3-2 is also a total order, even though the graph is not very linelike. Therefore we introduce a formal distinction and say that a graph G is *linear* if (*a*) the path relation ρ on G is a total order, and (*b*) G is a basic graph.

If P is any totally ordered set of elements, then by Theorem 1-8 there exists a unique linear graph G on P. Because linear graphs and linear data structures are so common in computer applications, one would like a better characterization of them. Again intuitively, a graph is linear if for each point x, there is a unique succeeding point y such that $(x, y) \in E$. The relation E can then be viewed as a kind of successor function. Formally stated in terms of our left- and right-neighbor notation, this becomes the following theorem.

> **Theorem 3-1** A finite graph G = (P, E) is linear if and only if
> (*a*) there exists exactly one point $x \in P$ such that $L(x) = \emptyset$,
> (*b*) for all $y \in P$, $|L(y)| \leq 1$, $|R(y)| \leq 1$, and
> (*c*) G is connected.
> That is, each point y has a unique "preceding" and a unique "following" point.

These two results define what we formally mean by a linear structure, whether we call it a sequence, vector, singly subscripted array, string, chain, or the more commonly used term of list. More precisely, a *simple list* L is any linearly ordered data structure. A *sublist* L' of L is any *connected* subgraph of L.† For the present we shall refer to simple lists as just lists. A more general list concept will be given in Chap. 8, but for now the distinction is unimportant.

The abstract model of any linear structure will always look like that of Fig. 3-3. The only variation can be in its number of elements and the nature of the

---

†The definition of *sublist* as a sequence of *consecutive* elements is standard in computer science; it also coincides with the normal meaning of a *substring*. However, it is distinct from the traditional meaning of a *subsequence*, which is used to denote any arbitrary subset of elements (with the same relativized ordering). Our concept of a sublist would be more likely called a *segment* or *interval* in mathematics.

$$(f_1, \ldots, f_n) \longrightarrow (f_1, \ldots, f_n) \longrightarrow \cdots \longrightarrow (f_1, \ldots, f_n) \longrightarrow (f_1, \ldots, f_n)$$

Figure 3-3 Prototype model of all lists.

assignment functions $f_1, \ldots, f_n$ defined on its point (or edge) set. Therefore, a declaration statement of the form

REAL X[1:10]

completely describes the linear structure X as consisting of 10 elements with a single assignment function into the set V of real numbers. (Note that the abstract models shown in Figs. 2-1 and 2-2 are also linear structures, but that S_M, shown in Fig. 2-3, is not. Why not?)

Linear structures are both so ubiquitous and so simple that there exist a wide variety of alternative computer representations. Recall that in Chap. 1 it was claimed that the "best" computer representation will normally be governed by the kinds of procedures that will be subsequently defined to operate on the data structure. For this reason, lists are often functionally classified according to their intended uses. In particular, one considers the operations of adding elements to, or deleting elements from, the linearly ordered set. Thus a simple list is called (depending on its use) a

1. n-*tuple* (or *vector,* or *singly subscripted array*) if elements can be neither added nor deleted; that is, its size is fixed;
2. *stack,* if all addition and deletion of elements occurs at *one* end;
3. *queue,* if all additions occur at one end, and all deletions occur at the other end;
4. *deque,* if additions and deletions can occur at the ends only.

Stacks are also known as LIFO (last-in, first-out) lists, and queues are called FIFO (first-in, first-out) lists. Both these terms, which are common in business data processing, arise from different accounting procedures used in inventory control processes. The value $f_i(x)$ of an assignment at any point or element of a list may be changed at will. In the case of n-tuples, most programming languages do this by means of an assignment statement; in other cases, a separate routine may be necessary. However, common conventions associated with the use of stacks often forbid, for formal reasons, the retrieval or alteration of assigned values save for those of the designated end element. The last term *deque* (which is pronounced "deck") actually is an abbreviation of "double-ended queue."

3-2 LINKED REPRESENTATION OF LISTS

The linked representation of lists is straightforward, since we need only allocate to each element $p_i \in P$ of S_M a single cell in S_R. Further, to represent the linear relation on P one needs, in general, only a single link field to link to the next element in the set. Figure 3-4 illustrates a linked list of four elements identified by the symbolic string LIST. Such identifiers are most easily established by declaring a one-word variable, say LIST, which is thereby

LIST

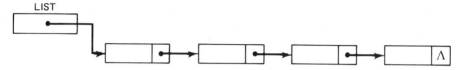

Figure 3-4 A simply linked representation S_R of a list S_M.

"known" to the program, and let it point to the least element of the linear structure. The program can thus access the least element by means of this reference pointer, and by following links it can access each succeeding element. Thus the pointer LIST really serves to identify the entire linear structure. Notice in Fig. 3-4 that each element is explicitly linked to the next following cell, but not to the immediately preceding cell. Such a list is said to be *simply linked*. If we were to add a second link field to each cell indicating the preceding cell, it would be called *doubly linked*.

The actual size of the representing cells depends on the amount and nature of the information to be associated with each element. Many times a single word is sufficient, with the information stored in the leftmost field of the word and the next link stored in the rightmost field. Alternatively one might need two or three word cells, as illustrated in Fig. 3-5. Any portion of any word of the cell can be used as the link field NEXT. But for the sample procedures of this section we will assume the lists are always linked through the rightmost field of the *first* word of the cell.

Let us now consider various operations on lists. In these procedures we will assume the existence of two special routines. The integer function GIVEME returns as its functional value the address of a cell that can be used in building data structures. The second procedure is a subroutine TAKEIT, which "gives back" a cell that is no longer needed. We are somewhat guilty of putting the cart before the horse, since we will carefully describe the implementation of these two routines, together with a general system to handle dynamic cell allocation, in the next section. But while they are easy to code, they are based on ideas that we first develop here. GIVEME and TAKEIT will be used throughout this text.

Assume that we will use a list as a stack, adding and deleting all elements at a single end. It is customary to call the "dynamic" end of the stack its top, and to visualize a structure as illustrated in Fig. 3-6. When we add an element to the end of a stack, we commonly say that we are "pushing an element down" on the stack. For this reason these are often called *pushdown stacks*. Deletion of

f_1	NEXT
f_2	
f_3	

Figure 3-5 A typical three-word cell in a linked list representation.

STACK

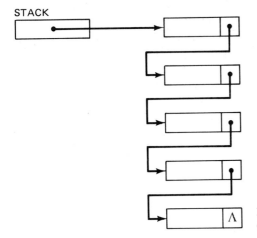

Figure 3-6 Configuration of a stack with five elements.

an element is frequently referred to as "popping" the "top" element. (This terminology arises, by analogy, from the spring-loaded stack of plates often found in cafeterias. New plates added to the top of the stack push the entire stack down. As plates are removed from the top, the stack pops up.) The following routines PUSHDOWN and POPTOP will respectively push down and pop off a single word of information, called VALUE, from the top of a stack whose name (reference pointer) is passed as parameter. Consequently the stack representation will require two word cells, as shown in Fig. 3-7. The left half of the first word is simply unused.

procedure pushdown$_1$ (stack, value);
pointer stack;
variable value;

This routine pushes the value of the scalar variable value down on the stack.

begin
    pointer cell;
    field   next, data;
α: cell ←giveme(celsiz);
β: next(cell) ←stack;
γ: data(cell) ←value;
δ: stack ←cell;
    exit;
    end

Unused	NEXT
DATA	

Figure 3-7 The cell format assumed by the procedures PUSHDOWN and POPTOP.

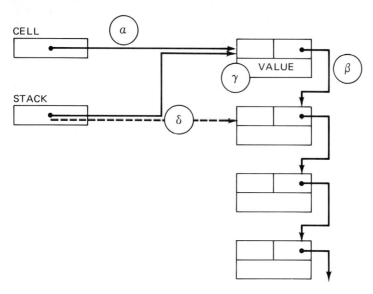

Figure 3-8 The configuration of the stack after executing PUSHDOWN.

In this simple procedure the value of the temporary variable **CELL** is the address of an available cell which has been allocated in statement α. Both statements β and γ indirectly store a link and the information in the corresponding fields of the cell. Figure 3-8 shows the configuration of the stack after executing PUSHDOWN. Edges have been labeled by the statement that created them. The procedure to pop the top element is nearly as easy.

function poptop$_1$ (stack);
pointer stack;

This (incomplete) procedure returns as its functional value the value stored in the top element of the stack. The element itself is released.

begin
    pointer cell;
    field next, data;
    cell ←stack;
    poptop ←data(cell);
ϵ: stack ←next(cell);
    call takeit (cell, celsiz);
    exit;
    end

As simple as this procedure is, close inspection will reveal that it will not always work! Suppose the stack is empty, that there are *no* elements in the stack. In this case the statements of the procedure are meaningless and their behavior unpredictable. Clearly we must check for the possibility of an empty stack and handle this case appropriately. First, however, we must determine how the procedure will recognize when the stack is empty, and then we must determine what will be an appropriate response.

To determine a condition to signal the existence of an empty stack, consider the application of the function POPTOP to a stack consisting of only a single element. From the configuration of Fig. 3-6 we see that its link field will contain the nullvalue, since there is no next element. Consequently POPTOP will first assign as its function value the value of this top, and only, element. Then statement ϵ assigns to the reference pointer STACK the value of the link field NEXT, which is in this case the nullvalue. Finally the cell is returned. Thus the stack will be empty if and only if the value of STACK is the nullvalue. This condition is easily tested.

Now suppose the procedure POPTOP finds that the stack is empty. What should it do? In particular, what function value should be returned? Several possibilities exist here. The procedure could simply terminate the run with an error condition. A more plausible action would be simply to return the nullvalue as its function value, thereby signaling the calling procedure that the stack was empty. That higher-level routine can then, and under these conditions *must,* test the returned value to decide appropriate action. We choose this latter course. The revised POPTOP becomes as follows:

function poptop$_2$ (stack);
pointer stack;

This function returns as its functional value, the value of the top element of the stack. The element itself is released.

begin
    pointer cell;
    field next, data;
    if stack = nullvalue
        then poptop ←nullvalue
        else cell ←stack;
            poptop ←data(cell);
            stack ←next(cell);
            call takeit (cell, celsiz)
    exit;
    end

Given this convention for handling empty stacks, we now look back to check our coding of PUSHDOWN. If we push a single element down on an initially empty stack, statement β will set in the link field of this only, and last, element of the stack the current value of the pointer **STACK**. Since it will contain by convention the nullvalue, so too will the link field, and a well-formed list will result.

Unlike many numerical algorithms, <u>virtually all procedures that operate on data structures must check for</u> *boundary conditions*. This admittedly imprecise term is used to denote a variety of situations in which a "well-formed" data structure is close to being an "ill-formed" structure. In particular, we will use the term *boundary condition* to refer to that state when the data structure is empty, or nearly so, and when it is full, or nearly so. Given the present state of the art, there is no known systematic way of checking for appropriate boundary conditions. Much of the current art of programming with data structures consists of including sufficient tests to discover all plausible boundary conditions— together with many implausible ones as well!† The discovery and handling of boundary conditions will be a recurrent theme; it is one of the most common oversights of beginning programmers.

Finally we emphasize the use of the *nullvalue* to denote the nonexistence, or the "emptiness," of something. It is used in the data structure to indicate that there is no next element. It was returned as a functional value to indicate that the function is undefined, given the current empty state of its argument. The nullvalue will be used so frequently in our procedures that it is invariably treated as a kind of system constant that is passed to all routines as a global variable, say through labeled common. Recall that the nullvalue must be small enough to fit into any link field and must be readily distinguishable from valid values. Unfortunately, in many applications these two constraints are incompatible. For example, the most commonly used nullvalue, zero, may be a perfectly valid functional value for a routine such as **POPTOP**. For this reason one often implements two distinct nullvalues—a partial-word nullvalue to be used in constructing the data structures themselves, and a whole-word nullvalue to be passed between procedures. While we will seldom distinguish between these two types of nullvalue, it is nevertheless a valuable programming habit.

Let us now examine the basic operations of adding and deleting elements when the list is treated as a queue. As a concrete example one can visualize people lined up at a serving counter waiting for service, or jobs queued up in a multiprogramming environment waiting for some resource to be allocated by the operating system. If we assume that the tasks (or people) enter the queue at the left (or rear) of the line, and gradually work forward to the right (or front) of the queue where they are finally served and leave the queue, then the abstract model might look like Fig. 3-9. Appropriate assignment functions that associate data with individual elements of the structure might be: f_1, an identification of the individual in the queue (e.g., a task number in a scheduling queue); f_2, the time of entry into the queue (for generating statistical analyses in a simulation

---

†A corollary to the well-known *Murphy's law* is: If a procedure can encounter an ill-formed data structure, it will.

Left : Rear : (f_i) ⟶ (f_i) ⟶ $\cdots$ ⟶ (f_i) ⟶ (f_i) Right: Front

Figure 3-9 The abstract model S_M of a queue.

model); f_3, a priority assignment; or other similar information. For concreteness we will assume only that an identification number (small enough to fit into a link field of the cell) is present.

As in the stack example, a reference pointer, say REAR, can be made to point to the left end and thereby access the entire list. But since we will be working with both ends, it would seem more reasonable to use two pointers that will give immediate access to either end without having to work through the list, element by element, to find the other end. Consequently we implement two separate pointer variables, say FRONT and REAR, each of which references its respective end. This representation is illustrated in Fig. 3-10. With this representation, the routine to add elements, which we now call ENTER, can be seen to be virtually identical to that of PUSHDOWN in the stack example.

procedure   enter₁ (idnum, rear);
integer   idnum;
pointer   rear;

This routine adds a new element, with assigned data value "idnum," to the rear of the queue.

begin
    pointer   cell;
    field   idfld, next;
    cell ←giveme(celsiz);
    idfld(cell) ←idnum;
    next(cell) ←rear;
    rear ←cell;
    exit;
    end

Inefficient queue system

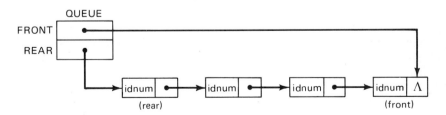

Figure 3-10 A computer representation S_R of the queue of Fig. 3-9.

The process of deleting elements from the queue, however, appears to be a much more involved operation than that of POPTOP.

integer function   serve$_1$ (front, rear);
pointer   front, rear;

This function deletes (or serves) the element at the front end of the queue by releasing the cell and returning the associated value as its functional value.

begin
      pointer   cell, nextcell, prev;
      field   idfld, next;
      cell ←front;
      serve ←idfld(cell);

      We must now "walk through" the elements of the list to find that cell immediately preceding the front of the queue, since that will be the new front.

α: prev ←loc(rear);
β: nextcell ←next(prev);
        if nextcell = cell **then go to** γ;
        prev ←nextcell;
        go to β;
γ: front ←prev;
      call takeit (cell, celsiz);
      exit;
      end

If the queue is at all long, say 20 or more elements, it is evident that the loop beginning at statement β to access the next-to-last element may be quite time-consuming. Moreover, we included a separate reference pointer to the front of the queue just to prevent this kind of exhaustive search! Something is drastically wrong with the "natural" way of representing queues!

But before we correct this major fault, it will pay us to examine this relatively inefficient process more closely. There will be situations where one cannot avoid accessing and examining each element of a list one by one, and it is important that the effect of each of the statements α through γ be clearly understood.† Note especially that the variable PREV always identifies the cell previously encountered before the cell NEXTCELL currently being examined. Consequently statement α initializes this loop by treating the pointer variable REAR *as if it were a cell in the list.* This very useful trick works, however, only if one has designed the data structure itself with some care; in particular, the NEXT field must be right-justified in the first word of the cell. Why? (The use of *header cells,* introduced in Sec. 4-2, will eliminate the need for such tricks.)

---

†If the reader is coding in a language that permits the **while** control statement, then the loop beginning with β can be replaced by the "cleaner" statement
    while next(prev) ≠ cell **do** prev ←next(prev);

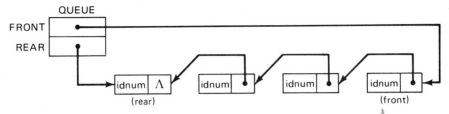

Figure 3-11 An alternative representation S_R of the queue of Fig. 3-9.

efficient queue configuration

We now return to the problem of efficiently accessing the next-to-last element of the list. Surprisingly this cannot be done by altering the process; we must instead redesign the computer representation of the queue itself. First we note that we are not really looking for the next-to-last cell, but rather the "next-to-front" cell. Such verbal misdirection can be fatal. The second major clue to the redesign lies in the observation that while ENTER sets the link field NEXT, corresponding to the next-in-line relation, neither procedure ever follows that link (save in the loop to find the preceding cell). We really want a computer representation such as Fig. 3-11, in which all the links are reversed. Although the computer representation S_R is no longer an exact replica of the "natural" abstract model S_M, shown in Fig. 3-9, it is a representation that facilitates computer processing. At the same time that we rewrite ENTER and SERVE to reflect this revised queue configuration we should consider the possible boundary conditions that were ignored in these early versions.

Since SERVE will remove elements only from the front of the queue and leave the rear unchanged, it is natural to code the SERVE process in such a way that no reference is made to the pointer REAR. But consider the nearly empty queue consisting of a single element as shown in Fig. 3-12a. Execution of the process SERVE would result in an "empty" queue as shown in Fig. 3-12b. The dashed lines indicate the released cell that has been returned to the "system" for possible use in some other data structure. But because REAR was not altered in SERVE, this variable still points to this nonexistent cell. Note that if SERVE were to be called again, the natural test for the empty boundary condition,

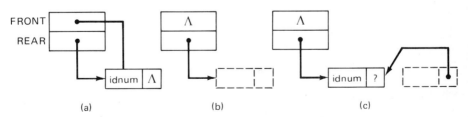

Figure 3-12 (*a*) Single element queue before executing SERVE. (*b*) "Empty" queue after executing SERVE. (*c*) "Singleton" queue after executing ENTER.

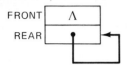

Figure 3-13 A configuration of reference pointers when the list is empty.

if front = nullvalue **then** . . .

will function correctly. But if ENTER were executed, the ill-formed singleton queue of Fig. 3-12 would result. Clearly a completely "natural" approach is dangerous.

SERVE, if called to remove an element from an empty queue, must check that the pointer FRONT is not null. Similarly, if ENTER adds an element to a previously empty queue, it must be aware of this condition so that it can reset the pointer FRONT (which it would normally leave strictly alone). It would suffice for ENTER to just check FRONT for the nullvalue and act appropriately. We will, however, play one more small trick. If the queue is empty, the pointer FRONT will contain the nullvalue, but the pointer REAR will be set to point to itself, as shown in Fig. 3-13. Convince yourself that the following versions of ENTER and SERVE will now work correctly—especially statement δ in ENTER. (Note that this trick again works *only* because NEXT is right-justified in the first word of the cell.)

procedure   enter₂ (idnum, front, rear);
integer   idnum;
pointer   front, rear;

This routine adds a new element, with assigned data value "idnum," to the rear of a queue.

begin
    pointer   cell;
    field   idfld, next;
    cell ←giveme(celsiz);
    idfld(cell) ←idnum;
δ: next(rear) ←cell;
    next(cell) ←nullvalue;
    rear ←cell;
    if front = nullvalue **then** front ←cell;
    exit;
    end

integer function   serve₂ (front, rear);
pointer   front, rear;

This function deletes (serves) the element at the front end of a queue by releasing the cell and returning the associated data value as its functional value. An empty queue is denoted by setting the "front" pointer to the nullvalue, and "rear" pointing to the variable itself.

```
begin
     pointer   cell, nextcell;
     field     idfld, next;
     cell ←front;
     if cell = nullvalue
          then   serve ←nullvalue
          else   serve ←idfld(cell);
                 nextcell ←next(cell);
                 call takeit (cell, celsiz);
                 front ←nextcell;
                 if nextcell = nullvalue then rear ←loc(rear);
     exit;
     end
```

The implementation of these processes points up the following important principle, which will become even more apparent in successive chapters: *The obvious abstract structure* S_M *should not always be translated literally when designing a computer representation* S_R. They also demonstrate the importance of checking the behavior of *all* processes and the status of *all* pointers at, or near, the boundary conditions.

It has been suggested that the queue and the processes of the preceding discussion might be viewed as part of a simulation of an operating system, with its scheduling and resource allocation queues. Another characteristic feature of operating systems is the *interrupt* facility, by which certain tasks take precedence in processing queues over other tasks that have been waiting in line. (If we are modeling people waiting in a service line, this undignified process is simply called "butting into line.") Let us consider how we can implement an interrupt process in the simulation. (Of course the linear data structure should technically no longer be called a queue, since we will be adding elements "in the middle" as well as at one end. It is simply a list. Nevertheless it is often customary to continue calling these structures queues.)

If we know the cell address of that element in the queue, next to which the new task element is to be inserted, and if the new task is to be inserted following that element, then the implementing process is quite simple. Verify that the next procedure inserts the new element into the queue (list), as shown in Fig. 3-14, by only altering two link fields.

```
procedure   interrupt (idnum, cell);
integer     idnum;
pointer     cell;
```

This routine inserts a new element into the list immediately following the specified cell.

```
begin
     pointer   newcell;
     field     idfld, next;
     newcell ←giveme(celsiz);
     idfld(newcell) ←idnum;
```

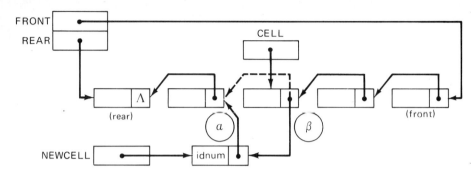

Figure 3-14 Insertion of a new element into the "middle" of a queue (list) by the process INTER-RUPT.

α: next(newcell) ← next(cell);
β: next(cell) ← newcell;
   exit;
   end

Notice that the order of execution of the two statements α and β is crucial. Reverse them and the process will yield an ill-formed data structure. Notice also that we did not pass as a parameter to this process a pointer to either end of the list. This seems somewhat suspicious, and closer inspection of the routine reveals that it will not work in the special case when CELL denotes the "rear" cell of the queue (a kind of boundary condition). Correction to handle this case, which is not really an interrupt, is in any case straightforward and is left as an exercise.

   Execution of the INTERRUPT procedure is conditional on two strong assumptions. One assumption was that the new cell would be inserted immediately following the specified cell of the list. Were the new cell to precede the specified cell, then INTERRUPT would have to "walk" through the list, with code identical to that of our initial SERVE$_1$ routine, simply to locate the cell PREV that immediately precedes CELL in the list. These remarks, together with problems encountered in adding and deleting elements from the ends of the queue, point out a very strong asymmetry associated with processes that operate on simply linked lists.

   The other assumption, on which the process INTERRUPT was based, is that the location of the new element (in terms of the cell address of an existing element) would be known. This is a very strong condition, and a somewhat dubious one. It seems much more likely that INTERRUPT would be passed as parameter only the identification number of the task that the new task is to precede or follow. It seems even more reasonable to expect that INTERRUPT would be passed the id number and priority (assuming that such values are assigned to elements of the queue) of the new task, and that it would be inserted in the queue immediately preceding all tasks with lower priority (see Exercise 3-3). In either case it will be necessary to "walk through" the list in order to locate the proper position of the new element. And given such a search, it becomes irrelevant whether the new cell is inserted preceding or following the located cell.

EXERCISES FOR SECTION 3-2

3-1 Code a routine PUSHDN and a function POPTOP. (Assume the existence of GIVEME and TAKEIT, which will be given in the next section.) Code a routine TOP(STACK) that merely returns the value of the "top" element, but does not alter the stack itself. Suppose that two or more values (assignment functions) were associated with each element of the stack. How would these routines have to be modified?

3-2 Recode the procedure INTERRUPT so that it will function correctly in the boundary situation where the value of the parameter CELL is the address of the "rear" cell in the queue.

3-3 Code an interrupt process with calling sequence

INTERRUPT (FRONT, REAR, PRIORITY, IDNUM, TIME)

which will enter a new task with specified priority, identification, and time of entry into the queue in its proper position as shown in the accompanying figure.

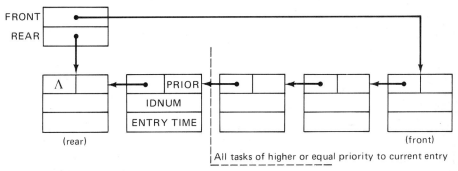

Ex. 3-3

*****3-4** Write a short procedure REVERSE(FIRST, LAST) that will accept as input any list that is simply linked, as shown below, and reverse the order of the elements. Note that the list may be empty, consist of a singleton element, or consist of two or more cells.

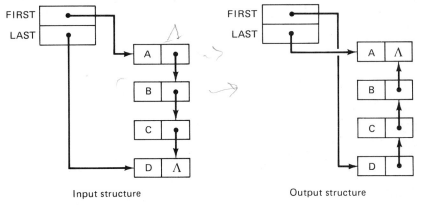

Input structure   Output structure

Ex. 3-4

3-3 APPLICATIONS OF SIMPLY LINKED LISTS

Cells are the building blocks of linked data structures. To design useful data structures, and to implement processes that will operate on them, one needs a source (or pool) of available cells from which individual cells may be requested as needed and to which they may be returned. While some operating systems offer the user this kind of dynamic memory allocation facility, most do not. But this is not essential. Applications programmers may easily code their own cluster of dynamic allocation routines and include them with their own programs. Indeed, considering the ease with which this is done, it is surprising that this technique is not seen more often in practice. In this initial effort we will design a package to allocate only cells of a single fixed size. It will be sufficient for many of the problems that will be encountered in this text, as well as most applications found in practice. Later, in Chap. 10, we will investigate modifications which will permit dynamic allocation of variably sized cells.

Initially a large block of consecutive words must be reserved from which the pool of available cells, or simply *free pool*, may be created. This is most simply done by dimensioning a singly subscripted array in the main program (which "knows" the presumed size of the data structures) and passing both the name and dimension of the array to an initializing routine of the allocation cluster—call it SETUP—which subdivides the words of the array into cells. The array is never again referenced by any program.

Suppose one has a collection of cells, some of which have been allocated to other processes and some of which are unused and are free to be allocated. Some way must be devised to keep track of those that are unused and that may be allocated on request. Perhaps the easiest management scheme is to link all available cells together in the form of a list. For this reason the free pool is often called the *list of available space* or the LAVS. Since cells will be removed from, or returned to, this list one at a time, the list may be organized as either a stack or a queue. In some kinds of list-processing applications there is a slight advantage to organizing the free-pool list as a queue. For this reason we will use a queue organization in contrast to a stack organization.

Three subprocesses are required in the dynamic allocation cluster. An initializing procedure SETUP, which is called but once in any execution, creates an initial queue of appropriately sized cells in the array of consecutive words that was reserved by the main program and passed as parameter to the process. The function GIVEME allocates a single cell by removing it from the end of the list and returning its address as functional value. The subroutine TAKEIT accepts as its parameter the address of a cell to be returned to the free pool and adds it to the other end of the queue.

Three design questions remain. Through what field should we link the free-pool queue? Our choice will be the rightmost link field of the first word. How shall the reference pointers be handled? This is a fairly important question, since to maintain the integrity of the free pool, *only* these three routines should ever have access to its cells. All allocation and deallocation should be handled by these two procedures alone. Our preference is to place the reference pointers in a private block in labeled common, to be shared by only these three procedures. An alternative (if you have a compiler that will permit it) is to include all three procedures in a single subprogram with separate entry points. Finally there is the question of how GIVEME should handle an allocation request if the queue is empty. Such a condition is called *overflow*, in that the amount of storage requested has overflowed what is available. One possibility would be to pass back the nullvalue and let the requesting process decide on appropriate action. But in practice, the only appropriate action is invariably to terminate the run. On overflow we prefer to let GIVEME print some nasty message and terminate execution itself.

Dynamic allocation of cells can thus be implemented by the following three procedures.

procedure setup   (array, dim, celsiz);
integer array   array [1:dim];
integer   dim, celsiz;

This procedure creates a free pool of available cells (each cell consisting of "celsiz" words) in the specified "array" that has been reserved by the main program. The cells are linked in the form of a queue. Cells are taken from the top and returned to the bottom. The pointers "top" and "bottom" in labeled common serve as the bookkeeping links between the three routines that access the free pool.
top   = first available free cell,
bottom = last available free cell.

begin
      pointer   bottom, cell, first, last, nextcell, top;
      integer   size;
      field   next;
      common/nulval/null;
      common/frpool/bottom, top, size;
      if dim < celsiz **then print** "error message";
      size ←celsiz;
      nextcell ←null;
      last ←cell ←loc(array [dim]) − (celsiz − 1);
      first ←loc(array[1]);

      Link cells in descending order of their addresses.

α: **if** cell < first **then go to** β;
            next(cell) ←nextcell;
            nextcell ←cell;
            cell ←cell −celsiz;
            go to α;

      Set the top and bottom pointers.

β: top ←nextcell;
      bottom ←last;

```
        exit;
        end
```

integer function giveme   (celsiz);
integer   celsiz;

This function removes the top cell from the queue of available cells and delivers its address as function value. Note that the link field of the cell is set to null before returning it, so that the requesting process will not get an entry into the free pool.

```
begin
        pointer      bottom, cell, nextcell, top;
        integer      size;
        field        next;
        common/frpool/bottom, top, size;
        common/nulval/null;
        if celsiz ≠ size then print "error message";
        cell ←top;
        if cell =null
            then print "overflow message";
                    stop execution;
        nextcell ←next(cell);
        if nextcell =null then bottom ←loc(bottom);
        top ←nextcell;
        next(cell) ←null;
        giveme ←cell;
        exit;
        end
```

procedure   takeit (cell, celsiz);
pointer cell;
integer celsiz;

This procedure returns a single cell, whose address is passed as parameter, to the bottom of the queue of available cells.

```
begin
        pointer      bottom, top;
        integer      size;
        field        next;
        common/frpool/bottom, top, size;
        if celsiz ≠ size then print "error message";
        if top =null then top ←cell;
        next(bottom) ← cell;
        next(cell) ←null;
        bottom ←cell;
        cell ←null;
        exit;
        end
```

Not surprisingly, these procedures, GIVEME and TAKEIT, bear a striking resemblance to SERVE and ENTER, which were developed in the preceding section. Figure 3-15 illustrates a typical Fortran program that might be used to test the execution of these three allocation routines. Note the use of SETUP, GIVEME, TAKEIT, and the primitive field manipulating routines. An additional routine DUMPFS has been included to dump snapshots of the cells in the free pool, both those that are in use and those available for allocation. Figure 3-16 shows one such dump. (This dump was generated on a CDC 6400 with 60 bit words, so it is unlikely to be identical to dumps generated by your own system.) The hand-drawn links indicate its current configuration after a number of cells have been allocated, returned, and reallocated.

Figure 3-15 A sample Fortran program to test the procedures GIVEME and TAKEIT. (A representative version of SETUP and a dump procedure are also shown.)

```
          SUBROUTINE SETUP (SPACE, DIM, CELSIZ)
          INTEGER    SPACE(DIM),DIM,CELSIZ
C
C         THIS SUBROUTINE CREATES A FREE-POOL OF AVAILABLE CELLS (EACH CELL
C         CONSISTING OF *CELSIZ* WORDS EACH) IN THE ARRAY *SPACE* WHICH
C         HAS BEEN RESERVED BY THE CALLING ROUTINE.
C
C             THE CELLS ARE LINKED (THROUGH RIGHT FIELD OF THE FIRST WORD
C             OF EACH CELL) IN THE FORM OF A QUEUE.  CELLS ARE TAKEN FROM
C             THE TOP AND RETURNED TO THE BOTTOM.
C
C             THE POINTERS *TOP* AND *BOTTOM* IN LABELED COMMON SERVE
C             AS THE BOOKKEEPING LINK BETWEEN THE PRIMITIVE ROUTINES
C             WHICH ACCESS THIS FREE POOL OF AVAILABLE CELLS.
C             IN ADDITION THE RELEVANT FIELD DESCRIPTORS ARE ALSO PASSED.
C
          INTEGER    BOTTOM,CELL,LAST,NULL,NXTCEL,SIZE,TOP
          INTEGER    FIELD,NEXT
          COMMON /FRPOOL/ NEXT,TOP,BOTTOM,SIZE
          COMMON /NULVAL/ NULL
          COMMON /FPDUMP/ SIZEFP,FIRST
          INTEGER    FIRST,SIZEFP
C
C         ESTABLISH FIELD DESCRIPTION OF FREE POOL LINKS
C
          NEXT = FIELD(1, 0, 18)

          IF(DIM .LT. CELSIZ) GO TO 901
          SIZE = CELSIZ
          NXTCEL = NULL
          LAST = CELL = LOC(SPACE(DIM)) - (CELSIZ-1)
          FIRST = LOC(SPACE(1))
C
C         LINK CELLS IN DESCENDING ORDER OF THEIR ADDRESSES
C
   101        IF(CELL .LT. FIRST) GO TO 102
              CALL STORE (CELL, NEXT, NXTCEL)
              NXTCEL = CELL
              CELL = CELL-CELSIZ
              GO TO 101
C
C     SET TOP AND BOTTOM POINTERS
C
   102 TOP = NXTCEL
       BOTTOM = LAST
C
C     ESTABLISH VALUES IN /DEBUG/ THAT CONTROL DUMPFP
C
       FIRST = TOP
       SIZEFP = BOTTOM - TOP + CELSIZ
       RETURN
C
```

```
    901 WRITE (6,902) DIM,CELSIZ
    902 FORMAT (1H0,*ARRAY SIZE OF *,I3,* WORDS IS INSUFFICIENT TO *,
      1          *CREATE A FREE POOL OF *,I3,* WORD CELLS*)
        STOP
        END


        SUBROUTINE DUMPFP
C       THIS ROUTINE DUMPS THE FREE POOL OF AVAILABLE CELLS .
C       ITS PRIMARY USE IS FOR DEBUG PURPOSES.
C
        COMMON /FPDUMP/ DIM,FIRST
        COMMON /FRPOOL/ NEXT,TOP,BOTTOM,CELSIZ
        INTEGER   CELSIZ,DIM,FIRST
        INTEGER   ADDR

        WRITE (6,1)
      1 FORMAT (1H0,*DUMP OF THE WORDS IN THE FREE-POOL, IN OCTAL*)
        WRITE (6,2) TOP,BOTTOM
      2 FORMAT (1H ,*FREE POOL POINTERS = *,O6,2X,O6,/)
        DO 103 K=1,DIM
            ADDR = FIRST + K - 1
            IF(MOD(K-1,CELSIZ) .NE. 0) GO TO 102
    101         WRITE (6,3) ADDR,CONT(ADDR)
      3         FORMAT (5X,O6,2X,O20)
                GO TO 103

    102         WRITE (6,4) CONT(ADDR)
      4         FORMAT (13X,O20)
    103     CONTINUE
        RETURN
        END


        PROGRAM TEST (TAPE5, TAPE6)
C
C       TEST OF SETUP, GIVEME, AND TAKEIT ROUTINES
C           IN THIS TEST PROCEDURE WE RESERVE A BLOCK ≠SPACE≠ FOR THE
C           POOL OF FREE CELLS.  WE CALL ≠SETUP≠ TO ORGANIZE THE SPACE
C           AS A POOL OF TWO WORD CELLS.
C
C           A STRING OF ALPHABETIC CHARACTERS IS READ, THEN STORED AS
C           A LINEAR LIST, ONE LETTER PER CELL.  THE PROGRAM THEN
C           WORKS THRU THE LIST, EXAMINING EACH CELL, PRINTING ITS
C           CONTENTS, AND RETURNING IT TO THE FREE POOL.
C
        DIMENSION SPACE(19),LETTER(70)
        INTEGER   ALPHA,CELL,CELSIZ,DIM,NEXT,NULL,OLDCEL,STRING
        INTEGER   CONT,FETCH,FIELD,GIVEME
        COMMON /NULVAL/ NULL
        DATA NULL / 377777B /
C
C       DEFINE LINK FIELD TO NEXT CELL OF LIST
C
        LINK = FIELD(1, 0, 18)
C
C       ZERO WORKSPACE.  THIS IS TOTALLY UNNECESSARY, BUT IT MAKES IT
C       MUCH EASIER TO READ DUMPS OF THE FREE-STORE.
C
        DO 100 I=1,19
            SPACE(I) = 0
    100     CONTINUE
        CELSIZ = 2
        DIM = 19
        CALL SETUP (SPACE, DIM, CELSIZ)
        CALL DUMPFP
C
C       READ A STRING OF ALPHABETIC CHARACTERS, ECHO IT, AND STORE THE
C       INPUT STRING AS A LIST WITH ONE CHARACTER PER CELL.
C
    101 READ (5,1) N,(LETTER(I),I=1,N)
      1 FORMAT (I2,70A1)
        IF(N .LE. 0) STOP
        WRITE (6,2) (LETTER(I),I=1,N)
      2 FORMAT (1H0,*INPUT STRING IS *,70A1)
C
```

```
C      CREATE THE LINKED LIST OF INPUT CHARACTERS.
C
       OLDCEL = NULL
       DO 102 I=1,N
            CELL = GIVEME(CELSIZ)
            CALL STORE (CELL, LINK, OLDCEL)
            CALL STOREW (CELL+1, LETTER(I))
            OLDCEL = CELL
  102       CONTINUE
C
C      LET *STRING* BE A FIXED REFERENCE POINTER TO THIS LIST
C      FOLLOW THE LINKS OF THE LIST, PRINTING CELL CONTENTS IN THE
C      PROCESS, AND RETURNING CELLS.  NOTE THAT THE STRING SHOULD BE
C      PRINTED WITH THE CHARACTERS IN THE REVERSE ORDER
C
       STRING = CELL
       WRITE (6,3) STRING
    3 FORMAT (5X,*STRING = *,O6)
       CALL DUMPFP
       CELL = STRING
  103       IF(CELL .EQ. NULL) GO TO 104
            ALPHA = CONT(CELL+1)
            WRITE (6,4) ALPHA
    4       FORMAT (10X,A1)
            NEXT = FETCH(CELL, LINK)
            CALL TAKEIT (CELL, CELSIZ)
            CELL = NEXT
            GO TO 103
  104 CALL DUMPFP
       GO TO 101
       END
```

To ensure that these fundamental linked storage techniques are completely understood, let us examine two concrete applications: one from formal language theory, and one from operating systems. As with the algorithms for allocating and maintaining the free pool of available cells, we will illustrate processes by examples of Fortran code, a language with which most readers will be familiar. The use of Fortran is only exemplary. But it is worthwhile to see how these kinds of procedures might be implemented in an actual programming language.

In automata theory, a *finite-state machine* is an abstract model of a computer (CPU) with only a finite amount of memory. A more powerful class of computational devices, called *pushdown store automata,* can be created by adding to a finite-state machine a potentially infinite pushdown stack. But use of the stack is restricted. Information can be written on, or erased from, this stack memory only at the top. In addition the CPU may only reference the information in the top element; it may not "look at" other elements in the stack. In formal language theory, languages (which are simply sets of strings or sets of lists) are characterized in terms of the kinds of grammar that can generate all possible strings in the language. These same languages (or sets) may also be characterized by the kinds of automata (computational processes) necessary to accept or to recognize which strings belong to the language and which strings do not.† An important theorem relating these two kinds of characterizations is

---

†Much of automata theory may be regarded as an effort to formalize, then answer, the question, "How hard is it to recognize members of various classes of sets?" It seems natural to extend this theory to questions concerning the difficulty of recognizing various classes of data structures.

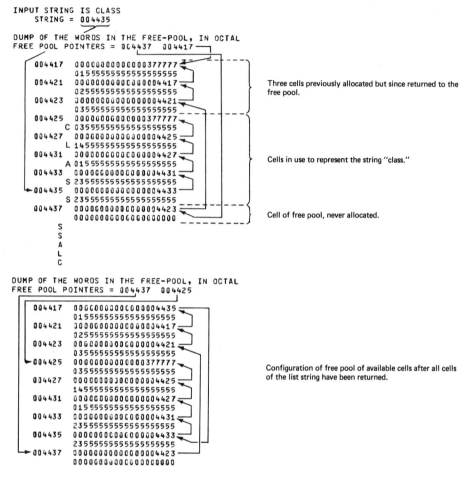

INPUT STRING IS CLASS
     STRING = 004435

DUMP OF THE WORDS IN THE FREE-POOL, IN OCTAL
FREE POOL POINTERS = 0C4437   004417

Three cells previously allocated but since returned to the free pool.

Cells in use to represent the string "class."

Cell of free pool, never allocated.

DUMP OF THE WORDS IN THE FREE-POOL, IN OCTAL
FREE POOL POINTERS = 004437   004425

Configuration of free pool of available cells after all cells of the list string have been returned.

Figure 3-16 Sample output from the test program of Fig. 3-15.

as follows: A language is context-free if and only if it can be accepted by a pushdown store automata (Hopcroft and Ullmann, 1969).

The language $\mathscr{L} = \{a^n b^n | n \geq 0\}$ consisting of n instances of any symbol (not only the letter a) followed by precisely the same number of instances of a second symbol is a classic context-free language.† According to the theorem, a pushdown store acceptor should be able to identify strings belonging to this set. Figure 3-17 shows such a program, which employs various data structures that have been developed so far. In this program the string to be recognized is first

---

†A string is a linear structure with assignment function f into some alphabet or vocabulary V. Language membership is an assertion about these assignments values. For example the string $\langle x_1, \ldots, x_n \rangle$ is in $\mathscr{L}$ above if (1) n is even, and (2) letting m = n/2, for all $i \leq m$, $f(x_i) = f(x_1)$ and for all $j > m$, $f(x_j) = f(x_{m+1})$.

Figure 3-17 A sample Fortran program and subroutines that employ both lists and stacks to recognize strings of symbols. A few examples of its output are shown.

```
        PROGRAM PARSE (TAPE5, TAPE6)
C       THIS MAIN PROGRAM READS, FROM INUPT UNIT 5, A STRING OF SYMBOLS
C       OVER SOME VOCABULARY ((V1,V2,...,VN). (BLANK IS ASSUMED TO BE
C       THE END-OF-STRING DELIMITER.)
C       THE STRING IS THEN PASSED TO AN ACCEPTING ROUTINE TO DETERMINE
C       IF IT IS WELL-FORMED (THIS, OF COURSE, DEPENDS ON WHAT KINDS
C       OF STRINGS THE ACCEPTING SUB-PROCESS HAS BEEN PROGRAMMED TO
C       ACCEPT).
C
        INTEGER   ARRAY(100),CELL,LISTEND,NULL,PREV,STRING,SYMBOL(80),
       1          V(20)
        INTEGER   FIELD,GIVEME,LOC
        LOGICAL   ACCEPT
        COMMON /NULVAL/ NULL
        COMMON /FIELDS/ NEXT,DATA
        COMMON /STACKF/ STKLNK,STKDAT,STKSIZ
        INTEGER   DATA,NEXT,STKLNK,STKDAT
C
C       INITIALIZE FIELD DESCRIPTORS, NULL SYMBOL, AND FREEPOOL,
C       (NOTE THAT WE HAVE DEFINED THE FIELDS USED IN STACK STRUCTURES
C       SEPARATELY FROM THOSE OF THE LIST STRUCTURE, EVEN THOUGH THESE
C       FIELDS REPRESENT PRECISELY THE SAME PORTIONS OF THEIR
C       CORRESPONDING CELLS.)
C       THEN BEGIN READING INPUT STRINGS.  ECHO BACK EACH AFTER IT IS READ
C
        NEXT = STKLNK = FIELD(1, 0, 18)
        DATA = STKDAT = FIELD(2, 0, 60)
        NULL = 377777B
        DO 100 I=1,100
            ARRAY(I) = 0
  100       CONTINUE
        CALL SETUP (ARRAY, 100, 2)

  101 READ (5,1) (SYMBOL(I),I=1,80)
    1 FORMAT (80A1)
            IF(EOF(5)) 301,102
  102 WRITE (6,2) (SYMBOL(I),I=1,80)
    2 FORMAT (1H0,*INPUT STRING - *,80A1)
C
C       THE STRING OF INPUT SYMBOLS IS CONVERTED INTO A SIMPLE LINKED
C       LIST.  AT THE SAME TIME THE COMPONENT SYMBOLS ARE EXAMINED TO
C       DETERMINE THE VOCABULARY, V, OVER WHICH THE STRING HAS BEEN
C       DEFINED.
C
        V(1) = SYMBOL(1)
        N = 1
        PREV = LOC(STRING)
        DO 105 I=1,80
            IF(SYMBOL(I) .EQ. 1H ) GO TO 106
            DO 103 J=1,N
                IF(SYMBOL(I) .EQ. V(J)) GO TO 104
  103           CONTINUE
            N = N+1
            V(N) = SYMBOL(I)
  104       CELL = GIVEME(2)
            CALL STORE (PREV, NEXT, CELL)
            CALL STORE (CELL, DATA, SYMBOL(I))
            PREV = CELL
  105       CONTINUE
  106 CALL STORE (PREV, NEXT, NULL)
      LISTEND = PREV
C
C       IS THIS STRING WELL FORMED
C
        IF(.NOT. ACCEPT(STRING,V,N)) GO TO 201
        WRITE (6,3) (V(J),J=1,N)
    3 FORMAT (16X,*IS A WELL-FORMED STRING OVER THE VOCABULARY, V = *,
       1          20(A1,2X))
        GO TO 202
  201 WRITE (6,4)
    4 FORMAT (16X,*IS ILL-FORMED.*)
C
C       RETURN THE INPUT STRING TO THE FREE POOL.  (NOTICE THAT SINCE
C       THIS STRING IS LINKED THROUGH THE SAME FIELDS AS THE FREE POOL
```

```
C       ITSELF, WE CAN RETURN THE ENTIRE STRING BY A SINGLE OPERATION
C       RATHER THAN RETURN IT CELL BY CELL.)
C
    202 CALL ERASE (STRING, LISTEND)
        GO TO 101
    301 STOP
        END


        LOGICAL FUNCTION ACCEPT (STRING, VOCAB, N)
        INTEGER    STRING,VOCAB(N),N
C       THIS PROCEDURE SIMULATES A PUSH-DOWN STORE ACCEPTOR WHICH
C       RECOGNIZES STRINGS OF THE FORM
C            N INSTANCES OF A SYMBOL FOLLOWED BY EXACTLY N INSTANCES OF
C            ANY OTHER SYMBOL.
C       IT USES TWO STACK ROUTINES *PUSHDN* AND *POPTOP*.
C
        INTEGER    CHAR,NULL,NXTCEL,STACK,STATE,Y
        INTEGER    FETCH,POPTOP
        COMMON /NULVAL/ NULL
        COMMON /FIELDS/ NEXT,DATA

        STATE = 1
        STACK = NULL
        NXTCEL = STRING
C
C       FETCH THE NEXT CHARACTER FROM THE INPUT STRING.
C
    101 IF(NXTCEL .EQ. NULL) GO TO 201
        CHAR = FETCH(NXTCEL, DATA)
        NXTCEL = FETCH(NXTCEL, NEXT)
C
C       GO TO STATE1 OR STATE2 OF THE ACCEPTOR.
C
        GO TO (102, 104), STATE
C
C       ACCEPTOR IS IN STATE 1 (IT HAS BEEN SCANNING THE SUBSTRING OF
C       INITIAL SYMBOLS).  IS THE CURRENT CHARACTER IN THIS INITIAL
C       SEGMENT,
C
    102 IF(CHAR .NE. VOCAB(STATE)) GO TO 103
C
C           YES IT IS, SIMPLY PUSH IT DOWN ON THE STACK.
C
            CALL PUSHDN (STACK, CHAR)
            GO TO 101
C
C           NO ITS NOT, TRANSFER TO STATE 2 AND BEGIN POPPING ELEMENTS
C                       OFF THE STACK.
C
    103     STATE = 2
C
C       ACCEPTOR IS IN STATE 2 (IT IS SCANNING THE SECOND SUBSTRING).
C       IS THE CURRENT CHARACTER IN THIS SET
C
    104 IF(CHAR .NE. VOCAB(STATE)) GO TO 202
C
C           YES IT IS, POPOFF (IF POSSIBLE) THE CORRESPONDING CHARACTER
C                       IN INITIAL SUBSTRING FROM THE STACK.
C
            IF(STACK .EQ. NULL) GO TO 202
            Y = POPTOP(STACK)
            GO TO 101
C
C       EMPTY INPUT STRING,  STRING IS WELL-FORMED IF AND ONLY IF
C       STACK IS ALSO NULL.
C
    201 IF(STACK .NE. NULL) GO TO 202
        ACCEPT = .TRUE.
        RETURN
C
C       STRING IS ILL-FORMED.
C           (NOTE THAT THIS ACCEPTOR ONLY INDICATES THAT THE STRING IS
C           NOT WELL-FORMED.  A SUPERIOR RECOGNIZER WOULD AT THIS POINT
C           ALSO INDICATE WHY IT IS ILL-FORMED.  IT COULD EITHER
C           1.   PRINT A DIAGNOSTIC MESSAGE, OR
C           2.   PASS AN ERROR CODE BACK TO THE CALLING ROUTINE,
C           TO INDICATE THE NATURE OF THE TROUBLE.)
```

```
C     EMPTY STACK (IF NECESSARY) BEFORE RETURNING
C
  202 ACCEPT = .FALSE.
  203 IF(STACK .EQ. NULL) RETURN
          Y = POPTOP(STACK)
          GO TO 203
      END


      SUBROUTINE ERASE (FIRST, LAST)
      INTEGER    FIRST,LAST
C     THIS PROCEDURE RETURNS A LIST THAT MUST BE SIMPLY LINKED
C     THRU A LINK FIELD IN WORD1, TO A FREE STORE, THAT MUST BE
C     SIMILARLY LINKED, AS ONE SINGLE UNIT RATHER THAN CELL BY CELL.
C
C     (NOTE HOWEVER THAT IT IS A DANGEROUS ROUTINE TO ADD TO THE FREE
C         POOL CLUSTER, SINCE IF THE STRING IS IN ANYWAY ILL-FORMED
C         IT MAY CAUSE THE FREE-POOL TO BE ILL-FORMED.)
C
      INTEGER    TOP,BOTTOM
      COMMON /FRPOOL/ NEXT,TOP,BOTTOM,CELSIZ
      COMMON /NULVAL/ NULL

      IF(FIRST .EQ. NULL) RETURN
      IF(TOP .EQ. NULL) TOP = FIRST
      CALL STORE (BOTTOM, NEXT, FIRST)
      BOTTOM = LAST
      FIRST = LAST = NULL
      RETURN
      END


INPUT STRING - AAAAAAAAAABBBBBBBBBB
              IS A WELL-FORMED STRING OVER THE VOCABULARY, V = A   B

INPUT STRING - GGGQQQ
              IS A WELL-FORMED STRING OVER THE VOCABULARY, V = G   Q

INPUT STRING - AAABBBB
              IS ILL-FORMED.

INPUT STRING - AAAABBB
              IS ILL-FORMED.

INPUT STRING - AAAACBBBB
              IS ILL-FORMED.

INPUT STRING - CCCCQQQCQQ
              IS ILL-FORMED.

INPUT STRING - $$$$$$$$,,,,,,,,
              IS A WELL-FORMED STRING OVER THE VOCABULARY, V = $   ,
```

input as a sequential array SYMBOL(80). This is used to create an explicitly linked list whose "name" is passed to the accepting subprocess. The acceptor itself scans the string in a left-to-right fashion to determine whether or not the string is well formed (in the set). Creation of such a list to represent the string is not really necessary. Sequential representation as a singly subscripted array would have been perfectly adequate, and in this instance, superior. This particular representation was included solely to provide more examples of list manipulating techniques. Figure 3-18 illustrates the configuration of the two data structures at one stage in the recognition process.

One of the earliest applications of linked data structures was the use of buffer chains in multiple input/output buffering. A major problem in the design of computers, and of the operating systems that oversee their execution, is the

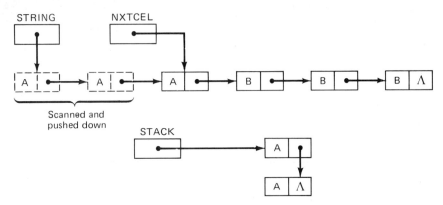

Figure 3-18 Configuration of the pushdown store acceptor after the first two characters of a string have been scanned.

large disparity between the rate at which information can be processed by the completely electronic central processing unit and core memory, and the rate at which it can be input from, or output to, a largely mechanical peripheral device. Card readers, punches, and line printers are notoriously slow, but even high-speed magnetic tape and disk units still operate at data rates well below that of the CPU. The problem is to synchronize the interface between these units.

To begin, let us consider only the output process associated with a line printer. Assume that a process, executing in the CPU, has generated a record of k characters that is to be printed. The easiest way to handle this output is to reserve a block in core memory, called a *buffer*, that may be accessed both by the central processing unit that will generate the record and by a channel, peripheral processor, or line printer itself, that will dispose of the record. Execution of an output command, say a WRITE statement in a user's program, causes the record to be placed in the buffer. Then a signal is sent to the independent output processor that the buffer now contains a record to be disposed. From the executing program's point of view the record has now been written—it may continue processing successive statements—*but* it may not execute another WRITE operation until the output processor has cleared the buffer. If the executing process would perform a second WRITE operation before the buffer is cleared, it must wait and idle the CPU.

Unfortunately, it is a characteristic of many programs that they perform a series of calculations, then follow it with a burst of output operations, say half a dozen records or so. Idling the CPU while all the records are disposed becomes intolerable in a high-throughput operation. An alternative solution, called *multiple buffering,* is to reserve several additional buffers into which subsequent records can be placed. In this situation the process executing on the CPU need not idle unless all the buffers are *full.* Now, however, we must organize these additional buffers. Clearly we want the records to appear on the line printer in the same order in which they were generated by the program, that is, in a first-in, first-out basis. Hence, conceptually we want a queue (actually, as it turns out, two queues) of buffers. The generating CPU process enters a record to be written into the buffer that is currently at the rear of the queue. The output processor disposes (or serves) the record in the buffer that is currently at the front of the queue. When the output processor has disposed of a record in a buffer, that buffer becomes available for reuse. Conversely, the writing process must first secure an available buffer (if any) before entering the record to be written. The list of available buffers can be organized as either a stack or as a queue; in this case the latter is preferable.

In practice the n output buffers that will be assigned to a particular process are reserved and "circularly" linked in a manner shown in Fig. 3-19a. For this reason one often hears them called a *buffer ring* or *buffer pool*. Reference pointers indicate the front and rear buffers in the queue. With this organization we can now write the procedures WRITE and OUTPUT. The former will be executed by the CPU, while the latter will be executed by the output processor.

procedure write (record);
data   record;

This process secures an available buffer in the buffer pool (if any), and inserts it at the rear of the queue of records to be disposed by the output processor.

begin
     system pointer   front, rear;
     field   next;
α: **if** next(rear) = front **then go to** α;
     cont(rear + 1 **thru** rear + k) ← record;
     rear ← next(rear);
     exit;
     end

procedure output;

This process disposes of the contents of the front of the output queue on the assigned output device. On completion it returns the buffer to the available queue, and proceeds to dispose of the next record (if any). If the output queue is empty, this process simply idles in a do-nothing loop.

begin
     system pointer   front, rear;
     field   next;
β: **if** front = rear
         then go to β
         else dispose of cont(front + 1 **thru** front + k);
            front ← next(front);
            go to β;
     end

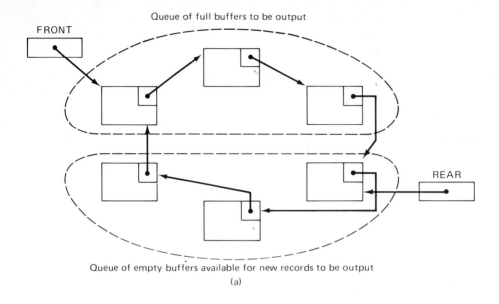

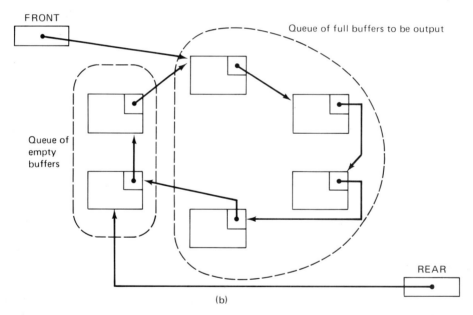

Figure 3-19 (*a*) A ring of output buffers. (*b*) The configuration of the buffer ring after two insertions by WRITE and one removal by OUTPUT.

Figure 3-19*b* illustrates the changed configuration of the buffer pool as a result of two insertions by WRITE and one removal by OUTPUT. Apparently the net effect of these two processes is to have the two reference pointers "chase" one another around the ring. In fact, the OUTPUT process simply strives to keep the output queue in an empty condition (FRONT = REAR), since the process is never exited.

Statements α and β are of special interest. The former idles the executing program if the available queue is empty, while the latter idles the output processor if the output queue is empty. This is normal procedure in a dedicated single-process environment, but it is quite unsatisfactory in a multiprocessing environment. In practice, when statement α discovers a full or nearly full output queue, it should store the current output record, but instead of returning normally to the executing program it should generate an interrupt to the system monitor so that a different program can make use of the CPU. In a similar manner, discovery of an empty output queue at statement β should cause a similar interrupt so that the output processor can be reassigned to dispose of the records in the output queue of some other program. Handling of such interrupt messages, however, is beyond the scope of this text. The interested reader may wish to consult a reference such as Donovan (1972).

The careful reader is likely to have noticed two discordant facts about this configuration and its processes. First, it should have been evident that statement α treats the available buffer queue as empty even though there is in fact a single available buffer. A more efficient buffering procedure would make use of *all* available buffers, but at the cost of more complex handling of the reference pointers (see Sec. 4-2). Secondly, the explicit links in the first word of each buffer are never altered. The individual buffers always stand in the same relative position with one another. It is reasonable to ask if the explicit linkage is really necessary. In this particular situation, the answer is no; in fact, an implicit sequential linkage would be far superior. In practice, pools of fixed-size buffers are sequentially represented, and we will consider this kind of representation in the next section. Pools of variably sized buffers would most likely be explicitly linked.

Multiple buffering of input processes is handled in an analogous fashion. An input queue of records to be read by the program is maintained. But there is one striking difference. The output processor strives to keep the output queue empty, while the input processor strives to keep the input queue full! One may reasonably ask, "How can an input processor fill a buffer queue with records that an executing program has not as yet requested?" The underlying assumption that governs the multiple buffering of input is that an executing process will eventually read all the records in the input file *in the sequence that they appear in that file*. Under this assumption the input processor reads the records of the file as fast as it can and stuffs them into the input buffer queue. *But* the sequence of input may be altered by the executing program, as for example by a BACKSPACE or REWIND command to a tape or disk file. In this case the input processor must first purge the input queue and begin filling it anew. It is this additional logical complexity, which cannot arise in the case of output, that led us to look at buffered output in detail.

More importantly, even though one may buffer output to a randomly organized data file, it is *logically* impossible to buffer input. There is no way that the input processor can predict the next record that the executing program may want to read. For this reason random access and retrieval must necessarily be less efficient than sequential access—even though the files themselves may be identically represented on identical peripheral devices, as in the case of indexed sequential files on a magnetic disk or drum.

EXERCISES FOR SECTION 3-3

*3-5 Code the two routines GIVEME and TAKEIT, which are necessary to complete the dynamic allocation cluster. (Note that object versions of these routines will have to be loaded with virtually every subsequent programming assignment encountered in this text. *Keep your own copy of the object deck, or else keep a version in a permanent system file.*)

3-6 Implement a free-pool cluster using a stack organization. (Note that SETUP remains virtually unchanged, but new versions of GIVEME and TAKEIT must be coded analogous to PUSHDN and POPTOP.) These routines should be slightly more efficient, since fewer statements need be executed. What is the savings? Can you devise a criterion for *measuring* the resultant increase in processing efficiency?

3-7 There are a number of additional internal checks that might be incorporated in GIVEME and TAKEIT to further guarantee the integrity of the free pool. Some of these are:

(*a*) Distinctively mark the tag field of the first word of every cell in the free pool; let GIVEME test for this tag and remove it before returning.

(*b*) Let TAKEIT test the address passed it as parameter to insure that (1) it is within the array bounds, (2) it is the first word of a cell, and (3) it is not already an available cell in the free store.

Code some of these additional safeguards. What is the additional computational expense? Is it worth it?

*3-8 An unwanted list is normally returned to the free pool one cell at a time. But

(*a*) *if* the list is linked through the same field as the free pool, and

(*b*) *if* the list is well formed, then the entire list can be returned to the free pool by resetting at most two fields. Code a routine

ERASE (LBEGIN, LEND)

that will return all the cells of the list in the accompanying figure in one operation. (The routine ERASE has not been included in our dynamic allocation cluster because there are too many dangers associated with its use. But it is well worth including in one's own private system where it will be properly used.)

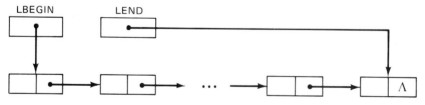

Ex. 3-8

3-9 (*a*) Use the versions of PUSH and POPTOP coded for Exercise 3-1 to complete the pushdown store acceptor of Fig. 3-17.

(*b*) Verify that $\mathscr{L}' = \{a^n b^n c^n | n \geq 0\}$ cannot be recognized in the same way with a single stack. Why? So it is not a context-free language.

(*c*) Code a two-stack acceptor that will recognize this language $\mathscr{L}'$.

*3-10 In the buffer configuration we have illustrated, the pointer REAR does not point to the last buffer in the output queue, but rather to the first available buffer. Suppose REAR did point to the last buffer in the output queue. How would this affect WRITE and OUTPUT?

3-11 Recode WRITE and OUTPUT so that every buffer can be used. (Note that you will have to first decide on appropriate and distinct criteria to signify an empty and a full output queue.)

3-12 Design a multiply buffered input system. Write the procedures READ and INPUT analogous to WRITE and OUTPUT. Include as well a procedure BACKSPACE (N) that backspaces the sequential file by n records. (Note that if N is less than or equal to the number of records currently in the input queue, there is no need to physically backspace the external device and actually reread any records; the backspacing can be simulated by simply resetting the pointers FRONT and REAR. Include this capability in the procedure.)

FOUR

ALTERNATIVE REPRESENTATIONS OF LINEAR STRUCTURES

In the preceding chapter we considered only one basic method of representing linear structures—by means of a simply linked list. In this chapter a variety of alternative representations and applications of this same abstract data structure are examined.

4-1 SEQUENTIAL REPRESENTATION OF LINEAR STRUCTURES

Since computer storage is totally ordered by its integer addressing scheme, the cells of a linear data structure can be located in such a fashion that the next cell in the order may be accessed by merely incrementing (or decrementing) the address of the current cell. Such *sequential* (from the sequential ordering of the storage registers) *representations* eliminate the need to explicitly indicate the next cell by means of a link field. In addition to the more efficient use of storage, sequential representation may also yield more efficient processing routines. In this text we will emphasize linked representations because the techniques are more easily generalized to more complex structures, and because many applications programmers seem unfamiliar with their use. But once the utility of linked storage is perceived, many programmers seem unable to consider any other kinds of representation. This is unfortunate, especially in the case of linear structures, since if a sequential representation is satisfactory for the task at hand, it is almost always superior to any other representation. In this section we will investigate sequential representation in considerable detail, and in the process discover many of its strengths and its weaknesses.

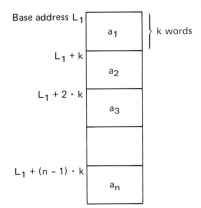

Figure 4-1 Standard sequential representation of a singly subscripted array.

The most basic linear structure is a vector, or singly subscripted array. It is presumed that the reader is already familiar with the standard representation of these arrays, but for completeness we will include a brief review. (Multiply subscripted arrays, which may or may not be regarded as linear structures, depending on one's point of view, are discussed in Chap. 7.)

Let $S_M = \langle a_1, a_2, \ldots, a_n \rangle$ denote any vector of n elements. The values assigned to each element are most commonly real or integer numbers, and occasionally complex values or some other kind of data. In the former cases we will require only one word per cell in the representation; in the latter cases we may need two or more words of storage per cell. In general let k denote the number of words necessary to represent the assigned value of any element, so that k will also denote the cell size. To represent the array, $k \cdot n$ consecutive words must be reserved. The assigned value of the first element is stored in the first cell, the value of the next in the second cell, and so on. The location of the first element a_1 is called the *base address* of the array and may be denoted by L_1. (The base address may also be regarded as the address of the array as a whole; and when the "name" of an array is passed as parameter to a subroutine or function, it is this base address that is passed.) Figure 4-1 illustrates this standard array representation.†

Given the base address L_1, it is easy to calculate the location of any desired element in the array, say a_i, by means of the formula, called an *accessing function*

$$\text{address}(a_i) = L_1 + (i-1) \cdot k \qquad (4\text{-}1)$$

If the address of any cell in the array is known, the address of the next, or the preceding, cell may be determined by merely incrementing or decrementing by k.

---

†The representation shown is sometimes called *forward storage*. An alternative *backwards storage*, in which the first element is stored in the last cell, was used in some early computers whose unsigned hardware index registers could only be used to decrement core addresses.

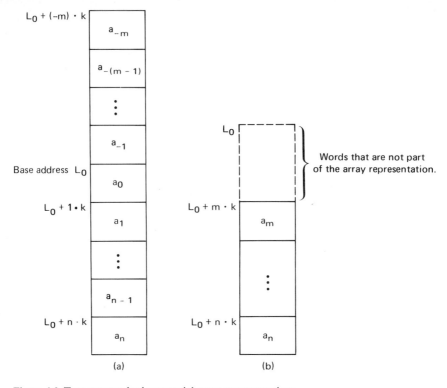

Figure 4-2 Two nonstandard sequential array representations.

The accessing function (4-1) is not aesthetically pleasing. One would much prefer a formula of the form

$$\text{address}(a_i) = \text{base address} + i \cdot k \qquad (4\text{-}2)$$

This latter accessing function requires the base address of the array, call it L_0, to be the address of the (possibly imaginary) element a_0. Readily, $L_0 = L_1 - k$. With an accessing function such as (4-2) it becomes evident that one need not restrict oneself to the representation of arrays with subscripts in the range $[1, n]$ (as is required by standard Fortran). There is no reason why the subscripts may not be constrained to the range $[m, n]$ where $1 \le m < n$, or extended to include negative subscripts in the range $[-m, n]$. Both configurations are illustrated in Fig. 4-2. Notice that in the former case, the base address L_0 denotes a word of storage that is not actually part of the array representation.

It should be apparent that the address of any cell in the array (or outside the array) can be chosen as the base address, although L_0 and L_1 seem the most natural ones, and the accessing function then designed in conformity. If one is using one's own representation and coding one's own accessing function, then

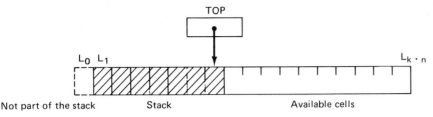

Figure 4-3 A sequential representation of a single stack.

the choice is irrelevant. But when programming within the constraints of a high-level language, then the twin questions, "What accessing function will the compiler assume?" and "What base address will be passed when an array name is used as a subprogram parameter?" can be quite crucial.

Stacks may be sequentially represented in much the same way as arrays of fixed length. Let k be the cell size as before. Then (1) allocate (or reserve) a block of $k \cdot n$ consecutive words in locations L_1 through $L_{k \cdot n}$; (2) choose a name (or reference pointer) for the stack, say TOP or STACK; and (3) set $TOP = L_0 = L_1 - k$. Given this configuration, shown in Fig. 4-3, the processed PUSHDOWN and POPTOP may be easily coded as follows.

procedure pushdown$_3$ (top, data);
pointer   top;
variable   data;

This routine pushes the k words of "data" down on the sequential stack referenced by "top." It becomes the new "top" element.

begin
        top ← top + k;
        if top > $L_{k \cdot n}$ **then** "overflow";
        cont(top **thru** top + (k − 1)) ← data;
        exit;
        end

function poptop$_3$ (top);
pointer   top;

This function deletes the "top" element of a sequential stack and returns its contents as functional value.

begin
        common /nulval/ null;
        if top ≤ L_0
                then poptop ← null
                else poptop ← cont(top **thru** top + (k − 1));
                        top ← top − k;
        exit;
        end

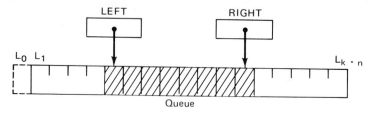

Figure 4-4 A sequential representation of a single queue.

Notice that cells are added or deleted from the stack merely by increment-ing or decrementing the value of TOP. Consequently the stack "pulsates" within its block of reserved storage as the top moves to the left or to the right. If one uses array indices instead of core addresses to reference cells of the stack, then it becomes an almost trivial task to implement these routines in any higher-level language.

It seems evident that we can implement a sequential queue in much the same manner; by allocating $k \cdot n$ consecutive words; by setting up two point-ers, LEFT and RIGHT; and by letting the deletion operation increment the left-most pointer. Check the operation of the following two procedures on the con-figuration illustrated in Fig. 4-4.

procedure add$_1$ (right, data);
pointer   right;
variable   data;

This routine adds a new element to the "right" of a sequential queue, and assigns "data" as the value of that element.

begin
    right $\leftarrow$ right $+$ k;
    if right $> L_{k \cdot n}$ **then** "overflow";
    cont(right **thru** right $+(k-1)$) $\leftarrow$ data;
    exit;
    end

function delete$_1$ (left, right);
pointer   left, right;

This function deletes the leftmost element of a sequential queue and returns its assigned value.
begin
    common /nulval/ null;
α: **if** left $>$ right
        then delete $\leftarrow$ null
        else delete $\leftarrow$ cont(left **thru** left $+(k-1)$);
           left $\leftarrow$ left $+$ k;
    exit;
    end

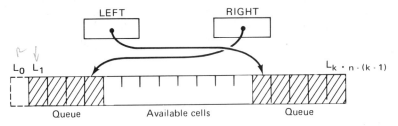

Figure 4-5 A queue circularly "wrapped around" its allocated block of sequential storage.

We may test the validity of the "empty queue" boundary condition (statement α) by considering the queue consisting of a singleton element. In this case LEFT = RIGHT since both point to the same cell. If that cell is deleted to create an empty list, then LEFT will be incremented to leave LEFT > RIGHT. Since the queue will be initially empty, L_1 and L_0 are reasonable initial values for LEFT and RIGHT, respectively.

If we examine the operation of these two procedures on the queue of Fig. 4-4, we see that it moves steadily from left to right through its allocated block instead of pulsating, as did the stack representation. This should lead us to question the overflow or "queue full" boundary condition. Even though RIGHT has passed $L_{k \cdot n}$, the queue need not be full. Cells may have been released from the left end that could be used again in the queue. A reasonable approach that will permit maximum utilization of the allocated storage is to <u>let the queue</u> <u>"wrap around" the block, and treat the addressing as if it were circular.</u> Figure 4-5 illustrates such a wrapped-around queue. The following modifications of ADD and DELETE handle this wrap around addressing.

procedure add$_2$ (left, right, data);
pointer　left, right;
variable　data;

This routine adds a new element to the "right" end of a queue that is circularly wrapped around its sequential storage. "Data" is assigned as the new element.

begin
　　if right $= L_{k \cdot n} - (k-1)$
　　　　then　right $\leftarrow L_1$
　　　　else　right $\leftarrow$ right $+ k$;

Check whether this new cell is really the leftmost cell of the queue.

β:　**if** right $=$ left **then** "overflow";
　　cont(right **thru** right $+ (k-1)$) $\leftarrow$ data;
　　exit;
　　end

function delete$_2$ (left, right);
pointer　left, right;

This function deletes the leftmost element of a circularly represented queue and delivers its contents as functional value.

```
begin
      common /nulval/ null;
γ:   if left > right
          then delete ←null
          else delete ←cont(left thru left +(k − 1));
                left ←left +k;
                if left > L_{k·n} −(k − 1)
                    then left ←L_1;
      exit;
      end
```

To avoid a premature and unnecessary overflow condition we wrapped the queue around its storage area. (It should be evident that this treatment of a sequential queue is conceptually equivalent to the circularly linked buffer pool of Sec. 3-3.) But now we must reconsider the way boundary conditions are recognized. The test for the empty queue (statement γ) is patently in error. The condition LEFT > RIGHT will hold any time the queue has been wrapped around its storage! This must be corrected by replacing statement γ with a more precise test, viz.,

γ':   if left = right + k then ...

since deletion of a singleton cell will yield this configuration. The initial setting of LEFT = L_1 and RIGHT = L_0 would then be left unchanged since this will signify the initially empty queue.

Now assume that a cell has been added to the initially empty queue, incrementing RIGHT. If a second cell is added, the overflow boundary condition will be found because now LEFT = RIGHT (statement β), even though the queue contains only a single element! Revision of ADD and DELETE, together with an appropriate choice of initial values for LEFT and RIGHT, is left as an exercise for the reader (Exercise 4-2). It is not difficult (although some care must be taken when performing the wrap-around) *provided* the following two conventions are assumed:

1. RIGHT points to the first available cell, not the actual rightmost cell of the queue (or alternatively, LEFT points to the cell immediately preceding the actual leftmost cell), and
2. One unused cell will always be kept as a "buffer" between the two ends of the queue.

If the cell size k is small relative to the total storage allocated for the queue, then the use of one cell to function as a buffer in (2) above is a small price to pay for the resultant simplification of the processes. If, however, the cells are relatively large (as in the case of input/output buffer pools), then reservation of a single cell may waste a significant portion of the total allocated storage, and the practice becomes extravagant. The reader is encouraged to try to devise processes that will permit the full utilization of every cell in the representation. It will be discovered that simple tests on the value of the pointers LEFT and RIGHT alone will not be sufficient; at least one extra "flag" must be created, set, and tested by the routines.

The preceding queue examples graphically demonstrate that the sequential representation of even simple dynamic data structures normally involve moderately complex procedures. It is easy to introduce logical programming errors. This need not be a condemning criticism, since even fairly involved arithmetic operations may be computationally more efficient than setting, following, and erasing explicit links. A more serious problem arises when one considers the problem of representing *several* dynamic structures in a sequential fashion.

In the development so far, a fixed number of cells have been initially allocated for the creation of these dynamic stacks and queues, independent of whether they were represented sequentially or by linked structures. Consequently our primary concern, after ensuring that all processes are without logical errors, should be whether an overflow condition will force a premature and unwanted termination of the procedure. Although some lists may be longer and some shorter, it should be possible, based on a knowledge of the problem at hand, to predict the *expected* (in a probabilistic sense) length of each list involved. Let us denote this expected value by E. (Unfortunately, in some practical situations even a crude approximation of E may be surprisingly difficult.) Further, it seems reasonable to assume that while the length n of a list may well exceed E, longer lists are significantly less likely than shorter lists. That is, $\text{prob}(n \geq E + i) \to 0$ as $i \to \infty$. In lieu of more concrete knowledge about the nature of the problem and its associated lists, Eq. (4-3) appears to be a reasonable probabilistic statement:

$$\text{prob}(n \geq E + i) = a/i \quad \text{where } a \in (0, 1) \tag{4-3}$$

(Possibly a more general form of equation, say $\text{prob}(n \geq E + i) = a(n)/i^p$, $p > 0$, would be more realistic. However, the conclusions of this section are largely independent of the precise form of the distribution, provided only that it is a decreasing function of the length n.)

If only a single dynamic list is used in the program and $N > E$ cells have been allocated for its representation, then the probability of a disastrous overflow occurring is simply

$$\text{prob(overflow)} = \text{prob}(n > N) = a/(N - E) \tag{4-4}$$

The probability of overflow may be made vanishingly small, though seldom zero, simply by allocating many more cells for the list than are thought to be necessary; that is, by letting $N \gg E$ (where $\gg$ denotes "very much greater than"). But such a solution of the overflow problem is both unelegant and expensive. Most programmers would choose N as small as possible while still keeping the probability of overflow acceptably small.

Now consider a program that involves two dynamic lists, list_1 and list_2. Let E_1 and E_2 denote their respective expected lengths. If we allocate two *separate* blocks of cells, of size N_1 and N_2, for their respective representations, we can calculate the probability of fatal overflow to be:

$$
\begin{aligned}
\text{prob(overflow)} &= \text{prob(list}_1 \text{ overflows } or \text{ list}_2 \text{ overflows)} \\
&= \text{prob}(n_1 > N_1) + \text{prob}(n_2 > N_2) \\
&= \frac{a}{N_1 - E_1} + \frac{a}{N_2 - E_2} \\
&\approx 2 \cdot \frac{a}{N - E} \qquad \text{provided } N_1 \approx N_2 \text{ and } E_1 \approx E_2
\end{aligned}
$$

Thus if one represents k separate lists, each with its own allocated cells, we find, using the natural generalization of the argument above, that the probability of fatal overflow is roughly k-fold more likely.

Now suppose, instead of allocating separate blocks for the representation of each list, we allocate a single block of $N_1 + N_2$ cells and let the two lists "share" these cells. The calculation of the probability of fatal overflow now becomes:

$$
\begin{aligned}
\text{prob(overflow)} &= \text{prob}(n_1 + n_2 > N_1 + N_2) \\
&= \text{prob}(n_1 > N_1 + i) \cdot \text{prob}(n_2 > N_2 - i) \\
&= \frac{a}{(N_1 + i) - E_1} \cdot \frac{a}{(N_2 - i) - E_2} \\
&\approx \frac{a^2}{(N^2 - i^2) - 2NE + E^2} \qquad \text{if } N_1 \approx N_2, E_1 \approx E_2 \\
&\approx \frac{a^2}{((N - i) - E)^2} \\
&\approx \left(\frac{a}{N - E} \right)^2
\end{aligned}
$$

The preceding calculations, which (1) assume that the lists grow independently of one another, and (2) involve some rather gross approximations in the last three steps, show that the representation of several lists in shared storage actually decreases the probability of overflow. This agrees with intuition, since if the behavior of the two lists is independent, even though list_1 becomes long it is likely that list_2 may be short, so that some of the cells that were allocated for list_2 can be used instead for list_1. If k lists are represented in a shared storage, then the probability of fatal overflow, relative to the single-list probability, is reduced roughly by a power of k.

It is clear therefore that any process that will employ several dynamic data structures should strive to allocate available cells in such a way that they may

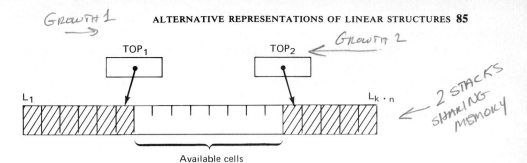

Figure 4-6 Two sequential stacks represented in a common block of consecutive cells.

be used to represent any of the possible structures. Linked representations using a free-pool allocation package automatically share cells between data structures. The important question is: "Can several sequentially represented lists be organized so that they share a common block/of/allocatable cells?" The answer is yes; but save for one exception, at some computational cost.

Let us consider the exception first. Two stacks may be represented in shared storage with no additional processing overhead. The trick is quite easy. Let the two stacks grow toward each other from either end of the block, as illustrated in Fig. 4-6. While separate routines to push down (and pop off) $stack_2$ must be written (since it must decrement TOP_2, whereas the other increments TOP_1, and vice versa), there is no real additional complexity.

Now assume that we wish to represent m $\geq$ 3 independent sequential stacks in a common block of storage. At least some of the lists must "float" in the center of the block. Therefore, two reference pointers will be required for each stack, one to the TOP of the stack as before, and another to the BASE of the stack. The configuration is shown in Fig. 4-7. Note that the BASE pointer indicates the cell immediately preceding the first cell of its stack. $Stack_i$ will be empty if $TOP[i] = BASE[i]$. Similarly, $stack_i$ is "full" if $TOP[i] = BASE[i+1]$ as shown in the figure. An attempt to push another element down on $stack_i$ will cause an overflow condition. *But it need not be a fatal*

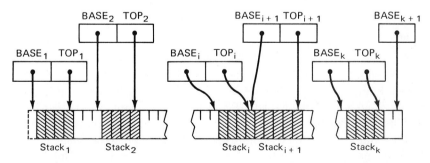

Figure 4-7 k stacks sequentially represented in a common block of consecutive cells. (Note the extra pointer $BASE_{k+1}$, indicating the last cell in the block.)

overflow. Although there is no available cell between stack$_i$ and stack$_{i+1}$, there may well be available cells somewhere within the block. Possibly the positions of the stacks can be shifted, or *repacked,* so as to create an available cell between these two stacks. Since the routines to push down and to pop off are largely duplicates of those given earlier, we sketch below only portions of code associated with the repacking process.

```
procedure pushdown (i, data);
            .
            .
            .
            if top [i] = base [i + 1] then go to full;
            No "local" overflow, push down data on stack.
push:       top [i] ←top [i] +celsiz;
            .
            .
            .
            exit;
            Search for an available cell "above" stack_i.
full:       for k =i + 1 thru m do
                if top [k] < base [k + 1] then go to shiftup;

            No free cells exist "above" stack_i. Check for an available cell "below" stack_i.
            .
            .
            .
            A free cell has been found between stack_k and stack_k+1. Shift stack_i+1 thru
            stack_k up one cell. Note that the actual shifting must be done in reverse order to
            avoid overwriting existing values.
shiftup:
            for cell =top [k] thru base [i+1] do
                cont(cell +celsiz) ←cont(cell);
            Now reset the shifted stack pointers.
            for j =i+1 thru k do
                base [j] ←base [j] +celsiz;
                top [j] ←top [j] +celsiz;
            go to push;
            .
            .
            .
            end
```

Figure 4-8 shows the repacked stack configuration resulting from the "shift up" process. It should be evident that a considerable amount of effort has been expended just to make one cell available to stack$_i$. Since stack$_i$ is currently active, it is reasonable to predict that more elements are likely to be pushed down on stack$_i$ in the near future. Based on the reasonable expectation, an intelligent repacking procedure might well provide several available cells between stack$_i$ and stack$_{i+1}$. Following this train of thought, it appears that with a little addi-

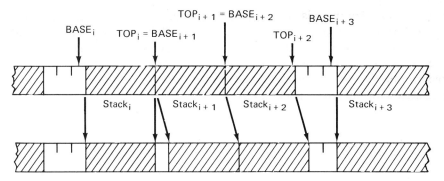

Figure 4-8 Repacking by "shifting up" one cell to provide space between stack$_i$ and stack$_{i+1}$.

tional effort an intelligent repacking algorithm might work through the entire block redistributing at least one cell (if possible) to every stack, and more cells (if possible) to the currently most active stacks. [Knuth (1969) offers one such routine, which, although long, is well worth looking up. See also Exercise 4-5.]

Repacking algorithms, especially intelligent ones, tends to be fairly complex, so that many programmers when faced with this situation simply turn to linked representations (which, of course, never need repacking). This is often justified on the additional grounds that repacking tends to be relatively inefficient in terms of computation time. But is it? The important issue is not how much time a single repacking of the lists requires, but rather how often the process will be invoked. If the block of consecutive locations is only partially full, say 50 percent, and if the relative demand on the lists is fairly constant over the period of execution, then a good repacking algorithm may be called but a few times in the course of a lengthy run. The much more efficient execution of sequential versions of **POPTOP** and **PUSHDOWN** may more than compensate for the cost of an occasional repacking. If, however, the block is nearly full, say 95 percent of the locations are utilized in lists, then the procedure may be frequently called to redistribute the few remaining cells. Such *thrashing* is clearly inefficient. In fact, it is usually wise to set a threshold, say 95 percent of the total reserved block, above which any local overflow is treated *as if it were* a fatal overflow. The rationale is that a reserved block which is so nearly full is almost certain to overflow in a few more iterations in any case, so there is little profit in performing the relatively expensive repacking procedure a few more times.

In contrast, a linked representation employing a free-pool approach never needs repacking. More importantly, the code itself is much more straightforward and less prone to insidious logical errors. Consequently, the initial implementation of dynamic data structures is normally an order of magnitude faster if a linked representation is employed. It would also appear that the linked representation is more efficient in terms of storage, since a free pool will not overflow until it is completely exhausted, while a sequential representation should set some lower threshold to avoid thrashing. This is not necessarily so. The extra words needed to just represent the explicit links often exceed that unused surplus included to prevent excessive sequential repacking.

As a general rule, *if* the process will be used sufficiently often, and *if* one can afford the additional programming expense, then a sequential representation is usually the more efficient of the two. But for the initial research and development of a system involving dynamic data structures, the author prefers linked representations.

EXERCISES FOR SECTION 4-1

4-1 The procedure $POPTOP_3$ contains the statement

$$poptop \leftarrow cont(top \text{ thru } top + (k - 1));$$

which although logically reasonable, should seem absurd to most programmers. Is there any way, given the conventions of your programming language, that a function can return more than a single word of information? Code versions of $PUSHDOWN_3$ and $POPTOP_3$.

*4-2 Set up adequate boundary condition tests for a circular representation of a sequential queue, and recode the ADD and DELETE procedures so that they will work correctly;

(*a*) assuming an unused buffer cell between the ends of the queue (quite easy if suggestions of the text are followed), or

(*b*) making use of every available cell.

What should be the initial values of the pointers, LEFT and RIGHT? Test your procedures with several concrete examples.

4-3 Implement a system whereby two stacks "grow toward" each other, as in Fig. 4-6. Let the stacks be designated $stack_1$ and $stack_2$ with procedures

$$\left. \begin{array}{c} PUSHDN(I, DATA) \\ POPOFF(I) \end{array} \right\} I = 1, 2$$

What is the overflow condition?

*4-4 Complete the procedure PUSHDOWN so that it will handle the repacking of $m \geq 3$ stacks. If local overflow occurs at $stack_i$, a *fixed* number of cells should be made available (if possible) between $stack_i$ and $stack_{i+1}$. Would any changes be required to handle queues instead of stacks?

4-5 Devise and code an intelligent repacking scheme that

(*a*) counts the total number of unused cells available in the block,

(*b*) allocates one (or more) of these cells to each stack, and

(*c*) proportionally allocates the remainder among the most "active" stacks.

Note that this will require an additional variable associated with each stack to record its activity or growth since the last repacking. (It may be either an incremental counter or a pointer to the location of the old top element just after the last repacking.) Also note that some lists will be shifted up and others shifted down. This must be done carefully to avoid overwriting information.

4-6 Similar procedures to repack $m \geq 2$ queues sequentially represented in a shared block of storage can be written. But they tend to be less effective, because as we have seen, they tend to move through the storage forcing frequent repacking.

(*a*) Modify ADD with a simple repacking process so that it can operate on several queues in a block of common storage.

(*b*) Would an intelligent repacking process be worthwhile? Why, or why not?

(*c*) Implement the procedure and count the number of times a cell must be shifted relative to the number of additions and deletions.

(*d*) Would it pay to simply shift an entire queue one cell to the left on each deletion (in which case there is no need to "wrap around" storage)?

*4-7 Some qualitative assertions comparing linked with sequential representations close this section. Can they be defended with any quantitative evidence? What would constitute such evidence?

One may seek answers to this kind of comparative question by employing simulation techniques. One useful kind of simulation involves writing a "driver" program to generate a series of "typical" subprogram requests and to keep statistics about the performance of the implemented subprograms.

(*a*) Code the most efficient linked and sequential procedures (either stack or queue is satisfactory) and simulate their use by a main program.

While such a simulation is invaluable to gain insight into the behavior of these processes, there are some very knotty questions concerning what real information has been gained. After completing a number of simulation runs, can you state which technique is better? What are the relevant properties that contrast sequential with linked representations? Are they of a measurable nature?

(*b*) Describe the meaningful parameters that differentiate linked versus sequential representations, and explain how you would measure them.

Finally, one may question whether the demand load on these lists that has been generated by the main simulation procedure (usually a uniform probability distribution) is at all typical of a real-life situation.

(*c*) How could a mix of real-life demands on a collection of lists be determined? How should it be described so that it can be later replicated in a simulation?

4-2 OTHER LINKED REPRESENTATIONS OF LINEAR STRUCTURES

The last cell of a simply linked list always contains the nullvalue. To many it has seemed a waste not to make better use of this field. Why not let it point back to the first cell of the list? If this is done, the resulting representation, shown in Fig. 4-9, is called a *circularly linked* list. There are two evident problems associated with the use of circular list representations. First suppose we code a process to "walk through" the list, as in Sec. 3-2; how will the process know when it has reached the end? (The procedures we presented earlier would simply keep going around and around without stopping.) Two solutions suggest themselves. The process can keep as a temporary pointer the address of the first (entry) cell of the list and compare the address of each newly accessed cell against it. A second more commonly used technique is to *mark* the

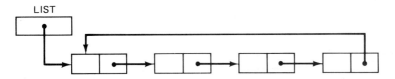

Figure 4-9 A circularly linked list.

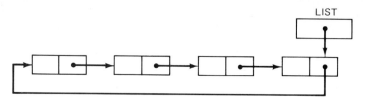

Figure 4-10 The circularly linked list of Fig. 4-9, with the pointer LIST referencing the "last" cell of the list.

first or the last cell in some distinctive fashion. Such marks are often called *tags*. On most computers with words of more than 16 bits, it is usually possible to "carve out" a tiny field of 1 to 6 bits called a *tag field,* and still leave sufficient bits to represent one or more link fields.

The second problem with circularly linked lists is a functional one. In practice, it is generally the last cell we want to be able to access directly from the first, not the reverse. If a process must "walk through" the entire list in order to access the last cell, it seems a bit superfluous to then have a link back to the beginning. Circularly linked lists are more useful if the reference pointer links to the last cell of the list rather than the first, as shown in Fig. 4-10. In this configuration, two rather than just one link must be followed to access the first cell of the list. But for the cost of following that extra link, the cells at each end of the list are "known" immediately with just a single pointer.

Note that Fig. 4-10 is actually *identical* to Fig. 4-9 if they are viewed solely as data structures. They are only drawn differently. The real distinction between them is purely a matter of programming convention. If a process operating on them assumes that LIST points to the first element, then Fig. 4-9 is more natural; if the process will follow an additional link to reach the first element, then Fig. 4-10 is a more appropriate drawing. Naturally all processes operating on the data structure must be coded with respect to the same convention.

The utility of circular linking can be demonstrated by a small example. In a string processing application, let the strings themselves be circularly linked as shown in Fig. 4-11. An important operator in string processing is that of *concatenation,* which "joins" two strings, $\chi = \langle x_1, x_2, \ldots, x_m \rangle$ and $\psi = \langle y_1, y_2, \ldots, y_n \rangle$, "end to end" in a left-to-right fashion to form a new string $\phi = \chi \circ \psi = \langle x_1, x_2, \ldots, x_m, y_1, y_2, \ldots, y_n \rangle$. (The concatenation operator is frequently denoted by simply juxtaposing its two argument strings, as in $\chi\psi$.) Given the representation of Fig. 4-11, a concatenation procedure can be written as follows:

pointer function concatenate (x, y);
pointer   x, y;

This procedure concatenates the two strings x and y, represented as circular lists, and

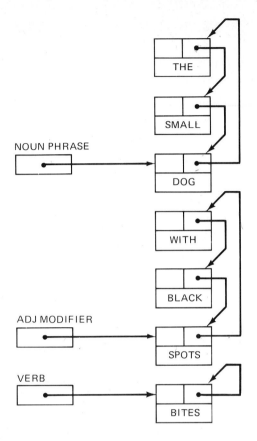

Figure 4-11 Three circularly linked strings.

returns as its functional value a pointer to the new string. Note that the operation is not commutative, and that the order of its parameters is crucial.

begin
      pointer   z, xfirst;
      field   next;
      common /nulval/ null;
      z ← y;
      xfirst ← next(x);
      next(x) ← next(y);
      next(y) ← xfirst;

      "Destroy" the passed reference pointers.

      x ← y ← null;
      concatenate ← z;
      exit;
      end

If a fragment of the rewrite rules of a grammar to generate well-formed English sentences looks like:

⟨sentence⟩ ::= ⟨subject⟩⟨verb⟩|...
⟨subject⟩ ::= ⟨noun phrase⟩⟨adj modifier⟩|...

then execution of the following two statements (which might have been chosen by a process that searches some tabular representation of the rewrite rules)

subject ← concatenate(noun-phrase, adj-modifier);
sentence ← concatenate(subject, verb);

will generate a well-formed English sentence, "The small dog with black spots bites."

The data structure shown in Fig. 4-11 has a serious weakness. In the illustrated cell format, only a single word has been allocated to store the value of that element in the string, i.e., the word itself. This limits the size of allowable words in the string to a maximum length of from 4 to 10 letters, depending on the implementing computer and the internal character coding scheme used. But whatever their maximum length, it is inevitable that words of more letters will be wanted. One possible approach would be to assign only individual characters as values of the elements of the string. Then each word is itself a string and may be of indefinite length. Such a representation, however, requires many more cells, together with the necessary link fields, to represent a sentence. In our small example, 36 cells would be required to represent all the letters and intervening blanks. That is a high price to pay in terms of storage and in terms of processing overhead, since at least 36 link fields must be set (and probably followed) sometime during the generation process.

An alternative approach would not store any of the assigned element values in the cells at all. Instead, a large lexicon of all possible words (together, perhaps, with other lexical information such as "part of speech," "plural suffixes," etc.) would be set up as a separate data structure. (If the lexicon is relatively static, a sequential representation of its constituent parts would seem appropriate.) In this case the "assigned value" field of the cells of the string would simply point to the appropriate entry in the lexicon, as illustrated in Fig. 4-12.

With this latter representation, if a word appears several times in the same or different strings, it is still written out only once. But multiple references are made to it; that is, the assignment function

f(string element) → {English words}

need not be a 1-1 function. Notice that the procedure CONCATENATE need not be changed, even though the data structure has been. It does not refer to the assigned values. Further, the data structure of Fig. 4-12 allows greater flexibility in the design of other processes. The lexicon can be treated as an independent structure, and processes to modify it (for example, an update process to correct some discovered error) can be applied to it alone. But this will automatically update all strings defined over the lexicon. Similarly, the entire lexicon

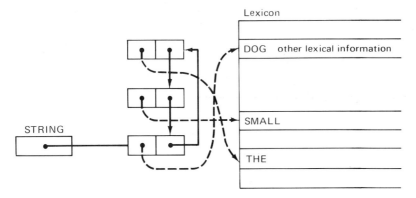

Figure 4-12 A circularly linked string, in which each cell references a word in a lexicon as opposed to storing the value of the word itself.

need not be in immediate core storage; the bulk of it may reside in a low-cost peripheral store as a sequential file to be accessed only as needed.

In the preceding example we see that the string representation may be regarded as little more than an entry device to some other data structure. While this is the first such example of this usage, we shall see many more. Indeed it may be correct to say that the prime use of linked data structures is solely as a dynamic way of gaining access or entry to some other data structure that is most often sequential.

Is a list with no elements a list? The preceding question is not a fatuous one. In set theory a set S with no elements is called an *empty set,* denoted by $\emptyset$. (There are several curious properties associated with the empty set. For instance, one may construct a set whose elements are themselves sets, as in $\mathscr{S} = \{S_1, S_2, \ldots, S_n\}$. Consider a set $\mathscr{T}$ whose single element is the empty set, so that $\mathscr{T} = \{\emptyset\}$. The set $\mathscr{T}$ is not empty since it contains a single element.) Since we have defined a simple list to be no more than a totally ordered set P of elements, it is apparent that one can easily have an "empty" list, if $P = \emptyset$. How should such an empty list be represented? If the cells of the representation correspond to the elements of the list, then there can be no cells, and hence no representation.

There are two possible approaches to this conundrum. One may simply set the reference pointer to the nullvalue whenever the data structure is empty. This solution has several shortcomings,† and most data structure designers prefer to use header cells. A *header cell* in a representation S_R is a unique cell

---

†If a null reference pointer is encountered, there may be some ambiguity as to whether the list is undefined or merely empty. A more serious drawback arises if there are several pointers (often in different procedures) to the same structure. If the structure is initially empty, then all pointers will be null. If elements are subsequently added to the structure, say by one of the processes, it is normally impossible to change all pointers which may reference it. The same problem arises if an initially nonvoid structure is emptied.

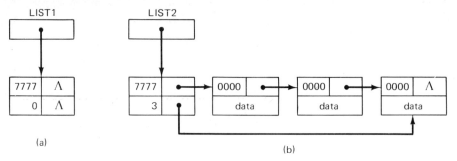

Figure 4-13 Two list representations with header cells.

which (1) is always present in the representation, and (2) is distinguishable from all other cells in the representation. Normally the header cell is not regarded as corresponding to any of the elements of the abstract data structure S_M. If anything, it is thought of as representing the entire structure as a whole. Figure 4-13 illustrates two list representations employing header cells. The first is an empty list. With header cells, there is always at least one cell in the representation of any list, even the empty list.

The leftmost field of the first word (all binary 1s, or octal 7s) is used to distinguish the header cell from the normal list cells (all binary zeros). In this situation the existence of a shorter tag field would be invaluable. It is not uncommon for the header cell to have a different cell format from the other cells of the representation. In the example of Fig. 4-13, the second word of "normal" cells is undivided to contain a whole-word assigned value, while the second word of the header cell has been divided into two fields. The right field has been used to provide an extra link to some special cell in the list. [In this case it links directly to the last element of the list, but it might be set to link to any other element, say one currently being (or about to be) manipulated by some process.]

Since the header cell may be considered to represent the data structure as a whole, it is common to use it to store global information about the whole structure. In the example, the left field of the second word of the header contains a count of the number of elements in the list, that is, its length. Such global information can be used in manifold ways; for instance, a much more efficient substring matching algorithm (see Exercise 4-11) can be devised if the length of both strings is known. Global information about an entire list is often called an *attribute* (or property) of the list. If the number of attributes is indefinite, or exceeds that which can be comfortably stored in a single cell, it is common practice to create a separate list of these global attributes, called an *attribute list*.† Naturally the header cell would provide a link to this separate, but dependent, list.

†An attribute A_j is a function that maps members of a *set of lists* into a set of values. Thus the terms *assignment, attribute,* and *property* are really synonyms for the same functional concept. If a point of a list, or any structure S_M, had an indefinite number of assignments, then it would be natural to represent them using an *assignment* list.

In many list operations, such as search and arbitrary cell addition or deletion, one must know (and usually reset a link of) the preceding cell. But there will be no preceding cell when the process is looking at the first cell of the list. Consequently when writing such processes, one must either include a small section of code to handle this special case, or else treat the list pointer *as if it were the preceding cell,* as we did in Sec. 3-2. Both are undesirable. If the list begins with a header cell, there is always a preceding cell. Their use greatly simplifies the coding of such procedures at small cost. (Redo Exercise 3-3, but now assuming a header cell.)

Finally, the list itself may be an element of some higher-level data structure, say as a linearly ordered set of lists (or list of lists). It is reasonable to let the header cell represent the list in this other structure, and link to the other elements (lists) in it.

Header cells have many uses. The discussion above has indicated five: representing an empty structure, providing additional links into the structure, providing global information about the structure, simplifying procedure code and representing the entire structure if it is treated as an element of some other data structure. Their free use is encouraged. (Because they need a distinguished cell anyway, circular lists invariably include a header cell.) Even though an extra cell of storage is required, the author routinely includes a header cell in the design of all linked data structures, because he has found through experience that, sooner or later, he will wish one were there.

Before we develop the next application, symbolic manipulation of polynomial expressions, which will make use of circularly linked lists and the header cell concept, we must introduce a new kind of total ordering.

Let $S_1, S_2, \ldots, S_n$ be sets, each of which is totally ordered by a relation $\leq_i$, $1 \leq i \leq n$. The *cartesian product* $S_1 \times S_2 \times \cdots \times S_n$ is the set of all possible n-tuples (or vectors) $\{(x_1, x_2, \ldots, x_n) | x_i \in S_i\}$. We may totally order this new set by saying that $x \leq y$, where $x = (x_1, x_2, \ldots, x_n)$ and $y = (y_1, y_2, \ldots, y_n)$. x_i, $y_i \in S_i$, if for some j, $1 \leq j \leq n + 1$,

$$(a) \quad x_i = y_i \quad \text{for all } i < j$$
and
$$(b) \quad x_j < y_j \quad \text{if } j < n.$$

Such a total order is said to be a *lexicographic ordering*.

Normally the component sets S_i are all identical, as are the total orders $\leq_i$ on them. Three familiar examples of lexicographic orders are given below:

$$(4, 7, 2, 5, 9) < (4, 7, 3, 1, 2)$$
$$\text{COMPUTATIONAL} < \text{COMPUTER}$$
$$\text{THE} < \text{THERE}$$

The latter two are simply examples of alphabetic sorting—from which this ordering derives its name—where one compares the two words (or strings) letter by letter, using the normal alphabetic ordering on $S = \{$blank, A, B, $\ldots$, Z$\}$. (Note that it is customary to regard the "blank" symbol as preceding all other symbols in the alphabetic sequence.†) While it has been implicitly assumed, one would want to prove the following:

Theorem 4-1 A lexicographic ordering defined on the cartesian product $S_1 \times S_2 \times \cdots \times S_n$ is a total order relation.

Let $P(x_1, x_2, \ldots, x_n)$ denote a polynomial expression in n different variables x_i. Then P may be expressed as a generalized sum of the form

$$P(x_1, x_2, \ldots, x_n) = \Sigma a_{i_1, i_2, \ldots, i_n} (x_1^{i_1})(x_2^{i_2}) \cdots (x_n^{i_n})$$

where the summation is taken over all $(i_1, i_2, \ldots, i_n)$ with $0 \leq i_j \leq d$. (Here we let d denote the largest permissible exponent value.)

The notation used above may seem unfamiliar and confusing to you at first. For polynomials in a few variables, say three or less, it is more common to denote the variables by distinct symbols, for instance to let $x = x_1$, $y = x_2$, and $z = x_3$. Then one might write the polynomials $P(x, y, z)$ and $Q(x, y, z)$ in a more familiar fashion as:

$$P(x, y, z) = -3.0x^2yz + 2.5xy^2 - 17.0x + 14.0yz \tag{4-5}$$

$$Q(x, y, z) = 4.0x^2y^2 - 2.5xy^2 + 3.0x - 2.5z + 8.0 \tag{4-6}$$

While this latter notation seems to be more quickly understood by humans, the more formal notation given above provides an abstract model that will greatly simplify the problem of devising a useful computer representation. For this reason the reader should verify that

$$P(x_1, x_2, x_3) = a_{211} \cdot x_1^2x_2x_3 + a_{120} \cdot x_1x_2^2 + a_{100} \cdot x_1 + a_{011} \cdot x_2x_3$$

where $\quad a_{211} = -3.0$, $a_{120} = 2.5$, $a_{100} = -17.0$, and $a_{011} = 14.0$

is completely equivalent to the polynomial expression (4-5).

The real numbers $a_{i_1, i_2, \ldots, i_n}$ are called the *coefficients* of the monomial term in which the variables $x_1, x_2, \ldots, x_n$ have the integer exponents (or powers) $i_1, i_2, \ldots, i_n$, respectively. Of course any variable raised to the zero power is simply 1, so it can be ignored, as in the expression (4-5). The special coefficient $a_{0,0,\ldots,0}$ is called the *constant* term of the polynomial.

To represent a polynomial expression in computer storage, it seems natural to let a single cell represent a single monomial term. Each monomial term is completely characterized by its coefficient and by the exponents $i_1, i_2, \ldots, i_n$ of its variables, so these are the only values that need be included in the cell. Figure 4-14 therefore illustrates an acceptable cell structure. Notice that the link field (to the next monomial term) has been put into the second word, rather than

---

†There is no customary ordering for the symbols in a computer's character set (other than for the digits and letters). Should # be "less than" $? The particular order implemented by the manufacturer is called the computer's *collating sequence*. Most are different, and some contain apparently irrational incongruities. Knowing one's own collating sequence is important.

COEFFICIENT	
i_1	LINK
i_3	i_2
...	...
i_n	i_{n-1}

Figure 4-14 A cell format of a monomial term in the representation of a polynomial.

the first. (We have done this primarily to give some variety to our list examples.) Notice also that the cell size is indefinite, since we may not know the number of variables over which the polynomial is defined.

Instead of linking the individual monomial cells arbitrarily, we want a well-defined ordering, so that the monomial terms will always appear in the same relative position in any representation of the polynomial. For this reason we order these terms lexicographically in *descending* order with respect to their exponent sequences $\langle i_1, i_2, \ldots, i_n \rangle$. Expressions (4-5) and (4-6) are in lexicographic order. One more convention will be imposed on the computer representation. All monomial terms with a zero coefficient will be omitted from the list, *except for the constant term that will always be included, whether or not its coefficient is zero.* In this way we can let the constant term serve as a distinguished header cell (all the i_j fields equal zero). With these conventions, the computer representation of the polynomial P(x, y, z) of (4-5) is shown in Fig. 4-15.

Polynomials are widely used in numerical calculations because they are easy to represent and evaluate, both differentiation and integration are nearly trivial, and they may be used to closely approximate any continuous function in n variables. However, most numerical techniques do not work with the polynomials themselves, but rather with their polynomial values. For example, a typical numerical procedure to add the two polynomials P(x, y, z) and Q(x, y, z) would first evaluate them for fixed values of x, y, z and then just add

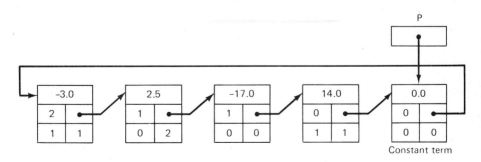

Figure 4-15 A linked representation of the polynomial P(x, y, z).

the resulting values. It would not normally return a new polynomial as the result of the addition.

In a system that performs symbolic calculation, it is the expressions themselves, not their values, that are manipulated. In such a system, the sum of two polynomial expressions, say $P(x, y, z) + Q(x, y, z)$, is a new polynomial

$$R(x, y, z) = 4.0x^2y^2 - 3.0x^2yz - 14.0x + 14.0yz - 2.5z + 8.0 \qquad (4\text{-}7)$$

The following procedure symbolically adds two polynomials, represented as in Fig. 4-15.

procedure   polyadd (p, q, n);
pointer   p, q;
integer   n;

This procedure creates the algebraic sum of two polynomials P and Q in n variables. On exit q is left pointing to the resultant sum, while the pointer p and its polynomial are left unaltered.

begin
    real   a;
    integer   celsiz, i, j;
    pointer   header, lastq, newq, oldq;
    field   link, coef, exp[1:n];

Initialize pointers p and q to the first term of each polynomial. The additional pointer lastq always follows q as it successively points to each cell in Q in turn.

    celsiz $\leftarrow \lfloor n/2 \rfloor + 2$;
    p $\leftarrow$ link(p);
    header $\leftarrow$ lastq $\leftarrow$ q;
    q $\leftarrow$ link(q);

Compare the exponent sequences $\langle i_1, \ldots, i_n \rangle_P$ and $\langle j_1, j_2, \ldots, j_n \rangle_Q$ of the current monomial terms in P and Q, respectively.

compare:
    for k = 1 **thru** n **do**
        i $\leftarrow \exp_k(p)$;
        j $\leftarrow \exp_k(q)$;
        if i < j **then go to** lessthan;
        if i > j **then go to** greaterthan;

The exponent sequences $\langle i_1, i_2, \ldots, i_n \rangle_P$ and $\langle j_1, j_2, \ldots, j_n \rangle_Q$ are equal. Add these two monomial terms.

    a $\leftarrow$ coef(p) + coef(q)
    if q = header **then go to** constant;
    if a $\neq$ 0.0
        then *New coefficient is non-zero, alter coefficient of corresponding monomial*
            term in Q.
            coef(q) $\leftarrow$ a;

```
        p ←link(p);
        lastq ←q;
        q ←link(q);
        go to compare;
     else  New coefficient is zero. Delete this monomial term from the represen-
           tation of Q.
        oldq ←q;
        q ←link(q);
        p ←link(p);
        link(lastq) ←q;
        call takeit (oldq, celsiz);
        go to compare;
```

$\langle i_1, i_2, \ldots, i_n \rangle_P$ *is lexicographically less than* $\langle j_1, j_2, \ldots, j_n \rangle_Q$. *Advance to next monomial term in Q.*

```
lessthan:
     lastq ←q;
     q ←link(q);
     go to compare;
```

$\langle i_1, i_2, \ldots, i_n \rangle_P$ *is lexicographically greater than* $\langle j_1, j_2, \ldots, j_n \rangle_Q$. *Insert a copy of the monomial term of P into the list representation of Q. Fetch next term in P only.*

```
greaterthan:
     newq ←giveme(celsiz);
     for k =0 thru celsiz-1 do
         cont(newq +k) ←cont(p +k);
     link(newq) ←q;
     link(lastq) ←newq;
     lastq ←newq;
     p ←link(p);
     go to compare;
```

This is the constant cell of both lists. Insert the new coefficient in the cell of Q, whether zero or not, and the procedure is done.

```
constant:
     coef(q) ←a;
     exit;
     end
```

Although moderately long, this procedure should be studied in detail. The handling of the pointers P, Q, and LASTQ is particularly worth examining. Readers should desk check the operation of this process using the polynomials P and Q given in Eqs. (4-5) and (4-6) [the result should be R given in Eq. (4-7)], and preferably code their own version to be tested with a main program.

Figure 4-16 illustrates the configuration of the two lists, $P(x_1, x_2, x_3)$ and $Q(x_1, x_2, x_3)$, together with their respective pointers just after a copy of the cell corresponding to the polynomial term $-3.0x^2yz$ of P has been inserted into the

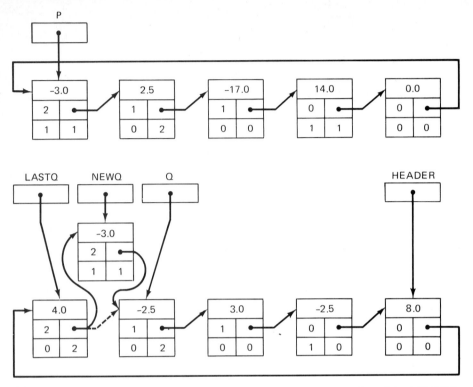

Figure 4-16 Intermediate configuration of the argument lists during execution of the POLYADD routine.

list representation of Q. The pointer P has not yet been advanced to the next cell.

From a purely practical standpoint, POLYADD would have been superior if it had been implemented as a nondestructive function that creates an entirely new list representing the resultant polynomial sum, and returns as its functional value a pointer to the list. Generally one eschews processes that destroy their input arguments, as POLYADD destroys the original polynomial Q. However, the handling of cell deletion when the new coefficient is zero makes this version more interesting from a pedagogic point of view.

In Sec. 3-1 we defined a *deque* as a simple list to which additions and deletions may be made at either end; but we have shown no representations of a deque. Of course, a deque can be represented by a simply linked list with pointers to each end, just as we represented simple queues. Addition of new cells at either end is easy and is left as an exercise for the reader. Similarly, deletion of cells at one of the ends is equally easy. But deletion of a cell at the other end requires the address of the preceding cell in the list so that the pointer can be reset to this preceding cell and its "next" link can be set to the nullvalue. This in turn requires a process that will "walk through" the entire list.

LIST

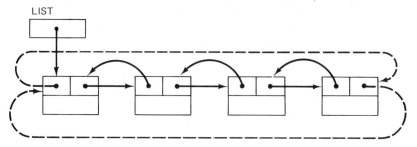

Figure 4-17 A doubly linked list. ⇢ denotes optional "circular" links.

To avoid this time-consuming "walk-through" process, <u>many deques are doubly linked.</u> Each cell in a *doubly linked list* contains a link to the next following cell and a second link to the immediately preceding cell, as shown in Fig. 4-17. Insertion or deletion of cells in a doubly linked representation is equally easy at either end of the list. Indeed, with double linking one can add or delete cells from the middle of the list with little more effort than addition or deletion at the ends. Consequently, little is gained by restricting these operations to the ends, so that it may be called a deque. <u>In terms of computer representation, a deque is virtually indistinguishable from an arbitrary list.</u>

Recall that a marked asymmetry was found in the simply linked queues of Sec. 3-2. Doubly linked lists do not exhibit such asymmetry, and they have been called *symmetric lists* by some authors (Weizenbaum, 1963). The symmetry is further enhanced if they are circularly linked as shown in Fig. 4-17.

Double linking is an important and frequently used representational technique. It belongs in any programmer's bag of tricks. Its use conveys considerable flexibility with regard to structural operations, addition, deletion, or reconfiguration. But double linking may require additional storage to represent the additional link, and always involves additional processing overhead, since normally twice as many links must be set or reset. Because of its power, there is an unfortunate tendency, especially among students, to overwork double linking. Surprisingly, the author knows of few applications where double linkage of the data structure is essential, or even particularly advantageous. One clear exception to this observation is <u>certain real-time applications, for example, graphic display.</u> Here the ability to rapidly move back and forth through the data structure is often of utmost importance, and double linking may be well worth considering.

EXERCISES FOR SECTION 4-2

4-8 Code an implementation of the process CONCATENATE.

4-9 A program to randomly generate well-formed sentences using a table of syntactic rewrite rules demands some time and effort; but if the lexicon is well chosen, the results can be hilarious.

[The output of a simple program of this nature fooled an undergraduate English class into thinking it was legitimate blank verse. A fascinating system along this line was the ELIZA project (Weizenbaum, 1966).]

4-10 Suppose the lexicon of Fig. 4-12 is implemented as a doubly subscripted array. Should the assignment pointer in the left field of each cell be a storage address or an array index? Why?

*4-11 (a) Design a logical procedure SAME (X, Y) that will test whether the two strings X and Y are identical. (Assume a representation as in Fig. 4-11.)

(b) A more difficult process to write, but more important in practice, is a logical procedure SUBSTRING (X, Y, ADDR) that returns **true** if X is a substring of Y, and **false** otherwise; code it. If **true**, SUBSTRING should also return with ADDR pointing to the cell of Y where the match begins. Test your procedure with the following strings

$$X = \text{abbca}$$
$$Y = \text{cabbababbcabbcab}$$

(where each letter is treated as a single element of the string).

(c) How would the global information "string length," stored in a header cell of the representation, simplify these two procedures?

4-12 There is an intriguing analogue to the concept of a lexicographic order which, to the author's knowledge, has never been fully investigated. Suppose the component sets P_i are partially ordered, not totally ordered. Can one define a concept of an induced partial ordering on $P_1 \times P_2 \times \cdots \times P_n$? Actually it is clear that one can define such a partial order in several ways; the real questions are "What are its properties?", "Is the definition natural?", and "Is it of any use?"

*4-13 (a) Code an implementation of POLYADD and test it. (Clearly, subtraction of polynomials is identical, and the same routine with multiple entry points can do both.)

(b) To effectively test the polynomial add procedure you will want procedures to read, to print, and to evaluate polynomials, say RDPOLY(P, N), PRPOLY(P, N), and VALUE(P, N, X), where N denotes the number of variables. Code them. Having done this, you will be well on your way to implementing a small symbolic manipulation package.

(c) Design and code a program POLYMULT to multiply two polynomials P and Q. Although longer, it is not really much more difficult than addition. (Since the set of all polynomials in n variables is only a ring, not a field, it is impossible to design a general polynomial division procedure.)

(d) Design and code procedures to symbolically differentiate and integrate polynomial expressions.

4-14 Figure 4-14 shows the cell format used in the text for polynomial representation. On many machines the cell format shown in the accompanying figure is superior because it allows a more rapid comparison of the exponent sequences. Why? Recode the comparison test of POLYADD using this new format.

COEFFICIENT	
LINK	I_1
I_2	I_3
⋮	
I_{n-1}	I_n

Ex. 4-14

4-15 Rational functions of the form

$$R(x_1, x_2, \ldots, x_n) = \frac{P(x_1, x_2, \ldots, x_n)}{Q(x_1, x_2, \ldots, x_n)}$$

are widely used in numerical applications. The representation of polynomials given in the text is easily extended to rational functions by providing a header cell with two fields, one of which links to the numerator P, the other linking to the denominator Q.

Both multiplication and division (the set of rational functions is a field) are nearly trivial, since one merely performs a polynomial multiplication of the numerators and denominators independently. Addition is the more difficult process, since to add the functions $R_1 = P_1/Q_1$ and $R_2 = P_2/Q_2$, three products and a sum, $(P_1 \cdot Q_2 + P_2 \cdot Q_1)/(Q_1 \cdot Q_2)$, must be determined. The most serious problem in the implementation of a system to manipulate representations of rational functions is that of storage. Most algebraic operations tend to result in expressions consisting of inordinately long polynomials in both the numerator and denominator that gobble up storage. Absolutely essential to such a system is a simplification procedure that will reduce the size of rational expressions by discovering, and canceling out, all factors common to both the numerator and denominator. Since the ring of monic polynomials is a euclidean domain it is possible, in theory, to apply Euclid's algorithm to find the greatest common factor of any two polynomials and "divide" it out. But in practice, accumulated round-off in the real coefficients makes it difficult to implement—how small must the coefficient be before it is considered to be zero?

But in spite of the fact that the implementation of a truly practical system is unlikely, the design and coding of a system to manipulate rational functions is both interesting and rewarding.

*4-16 Given a doubly linked list as shown in Fig. 4-17, write procedures to:

ADDLFT(LIST,DATA) ⎫	add an element to the left
ADDRGT(LIST,DATA) ⎭	(or right) end
DELLFT(LIST) ⎫	delete left (or right) most
DELRGT(LIST) ⎭	element, and return value
INSERTLFT(LIST,CELL,DATA) ⎫	insert element to left (or
INSERTRGT(LIST,CELL,DATA) ⎭	right) of specified cell
DELETE(CELL)	delete specified cell

Watch the boundary conditions. Would header cells be advantageous?

4-17 Although none of the situations examined so far motivate this assertion, there are nevertheless examples where a process "knows" the address of a single cell within a list, but nothing else. In particular, it would like a link to the header cell or to either end. Under these circumstances a list might well be "doubly linked" as shown in the accompanying figure.

(*a*) Design procedures PRECEDE(CELL), LFTEND(CELL), RGTEND(CELL), and HEADER(CELL), which—given the address of a cell in the list—return the address of the corresponding cells.

(*b*) Design procedures to dynamically add and delete elements from such a list (as in the preceding exercise). Note that special care must be taken to ensure that the cells with the two different kinds of links are always in some sense "interleaved," or else the procedures of (*a*) may not work. What configuration should the singleton, doubleton, and three element lists have?

Ex. 4-17

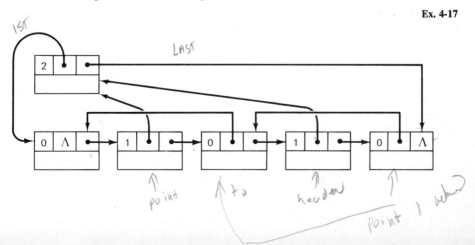

*4-18 A linked data structure is constructed of cells with only one link field per cell, so each cell has a unique "next" cell, save for exactly one in which the link field is null. Must the data structure be a linear structure? Prove (by means of a rigorous demonstration) or disprove (by means of a counterexample).

This exercise is important, because if a computer representation is supposed to be linear, then we would like a practical means of testing whether it is really well formed. If the assertion is true, then only a count of the null links need to be kept; if it is false, some other test must be devised.

4-3 LINKED REPRESENTATION OF SETS

In this section we will develop a representation of sets, and implement standard set-theoretic operations using it, that will be of considerable value in subsequent chapters. The approach taken is quite straightforward and naïve compared to some set representations. Still it will be sufficient for a variety of interesting applications.

Let X denote any finite set of elements $\{x_1, \ldots, x_n\}$. We will assume that each element x_i is also part of a data structure that is represented by a cell and may be identified by its cell address c_{x_i}. The elements may be simple variables, points of a graph, or composite data structures such as arrays, lists, or trees. (In the latter cases, c_{x_i} would be the base address of the array, the address of a reference pointer, or the address of a header cell denoting the entire structure.)

Now the cells representing the elements of the set could be simply chained in any order as a linked list, so as to represent the set. But such an approach has two serious drawbacks. First, a cell may be an element of many such sets. It is patently impractical to include a link field in the cell format for every possible set of which it might be a member. Further, we do not want to link the elements of a set in any old order, because it will make the important set operators, union, intersection, and relative complement incredibly inefficient. Consequently we will adopt the following representation.

A set will be represented by a simply linked list of one-word cells, together with a header cell.† In these cells, which denote elements of the set, the *element* field (left field in figures) will link to the element c_{x_i} being included as a member, and the *link* field will link to the next element cell in the list. This format is shown in Fig. 4-18. The link field of the header cell links to the first element cell in the list (provided the set is nonempty). The remaining left field of the header is called the *current* field and may link to any cell in the set list.

Moreover, all element cells of a set list will be linked in *ascending order on the value of their element fields,* that is, in ascending order of the cell addresses c_{x_i}.

---

†The cells representing elements of the data structure itself will almost certainly be of a different size, so there is some problem in the dynamic allocation procedure, GIVEME. One solution is to maintain two separate free pools, one with cells of size 1, the other with cells of size n. A better, and actually simpler, approach is given in Sec. 10-1, by which a minor modification to GIVEME will handle requests for cells of several sizes. For purposes of this section it is irrelevant how allocation is handled.

CELL$_x$ | LINK

Figure 4-18 A cell format for set elements.

Figure 4-19 illustrates the representation of a typical set, with reference pointer SET. The value of insisting that the cells of a set list be linked in ascending (or descending) order of the cell addresses of the elements belonging to the set is readily shown by the following procedure to create the intersection of two sets. Each cell of a set list is examined at most once.

pointer function meet (seta, setb);
pointer seta, setb;

Given two sets, with reference pointers seta and setb, this routine creates a new set which denotes their intersection.

begin
　　pointer　cell, cella, cellb, newcell;
　　field　　current, element, link;
　　common /nulval/ null;

　　Create an initially empty set, consisting of the header cell alone.

　　meet ←cell ←giveme(1);
　　current(cell) ←cell;
　　link(cell) ←null;

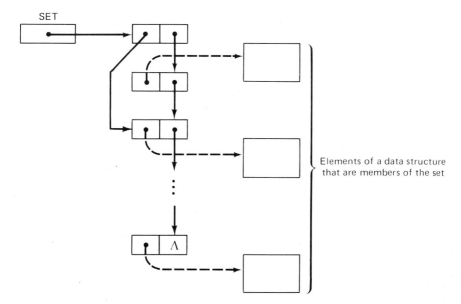

Figure 4-19 A representation of a set.

Work through both lists comparing element addresses, one at a time.

```
    cella ←link(seta);
    cellb ←link(setb);
compare:
    if cella =null or cellb =null then exit;
    if element(cella) < element(cellb) then go to less;
    if element(cella) =element(cellb) then go to equal;
```

Element$_a$ is greater than element$_b$. Get next cell from set$_b$.

```
    cella ←link(cella);  ₹ backward
    go to compare;
```

Element$_a$ is less than element$_b$. Get next cell from set$_a$.

```
less:
    cella ←link(cella);
    go to compare;
```

The element is common to both sets. Add a cell to the resultant list that also points to this element. Get next cells from both sets.

```
equal:
    newcell ←giveme(1);
    element(newcell) ←element(cella);
    link(newcell) ←null;
    link(cell) ←newcell;
    cell ←newcell;
    cella ←link(cella);
    cellb ←link(cellb);
    go to compare;
    end
```

This procedure is easily coded. It could be invoked with a statement such as

$$X = MEET(Y, Z)$$

where the variables Y and Z serve as reference pointers to their respective sets. The address returned by MEET will be the address of the header cell of the set list, so X will become a pointer to their intersection. Similarly the implementation of the set routines UNION and RCOMP (relative complement of two sets) are reasonably straightforward and are left to the reader. See, however, Exercise 4-19. One would also expect routines such as NEWSET (to create an initially empty set), INSERT (to add an element to an existing set), and RELEASE (to return the representation of a set to the free store), together with logical functions SUBSET, MEMBER, and EMPTY that return TRUE if the indicated condition holds, and possibly an integer-valued function SIZE that returns the cardinality of the set.

So far no use has been made of the left field in the header cell, which was called the current link. Why was it included? An important concept of program control in any programming language is the ability to execute some block of code for all the members of a set. DO loops in Fortran belong to this class; so also are the **for** and **do** . . . **while** constructions of Algol.† We would naturally want a process that will allow the explicit construction of a set coupled with the ability to perform a block of code using every member of that set. The following process NXTELM increments through a set on each call returning a new element from the set. It uses the current link, which always points to the last element that had been returned by NXTELM.

pointer function nxtelm (set);
pointer set;

This process returns as its functional value the internal identifier (cell address c_x) of the next element in the "set," if any. If the set has been exhausted, it returns the nullvalue.

begin
    pointer setcel;
    field current, element, link;
    common /nulval/ null;

    Get the next cell in the set list, which points to the next element of the set.

    setcel ←link(current(set));
    if setcel =null
        then *Set is exhausted.*
            nxtelm ←null
        else *Return pointer from element field.*
            nxtelm ←element(setcel);
            current(set) ←setcel;
    exit;
    end

The preceding process NXTELM, which steps (increments or indexes) through the list representing a set, is a *reentrant* process. The CURRENT link that "remembers" the position of the process within the set is associated with the set itself, not the process. Consequently the process could begin searching through one set, say SETA, pause and begin incrementing through another set SETB, and then return to complete its search of SETA.

---

†In DO loops the set (of integers only) is defined by giving its upper and lower bounds, and possibly an increment parameter. It would be a more explicit set operation if it were coded as

for all i ∈ [1, n] **do**

The "for list" concept of Algol permits more varied definition of the index set. The elements of the set may be explicitly enumerated, may be defined by a characteristic property (the **while** construction), or may be defined by giving the upper and lower bounds of an interval, as in DO loops.

To be used effectively, a process that initializes this set retrieval procedure, say INITSET, must also be coded. It need only set the CURRENT link in the header cell pointing to the header cell itself (left as an exercise for the reader). With INITSET and NXTELM one can now implement programs that used the following control statements to index over arbitrary sets.

```
        ⋮
    call initset (set);
loop:
        x ←nxtelm(set);
        if x = null then go to α;
            ⋮
        Block of code to be executed, possibly involving other calls to nextelm
            ⋮
        go to loop;
α:   Next block of code
            ⋮
```

Since this preceding section of code is quite lengthy, and since it will be used in a number of subsequent processes, we will abbreviate it with the following control statement

$$\textbf{for all } x \in \text{set } \textbf{do} \tag{4-7}$$

Notice the striking similarity between the implementation of the preceding control statement and the implementation† of an ordinary Fortran DO loop

$$\text{DO 201 } I = J, K, L$$

which follows.

```
        ⋮
    I = J − L              initialize I to precede first element
β   I = I + L              increment index variable, I
    IF(I .GT. K) GO TO γ   test for termination of loop.
        ⋮                  Block of code to be executed possibly
                           involving other DO loops but not on same
                           index variable.
```

---

†This is a "correct" implementation of the DO loop concept. Many actual compilers, for archaic compatibility reasons, initialize by setting I = J, then increment and test *after* executing the body of the loop at least once. That is, they do not admit indexing over the empty set.

GO TO β

γ next statement

$$\vdots$$

Even if an actual compiler does not recognize the explicit expression of the loop construct in its language, it is clear that indexing through a set is still an important control concept in the design of computational processes. Further, the construct can be used in the abstract description of such processes, even though its implementation may require a hand expansion into the statements of the actual programming language being used. This is precisely the way we will regard the "new" control expression (4-7) that we have introduced above.

Since by adding the control statement

for all x $\in$ set **do** ...

we have begun to modify the Algol-like language that we use to describe procedures that operate on data structures, we might point out another useful modification. Variables that serve as pointers, and whose assigned values must thus be valid cell addresses, we have been declaring to be of type **pointer.** This declaration serves mostly to remind the reader of the intended use of these variables; although in an implemented programming language, they could provide the basis for various forms of syntactic and run-time error detection. This form of declaration may be refined by indicating not only that the variable is a *pointer,* but by designating the kind of structure to which it points. Thus we might declare **list pointer, stack pointer,** or **set pointer** variables, or more simply, just variables of type **list, stack,** or **set,** respectively. For various reasons we choose not to adopt this intriguing linguistic convention—save in the case where the variable is a set pointer. In this case we will declare the variable to be of type **set.**

EXERCISES FOR SECTION 4-3

4-19 Although the procedure MEET as written will always work, its implementation as a *function* subprogram may introduce undesirable side effects. Suppose the process is invoked by the statement X = MEET(Y, X). The reference pointer X will be left pointing to the intersection set as expected. But what will happen to the original set X that served as argument? Its list representation will be left without a reference pointer as "garbage" that can never be used. Clearly we would like the process to return the cells of this argument list before exiting. One solution is to implement the process as a subroutine and pass the result pointer, say SETC, as parameter as well. Then a test for "identity," viz.,

if loc(setc) = loc(seta) **then call** release (seta);

can be used to trigger the return of these representations. [If one is operating in a garbage-collecting environment (see section 10-3), or the language has its own compiler, this problem may vanish.] Redesign MEET (and UNION, RCOMP) to provide for this kind of release.

*4-20 Write and implement the set processes UNION, RCOMP, NEWSET, INSERT, SUBSET, MEMBER, EMPTY, SIZE, and INITSET. With the possible exception of UNION, all are virtually trivial.

4-21 Note that these set lists cannot be erased in a single operation since there is no link to the other end. Suppose instead that they were circularly linked; then return would be trivial. How would the processes MEET, NXTELM, and those above, need to be changed if a circularly linked representation were used?

4-22 A partition is a collection (or set) of sets. First draw the data structure that would represent such a set of sets; then design a logical function PARTITION(P, SET) that will test whether or not the collection P is a partition of the set SET.

4-23 Reexamine the procedures given in this text and redeclare those variable of type **pointer** to be of type **list, stack,** or **set** as appropriate. Temporary local pointers which are used to keep place as processes "wander" through the structure might be declared to be of type **point** or **element.** Do these changes make the processes easier to understand?

*4-24 In addition to making the interpretation of a process more clear, declarations can be used to provide for error detection. For example, a compiler might (1) check that field identifiers were always used in conjunction with pointer variables, or (2) that the arguments of a set-valued function such as UNION were themselves sets. Further run-time checks could be made to ensure that values assigned to pointer variables lie in the range of valid addresses, that the structure identified by a set variable is actually a well-formed set, etc. Devise and implement such run-time tests for some of the procedures you have already implemented. You may find it helpful to modify the data structure and include a distinctive tag field in each cell. (The author has found that this kind of run-time error detection, although costly in terms of overhead, is invaluable in the development of applications that make extensive use of data structures. Conditional compilation techniques permit their suppression in the fully debugged system.)

4-25 All the procedures of this text are to some degree dependent on the representation of the data structure, even though we have employed several techniques to minimize such dependency. As distributed networks and data bases become more widespread, it becomes increasingly desirable to express procedures in a form that is totally independent of any particular representational structure. To what extent can an appropriate choice of type declarations help to achieve this independence? [Note that this is a large and open-ended question. Both Hoare (1972) and Date (1975) offer interesting insights to this issue.]

TREES

In this chapter we examine a class of acyclic structures, called *trees,* which may in some sense be regarded as the next step up in a hierarchy of structural complexity. These structures are widely used in computer science as evidenced by the following partial list: parse trees (compiler theory and formal languages), search trees (information retrieval), decision trees (artificial intelligence, systems analysis), and directory trees (file manipulation, operating systems). The tree concept has a rather natural intuitive formulation in the assertion that a tree is a connected graph without circuits (cf. Exercise 1-17). Recalling the definition of a circuit (page 24), the reader can see that the five graphs of Fig. 5-1 we would want to call trees, whereas the five graphs of Fig. 5-2 we would designate nontrees.

There is nearly as rich a variety of techniques for the computer representation of tree structures as was found for the representation of linear structures. We could proceed to explore them armed only with this intuitive concept. But it will be profitable in the long run if we first pin down more formally some of the properties of trees.

5-1 FORMAL PROPERTIES OF TREES

We choose to express the tree concept somewhat differently by saying that a *tree* is a finite connected graph $G = (P, E)$ such that

$$|P| = |E| + 1$$

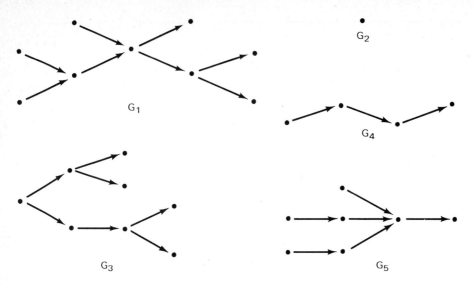

Figure 5-1 Trees.

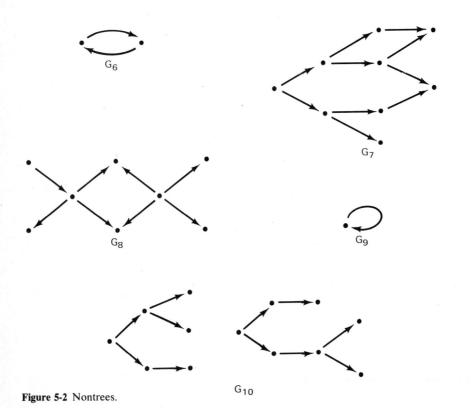

Figure 5-2 Nontrees.

The reader should convince himself that all the graphs of Fig. 5-1 satisfy this definition, and hence should be called trees, while all the graphs of Fig. 5-2 fail to satisfy this definition. Intuitively, it characterizes the tree concept as we think it should. The graph G_{10} of Fig. 5-2 is not a tree because it is not connected, but each of its connected components is a tree. Such disconnected graphs, whose connected components are all trees, are called *forests*.

Theorem 5-1 follows as an almost immediate corollary of this definition and Theorem 1-10.

Theorem 5-1 A graph is a tree if and only if every edge is a disconnecting edge (that is, its removal disconnects the graph).

Consequently every tree must be loop-free. One can then show the following:

Theorem 5-2 A connected graph G is a tree if and only if every connected subgraph H is a tree.

In classical algebra (e.g., lattice theory, group theory, and field theory) it is customary to require that important substructures possess the essential properties of the structure as a whole. For example, subgroups of a group must themselves be groups; sublattices are lattices. In this tradition we say that a subgraph T', of a tree T, is a *subtree* if T' is connected (or, in view of the preceding theorem, if it is itself a tree).

Theorem 5-3 (Tutte, 1967) A graph G is a tree if and only if between any two points x and z there exists a unique walk $\omega(x, z)$.

From this characterization, the following properties of trees, which we express as corollaries, readily follow.

Corollary 5-4 Every walk in a tree is simple.

Corollary 5-5 Trees are circuit-free.

Corollary 5-6 Trees are acyclic.

Corollary 5-7 Every tree T contains at least one minimal point x, with $L(x) = \emptyset$, and at least one maximal point z, with $R(z) = \emptyset$.

Corollary 5-5 asserts that trees are graphs without circuits. We would certainly expect to be able to prove this property from our chosen definition, since we had used it at the beginning of the chapter to create an intuitive image of what kinds of structures we wanted to call trees and what kinds we did not want to consider as trees. In fact, we can completely characterize trees according to the existence or nonexistence of circuits, as shown by the following theorem.

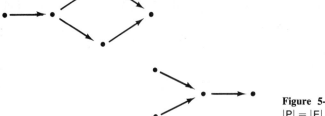

Figure 5-3 An acyclic graph, with $|P| = |E| + 1$, that is not a tree.

Theorem 5-8 (Harary, 1969) A graph G is a tree if and only if any one of the following equivalent assertions is true:

(a) G is connected and circuit free,

(b) G is circuit free, but any additional edge creates a circuit,

(c) G is circuit free, and $|P| = |E| + 1$.

In contrast to characterization (c) above, the reader should note that an acyclic graph need not be a tree, as shown in Fig. 5-3, even if $|P| = |E| + 1$.

So many various alternative characterizations of the tree concept have been stated—almost to the point of tedium—in order to bring out the extraordinary richness of this concept. Trees appear in a great many applications, but invariably it seems that the point of approach is different. In some cases it is the absence of circuits that is of paramount importance; in others, it may be the uniqueness of walks or the fact that every edge is disconnecting. But no matter how the tree concept gets introduced into the particular area of application, it is still a tree.

In many respects the absence of circuits may be considered to be the fundamental defining characteristic; it is certainly the way one *visually* checks whether a graphic representation of a graph is a tree or not. We surely do not count points and edges. In many graph theory texts it is given as the initial definition, and then the other characterizations are derived from it. In contrast, the expression (5-1) relating the cardinalities of the point and edge sets seems to be of secondary, and of almost contrived, importance. Yet we have chosen to give it as the fundamental definition because we feel that it is the more natural characterization given the context of computer data structures. A computer process that simply counts seems more basic than a process to discover circuits, or to determine whether a walk is unique.

So far our development of the tree concept has been that which might be found in any text on formal graph theory. But many texts in computer science would choose to call only the graphs G_3 and G_4 in Fig. 5-1 trees. It is precisely this more restricted form of tree that most often occurs in computer applications, and hence is of most interest.

Recall that the sets $\overline{L}(A)$ and $\overline{R}(A)$ were called left and right *ideals,* since they in fact constituted algebraic ideals with respect to the path relation, and

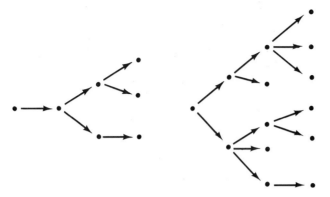

Figure 5-4 Right principal trees.

that in conformity to standard algebraic notation, the sets $\overline{L}(\{y\})$ and $\overline{R}(\{y\})$ were called *principal ideals*. We will now use this terminology to develop a characterization of the restricted class of trees that is of special interest to computer scientists. Let $T = (P, E)$ be a tree with $x \in P$. By the *right* (or left) *principal subtree* on x, denoted T_x, we mean the subgraph $\overline{R}(\{x\})$, (or $\overline{L}(\{x\})$). T itself is said to be a *right* (or left) *principal tree* if for some $x \in P$, $T = T_x$. The point x is called the *principal point* of the tree or subtree.

Readily, any ideal must be connected, so that by Theorem 5-2 these subgraphs really are subtrees. Further, the principal point x is clearly minimal, that is, $L(x) = \emptyset$. The maximal points $\{z_i\}$, for which $R(z_i) = \emptyset$, are called *end points* of the tree. Two right principal trees are illustrated in Fig. 5-4. They have been drawn "growing to the right" in our conventional way of drawing acyclic graphs in a left-to-right fashion, hence our reason for calling them "right" principal. Notice, however, that the two graphs of Fig. 5-5 are also right principal trees, even though they have been drawn differently. In fact, most authors illustrate trees by having them branch downward, as does Fig. 5-5a. On those occasions when it seems more appropriate we shall also.

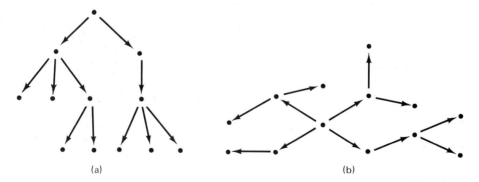

(a)   (b)

Figure 5-5 More right principal trees.

Right principal trees are called *rooted trees* by many authors.† Harary (1969) descriptively calls them *out-trees*. They are the kind of relation that one intuitively pictures as a directed tree, but in fact they are only a very restricted subset of the class of all directed trees (see Exercise 5-7). However, this very restriction makes them somewhat easier to characterize, and makes them extremely useful in so many practical applications.

Theorem 5-9 A graph G is a right principal tree if and only if
(*a*) it has a unique least point x, and
(*b*) $|L(y)| = 1$, for all $y \neq x$.

(It is worth comparing this characterization of principal trees with that of linear graphs given in Theorem 3-1; see also Exercises 5-5 and 5-6.)

Both the characterizing properties (*a*) and (*b*) above have important consequences. Every tree with a least element must be right principal, and every element of the structure is reachable from the least point. This means that with a single reference pointer, or entry point, one can still be certain of accessing all the elements of the representational structure. The fact that $|L(y)| \leq 1$ for all $y \in P$ both permits more effective representations and provides a test by which processes operating on a representation can guarantee that the resulting structure is well formed.

Left and right principality are dual concepts. A tree is left principal if and only if its inverse is right principal. For every statement (or theorem) about right principal trees, an analogous dual statement can be made about left principal trees. For the remainder of this chapter we will be concerned almost exclusively with right principal trees, and for brevity we will assume that the terms *tree* and *principal tree* mean a right principal tree unless explicitly modified to the contrary.

EXERCISES FOR SECTION 5-1

*5-1 In addition to the defining expression (5-1) of trees, empirically verify that the other important characterizations given in Theorems 5-1, 5-3, and 5-8 also separate the 10 graphs of Figs. 5-1 and 5-2 into the same sets of trees and nontrees. In short, convince yourself that you really understand the implications of these results about the nature of trees.

Alternatively, formally prove that these characterizations are mathematically equivalent.

*5-2 (*a*) Construct by trial and error all the distinct (nonisomorphic) right principal trees on four points. Let n_R denote the number of such distinct right principal trees. Clearly there are exactly the same number n_L of left principal trees (since a tree is right principal if its inverse is left principal).

(*b*) Construct by trial and error all arbitrary trees, that is, the set of left and right principal together with those which are neither (e.g., G_1 of Fig. 5-1). Let n_T denote this number.

---

†Those who continue this horticultural terminology normally call the principal point of a tree, or subtree, its *root;* maximal, or end, points may be called either *leaves* or *twigs;* paths in the tree are called *branches.*

(*c*) Show that $n_T \geq n_L + n_R = 2 \cdot n_R$, provided $|P| \geq 4$.

(*d*) By similar trial and error construction determine all right principal and all arbitrary trees on five points. (Note $n_T = 27$.)

5-3 Give a formal definition of *left principal tree;* then state a characterization analogous to Theorem 5-9.

5-4 Prove, using Theorems 3-1, 5-9, and the characterization above, that a structure is linear if and only if it is both a left and right principal tree.

5-5 Graphs for which $|L(y)| = 1$ (or $|R(y)| = 1$) are called *functional graphs.* Functional graphs need not be trees, nor acyclic, nor even connected. Draw some functional graphs that are not trees.

5-6 Trees are required by definition to be connected. Yet there is no explicit reference to connectivity in Theorem 5-9. What part of this characterization guarantees the necessary connectivity?

5-7 Consider the accompanying table, enumerating right principal and arbitrary trees on sets of few points.

$|P|$	n_R	n_T	n_R/n_T
3	2	3	0.666
4	4	8	0.500
5	9	27	0.333
6	20	91	0.219
7	48	350	0.137
8	115	1376	0.083
9	288	5743	0.050
10	719	24635	0.029
11	1842	108968	0.017

Readily, n_R and n_T are unbounded as $|P| \to \infty$. It is conjectured, however, that the ratio $n_R/n_T \to 0$. Prove it. [Solution of this kind of problem requires the symbolic expression of the "number of things" called an *enumeration series* as may be found in Riordan (1958, cf. page 138) or Knuth (1968). Note also the diversity of trees as $|P|$ becomes even moderately large.]

5-8 One can get a different perspective on the role that trees play in the spectrum of relational structures by considering the set $\mathscr{G}(P) = \{G_i = (P, E_i)\}$ of all *connected* graphs on a given set P of elements. We may partially order this set $\mathscr{G}(P)$ of graphs by edge inclusion, that is, $G_i \leq G_j$ if $E_i \subseteq E_j$. Since $(\mathscr{G}(P), \subseteq)$ is acyclic, we know (by Theorem 1-3) that it has minimal elements. We could now alternatively define a graph $G = (P, E)$ to be a *tree* if it is a minimal element in the set $(\mathscr{G}(P), \subseteq)$. Show that expression (5-1) and its corollary Theorem 5-1 follow from this definition.

Given this perspective, trees can be regarded as the simplest (in the sense of smallest or minimal) connected relation on any set P. (This is contrary to the opening statement of the chapter, which said that trees represent the next step up in relational complexity.) Justify the assertion that linear structures are more complex (in that their definition involves more mathematical constraints) than principal trees, which are in turn more complex than arbitrary trees. Is it true that the more complex (in terms of mathematical constraints) a class of mathematical objects is, the easier it is to represent the class? In addition to classes of graphs, you might consider such mathematical objects as functions, groups, and so on.

5-2 REPRESENTATION OF BINARY TREES

Principal trees are essentially characterized by the cardinality of the set of left neighbors of any point, that is, $|L(y)| \leq 1$ for all y. It seems very natural to further restrict this concept by imposing bounds on the cardinality of the set of

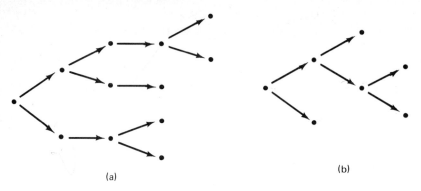

(a)

(b)

Figure 5-6 (*a*) Binary tree. (*b*) Complete binary tree.

right neighbors R(y). A principal tree is called an *n-ary tree* if for all y ∈ P, |R(y)| ≤ n. In those special cases when n = 2 or 3, it is called a *binary* or *ternary tree,* respectively. The tree is said to be *complete* if |R(y)| = n for all non-maximal points y. (If y is maximal, then of course |R(y)| = 0.) Figure 5-6 illustrates a binary tree and a complete binary tree.

Binary trees are particularly easy to represent by a linked structure, since no more than three link fields will ever be required. Two link fields are sufficient to link to the neighboring cells representing R(y) = {z_1, z_2}. In addition, we frequently doubly link the representation by including links back to those elements in L(y). But since the tree is principal, we know that |L(y)| ≤ 1, so that at most one additional link field will be necessary. Consequently, we can use fixed-size cells with a format as shown in Fig. 5-7. (This particular format, which we will use in our examples, can be easily changed to suit a problem at hand.)

Letting the cells of S_R correspond to the points of S_M, one gets a natural representation as shown in Fig. 5-8. Notice that in this case the structure of the representation almost perfectly mirrors that of the model. We will see representations where this is not so. In the graph S_M of Fig. 5-8 we have drawn the single right neighbor e of c below it, while the single right neighbor h of f was drawn above it. Clearly this makes no difference since one can draw a graph in any manner whatever without altering its essential relational structure. But turning to its representation S_R, we see that in those cases where R(y) is a singleton set {z} we sometimes used the R_1 field, and sometimes the R_2 field, to link to it. Would it make any difference if we had been more consistent and al-

LEFT LINK	R_1 LINK
data$_1$	R_2 LINK
data$_2$	

Figure 5-7 A cell format for a binary tree representation.

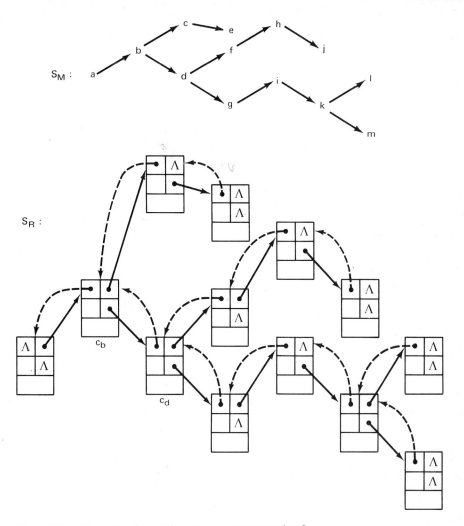

Figure 5-8 A binary tree S_M and its computer representation S_R.

ways used the R_1 field to link to singleton elements? Would it have made any difference if we had interchanged the R_1 and R_2 links in cell c_b or cell c_d? In both cases the answer is no. Had these changes been made, the resulting representation, call it S_R', would still represent the same *abstract* graph, because in abstract graph theory there is no ordering imposed on the elements of the sets $R(y)$.†

†These observations show that representational structures with very distinct differences may nevertheless represent the same abstract data structure. It points up the real problem of comparing two computer data structures to see if they represent the same thing.

But there may be practical applications in which we would like to impose an order on the right neighbor sets R(y), which is based on some property of the problem at hand. If this extra ordering is assumed, then the particular field used to link to a neighboring cell may be quite important. This idea can best be developed in the context of a concrete problem.

Let us assume that we have a set S = {w_i} of elements that can be totally ordered by some relation ≤. (In the concrete example we will let S be a set of English words that are lexicographically ordered, but the particular set or the particular order is really irrelevant.) Now suppose we have an arbitrary element w, and we wish to discover whether or not w already belongs to the set S. One way of solving this set membership problem is by an *exhaustive search* procedure, which compares w with each element w_i one at a time. We call w the *search key* of the procedure. If S consists of n elements, then it is fairly easy to see that *if w is an element of* S then the *expected* (or average) number of comparisons to ascertain this fact, which is denoted by E(comparisons|w ∈ S), will equal n/2. But if w is *not* an element of S, then w must be compared with every element of S and E(comparisons|w ∉ S) = n. For large sets, say a dictionary, this represents a lot of comparisons! If we are willing to make use of an ordering on S, then by simply examing the elements w_i in ascending (or descending) order, E(comparisons|w ∉ S) can be reduced to n/2; since if for some j, w_j > w, then we know that for all k ≥ j, w_k > w and we can stop searching.

Even this last improvement is not very efficient for large sets. Much more effective use may be made of the total ordering on S. A *binary search* technique is one based on the normal way of searching for an entry in an unindexed dictionary or telephone directory: (1) open the directory to the center; if the search key w is there, stop; (2) if w precedes the entries on the center page, then only the first half of the directory need be searched—open to the center page of that remaining half [i.e., go to (1)]; (3) if w follows the entries of the center page only the latter half need be searched—split that remaining half. In this process it is clear that with each comparison, either the key is located (or found to be missing) or else the remaining interval of entries to be searched is halved. It can be shown (cf. Sec. 9-1) that the expected number of comparisons required for this search technique approaches $\log_2 (n) - 1$, for large n. A more precise definition of the binary search process is given by the procedure below.

[handwritten in margin: binary tree traversal]

logical function bsearch₁ (key, w, size, index);
element   key;
element array w [1:size];
integer   index, size;

This procedure performs a binary search to determine if the element "key" is in the array of elements "w_i". If key = w_i for some i, it returns true, and sets "index" to i. If key ≠ w_i for all i, it returns false. Note that the elements w_i are indexed in ascending order according to some total order, that is i < j implies w_i < w_j.

begin
    integer first, last, m;
    first ←0;
    last ←size;

    "first" will always denote the index immediately preceding that of the first element
    in the current search interval. "last" denotes the index of the actual last element
    of the search interval. m is the index of the middle element.

findmiddle:
    m ←first + ⌊(last − first + 1)/2⌋;
    if key = w[m]
        then bsearch ←**true;**
            index ←m;
            exit;
    if key < w[m]
        then   *Search lower half interval, if nonempty.*
            if first = m − 1
                then   bsearch ←**false;**
                        exit
                else   last ←m − 1
        else *key > w[m]. Search upper half interval*
            if first = last − 1
                then   bsearch ←**false;**
                        exit
                else   first ←m;
    go to findmiddle;
    end

Consider a small set of 15 English words lexicographically ordered. Figure 5-9 graphically illustrates the binary search procedure by showing for each iterative step the interval(s) that would be searched at that step, together with the middle index associated with each interval. Notice that for this set *at most* four comparisons ever need to be made to determine whether a key is, or is not, a member of the set in contrast to the *expected* 7.5 (= 15/2) comparisons associated with a sequential search.

This binary search process can also be abstractly modeled by a binary tree as shown in Fig. 5-10. If this abstract binary tree is represented as in Fig. 5-8, using cells with format as shown in Fig. 5-11, then the following search procedure can be easily implemented.

logical function bsearch$_2$ (tree, key, point);
pointer   tree, point;
data   key;

This procedure searches the points of binary "tree" to see if "key" has been stored in

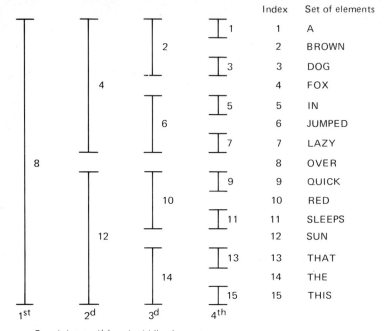

	Index	Set of elements
1	1	A
2	2	BROWN
3	3	DOG
4	4	FOX
5	5	IN
6	6	JUMPED
7	7	LAZY
8	8	OVER
9	9	QUICK
10	10	RED
11	11	SLEEPS
12	12	SUN
13	13	THAT
14	14	THE
15	15	THIS

1st 2d 3d 4th

Search interval(s) and middle elements

Figure 5-9 Schematic representation of the binary search process.

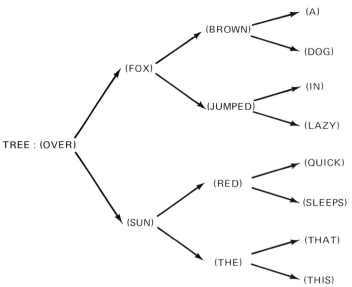

Figure 5-10 A binary search tree.

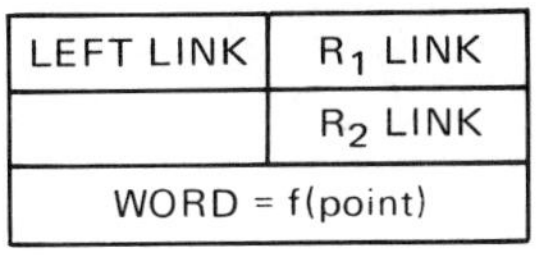

LEFT LINK	R₁ LINK
	R₂ LINK
WORD = f(point)	

Figure 5-11 A cell format for the binary search tree.

the tree (i.e., if f(point) = key). If so, it returns true and sets "point" to that element. If not, it returns false and (1) enters a new point into the tree with that assigned value and (2) sets "point" to indicate this new element.

begin
    pointer   cell, newcell;
    field   f, left, r1, r2;
    common /nulval/ null;
    cell ←tree;

    Compare f(cell) with the key. If equal, entry is found. If key < f(cell), follow R_1 edge of the tree; if key > f(cell) follow R_2 edge.

compare:
    if key = f(cell)
        then bsearch ←**true;**
              point ←cell;
              exit;
    if key < f(cell)
        then   *Follow R_1 link if any.*
              if r1(cell) ≠ null
                  then cell ←r1(cell);
                      go to compare
                else *Key is not in the tree, enter it.*
                    newcell ←giveme(celsiz);
                    r1(cell) ←newcell;
                    go to notfound
        else *This branch if key > f(cell), follow R_2 link, if any.*

              if r2(cell) ≠ null
                  then cell ←r2(cell);
                      go to compare
                else *Key is not in the tree, enter it.*
                    newcell ←giveme(celsiz);
                    r2(cell) ←newcell;
                    go to notfound;

    The key was not found. A new cell has been created and partially linked into the tree. Set remaining fields.

notfound:
    r1(newcell) ←r2(newcell) ←null;
    left(newcell) ←cell;
    f(newcell) ←key;
    bsearch ←**false;**

point ← newcell;
exit;
end

In this latter binary search process on a linked representation, the total order on the set determines which edge in the tree (link in the representation) will be followed in the search for the element. Thus we may call the tree an *ordered binary tree*. The order of elements in the set R(y) is crucial.

The ease with which new elements were added to the search set in this procedure makes it a valuable technique anytime one is working with dynamic sets, for example, building a lexicon of words encountered in a body of text (see Exercise 5-10) or the symbol table of a compiler. Were a new element to be added to the sequentially represented set of the first search procedure, then all elements following it in the set would first have to be "shifted down" one position. In a dynamic environment one would expect to shift n/2 elements in the sequential representation for each new element added. This compares unfavorably with the simple allocation of a new cell, which is then linked appropriately into the explicit binary tree.

On the other hand, if a linked binary search tree is "grown" in a dynamic fashion, then the structure of the tree is entirely dependent on the order in which new elements are encountered and entered. The resulting structure need not be optimal for retrieval purposes. Figure 5-12 illustrates a binary tree over the same vocabulary set as Figs. 5-9 and 5-10 that was created by **BSEARCH₂**

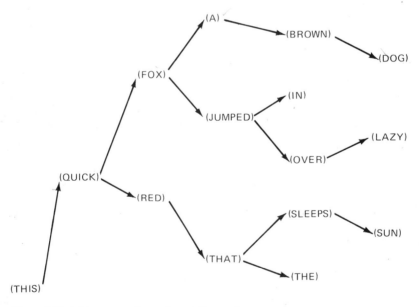

Figure 5-12 A binary search tree "grown" over the same vocabulary as that of Fig. 5-9.

as it scanned successive words in the sentence "this quick red fox jumped over a lazy brown dog that sleeps in the sun." This *unbalanced* tree contains paths of length 5 (to the entries "dog," "lazy," and "sun") so that as many as six comparisons may be made (and five links followed) to retrieve an item. In contrast, no more than four comparisons were necessary (three links followed) in the *balanced* trees of Figs. 5-9 and 5-10. (Path length and "balance" in trees are considered more fully in Chap. 9.)

This example illustrates a general rule of thumb: *Linked data structures are generally more appropriate for the representation of dynamic data structures; sequential representations tend to be superior for static, or nearly static, data structures.*

This example made use of an ordered tree. Let us more generally say that a graph G is *ordered* if there exists a linear order on each of the sets $\{y\} \cup L(y)$ and $\{y\} \cup R(y)$ for all $y \in P$. (Note that each set may be ordered separately, so one may be considering as many as $2 \cdot |P|$ distinct linear relations $\leq_i$.) There will be various occasions in which we will encounter several different relations, say E_1, E_2, ... on the same point set. Of primary interest will be those situations where E_1 and E_2 are in some sense comparable, or are themselves related in some regular fashion. In the example of this section, the individual linear relations $\leq_i = \langle z_1, y, z_2 \rangle$ were simply constrained to be a restriction of the overall lexicographic ordering. In the next section we will explore other ways in which linear relations L may be intertwined with a tree relation E.

Finally, we should note that the binary tree of Fig. 5-10 explicitly models a flow of control (or decision structure) that is *implicitly* present in the binary search process $BSEARCH_1$. In effect, *a data structure is used to implement a process*. In Chap. 1 we said that the distinction between the concepts of *process* and *data* was at best a fuzzy one; we will encounter more examples of this sort. For instance, in the following sequential representation of a binary tree we will use *a computational process to implicitly represent the edge structure of the tree*.

If a binary tree is static, and if it is *full* (with all endpoints at the same distance from the principal point), as in Fig. 5-10, then the following very effective sequential representation can be used. (If the tree is not full, then extra dummy points can be added, but for trees of any depth, this may be very costly in terms of storage.) Let the principal point x be the first element in the sequential representation. Let y_1, $y_2 \in R(x)$ be the second and third elements. Let z_1, $z_2 \in R(y_1)$ and z_3, $z_4 \in R(y_2)$ be the fourth, fifth, sixth, and seventh elements, respectively; and so on. The binary tree of Fig. 5-10, so represented in a sequential array, is shown in Fig. 5-13. One can then define the following elegant *accessing function* on the representation. Let y_i denote that point of the tree with index i in the sequential representation; then y_j is the unique element of $L(y_i)$ if $j = \lfloor i/2 \rfloor$, and y_k, y_m are the elements of $R(y_i)$ if $k = 2 \cdot i$ and $m = 2 \cdot i + 1$. (In these accessing functions, i, j, k, m must satisfy the constraint that $0 < i, j, k, m \leq |P|$, else the indicated location is not an element of the tree.) Consequently the entire structure of the tree relation can be

i	$f(x_i)$
1	OVER
2	FOX
3	SUN
4	BROWN
5	JUMPED
6	RED
7	THE
8	A
9	DOG
10	IN
11	LAZY
12	QUICK
13	SLEEPS
14	THAT
15	THIS

Figure 5-13 A sequential representation S_R of the binary tree of Fig. 5-10.

reproduced by simple arithmetic calculations with no need of explicitly stored links.

EXERCISES FOR SECTION 5-2

5-9 Implement the binary search process BSEARCH$_1$ over a sequentially stored set.

*5-10 Code an implementation of BSEARCH$_2$ for use with a main program that scans a body of text and builds a lexicon of all the words it encounters. But include the following modifications:

   (*a*) Use the left field of word 2 of the cell (or some other field) to store a count of the number of occurrances of that particular word in the text.

   (*b*) Have the search routine increment this count if the key is found, or set it to one when a new word is entered into the lexicon.

   (*c*) Keep a separate record of (1) the number of times the routine is executed, (2) the total number of all R$_1$ links followed, (3) the total number of all R$_2$ links followed (for consistency, count the addition of a new cell as if the R$_1$ or R$_2$ link to it had been followed), and (4) the maximum length path within the tree.

   (*d*) Provide a separate entry into the routine (or keep these values in common storage) so that they, and the average number of links followed per item, can be printed at the end of the run.

   This is the first of a number of exercises that are aimed at not only getting a process to work, but also trying to get information about the nature of the data structures involved and the effectiveness of the process. Too little is known about data structures and processes, and it is this kind of inquiry that should distinguish a computer scientist from a programmer.

*5-11 Write a simple process PATH(POINT) that will print out (in reverse order) that sequence of points that is the unique path from the principal point of the tree to POINT, given the representation of Fig. 5-8.

5-12 Write a procedure LIST(TREE) that will print out a list of all the elements of the tree in accordance with the total order (e.g., lexicographic order) imposed on the set. Note that this will involve "walking about" in the tree to pick up the elements in the correct order. Every point must be "visited" and listed at least once. Such a tour is called a *traversal* of the tree.

*5-13 Devise several variations of the linked binary tree and then rewrite portions of BSEARCH₂ so as to reflect these changes in the representation. In particular:

    (*a*) In the cell format of Fig. 5-11 only one computer word was used to store the assigned value of the cell, but on most computers several words of storage would be required to represent a 10-to-12-letter vocabulary word. Change the cell format to one appropriate for your computer. What must be done to the search key, "key"?

    (*b*) Store the actual words of the lexicon in a separate sequential array as in Fig. 4-12. Represent the tree with cells of only two words, with the index (or address) of the assigned value stored in the left field of word 2.

    (*c*) Replace the comparison of the key and the assigned value f(y), which is coded directly in BSEARCH₂, with a subprocess that returns −1, 0, or +1 to indicate the position of the key within the ordering. This is particularly useful if the ordering on the set involves extensive calculation.

5-14 Write a binary search procedure BSEARCH₃ to operate on sequential representations such as Fig. 5-13. The process should be completely equivalent to that of BSEARCH₁ in terms of the number of comparisons needed to locate any particular item. Is it simpler? Assuming BSEARCH₃ were to also add entries to the tree as did BSEARCH₂, how must the process be modified? How much additional work will be required?

5-3 TRAVERSAL OF BINARY TREES

In the syntax of standard algebraic programming languages, computational expressions are constructed by inserting binary operator symbols (e.g., $+$, $-$, $*$, $/$, and $**$) between two operand symbols (variables, constants, or other data items). This way of representing the expression of a sequence of computational operations is called *infix notation;* a typical example might be the familiar quadratic formula for finding one root of a quadratic equation,

$$(-\text{B} + \text{SQRT}(\text{B}**2 - 4*\text{A}*\text{C}))/2*\text{A} \tag{5-1}$$

In this expression parentheses are necessary to specify the order of evaluation. Alternative "parenthesis-free" representations of this expression place the operator symbol before or after, rather than between, its operands, as in

$$/ + -\text{B SQRT} - ** \text{B } 2 * 4 * \text{A C} * 2 \text{ A} \tag{5-2}$$

$$\text{B} - \text{B } 2 ** 4 \text{ A C} * * - \text{SQRT} + 2 \text{ A} * / \tag{5-3}$$

These are called *prefix* and *postfix* notation, respectively. (A fuller discussion of infix, prefix, and postfix notation can be found in numerous computer mathematics and programming languages texts.) The computational expression (5-1) can also be represented as a binary tree T as shown in Fig. 5-14. Note that the tree is drawn in a "top-down" orientation because it seems more natural in this application that the end points of the tree (maximal points) denote all, and only operands of the expression, and that T is *not* a parse tree of the expression. Its parse tree describes the decision structure involved in *recognizing* that the

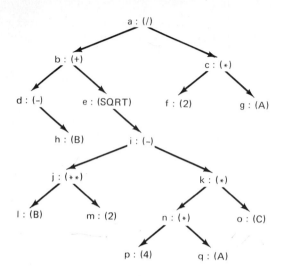

Figure 5-14 Expression (5-1) represented as a binary tree.

string is a well-formed expression. Although there is no accepted terminology, an *expression tree* might be an appropriate name for T.

Now $T = (P, E)$ is readily a graph (with assignment function f into the set of operator, function, variable, and literal symbols of the language), but the strings (5-1), (5-2), and (5-3) are also graphs. They are linear graphs $L_i = (P, E_i)$. Moreover, they are linear graphs over the same point set P as T.

A *traversal* of a graph $G = (P, E)$ is any *linear* relation E' on P. If in addition the traversal E' has the property that for any ideal $\overline{R}(y)$ of G, $E'|_{\overline{R}(y)}$ (that is, E' restricted to the ideal) is a traversal of $\overline{R}(y)$, then it is called a *restricted traversal*. Thus the strings (5-1), (5-2), and (5-3) are traversals of T—as indeed is any random listing of the points of P. But it is clearly preferable if the traversal E' reflects the edge structure E of the original graph. Intuitively the traversals (5-1), (5-2), and (5-3), which are all restricted traversals, are in some sense compatible with the relation E that defines the structure of the tree T. We will have to make this "intuitive feeling" more explicit.

By its very name, a traversal suggests a process which "walks through" the tree or graph, "visiting" every point in P. In this section we will first define three traversals of particular interest in terms of a recursive procedure; later we will provide more formal graph theoretic definitions of them.

We are taught in elementary logic and in English composition to avoid circular definitions (that is, explanations couched in the term that is to be explained) as if they were a form of the plague. Yet in mathematics and in computer programming this kind of circular approach to things is considered quite acceptable—provided it is subject to some rather strict standards. It is called *recursion.* A property (or process) $\mathscr{P}$ is said to be *recursively defined* on a finite set S if the definition of $\mathscr{P}$ is given in terms of $\mathscr{P}$ itself, *but always in terms of $\mathscr{P}$ acting on S', which must be a proper subset of S; that is, $S' \subset S$.* For sets S that have no proper subsets, especially singleton sets, a separate nonrecursive definition must be given. This is called the *terminal definition* (or condition).

As an example we may recursively redefine the concept of a principal tree as follows:

A subgraph $T = (P, E)$ is a principal subtree, denoted T_y, with principal point y

(*a*) if $P = \{y\}$ is a singleton set with $E_P = \emptyset$, or

(*b*) if each point $z_i \in R(y)$ is the principal point of T_{z_i} in a set $\{T_{z_i}\}$ of *disjoint* principal subtrees.

Figure 5-15 graphically illustrates this kind of definition.

The use of recursion, which we will encounter from time to time, is controversial. It is strongly endorsed by some and condemned by others. Its greatest asset is a kind of natural clarity, since in the explanation of complicated processes and properties the human mind is accustomed to subdividing the problem into smaller, more easily defined subprocesses and then explaining the whole in terms of these smaller pieces. The use of recursion has proven to be a boon in artificial intelligence. On the other side of the coin, recursive processes, although they may be clearly and compactly described (or coded), often execute inefficiently because of the overhead associated with maintaining the recursion and because it is easy to overlook redundant operations. Moreover, recursive definitions tend to be procedure-oriented and may not easily lend themselves to classical mathematical proof techniques. But regardless of its merits, recursion is a technique that belongs in the repertoire of any practicing programmer or computer scientist. Our policy will be to make sparing use of recursion in those situations where its clarity far outweighs any possible inefficiency.

We can now recursively define three important traversals in terms of a procedure defined on the set $\overline{R}(y)$.

Preorder traversal of $\overline{R}(y)$:

(*a*) Add y to the linear order.

Let $R(y) = \{z_1, z_2, \ldots, z_n\}$ be the set of right neighbors

(*b*) Traverse $\overline{R}(z_1), \overline{R}(z_2), \ldots, \overline{R}(z_n)$.

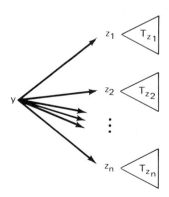

Figure 5-15 Recursive definition of principal tree. T_y is a principal tree if and only if $T_{z_1}, T_{z_2}, \ldots, T_{z_n}$ are principal subtrees.

Symmetric traversal of $\overline{R}(y)$: Let $R(y) = \{z_1, z_2\}$.
(This traversal is defined only if T is binary.)

(*a*) Traverse $\overline{R}(z_1)$.

(*b*) Add y to the linear order.

(*c*) Traverse $\overline{R}(z_2)$.

Postorder traversal of $\overline{R}(y)$: Let $R(y) = \{z_1, z_2, \ldots, z_n\}$ be the set of right neighbors.

(*a*) Traverse $\overline{R}(z_1), \overline{R}(z_2), \ldots, \overline{R}(z_n)$.

(*b*) Add y to the linear order.

If R(y) is empty, then the associated step is omitted, but y is always added to the linear order. If the tree T is regarded as an ordered tree, then the recursive traversals of $\overline{R}(z_1), \ldots, \overline{R}(z_n)$ must be performed in the same sequence as the order on R(y).

Using these procedural definitions, the reader can verify that the preorder, symmetric, and postorder traversals of the tree of Fig. 5-14 are, respectively,†

$$a\ b\ d\ h\ e\ i\ j\ l\ m\ k\ n\ p\ q\ o\ c\ f\ g \qquad (5\text{-}4)$$

$$d\ h\ b\ e\ l\ j\ m\ i\ p\ n\ q\ k\ o\ a\ f\ c\ g \qquad (5\text{-}5)‡$$

$$h\ d\ l\ m\ j\ p\ q\ n\ o\ k\ i\ e\ b\ f\ g\ c\ a \qquad (5\text{-}6)$$

Readers should be certain that they understand how these traversals were obtained, and should ensure their ability to generate similar traversals from binary trees such as Figs. 5-10, 5-12, and 5-14. If one replaces the point identifiers y_i in these traversal sequences with their assignment values $f(y_i)$, then they read respectively:

$$/ + -B\ \text{SQRT} - ** \ B\ 2 ** 4\ A\ C * 2\ A \qquad (5\text{-}7)$$

$$-B + \text{SQRT}\ B ** 2 - 4 * A * C / 2 * A \qquad (5\text{-}8)$$

$$B - B\ 2 ** 4\ A * C * - \text{SQRT} + 2\ A * / \qquad (5\text{-}9)$$

Comparison of these assignment value sequences with (5-2), (5-1), and (5-3) makes evident the choice of names for these traversals, and indicates a further point of contact between binary trees and computational expressions.

Given a computer representation S_R, as in Fig. 5-16 or Fig. 5-8, then implementation of a process that will generate these traversals and return a sequential (array) representation is trivial (as shown below), *provided* the programming language used supports recursive coding.

---

†These linear orders are represented as sequences (or lists) with the individual edges of E′ implicitly given by juxtaposition in the usual way. Between each point identifier an explicit directed edge could have been inserted.

‡The symmetric traversal is ambiguous in cases where $|R(y)| = 1$. Should the singleton element z be treated as if it were z_1 or z_2? Should h precede d in the order, or d precede h as shown? In this case we have followed the convention of treating z as if it were z_2.

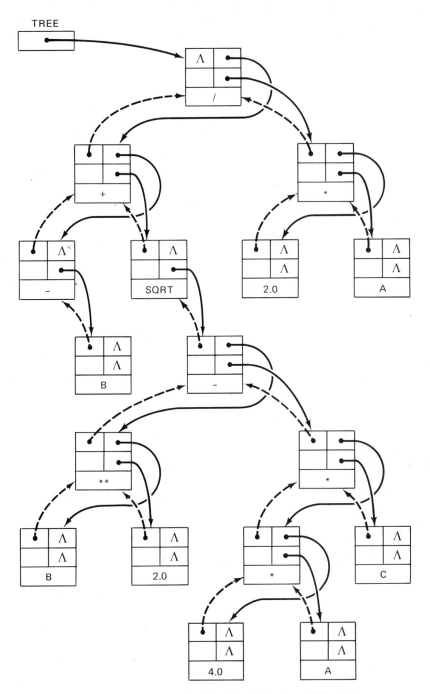

Figure 5-16 A computer representation S_R of the binary tree of Fig. 5-14.

procedure preorder$_1$ (point, sequence, index);
pointer   point;
pointer array   sequence[1:n];
integer   index;

This procedure traverses the binary tree (or subtree) with principal point "point" and inserts the traversed points into the array "sequence," beginning with sequence[index + 1], in the order they are encountered.

begin
    field r1, r2;
    common /nulval/ null;
    if point = null **then exit;**
    index ←index + 1;
    sequence[index] ←point;
    call preorder (r1(point), sequence, index);
    call preorder (r2(point), sequence, index);
    exit;
    end

Notice that this procedure is virtually an exact translation of the recursive definition of a preorder traversal.

Suppose a recursive programming language is not available, and in many cases it is not. It is well known that any recursive procedure can be implemented by the use of pushdown stacks. Indeed, recursive languages are commonly implemented by means of a run-time stack. We may do the same.

procedure preorder$_2$ (tree, sequence, i);
pointer   tree;
pointer array   sequence[1:n];
integer   i;

This process traverses the binary tree (or subtree) with principal point "tree" and places cell addresses as encountered in the preorder "sequence." On exit, i denotes the number of points in the tree.

begin
    pointer   cell, stack;
    field   r1, r2;
    common /nulval/ null;
    i ←0;
    stack ←null;
    cell ←tree;
    while cell ≠ null **do**
        Add "visited" cells to the linear sequence.
        i ←i + 1;
        sequence[i] ←cell;

```
    if r2(cell) ≠ null
        then Stack the principal point of the "untraversed" R₂ subtree.
            call pushdown (stack, r2(cell));
    if r1(cell) ≠ null
        then Continue traversing this R₁ branch.
            cell ←r1(cell)
        else This R₁ branch is exhausted. Back up and traverse the last R₂ sub-
            tree.
            cell ←poptop(stack);
exit;
end
```

Given a representation of the binary tree as in Sec. 5-2, this procedure is easily implemented using the stack routines developed in Chap. 3. Note, however, that in neither traversal routine was the link to the left neighbor of a point ever used. In PREORDER₂ the stack was used to work back through the tree. However, if a link exists to the left neighbor of each point, then a preorder traversál process can be written that needs no additional stack. The tree itself can be made to function as its own stack.

```
procedure preorder₃ (tree, sequence, i);
pointer         tree;
pointer array   sequence[1:n];
integer         i;
```

This process traverses the binary tree (or subtree) with principal point "tree" and places point addresses as encountered in the preorder "sequence." On exit, i denotes the number of points in the sequence.

```
begin
        pointer   cell, lnbhr;
        field     left, r1, r2;
        common /nulval/ null;
        cell ←tree;
        i ←0;
```

Insert this point into the sequence.

```
insert:
        i ←i+1;
        sequence[i] ←cell;
```

Follow the R₁ link, if possible.

```
    if r1(cell) ≠ null
        then cell ←r1(cell);
                go to insert;
```

Follow the R_2 link, if possible.

r2nbhr:
    if r2(cell) $\neq$ null
        then cell $\leftarrow$ r2(cell);
            go to insert;

No untraversed right neighbors of this cell. Back up to a left neighbor, if any. If the process "backs up" a R_1 link, check for R_2 neighbors only. If it "backs up" a R_2 link, then keep backing up.

backup:
    if cell $=$ tree **then exit;**
    lnbhr $\leftarrow$ left(cell);
    if r1(lnbhr) $=$ cell
        then cell $\leftarrow$ lnbhr;
            go to r2nbhr
        else cell $\leftarrow$ lnbhr;
            go to backup;
    end

The following is a similar "stackless" postorder traversal procedure. Coding of a symmetric traversal is left to the reader.

procedure postorder$_1$ (tree, sequence, i);
pointer   tree;
pointer array   sequence [1:n];
integer   i;

This process traverses the binary tree (or subtree) with principal point "tree" and inserts point addresses in a postorder "sequence." On exit, i denotes the number of points in the sequence.

begin
    pointer   cell, lnbhr;
    field   left, r1, r2;
    common /nulval/ null;
    cell $\leftarrow$ tree;
    i $\leftarrow$ 0;

Traverse this subtree. Follow chain of R_1 links as far as possible.

follow:
    while r1(cell) $\neq$ null **do**
        cell $\leftarrow$ r1(cell);

"cell" has an empty R_1 subtree (it can be regarded as having been traversed). Has it an R_2 subtree that must be traversed?

r2subtree:

    if $r2(cell) \neq$ null

        then cell $\leftarrow r2(cell)$;

            go to follow;

The R_1 and R_2 subtrees, if any, have been traversed. Insert this point into the sequence.

insert:

    $i \leftarrow i + 1$;

    sequence $[i] \leftarrow$ cell;

Back up to its left neighbor, if any. If we "backed up" an R_2 link, the "lnbhr" can be traversed. If not, then its R_2 subtree, if any, must be traversed.

    if cell = tree **then exit;**

    lnbhr $\leftarrow$ left(cell);

    if $r2(lnbhr) =$ cell

        then cell $\leftarrow$ lnbhr;

            go to insert

        else cell $\leftarrow$ lnbhr;

            go to r2subtree;

    end

All the preceding processes have represented the linear traversal relation E′ implicitly by means of a sequential array. Could not a linked representation have been used? Since it is a relation on the same point set P as the tree relation E, could the linked representation make use of the same cells? The answer to both questions is "yes." The left field of word 2 of the cells has been idle. It can be used to represent the traversal relation. A linear relation such as these, that runs "through" a data structure, is called a *thread*. If the thread is explicitly represented, the structure is said to be *threaded,* and the field used called a *thread link.* Figure 5-17 illustrates the tree, threaded with respect to the postorder traversal. Note that an extra reference pointer THREAD has been added to provide entry to the first point of the thread.

Preorder, symmetric, and postorder traversals have been defined in terms of computational processes that generate the traversing linear relation. We prefer to have a definition that is expressed solely in terms of properties of the original relation E and the linear relation E′, that is, in terms of the path relation on the given graph. Consequently we may redefine these by saying that a restricted traversal E′ of a tree T is called a

    (*a*) *preorder traversal* if $R(y) = \{z_1, \ldots, z_n\}$ implies that $\rho_{E'}(y, z_1)$, $\ldots$, $\rho_{E'}(y, z_n)$,

    (*b*) *symmetric traversal* (defined only on binary trees) if $R(y) = \{z_1, z_2\}$ implies that $\rho_{E'}(z_1, y)$ and $\rho_{E'}(y, z_2)$,

    (*c*) *postorder traversal* if $R(y) = \{z_1, \ldots, z_n\}$ implies that $\rho_{E'}(z_1, y)$, $\ldots$, $\rho_{E'}(z_n, y)$.

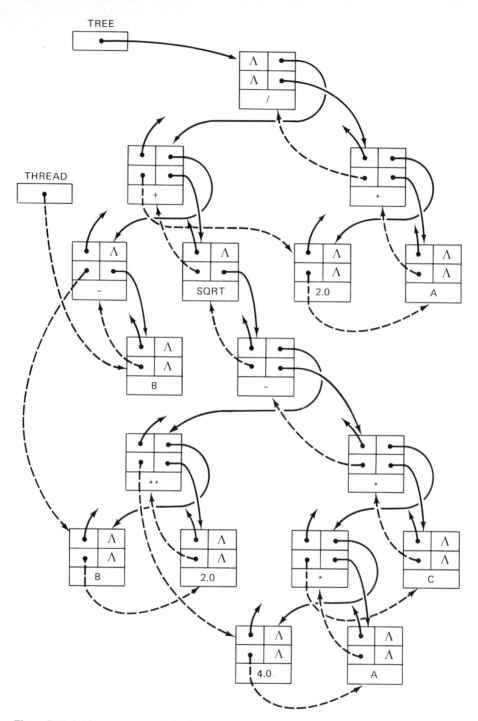

Figure 5-17 A binary tree threaded with respect to the postorder traversal. (Left neighbor links have been omitted for clarity.)

If T is assumed to be an ordered tree, then the traversal preserves the linear order of elements in R(y); that is z_i, $z_j \in R(y)$, $i \leq j$, implies that $\rho_{E'}(z_i, z_j)$.

Given these new definitions, it is now possible to rigorously prove the following:

Theorem 5-10 In an ordered principal tree T, the preorder, postorder, and symmetric (if T is a complete binary tree) traversals are unique.

Because they are unique, this theorem justifies describing these traversals by means of deterministic, single-valued algorithms, as we have done previously. Also the ability to prove a "known" result of some importance provides a measure of confidence that these definitions capture the essential properties of these concepts.

Since a traversal is a linear relation, it must be connected (its path relation is a total order). Consequently, in a restricted traversal the points of any principal ideal constitute a connected substring of the linear sequence. Test that this is really the case given the trees and traversals of Fig. 5-18. We shall see in the next section that this formal property is of considerable practical importance and accounts for much of the utility of these traversals. Restricted traversals can be defined on other than principal trees, as shown by the second tree of Fig. 5-18. This traversal is clearly neither preorder nor postorder. In the course of proving Theorem 5-10, one can simultaneously show that it is impossible to have a restricted preorder traversal [in which $\rho_E(x, z)$ implies $\rho_{E'}(x, z)$] unless the graph *is a principal tree.* Postorder traversals are similarly impossible. We shall find this a handicap when we study traversals, called *topological sorts,* of arbitrary acyclic graphs in Chap. 6.

In the remainder of this section we digress somewhat in an effort to put the linearization of data structures, of which the traversal concept is an example, into the perspective of several other themes in computer science.

The binary tree of Fig. 5-14 was informally called an expression tree; it

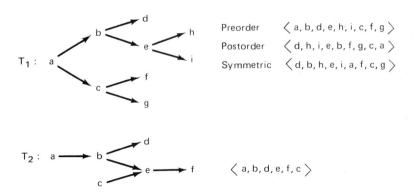

Figure 5-18 Restricted traversals on trees.

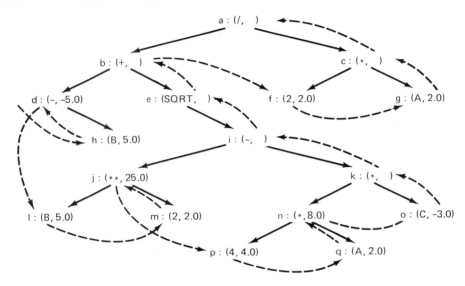

Figure 5-19 A threaded expression tree T, with two assignment functions:

$$f_1 : P \rightarrow \{\text{identifiers of } \mathcal{L}\}$$
$$f_2 : P \rightarrow \{\text{reals}\}$$

may be regarded as a representation of the logical relationships between the operators and operands of the expression. The usual interpretation of such a tree involves two assignment functions: f_1, which maps points into the set of identifiers of the language (operator symbols, legal variable identifiers, and literal identifiers) as was shown in Fig. 5-14†; and a second assignment f_2, which maps points into the field over which the expression is to be evaluated, commonly the real numbers. The value $f_2(y)$ associated with any point y is the value of the principal subtree (subexpression) of which it is the principal point. The values $f_2(y)$ of maximal points are assumed to be assigned—by the compiler, if $f_1(y)$ is a literal identifier, or by a previously executed assignment statement, if $f_1(y)$ is a variable identifier. Figure 5-19 illustrates such a tree after having executed the three assignment statements: A ← 2.0, B ← 5.0, and C ← −3.0.

Assuming that the f_2 values have been assigned to all maximal points, then clearly $f_2(y)$ can be assigned (or evaluated) if and only if for all $z_1, z_2 \in R(y)$, $f_2(z_1)$ and $f_2(z_2)$ have been assigned. By assigning f_2 values in accordance with a postorder traversal, precisely this condition will be assured. Consequently, if the points are traversed and subexpressions evaluated in postorder sequence, as shown by the thread in Fig. 5-19, then no point y will be encountered until all

---

†An operation associated with maximal points is a "fetch" operation that accesses the literal or variable value from storage. Thus f_1 might very well be a storage address rather than the symbolic identifier. At other points, f_1 might also be an address—an entry point to the operation that is denoted by the symbol and is to be performed.

$z_i \in R(y)$ have been evaluated. In the illustration, those points corresponding to the initial segment $\langle h, d, l, m, j, p, q, n, o]$ of the sequence (5-6) are shown with assigned f_2 values.

For this reason the thread in the expression tree can be treated as the *order of execution,* and a language translator would generate executable machine code that follows this thread sequence. Such threaded structures are often called *plexes.* Most compilers never create an explicit expression that is subsequently traversed; it would be far too inefficient. However, virtually all make use of the postorder sequence based on an *implicit* tree of this form.

Traversals are frequently used to linearize a nonlinear data structure so that it is compatible with some sequential process. The sequential order of evaluation of computational expressions is just one example. Standard input/output processes are also sequential. Each element of a structure to be output must be visited at least once; hence the structure must be traversed. If there is a unique correspondence between the structure and its linear form (as is the case with these traversals), then a traversal operator by itself is a sufficient input/output mechanism that converts principal trees into list notation, and vice versa. Parentheses, or some other form of delimiter (see Chap. 8), are used in the list representation to indicate those sublists that correspond to subtrees (ideals). On output one may employ other tricks [such as variable spacing across a printer line (see Exercise 5-32)] to more graphically convey the structure of the tree.

It is also fascinating to speculate about other examples of this linearizing process in a noncomputational context, especially that of natural language. It seems apparent that the structure of ideas—that is, the logical relationships between the components of an idea—need not be linear. But because of the inherent linearity of the audio communication channel, the verbal expression of them must be sequential. Forced linearization of logically "concurrent" segments of an idea are often signalled by special words or phrases such as "on the other hand," "meanwhile . . . ," or "if . . . then . . . else." As an oversimplified model of an idea one could propose a tree with actions (verbs) functioning as operators and objects (nouns) serving as operands. The normal word order of spoken English, subject-verb-object(s), then reflects a linearization by a kind of symmetric traversal of the idea structure. Spoken German also employs this normal word order, but it makes provision for a preorder traversal in the inverted form, time adverb-verb-subject-object(s), and for a postorder traversal in dependent clauses where the verb comes last.

EXERCISES FOR SECTION 5-3

5-15 Enumerate (by trial and error construction) all *ordered* binary trees on 4 points; there are 14. [Note that this is different from the set of all binary trees, since we consider as distinct ordered binary trees, even though they are isomorphic (see the accompanying figure).] Enumeration of the ordered binary trees on 5 points is much more difficult; there are 42. The author knows of no enumeration formula for the general case.

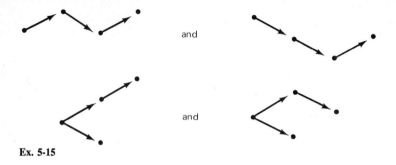

and

and

Ex. 5-15

5-16 A familiar example of a recursively defined mathematical function is that of the factorial function

$$n! = \begin{cases} 1, \text{ if } n = 0 \\ n \cdot (n-1)!, \text{ if } n > 0 \end{cases}$$

Write a recursive integer function FACT(N) that returns as its functional value n!.

Computation of the factorial function may be expressed as a simple iteration within a **for** loop. Write an iterative version of FACT(N). Which appears to be the more efficient? Why?

5-17 The value $\binom{n}{m}$, which denotes the number of ways in which a set of m distinct objects may be selected from a collection of n objects, is sometimes expressed by the following *recurrance relation* ("recurrance relation" is often a mathematical synonym for "recursive definition"):

$$\binom{n}{m} = \begin{cases} 1, \text{ if } m = 0 \\ \binom{n-1}{m} + \binom{n-1}{m-1}, \text{ if } n \geq m \geq 1 \\ 0, \text{ if } m > n \end{cases}$$

Write a recursive procedure COMB(N, M) that calculates and returns $\binom{n}{m}$ as its functional value.

[Note that there are many more "efficient" definitions of this "combination" function (Knuth,1968), (Liu,1968).] Rewrite COMB(N, M) as a nested iteration. Which is conceptually clearer?

*5-18 Generate the preorder, symmetric, and postorder traversals of the trees in the accompanying figure.

5-19 Work through the recursive code of the procedure PREORDER₁ assuming that the procedure is initially called by the statements

index ←0;
call preorder (tree, sequence, index);

where TREE denotes the tree of Fig. 5-16. In particular, identify each new entry to the procedure by the integers 1, 2, 3, ..., and for each element of the SEQUENCE indicate which entry to PREORDER generated it.

5-20 Write a process, in the procedural notation of the text, to generate a symmetric traversal of a binary tree. [Note that a routine to list the elements of a binary search tree in lexicographic order (Exercise 5-12) is nothing more than a symmetric traversal of the tree.]

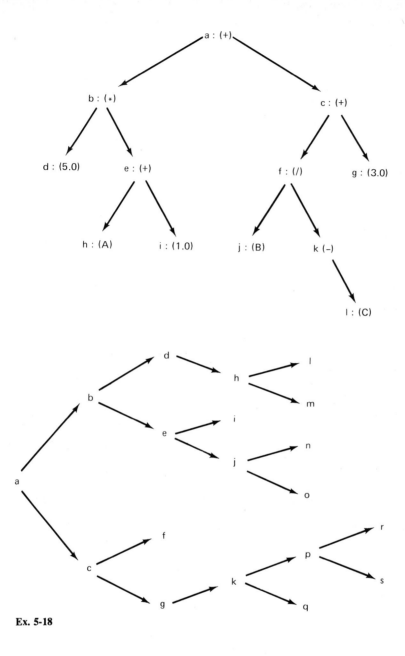

Ex. 5-18

5-21 Code implementations of the (*a*) preorder, (*b*) symmetric, and (*c*) postorder traversals that do not require an auxiliary stack.

5-22 Design a process that will generate a postorder traversal of a binary tree that is sequentially represented in the manner of either Fig. 5-9 or Fig. 5-13.

5-23 The traversal routines of Exercise 5-21 can be tested by using the routines of Exercise 5-10 that generated various binary search trees. One need only add a final sequence to the main test program such as:

```
call travrs (tree, seq, npts);
for i = 1 thru npts do
    f1 ←word(seq[i]);
    f2 ←count(seq[i]);
    print seq[i], f1, f2;
    format (O6,":(", A 10, ", ", I4, ") ");
```

where WORD and COUNT are the identifiers of the fields containing the word in the lexicon and the count of its occurrances in the text respectively.

*5-24 To test these traversal algorithms, one can alternatively write a program to generate random binary trees on n points. The easiest such random generation scheme is to begin with a principal point. For each additional point, generate a random sequence of 1s and 2s, as in 1221121121 ..., . Starting with the principal point, follow the R_1, R_2, R_2, R_1, ... links until a null link is encountered. Add the new point at that position.

(*a*) Code and run a program RNDTRE(NPTS).

(*b*) What is the expected length of the longest path in a tree so generated? (The average of longest path lengths over a set of generated trees is a good empirical approximation of the expected value.)

(*c*) What is the expected number of maximal points?

5-25 The ability to generate random data to test algorithms is an important research tool. From it one can begin to predict the expected behavior of various processes. But to be of statistical value, various properties of the random distribution must be known. For example, does the random tree generator of the preceding exercise generate a *uniform distribution* of ordered binary trees on n points, in which each tree on n points is *equally likely*? Show that the distribution generated is *not* uniform by considering the case n = 4. (*Hint:* Assuming that the distribution is uniform, use Exercise 5-15 to determine the true probability that $|R(t)| = 1$, where t is the principal point. Analytically calculate the probability that $|R(t)| = 1$ in the process as described.) The author knows of no way to *efficiently* generate members from a uniform distribution of ordered binary trees. Conversely the distribution of the generation algorithm described above has not been statistically characterized. Both are interesting open problems.

*5-26 In Fig. 5-17 the left neighbor links have been omitted for clarity. But they could have been omitted altogether from the computer representation S_R, since from any point it is possible to access its left neighbor by following the thread links. Write a procedure LNBHR(POINT) that will return the address of the left neighbor cell, given the address of any point cell as argument, by following only the thread links of a *postorder* traversal as in Fig. 5-17.

*5-27 Clearly a more compact representation, in terms of storage, of a threaded tree can be made by replacing the explicit left neighbor link with an implicit computation process such as LNBHR above. But there is the familiar "time vs. storage" trade-off. To get a rough measure of the increased processing cost, determine the expected (average) number of links that must be followed to access the left neighbor of any point y *in the case of Fig. 5-17*. (An alternative measure of computational cost might be expressed in terms of the number of comparisons required.)

5-28 Several variants of the traversal concept can be defined. For instance, E' can be called a *reverse preorder traversal* if the subtrees $\overline{R}(z_1), \ldots, \overline{R}(z_n)$ of $R(y) = \{z_1, \ldots, z_n\}$ are traversed in reverse order, that is, $\overline{R}(z_n)$ is traversed first, $\overline{R}(z_{n-1})$ next, and $\overline{R}(z_1)$ last. Similarly one can modify the threaded representation. The linear relation E' could be doubly linked, or it could be *backward threaded,* with each point linked to the point that precedes it in the traversal, rather than the *forward threading* we have shown. Show that a backward-threaded reverse preorder traversal is identical to the forward-threaded postorder traversal shown in Fig. 5-17. (*Note:* Backward threading is slightly easier than forward threading, and preorder traversal is slightly easier to generate if T need not be binary.)

5-29 Prove Theorem 5-10. (*Hint:* Suppose E_1' and E_2' are distinct preorder traversals, so that for some $x \neq z$, $\rho(x, z)$ in E_1' and $\rho(z, x)$ in E_2'. Can there be a path $\rho(x, z)$ in T? How must x and z be related in T?)

5-4 REPRESENTATION OF N-ARY TREES

A tree is said to be n-*ary* if for all points y, $|R(y)| \leq n$. Figure 5-20 shows a typical ternary (3-ary) tree. For review we observe that the preorder and postorder traversals of this tree are respectively

$$a\ b\ e\ f\ c\ g\ k\ l\ d\ h\ i\ m\ j \qquad (5\text{-}10)$$

$$e\ f\ b\ k\ l\ g\ c\ h\ m\ i\ j\ d\ a \qquad (5\text{-}11)$$

The symmetric traversal is not defined on T. A straightforward representation S_R, as in Sec. 5-2, is easily implemented: simply provide for three right neighbor links R_1, R_2, and R_3 in each cell. Unfortunately an immediate drawback becomes apparent. If the upper bound n on the cardinality of the right neighbor sets is at all large, and link fields $R_1, \ldots, R_n$ are set aside in each cell for the maximum possible out edges, then a considerable amount of storage will be wasted. Most of the link fields can be expected to be null. In fact, it is not hard to show (Exercise 5-30) that in such a straightforward representation of an n-ary tree, exactly $(n - 1) \cdot |P| + 1$ of the link fields will be null. In the case of the ternary tree of Fig. 5-20 on 13 points, 27 link fields would be null.

Alternatively one could represent the points by variably sized cells, each just sufficiently large enough to contain the nonnull right link fields associated with that point. But with dynamic structures, where the size of R(y) may vary widely during execution, this becomes very awkward. What we want is a method of representation that employs fixed-sized cells with a limited number of link fields that can nevertheless represent principal trees of arbitrary out degree.†

---

†There exist situations where just the reverse is preferable, where very large cells with many R links are superior. See the discussion of B trees in Chap. 11.

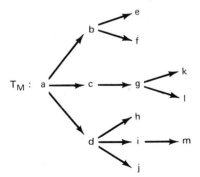

Figure 5-20 A ternary tree.

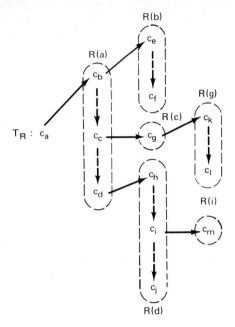

Figure 5-21 A Knuth transform of the ternary tree of Fig. 5-18.

Suppose we regard those points $z_1, z_2, \ldots, z_n \in R(y)$ as a set. This set is easily represented by chaining the cells $c_{z_1}, c_{z_2}, \ldots, c_{z_n}$ as a simply linked list. Now the mapping $y \leftarrow R(y)$ may be represented by a single link from the cell c_y to the cell c_{z_1} that denotes the first point in the set $R(y)$.† Figure 5-21 illustrates the resulting structure with dashed edges denoting the set relation and solid edges denoting the functional relation $y \rightarrow R(y)$. An appropriate cell format for a computer representation is shown in Fig. 5-22, and the resulting data structure itself is shown in Fig. 5-23. Several variants exist for the backward linking of cells to their left neighbors. In this example a single functional link is provided from y to the set $L(y)$, which, since T is a principal tree, is at most a singleton point.

†If the tree is regarded as an ordered tree, then the cells c_{z_i} can be linked in the same ordered sequence as the points z_i are ordered in $R(y)$. If T is just a garden-variety (unordered) tree, then the cells may be linked in any order.

LEFT link to L(y)	RIGHT link to R(y)
	NEXT link to $y_{i+1} \in R(x)$
Assigned values	

Figure 5-22 A cell format for Knuth representations.

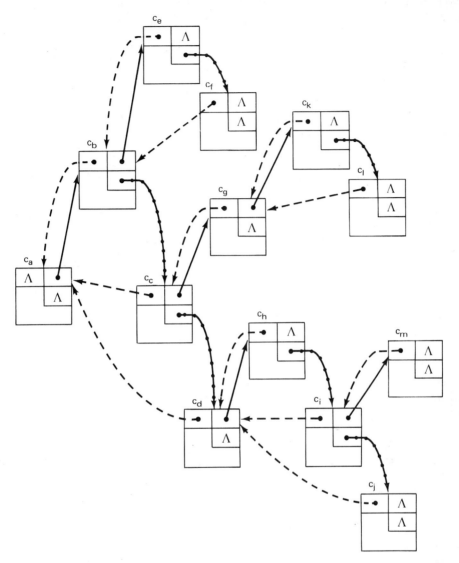

Figure 5-23 A representation T_R of the tree T_M of Fig. 5-20.

A *representational transformation* is a mapping φ that transforms the elements of a set $\{S_M\}$ of abstract data structures into a set $\{S_R\}$ of computer data structures in such a way as to preserve those features *of interest* in S_M.† Until now the transformation $\varphi:S_M \to S_R$ has invariably been a virtual one-to-one isomorphism. But Figs. 5-21 and 5-23 are not at all similar to the original tree of Fig. 5-20. Yet it should be evident that the representation S_R completely

†Normally one wants to preserve the complete edge structure of the abstract relation E, but one may be content with lesser amounts of information, such as the path structure or other homomorphic abstractions (see Chap. 8).

preserves all the structure that was present in the original tree relation E, since from S_R a simple computer process can retrieve L(y) and R(y) for any y and thereby uniquely recreate E itself. The preceding transformation we call the *Knuth transform* after Donald Knuth (1968), who first described it, although the technique itself was apparently a well-known bit of lore.†

Let's look more closely at the Knuth transform in Fig. 5-21. Since at each point there are no more than two "out" edges, it looks very much like a binary tree. In fact, if you turn back to Fig. 5-8 in the preceding section, you will note that, except for a bit of graphic distortion and a different treatment of the left links, that figure is identical to Figs. 5-21 and 5-23. It is therefore said that the Knuth transform maps the set of all right principal trees into the set of all binary trees.‡ This is suggestive, but also somewhat misleading. S_R really consists of two separate relations, E_1 denoting the functional relation y → R(y), and E_2 denoting a set relation. Both are defined over the same point set P. It is the union of these two relations, $E_1 \cup E_2$, that is tree structured.

There is a curious and important relationship between traversals defined on S_M and S_R. If S_R (Fig. 5-21) is regarded as a binary tree it can, of course, be traversed. [Many readers with a past association with binary expression trees will find it easier to trace the traversal if the tree is oriented in a top-down position. Figure 5-24 is identical to Fig. 5-21, but rotated slightly and reflected to

---

†Knuth calls the set R(y) = $\{z_1, \ldots, z_n\}$ the *descendents* of y. z_1 is called the *son* of y, while $z_2, \ldots, z_n$ are *brothers*. x = L(y) is called the *father*.

‡More precisely, the Knuth transform maps the set of all right principal forests *onto* the set of binary trees. However, the domain of the Knuth transform can be extended to include more than just principal trees (see Exercise 5-42 and also Sec. 6-4).

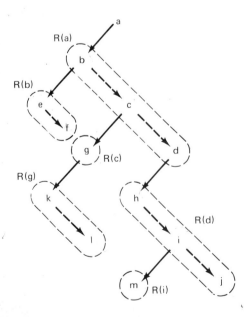

Figure 5-24 The tree of Fig. 5-21, repositioned with a top-down orientation and left-to-right ordering on the sets R(y).

give a "left-right" representation of the order on the right neighbor sets R(y).]
If we then compare the resulting traversals

Preorder:	a b e f c g k l d h i m j	(5-12)
Symmetric:	e f b k l g c h m i j d a	(5-13)
Postorder:	f e l k g m j i h d c b a	(5-14)

with those of the original abstract tree, Fig. 5-20, we discover that, *if* T_R *is the image of a tree* T_M *under the Knuth transform, then* (1) *a preorder traversal of* T_R *is a preorder traversal of* T_M, *and* (2) *a symmetric traversal of* T_R *is a postorder traversal of* T_M. (The postorder traversal of T_R has no apparent counterpart in T_M.) Thus, with slight modification due to the different handling of the left links, the traversal routines developed in Sec. 5-3 for binary trees are immediately extensible to Knuth representations of arbitrary principal trees. Consider, for example, the following preorder traversal procedure.

```
procedure preorder₄ (tree, sequence, i);
pointer        tree;
pointer array  sequence [1:n];
integer        i;
```

This process traverses the binary Knuth representation of a tree with principal point "tree" and places cell addresses in "sequence" according to the preorder sequence of the abstract model (which is also the preorder sequence of the representation). On exit, i denotes the number of points in the sequence.

```
begin
    pointer  cell;
    field    left, next, right;
    common /nulval/ null;
    cell ← tree;
    i ← 0;
```

Insert address of this cell into the sequence.

```
insert:
    i ← i + 1;
    sequence [i] ← cell;
```

Follow function link to the first element z_1 in $R(y_k)$, if it is nonempty.

```
    if right(cell) ≠ null
        then cell ← right(cell);
             go to insert;
```

$R(y_k)$ *is empty or has been traversed. Follow set link to next element y_{k+1} in this set.*

```
nextinset:
    if next(cell) ≠ null
        then cell ← next(cell);
             go to insert;
```

All points y_k of this set $R(x)$ have been traversed. "cell" was the last. Back up to x. It has been traversed, but the next point in the set of which x is a member has not.

```
if cell = tree then exit;
cell ← left(cell);
go to nextinset;
end
```

Compare this procedure with the process PREORDER₃ given in Sec. 5-3. Note that the code is identical up to the point where the process begins "backing up" in the tree. Note also that the comments describe what is taking place in *the virtual abstract tree T_M, not in its representation T_R.* This distinction is important. Many programmers design and write processes to operate on conceptual data structures that may exist only in the mind's eye.† Although it is purely a matter of personal preference, the author finds it much easier to describe blocks of code as if they are operating on the abstract model he visualizes, then make local modifications to the actual code that will reflect the properties of the actual representation.

Even if the original abstract model T_M is a binary tree, its representation T_R under the Knuth transform will be quite different—even though it is still a binary tree. Figure 5-25 illustrates the image of the binary expression tree (Fig. 5-14) tilted somewhat to emphasize its binary structure. Compare the traversals of this tree with Eqs. (5-1), (5-2), and (5-3), given in the preceding section.

The following procedure generates the postorder traversal of an arbitrary n-ary tree that has been represented under the Knuth transform. Compare it with POSTORDER₁, given previously; they are very different. Compare it with your own symmetric traversal procedure (Exercise 5-20). They should be quite similar, save again for the handling of the left links.

```
procedure postorder₂ (tree, sequence, i);
pointer        tree;
pointer array  sequence[1:n];
integer        i;
```

This process traverses the binary Knuth representation of a tree (or subtree) with principal point "tree" and places cell addresses as encountered in the postorder "sequence" of the abstract tree. On exit, i denotes the number of points in the sequence.

```
begin
    pointer  y;
    field    left, next, right;
```

†When programmers write the code X ← Y + Z, they visualize an addition operation on two real numbers, not the sequence of shifts and logical operations that actually occur on their binary representations. Indeed the whole thrust of programming languages is to create an environment that is conducive to solving problems in as abstract and as mathematical a context as possible.

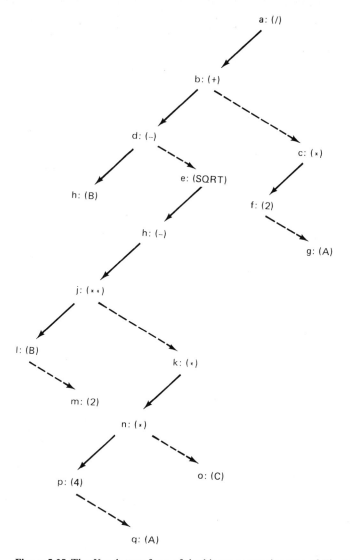

Figure 5-25 The Knuth transform of the binary expression tree of Fig. 5-14.

y ←tree;
i ←0;
Follow the path of functional R links as far as possible.

follow:
    while right(y) ≠ null **do**
        y ←right(y);

The set of right neighbors R(y) is empty. Insert this point into the sequence.

insert:
    $i \leftarrow i+1$;
    sequence $[i] \leftarrow y$;

Is y_k an element of some set $R(x)$? If so, traverse $\overline{R}(y_{i+1})$.

if next(y) $\neq$ null
    then $y \leftarrow$ next(y);
        go to follow
    else *y was the "last" point in some set $R(x)$. Back up to $x = L(y)$. It may be traversed.*
        if y = tree **then exit;**
        $y \leftarrow$ left(y);
        go to insert;
    end

In the computer representation T_R, shown in Fig. 5-23, a field has been allocated in *every* cell to provide a link to the left neighbor of that point *in the abstract tree* T_M. However, the careful reader will have noted that this link is never followed in POSTORDER$_2$ *unless* the NEXT link (right field of word 2) is null. Couldn't these two links be combined in some way so that they share the same field? Yes, *provided* there is some way of distinguishing the significance of the link contained within the field—whether it is a NEXT link or a LEFT link. If the word size of the implementing computer is large enough to squeeze in an extra tag field, then it can be used for just this purpose. Figure 5-26 illustrates such a representation. The function RIGHT link is stored in the right field of word 1 as before. The left field of word 1 now contains either the NEXT set link, or the LEFT neighbor link, depending on whether the tag field is 0 or 1, respectively.

A clear saving of computer storage has been gained, but at what cost? Consider a process that, given any point (cell address), returns its left neighbor. Were it to be implemented on the representation shown in Fig. 5-23, then it would merely follow the left link to immediately access the left neighbor. Its implementation on the representation shown in Fig. 5-26 demands a bit more complexity.

pointer function lnbhr (y);
pointer y;

Given any point identifier (cell address) in a tree, this process returns as its functional value that point x which is its left neighbor. The data structure representation is presumed to be that of Fig. 5-26.

begin
    pointer   cell;
    field   left, next, tag;†

†Note that LEFT and NEXT are different names for the same identical field.

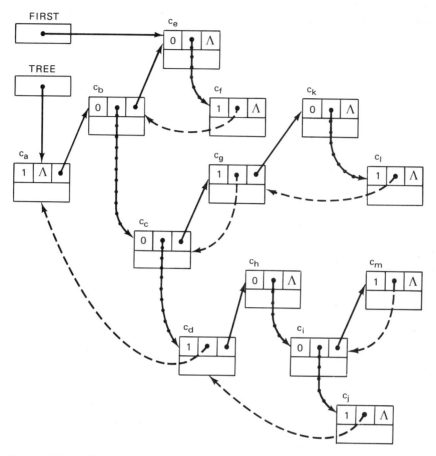

Figure 5-26 A different representation T_R of the tree of Fig. 5-20. Both LEFT neighbor links (dashed arrows) and NEXT set links (solid dotted arrows) share the same field.

```
cell ←y;
while tag(cell) =0 do
     cell ←next(cell);
lnbhr ←left(cell);
exit;
end
```

We see the familiar trade-off of storage versus processing time. However, the trade-off is not completely clear in this case, for we have also provided in the representation of Fig. 5-26 a partial threading with respect to the postorder traversal on T_M. Readily, a representation T_R could be explicitly threaded with respect to the postorder traversal by simply linking the cells through an additional link field. Then a process, given any point y in the tree, can return the next point in the postorder traversal by following only this explicit link to find that next element. At the other extreme, the representation shown in Fig. 5-23 can be considered to be *implicitly* threaded, since the same process can be implemented—it is POSTORDER$_2$. That Fig. 5-26 is partially threaded can be seen from the following procedure.

pointer function nextinsequence (y);
pointer   y;

Given a point identifier y belonging to a tree, this process returns the next point in the postorder traversal sequence defined on that tree. The data structure representation is that of Fig. 5-26.

```
begin
     pointer   cell;
     field      left, next, right, tag;
     cell ←y;
     if tag(cell) =0
          then Fetch the next point y_{i+1} in the set R(x). Find the first point in the sub-
               tree R̄(y_{i+1}) by following the functional R links.
               cell ←next(cell);
               while right(cell) ≠ null do
                    cell ←right(cell);
               nextinsequence ←cell
          else
               nextinsequence ←left(cell);
     exit;
end
```

Thus the ability to test the meaning of a field, which was obtained by the addition of a 1- or 2-bit tag field to the representation of the tree, has led not only to an overall saving in storage; it may reduce the effort to implement certain processes on the representation. Several variants of this example can be designed to partially thread the preorder traversal, or to partially doubly link any traversal thread. (See Exercise 5-34.)

For the remainder of this section we will assume a representation as shown in Fig. 5-23, even though it need not be the best possible one. Let us now assume that the data structure (tree) is dynamic and that points y and edges (x, y) will be both added and deleted. Remember that all such additions and deletions will always be defined in terms of the virtual data structure T_M even though the actual changes will take place in the representation T_R.

A new point y is created by simply issuing a call to GIVEME to allocate a representing cell as in

y ←giveme(celsiz);

But the point is an isolated point. Its relation to an existing structure is defined by creating one or more edges. The following simple procedure illustrates this process.

```
procedure edge (x, y);
pointer   x, y;
```

This process creates an edge (in the abstract structure S_M) between the point x and the point y. If R (x) is regarded as being ordered, then y is inserted as the first element y_1 of the set. Note that if S_M is a tree, then addition of extra edges may destroy its properties as a tree. This procedure does not check that the addition of the edge is legal.

```
begin
    field   left, next, right;
    next(y) ←right(x);
    right(x) ←y;
    left(y) ←x;
    exit;
    end
```

There is an implicit assumption that Y was a newly created isolated point that is being added to a tree structure by establishing the edge (x, y). But this need not be the case. Let Y denote the principal point of an entire tree T_y. Let G identify the point g in some other tree, say that of Fig. 5-20.† Then execution of the process EDGE(G, Y) effectively attaches the entire tree T_y to the tree T_A containing g, as shown in Fig. 5-27. If the data structures involved are principal

†Actually G identifies the cell in T_R corresponding to the point g in T_M.

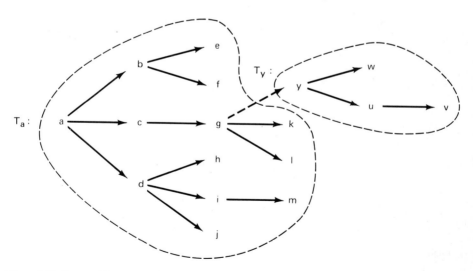

Figure 5-27 Composition of two principal trees T_a and T_y by the creation of the edge (g, y) (shown as a dashed line).

trees, then simple tests should be included in the EDGE process to ensure that the resulting structure is the representation of a principal tree. (See Exercise 5-36.)

An interesting question now arises. Suppose that the representations of the trees T_a and T_y are threaded, say with respect to the postorder traversal. Must the entire tree be retraversed to establish the new threading?

Because the postorder (or preorder) traversal is restricted, the traversal sequence of T_y can be simply "inserted" into the traversal sequence of T_a to yield the traversal sequence on their composition. The postorder traversal on the composed tree of Fig. 5-27 is

$$e\ f\ b\ (w\ v\ u\ y)\ k\ l\ g\ c\ h\ m\ i\ j\ d\ a$$

where the subsequence (w v u y) is the postorder traversal of T_y alone. Thus a threaded representation can be simultaneously maintained by the addition of at most two more links, from cell c_b to c_w and from cell c_y to c_k. Therefore, threaded representations of even large principal trees become practical in a dynamic environment.

The converse processes of point and edge deletion present different problems. If the data structure is a tree, then deletion of an edge (y, z) disconnects the structure (Theorem 5-1), leaving z as the principal point of one of the components. Implementing the process DELETE(Y, Z) is straightforward. Search through the set R(y) for the cell c_z; when found, delete it from that list by "linking around it"; finally, delete the left neighbor link in c_z. No cell is returned to the free pool, just as no cell was allocated in the creation of the edge.

Deletion of a point from a data structure is more of a problem solely because there is some question as to what the correct result should logically be. Let y be a point in T with $L(y) = x$ and $R(y) = \{z_1, \ldots, z_n\}$. If y is maximal in T [i.e., $R(y) = \emptyset$] there is no problem; simply delete the edge (x, y) as before and return the cell c_y to the free pool. If $R(y) \neq \emptyset$, one could simply delete the edges (x, y), (y,z_1), ..., (y, z_n) and then return the point cell. This will yield a disconnected data structure of $n + 1$ connected components. However, this is seldom the desired result in practice, as for example the removal of a term from a tree-structured lexicon. In the original connected data structure there existed paths $\rho(x, z_1), \ldots, \rho(x, z_n)$. It seems natural that they should exist in the reduced data structure T' as well.

procedure remove$_1$ (y);
pointer   y;

This process removes the point y from the abstract structure T_M. Let $x = L(y)$. For all $z_i \in R(y)$, z_i is inserted into R(x).

begin
    pointer   cell,x,z1;
    field   left, next, right;
    x ←left(y);

```
z1 ←cell ←right(y);
if z1 ≠ null
    then R(y) is not empty. Walk through, linking x as the left neighbor of each
        z_i. Link the last cell z_n to the remainder of R(x).
        while next(cell) ≠ null do
            left(cell) ←x;
            cell ←next(cell);
        left(cell) ←x;
        next(cell) ←next(y);
if y = right(x)
    then y is the first point of R(x).
        right(x) ←z1
    else y is not the first point. Find the preceding cell and link it to either z_1 or
        next(y).
        while next(cell) ≠ y do
            cell ←next(cell);
        if z1 ≠ null
            then next(cell) ←z1
            else next(cell) ←next(y);
call takeit (y,celsiz);
exit;
end
```

This somewhat involved process has two special characteristics. First, it "walks through" two simply linked lists in a manner that was eschewed in Sec. 3-2. Second, it requires careful attention to the boundary conditions on these lists, whether R(y) is empty and whether y is the first element of R(x), to ensure the correct relinking of the remaining structure. But even so, we find that it will fail in the boundary case where y is the principal point of the tree T. But what *should* the procedure do if y is the principal point? There is no logically reasonable way to reconnect the tree after deletion of its principal point. The author's approach would be to first test whether LEFT(Y) = NULL, and if so, print a warning diagnostic and exit immediately, without deleting the point.

The general problem of point deletion while still maintaining the essential properties of the data structure will be illustrated by one more example. Recall the binary tree representation of a lexicon of words developed in Sec. 5-2, and suppose we wish to delete the word "fox" from the lexicon. Figure 5-28 repeats the significant portions of Fig. 5-12. If the process above, which makes each right neighbor of the deleted cell a new right neighbor of its former left neighbor, is employed, then the points with assigned values "a," "jumped," and "red" will all be right neighbors of the point with value "quick." The resultant structure would no longer be a binary tree. It is not an appropriate deletion process, since it does not preserve its binary property. Whatever deletion process is invoked must preserve this as well as the total ordering on the assigned values of the points (the words of the lexicon).

First we observe that if either the R_1 or the R_2 link of the cell to be deleted

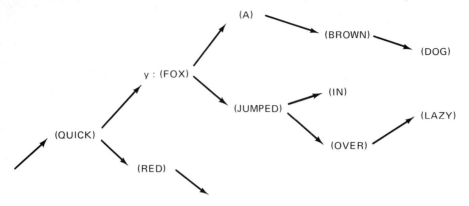

Figure 5-28 A portion of the binary retrieval tree of Fig. 5-12.

is null, then there is no problem. Consequently we write a small subprocess to handle this simple deletion.

procedure simpleremove (cell);
pointer   cell;

This procedure deletes a cell from a binary tree for which it is known that (1) either the R_1 link or the R_2 link is null, and (2) "cell" is not the principal point.

begin
    pointer   lnbhr, rnbhr;
    field   r1, r2;
    if r1(cell) = null
        then   rnbhr ←r2(cell)
        else   rnbhr ←r1(cell);

    Fix correct link to its left neighbor.

    lnbhr ←left(cell);
    if cell =r1(lnbhr)
        then   r1(lnbhr) ←rnbhr
        else   r2(lnbhr) ←rnbhr;
    call takeit (cell, celsiz);
    exit;
    end

Next we observe that if the cell y to be deleted has nonnull R_1 and R_2 links, then the cell z in the tree whose assignment value f(z) immediately follows (or precedes) f(y) in the total order must have a null R_1 (or R_2) link. We can simply "exchange" the assigned values of these two cells and delete z. Further, everything in the R_2 (or R_1) subtree of y, whose values followed f(y) in the total order,

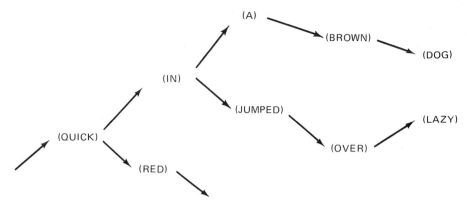

Figure 5-29 The restructured tree after deletion of the point y : (FOX).

must also follow f(z) in the total order, so this property will be preserved. Figure 5-29 shows the restructured binary tree after execution of the following process.

procedure remove₂ (tree, word);
pointer   tree;
data   word;

This process removes the cell with f(cell)="word" from the binary structured lexicon "tree."

begin
     pointer   x, y, z;
     field   f, left, r1, r2;

     First find the cell y to be removed.

     if bsearch₂ (tree, word, y) = **false**
          then *The word is not in the lexicon; do nothing.*
               exit;

     Locate the left neighbor x of y.

     if left(y) = null
          then *y is the principal point of the tree.*
               if r2(y) ≠ null
                    then   **go to** findz
                    else   *Special case.*
                         tree ←r1(y);
                         call takeit (y, celsiz);
                         exit;
     x ←left(y);

     If either R_1 or R_2 link is null, then simply delete the cell.

if r1(y) = null **or** r2(y) = null
   then call simpleremove (y);
         exit;

Find the cell z whose value immediately follows "word" in the total ordering. Its R_1 link must be null. First follow the R_2 link (known to be nonnull), then follow R_1 links as far as possible.

findz:
   z ← r2(y);
   while r1(z) ≠ null **do**
      z ← r1(z);

Replace y with z, and delete z from the tree.

   f(y) ← f(z);
   call simpleremove (z);
   exit;
   end

This point deletion process raises several tantalizing questions. If the cell to be deleted has nonnull R_1 and R_2 links, then it serves as a kind of balance point (or midpoint) of its subtree. There is clearly the option of exchanging it with either the point immediately preceding it in the total order, or the one immediately following it (as the procedure *always* does). It is clearly desirable to shift the balance point in such a way that subsequent binary searches in the tree are optimized. Is it possible to efficiently decide the best way to shift the balance? The answer to this question is quite involved, and we defer its consideration until Chap. 9, when we discuss one class of balanced trees, called *height-balanced* trees.

With these structure-manipulating procedures available, one can employ trees in normal programming applications in a variety of ways. A moderately powerful extension to Fortran, called *Treetran,* is described in Findler (1972). It is based on precisely this representation and employs these tree manipulation principles. Applications described there, in exercises and in following sections, give an indication of the computing power that is obtained by the addition of a few such structure-manipulation procedures.

EXERCISES FOR SECTION 5-4

5-30 Show that if n right neighbor links are allocated in each cell of a representation of n-ary trees, then exactly (n − 1) · |P| + 1 of these link fields will be null; regardless of the kind of tree actually represented. (*Hint:* Run a simple induction on |P| and add another point to the tree.)

∗**5-31** Code a program that will generate a preorder traversal of an abstract tree T_M represented by a Knuth transformation T_R, as shown in Fig. 5-23.

∗**5-32** (*a*) Write a procedure PRTREE(TREE) that displays a principal tree (represented under the Knuth transform) by simply printing on successive printer lines the assigned values of points of the tree in preorder sequence.

(*b*) The display qualities of this routine will be much more effective if each point is shifted horizontally on the print line according to its distance (or depth) from the principal point, as shown in the accompanying figure. (Given variable formatting this is easy; a bit tricky without it.)

(*c*) Trees too "deep" to fit across the page can still be displayed by creating a list of those points whose subtrees would exceed the right margin, and subsequently using PRTREE to print each subtree as a "continuation."

(*d*) If the tree is a binary tree, as in Fig. 5-8, then a display as in (*b*) above is more effective if the symmetric traversal is followed. Why?

Such display routines are a must for most applications. For debugging purposes you may also wish to identify each point with its representing cell address.

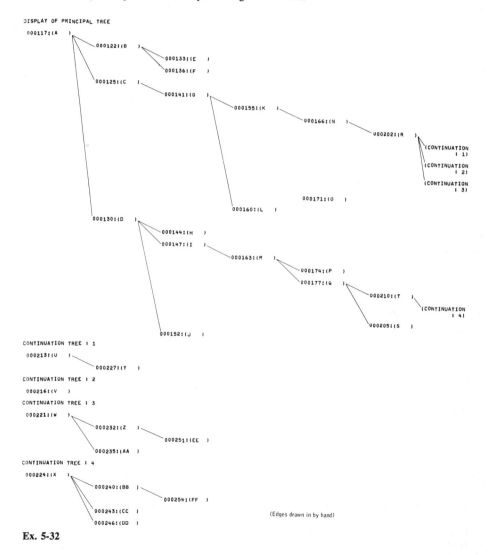

Ex. 5-32

5-33 Header cells can profitably be used in the representation of trees as well as simple lists—and for much the same reasons. Draw the representation of a tree with header cell, in which the cells are also circularly linked (through the header cell) with respect to

(a) the preorder traversal, and

(b) the postorder traversal.

Give a measure of the link redundancy of these representations. Is one better than the other?

5-34 Figure 5-26 illustrates a representation in which the right neighbor set link is shared with the left neighbor link to yield a representation that is partially threaded with respect to the postorder traversal. Suppose it were to be partially threaded with respect to the preorder traversal. Which links should share a common field? If an explicit left neighbor link is not included in the representation, can the left neighbor nevertheless be accessed? (It will be necessary to assume that the preorder traversal begins and ends at a header cell.) Write a procedure to access the left neighbor using this representation.

5-35 In the procedure NEXTINSEQUENCE, if the argument point is the "last" point of the traversal sequence (the principal point of a postorder traversal), then what value should be returned?

Suppose we were interested only in those points of the traversal restricted to a principal *subtree*. What changes must be made to the formal parameters of the procedure? How must the code itself be changed?

*5-36 Implement a small interpretative language of imperative commands that manipulate tree structures. A main driver program should read the commands NEWPOINT, EDGE, PRTREE, THREAD, DUMP, and DONE (together with other required parameters) from an input file, then generate calls to corresponding routines to execute the operation. *Note:*

(a) EDGE should include tests that will prohibit the creation of any edge that will result in a structure that is not a principal tree. Given such an "illegal" command, an appropriate response would be an error diagnostic explaining *why* the edge is illegal, then treating the command as if it were a "no-operation."

(b) In the absence of a DECLARE command, a fixed number of assignment functions must be associated with each point.

(c) See the following exercise.

5-37 In the preceding interpretative system, commands are of the form

$$\text{EDGE} \quad \text{X} \quad \text{Y}$$

where the symbols X and Y identify points in the abstract tree T_M. They are the way the user of the language identifies the points of the structures and are called *external identifiers*. But the corresponding cells c_x and c_y are identified by their cell addresses, which may be called *internal identifiers*. Since the command sequences are not compiled, the implementing interpreter must maintain the correspondence $X \leftrightarrow c_x$ between external and internal identifiers at run time. A simple lookup procedure in a sequential array will suffice. A binary-tree structured symbol table, similar to that of Sec. 5-2, would be better. (This is the tip of a problem that is more thoroughly examined in Sec. 9-3.)

5-38 Extend the preceding interpretative language with commands LNBHR, RNBHR (which list the left and right neighbors of a point), DELETE, and REMOVE. If the tree has been threaded, how should DELETE and REMOVE handle the thread?

5-39 Recode EDGE above so that the representation of the tree is *always* threaded with respect to the postorder traversal.

5-40 Consider a partially threaded representation of an arbitrary principal tree as in Fig. 5-26. Modify the algorithm EDGE so that the composed graph (e.g., representation of Fig. 5-27) is also partially threaded with respect to the postorder traversal. Would this process be simpler if the representation of every tree included a header cell as in Exercise 5-33?

5-41 Extend the programs of Exercise 5-10 to include the removal of terms from the binary structured lexicon.

5-42 Shown in the accompanying figure is a nonprincipal tree (it has two minimal points) that can nevertheless be represented using the Knuth transform, with a functional link $y \rightarrow R(y)$ and a next link from $z_i \in R(y)$ to z_{i+1}. It can be easily verified that a process RNBHR, such as that in Exercise 5-38, will return all and only cells c_{z_i} corresponding to the elements $z_i \in R(y)$, given the cell address c_y. But not every arbitrary tree can be so represented with the assurance that RNBHR will return precisely the right neighbor set $R(y)$ of every point. Construct, by trial and error, a nonprincipal tree that *cannot* be represented in this fashion.

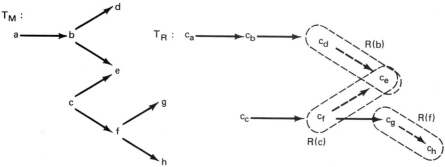

Ex. 5-42

UNRESTRICTED DIRECTED GRAPHS
AND NETWORKS

In the preceding chapters we examined the representation of special kinds of graphs, the class of linear graphs and the class of principal trees. There are two reasons for treating these special classes of graphs in a separate fashion. First, many applications are expressed in terms of linear- or tree-structured relations with operation particular to this kind of data structure; it makes sense to design representations that simplify the implementation of these operations. Second, these restricted classes of graphs have unique graph theoretic properties that guarantee the existence of "superior" representations (just as the subclass of integers has distinct properties that justify a different computer representation from that of all the real numbers). In this chapter we consider the representation of all other directed graphs. While there exist other subclasses with structural properties that can be exploited in their representation (e.g., acyclic graphs and two-terminal networks), none seems as important as do those of trees and linear lists.

6-1 COMPARISON OF NAÏVE LINKED AND SEQUENTIAL REPRESENTATIONS

Before considering their representation, it might be wise to examine a few typical examples of the kinds of abstract structures that will be of interest. Until now, all the data structures S_M that we have considered consisted of a point set

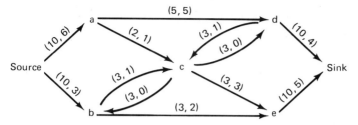

Figure 6-1 A flow graph.

P, a relation E on those points, and one or more assignment functions $f_i:P \rightarrow V_i$; that is, they were graphs with point assignments only. Consequently it has been appropriate in S_R to use cells to represent the individual points of P, to use links to represent the elements (edges) of E, and to use fields within each cell to represent the assigned values $f_i(x)$. Many of the directed graphs we will now consider will have, in addition, edge assignment functions $g_j:E \rightarrow V_j$. Figures 6-1 and 6-2 are typical.

A common interpretation of edge assignment values is that they denote the "flow" of something through the graph. One frequently sees references, particularly in the literature of operations research, to the concept of a *flow graph* or *transport network*. Figure 6-1 may be interpreted as the flow (of say a liquid) through the pipes (edges) of a system from the least point, called a *source,* to the greatest point, called a *sink*. If we let e_k denote any arbitrary element of E, then we may interpret the values of the first edge assignment function $g_1(e_k)$ to

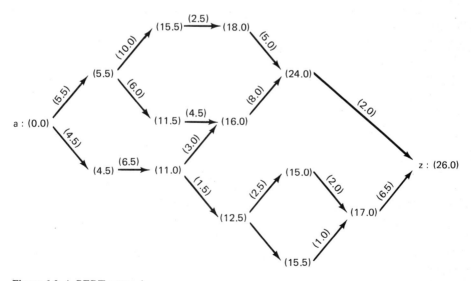

Figure 6-2 A PERT network.

be the capacity or potential of the pipe, and we may interpret $g_2(e_k)$ to be the actual flow occurring in the pipe.†

Of course, the edge assignment values need not denote flows. We may take Fig. 6-2, which has both point and edge assignments, to be a PERT (for Performance Evaluation and Review Technique) network that abstractly models the completion of a process occurring in time. Then a rather different interpretation of the significance of points, edges, and assignment values must be made. The points $p_i \in P$ are taken to denote points in time, called *events:* they denote the occurrence of something. The edges $e_k \in E$ denote subtasks or subprocesses, called *activities,* which have a distinct time of initialization and time of completion. Each edge assignment value $g(e_k)$ represents a *time interval,* the expected time required to complete the subtask. Each point assignment value $f(p_i)$ denotes a specific *point in time,* the time at which the event occurs. Taken together, the network represents an entire process which originates with event a and is completed at event z.

These two examples illustrate how data structures are employed in a large class of theoretical problems that take the form "Given a graph with one or more assignment functions, determine the functional values of a remaining assignment that will be consistent with the structure of the graph and the values of the existing assignments." In the case of the flow graph, g_1 (edge capacity) is normally an arbitrary function, and one is to assign values $g_2(e_k)$ such that the function g_2 is a flow assignment and is maximal. In the case of PERT networks, the activity duration $g(e_k)$ is normally arbitrary, and one is to determine event assignments $f(p_i)$ that are consistent with the dependence structure E.

It is worth special emphasis to note that *the interpretation of the meaning, or significance, of an abstract data structure is the province of various individual disciplines*—operations research, electrical engineering, linguistics, and physics, to name a few. *Normally the computer scientist will be concerned only with its representation in the computing environment.* We sketch occasional applied interpretations, as in the preceding paragraphs, solely to provide intuitive insight into the kinds of data structures that may be encountered.

The important lesson from the preceding two examples is that in general the representation must provide some mechanism by which values may be associated with individual edges of the relation, and that in general the representation of the relation by links alone will not be sufficient. We have hitherto ignored this issue in the case of tree and linear structures because it posed no real problem. (See Exercise 6-2 for a justification of this assertion.)

Perhaps the simplest way of representing arbitrary graphs is to allocate cells that will correspond to the elements of E as well as cells to correspond to the elements of P. Then the values of assignment functions defined on P and E may be treated as fields of the representing cell. (Since there need not be the same number of assignment functions defined on these two sets, one will nor-

---

†Not every arbitrary edge-assignment function can be called a flow (just as not every function of the reals can be called continuous). See Exercise 6-1 for additional characteristics of flow-assignment functions.

LEDGES	REDGES
f_1	
f_2	

LPOINT	RPOINT
LLINK	RLINK
g_1	
g_2	

(a) (b)

Figure 6-3 Typical cell formats for (*a*) a point cell, and (*b*) an edge cell.

mally want to modify the allocation procedure GIVEME so that it will deliver cells of varying size. Exercise 6-3 suggests one approach; several more elegant, but nearly as simple, modifications are developed in Sec. 10-1.) The set of *out edges* incident to any point y, that is, $\{(y,z)|z \in R(y)\}$, may be chained in the form of a simple linked list in the manner that sets were represented in Sec. 4-3. The set of *in edges*, $\{(x,y)|x \in L(y)\}$, may be similarly linked. Using cell formats as shown in Fig. 6-3, one can easily build a linked representation of the flow graph of Fig. 6-1 as shown in Fig. 6-4.

Admittedly this representation looks excessively complex, with links pointing every which way. But in reality it is not at all difficult to work with.

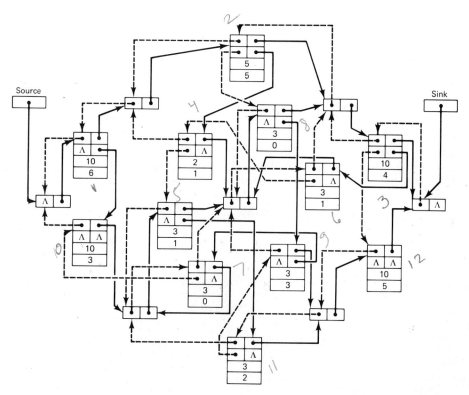

Figure 6-4 A linked representation of Fig. 6-1. Solid lines denote REDGES, RPOINT, and RLINK links. Dashed lines denote LEDGES, LPOINT, and LLINK links.

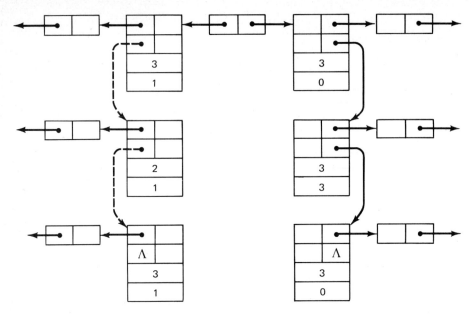

Figure 6-5 A portion of Fig. 6-4.

The trick is to look at only a single cell, together with those neighboring cells to which it is linked, and to totally ignore all the rest of the structure. This kind of microscopic local vision is, after all, the view of the data structure as "seen" by a standard sequential procedure, which only works with one element at a time. Figure 6-5 shows in this fashion a small portion of the structure surrounding the "center" point of the graph. By taking such a local view of the representational structure, it becomes straightforward to write those primitive operators on which more complex procedures can be based. As an example, consider the following procedure, which implements the right neighbor operator R(y) as defined on the abstract model.

set function rnbhr (y);
pointer y;

This procedure finds the set of right neighbors of the point y, forms a linked representation of this set (with elements ordered in ascending order of their storage locations) and returns as function value a pointer to the set.

begin
      pointer   edgecell, header, nextcel, prev, setcell;
      field   current, element, redges, rlink, rpoint, setcell;
      common /nulval/ null;

Create an initially empty set consisting of only a header cell.

```
rnbhr ←header ←giveme(celsiz);
setlink(header) ←null;
current(header) ←header;
```

Examine each edge cell denoting (y, z), if any, and insert an element into the set pointing to the point z.

```
edgecell ←redges(y);
while edgecell ≠ null do
     z ←rpoint(edgecell);
     setcell ←giveme(celsiz);
     element(setcell) ←z;
```

Insert this cell into the linked representation of the set according to the value of z.

```
     prev ←header;
     nextcel ←setlink(header);
     while nexcel ≠ null and element(nextcel) < z do
          prev ←nextcel;
          nextcel ←setlink(prev);
     setlink(prev) ←setcell;
     setlink(setcell) ←nextcel;
     edgecell ←rlink(edgecell);
exit;
end
```

A routine that returns as function value the set of left neighbors can be similarly written, as can functions that return pointers to those cells representing the initial and terminal points x and y, given a pointer to that cell representing the edge $e_k = (x, y)$. By coding and implementing such basic routines one can develop programming languages (or a system of procedures that approximate a language) in which algorithms and processes can be written that appear to be operating on the abstract data structure S_M, not on any particular representation. (See Exercise 6-5.) In following sections we will assume the existence of such a system, and all procedures will be expressed in terms of these higher-level abstract operators.

There already exists a wide variety of such languages and systems that have been independently developed by different authors. A partial list would include systems with names such as AMBIT-G, GRAAL, GRAPHSYS, GRASPE, and LEAP. Each has been developed with respect to a slightly different philosophy, and a different formal notation reflecting its author's approach to computer data structures. [Descriptions of these systems can, for the most part, be found only in the report literature. GRAAL and LEAP will be discussed quite thoroughly in this text (Secs. 6-2 and 9-5).] Other approaches can be found in articles such as Crespi-Reghizzi (1970), Early (1971), or

Sibley and Taylor (1973).] A recognition of these differences and a comparative evaluation of their relative merits and disadvantages are well worth the effort.†

The representation illustrated in Figs. 6-3, 6-4, and 6-5 is adequate to form the data base of a general purpose system; however, two modifications would be recommended to increase its utility. It is worthwhile to add one additional field in each of the point- and edge-cell formats. All those cells denoting points of a single structure may then be linked as a simple list so that it is easy to retrieve the set P. Similarly all edge cells may be linked so that the set E is readily accessible. A single cell may serve as the header of both of these simple lists. This header cell may be treated as if it represents the structure as a whole and may be used to reference, or name, the entire structure. There are at least three different kinds of cells employed in this representation—four, if one adds the recommended header cell to denote the entire structure itself. This variety provides an excellent opportunity for programming errors. It is especially recommended that a tag field be added to each cell to provide a mechanism by which one can test for internal consistency. For example, given such a modification, the first executable statement of the process LNBHR would become

if tag(y) $\neq$ pointtag **then execute** error exit

While the linked structure that has been developed is a satisfactory basis for representing abstract data structures, one may question if it is in any sense the best. One evident drawback that has already been noted is the plethora of links and pointers involved. These must be set when the representation is created; reset if it is modified; and followed in the course of normal procedures that reference parts of the structure. The consequent overhead appears to be high and it is reasonable to look for a "cleaner" representation, possibly a sequential rather than a linked representation.

Let G be a graph with point set $P = \{p_i\}$ and edge set $E = \{e_k\}$. Recall that in its 0-1 _adjacency matrix_ A_G, $a_{ij} = 1$ if and only if $(p_i, p_j) \in E$. Since the essential information as to whether the edge (p_i, p_j) exists or not is determined by whether the array element a_{ij} is nonzero or not, it is possible to relax the normal assumption that A_G is a 0-1 matrix and let the value of the array entry convey additional information. Frequently one considers integer-valued adjacency matrices in which the value a_{ij} denotes the length of a path from p_i to p_j (see Sec. 6-3). For now it will be convenient to let A_G be a real-valued matrix and let the value of a_{ij} denote the value of an edge assignment function $g : E \rightarrow R$. For ex-

---

†Several well-known languages and systems, e.g., LISP, SLIP, COMIT, FORMAC, have been omitted from this list on the grounds that they are primarily designed to work with only a restricted class of data structures. Similarly systems such as SPIRES, MULTICS, AED, which have been used to support data retrieval and manipulation systems have been regarded as more general purpose operating and file processing systems. To distinguish between these categories is an admittedly arbitrary exercise.

	Source	a	b	c	d	e	Sink
Source	0	10.0	10.0	0	0	0	0
a	0	0	0	2.0	5.0	0	0
b	0	0	0	3.0	0	3.0	0
c	0	0	3.0	0	3.0	3.0	0
d	0	0	0	3.0	0	0	10.0
e	0	0	0	0	0	0	10.0
Sink	0	0	0	0	0	0	0

Figure 6-6 A representation of the graph G of Fig. 6-1 and its assignment function $g_1 : E \to R$, by its adjacency matrix A_G.

ample, Fig. 6-6 shows an adjacency-matrix representation of the flow graph of Fig. 6-1 that simultaneously represents the capacity assignments g_1. (Note that if 0.0 were a valid assignment value, then some other value, possibly the nullvalue, would have to be used to denote the nonexistence of edges.)

An integer array $B_G = [b_{ki}]$ is called the *incidence matrix* of the graph G if for each element $e_k = (p_i, p_j) \in E$, the array elements $b_{ki} = -1$, $b_{kj} = +1$ and $b_{km} = 0$ for all $m \neq i,j$. That is, the element b_{ki} is nonzero if and only if the point p_i is incident to the edge e_k; hence its name. Figure 6-7 shows an incidence matrix representation of the flow graph of Fig. 6-1.

Since in both representations the elements of each row and column are used to denote the local structure about a single point or edge, it is customary to identify points and edges with integers instead of symbolic identifiers, as has been the rule in this text. Then one can use the identifier as an index and more simply say that the edge (i, j) exists if and only if a_{ij} is nonzero, or if for some k, $b_{ki} = -1$ and $b_{kj} = +1$.

The integer point (or edge) identifier can similarly be used as an index to

	Source	a	b	c	d	e	Sink
e_1	-1	+1	0	0	0	0	0
e_2	-1	0	+1	0	0	0	0
e_3	0	-1	0	0	+1	0	0
e_4	0	-1	0	+1	0	0	0
e_5	0	0	-1	+1	0	0	0
e_6	0	0	+1	-1	0	0	0
e_7	0	0	-1	0	0	+1	0
e_8	0	0	0	-1	+1	0	0
e_9	0	0	0	±1	-1	0	0
e_{10}	0	0	0	-1	0	+1	0
e_{11}	0	0	0	0	-1	0	+1
e_{12}	0	0	0	0	0	-1	+1

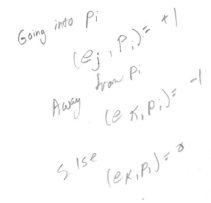

Going into P_i
$(e_j, P_i) = \times 1$
from P_i
Away $(e_k, P_i) = -1$
5 lse $(e_k, P_i) = 0$

Figure 6-7 A representation of the graph G of Fig. 6-1 by its incidence matrix E_G.

represent point (or edge) assignment functions by sequential arrays. Given an incidence matrix representation of the relation, auxiliary singly subscripted arrays f1 [i], f2 [i], etc., can denote the values of $f_1(p_i)$ and $f_2(p_i)$, while g 1 [k] and g2 [k] would denote $g_1(e_k)$ and $g_2(e_k)$. On the other hand, if one employs an adjacency matrix as the basis for representing the relation, then since the edges themselves are not explicitly identified, a separate matrix must be constructed for each edge assignment function. The values of point assignment functions may be handled as before with singly subscripted arrays f1 [i] and f2 [i].

Notice that the set of right neighbors of the point p_i, given the commonly used adjacency matrix representation, is precisely those nonzero entries in row i of the matrix; and the set of left neighbors is denoted by the $i th$ column. Consequently in most processes the procedure RNBHR(p_i) can be replaced by the simple loop

for i = 1 **thru** npts **do**
  if a[i, j] $\neq$ 0   (6-1)
      then $\begin{cases} \text{code to be executed if point} \\ p_j \text{ is an element of R}(p_i) \end{cases}$

which examines each element in the $i th$ row in turn, then performs some appropriate operation if it is nonzero.

For the remainder of this section we are going to carefully compare the relative storage and computational costs of these three different representations. While lengthy, this provides a good exercise in an important aspect of the design of representational structures. It is not difficult to derive expressions that calculate the storage needed for each of the preceding representations. Let $S_M = (P, E, f_1, \ldots, f_m, g_1, \ldots, g_n)$ be a relational structure with m point assignment functions and n edge assignments. We will assume that a single computer word is needed for each array element.† Then the storage required to represent S_M by an adjacency matrix is given by

$$n \cdot |P|^2 + m \cdot |P| \qquad (6\text{-}2)$$

while that needed for an incidence matrix representation is

$$|P| \cdot |E| + m \cdot |P| + n \cdot |E| \qquad (6\text{-}3)$$

The storage requirements of a linked representation is dependent on the number of link fields that can be packed into a single word. This in turn is a function of the individual computer and its word length and addressing scheme, together with the inclinations of the system designer. (Many programmers prefer to store only one link per word on the grounds that the computational overhead of packing and unpacking link fields is not justified by the storage sav-

---

†A technique for compacting array representations is given in Exercise 6-38. While the use of it or other representations would modify the precise values of these expressions, they would not alter their general form, nor significantly alter the general conclusions of this section.

ings thus obtained.) In any case we will let α denote the number of words used to store the link and tag fields associated with a point cell, and let β denote the number of words needed for the link and tag fields of an edge cell. Then the total storage required is

$$(\alpha + m) \cdot |P| + (\beta + n) \cdot |E|$$
$$= \alpha \cdot |P| + \beta \cdot |E| + m \cdot |P| + n \cdot |E| \qquad (6\text{-}4)$$

Now to compare the storage efficiency of a linked representation with that, using an incidence matrix, we may ignore the last two terms of both (6-3) and (6-4), since they are common to both. Then a linked representation will be superior whenever

$$\alpha \cdot |P| + \beta \cdot |E| \leq |P| \cdot |E| \qquad \longleftarrow \text{ INcidence-link}$$

Similarly one sees that the linked representation will be superior to an adjacency matrix whenever

$$\alpha \cdot |P| + (\beta + n) \cdot |E| \leq n \cdot |P|^2 \qquad \longleftarrow \text{ adjency-link}$$

Since the storage requirement for a linked representation is a linear function of the size of the structure, that is, $|P|$ and $|E|$, whereas both the matrix representations involve products of these values, a linked representation of a "sparse" relation is nearly always more efficient, regardless of the constant factors α and β. (This should not be surprising, since it should seem intuitively wasteful to store the zero elements in A_G and B_G for all those instances where there is no relation.)

It is more difficult to compare these representations in terms of computational efficiency; so much depends on (1) the particular operations to be performed on the structure, (2) the frequency of these operations, (3) the local implementation of low-level procedures that access array elements and cell fields, and (4) the density of the structure. The *density* d of a structure $G = (P, E)$ is the ratio $|E|/|P|$. Since virtually all computer structures are connected, we may assume that $d \geq 1.0$. ($d = 1.0 - \epsilon$ if and only if G is a tree, when other representational techniques would be used. See Exercise 6-9.) If G is a *complete* graph, then there is an edge from any point y to each of the remaining $|P| - 1$ points z_i. Consequently $|E| \leq |P| \cdot (|P| - 1)$ and $d \leq |P| - 1$, or if G is acyclic, $d \leq \frac{1}{2}(|P| - 1)$.

In spite of these indeterminate variables, a rough measure of relative computational efficiency may be obtained by comparing the computational costs of implementing a RNBHR procedure using either linked or sequential representations. This single procedure is invoked by the vast majority of processes that operate on data structures. Readily, if G is sequentially represented by means of an adjacency matrix

$$\text{cost}(R(y)) = \gamma \cdot |P| \qquad (6\text{-}5)$$

where γ denotes the fixed overhead involved in incrementing through the loop of (6-1), accessing a single array element, and comparing it to zero. In contrast the procedure RNBHR, described previously with the linked structure, must (1) allocate and create a header cell for the set, (2) follow links through the chain of edge cells, and for each allocate and create a set cell, then (3) insert it in the list of set cells in its proper position. But while the computational overhead of these separate operations is considerably more than that of simply incrementing through a loop, steps (2) and (3) may have to be executed only a few times, that is, $|R(y)|$ times. Thus in large data structures, if $|P|$ is significantly greater than $|R(y)|$, it may be more economical to perform these relatively expensive steps a few times than to repeatedly increment through the loop.

We can make this comparison somewhat more precise. It is easily shown (Exercise 6-10) that the average, or expected, value of R(y) is precisely d, the density of the graph. Let δ, ϵ, and ζ denote the computational cost of steps (1), (2), and (3), respectively. Then,

$$\text{cost}(R(y)) = \delta + \sum_{i=1}^{d} \left(\epsilon + \sum_{j=1}^{i/2} \zeta \right)$$

$$= \delta + \epsilon \cdot d + \sum_{i=1}^{d} \sum_{j=1}^{i/2} \zeta \qquad (6\text{-}6)$$

$$= \delta + \epsilon \cdot d + (\zeta/4) \cdot (d^2 + d)$$
$$= (\zeta/4) \cdot d^2 + (\epsilon + \zeta/4) \cdot d + \delta$$

Note that expression (6-5), the cost of accessing the right neighbors given a sequential representation, is solely a function of $|P|$, the total size of the structure; while expression (6-6) shows that the cost when using a linked representation is solely a function of the density d, and independent of the overall size of the structure.

Expressions (6-5) and (6-6) acquire practical significance only after real values are determined for the constant coefficients γ, δ, ϵ, and ζ. These will vary considerably according to the particular language used to code the procedures and the machine and operating system used to execute them. Some may be determined by summing the incremental execution times of constituent low-level instructions; others must be determined empirically. Often it is easier to directly measure the total cost of determining R(y). Figure 6-8 shows the results of one such set of direct measurements.

The solid and dashed curves, denoting the cost of determining R(y) given a sequential array representation and a linked representation respectively, illustrate clearly that the former is a linear function of $|P|$, while the latter is a polynomial function of d. However, the reader is warned to regard the actual CPU times given in this plot with considerable circumspection. First, they are values associated with a specific computer and procedure encoding, both of which are unlikely to be that of the reader. More importantly, we are to some extent comparing apples with oranges, since the R(y) defined on the sequential array merely loops through and examines each element of the column, while R(y) defined on the linked representation actually creates a linked set that has individual existence and may be used subsequently without recomputation.

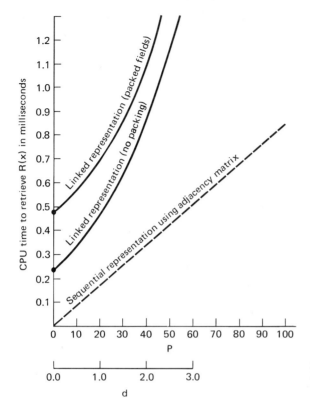

Figure 6-8 A comparison of retrieval costs for linked and sequential representations.

Consequently their relative efficiencies may be decided by the anticipated use of R(y) in further computation.

In spite of all the preceding caveats, Fig. 6-8 provides useful information. It establishes that there exists a definite trade-off point in terms of computational efficiency between sequential and linked structural representations, even though the particular location of that balance point (for structures of relatively low density) in the range $70 \leq |P| \leq 90$ may be argued. Before embarking on the implementation of a large data system, you should conduct a number of your own simulations using contending representations and algorithms with anticipated data sets to derive similar curves appropriate for that particular application.

We reexamine Fig. 6-8 once again. There are two curves denoting the cost of determining R(y) given a linked representation. A characteristic of many algorithms operating on linked structures is the frequent accessing and setting of link fields. If several link fields are packed in a single word, the overhead of just packing and unpacking can be considerable. The extent of such packing overhead is indicated by the area between these two curves.† Finally we note

---

†Packing would be employed only to conserve storage in computers of relatively large word size. In byte-addressable computers (e.g., IBM 360/370 series) there is little reason to pack fields.

that even if R(y) is empty, there is a fixed computational cost associated with the calculation of the set. δ in (6-6) denotes this fixed overhead, creating the initially empty set, allocating a header cell, etc. The value of δ can thus be derived directly from the plot. The values of ϵ and ζ can be derived with a minimal application of analytic geometry. (See Exercise 6-15.)

EXERCISES FOR SECTION 6-1

6-1 Consider a physical interpretation of a flow graph in which edges literally denote pipes through which there is a flow of liquid $g_2(e_k)$. Then the amount flowing into a point y must equal the amount flowing out, or

$$\sum_{x \in L(y)} g_2(x, y) = \sum_{z \in R(y)} g_2(y, z) \quad \text{for } y \neq \text{source, sink}$$

Now we may call any graph whose edge assignments satisfy this equality a flow graph.

(a) Is Fig. 6-1 a flow graph with respect to g_1? With respect to g_2?

(b) Assign another nontrivial flow g_2 on the graph of Fig. 6-1 such that $g_2((c, b)) = 1$.

6-2 Let T_M be a principal tree with edge assignment functions $g_1, \ldots, g_n$. We may use fields of the cell c_y (where c_y is a cell representing the point $y \in P$) to denote the functional value of $g_i(x, y)$ where $(x, y) \in E$. Consequently, the techniques of Chaps. 4 and 5 are valid.

(a) Use the fact that in a right principal tree, $|L(x)| \leq 1$ for all x to justify such a representational technique.

(b) If t is the principal point, what values will be assigned to the fields of the cell c_t? (Note that $|P| = |E| + 1$, what is the significance of this equality?)

(c) Sketch a representation of the data structure in the accompanying figure.

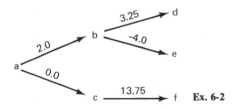

Ex. **6-2**

6-3 In Sec. 4-1 the technique was discussed in which two sequential stacks of cells could be implemented at opposite ends of a block of storage and allowed to "grow toward each other." Implement a version of GIVEME that employs this mechanism to return either of two distinct-sized cells. Is such a procedure superior to simply establishing two distinct free pools, one for point-sized cells and one for edge-sized cells, with separate allocation and deallocation routines? Why, or why not?

6-4 The procedure RNBHR seems a bit superfluous, since those points z_i constituting the right neighbors of y are already represented as a set that is denoted by the linked list of edge cells. RNBHR, in effect, is merely copying this set (and possibly reordering its elements). Yet the creation of such redundant copies is essential if one is to effectively use sets associated with the data structure. Why?

* **6-5** A fairly complete system of procedures to process arbitrary directed data structures can be built up using the set manipulation procedures of Sec. 4-3 and the following procedures:

To create data structures:

EDGE (x, y)	creates an edge between points x and y
POINT (graph)	creates a new point and adds it to the graph
ASSGNP (x, k, value)	sets $f_k(x) =$ value
ASSGNE (x, y, k, value)	sets $g_k(x, y) =$ value
GRAPH	creates a new graph, of no points

To work with data structures:

P(graph)	returns pointer to the set of points P constituting the graph
E(graph)	returns pointer to the set of edges E of the graph
L(y)	returns pointer to the set of left neighbors
R(y)	returns pointer to the set of right neighbors.
TAIL(edge)	returns pointer to point x, given edge (x, y)
HEAD(edge)	returns pointer to point y, given edge (x, y)
PDATA(x, k)	returns $f_k(x)$
EDATA(edge, k)	returns $g_k(edge)$

Implement these routines.

6-6 Let min(S) denote those points of a subset S that are minimal with respect to the relation E, that is,

$$\min(S) = \{y \in S | (x, y) \in E \text{ implies } x \notin S\}$$

It is easy to implement such a minimal set operator if the argument set S is P (that is, the whole graph); the procedure simply looks at each point cell and checks if the left link is null. It is somewhat more involved if S may denote an arbitrary subset of points. Write algorithms to find min(S) that use

(*a*) the basic operators L(A) and ∩.

(*b*) work directly on the low-level data structure. Which is preferable? Why?

* **6-7** Consider a set P of 50 elements, with *two* relations E_1 and E_2 defined on P in which $|E_1| = 75$ and $|E_2| = 65$. Assume that there are two assignment functions f_1 and f_2 defined on P, and one assignment function defined on each of the relations, say g_1 and g_2. Calculate the amount of storage needed to represent this structure using

(*a*) a linked representation,

(*b*) an adjacency matrix representation, and

(*c*) an incidence matrix representation.

(Assume that the assignment values are all real. For many implementations it is reasonable to assume that $\alpha = 4$ and $\beta = 3$. Otherwise you may determine the actual overhead required in a representation of your own design.)

6-8 (*a*) Determine an expression that represents the cost of accessing the set R(y) of right neighbors if S_M is represented as an incidence matrix.

(*b*) Compare it to the other expressions derived in this section.

(*c*) Under what conditions might the sequential representation of a relation by its incidence matrix be superior to its representation by its adjacency matrix?

6-9 Show that if $S_M = (P, E)$ is a tree, then $d = 1.0 - \epsilon$, where $\epsilon = 1/|P|$. What theorem justifies the assertion that $d \geq 1.0$ implies S_M is not a tree?

6-10 It is readily apparent that

$$|E| = \sum_{y \in P} |L(y)| = \sum_{y \in P} |R(y)|$$

Use this to show that expected $(|L(y)|) =$ expected$(|R(y)|) = d$.

* **6-11** It is claimed that most structures encountered in computer science are of relatively low density. While this is an unprovable assertion, one can make some intuitive tests of its general validity.

   (*a*) Pick structures at random from this text and calculate their density. Repeat with any other known structures.

   (*b*) Randomly draw three graphs $G_i = (P_i, E_i)$ with $|P_i| \geq 10$ such that $d = 2.0$. Are they "reasonable"? Are they "basic"?

6-12 In expression (6-6), denoting the computational cost of retrieving R(y) using a linked structure, the second summation

$$\sum_{j=1}^{i/2} \zeta$$

represents the cost of inserting the i*th* right neighbor into its correct position in the set, sorted by cell storage location. Why is the upper limit of the summation i/2 and not i? This assumes the "crude" *sort by insertion*. There are many faster sorting algorithms. Would any of these be better in this case? Why, or why not?

6-13 It is sometimes the case that there are several different relations $E_1, E_2, \ldots, E_n$ on the same point set P. Devise and compare the best representations using

   (*a*) linked point and edge cells,
   (*b*) adjacency matrices, and
   (*c*) incidence matrices.

What changes would have to be made to the procedure RNBHR, given your linked representation?

6-14 A criticism of the RNBHR operator implemented on a linked representation is that its computational cost is a second-degree polynomial function of d. This in turn is caused by sorting the points of the set R(y) in ascending order of their cell addresses. It is more efficient to initially sort the edge cells once when the structure is created, rather than repeatedly sort them every time the set R(y) is retrieved. Is this possible? If so, how must the routine EDGE be changed?

6-15 Using values as given in Fig. 6-8, determine the values of γ, δ, ϵ, and ζ in expressions (6-5) and (6-6), that is, fit a second-degree polynomial to the observed data. Determine the same values by a detailed timing analysis, instruction by instruction. Do these values match? (There is often enough discrepancy to encourage a healthy skepticism of one's results.) If not, why not?

6-2 SOME DIFFERENT REPRESENTATIONS

It is always dangerous for a student to examine a subject matter from only a single perspective, and in the development of this text there have been definite author biases. This is natural, even though it may be somewhat undesirable. To counteract this tendency we will now consider computer representations developed by the University of Maryland in the course of implementing the graph manipulation language GRAAL.† The structure underlying the implementation employs the basic techniques of both linked and sequential representation that we have been studying, but combines them in new ways.

The fundamental data structure is the set, and the representation of sets un-

---

†GRAAL, GRAph Algorithmic Language, is a linguistic variant of Algol, or Fortran, which requires either the implementation of a new compiler or the modification of an existing one. We will make no attempt to describe its linguistic features; Rheinboldt (1971) is recommended for those interested in pursuing this aspect. We will examine key aspects of its structural representations, but our description will be in no way complete; Mesztenyi (1972) is a source of detailed information.

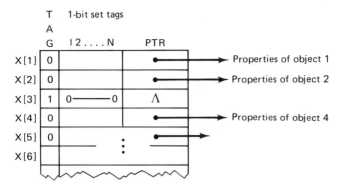

Figure 6-9 The sequential representation of the universe of all objects or items.

derlies all other representations in GRAAL. In naïve set theory there is a *universe* X consisting of all elements x_i that may be members of one or more sets. Elements x_i in the universe X may be any kind of identifiable object, they may be integer or real numbers, they may be points or edges of a graph, or they may be entire graphs or sets themselves. But for now we will regard these elements as objects of an unspecified nature. The universe is represented by a sequential array—call it X[i]—of one-word pointers, as shown in Fig. 6-9.† The leftmost TAG field is set to 1 if the object formerly referenced by this word is no longer a valid element of the universe, otherwise it is zero. The rightmost PTR field is a link to the associated properties (if any) of the object. These properties depend on the nature of the object and may be ignored for the present. The remaining portion of the word is subdivided into n one-bit fields which are used to denote set membership as explained below. The index i of the object in the array X is used as its *internal name*.

We have usually employed a cell, say c_x, to denote an element x in a representation. Several times we have found it advisable to tag the cell so as to indicate just what kind of an element it denotes. For example, in the preceding section we recommended that point cells be tagged with a 1, that edge cells be tagged with a 2. It is important to note that tagging is simply another way of representing set membership, although we have not heretofore explicitly said so. By tagging a point cell with a 1, we are indicating its membership in the set P. A cell tagged with 2 is shown to be a member of the set E.

The representation of sets as a linked chain of referencing pointer cells, as developed in Sec. 4-3, is a completely general technique. There is no a priori upperbound on either the number, size, or kinds of sets that can be so represented. But for this reason it may also be relatively inefficient. The representations must be sorted in ascending (or descending) order of internal storage

---

†This description is given with respect to the terminology of this text. The documentation of GRAAL refers to *nodes* and *arcs,* instead of *points* and *edges.* The universe is called the *universal sequence* and referenced by D(i) not X[i]. These idiosyncratic variations become unimportant, once the method itself is understood.

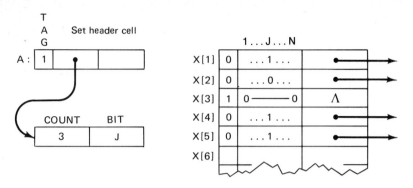

Figure 6-10 A tagged representation of the set $A = \{x_1, x_4, x_5\}$ as employed by GRAAL.

location in order to allow reasonable implementation of the union, intersection, complement, or other set operators. And it was precisely this sorting operation that was seen to dominate the computational efficiency of the right neighbor procedure RNBHR of the preceding section. If relatively few sets will ever be defined at one time—and this is the case in most applications—then a tagged representation of set membership can be employed that eliminates most of the computational overhead. For this reason the designers of GRAAL chose to use a tagged representation of set membership.

Suppose that members of the set A have bit_j set to 1, and that members of set B are tagged by bit_k. Then an element $x_i \in X$ is a member of the set $C = A \cap B$ if and only if both bits j *and* k are set to 1. Testing for such boolean combinations of bits is not hard; on many computers it can be performed with highly efficient hardware instructions. The complete representation of a set, say the set A, is shown in Fig. 6-10. A set header cell, denoted by the identifier A, links to a second cell that serves to specify how the set is defined, that is, which bit j is used to tag those elements of the universe that belong to the set.† Given this representation, a straightforward procedure to define a set C in terms of the intersection of two sets A and B can be written as follows

procedure meet (a, b, c);
set   a, b, c;

This procedure using the tagged set representation of GRAAL defines the set c to be the intersection of sets a and b. Note that it does not create the set c.

---

†One may regard the tagged representation of sets in light of the following formal model. A set S_j may be defined in terms of its boolean *characteristic* function χ_j in which for all $x \in X$, $\chi_j(x) = 1$ if $x \in S_j$, $\chi_j(x) = 0$ if $x \notin S_j$. Using our earlier notation, we would call χ_j an assignment function defined on all of X. Since χ_j is a boolean assignment function, the field allocated to represent its value x need be only one bit in length—and may be called "bit_j." The introduction of the characteristic function concept in the treatment of sets seems to be largely a pedantic exercise, except that it suggests a way of implementing the concept of *fuzzy sets* and *fuzzy graphs* (Zadeh, 1975), which are defined in terms of real-valued characteristic functions.

```
begin global x[1:sizeofuniverse];
    integer i, j, k, m;
    j ←defbit(a);
    k ←defbit(b);
    m ←defbit(c);
    for i = 1 thru sizeofuniverse do
        if bit(x[i], j) ∧ bit(x[i], k) = 1
        then bit(x[i], m) ←1
        else bit(x[i], m) ←0;
    exit;
    end
```

In this procedure DEFBIT is assumed to be a process which, given the set header cell, determines the tag bit used to define the set. Its coding, given a structure such as Fig. 6-10, appears evident. It is worth noting the simplicity of this procedure in comparison to that of MEET defined in Sec. 4-3 that operates on a linked representation. The one apparent criticism that can be raised is that every element of the universe X is examined for possible membership. If the size of X is at all large, this may be relatively inefficient. However, GRAAL employs a simple, but elegant, trick that minimizes this drawback considerably. See Exercise 6-18.

The one-word pointer cells in the universe array allow only n distinct set tags (n = 15 in the version of GRAAL implemented on a Univac 1108). Some provision must be made in case more than n sets are required in a given application. Two different set representations are used by GRAAL†, the first in terms of tag bits has been described; the second is a straightforward linked representation, as shown in Fig. 6-11. The tag bit of the header cell indicates which

---

†Actually it employs four different set representations. For the sake of efficiency empty sets and "atomic" sets (consisting of just a singleton element) are given special representations which use the rightmost field of the set header cell. See Exercise 6-21.

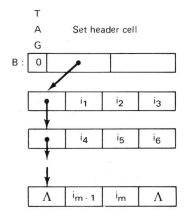

Figure 6-11 A linked representation of the set B. The element indicies are ordered $i_1 < i_2 < \cdots < i_m$.

representation is being used. The element links i_1, i_2, . . . , i_m are the array indices of the corresponding elements in the universal array X. They are ordered in ascending order. Notice that to conserve storage, each cell of the set representation denotes up to three distinct elements of the set.

All set operations are defined in terms of the tagged representation; the linked representation serves solely as a kind of secondary storage in which the definition of currently unused sets is preserved. Consequently the process DEFBIT used by set operation procedures such as MEET may have to do more than just ascertain the defining tag bit. If the referenced set, say B, is currently defined by a linked representation, it must first be converted into a tagged representation. This is not difficult since the index fields in the linked cells show just which elements of $X[i]$ are to be tagged. But of course, all the n bits allocated for set representation are likely to be in use (otherwise there is no reason for B to have been defined in the secondary linked fashion). Some set, say S, which is currently defined by bit_k, must be "mapped out" into a linked representation so that bit_k can be freed to represent the set B. This operation is not difficult either. Only a mechanism for deciding which set S would be best to map out into the secondary representation is of significant interest (see Exercise 6-20).

Close examination of these procedures that convert representations is of value because they illustrate on a small, and relatively manageable, scale those techniques needed to handle a problem that increases in severity and magnitude as one begins to work with large data structures. Given a data structure of reasonably large size, it is unlikely that all of it can reside in immediate core storage at any given time.† Some part of it must reside in secondary storage, say a disk file. As references occur to various elements of the structure, certain parts of it must be swapped between core and secondary storage. And in the course of swapping these parts, some transformation of their respective representations must take place, since the addressing schemes of the two devices are invariably different.

Functions that associate data with individual elements of the structure we have called *assignment functions;* in GRAAL they are called *properties,* a term that is widely used by many authors. Both denote functions f_i defined on a set S of elements. We have suggested that assignment functions, or properties, be represented by allocating fields in the cells representing the elements and letting the value of each field denote either the functional value itself or a link to where the functional value can be found. This method of representation is fine *if* it is known a priori how many assignment functions will be defined, and their nature. GRAAL makes no such assumption, and represents assignment functions by means of a linked "property ring," as shown in Fig. 6-12. Each cell in the property ring has a link to the next cell in the ring (the last property cell of

---

†Even if an entire data structure can be made to fit into core storage, it is often economically desirable to map only small portions in and out, since most processes reference only locally related parts of the structure at any given time.

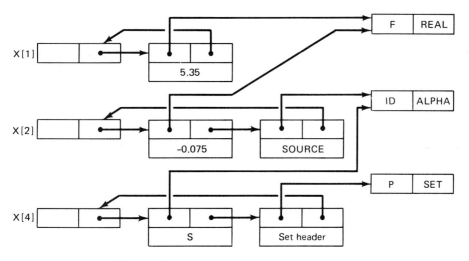

Figure 6-12 Property rings associated with the elements x_1, x_2, and x_4.

the ring is indicated by a tag in the link field), and a link to a cell that describes
the nature of the property (or equivalently the range of the function)—that is,
whether the value of the property is real, integer, alphabetic, a set, or some
other data structure. It is used to interpret the second word of the cell, which
may be the functional value itself or a pointer to the functional value. In the figure, the elements x_1 and x_2 both have an associated real assignment function f.
x_2 further has an associated alphabetic assignment which very likely serves as
a symbolic identifier of the element. x_4, which is symbolically identified by the
string S, is associated with a set. The second word of the property cell serves as
the set header word. Whether the element x_4, or S, is itself a set, or whether the
set is merely some derived set somehow associated with the element, is strictly
a matter of interpretation. In some cases these assigned values will be regarded
as properties of the element itself; in other cases they may be regarded as "associated" values.†

   So far in our description of GRAAL we have discussed the representation of
arbitrary elements in a universe, of sets, and of properties associated with elements; but we have not even mentioned relations or graphs. In fact it is unnecessary. In Chap. 1 we define a relation as being merely a set E associated with a
different set P. The notation $(x, y) \epsilon E$, (instead of the more commonly seen

---

†This difference of possible interpretation helps to justify differences in terminology. If the element x_1 is regarded as representing a real number, one might say it has the "property of being a real
number" with value 5.35. In this case the term *property,* or possibly *type,* seems most appropriate.
On the other hand, if x_1 also has the "property of being a point in a graph," then it might seem more
natural to refer to 5.35 as the value of an *assignment function.* But regardless of what seems most
natural, both interpretations are logically identical concepts, and to try to systematically differentiate between them is dangerous.

infix xEy) has been used to reinforce this set-theoretic approach.†
Consequently, it is possible to represent graphs and relations in terms of a variety of set-theoretic notations. For example, with each element y in the universe we could associate two set-valued assignment functions, L and R, whose values are the set of left and right neighbors of y, respectively. These are easily representable in terms of the GRAAL data structure. (See Exercise 6-23.) With such an approach, only the points y ∈ P are ever actually represented in the structure. The set E is only implicitly defined. The existence of the edge (y, z) ∈ E may be inferred if z ∈ R(y), but it is not a represented element of the structure and has no separate existence or identity. In particular, there is no way of associating an assignment function with the edge.

If one chooses to regard both the points of P and the edges of E as distinct identifiable elements of the universe, one may still represent the structure of a directed graph by means of four *incidence* (or boundary) *operators* defined as follows:

For all $e_i = (x, y) \in E$:

$$\partial_L(e_i) = x$$
$$\partial_R(e_i) = y$$

For all $y \in P$:

$$\delta_L(y) = \{e_i \in E \mid \partial_R(e_i) = y\}$$
$$\delta_R(y) = \{e_j \in E \mid \partial_L(e_j) = y\}.$$

Notice that for all elements $e_i \in E$, ∂_L and ∂_R are well-defined single-valued functions whose range is P. δ_L and δ_R, on the other hand, are set-valued functions whose range is the power set of E, that is, $\mathscr{P}(E)$. It is not hard to verify that the left and right neighborhood operators L and R, which we have used extensively, can be defined in terms of these incidence operators as follows:

$$L(y) = \partial_L[\delta_L(y)]$$
$$R(y) = \partial_R[\delta_R(y)]$$

Moreover, the ∂ and δ operators can be shown to be boundary and coboundary operators in the usual topological sense, and the notational symbolism has been chosen to suggest this fact.

Thus GRAAL, with just the representational structures so far described, is capable of representing any abstract relational structure S_M. But it must employ

---

†Nevertheless, our development has suggested that the sets P and E are fundamentally different, and elements of these sets have been differently represented. For the purposes of most computer applications and for good pedagogy this is normally a wise distinction to make. But it is unnecessary in theory, and can lead to representational problems. An element x can be a point in one structure, say G_1, and simultaneously serve as an edge in another structure, say G_2. Thus $x \in P_{G_1}$ and $x \in E_{G_2}$. (See Exercise 6-28, for example.) The design of the GRAAL representation permits this kind of dual interpretation.

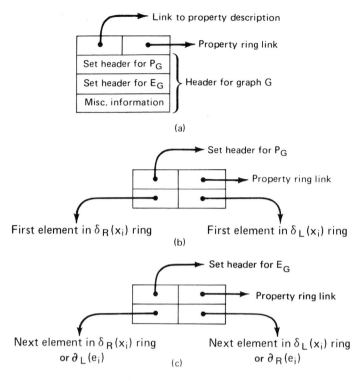

Figure 6-13 Formats of (*a*) graph, (*b*) point, and (*c*) edge property cells in a GRAAL representation.

an abundance of sets to do so, and the resulting representation will be relatively inefficient, in terms of both computation time and storage. In recognition of this, the designers of GRAAL have included three additional special properties: *graph, point,* and *edge.* If an element x_i may be interpreted as an entire graph G, then a *graph cell,* as shown in Fig. 6-13, will be included in its property ring. The graph cell contains set header words for both P_G and E_G, together with a word of other information about the graph, for instance, the type of graph (GRAAL admits representations of four different types of graph, only one of which we will describe). If x_i is a point, then a *point cell* will be included in its property ring. The link to the set header for P_G denotes that x_i is to be regarded as a point with respect to the graph G; it may well have different properties that are independent of its association with G. Those edge elements that constitute the left and right coboundary in G of this point are linked as a ring *through the property cells* (see Fig. 6-13). If x_i is to be interpreted as an edge in G, its property ring will contain an *edge cell.* One field links to the set header of E_G (in a graph cell). Other fields continue the ring of coboundary edge elements δ_R and δ_L, or if it is the last element in the ring, to the boundary points ∂_L and ∂_R.

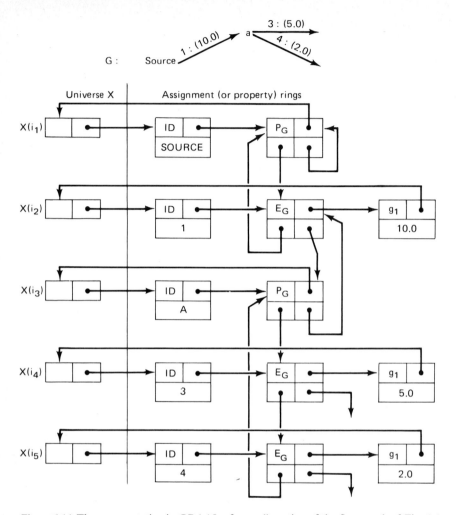

Figure 6-14 The representation in GRAAL of a small portion of the flow graph of Fig. 6-1.

A clearer understanding of the interdependence of point and edge cells can be seen in Fig. 6-14, which shows the GRAAL representation of a small portion of Fig. 6-1. Links to property description words have been replaced with symbolic indicators of the kind of property, e.g., ID, P_G, E_G, and g_1.

In this presentation, many of the details of GRAAL have been intentionally omitted. Its documentation describes a number of lovely representational techniques, some of which might be called representational tricks. Consequently it is easy to lose sight of the forest for the trees. We have tried to show that the total system involves only a few standard well-known representations which are then put together to form a consistent whole. Readers will find the cited references a fascinating study of how one group "put it all together."

EXERCISES FOR SECTION 6-2

6-16 Write procedures that will

    (*a*) define the union, relative complement, and symmetric difference of two sets,

    (*b*) increment through the elements of a set, using a function NXTELM that returns new elements in a successive fashion, and

    (*c*) pick at random, and with uniform probability, one element from the set, using a tagged representation of the set as in GRAAL.

6-17 Implement a small system that represents sets by means of a universal array X[i] and a collection of tag bits. Implement the basic set operations on this representation.

6-18 A set operation, say one to define the intersection, need not examine all the elements of the universe if the index of the first and last elements belonging to a set is known. At worst, only those elements in the interval $[x_{first}, x_{last}]$ need be examined. The full specification of a tagged set used by GRAAL is shown in the accompanying figure; it provides this information.

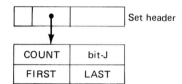

Set header

COUNT	bit-J
FIRST	LAST

Ex. 6-18

    (*a*) Modify the procedure MEET so that it most effectively makes use of this knowledge.

    (*b*) The computational efficiency of such set operations is based on the expected length of the interval $I_S = [x_{first}, x_{last}]$. Assuming that the elements of a set S are uniformly distributed in the universe X[i], calculate the expected length of the interval I_S as a function of $|S|$.

    While one can derive theoretical results based on the preceding expression of expected interval length, the underlying assumption that the occurrence of elements $x \in S$ in the array X[i] is uniform is at best a dubious one. In practice, in the execution of relatively short applications there is a marked tendency for the elements of individually created sets to be clustered.

    (*c*) Add data-collecting routines to the implementation of Exercise 6-17 and obtain an empirical measure of the expected length of intervals I_S.

6-19 Write procedures SWAPIN and SWAPOUT that will convert a linked representation of a set to a tagged representation, and vice versa. Assume GRAAL representations as illustrated in Figs. 6-10 and 6-11.

6-20 Normally the procedure SWAPIN must first execute SWAPOUT in order to free a tag bit, say bit_k, for use in the representation. It is clearly better to swap out a set that will not soon be referenced by any process. But few processes have such foresight. At best it can estimate what sets are least likely to be referenced on a basis of past usage. Normally, total past usage and most recent past usage are the best estimators. GRAAL associates with each tag bit_k the two words shown in the accompanying figure.

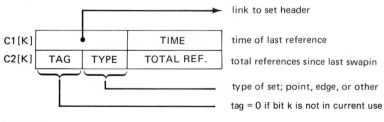

link to set header

time of last reference

total references since last swapin

type of set; point, edge, or other

tag = 0 if bit k is not in current use

Ex. 6-20

(a) Devise a choice algorithm based on this information that picks the best set to swap out of tagged representation. Modify **SWAPIN** above to use your algorithm.

Of course, every process that operates on tagged set representations must update these information words to keep them current. Such computational overhead is totally wasted if few sets are ever swapped, but it may be invaluable if there are many sets in the system.

(b) Devise an experimental test that will try to measure the overhead cost of maintaining this information versus the cost of unnecessary swapping if it is not present.

(c) Can one express this trade-off in the form of a closed mathematical expression?

6-21 GRAAL employs, in addition to the tagged and linked set representations described in this section, two additional special representations for empty and singleton sets as shown in the accompanying figure.

Ex. 6-21

(a) How must procedures to determine set membership, to define unions, intersections, etc., be modified to handle these additional representations?

Readily, if $|S| \leq 1$, there is no need to examine all elements of the universe to determine if $x \in S$, or to form $S \cup T$, $S \cap T$, etc., so the computational cost is reduced below even that predicted by Exercise 6-18. But the actual reduction depends on the probability that a set S is empty or a singleton, and this in turn depends on the particular application area.

(b) Assuming $\mathrm{pr}(|S| \leq 1) = \sigma$, rederive the expected computational cost of executing $S \cap T$

(c) Empirically determine σ for some application area of interest.

*6-22 Given the graph (see accompanying figure) $G = (P, E)$ with $|P| = 7$, $|E| = 8$, determine the values of

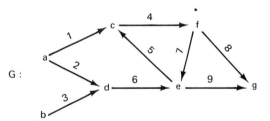

Ex. 6-22

(a) $\partial_L(7)$
(b) $\partial_R(2)$
(c) $\delta_L(a)$
(d) $\delta_R(e)$
(e) $\delta_R(d)$

(*Note:* letters are point identifiers; integers are edge identifiers.)

6-23 It is asserted in the text that only set and assignment function representations are necessary to represent arbitrary directed graphs. Using the techniques of this section, sketch the structures S_R that would represent the graph S_M in the accompanying figure, assuming

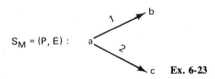

Ex. 6-23

(*a*) only the left and right neighborhood operators L and R are defined on the set P, and
(*b*) the incidence operators ∂_L, ∂_R, δ_L, and δ_R are defined on the sets P and E.

6-24 The representation of graphs by a circular linking of point and edge property cells in GRAAL is actually based on the formal mathematical observation that

for all e_i, e_j ϵ $\delta_R(y)$, $\partial_L(e_i) = \partial_L(e_j) = y$

(*a*) Prove this assertion.
(*b*) Prove that the assertion made in the text that for all y ϵ P

$$L(y) = \partial_L[\delta_L(y)]$$

$$R(y) = \partial_R[\delta_R(y)]$$

6-25 Two arbitrary sets P and E, together with four arbitrary functions $\partial_{L/R}:E \rightarrow P$ and $\delta_{L/R}:P \rightarrow \mathscr{P}(E)$ need not describe a well-defined directed graph.

(*a*) For example, it is claimed that the sets and functions below do not describe a graph. Why?

$$P = \{a, b\} \quad E = \{x, y\}$$

$$\partial_L(x) = \partial_L(y) = \partial_R(y) = a$$
$$\partial_R(x) = b$$
$$\delta_R(a) = \delta_L(b) = \{x, y\}$$
$$\delta_L(a) = \delta_R(b) = \emptyset$$

(*b*) Give necessary and sufficient conditions on P, E, ∂_L, ∂_R, δ_L, and δ_R to ensure that together they do describe a directed graph.

These conditions become, in effect, axioms of a graph theory couched in this terminology. And a system that represents directed graphs using only set and assignment function representations must verify that these axioms hold on completion of any process that creates or modifies a graph, if it is to guarantee any form of internal consistency.

(*c*) Write procedures to test for these conditions using the data representation of Exercise 6-23.

(*d*) Contrast these procedures with similar verification procedures that would be employed, given the GRAAL representation as shown in Fig. 6-13.

6-26 Compare the GRAAL representation of Fig. 6-13 with that shown in Fig. 6-5. Are they essentially the same, or are there fundamental differences? Justify your answer.

6-27 Directed graphs may be defined by four boundary (or incidence) operators ∂_L and ∂_R, which are single-valued, and δ_L and δ_R, which are set-valued. Show that *undirected* graphs may be similarly described in terms of two set-valued boundary operators ∂ and δ.

6-28 Consider the *undirected* graph G = (P, E) shown in the accompanying figure. We may define a second relation E* on the set of edges E = $\{e_1, e_2, e_3, e_4, e_5\}$ as follows: (e_i, e_j) ϵ E* if and only if e_i and e_j are incident to the same point in G. The resulting graph L(G) = (E, E*) is called a *line graph* (see the accompanying figure). Line graphs occur in the theory of undirected graphs (Harary, 1969). There is no real equivalent counterpart in directed graphs.

(*a*) How might both G and L(G) be represented in GRAAL?
(*b*) Draw L(L(G)).

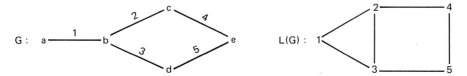

Ex. 6-28

6-3 TOPOLOGICAL SORTS; PATH FINDING

The concept of a path $\rho(x, z)$ between two points was introduced in Chap. 1 as a sequence of points $\langle y_0, y_1, \ldots, y_n \rangle$ such that $y_0 = x$, $y_n = z$, $y_{i-1} \neq y_i$, and $(y_{i-1}, y_i) \in E$, but it has hardly appeared in the intervening pages. The concept, however, is of both theoretical and practical interest. Its theoretical interest stems from the fact that many formal properties of structures may be expressed in terms of the path relation. Practically, a path may be viewed as the process by which edges (or links) may be followed in a representation in order to access some element of interest in a data structure. In this section we will look at two important kinds of processes that operate on data structures. The first, topological sorting, is defined in terms of paths; the second is concerned with the actual discovery of paths and definition of the path relation itself.

Let $G = (P, E)$ be a graph. A *linear* relation E_S defined on P is said to be a *topological sort*† of P with respect to E if $\rho_E(x, z)$ implies $\rho_{E_S}(x, z)$.

Verify that S_1 in Fig. 6-15 is a topological sort of G, as is S_2. In these figures we show the topological sorts as explicit linear graphs. Alternatively, they may simply be presented as a sequence of elements as in:

$$S_3 = \langle a, b, c, d, e, f, g, h, i \rangle$$

Note that a topological sort is a traversal of G, and that only the preorder traversal of a principal tree is a topological sort.

One should immediately ask whether, given an arbitrary graph G, there will necessarily exist a topological sort of G, and if so, whether it will be unique. It is not hard to show the following:

Theorem 6-1 Let $G = (P, E)$ be a finite graph. A topological sort $S = (P, E_S)$ exists if and only if G is acyclic. Furthermore, S is unique if and only if E is a total order relation, in which case S is the basic graph of G.

One can write a procedure, say TSORT, that will generate the topological sort of a structure G given as its argument. But as a consequence of the preceding theorem, TSORT will be defined only on the restricted class of acyclic, or partially ordered, structures. Also it will not properly be a function, in the sense that given a particular argument G, TSORT(G) will not denote a unique object. Instead it is a nondeterministic procedure that returns one member from the set of all possible topological sorts of G. (It is nondeterministic only in the sense that one cannot predict a priori which linear sequence will be generated. The computer program implementing the process will undoubtedly itself be deterministic.)

We may define one procedure to generate a topological sort as follows:

---

†It is reasonable to call E_S a *sort*, since sorting is simply the process of linearly ordering the elements of a set with respect to some chosen criterion. The reason for the adjective *topological* is less apparent. Intuitively one may say that the sorting criterion is based on the global structure, or topology, of the graph.

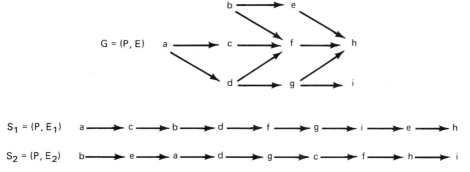

Figure 6-15 An acyclic graph G and two topological sorts S_1 and S_2.

Since G is acyclic, we know by Theorem 1-3 that there exists at least one minimal point, call it x_1. Since $L(x_1) = \emptyset$, it may be safely added to the sort sequence. Do so, and delete x_1 from G to form G_1. G_1 so reduced is still acyclic (Theorem 1-2). Hence G_1 also has at least one minimal point (call it x_2). (Of course, it may have several minimal points, in which case one is chosen arbitrarily.) x_2 can now be added to the sort sequence and deleted from G_1 to form G_2. Continuing this process, which gradually whittles away G until all its points have been added to the sequence, will clearly work, since G is finite. It can be used as the basis of a proof of Theorem 6-1 as well as a computer algorithm. But it is a destructive process, and a procedure which destroys its argument data structure is seldom acceptable in practice.

A nondestructive topological sort algorithm can be based on the observation that y can be added to the sort sequence if and only if the points of $\bar{L}(y)$ are already in the sequence, and thus effectively if and only if all the points of the left neighborhood $L(y)$ are in the sequence. The procedure can thus be written so that it sweeps through all the points of the structure examining each one by one, and if $L(y) = \emptyset$ (i.e., y is minimal) adding y to the sequence. But instead of removing y from the structure, it need only tag the point. Now, on successive sweeps, a point y will be added to the sort sequence if (1) y is untagged, and (2) for all $x_i \in L(y)$, x_i is tagged. While this procedure is easy to code (Exercise 6-33) and is nondestructive (if one final sweep removes all tags), it can also be extremely inefficient. Each point y_i of the structure, together with its set of left neighbors, may have to be examined as many as $|P|$ times. For even small structures, of say 100 elements, this is costly.

Rather than a blind examination of all points in repeated sweeps through the point set P, one can base an algorithm on the observation that, except for the minimal points, it is fruitless to examine any point for inclusion in the sort sequence unless at least one of its left neighbors has just recently been tagged and included. Consequently the preceding algorithm can be modified so that after adding an element y to the sort sequence and tagging it, its right neighbors $R(y)$ are immediately examined for possible inclusion in the sequence. Thus for each $z_i \in R(y)$, $L(z_i)$ would be examined to see if all its points are now tagged. If so, then z_i can be added to the sequence and tagged, and its right neighbors examined. But now we encounter a different kind of problem. Suppose both z_1 and $z_2 \in R(y)$ are now eligible to be added to the sort sequence. If we choose to add z_1, tag it, and examine $R(z_1)$, we must somehow remember that z_2 is still available for inclusion in the sort sequence. The following algorithm TSORT does this by inserting z_2 into a set of eligible elements. Also, instead of physically tagging the cell representation of a point to indicate that the point has been sorted, the point will be added to a set SORTED.†

```
procedure tsort   (graph, sort);
pointer           graph;
pointer array     sort[1:n];
```

The sequence of points, as denoted by the array of pointers "sort," is a topological sort of "graph," in the sense that for any points x, z of "graph" such that sort[i] = x and sort [j] = z, if the path ρ(x, z) exists, then i < j.

```
begin
      set       sorted, eligible, points;
      pointer   y, z;
      integer   i;
```

All minimal points of the graph are eligible for immediate insertion into the topological sort sequence.

```
      eligible ←minpts(graph);
      i ←0;
```

Any element of the set "eligible" may be appended to the sort sequence; pick one and do so. Also test whether any of its right neighbors are now eligible.

```
      while eligible ≠ ∅ do
            begin
            set   rset
            y ←pick(eligible);
            eligible ←eligible ~ {y};
            i ←i +1;
            sort[i] ←y;
            sorted ←sorted ∪{y};
            rset ←rnbhr(y);
            for all z ∈ rset do
                  begin
                  set   lset;
                  lset ←lnbhr(z);
                  if lset ⊆ sorted then eligible ←eligible ∪ {z};
```

†Tagging and set membership are equivalent concepts. In fact, tagging cells is simply one way by which a computer representation of a set can be implemented, as we saw in the preceding section. By expressing the procedure in terms of set notation, we leave it open to the implementor whether they should be represented by (1) tagging individual cells, (2) by methods given in Sec. 6-2, or (3) by creating explicitly linked sets as described in Sec. 4-3.

```
ψ:              end;
ω:        end;
       points ←p(graph);
       if points ⊄ sorted then execute error exit;
       exit;
       end
```

The preceding algorithm is of interest for several reasons. It assumes the implementation of several fundamental processes that operate on graphs and sets: MINPTS, which returns the set of minimal points of the designated graph; PICK, which randomly chooses any element of a set; the right and left neighbor operators, RNBHR and LNBHR; and P, which returns the set of points of G.· Once a representational structure has been decided on, it is not hard to code any of the routines. Further, there are expressions in this procedure that denote a variety of set operations; <u>the operator symbols ∪ and ~ that denote union and relative complement respectively; tests</u> for set containment and emptiness; and a control statement that increments through the elements of a set. Unless your programming language admits these kinds of expressions, which it undoubtedly does not, they must also be coded into the form of functions and subroutine calls. But again, it is not hard, particularly if a linked representation of sets such as given in Sec. 4-3 is employed.

Because the TSORT algorithm is expressed in terms of these fundamental operations, most of which denote sets of elements that have been derived from the relational structure itself, it reads far more like a proof of formal constructive mathematics than the traditional computer program. In fact, unlike any of the preceding procedures, there are no field declarations; there is no description of the computer representation itself. The process only references (1) the entire structure by name, GRAPH, (2) individual points of the structure by the variable names Y and Z, and (3) the derivative sets MINPTS(GRAPH), RNBHR(Y) and LNBHR(Z), which can be implemented with respect to any particular computer representation. (However, some representations may make its implementation easier and/or cleaner.) More and more the procedures of this text will be expressed in this fashion, with the reader expected to fill in those intermediate processes which are to operate directly on his or her chosen representation.

Finally, the reader should note a third programming convention which has not previously appeared in any of the formal procedures: the use of an explicit block structure. Recall that a *block,* as defined by Algol and several subsequent languages, is a sequence of statements (delimited by **begin** and **end**) that may be treated as if they constituted a single statement, *and* which include at least one locally declared variable. The latter condition distinguished blocks from *compound statements* which may similarly be delimited by **begin** and **end.**† The seg-

---

†In the conventions of this text, compound statements—that is, sequences of statements that are to be regarded syntactically as single statements—have been implicitly delimited by indention rather than the explicit delimiters **begin** and **end.** They have been frequently used as the alternatives of conditional **if** ... **then** ... **else** statements, and in repetitive **for** and **while** loops.

ments **"begin set** rset; ..., **end;"** and **"begin set** lset; ...; **end;"** are genuine blocks. By declaring a variable local to a block, there is an implication that the object referenced is evanescent, that it is created only on entry to the block and is destroyed on exit from the block. This is precisely the implication intended with its current use. The sets referenced by this procedure are strictly temporary data structures, yet their representation may require considerable storage. Once their utility is finished, that storage—particularly if it is a linked representation—should be released for reuse. Such release is to be implicitly assumed with the use of block structure notation. In actual implementations, explicit statements of the form CALL RELEASE (LSET), CALL RELEASE (RSET), and CALL RELEASE (ELIGIBLE, P, SORTED) may have to be inserted prior to the END delimiters labeled ψ and ω, and prior to exit from the process as a whole. If this procedure is coded in any system that does not support automatic "garbage collection" (see Section 10-3), then explicit release commands of this nature will undoubtedly be necessary.

One application of the topological sort operator is in the implementation of the *critical path method* of PERT analysis, which we will briefly describe here. [More detailed descriptions can be found in several references, viz. Berztiss (1975).] Each subactivity (edge) of the entire project represented by the acyclic network is initially assigned a length of time (the expected time to complete that activity); call this $g{:}E \rightarrow R$. We must assign to each event (point) of the network a time of occurrence, which is the length of the *longest* path from the initial event, or least point, a to it. Path length here will be defined in terms of a sum of edge assignment values, that is,

$$|\rho(x, z)| = |\langle y_0, \ldots, y_n\rangle| = \sum_{i=1}^{n} g(y_{i-1}, y_i) \qquad (6\text{-}7)$$

Verify that the point assignments of Fig. 6-2 do indeed denote the longest path to that point. Given the dependence structure of the network, this time denotes the earliest possible time that all preceding activities can have been completed. It is called *early event time,* and we assign it as $t_1(y)$.

It should be evident that one can sequentially calculate t_1 (early event time) for the points of the network only if they are processed in accordance with a topological sort sequence. Then the assignment expression becomes simply

$$t_1(a) \leftarrow 0$$
$$t_1(y) \leftarrow \max_{x \in L(y)} (t_1(x) + g(x, y)) \qquad \text{if } y \neq a$$

Eventually the terminal point z will be assigned a value $t_1(z)$—the expected time of completion for the entire project. Now, by following a *reverse topological sort,* in which $\rho_G(x, y)$ implies $\rho_S(y, x)$, a similar process can assign *late event times* t_2 by using the assignment expression

$$t_2(z) \leftarrow t_1(z)$$
$$t_2(x) \leftarrow \min_{y \in R(x)} (t_2(y) - g(x, y)), \qquad \text{if } x \neq z$$

These times denote the latest possible time that the event y may occur without delaying the entire project. Points (events) such that $t_1(y) = t_2(y)$ are called *critical* points. They form one or more *critical paths* whose constituent activities (edges) are crucial to the overall completion of the project within the allotted time. The following procedure to perform a critical path analysis is easily implemented using techniques of this chapter.

```
procedure pert   (network, critical, ncp);
pointer          network;
pointer array    critical[1:ncp];
integer          ncp;
```

This procedure assigns early event (t_1) and late event (t_2) times to points of an acyclic network, in conformity to activity times (g) defined on its edge set. All critical points ($t_1 = t_2$) are returned in the sequential array "critical," although not necessarily in any path sequence.

```
begin
      pointer          initial, final, x, y, z;
      pointer array    sort[1:n];
      field            g, t1, t2;
      call tsort (network, sort);
      Assign early event times.
      initial ←sort[1];
      t1(initial) ←0;
      for i=2 thru n do
           begin
                set   lset;
                y ←sort[i];
                t1(y) ←0;
                lset ←lnbhr(y);
                for all x in lset do
                     t1(y) ←max(t1(x)+g(x, y), t1(y));
           end;
```

Now assign late event times, following the inverse of the topological sort sequence.

```
      ncp ←0;
      final ←sort[n];
      t2(final) ←t1(final);
      for i=n−1 thru 1 do
           begin
                set   rset;
                y ←sort[i];
                t2(y) ←t2(final);
                rset ←rnbhr(y);
                for all z in rset do
                     t2(y) ←min(t2(z)−g(y, z), t2(y));
```

```
          if t2(y) = t1(y)
              then ncp ← ncp + 1;
                    critical [ncp] ← y;
          end;
    exit;
    end
```

The problem of finding paths in a structure appears in many guises and many contexts. In contrast to the preceding application, which was concerned with the longest paths, one often wants to find the shortest path, or just the existence of any path. One encounters this problem in operations research, in artificial intelligence, in electrical engineering, and in data access. The goal may be to determine the existence of paths between *all* pairs of points (that is, to define the path relation ρ); to count the number of distinct paths between pairs of points; or to find the length of the shortest paths between all points. Instead of determining this information for all pairs of points, one point, say x, may be given and the goal may be to find all points z_i such that there is a path from x to z_i [that is, to define the set $\bar{R}(x)$]. Or two points may be given, say x and z, with the problem to find the shortest path, if it exists, from x to z. A different form of the problem involves the identification of all paths that are cycles, or more often fundamental cycles, in the structure. Consequently, there is an immense amount of literature on the question of finding paths in one form or another. We can at best provide a cursory introduction to some of the main lines of attack, with primary emphasis on the way that a particular representation may help or hinder an algorithmic approach.

Every edge relation E induces a path relation ρ; recall that, given G = (P, E), we called the induced graph $G^T = (P, \rho)$ its *transitive closure*. Figure 6-16 shows a graph (which will be used as a running example) and its transitive closure. The elements (x, z) of the path relation may be denoted by ρ as usual, or by E^T in the context of the explicit graph G^T. We can give an abbreviated procedure that will generate the set of edges in G^T (or ρ) as $E^T \leftarrow E$;

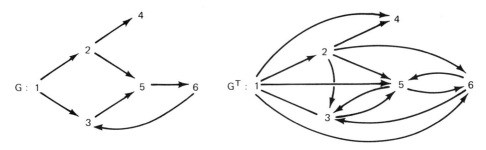

Figure 6-16 A graph G = (P, E) and its transitive closure $G^T = (P, \rho)$ or (P, E^T).

for all y ε P **do**
    for all x ε L(y) **do**
        for all z ε R(y) **do**   (6-8)
            $E^T \leftarrow E^T \cup \{(x, z)\}$

Apply this procedure to the graph of Fig. 6-16 and convince yourself intuitively that it will always yield the set E^T. A formal demonstration that expression (6-8) does in fact define the set E^T is not hard to prove. (See exercise 6-39.)

    Let us suppose that G is represented by its 0-1 adjacency matrix A_G, as shown in Fig. 6-17. (Integer point identifiers have been used in Fig. 6-16 so that the correspondence between elements of P and rows and columns in A_G is evident.) In this representation the jth row denotes R(j)—that is, for all k, $a[j, k] = 1$ implies $k \in R(j)$—while the jth column denotes L(j). Hence the constructive definition (6-8) above can be recast into matrix notation, where V and Λ denote the boolean operators "or" and "and," respectively.

for j = 1 **thru** n **do**
    for i = 1 **thru** n **do**
        for k = 1 **thru** n **do**   (6-9)
            $a[i, k] = a[i, k] \lor (a[i, j] \land a[j, k]);$

The procedure expressed in this form is normally known as *Warshall's Algorithm* (Warshall, 1962). Apply this algorithm to the 0-1 matrix of Fig. 6-17.

    Suppose we (1) replace the symbols V and Λ by the operator symbols + and ·, as is common practice; (2) regard A_G as being a 0-1 integer matrix instead of a boolean matrix; and (3) change the sequence of loops so that we index over j in the innermost loop. Procedure (6-9) then becomes

for i = 1 **thru** n **do**
    for k = 1 **thru** n **do**
        for j = 1 **thru** n **do**   (6-10)
            $a[i, k] = a[i, k] + (a[i, j] \cdot a[j, k]);$

This procedure should be immediately recognized as an expression of matrix multiplication, especially if we rewrite the innermost loop in the more recognizable form

$$a[i, k] = \sum_{j=1,n} (a[i, j] \cdot a[j, k]) \qquad (6\text{-}11)$$

A_G	1	2	3	4	5	6
1	0	1	1	0	0	0
2	0	0	0	1	1	0
3	0	0	0	0	1	0
4	0	0	0	0	0	0
5	0	0	0	0	0	1
6	0	0	1	0	0	0

Figure 6-17 The adjacency matrix representation A_G of the graph of Fig. 6-16.

$A_G^{(2)}$

	1	2	3	4	5	6
1	0	0	0	1	2	0
2	0	0	0	0	0	1
3	0	0	0	0	0	1
4	0	0	0	0	0	0
5	0	0	1	0	0	0
6	0	0	0	0	1	0

$A_G^{(3)}$

	1	2	3	4	5	6
1	0	0	0	0	0	2
2	0	0	1	0	0	0
3	0	0	1	0	0	0
4	0	0	0	0	0	0
5	0	0	0	0	1	0
6	0	0	0	0	0	1

Figure 6-18 Powers of A_G and corresponding edges in E^T.

Let's use superscripts to denote matrices raised to different powers. Thus the original adjacency matrix would be denoted $A_G^{(1)}$. Then $A_G^{(2)} = A_G^{(1)} \cdot A_G^{(1)}$ and $A_G^{(3)} = A_G^{(1)} \cdot A_G^{(1)} \cdot A_G^{(1)} = A_G^{(1)} \cdot A_G^{(2)}$ where $\cdot$ denotes ordinary matrix multiplication. Figure 6-18 illustrates these matrix powers, together with the corresponding edges of the graph G^T. Notice that these products are no longer 0-1 matrices because we are now performing addition and multiplication over the ring of integers. A little inspection should convince you that $a_{ik}^{(L)} \neq 0$ *if and only if there exists a path of exactly length L from* i *to* k. Moreover, the value $a_{ik}^{(L)}$ denotes the number of distinct paths $p(i, k)$ *of length* L.

Let $A_G^{(0)} = I$ be the identity matrix. This agrees with our definition of *path* which asserted the existence of a path of length zero from any point to itself. The matrix sum $A_G^{(1)} + A_G^{(0)} = \tilde{A}_G^{(1)}$ we will call the *augmented adjacency matrix*. It is not hard to show that $\tilde{a}_{ik}^{(L)} \in \tilde{A}_G^{(L)} = \tilde{A}_G^{(1)} \cdot \tilde{A}_G^{(L-1)}$ denotes the number of distinct paths $p(i, k)$ of length $\leq$ L.

Suppose, as is usually the case, that instead of the number of distinct paths from point i to point k, we wish to know the length of the shortest path. This may be represented by D, called *a distance matrix,* where d_{ik} is length of the shortest path $p(i, k)$. It is easy to see how, in the process of generating the sequence of matrices $A_G^{(L)}$ [or $\tilde{A}_G^{(L)}$] one can also construct D. Initially let d_{ik} equal infinity (actually any impossibly large number such as n^2), then simply add the following statement to the loop with index k:

if d [i, k] =infinite **and** a [i, k] $\neq 0$ **then** d [i, k] $\leftarrow$ L;   (6-12)

D	1	2	3	4	5	6
1	∞	1	1	2	2	3
2	∞	∞	3	1	1	2
3	∞	∞	3	∞	1	2
4	∞	∞	∞	∞	∞	∞
5	∞	∞	2	∞	3	1
6	∞	∞	1	∞	2	3

Figure 6-19 The shortest distance matrix D for the graph G of Fig. 6-16. (An alternate version, generated from $\tilde{A}_G$, would have all elements d_{ii} on the main diagonal with value zero.)

The distance matrix D for the graph of Fig. 6-16 is shown in Fig. 6-19.

Because of the natural correspondence between matrix multiplication and the definition of the path relation,[†] there is great appeal to the use of adjacency matrices as a representation of relations and data structures. Moreover, since important processes can be defined in terms of standard algebraic operations, they are easy to implement in the idiom of existing high-level programming languages. But there are also disadvantages to this approach.

Readily, storage must be allocated for three, or four if the distance matrix D is desired, $n \times n$ matrices; A_G, which represents the original relation; $A_G^{(L-1)}$ and $A_G^{(L)}$, which serve as temporary representations; and D. $4n^2$ storage locations is a fairly heavy price to pay, even in the case of small structures where $n \leq 100$. Of even more concern is the computational cost of generating D. Let α denote the cost of performing the statement of the innermost loop in expression (6-10); then since it is performed n^3 times we have a cost of $\alpha \cdot n^3$—to generate the elements a_{ik} of $A_G^{(L)}$ from $A_G^{(L-1)}$. Consequently the cost to generate D is given by

$$\text{cost (D)} = m(\alpha \cdot n^3 + \beta \cdot n^2) \qquad 1 \leq m \leq n \qquad (6\text{-}13)\text{‡}$$

where m denotes the value of the largest element $d_{ik} \in D$ (that is, the longest shortest path $\rho(i, k)$) and β denotes the cost of testing whether $a_{ik}^{(L)}$ has just become nonzero (6-12). In the worst case we may have $m = n$, so that $\text{cost(D)} = \alpha \cdot n^4 + \beta \cdot n^3$. Thus the computational efficiency of an algorithm to calculate D by means of matrix multiplication is said to be of *order* n^4, denoted $O(n^4)$, since the $\alpha \cdot n^4$ term effectively dominates the expression when n becomes large. Classification of a computational process in terms of its order provides an approximate measure of its computational cost and efficiency. It is particularly valuable as an indicator of how the cost will change as the process is applied to larger and larger data structures. Processes of order $O(n^4)$ are normally considered to be unacceptable since increasing the data structure by an order of magnitude, say, from a structure with 10 points to one with 100 elements, increases execution time ten-thousand-fold! Many commonly used

[†]Multiplication of the adjacency matrices is actually equivalent to the composition of the relations. The path relation is then regarded as the closure of E under the composition operator.

[‡]The cost of executing the control statements that increment and test the loop indices are regarded as negligible and have been ignored—a dangerous practice.

procedures are of order $O(n^2)$. These are considered acceptable, particularly if the coefficient α is small, but not really desirable. In the quest for computational efficiency one especially seeks those algorithms of linear order $O(n)$ or of order $O(n \log n)$.

About this point the reader is likely to smell a rat. The first expressions (6-8) and (6-9) given as constructive definitions of E^T are readily of order $O(n^3)$, where $n = |P|$. But by simply interchanging the sequence of control loops, so that we could describe the process in terms of matrix multiplications, the order was increased to $O(n^4)$. Can't we return to these original expressions and formulate an $O(n^3)$ algorithm to determine the shortest path matrix, D? The answer is yes, but first let's generalize the problem slightly. Assume that with each edge $(i, k) \in E$ we associate a length g_1. The value $g_1(i, k)$ may represent a real length as in the length of some link in a road network, or it may represent the time to perform some operation which takes us from point$_i$ to point$_k$, or the cost of such an operation. In any case, we will assume that g_1 is a real assignment function and that the length of a path is the sum

$$|\rho(i,k)| = |\langle y_0, \ldots, y_n \rangle| = \sum_{j=1}^{n} g_1(y_{j-1}, y_j).$$

as was previously given as expression (6-7). Note that our normal definition of path length follows if we assume that $g_1 = 1.0$ for all edges $(i, k) \in E$. As described in Sec. 6-1, we can also use the adjacency matrix A_G to represent g_1 by setting

$$a_{ik} = \begin{cases} g_1(i, k) & \text{if } (i, k) \in E \\ \text{infinity (any excessively large number)} & \text{if } (i, k) \notin E \end{cases}$$

The value "infinity" in this case serves as the nullvalue. Given this formulation, we can now examine an $O(n^3)$ shortest path algorithm due to R. Floyd (1962).

procedure shortestpath (a, n);
real array a[1:n, 1:n];
integer n;

Initially a_{ik} is the length of the direct edge $(i, k) \in E$, if it exists, and "infinite" otherwise. On exit, a_{ik} will denote the length of the shortest path $\rho(i, k)$ if it exists, and be "infinite" if no path exists.

begin
    integer   i, j, k;
    for j = 1 **thru** n **do**
        for i = 1 **thru** n **do**
            if a[i, j] < infinite
                then for k = 1 **thru** n **do**
                    if a[j, k] < infinite
                        then a[i, k] ← min(a[i, j] + a[j, k], a[i, k]);
    exit;
    end

Throughout this algorithm, $a[i, k]$ denotes $|\rho(i, k)|$ where $\rho(i, k)$ is a path of minimal length *so far discovered*. That Floyd's shortest path algorithm and expression (6-8) are effectively equivalent can be made somewhat more evident by the following expression of his algorithm in a more abstract notation:

for all $j \in P$ **do**
    for all $i \in P$ **do** $\quad\left.\right\}$ **for all** $i \in L(j)$ (of E^T)†
      if $\rho(i, j)$ **exists**
      then   (6-14)
          for all $k \in P$ **do** $\quad\left.\right\}$ **for all** $k \in R(j)$
            if $\rho(j, k)$ **exists**
            then $|\rho(i, k)| = \min(|\rho(i, k)|, |\rho(i, j)| + |\rho(j, k)|);$

There has been considerable interest in shortest path algorithms. Both equivalent algorithms and generalizations (Minicka, 1974) exist. Similarly, there is a large body of literature on the computation of all the *fundamental cycles* of a graph [e.g., Tiernan (1970) and Weinblatt (1972)]. These are fascinating areas, but to follow them would lead us into the areas of formal graph theory and algorithmic analysis and away from our prime question of the effect of data representation on processes using it. All these papers assume that the relation is represented by its adjacency matrix, and all subsequent analysis reflects it.

The procedures that have been presented all determine the existence of paths, or lengths of shortest paths, between *all* pairs of elements of the structure. Since they are generating n^2 items of information (the nonexistence of a path is information about the structure), it is not surprising that they are of order $O(n^3)$. But in practice one more often wants to find the shortest path, if it exists, between two known elements of the structure, say x and z. For example, in a dynamic system that operates on acyclic structures a routine EDGE that adds the edge (z, x) to the relation E should first determine whether $\rho(x, z)$ exists, if it is to guarantee the integrity (acyclicity) of the structure. Similarly, when using a road map, one seldom wants the distances between all cities, but only the shortest path (and distance) between the starting point and destination. This is almost certainly the case if the structure is at all large, say $n > 100$.

But if the relation is represented by its adjacency matrix, then the algorithm *must* effectively determine all possible path relations, because to discover $R(y_i)$ it must look at all elements of the ith row, and for $L(y_i)$ all elements of the ith column. If, however, the structure S_R is represented using the techniques of either of the preceding sections, then other kinds of algorithms become practical. The following procedure determines the existence of a path $\rho(x, z)$ between the two specified points, and if found returns the actual path sequence $< y_i >$.

---

†Recall that (1) $\rho(i, j)$ implies $(i, j) \in E^T$ and (2) in this algorithm E^T is being constructed so that edges are being added to E^T as paths are discovered.

boolean procedure path₁(x, z, y, length);
pointer   x, z;
pointer array   y[0:n];
integer   length;

This straightforward brute-force boolean procedure searches for a path from point x to point z in a relation. If found, it returns **true** *as its functional value and leaves pointers to one such path in the array* y_i. *If no path exists, it returns* **false**. *A depth-first search strategy is employed.*

```
begin
      integer    i;
      set array  rset[0:n];
      i ←0;
      y[i] ←x;
followpath:
α:   if y[i] =z
            then This trial path was successful.
                 length ←i; path ←true; exit;

      Try to extend the trial path through yᵢ.
      rset[i] ←rnbhr(y[i]);
      if rset[i] ≠∅
            then Continue along this trial path, getting yᵢ₊₁ from R(yᵢ).
                 y[i+1] ←nxtelm(rset[i]);
                 i ←i+1;
                 go to followpath;

      This trial path was a dead end. Back up and try another point in R(yᵢ₋₁), if any.

backup:
      if i=0 then path ←false; exit;
      if rset[i−1] =∅
          then   i ←i−1;
                 go to backup;
      y[i] ←nxtelm(rset[i−1]);
      go to followpath;
      end
```

The preceding algorithm searches for the point z in the right closure of x, $\bar{R}(x)$. If found, it will stop, but if $z \notin \bar{R}(x)$, then every point of $\bar{R}(x)$ must be accessed and examined at least once. It is called *depth-first search*, because if w_j, w_{j+1} are elements of $R(y_i)$, the entire set $\bar{R}(w_j)$ is examined before w_{j+1} is even considered. A simple example may help clarify the behavior of this procedure. Figure 6-20 shows the right closure of the point x. (Assume that the order of points in the right neighbor sets is alphabetical.) Iteration of the step **followpath** yields the initial trial path

$$\langle x, a, d, f, i, m \rangle$$

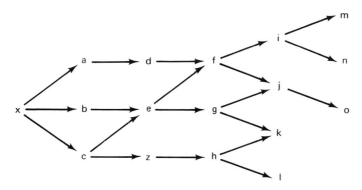

Figure 6-20 The right closure $\bar{R}(x)$ of x.

Since m is maximal, R(m) = ∅, the procedure must back up and try n, the next right neighbor of i. This too fails, so it backs up once more to consider the next right neighbor of f, which is j. This yields the trial path

$$\langle x, a, d, f, j, o \rangle$$

It too fails, so the algorithm must back up all the way to the initial point x, and begin searching along the trial path

$$\langle x, b, e, \ldots \rangle$$

But notice that with this representation, f is the "first" right neighbor of e. The procedure will once again examine all of $\bar{R}(f)$—with no more success than before. After considerable labor, the procedure will back up to e and begin searching for z in $\bar{R}(g)$: the point j, together with its right closure $\bar{R}(j)$, will be examined for yet a third time. When finally the trial path

$$\langle x, b, e, g, k \rangle$$

is shown to fail, the algorithm will back up once more to the initial point x, and begin a trial path through c. Unfortunately, e once again precedes z in the representation of R(c), so $\bar{R}(e)$ must again be searched. Verify that the point j together with its right closure $\bar{R}(j)$ (which could be very much larger than in this example), will be exhaustively searched exactly five times! Only the points h and l will not be examined.

It should be evident why this procedure was called a brute force approach!

Yet we can make a simple modification to the process that will ensure that $\bar{R}(y_i)$ need be examined at most once in the process of determining the existence of a path $\rho(x, z)$. Backup to the next point in $R(y_{i-1})$ occurs only if it is known that y_i cannot be a point in any *possible* path to z. It is not difficult to create a set, call it NOWAY, which is initially empty. If the procedure must back up, y_i is put into NOWAY. In the segment of code labeled FOLLOWPATH, we now need only check each new trial point y_i for membership in NOWAY. (see Exercises 6-44 to 45). At the cost of slightly increased overhead, the number of points accessed and examined, in this example, is reduced from 34 to 17.

One reason for considering such a horrendous algorithm is to illustrate a significant danger in the use of recursive programming. An elegant mathematical definition of the path relation may be given recursively as follows: Let $G = (P, E)$ and let $x, z \in P$. Then $(x, z) \in \rho$ if (a) $x = z$, or (b) for some $y_i \in R(x)$, $(y_i, z) \in \rho$.

Given a recursive programming language, it would be natural to follow this definition and code the following short and mathematically elegant procedure.

boolean procedure path$_2$ (x, z)
pointer   x, z;

This boolean procedure returns **true** *if there exists a path from x to z, and* **false** *otherwise.*

```
begin
    if x = z then path ← true; exit;
    for all y ∈ rnbhr(x) do
        if path(y, z) then path ← true; exit;
    path ← false;
    exit;
end
```

It should be evident that in terms of actual work performed, PATH$_2$ is equivalent to the brute-force version of PATH$_1$. But because of its apparent coding simplicity, this is likely to be overlooked. Further, even if its inherent inefficiency is perceived, it is awkward to create a global set of "impossible" points and share it between all the recursive versions of the procedure. Because of this, and other examples, the author tends to avoid recursive algorithms in connection with general data structures.

An analysis of the computational cost of PATH$_1$, whether modified to eliminate redundant reexamination of "impossible" points or not, is difficult to perform. (See Exercise 6-45.) It is a function of expected path length and of expected out-degree $|R(y)|$. But it should be evident, at least intuitively, that the linked representation offers the possibility of significant savings in computational cost, since at most $\overline{R}(x)$ need be examined, and in a large network this may represent only a fragment of the total structure. Other representations can be designed on which even more optimal path-searching algorithms can be designed; one such is discussed in Chap. 8.

Since the depth-first search of PATH$_1$ has the potential of searching nearly all of $\overline{R}(x)$, even when the target point z is fairly close to x, a strategy of extending all trial paths a step at a time may seem more reasonable. Such a strategy is commonly called a *breadth-first search*. Figure 6-21 suggests graphically the difference between these two approaches. But even a breadth-first search pro-

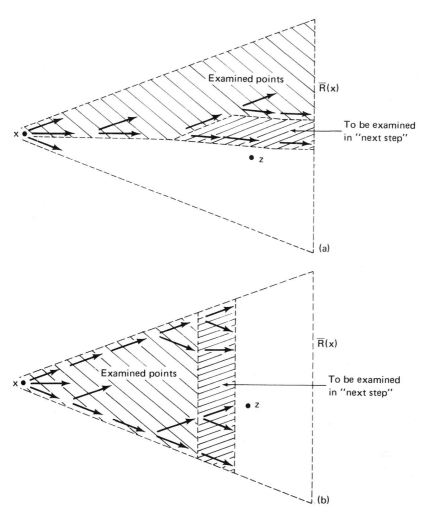

Figure 6-21 Schematic representations of (*a*) depth-first search, and (*b*) breadth-first search.

cess has the potential of searching all of $\overline{R}(x)$, although in a different sequence. If the target point z is known, as we have been assuming, then it would appear that we could materially reduce the number of points that must be examined in the search for a path $\rho(x, z)$ if the process would simultaneously expand "back" from z. Such *bidirectional* search techniques are frequently called *dynamic programming* (Bellman, 1972). Figure 6-22, in which $\overline{R}(x)$ and $\overline{L}(z)$ are visualized as "cones," graphically illustrates the concept behind this approach. Clearly the portion of the structure that must be examined, $\overline{R}(x) \cap \overline{L}(z)$, is very much reduced—*provided the path* $\rho(x, z)$ *exists;* otherwise the procedure may have to examine $\overline{R}(x) \cup \overline{L}(z)$. In our last algorithmic example we will illustrate both the techniques of breadth-first search and dynamic programming.

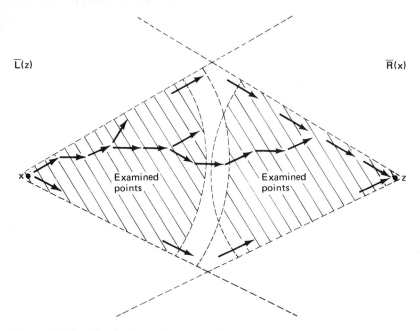

Figure 6-22 Search using dynamic programming.

By the *left* k-*neighborhood* of y let us mean that set $L^k(y) = \{x \mid \rho(x, y)| \leq k\}$ of points of distance less than or equal to k from y. We will call the set of points for which the path $\rho(x, z)$ of minimal length is precisely k its *left boundary*, bndy$(L^k(y))$. Right k-neighborhoods and boundaries can be similarly defined. Readily, $L^0(y) = R^0(y) = \{y\}$, and $L^k(y) \subseteq \bar{L}(y)$. Further, one can establish the following two theorems on which dynamic search procedures are predicated.

Theorem 6-2 $\rho(x, y)$ *exists if and only if* $\bar{R}(x) \cap \bar{L}(z) \neq \emptyset$.

Theorem 6-3 $\rho(x, z)$ *exists if and only if for some* $k \geq 0$,
(*a*) bndy$(R^k(x)) \cap$ bndy$(L^k(z)) \neq \emptyset$, or
(*b*) bndy$(R^{k+1}(x)) \cap$ bndy$(L^k(z)) \neq \emptyset$.

boolean procedure path$_3$(x, z);
pointer x, z;

*This procedure, which employs both breadth-first search and dynamic programming techniques, returns **true** if the path $\rho(x, z)$ exists, and **false** otherwise.*

begin
    pointer w, y;
    set   leftbndy, newleftbndy, lcone, rightbndy, newrightbndy, rcone;
    rightbndy ←rcone ←{x};
    leftbndy ←lcone ←{z};

searchstep:
    if rightbndy $\cap$ leftbndy $\neq \emptyset$ **then** path $\leftarrow$ **true; exit;**
    if rightbndy $= \emptyset$ **then** path $\leftarrow$ **false; exit;**

Enlarge the right neighborhood of x to form $R^k(x)$ from $R^{k-1}(x)$.

newrightbndy $\leftarrow \emptyset$;
for all y **in** rightbndy **do**
    for all w **in** rnbhr(y) **do**
        if w **not in** rcone
            then newrightbndy $\leftarrow$ newrightbndy $\cup \{w\}$;
                rcone $\leftarrow$ rcone $\cup \{w\}$;
rightbndy $\leftarrow$ newrightbndy;
if rightbndy $\cap$ leftbndy $\neq \emptyset$ **then** path $\leftarrow$ **true; exit;**

Enlarge left neighborhood of z to form $L^k(z)$ from $L^{k-1}(z)$.

newleftbndy $\leftarrow \emptyset$;
for all y **in** leftbndy **do**
    for all w **in** lnbhr(y) **do**
        if w **not in** lcone
            then newleftbndy $\leftarrow$ newleftbndy $\cup \{w\}$;
                lcone $\leftarrow$ lcone $\cup \{w\}$;
leftbndy $\leftarrow$ newleftbndy;
go to searchstep;
end

Underlying the preceding discussion of path finding has been two fundamental assumptions: that the identity of the terminal point z of the path is known, and that an explicit representation of the relation exists—either in linked or matrix form. Neither need be true.

In information retrieval the path-finding problem is often stated as "from the element x does there exist a path to some point z with a specified property, say $a \leq f_j(z) \leq b$?" In this context z might denote a cell, or record, in a relational file system with the assignment value f_j denoting either the retrieval key or the actual bit of information to be retrieved. In either case it is evident that $PATH_1$, or some variant of it, can be modified by replacing statement α with

if $f_j(y[i]) =$ targetvalue
    then *This trial path was successful. . . .*

However, a dynamic programming approach, as illustrated by $PATH_3$, cannot be employed.

In artificial intelligence, for instance game playing, the goal of the path finding process is also often specified in terms of a property f_j. For example, the assignment f_j may represent the configuration of a game at some state y_i of its play. The procedure, given an initial configuration $f_j(x)$, seeks to find a state z with a winning configuration $f_j(z)$. Edges (x, y) between states correspond to legal moves within the rules of the game, and the path, if found, is said to be a *solu-*

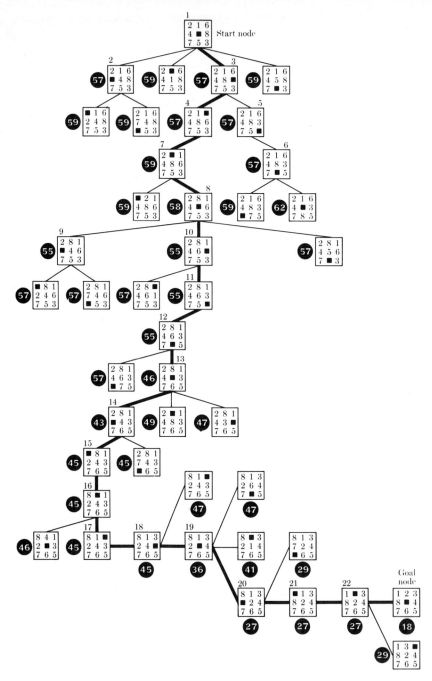

Figure 6-23 A portion of the structure S_M which models the 8-puzzle problem.

$f_1:P \to$ {possible configurations, eg., $\begin{smallmatrix} 2 & 1 & 6 \\ 4 & \blacksquare & 8 \\ 7 & 5 & 3 \end{smallmatrix}$ }

$f_2:P \to$ {reals, a heuristic measure of the likelihood that the point lies on a path to the final desired configuration}

(Reprinted from Nilsson, *Problem-Solving Methods in Artifical Intelligence*, McGraw-Hill, 1971.)

tion of the problem, where the abstract structure itself is regarded as the *problem*. Figure 6-23, which has been taken from Nilsson (1971), shows such a solution (path) in a tree which models the play of the 8-puzzle, a board game where one tries to slide numbered tiles so as to achieve some certain pre-specified configuration. Search, or path-finding, processes that involve properties f_j assigned to the elements of the structure (in both information retrieval and artifical intelligence) frequently employ *heuristic* strategies to reduce the expected computation cost. Although fascinating, a discussion of heuristic search is beyond the scope of this text. Of more relevance is the fact that the abstract structure S_M, as shown in Fig. 6-22, is seldom explicitly represented as a complete data structure S_R. Instead, the relation E is implicitly defined by a set of rules—the rules of the game—and a procedure R, which given some state y with assignment $f_j(y)$, generates the assignments of its set of right neighbors $\{f_j(z_k) | z_k \in R(y)\}$.

The procedures of these sections have assumed a representation S_R and implementation of a procedure RNBHR. Yet in many applications there is a conceptual data structure S_M about which one makes definitions, asserts statements, proves theorems, and which can be implemented by a compact *operator representation* (in terms of a right neighbor procedure) that is far superior to any explicit representation in terms of linked or sequential structures. However, such a definition is invariably embedded in the statement of the application itself, and the author knows of no theory by which such representations can be made generally applicable.

EXERCISES FOR SECTION 6-3

*6-29 Produce two more topological sorts of the graph of Fig. 6-15.

*6-30 Show that the graph in the accompanying figure can have no topological sort.

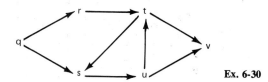

Ex. 6-30

6-31 Give a "constructive" proof of Theorem 6-1.

6-32 Instead of a routine that generates only one topological sort, as does TSORT, one might want to generate the set of *all* topological sorts. We know in the case of the graph of Fig. 6-15 that there are at least three. But how large is the set of all sorts? The initial element of the sequence can be either a or b. If a is chosen to be the first element, then b, c, or d can be the second element. If ⟨a, c⟩ is taken to be the initial segment of the sequence, then either b or d can be the third element, and so on. This dependency is illustrated by a forest of two principal trees of which a portion is shown in the accompanying figure. Notice that each path from principal point to an end point denotes a unique topological sort, so one need only construct this forest and count end points! Unfortunately, construction of the entire forest is somewhat tedious; there are over 300 end points (topological sorts) alone. However, enumeration can be simplified by observing that the entire tree need not be constructed. If two topological sorts have initial segments that contain the same points (though not

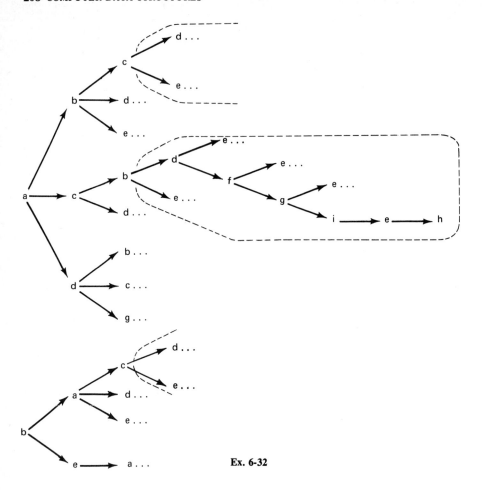

Ex. 6-32

in the same order), then any terminal segment that is valid for one will be valid for the other. For example, ⟨a, b, c, ...⟩ and ⟨a, c, b, ...⟩ have initial segments with common elements, and hence may have identical terminal segments. Thus the three subtrees enclosed by dashed lines must be identical, and only one need be constructed.

How many distinct topological sorts of the graph G of Fig. 6-15 exist?

6-33 Assume that GRAPH is represented by a sequential adjacency matrix EDGE[i, j]:

(*a*) Code the nondestructive TSORT algorithm that repeatedly sweeps through all points y in P, examining L(y) and tagging those added to the sequence.

(*b*) Add a modification that will terminate the procedure if a cycle is discovered. Does this change necessarily isolate or identify the cycle?

(*c*) The text states that a maximum of |P| sweeps may be necessary. The actual number of sweeps required is dependent on:

(1) the configuration of the structure itself—that is, the relation E—and

(2) the order in which points y_i are encountered in the process of sweeping through P.

Construct the worst case example where the number of sweeps = |P|. (It is unique.) Try to estimate the average number of sweeps that will be necessary if

(1) S_M is a linear structure, and

(2) S_M is a tree.

This is an example of a procedure whose computational efficiency is highly dependent on its particular representation.

*6-34 Implement TSORT using a linked representation of GRAPH similar to that described in Sec. 6-1.

6-35 Derive an expression for the computational efficiency of TSORT in terms of $|P|$ and d equals the density of GRAPH. Recall that d also denotes the average $|R(y)|$ and average $|L(y)|$, and note that a point z in R(y) will be fruitlessly examined (in the innermost block) a total of $|R(y)| - 1$ times before it too can be added to the sort sequence.

6-36 Show that if S is a topological sort of G, then its inverse S^{-1} is a reverse topological sort; that is $\rho_G(x, z)$ implies $\rho_{S^{-1}}(z, x)$. Which of the tree traversals of Sec. 5-3 is a reverse topological sort?

6-37 It is known that *if* G *is acyclic, then there exists an ordering of its points* $p_i = P$ *such that its adjacency matrix representation* A_G *is an upper* (or lower) *triangular matrix.* Use the concept of a topological sort to prove this assertion, and show how a TSORT procedure can be used to transform any acyclic graph into this representational form. Consequently, if all the structures are known to be acyclic, the discussion of storage requirements in Sec. 6-1 can be modified; only half as much storage will be needed in the case of adjacency matrix representations. Normally the representation of two acyclic structures is packed into a single $(n \times n + 1)$ array as shown in the accompanying figure (one in upper triangular, the other in lower triangular form). How must the routine RHBHR be modified, given this representation?

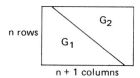

n rows

G_2

G_1

n + 1 columns   **Ex. 6-37**

*6-38 Figure 6-2 shows a PERT network with early event times (t_1) assigned to the points. Following the procedure PERT, assign late event times (t_2) and determine the critical points and critical path.

6-39 Show that expression (6-8) is a constructive definition of the set E^T in the transitive closure of $G = (P, E)$. Such a proof involves showing that for any path $\rho_E(x, z) = \langle y_0, \ldots, y_n \rangle$, $(x, z) = (y_0, y_n) \in E^T$. (*Hint:* Run an induction on paths of length n such that all "interior" points y_i, $0 < i < n$ have been examined in the outer loop.)

6-40 Implement Floyd's shortest-path algorithm. If you have developed a set of structure manipulating routines (as in Exercise 6-5), code an implementation suggested by its expression in Eq. (6-13).

6-41 The order of a computational algorithm is always a measure of its "worst case" performance; but it is clear that from a practical point of view one would much prefer an expression for the expected, or average, cost of computation. Consider the constructive expression (6-8). The two inner loops will be executed only $|L(y)|$ and $|R(y)|$ times, respectively. While it is possible that $|L(y)| = |R(y)| = n - 1$, so that the process can be of order $O(n^3)$, in practice these quantities are normally very much lower.

(*a*) Apply this constructive process to the graph of Fig. 6-16 and count the number of times that the innermost statement is actually executed.

It is clear that a sharper upper bound for the computational cost of this process is given by $\text{cost}(G^T) = |P| \cdot d(G^T)^2$, where $d(G^T)$ denotes the density of G^T.

Consequently, one could predict an expected upper bound, given $G = (P, E)$, if one could predict the expected number of edges in G^T, that is, $|E^T|$.

(*b*) Empirically estimate $|E^T|$ for a selection of
   (1) linear graphs,
   (2) trees, and
   (3) acyclic structures.

(*c*) What happens if you add one more edge to E so as to create a cycle?

(*d*) Try to derive a closed expression for $\exp(|E^T|)$. The author knows of none. Clearly this expression should be a function of $|P|$ and $|E|$; but as shown above other graph theoretic information about G, such as whether or not G is (1) acyclic, (2) a tree, (3) the numbers of minimal and maximal points (i.e., $|m_G|$, $|M_G|$), and (4) average path length could all be introduced as additional parameters which influence $exp(|E^T|)$.

6-42 Are the innermost statements of Floyd's shortest-path algorithm always executed n^3 times? Notice the conditional **if** statements. Add counters to the implementation of Exercise 6-40 to yield an empirical estimate for the expected cost for a sample selection of structures.

6-43 Suppose one wants to discover the length of the shortest *cycle* through each point. Which adjacency representation A_G or $\tilde{A}_G$ should be used?

* 6-44 Code the procedure PATH$_1$, but modify it so that as points are discovered that cannot possibly lie on the desired path, they are entered into a set for later testing. (Search algorithms in which a set of impossible solutions is developed in the course of the search process, and is subsequently used to terminate other impossible search sequences. These fall into a class that is commonly called *branch and bound* algorithms. Such algorithms have been widely used, and with great success, in integer programming and in a variety of artificial intelligence applications. In this terminology, *bound* refers to a bound (normally numerical) within which the solution, if it exists, must lie. If the bound is encountered in the search process rather than search in some impossible, or *unfeasible,* region, the algorithm "branches" and attempts some other alternative search sequence.)

6-45 One can easily construct examples in which construction of the set NOWAY to serve as a bound of impossible solutions is just so much needless overhead—for instance, if the target point z lies on the first path examined, or if the structure to be searched is a tree.

(*a*) Why is this mechanism unnecessary in a tree search? Prove it.

An important question is: How much search time can it be "expected" to save? or: How hard are we willing to work to avoid "work"? Probably the best answer to this question must be empirically obtained.

(*b*) Generate a number of random graphs, pick a random pair of points in the graph, and call both the brute force and modified versions of PATH$_1$. Keep a running total of the numbers of points accessed in both cases to provide a basis for comparison.

6-46 One possible disadvantage of PATH$_1$ as presented in the text is that the sequential array Y must be dimensioned with some finite upper bound. The recursive procedure PATH$_2$ used no such array. Instead, the points y_i were stacked by means of the run-time recursion stack. PATH$_1$ may also be recoded to make use of a linked stack rather than a sequential array. Try it.

* 6-47 A more serious defect of PATH$_1$ and PATH$_2$ shows up if the graph is cyclic. The process may get trapped into a cycle and trace around its edges indefinitely. Modify each to correct this defect. (*Note:* This cannot happen in PATH$_3$. Why?)

6-48 The text raises the question of whether a breadth-first or depth-first search is more efficient. Show that, *assuming no additional information about the location of the point z* in a procedure PATH(X, Z), the expected number of points examined given a breadth-first search is equal the expected number of points examined given a depth-first search. (*Hint:* Begin by noting that both search strategies will potentially examine all points in the ideal $\bar{R}(x)$, but with respect to different linear orders.)

6-49 Neither of the depth-first path-finding algorithms need return a path of minimal length.

(*a*) Construct an example in which PATH$_1$ (or PATH$_2$) returns a path $\rho(x, z)$ that is not of minimal length.

(*b*) Can these procedures be modified so that they will always find a minimal length path? How, or why not?

In contrast, the breadth-first search (as in PATH$_3$) always finds a path of minimal length.

(*c*) Justify this assertion.

(*d*) Modify PATH$_3$ so that:

(1) it returns the length of the minimal path, if it exists. (Assume all edges are of length 1.)

(2) it returns the sequence of points $\langle y_i \rangle$ that constitute a minimal path. (*Hint:* Each point added to either LEFTBNDY or RIGHTBNDY must link to the point from which it was accessed.)

6-50 Assume the existence of an edge weight function $g_1:E \to \{reals\}$, and summative definition of path length as in Eq. (6-7). Design a kind of breadth-first search algorithm that will find a path $\rho(x, z)$ of minimal length. Can you demonstrate that your process is really an algorithm (i.e., always finds a path of minimal length)? Suppose $g_1(y_{i-1}, y_i)$ can be negative.

6-51 The 8-puzzle is a set of eight numbered movable tiles in a 3×3 matrix. Any tile that is adjacent to the blank (or empty) element may be moved there, effectively interchanging that tile and the blank. The goal of the game is to transform some initial configuration of the tiles by a sequence of moves or interchanges into some desired final configuration. Suppose that we represent a configuration by a sequential array of nine integers (zero denoting the blank) as shown in the accompanying figure.

Configuration   Representation

1	2	3
4	5	6
7	8	■

$<1, 2, 3, 4, 5, 6, 7, 8, 0>$

2	1	6
4	■	8
7	5	3

$<2, 1, 6, 4, 0, 8, 7, 5, 3>$

Ex. 6-51

(a) Write a procedure RNBHR (C0, N, C1, C2, C3, C4) that, given a configuration C0 of tiles, generates the N $(1 \le n \le 4)$ configurations into which C0 can be transformed.

(b) Use RNBHR above and routines such as those developed in Exercise 6-5 to create an explicit representation of a portion of the game structure similar to that of Fig. 6-23.

(c) The abstract structure S_M of Fig. 6-23 need not be a tree since there may be two or more sequences of moves that lead to the same state y with configuration $g_1(y)$. Will the generation process of (b) above always yield a tree? Why?

(d) In lieu of actually generating such a structure, sketch a representation S_R that could be generated.

6-4 REPRESENTATION OF STRUCTURES BY A KNUTH TRANSFORMATION

In Sec. 5-4 a technique, using the Knuth transform, was presented by which any arbitrary principal tree could be represented as a binary tree structure. The advantage of this representation lay in the fact that at most two link fields, RIGHT and NEXT, were necessary to represent all the edges $(y, z_i) \in E$, independent of the size of $R(y) = \{z_i\}$. Exercise 5-41 illustrated application of the transformation to a nonprincipal tree, but asserted that it was not always applicable. Assuming that no independent representation of individual edges is necessary (e.g., there are no edge assignment functions g_i), then extension of the Knuth transformation to more general structures might be a very attractive representational technique. At least, it is worth exploring the extent of its applicability.

Recall that in Sec. 5-4, the Knuth transformation $\varphi:S_M \to S_R$ was informally described as follows: For each point y in S_M, associate a corresponding cell c_y in S_R. If $\{z_1, z_2, \ldots, z_n\} = R(y)$, then link $c_{z_1}, \ldots, c_{z_n}$ as a linear set using

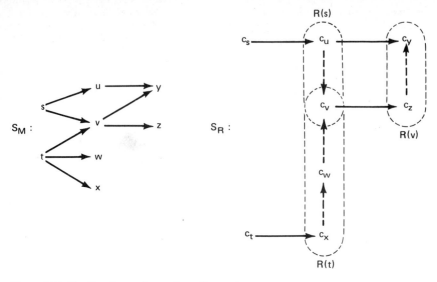

Figure 6-24 The Knuth transform of acyclic graph.

the NEXT field. Link the cell c_y to the set (list) representing $R(y)$ using the RIGHT field. Figure 6-24 illustrates this transformation applied to an acyclic graph, where dashed edges have been used to denote set links and solid edges to denote those links that represent the functional relation $y \rightarrow R(y)$. While the transformation clearly works in this case, we need only consider Fig. 6-25 to see an instance when it fails, even though S_M is a tree. Either the cell c_y must contain an additional link field to distinguish its membership in the sets $\{x, y\} = R(u)$ and $\{y, z\} = R(v)$, or else x will "appear" (as shown) to be an element of $R(v)$. The representation is not *faithful*, in the sense that computer procedures using S_R alone cannot reproduce the information contained in the relation of S_M.

The informal presentation of this transformation was satisfactory in Sec. 5-4 because it clearly worked, and because we made no real assertions about it that needed proof. Since our goal now is to map out precisely those structures for which it is applicable and those for which it is not, we will have to work from a more formal definition. First we note that the representations S_R are not really graphs as we have been using the term—since they have two distinct kinds of edges. Let us call a point set P with two or more relations $E_1, \ldots, E_k$ defined on it a *hypergraph*†, and denote it by $G = (P, E_1, \ldots, E_k)$. Then by an E_i *path*, $\rho_{E_i}(x, z)$ we will mean a sequence of points $\langle y_0, \ldots, y_n \rangle$ such that $(y_{j-1}, y_j) \in E_j$. (That is, an E_i path is simply a path restricted to the relation E_j.)

Now we may say that a hypergraph $G' = (P', E_1', E_2')$ is a *Knuth transform*

†The term *hypergraph* has other meanings; among them, a set P with an n-ary relation defined on it.

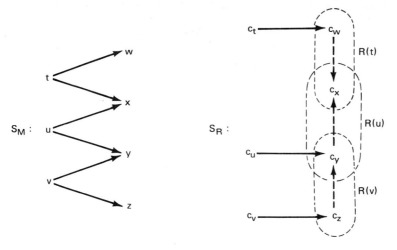

Figure 6-25 An abstract structure for which application of the Knuth transform yields an unfaithful representation.

of the graph $G = (P, E)$ if there exists a 1-1 onto function $\varphi: P \rightarrow P'$ [we will let y' denote $\varphi(y)$] such that:

1. $(y, z) \in E$ implies that for some *unique* $z_0 \in R(y)$ $(y', z_0') \in E_1'$ and $\rho_{E_2'}(z_0', z')$,
2. $(y', z_0') \in E_1'$ and $\rho_{E_2'}(z_0', z)$ implies that $z = \varphi^{-1}(z') \in R(y)$, and
3. E_1' and E_2' are partial functions.

It is not hard to verify that this definition includes the transform as informally described above. Further, any representation of S_M by such a transform must be faithful, since conditions (1) and (2) imply that a computer process that traverses the E_1' link (RIGHT link, if nonnull) in the cell c_y to the cell c_{z_0}, and then follows E_2' links (NEXT links, if any) will retrieve *all and only* those cells corresponding to points in $R(y)$. Thus all edges (y, z) of the original relation E are reconstructable. Finally, since E_1' and E_2' are partial functions, for any $y_j' \in P'$ there exists at most a single $z' \in P'$ such that $(y_j', z') \in E_1'$, and a single y_{j+1}' such that $(y_j', y_{j+1}') \in E_2'$. Hence E_2' paths from any cell c_y must be unique (thereby making the path-following procedure trivial), and no more than two link fields per cell will be needed in the representation of the hypergraph G'.

Let $S_M = (P, E)$ be any abstract data structure. S_M induces a second graph S^* that can be defined as follows: Let $\mathscr{R}$ be the collection of all sets $\{R(y) \mid y \in P\}$. Augment $\mathscr{R}$ with all finite intersections of elements of $\mathscr{R}$ (in the same manner that one forms a topological base from a subbase) to form $\mathscr{R}^*$. The set $\mathscr{R}^*$ is partially ordered by set inclusion to form $S^* = (\mathscr{R}^*, \subseteq)$. (Recall the example in Sec. 1-5.) Since the empty set $\emptyset \subseteq R(y)$ for all y, $\emptyset$ is a least element of S^*, implying that S^* is connected, whether or not S_M was. With these definitions it is now possible to prove (Pfaltz, 1975) that:

$$\mathcal{R}^* = \left\{ \begin{array}{l} R(s) = \{u, v\}, \ R(t) = \{v, w, x\}, \ R(u) = \{y\}, \ R(v) = \{y, z\}, \\ R(w) = R(x) = R(y) = R(z) = \phi, \ X = R(s) \cap R(t) = \{v\} \end{array} \right\}$$

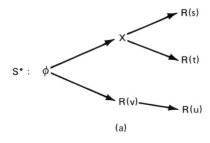

(a)

$$\mathcal{R}^* = \left\{ \begin{array}{l} R(t) = \{w, x\}, \ R(u) = \{x, y\}, \ R(v) = \{y, z\}, \\ R(w) = R(x) = R(y) = R(z) = \phi, \\ X = R(t) \cap R(u) = \{x\}, \ Y = R(u) \cap R(v) = \{y\} \end{array} \right\}$$

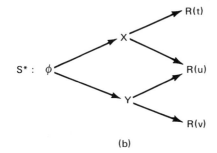

(b)

Figure 6-26 $\mathcal{R}^*$ and induced graphs S* associated with Figs. 6-24 and 6-25.

Theorem 6-4 The Knuth transform, $\varphi : S_M \to S_R$ of a finite graph $S_M = (P, E)$ exists if and only if $S^* = (\mathcal{R}^*, \subseteq)$ is a principal tree.

Figure 6-26 illustrates this theorem by presenting the induced graphs S* of the graphs of Figs. 6-24 and 6-25. In the first case S* is a tree and S_M is representable under a Knuth transform; in the latter case it is not.

To a computer scientist the statement of Theorem 6-4 should be most unsatisfactory. Given a data structure S_M to be represented, one is hardly willing to create $\mathcal{R}^*$ by forming the sets R(y), creating all possible finite intersections of them, testing this collection for all possible inclusions to form a partial order relation, and then testing whether the resulting relation is a tree. Clearly we should want a characterization of Knuth representability in terms of "local" properties of S_M itself, without involving S*. Using established results about principal trees, it is not hard to prove the following corollaries, which provide the desired "local" characterization.

Corollary 6-5 A Knuth transform of $S_M = (P, E)$ exists if and only if for all

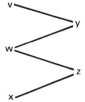

Figure 6-27 The "forbidden" subgraph of Theorem 6-7.

x, y, z $\in$ P, R(x) $\cap$ R(y) and R(x) $\cap$ R(z) nonempty implies that either (*a*) R(x) $\cap$ R(y) $\subseteq$ R(x) $\cap$ R(z), or (*b*) R(x) $\cap$ R(y) $\supseteq$ R(x) $\cap$ R(z).

Corollary 6-6 If S_M is a principal tree (or forest of principal trees) then the Knuth transformation of S_M exists.

The latter corollary (which follows from the observation that in principal trees R(x) $\neq$ R(y) implies R(x) $\cap$ R(y) = $\emptyset$) justifies the use of this transformation in Sec. 5-4. Corollary 6-5 may be restated in the form of a "forbidden subgraph" theorem of similar vein to the classic Kuratowski theorem that characterizes those graphs admitting a planar representation.

Theorem 6-7 A structure S_M is Knuth representable if and only if it does not contain the graph of Fig. 6-27 as a subgraph.

But there is an important difference. In most such characterizations, the forbidden subgraph may not exist as a homeomorph.† In this case, because of the local nature of Corollary 6-5, the literal subgraph itself must not exist. The graph of Fig. 6-25 contains this forbidden subgraph, but by adding the single point α to the graph, one gets the graph of Fig. 6-28. The two graphs are homeomorphic, but the latter is Knuth representable! This observation

---

†Two subgraphs H_1 of G_1 and H_2 of G_2 are *homeomorphs* if there exists a 1-1 onto function $\phi : H_1 \rightarrow H_2$ such that for all x, z $\in$ H_1

$$\rho_{G_1}(x, z) \qquad \text{if and only if} \qquad \rho_{G_2}(\phi(x), \phi(z))$$

An alternative definition of this concept is based on the subdivision of edges.

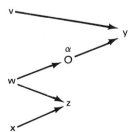

Figure 6-28 The "forbidden" subgraph of Fig. 6-27, "broken" by the addition of the extra point α.

provides an effective method of extending the technique of Knuth representation to include *all* directed graphs. Forbidden subgraphs in S_M may be "broken" by simply adding dummy points. The corresponding cells in the representation S_R are then tagged, and routines that operate on S_R may be modified in a straightforward way to treat these extra points as if they were invisible. Thus, at the cost of a few extra cells and some additional complexity to processing routines, the ability to represent any graph with cells containing a fixed number of link fields is obtained.

EXERCISES FOR SECTION 6-4

*6-52 Construct a Knuth transform of
    (*a*) Fig. 6-2 (assume no edge assignments),
    (*b*) Fig. 6-15,
    (*c*) Fig. 6-16 (do cycles invalidate the transform?)

6-53 Write a topological sort algorithm that will operate on a Knuth representation of this section. Test it using part (*b*) above.

6-54 Write and test a procedure PATH(X, Z, Y, LENGTH) that searches a Knuth transform S_R for the existence of a path $\rho(x, z)$ in S_M and returns it in Y [0:LENGTH] if found. (Note that because of the nature of the Knuth representation, a depth-first search can be implemented that requires no additonal sets, stacks, or arrays for the temporary storage of trial paths. Does this procedure traverse $\bar{R}(x)$? Use PREORDER₄ of Sec. 5-4 as a suggestive guide.)

6-55 Prove Theorem 6-4. This will have to be a constructive proof, and while the construction is fairly intuitive, it is hard to state with rigor.

6-56 This transformation was developed solely in terms of the right neighbor sets R(y). Knowledge of these alone is sufficient to completely characterize the relation. But it is often desirable to be able to directly access the set of left neighbors L(y) from the cell denoting y (similar to doubly linked lists). Clearly a symmetric development of the Knuth transform can provide for this.
    (*a*) Sketch a representation of the graph of Fig. 6-24 that explicitly represents both L(y) and R(y). Assume each cell contains four link fields, LEFT, NXTLFT, RIGHT, and NXTRGT.
    (*b*) This was unnecessary in the case of principal trees. Why?
    (*c*) Can the cells of R(y) be circularly linked so as to include the cell representing y in a ring structure? Why?

6-57 If the structures of a dynamic system were to be represented using the Knuth transformation, then one would need routines EDGE(Y, Z) and DELETE(Y, Z) to add and delete edges (in the abstract structure S_M), respectively. Each time an edge is added, the structure must be examined to detect whether a forbidden subgraph will be created, and if so, appropriately handled. Similarly, deletion of an edge may eliminate the need for an invisible point in the representation.
    (*a*) Write these procedures, and
    (*b*) estimate the expected computational overhead.

6-58 Ordered principal trees are representable under this transformation because for all $x \neq y$, $R(x) \cap R(y) = \emptyset$, so there is no conflict in ordering these right neighbor sets. There are other classes of graphs for which $R(x) \neq R(y)$ implies $R(x) \cap R(y) = \emptyset$. The best known class of graphs with this property are the *two-terminal parallel-series networks* (Liu, 1968). A graph is said to be *two-terminal* if it has unique least and greatest points that are its *terminals*. (Figures 6-1 and 6-2 are two-terminal, but not *parallel-series*.) The class of *basic* two-terminal series-parallel networks, or TTSPNs, is most easily defined as follows:
    (1) Any linear graph is a TTSPN (in this context it is sometimes called a *series* graph);

(2)   Any graph with $P = \{x, y_1, \ldots, y_n, z\}$ such that $R(x) = \{y_1, \ldots, y_n\} = L(z)$ is a TTSPN (these, as shown in the accompanying figure, may be called *parallel* graphs);

(3)   Any edge of a TTSPN may be replaced by an entire TTSPN, and the resulting graph will be a TTSPN.

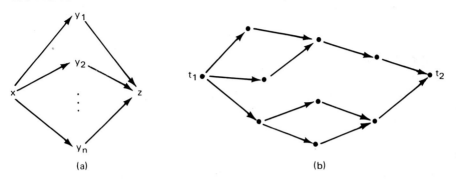

(a)   (b)

Ex. 6-58

(*a*) Construct one or two additional TTSPNs.
(*b*) Show that in any basic TTSPN, $R(x) \neq R(y)$ implies that they must be disjoint.
(*c*) Construct the Knuth transform of the graph of the figure.
(*d*) How would you represent left neighbor sets?

CHAPTER SEVEN

ARRAYS

An *array* is an ordered collection of similar elements, cells, or records. Those readers who have been primarily engaged in scientific programming using an algebraic language will be familar with the synonyms—*vector* and *matrix*—which normally mean arrays of scalar real, integer, and occasionally complex, numbers. Those who use a business-oriented language to solve commercial applications will probably call them *tables,* whose elements may be scalars but more frequently are records which are themselves composed of fields and elements. In either case the distinguishing characteristics of an array are: (1) the homogeneity of its elements, and (2) an ordering imposed on the elements. Linguistically, these two features permit the description of an array by simply describing one of its typical elements, followed by an indication of the number of such elements that belong to the collection.† And they allow subsequent reference to individual elements, that is the first element, second element, etc., by means of a *subscript* or *index* convention. In this chapter we will essentially use scientific terminology, but it is important to note that an array is not just a scientific, or a mathematical, concept. It may be used with any homogeneous collection of data whatsoever.

7-1 SEQUENTIAL REPRESENTATION OF ARRAYS

When an array is sequentially represented, the ordering of its elements is implicitly indicated by the addresses of its (element's) representational cells in a regular systematic storage schema. Associated with the schema there is a

---

†A declaration of the form *real array* a[1:m, 1:n] describes an array of m × n real scalar elements. A description of the form 02 INVENTORY-ITEM, OCCURS 20 TIMES, where the typical record "inventory-item" is subsequently described, similarly defines an array of 20 elements.

$$
A_{m \times n} = \begin{pmatrix}
a_{11} & a_{12} & a_{13} & \cdots & a_{1n} \\
a_{21} & a_{22} & a_{23} & \cdots & a_{2n} \\
a_{31} & a_{32} & a_{33} & \cdots & a_{3n} \\
\vdots & \vdots & \vdots & & \vdots \\
a_{m1} & a_{m2} & a_{m3} & \cdots & a_{mn}
\end{pmatrix}
$$

(a)

$$
A_{m \times n} = (\vec{a}_1, \vec{a}_2, \ldots, \vec{a}_m) = \left(\begin{pmatrix} a_{11} \\ a_{21} \\ \vdots \\ a_{m1} \end{pmatrix} \begin{pmatrix} a_{12} \\ a_{22} \\ \vdots \\ a_{m2} \end{pmatrix} \cdots \begin{pmatrix} a_{1n} \\ a_{2n} \\ \vdots \\ a_{mn} \end{pmatrix} \right)
$$

(b)

Figure 7-1 An m × n array represented as (a) a two-dimensional matrix of scalar elements, (b) a one-dimensional vector whose elements are themselves column vectors.

mathematical formula, or _accessing function,_ by which we can calculate the corresponding cell address given the subscript of an individual element. The case of singly subscripted or one-dimensional arrays was considered in Sec. 4-1, so let us immediately look at arrays of higher dimension. Figure 7-1a shows a typical two-dimensional mathematical matrix as it is commonly visualized. It consists of m rows and n columns. Each element a_{ij} is identified by a pair of subscript integers (i, j), which denote respectively the row and the column to which the element belongs. But array elements need not be only scalar values—they may be any unit of information; in particular, they may themselves be arrays. Figure 7-1b shows the same array, but this time regarded as a one-dimensional linear array of elements, each of which is a _column vector._† The first subscript denotes the position of the element within a column vector, the second subscript denotes the position of the column vector within the higher-order array.

Since the representation of one-dimensional singly subscripted arrays is familiar, and since all the components of the data structure shown in Fig. 7-1b are one-dimensional, let us simply use our existing representational machinery. First assume that each individual element will be represented by a cell of _celsiz_ consecutive words, bytes, or addressable storage locations. (If L_{i-1} is the address of $cell_{i-1}$, then L_{i-1} + celsiz will be the address L_i of $cell_i$.) Since each column vector is an element of the linear array $(\vec{a}_1, \vec{a}_2, \ldots, \vec{a}_n)$, each should be a

---

†Regarding an "essentially two-dimensional" matrix of values abstractly as a linear vector of column vectors is common and convenient in mathematics. For example, in the solution of the linear system $A_{m \times n} \cdot X_{n \times 1} = B_{m \times 1}$, if we regard the _coefficient matrix_ $A_{m \times n}$ as $(\vec{a}_1, \ldots, \vec{a}_n)$, then one may simply append the constant vector B to get the _augmented matrix_ $\bar{A} = (\vec{a}_1, \ldots, \vec{a}_n, \vec{b})$.

cell of that array, that is, should be also stored in consecutive locations. Consequently, if we let $\vec{L}_j$ denote the base address of the jth column vector, then the address of the ith cell (or element) within that vector will be given by

$$L_i = \vec{L}_j + (i - 1) \cdot \text{celsiz} \tag{7-1}$$

Compare this expression with that of (4-1). As there, we are tacitly assuming that the base address $\vec{L}_j$ of the jth column is the address $L(a_{1j})$ of its first element. Now we need only be able to calculate the address of $\vec{a}_j$ in $A = (\vec{a}_1, \vec{a}_2, \dots, \vec{a}_n)$, that is, the base addresses $\vec{L}_j$. As before, we will follow the convention that assigns as base address of A, L_A, the address of its first element, $\vec{L}_1$. But we note that now we are working with cells of size $m \cdot \textbf{celsiz,}$ since each cell (column vector) itself consists of m cells of size **celsiz.** Consequently

$$\vec{L}_j = \vec{L}_1 + (j - 1) \cdot m \cdot \text{celsiz} \tag{7-2}$$

By simply combining expressions (7-1) and (7-2) we get

$$
\begin{aligned}
L(a_{ij}) &= \vec{L}_j + (i - 1) \cdot \text{celsiz} \\
&= \vec{L}_1 + (j - 1) \cdot m \cdot \text{celsiz} + (i - 1) \cdot \text{celsiz} \tag{7-3} \\
&= L(a_{11}) + [(j - 1) \cdot m + (i - 1)] \cdot \text{celsiz}
\end{aligned}
$$

Notice that the base address L_A of the entire array A is simply the address of its first element a_{11}. Figure 7-2 illustrates the physical column-wise representation of the doubly subscripted array A in storage associated with the accessing function (7-3). Verify that, given a representation as in this figure, one can use expression (7-3) to calculate the address of any element a_{ij} and thus retrieve it. Also note that with this sequential representation, the array A is stored in consecutive locations and hence can itself be considered to be a cell, and perhaps an element of some other array or data structure.

Having derived the accessing function for the column-wise representation of doubly subscripted arrays, we may proceed to consider its implications and variations of it. First, it is evident that we could have chosen to regard the matrix A as a linear array of row vectors, in which case all the cells representing the elements of row i would have been stored contiguously and the accessing function would be expressed by

$$L(a_{ij}) = L(a_{11}) + [(i - 1) \cdot n + (j - 1)] \cdot \text{celsiz} \tag{7-4}$$

(See Exercise 7-1.)

Examination of expression (7-3) shows that two subtractions, two additions, and two multiplications must be performed every time a program accesses an array element using its subscript notation. We would particularly like to eliminate the subtractions in the factors $(j - 1)$ and $(i - 1)$. These arose from the convention which assumes that a cell address is the address of the first word, or byte, of the cell, and from the very natural convention of referring to the first element of a vector as $\vec{a}_1$ or a_{1j}. Consequently, we used L_1 as base address of the entire array (cell), and $\vec{L}_j$ as base address of the jth column vector

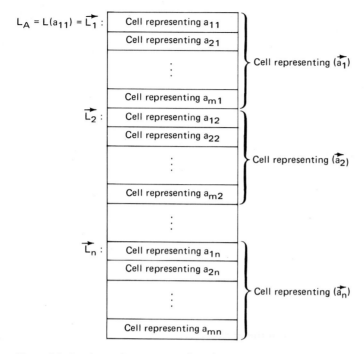

Figure 7-2 A columnwise representation of the doubly subscripted m × n array A.

(cell). Thus, when we reference the first (and any other) element, we must subtract one from the index. Alternatively, we could regard the subscripts as beginning with zero, that is, $0 \le i \le m - 1$, $0 \le j \le n - 1$. Then $L(a_{00})$ will be used as the base address, and the accessing function becomes

$$L(a_{ij}) = L(a_{00}) + (i \cdot m + j) \cdot \text{celsiz} \qquad (7\text{-}5)$$

which avoids the subtractions of expression (7-3).

Of course, in many mathematical applications it is not natural to use a zero subscript. Most problems are abstractly stated with subscripts in the range $1 \le i \le m$ and $1 \le j \le n$, so that this is a natural way to reference them within a program. But it is not hard to employ the same trick that was used in Sec. 4-1 and create an imaginary element a_{00} and use it as the base address. Figure 7-3 illustrates this representation, which must be used with the accessing expression

$$L(a_{ij}) = L_0 + (i \cdot m + j) \cdot \text{celsiz} \qquad (7\text{-}6)$$

where
$$L_0 = L(a_{11}) - (m + 1) \cdot \text{celsiz}$$

The preceding discussion has explored only a few of the possible ways of sequentially representing two-dimensional arrays and tailoring accessing functions that will arithmetically calculate the address of any individual element,

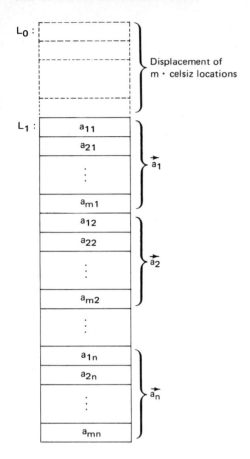

Figure 7-3 Columnwise representation of a doubly subscripted array $A = (a_{ij})$, with base address displaced.

given the name (or base address) of the array and identifying subscripts. The exercises will suggest a few more. Because of the manifold variations that are possible, some experienced programmers never use multiply subscripted arrays (even when coding in a higher-level language that permits them), but instead employ only singly subscripted arrays combined with explicit accessing expressions that convert multiple subscripts into a single subscript. They feel that this gives them more control over the sequential representation and an ability to fit it more closely to the application, and sometimes faster execution based on an overall knowledge of the process (e.g., saving the address, or index, of an element that will be used repeatedly in a series of calculations). They may be right. But program clarity and comprehension often suffer.

The design of a compiler for a higher-level algebraic language involves choosing one particular representational format for subscripted arrays together with its associated accessing formula. Any representation may be chosen, but once decided it becomes an essential implementing convention that must be consistently observed. Each time the compiler encounters a statement such as

$$c[i, k] \leftarrow a[i, j] + b[j, k];$$

it must generate a sequence of instructions that will calculate at run time the addresses of $C[I, K]$, $A[I, J]$, and $B[J, K]$ in accordance with the agreed accessing formula. Almost all systems employ sequential storage. But as we have seen, all the corresponding accessing expressions involve the upper bound (m or n) of at least one of the subscripts. This in turn makes the implementation of variably dimensioned arrays, especially the passing of variably dimensioned arrays to subprocedures, quite difficult. To execute the process correctly, the bounds of the array being passed must be known, and these are usually passed as additional parameters. But to implement the accessing expression the upper bounds of the largest possible array must be known, since it is this value that determines the cell size of allocated storage. To pass this bound explicitly as yet another parameter is aesthetically awkward. To pass it implicitly with the array identifier complicates the system's subroutine linkage conventions. In the next section an array representation which completely eliminates this problem will be considered.

Once having developed a representation for doubly subscripted arrays, it is not hard to extend the development to arrays with more subscripts. Since a doubly subscripted array is represented sequentially in a contiguous block of storage, it may be regarded as a single cell in a triply subscripted array. The entire array is then just a linear sequence of these rather large cells (which are in turn sequences of smaller cells). Figure 7-4 presents a schematic view of a

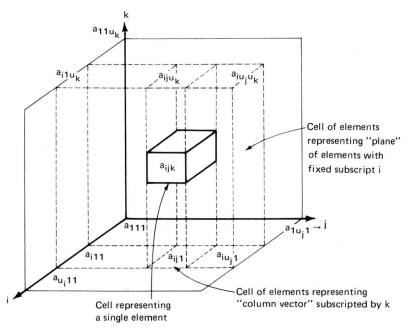

Figure 7-4 A schematic view of the sequential representation of a three-dimensional array with upper bounds u_i, u_j, and u_k.

triply subscripted, or three-dimensional, array decomposed into its constituent sequential cells. Convince yourself that

$$L(a_{ijk}) = L(a_{111}) + \{[(i-1) \cdot u_i + (j-1)] \cdot u_j + (k-1)\} \cdot celsiz \qquad (7\text{-}7)$$

where u_i and u_j denote the upper bounds on the first and second subscripts respectively

is an appropriate accessing function given a representation as shown in the figure. This sequentially represented three-dimensional array may in turn constitute a single cell in a four-dimensional array—and so on.

So far there has been a tacit assumption that all arrays have been sequentially stored in immediate random-access core memory, and that the function of accessing expressions is to calculate the core addresses of individual cells. So long as one is considering relatively small two-dimensional arrays, this assumption is perhaps justifiable. But consideration of multiply subscripted arrays soon makes such an assumption questionable. Even a single relatively small $20 \times 20 \times 20$ triply subscripted array requires 8000 individual cells. Core storage may be unavailable, or at least prohibitively expensive.† Some provision for peripheral storage must be made. To a programmer using a high-level algebraic language such as PL/1 or Fortran in a paged virtual-memory environment, this may seem unimportant; the system will handle it. But the user has little control over the accessing conventions of the system. Suppose that a triply subscripted array, such as shown in Fig. 7-4, is stored with one j-k plane per page. Suppose further that i is the index of some tight inner loop. One, and possibly more, page faults will occur for each execution of the loop. Although probably hidden in overhead charges, the cost of data representation will be borne by the user.

It may be possible to tailor the process to the accessing conventions (if they are known), or it may be more reasonable to construct one's own accessing conventions that are tailored to the process. While expressions (7-1) to (7-7) ostensibly calculate storage addresses, they in fact simply map multiply subscripted identifiers into singly subscripted, or linear, arrays. The array itself may be physically represented in peripheral storage, such as magnetic disk or tape, and the accessing expression used to calculate a disk address—or if a tape representation is used, to determine a series of tape reads, backspaces, or rewinds. To access each element individually from peripheral storage is clearly inefficient. Most often a portion of the array is kept in a kind of working storage in core, and the accessing expressions implemented by subroutines that "remember" the currently available portion so as to minimize the number of external storage accesses. Further, since many array operations are sequential processes that follow a predictable sequence (e.g., matrix multiplication), the accessing procedures may anticipate future requests and incorporate buffering features, as described in Sec. 3-3. Such an approach is identical to that of pag-

---

†Some installations charge more for a second's use of 20K of core storage than one second's use of the CPU. Shaving core storage may be as important as shaving microseconds.

ing in a virtual-memory environment except that the paging, especially the partitioning of the array into cells and physical records, is now under the control of the user instead of the system.

EXERCISES FOR SECTION 7-1

*7-1 Sketch the layout of a doubly subscripted array $A = (a_{ij})$ that is sequentially represented row-wise. Verify that expression (7-4) correctly calculates the address of the cell denoting the element a_{ij}.

7-2 A natural way of linearly ordering the elements of an array is by the lexicographic ordering of their subscript sequences. For instance, a_{ij} precedes $a_{i'j'}$ if $(i, j) < (i', j')$ in the lexicographic ordering. Which storage convention of two-dimensional arrays, column-wise or row-wise, preserves this natural lexicographic ordering?

7-3 In expression (7-6)—which assumes a *dummy element* a_{00} to serve as base address—m, not $m + 1$, is used as the constant multiplicative factor, even though $0 < i \leq m$. Further, L_0 is not really the address that a_{00} would occupy if it were represented, and there is no dummy element corresponding to a_{0j} preceding each column vector in Fig. 7-3. What is going on here? What would the storage format look like if one allowed the zero subscript? Sketch it. What would be the appropriate accessing expression?

7-4 Suppose one wanted to represent a doubly subscripted array whose subscripts were constrained to the ranges $4 \leq i \leq 7$ and $3 \leq j \leq 6$.
  (*a*) How many elements comprise the array?
  (*b*) How would you represent this array? What accessing function would you use?
Suppose instead that the first subscript had a range of $-2 \leq i \leq 5$.
  (*c*) Now what representation and accessing expression is appropriate?
  (*d*) Devise appropriate storage conventions and accessing expression for arbitrary two-dimensional arrays that may be declared by expressions of the form

real array a$[i1:i2, j1:j2]$;

where i1, i2, j1, j2 may be arbitrary integers subject only to the constraint that i1 $<$ i2 and j1 $<$ j2.
  (*e*) Generalize the above to n-dimensional arrays, n > 1.

*7-5 Assume that the elements of an array are not real or integer scalars (as is usually the case), but rather
  (*a*) complex numbers,
  (*b*) character strings of fixed length L, L $\geq$ 40 (e.g., fixed length records familiar in business applications), or
  (*c*) character strings of variable length.
What array representation and accessing expressions would you use in each case?

7-6 Write processes (they should be subroutines with runtime memory, not just expressions) that access elements of an n-dimensional array with fixed bounds—that is, represented in peripheral storage (either disk or tape, or both). The important design decision in the partitioning of the array into cells will be the choice of which cells correspond to physical records of the storage device. How do these accessing processes differ if the fundamental cell (physical record) is
  (*a*) an individual element of the array,
  (*b*) a column of the array (elements have same last subscript),
  (*c*) a row of the array (elements have same first subscript), and
  (*d*) a plane of the array.
Using the timing and pricing information for your own system, determine the computational and storage costs of accessing elements in a 50 $\times$ 50 $\times$ 50 array.

7-7 Assume that the dominant operation in some task is the multiplication of two large matrices A · B. Buffer the accessing routines of the preceding exercise so as to optimize this operation. Will it pay to represent the two arrays in different fashions using different accessing conventions? How would these same buffering conventions affect execution of a matrix transposition operation? A matrix assignment statement (A ← B)? A matrix inversion procedure?

7-8 A *lower triangular matrix* is one for which only elements on or below the main diagonal are nonzero, that is, those elements a_{ij} where $i \geq j$. An $n \times n$ lower triangular matrix is shown in the accompanying figure, together with its column-wise sequential representation.

$$
\begin{array}{ccccc}
a_{11} & 0 & 0 & \cdots & 0 \\
a_{21} & a_{22} & 0 & \cdots & 0 \\
a_{31} & a_{32} & a_{33} & \cdots & 0 \\
\vdots & \vdots & \vdots & & \vdots \\
a_{n1} & a_{n2} & a_{n3} & \cdots & a_{nn}
\end{array}
$$

a_{11}
a_{21}
a_{31}
$\vdots$
a_{n1}
a_{22}
a_{32}
$\vdots$
a_{n2}
a_{33}
$\vdots$
a_{nn}

Ex. 7-8

(*a*) Verify that

$$
L(a_{ij}) = L(a_{11}) + \frac{i(i-1)}{2} - 1 - (i-j) \qquad i \geq j \geq 1
$$

is an appropriate accessing function.

(*b*) Derive the accessing expression for a lower triangular array stored row-wise. It is much simpler (as is that of an upper triangular array stored columnwise) and does not involve the array bound N.

(*c*) How might two lower triangular arrays be compactly stored?

(The adjacency matrix of acyclic, and undirected, graphs may be put into lower (or upper) triangular form. Similarly, symmetric matrices in which $a_{ij} = a_{ji}$ may be stored this way.)

7-2 LINKED REPRESENTATIONS OF ARRAYS

In the preceding section a representation of multiply subscripted arrays was developed by regarding the entire array as a linear, or singly subscripted, structure each of whose elements could be arrays. This led to a decomposition of the array into *planes, columns,* and finally *elements,* whereby the sequential representation of each smaller "piece" was treated as a cell of the next larger piece.

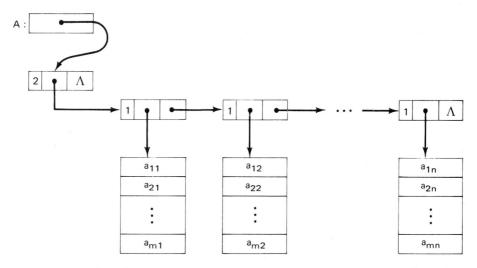

Figure 7-5 A partially linked, partially sequential representation (with header cell) of a doubly subscripted m × n array A.

This widely used representation is very efficient,† provided the arrays are relatively small and of fixed dimension. As one begins to consider larger, or variably dimensioned, arrays there appear potential deficiencies with such a pure sequential representation. But linear structures need not be only sequentially represented. We open this section with a very effective partially linked array representation that is used by some computer software (especially Burroughs systems) and then examine representations that are totally linked.

Assume that we wish to represent an m × n array A. As before, we can regard A as a linear sequence of column vectors $(\vec{a}_1, \vec{a}_2, \ldots, \vec{a}_n)$. Each of the m element column vectors will be represented as a sequential array, but the linear relation on the column vectors will be represented as a simply linked list with a header cell. In Fig. 7-5, which illustrates the representation, each cell of the list has two fields; one points to the sequential representation of the column, and the other links to the next cell in the linear list. It should not be hard to verify that the following procedure LOCATE serves as an accessing function by returning the location $L(a_{ij})$ of the specified array element.

pointer procedure locate (a, i, j);
pointer   a;
integer   i, j;

This procedure returns the address (pointer) of the cell representing the element a_{ij}

† Because only values assigned to the array elements are actually stored and because elements are accessed by a fairly simple arithmetic calculation.

```
begin
      pointer   cell, header;
      integer   column;
      field     data, next;
      header ←a;   an unnecessary statement
      cell ←data(header);
      column ← 1;
      while column <j do
            cell ←next(cell);
            column ←column + 1;  end
      locate ←data(cell) +(i − 1)*elementsize;
      exit;
      end
```

Compared to the arithmetic expressions of the preceding section, this accessing procedure seems quite cumbersome. Of course, a compiler could be expected to generate a highly optimized compact sequence of machine instructions to "walk down" the linked list; but still it is relatively slow.

In contrast, notice that this procedure will handle access in variably dimensioned arrays without modification, since there is no reference to the subscript bounds. Access of elements in arrays with lower bounds other than 1 requires only trivial modifications to LOCATE and to the representation itself. (See Exercise 7-14.)

The NEXT link field of the header cell in the representation of Fig. 7-5 is null. But this field can be used in a representation of a triply subscripted array, as shown in Fig. 7-6. Here each of the two-dimensional subarrays is linearly ordered by linking their header cells (through the NEXT field) as a linked list. Note that in this representation the value of the tag field denotes the dimension of the subarray indicated by the DATA field of that header cell. It is not hard to extend the procedure LOCATE to this triply subscripted case, and then generalize it to an arbitrary number of subscripts.

Numerous variations on this partially linked representation are possible. The initial partition of the array can be row-wise, or lexicographically by subscript sequence. Other fields, in addition to the tag field that signifies the dimension of the subarray, can be included in each header cell. For example, one might store the upper and lower bounds of the single subscript whose ordering is represented by the list of that header. (Note that every cell in the linked portion of the representation serves as header to some linear list.) Exercise 7-14 explores these variants in more detail.

A matrix is said to be *sparse* if the value of most of its elements is zero.†

---

†There is no firm criterion for how few nonzero elements an array should have to be called *sparse*. With fewer than 0.20 nontrivial elements, the matrix of Fig. 7-7 would appear to be sparse by any definition. See Pooch and Nieder (1973) for a source of sparse-matrix literature.

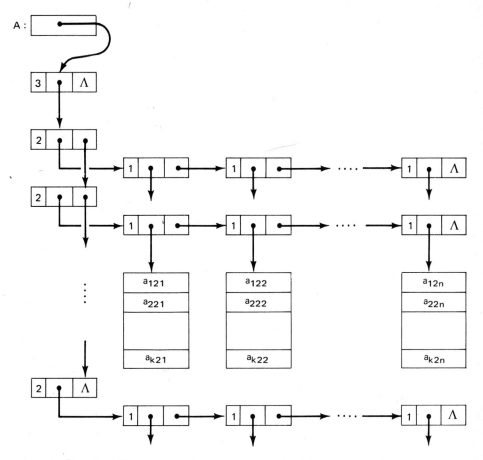

Figure 7-6 A partially linked representation of a triply subscripted k × m × n array.

Figure 7-7 illustrates a representative 8 × 8 sparse matrix. With so few significant nonzero elements—in this case only 12—it seems unnecessarily extravagant to allocate storage for 64 cells. Rather than represent every element, it is

A	1	2	3	4	5	6	7	8
1	0	1	0	0	0	0	5	0
2	0	0	0	0	0	0	0	0
3	-3	0	0	0	4	0	0	0
4	0	0	2	0	0	0	0	0
5	0	2	0	0	0	0	0	0
6	1	0	0	0	0	0	0	-3
7	0	0	0	0	7	0	0	4
8	0	0	7	0	5	0	0	0

Figure 7-7 A sparse matrix.

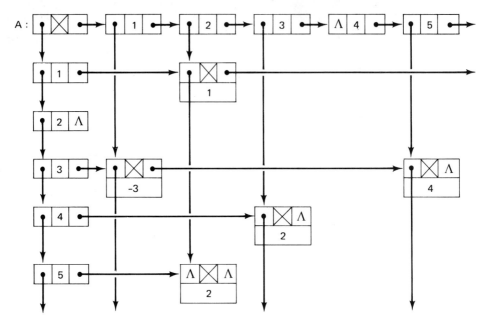

Figure 7-8 A linked representation of the sparse matrix of Fig. 7-7.

sufficient to merely allocate cells for the nonzero elements, then link each to those cells denoting the next nonzero entries in its row and column, respectively. Figure 7-8 shows a very straightforward linked representation. The nonzero elements of each row and each column are represented as a simply linked linear list preceded by a header cell containing the row, or column, index respectively. Such representations are frequently called *multilinked structures,* since each cell is linked into several distinct structures; in this case each cell belongs to two separate linear lists. We would prefer to regard this as a representation of a hypergraph $G = (P, R, C)$ where P is the set of nonzero values, R is the row relation, and C is the column relation; and then simply remark that the representation of any hypergraph is nearly always multilinked. The Knuth representations of Secs. 5-4 and 6-4 were certainly multilinked structures, and the binary trees of Sec. 5-2 may be so regarded.

In many respects this linked representation of arrays seems more natural than do the previous representations. Certainly one visually perceives an array as consisting of m distinct rows (m linearly ordered connected components of a row relation) and n distinct columns, with array elements located at the points of intersection. This representation faithfully models this view.†

---

†In contrast, the preceding sequential and partially linked representations algebraically decompose the array relation into a direct product of linear relations. Direct product decomposition is a powerful algebraic tool for the concise description of regular structures. It should perhaps be more widely used. But to many people it is not a "natural" descriptive mechanism.

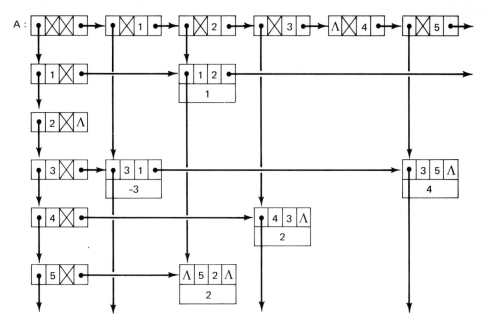

Figure 7-9 A "better" linked representation of a sparse matrix.

In fact, there is only one serious deficiency with the representation of Fig. 7-8. It is nearly unusable. The reader is invited to try writing a basic accessing procedure VALUE (A, I, J) that returns the assigned value of the element a_{ij}.†

Addition of explicit row and column index fields to each element cell, as shown in Fig. 7-9, produces a usable representation. An accessing procedure VALUE (A, I, J) need only walk down to row list $_i$ (or across to column list j), then across until it finds an element with column index j. If no such element is found, VALUE returns 0.0 by default. Processes to implement other matrix operations also may be coded, for example, value assignment (which involves changing an existing element value or possibly inserting a new cell into the two separate lists), matrix addition, multiplication, inversion, etc.‡ The latter procedures may become somewhat involved (we give a sample procedure MULTIPLY below), yet still be more efficient than their more easily coded sequential counterparts.

---

†Frequently, the cells of multilinked structures must include within the representing cell itself some identification that describes its role with respect to the other relations. This issue is considered more carefully in Chap. 9, on data access.

‡Since this representation is effective only for arrays in the domain of sparse matrices, there arise interesting questions as to whether these operations are closed over the domain. By and large, addition of two sparse matrices generates a matrix which is less sparse, while multiplication generates one which is more sparse. See Exercise 7-22 for one approach to the analysis of these operations.

pointer procedure multiply (a, b);
pointer   a, b;

This procedure forms the matrix product A · B *of the two arrays* a *and* b, *given a linked representation as shown in Fig. 7-9. It returns a pointer to the representation of the product. Note that there is no test to determine if the two arrays are conformable—in effect, array* a *is padded with additional columns (or* b *with additional rows) of zero elements to create conformability.*

begin
    real   sum;
    integer i,k,headersize, cellsize;
    pointer rowheadera, colheaderb, c, rowheaderc, colheaderc,
                rowprev, colprev, rowelement, colelement, newcell;
    field   colindex, rowindex, value, nextcolheader,
                nextrowheader, nextinrow, nextincol;

Create initial skeleton of the representation of the product array c. Allocate an array header cell, and a column header cell corresponding to each column in b.

    multiply ←prev ←c ←giveme(headersize);
    colheaderb ←nextcolheader(b);
    while colheaderb ≠ nullvalue **do**
        colheaderc ←giveme(headersize);
        colindex(colheaderc) ←colindex(colheaderb);
        rowindex(colheaderc) ←nullvalue;
        nextcolheader(prev) ←colheaderc;
        prev ←colheaderc;
        colheaderb ←nextcolheader(colheaderb);
    nextcolheader(colprev) ←nullvalue;
    prev ←c;
    rowheadera ←nextrowheader(a);
    For each row i=lbound to ubound in array a.
α: **while** rowheadera ≠ nullvalue **do**

        Create corresponding rowheader in representation of c.

        rowheaderc ←giveme(headersize);
        rowindex(rowheaderc) ←i ←rowindex(rowheadera);
        colindex(rowheaderc) ←nullvalue;
        nextrowheader(prev) ←rowheaderc;

        Now for this row of a consider every column k=lbound to ubound of b to determine values of the elements c_{ik} in the ith row of c.

        colheaderb ←nexcolheader(b);
        colheaderc ←nextcolheader(c);
β: **while** colheaderb ≠ nullvalue **do**
           sum ←0.0;
           k ←colindex(colheaderb);
           rowelement ←nextinrow(rowheadera);
           colelement ←nextincol(colheaderb);

Compare each element of i in a with each element of column k in b to find if any have common index j. If so, form $c_{ik} = \Sigma\, a_{ij} \cdot b_{jk}$

γ:

    while rowelement **and** colelement ≠ nullvalue **do**
        if colindex(rowelement) < rowindex(colelement)
           then rowelement ←nextinrow(rowelement);
               go to δ;
        if colindex(rowelement) > rowindex(colelement)
           then colelement ←nextincol(colelement);
               go to δ;

Add product $a_{ij} \cdot b_{jk}$ to sum.

    sum ←sum + value(rowelement)∗value(colelement);
    rowelement ←nextinrow(rowelement);
    colelement ←nextincol(colelement);
    continue   *End of while loop γ.*

δ:

Is c_{ik} a nonzero element? If so, add a cell to the representation of c.

    if sum ≠ 0.0 **then**
        newcell ←giveme(cellsize);
        value(newcell) ←sum;
        rowindex(newcell) ←i;
        colindex(newcell) ←k;
        nextinrow(newcell) ←nextincol(newcell) ←nullvalue;

There is now trouble linking this cell from the previous cell in the row list of c, but the previous cell in the kth column list must be found by search.

        nextinrow(rowprev) ←newcell;
        rowprev ←newcell;
        colprev ←colheaderc;

ε:

        while nextincol(colprev) ≠ nullvalue **do**
           colprev ←nextincol(colprev);
           nextincol(colprev) ←newcell;
    colheaderb ←nextcolheader(colheaderb);

End of while loop β.

  rowheadera ←nextrowheader(rowheadera);

End of while loop α.

exit;
end

    This procedure is not fully optimized, and the exercises will suggest several lines of improvement. Of more interest are various observations regarding the nature of the representation and operation itself. In Sec. 6-3 directed graphs G were represented by their adjacency matrix A_G and matrix multiplication used to generate the path relation. In an adjacency representation A_G, only the non-

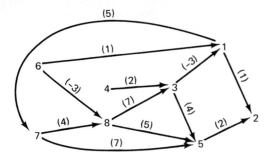

Figure 7-10 The graph represented by the sparse matrix of Fig. 7-7.

zero entries are of significance, and for the most part the representations are sparse. Consequently, the sparse array of Fig. 7-7 and its linked representation, shown in Fig. 7-9, can be regarded as a representation of the graph with edge assignment, shown in Fig. 7-10. Row i of Fig. 7-9 is simply a linked representation of the set R(i), while column k is a representation of the set L(k). Compare this representation of the graph with the linked representation developed in Sec. 6-1. Is there any essential difference? (Note that one would want to combine the cell that is the header of row j with the cell that is the header of column j into a single cell, since it is now regarded as denoting a single point rather than the same value in two separate index sets.)

By regarding the data structure in this light, one can then regard the MULTIPLY procedure as a *path extension* operation rather than an essentially numerical operation. And the key **while** loop γ of the procedure is seen to be merely an intersection operation, virtually identical to that given in Sec. 4-3. Graph theoretic interpretations can be used in the analysis of a number of matrix operations. While it can be misleading to attempt to push the correspondence too far, it is nevertheless valuable to perceive common threads in the representation of, and operations on, different data structures. Generalization of such common themes allows one to then emphasize those essential areas of difference that are characteristic of the particular application or context.

In the representations of this section the sets of row and column elements have been linked as simple lists. Some authors prefer to link them circularly, thereby creating a kind of multilinked ring structure. With such circularity, a process given only the cell address of an element can access the header, together with all other element cells of its row and/or column. This can be exploited in some applications, viz., pivoting in a matrix inversion procedure, but does not change the essential nature of either the representation or the procedure. In a similar vein, unused fields of the header cells may be used to store information, say the number of nonzero elements in the row or column. The reader should have no trouble making similar modifications to suit his or her particular needs.

Throughout this chapter we have tacitly assumed that all arrays were numerical matrices and that the operations defined on them would be algebraic operations. This need not be so. Visual images and spatially distributed data

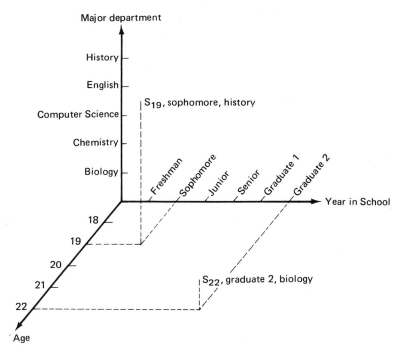

Figure 7-11 A triply subscripted array with nonnumeric index sets.

may be represented by arrays. While the element values and index sets are still numerical, the common operations of image processing or spatial analysis are sufficiently different that the representations of this section may no longer appear attractive (Rosenfeld, 1969, and Davis, 1975). As a more extreme example, we may consider an array whose element values are nonnumeric and whose index sets are also nonnumeric.

Consider the collection of students attending a college. Their names may be organized into a three-dimensional array whose subscript (or index) sets are AGE = {18, 19, ...} STATUS = {freshman, sophomore, junior, senior, graduatel, ...}, and MAJOR DEPT. = {biology, chemistry, computer science, English, ...}. Such an array is shown in Fig. 7-11. Just as elements of numeric matrices are identified by specifying some set of subscript values, individuals (or more correctly, subsets of individuals) of this collection are identified by a set of index† values. For instance, the element $S_{19,\text{sophomore, history}}$ denotes that subset of students who are 19, sophomores, and majoring in history.

This array could be represented by either of the partially linked or multilinked methods developed in this section. (The value assigned to an array element would probably be a pointer to a representation of the set of individu-

---

†*Index* and *subscript* are synonyms in most mathematical and programming languages, but in this particular context the term *index* is almost always used.

als stored elsewhere. However, a sequential representation using an accessing expression that is an arithmetic function of the index values is impossible.) But in practice they are seldom used, because often (1) the collection of array elements is very large, (2) the number of index sets (dimensions) is greater than three or four, (3) there may be no clear upper or lower bounds on the index sets, and (4) characteristic operations on the array involve retrieval of at most a small number of elements; these arrays are usually physically represented as files in low-speed storage. Thus, other representational mechanisms are used that we will examine in Chap. 11 under file retrieval. Still, even the brief introduction in this chapter is worthwhile because the use of arrays as an abstract model is of value in information retrieval, and appears in the terminology (viz., index set), because it helps to prevent a too restricted view of arrays, and especially because it questions a major consideration in the preceding discussions. Since algebraic operations on arrays often access *every* element of the array in tight loops, we became quite concerned about the possibility of excessive paging overhead when large arrays could no longer be wholly contained within core storage. But if the array is to serve primarily as just a way of organizing a collection from which only a few elements will be retrieved [as is the case in many arrays (tables) in Cobol programs], then this aspect becomes far less critical in the design of variably dimensioned arrays.

EXERCISES FOR SECTION 7-2

7-9 None of the array accessing expressions we have developed have included any run-time tests to ensure that the subscript values I, J, are actually within the defined bounds.

(*a*) What additional statement in the procedure LOCATE would provide such error detection for the subscript J, even though the upper bound is unknown?

(*b*) How would similar run-time error detection be implemented, given a sequential representation of the preceding section?

(*c*) Many run-time checks on subscript bounds can fail when arrays are specified as formal parameters with variable dimensions in subprocedures. Why? Give examples.

7-10 Hand-code in the assembly language of your system the kind of accessing sequence (for a partially linked array representation) that compiler might be expected to generate. What is the expected access time in a 20 × 20 array? Express access time as a function of N.

*7-11 Modify the procedure LOCATE so that it reflects the convention that the lower bound of all subscripts is zero, not 1.

*7-12 Rewrite the procedure LOCATE to access elements in a triply subscripted array, in arrays with arbitrary subscripts.

7-13 Redesign the partially linked representation so that the sequentially represented cells are rows of the array—that is, reflect the linear ordering denoted by the last subscript of the subscript sequence, rather than the first. How must LOCATE be changed? Does this revision have any significant effect on generalizations of the partially linked accessing mechanism? How? Why?

*7-14 Each list, whether linked or sequentially represented, denotes the linear order on one of the subscripts with certain of the other subscript values held fixed—all following subscripts in the illustrated representations. The header cell, whose DATA field links to that list, can be augmented with the fields LBOUND and/or UBOUND whose values denote these subscript bounds, respectively. Sketch such a representation and give the associated accessing procedure LOCATE. Test your design on the following examples:

    (*a*) the arrays A[4:7, 3:6] and B[−2:5, 3:6] (compare with Exercise 7-4),

    (*b*) the lower triangular matrix illustrated in Exercise 7-14, and

    (*c*) a similar upper triangular matrix.

Analogous to upper and lower triangular arrays, one might wish to consider *parallelogram* arrays, such as shown in the accompanying figure. (The author knows of no practical use for such arrays, but readily they do exist as abstract structures.)

    (*d*) Represent this kind of array structure

    (*e*) Suppose it were the second subscript that had the varying bounds (all rows were of fixed length), would the same representation work?

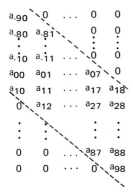

Ex. 7-14

7-15 Calculate the increased storage costs associated with a partially linked array representation. (In the two-dimensional m × n case, we note that all m∗n elements must be stored as in the sequential representation, but that n + 1 additional linked cells must be added.) Derive a general expression for the storage requirements of an array with arbitrary number of subscripts.

7-16 To define a *rectangular* array, the subscript values must belong to a totally ordered finite set. A subset of all such sets (there is an isomorphism between any such set and a subinterval of the integers) and they are easily used in numerical calculations. But other sets might be used. (In principle, both Algol and PL/1 permit subscript values of the set of real numbers.) Suppose we wish to use character strings (e.g., English words) as subscript values for all but the first subscript. How can this representation and LOCATE be modified to accommodate it?

7-17 It is assumed when discussing arrays that the sets of subscript values are linearly ordered; but suppose one or more of the subscript sets were to be partially ordered (say the last). One can visualize abstract structures, as shown in the figure on the following page, that may be defined in terms of direct products of relations. The problem is not of representation, which is quite straightforward; but rather are they of any practical use?

7-18 The fact that the cells of a representation have several different link fields does not by itself make the relation multilinked. It must be the representation of an abstract structure S_M that is a hypergraph with two or more relations. Thus the representation of a structure $S_M = (P, E)$ which is a tree would not normally be considered multilinked, while the representation of its Knuth transformation would be. However, the binary search trees developed in Sec. 5-2 *may* be regarded as the representation of a hypergraph $S_M = (WORDS, E_1, E_2)$. What are the two distinct relations E_1 and E_2 in this abstract formulation?

*7-19 The representation of Fig. 7-8 shows header cells even for rows and columns with no elements, e.g., row_2 and $column_4$. These redundant cells could easily be eliminated. Verify that their elimination would not affect the procedure MULTIPLY. Why not? But the product matrix C may have redundant header cells. Why? Modify the procedure to operate in the domain of nonredundant representations.

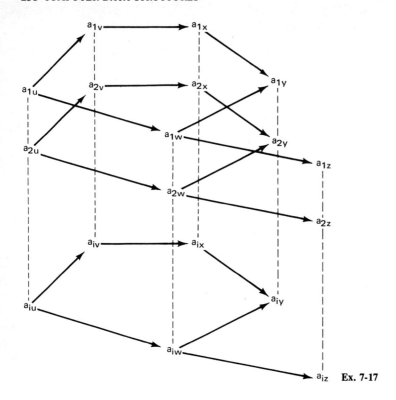

Ex. 7-17

7-20 One way that the procedure MULTIPLY can be optimized is by the elimination of the **while** loop ϵ that finds the previous column cell from which to link a new element cell added to C. One approach is to let the column header cells of C point to the last element cell added to that column rather than the first. This in turn demands that the procedure run through the row loop α in reverse order, that is, the links in the list of row headers of A must be reversed on entry and re-reversed on exit (see Exercise 3-4). Rewrite the procedure to incorporate this change. What is the expected increase in efficiency, if any?

7-21 Suppose that the arrays are represented as multilinked ring structures.

(a) Draw such a representation.

(b) How will this affect the operation of MULTIPLY? What changes will be necessary?

(c) What should be the configuration of a row (or column) header cell with no elements in the row?

(d) Rewrite MULTIPLY so that the generated array C is a well-formed ring structure. (Note that the approach of the preceding exercise is of value here.)

*7-22 Assume that the probability that any given element a_{ij} of a sparse $n \times n$ array is non-zero is expressed by the ratio

$$pr(a_{ij} \neq 0) = \frac{\text{no. of non-zero elements}}{n^2}$$

(a) In $C = A + B$, express $pr(c_{ij} \neq 0)$. ⎰ Assume that a sum of

(b) In $C = A \cdot B$, express $pr(c_{ik} \neq 0)$. ⎱ non-zero elements will never be zero.

(c) How does this expression change if elements a_{ii}, b_{ii} on the main diagonal are known to be zero? To be nonzero?

(d) Interpret (b) assuming $A = A_G^{(1)}$ and $B = A_G^{(m)}$ are adjacency matrices. Suppose G is known to be acyclic (so A may be assumed upper or lower triangular); are the expressions still valid?

(e) Using some randomly generated samples, test your expressions.

7-23 In the sequential process to form the product of sequentially represented arrays,

```
for i = 1 thru n do
    for k = 1 thru n do
        sum ← 0.0;
        for j = 1 thru n do
            sum ← sum + a[i, j] * b[j,k];
        c[i, k] ← sum;
```

let c_α denote the cost of incrementing and testing a **for** loop; c_β denote the cost of executing the two assignment statements (sum ← 0.0 and c[i, k] ← sum); and c_γ denote the cost of the innermost sum, multiplication, and assignment operations. Then

$$\text{cost(product)} = (c_\alpha + c_\gamma) \cdot n^3 + (c_\alpha + c_\beta) \cdot n^2 + c_\alpha \cdot n$$

(a) Derive a similar expression assuming sparse matrices and the procedure MULTIPLY. (Note that this is far more difficult and you may have to settle for an approximate expression. Also, you will need the results of Exercise 7-22b.

(b) Is this computational cost still of order $O(n^3)$?

(c) Empirically verify your expression by executing a version of MULTIPLY in which key parameters are explicitly counted.

7-24 If as claimed in this section, the rows of the array can be interpreted as a set R(i), the columns as a set L(k), and the **while** loop γ as a form of set intersection; then why not treat them as unordered sets? Why require that the subscript sets be ordered? What happens to the **while** loop γ if the row and column sets are not ordered on the index j? Why were the representation of sets in Sec. 4-3 given an arbitrary ordering? The index sets of the array shown in Fig. 7-11 are not inherently ordered; would you order them for representational purposes?

7-25 Write processes to perform a range of standard operations using sparse matrix representations. For instance,

(a) matrix addition, transposition, scalar multiplication;

(b) element assignment, test of equality;

(c) determinant evaluation;

(d) inversion.

*7-26 Flesh out the abstract array S_M given in Fig. 7-11 with a computer representation S_R of your own design for a small school (with say 20 students). Do this in detail. What will be the effect on your representation if the school expands to 200 students (and doubles the number of departments)? To 2,000 students? To 20,000 students?

EIGHT

HOMOMORPHIC STRUCTURES

8-1 ABSTRACTION; HOMOMORPHISM CONCEPTS

The process of *abstraction* is one in which a single entity is chosen to replace, denote, or name a collection of entities, be they real objects or concepts. The word *house* is a token which is used to abstractly represent any element in the collection of all real houses. Normally all elements x_i of the collection being denoted share some common property; call it $P(x_i)$. Further, it is normally assumed that in all important relations R between objects of the collection and other entities of the universe of discourse, one may substitute the abstract token for the object and the relation should still remain true. In our simple example, the word *house* may be regarded as denoting the entire collection (or possibly an abstract concept of "houseness," the property which defines the collection). There exist objects, say "apples," in the universe which do not belong to the collection denoted by *house* because that token when substituted into the relational assertion "*houses* can be cooked to make a tasty pie" is no longer true.

The process of abstraction is of crucial importance in intellectual thought because by describing relations between tokens denoting sets of objects rather than the myriad relations between numerous individual objects, one can reduce a problem, or its description, to comprehensible size and can focus on only those relations that are considered to be essential. Although the development of the preceding paragraph is overly simplistic, it nevertheless captures the spirit of what one is trying to do in an abstraction process.

Many times in the preceding chapters we have denoted a collection of points in a graph—that is, a subgraph—with an identifying token, often H. In a homomorphism we denote it by a point in a different graph. More formally, a *homomorphism* defined on the graph $G = (P, E)$ is a function φ which maps P onto the set of points P' in the graph $G' = (P', E')$ such that:

1. $(x, y) \in E$ implies $(\varphi(x), \varphi(y)) \in E'$, provided $\varphi(x) \neq \varphi(y)$,
2. $(x', y') \in E'$ implies there exist $x_i \in \varphi^{-1}(x')$ and $y_j \in \varphi^{-1}(y')$ such that $(x_i, y_j) \in E$.

The graph G' is said to be the *homomorphic image* of G. Figure 8-1 illustrates some homomorphic maps. In each, G_i' is the image of G_i. For brevity we will often use the notation $\varphi: G \to G'$ and let x' denote $\varphi(x)$ in G'.

Corresponding to any function φ defined on some set P is the partition $\mathscr{P}$ which is induced by the inverse image relation φ^{-1}. That is, $x, y \in S_i \in \mathscr{P}$ if and only if $\varphi(x) = \varphi(y)$. The homomorphism therefore may be regarded as "condensing" each of these subsets (or subgraphs) S_i of $\mathscr{P}$ and preserving only the edge structure "between" the sets. It is well known that functions uniquely

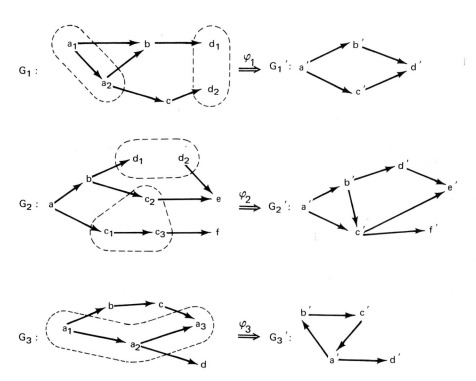

Figure 8-1 Three homomorphisms defined on different graphs G_i. [Note that we use x' to denote $\varphi(x)$.]

induce partitions of their domain, but if the function is a homomorphism we can prove the following stronger result.

Theorem 8-1 If $G = (P, E)$ is a graph and $\mathscr{P}$ is a partition of P, then there exists a unique homomorphic image $G' = \varphi(G)$ for which $\mathscr{P}$ is the inverse image partition.

One may construct G' by simply letting each equivalence class (element of the partition) $S_i \subseteq P$ be denoted by a point $p_i' \in P'$; then setting $(p_i', p_j') \in E'$ if and only if there exist $x \in S_i$ and $y \in S_j$ such that $(x, y) \in E$. Consequently one can regard the concepts of *partition* and *homomorphism* as synonymous (see Exercise 8-1). We will frequently describe homomorphisms in terms of their preimage partition on P.

It should be pointed out that just as the concept of abstraction is sufficiently complex that no single definition is likely to satisfy all interpretations, so too there are different definitions of homomorphism that the reader is likely to encounter. It would be well to point out the significance of each of the conditions in our definition. All definitions of homomorphism (which means "of the same form" or structure) include condition (1), that $(x, y) \in E$ implies $(\varphi(x), \varphi(y)) \in E'$. Homomorphisms are edge-preserving in that for every edge in the domain there is a corresponding edge in the image. But many authors do not add the extra condition "*provided* $\varphi(x) \neq \varphi(y)$." If $\varphi(x) = \varphi(y)$ and $(x, y) \in E$, then the edge $(\varphi(x), \varphi(x))$ would be included in E'. But we have found in previous work that the presence of loops is a nuisance in most computer structures. For this reason we give a definition that will prevent the creation of extraneous loops.

Condition (2), that corresponding to each edge in the image there must exist at least one edge in the domain that maps onto it under φ, seems natural; but it is not always used. Without it the preimage partition does *not* uniquely characterize the image G', but rather a class of homomorphic images (see Exercise 8-2). More importantly, one would expect that every 1-1 homomorphic mapping be an isomorphism. Condition (2) is necessary to ensure Theorem 8-1 and hence the following corollary.

Corollary 8-2 If the homomorphism $\varphi: G \rightarrow G'$ is a 1-1 function of P onto P', then φ is an isomorphism.

As we have already noted, given any point function defined on P (or any partition of P), there is a unique graph G' that is the homomorphic image of G under φ. Consequently, if G is any graph on n points, there exist

$$h_n = \sum_{i=1}^{n} \begin{Bmatrix} n \\ i \end{Bmatrix} \quad \text{where } \begin{Bmatrix} n \\ i \end{Bmatrix} \text{ denote Stirling numbers of the second kind} \tag{8-1}$$

distinct homomorphic mappings φ_i defined on G.† If n is only 6, then $h_n = 203$. This is simply "too many." By stating that G′ is a homomorphic image of G, "too little" information is conveyed. For practical use, the preservation of only the edge structure does not sufficiently restrict these maps. Invariably we find it necessary to further modify the homomorphic concept so that it preserves some other feature, or property, of interest that is to be found in G. For example, we may require that φ also preserve acyclicity (if G is acyclic) or the presence of cycles, if they are important. In each of the following sections we will further limit in some way the homomorphic concept, although not always in the same fashion. Under any definition, we know that homomorphisms always preserve paths:

Theorem 8-3 If $\varphi : G \rightarrow G'$ is a homomorphism then $\rho_G(x, z)$ implies $\rho_{G'}(x', z')$.

By the *composition* of the relation R_1 from X to Y, and the relation R_2 from Y to Z, denoted $R_1 \circ R_2$, we mean the relation from X to Z defined:

$$R_1 \circ R_2 = \{(x, z) \mid \text{ there exists } y \in Y \text{ such that } (x, y) \in R_1 \text{ and } (y, z) \in R_2\}$$

(The special case where R_1 and R_2 are both relations on the set S was given in Exercise 1-8.) Functions—say f and g—are relations, and the classical definition of the composition of functions $(f \circ g)(x) = g[f(x)]$ is a special case of that above. It is well known that the composition of functions is itself a function. Homomorphisms are special edge preserving functions and one can show the following:

Theorem 8-4 If $\varphi : G \rightarrow G'$ and $\psi : G' \rightarrow G''$ are homomorphisms, then their composition $\varphi \circ \psi$ is a homomorphism of G onto G″.

This suggests that it may be possible to "decompose" a given homomorphism φ into "simpler" homomorphisms $\varphi_1, \varphi_2, \ldots, \varphi_n$ such that $\varphi = \varphi_1 \circ \varphi_2 \circ \ldots \circ \varphi_n$, where each of these component mappings is more easily studied and analyzed. Let us call a homomorphism φ *simple* if, except for a single subgraph H, the preimage partition is trivial. (That is, φ condenses the subgraph H to a single point in G′, but is a 1-1 isomorphism on G ∼ H.) We will call H the *kernel* of the simple homomorphism, where this terminology is suggested by the concept of a kernel in homomorphisms of algebraic systems—the set of those elements which map onto the identity element of the image. The two concepts are similar, but they are not in any sense equivalent. Simple homomorphisms are denoted φ_H, where in this convenient notation the

---

†Note that while $\varphi_1 : G \rightarrow G_1'$ and $\varphi_2 : G \rightarrow G_2'$ may be distinct as functions, their homomorphic images G_1' and G_2' need not be distinct. They may be isomorphic. See Exercise 8-3.

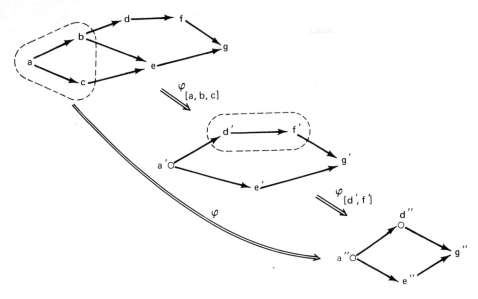

Figure 8-2 The homomorphism regarded as the composition of two simple homomorphisms $\varphi_{[a,b,c]}$ and $\varphi_{[d',f']}$.

subscript H completely characterizes the mapping. Figure 8-2 illustrates a homomorphism composed of two simple homomorphisms.

EXERCISES FOR SECTION 8-1

8-1 (*a*) Reconstruct and draw the partition P that must be induced on the point set of G by the homomorphism in the accompanying figure, given only that $\varphi^{-1}(d') = \{d\}$.

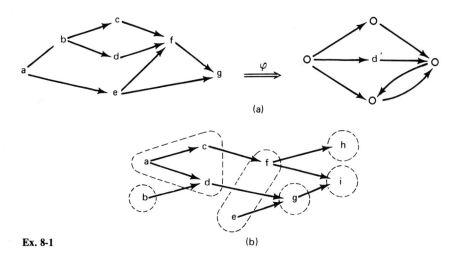

Ex. 8-1

(*b*) Given the graph G and the indicated partition $\mathscr{P}$ of its point set, construct the unique homomorphic image G' for which $\mathscr{P}$ is the preimage partition (see accompanying figure).

8-2 Because of condition (2) in the definition of a homomorphism, any point map $\varphi : P \to P'$ defines a unique homomorphic image $G' = \varphi(G)$ of G. Given G in the accompanying figure and the *point map* φ defined by the preimage partition, construct three graphs G'_1, G'_2, and G'_3 which are homomorphic images under φ *if condition* (2) *is ignored*.

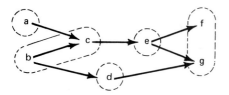

Ex. 8-2

8-3 The two partitions in the accompanying figure of the graph G define distinct homomorphisms φ_1 and φ_2. Show that their homomorphic images $\varphi_1(G)$ and $\varphi_2(G)$ are, however, identical (that is, isomorphic).

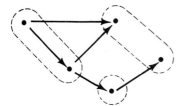 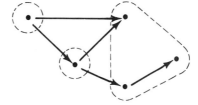

Ex. 8-3

8-4 In Fig. 8-1 G_2 is a tree, yet its image G'_2 under φ_1 is not a tree. G_3 is acyclic, yet G'_3 is not. Let φ_H be a simple homomorphism. Find necessary and sufficient conditions on H such that
(*a*) if G is a right principal tree, then G' will be a right principal tree, and
(*b*) if G is acyclic, then G' will be acyclic.

8-5 The Stirling numbers of the second kind $\left\{ \begin{matrix} n \\ i \end{matrix} \right\}$ may be defined by the recurrence relation

$$\left\{ \begin{matrix} n \\ i \end{matrix} \right\} = i \cdot \left\{ \begin{matrix} n-1 \\ i \end{matrix} \right\} + \left\{ \begin{matrix} n-1 \\ i-1 \end{matrix} \right\}$$

where for all n we have $\left\{ \begin{matrix} n \\ 0 \end{matrix} \right\} = 0$, $\left\{ \begin{matrix} n \\ 1 \end{matrix} \right\} = 1$, and $\left\{ \begin{matrix} n \\ i \end{matrix} \right\} = 0$ if $i > n$.

Use induction to show that this recurrence relation also denotes the number of ways of partitioning a set with n elements into a collection of i sets ($i \leq n$). Thus the number of ways of partitioning a set with n elements is that given in (8-1).

8-2 STRINGS, LISTS, AND LIST STRUCTURES

Strings are linear structures with an assignment function into some set V called a *vocabulary*, or *alphabet*. The linear relation E is often only implicitly represented by concatenation of elements of the string, or more precisely, by concatenation of their assigned values. In Sec. 4-2 we considered the following string over the set V of English words:

THE SMALL DOG WITH BLACK SPOTS BITES

In that section we created the string by concatenating three smaller *substrings* as shown below:

(THE SMALL DOG)   (WITH BLACK SPOTS)   (BITES)

Each of these smaller substrings was given a name. In the example of Sec. 4-3 (Fig. 4-11), they were called NOUN PHRASE, ADJECTIVE MODIFIER, and VERB, respectively. Such a naming procedure is precisely an example of the homomorphic abstraction process. The substring (THE SMALL DOG) is one member of a set of substrings generally called a noun phrase, in the same way that an individual dwelling may be considered one instance of a house. We can then model this abstraction process by a sequence of simple homomorphic maps, as illustrated in Fig. 8-3.†

†Each point in the image strings G′ through G^V also has an assigned value in some additional set which is disjoint from the set over which the original string was defined. Notation varies from author to author, but it is reasonably common to call the set in which the original string has assigned values the *terminal vocabulary* denoted V^T, and let homomorphic images have assigned values in V^N called the *nonterminal vocabulary*. V^N is therefore a set of *abstract names*.

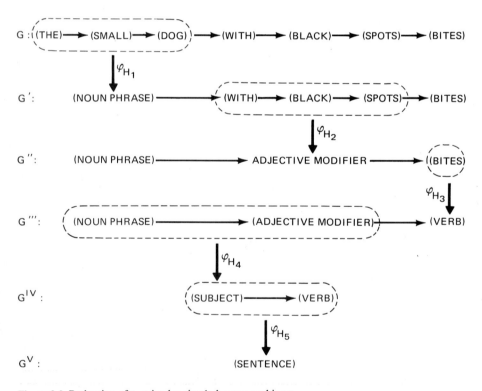

Figure 8-3 Reduction of a string by simple homomorphisms.

In formal language theory, the reduction of a string to a single point by successive simple homomorphisms (subject to the additional constraint that the kernel H must itself be a string) is called a *parse* of the string. A fundamental issue is: Under what conditions can a particular subgraph (or substring) H be homomorphically reduced or contracted?. In later sections we will look for properties in the relational structure defined on H (and possibly the "context" surrounding H) to decide whether or not H can be homomorphically contracted. But since the relational structure of strings is essentially trivial, the issue of *contractibility* in formal languages is normally based on the values $f(x_i)$ assigned to the elements x_i of the substring. The *productions* or *rewrite rules* of a formal grammar may be regarded as simply specifications of permissible homomorphic contractions, where the string or strings on the right-hand side of the production describes those substrings that may serve as kernels, while the left-hand side of the production gives the nonterminal name that should be assigned to its image. One can now pose several standard questions, such as: under what conditions can two different sequences of simple homomorphisms, $\varphi_1, \varphi_2, \ldots, \varphi_m$ and $\psi_1, \psi_2, \ldots, \psi_n$ be considered to be equivalent?, can one apply the homomorphic contractions in a left-to-right order on the string?, and how should permissible homomorphisms be specified so that some automatic process will always find the correct one to apply?. Consideration of this kind of question would lead us rather far afield into the theory of formal languages. There are many such linguistic nuances that must be considered in the practical application of contraction processes—for instance, compiler design, which we are not prepared to explore. These details are well handled in several excellent articles and texts (Aho, 1974; Feldman, 1968; Gries, 1971), which the reader is encouraged to pursue. However, so much of the theory of data structures, and especially list structures, has been influenced by formal language theory that it cannot be totally ignored.

In Fig. 8-3 an entire sublist was treated as a single entity, named, and then included as an element in subsequent lists. This suggests a way that the definition of a *simple list* given in Chap. 3 can be generalized. A *list over a set* P is a linear order on a set of elements, each of which may be either: (1) a point in the set P, or (2) itself a list over P.

If the element x is a member of P, it is called an *atomic* element, or an *atom*. If the element x is a list, we call it a *sublist*. A list is *simple* if all of its elements are atomic. The representation of a list is called a *list structure*. When this latter term is used there is a strong presumption that the list is not simple.

A list may directly contain itself as a sublist element, or it may indirectly serve as a sublist element of one of its sublists. (See Exercise 8-6.) Such a list is said to be *recursive*. Otherwise it is nonrecursive.† For the most part we will consider only nonrecursive lists.

---

†*Recursive* is used here in the sense of "self-referent," just as a self-referent definition or function is said to be recursive (as is the definition of a list). But they are not quite identical, since the latter includes some terminating criterion. One might also call recursive lists *cyclic*, but that does not seem to convey the self-referencing connotation.

Historically, the techniques of representing list structures have preceded the definition of the formal models they represent. Because of their power and generality it is sometimes difficult to pin down just what class of abstract structures they do represent. Probably our best approach will be to simply consider various examples and their representations.

Consider the following list L1, whose elements consist of both atomic points and lists.

$$\text{L1: (a, (b, a, b), c, (d, (e)))†} \qquad (8\text{-}2)$$

By the *length* of a list we mean simply the number of elements in the list. The list L1 above has length 4. This is more apparent if we name the sublists appearing in L1 as follows:

$$\text{L2: (b, a, b)}$$
$$\text{L3: (d, (e))}$$
$$\text{L4: (e)}$$

Then an alternative representation of the list L1 is

$$\text{L1: (a, L2, c, L3)} \qquad (8\text{-}3)$$

Readily, this list consists of but four elements.

L1 can now be represented, in much the same way that we represented simple lists in Chap. 4, using cells as shown in Fig. 8-4. The right-hand field is a link to the NEXT element in the list. If the element is an atomic element, then as before the assigned value may be simply stored in the left-hand field (or possibly a pointer to the assigned value which has been represented somewhere else in storage). If, however, the element is itself a list, it seems reasonable to store a pointer to its representation in this left-hand field. For this reason the field has been denoted as the F or SUBLIST field in Fig. 8-4, depending on its usage. Finally one extra field, a TAG field, must be added to indicate how the left field is being used. If TAG $= 0$, then the field denotes an assigned value, and the cell itself called an atom or *atomic cell*. If TAG $= 1$, then the field points to a sublist and the cell is called a *name cell* since it refers to, or names, a list. Figure 8-5 illustrates a list structure that represents L1.

Suppose now we want a simple enumeration, or listing, of the original list as given in (8-2) from the representation of Fig. 8-5. Clearly the process would follow the reference pointer L1 to access the first element, print it (or perform some other operation using it) and follow the NEXT link to the next element.

---

†The symbols a, b, c, d, e are to be regarded as assigned values associated with the element, not as element identifiers. A technically more "correct" representation of L1 would be

$$\text{L1: } (w_1, (x_1, x_2, x_3), w_2, (y_1, (z_1)))$$

where $f(w_1) = f(x_2) = a$, $f(x_1) = f(x_3) = b$, etc. While the distinction is important and is worth noting, virtually all the literature on lists uses the traditional linguistic notation, in which elements of a list (or string) are denoted by their assigned values, not some additionally supplied identifier.

Figure 8-4 A cell format for list structures.

This cell is a name cell denoting a sublist, so the process must follow the link in the SUBLIST field to access the first element of the sublist. The sublist is traversed in a simple fashion, but then a problem arises. How will the process "get back to" the name cell in the higher-level list to continue traversing it? One easy method, employed by the following procedure, is to stack the addresses of name cells each time the SUBLIST link is followed, then return to the cell whose address is on the top of the stack each time a sublist is terminated.

procedure printlist (list);
pointer   list;

This process displays the assigned values of list elements of a list represented as a list structure without header cells. It also delimits its sublists with open and close parentheses.

begin
      pointer   cell, stack;
      field   f, next, sublist, tag;
      cell ←list;
      stack ←null;
      print "(";

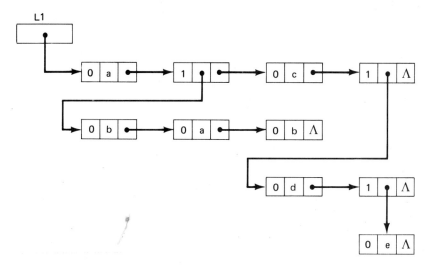

Figure 8-5 Representation S_R, of the list L1: (a, (b, a, b), c, (d, (e))).

continuetraversal:
```
    while cell ≠ null do
        if tag(cell) = 0
            then Atomic cell. Display it.
                print f(cell);
                cell ←next(cell)
            else Name cell. Follow link to sublist and begin displaying the sublist.
                print "(";
                call pushdown (stack, cell);
                cell ←sublist(cell);
```

No more cells in this list. Return to the higher level list, if any.

```
    print ")";
    if stack =null then exit;
    cell ←next (poptop(stack));
    go to continuetraversal;
    end
```

The preceding process "traverses" the list structure in the sense that it visits every element and puts them in a linear order. It is easily implemented using our existing stack procedures (Exercise 8-10). A more useful traversal procedure is a function which returns the address of the next cell in the traversal each time it is called, in the same fashion that NXTELM returns elements of a set, one at a time. This would allow one to "index" over a list structure, as well as over sets. Weizenbaum (1963) provided such indexing functions in his list-processing language SLIP by using a mechanism which he called a *reader*. Closer examination of his reader concept will reveal that it is little more than the stack employed above. The top element of the stack is a pointer to the "last" element that had been returned in the sublist currently being traversed. A separate reader (or stack) can be assigned to different traversals so that the functions themselves become reentrant.

The introduction of the auxiliary stack structure to control the traversal in PRINTLIST seems both inelegant and unnecessary. Can it be eliminated? One approach might be to circularly link each list "through" the name cell that references it, as in Fig. 8-6. Such a representation is called a *ring structure*—for obvious reasons. With a ring structure representation, when the traversal process reaches the end of a sublist it has an immediate link back to its place in the higher-level list. But surprisingly, given the ring structure *as shown,* a traversal process would still require an auxiliary stack. The problem is that when the process follows the NEXT link and encounters a name cell, it does not know whether it is simply the "next" element in the list (or sublist) it is currently following, in which case it should descend to the sublist it references by following the SUBLIST link, or if it has just ascended from the last element of its sublist, in which case it should follow the link in the NEXT field. To be useful, a ring structure must effectively tag, or mark, the *last* element in any list. If the last cell in every list is tagged, say with 2 if it is an atomic cell, with 3 if it is a name cell, then it is straightforward to implement a "stackless" traversal process.

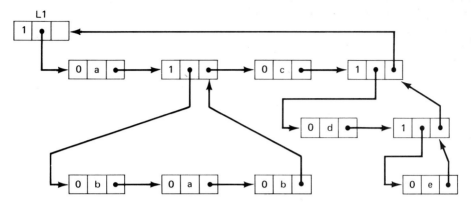

Figure 8-6 A ring structure representation of the list L1: (a, (b, a, b), c, (d, (e))).

In Chap. 4 we found it useful to add an extra header cell to circularly linked lists so that search processes would be able to recognize the beginning and end of a list. As shown above, the referencing name cell, even though it is tagged differently, cannot be used for this purpose. Figure 8-7 shows a list structure representation using header cells in which a search process can easily work both "up" and "down" through the subgraph structure. In fact, there are several different ways of representing list structures with this property; readers can probably devise a few of their own. While the author generally prefers to use header cells in the manner of Fig. 8-7, each has its proponents and each has its drawbacks.

Let us now return to the homomorphic reduction of the string THE SMALL

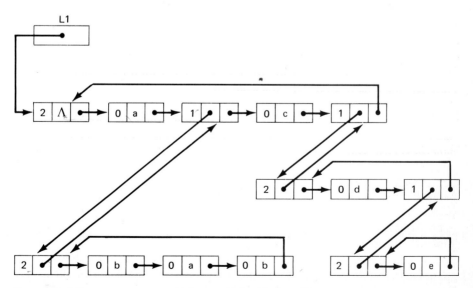

Figure 8-7 A list structure representation employing header cells.

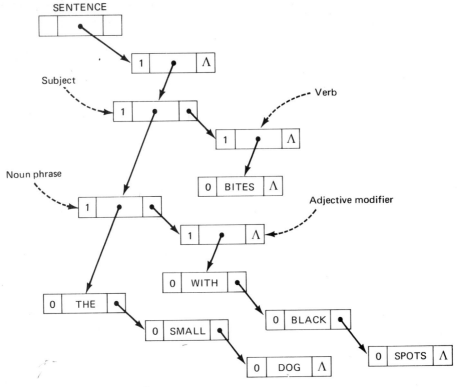

Figure 8-8 Representation of
(((THE SMALL DOG)(WITH BLACK SPOTS))(BITES))
as a list structure.

DOG WITH BLACK SPOTS BITES as shown in Fig. 8-3. It can be represented as a list structure in the manner shown in Fig. 8-8.

Figure 8-8 is very similar to Fig. 5-23, which is a Knuth representation of a principal tree. We can certainly interpret the list structure of Fig. 8-8 *as if it were* the Knuth representation of a tree. The abstract tree T_M that would correspond to it is shown in Fig. 8-9. In formal language theory this tree T_M is called the *parse tree* of the string. Any left-to-right traversal of the tree (it may be preorder, symmetric, or postorder) that prints only its endpoints will recreate the original string.

The correspondence above is not simply fortuitous, nor is it unexpected. Historically the development and application of list structures have occurred within a linguistic context, although their applications have since been extended. The concepts of list structure, homomorphism, and tree are thoroughly interrelated. In fact, each may be regarded as simply a different conceptual approach to a single common theme. But care must be exercised in such unification since each of these three concepts has extensions and subtleties that are not expressible in terms of the other two. The unification can be pushed too

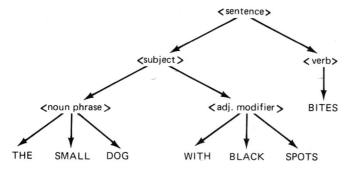

Figure 8-9 A parse tree of the string
THE SMALL DOG WITH BLACK SPOTS BITES

far. In the remainder of this section we will explore both the interrelation of these three concepts and some of their inherent differences.

The following theorem has long been known

Theorem 8-5 Every nonrecursive list structure can be uniquely represented by a principal tree, and vice versa.

For example, the list (8-2) and tree of Fig. 8-10 may be considered equivalent. The representational correspondence is easily established as follows:

1. x is an atomic element of the list if and only if it is an end point (maximal point) of the tree. (8-4)
2. Each interior point y of the tree corresponds to a sublist element whose elements $z_1, \ldots, z_n$ belong to $R(y)$.

It should be evident that the procedure PRINTLIST is nothing more than a process to convert a tree representation of a list structure into a linear repre-

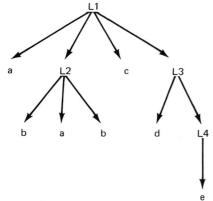

Figure 8-10 The list (a, (b, a, b), c, (d, (e))) regarded as a tree.

sentation whose sublists are parenthesized. Conversely, given a linear representation of a list in which every sublist is delimited by parentheses (or any other recognizable delimiter symbol), then it is equally straightforward to construct a tree representation (Exercise 8-8).

However, the sublists of a string representation are seldom explicitly delimited. Most often their existence and extent must be determined from the context of the linear list itself in accordance with some established convention. If the convention is moderately complex, then its rules may be spelled out in the form of a grammar and the subsequent recognition of sublists would be regarded as a parsing procedure.† Frequently a rather simple convention may be employed, together with a reasonably straightforward recognition and conversion procedure. For example, we might agree to explicitly delimit only the beginning of each sublist and follow the delimiter with a count of the number of elements in that sublist (or list). Using this convention, a linear representation of Fig. 8-10 would be

$$(_4 \text{ a } (_3 \text{ b a b c } (_2 \text{ a } (_1 \text{ e}$$

As an additional example, consider the expression tree of Fig. 8-11, which we have previously seen in Sec. 5-3. Using the same convention, its representation as a linear list would be

$$(_2 (_2 (_1 \text{ B } (_1 (_2 (_2 \text{ B } 2 (_2 (_2 \text{ 4 A C } (_2 \text{ 2 A}$$

Instead of the single symbol (open parenthesis) to denote the "begin sublist" delimiter, we can use a variety of symbols, say operator symbols associated with the internal points of the expression tree. In this case the linear representation becomes

$$/_2 +_2 -_1 \text{ B SQRT}_1 -_2 \uparrow_2 \text{ B } 2 *_2 *_2 \text{ 4 A C } *_2 \text{ 2 A}$$

This list is readily recognizable as the prefix representation (preorder traversal) of the expression. The subscript values associated with the operator (or sublist delimiter) symbols denote the *scope* of the operator. They are essential whenever a single symbol may denote two or more distinct operators with different scopes (sublists with different numbers of elements), as in the case of "minus," which may be interpreted as either a unary or binary operator. If we had chosen to delimit the ends of sublists, then a corresponding postfix representation would have resulted. The correspondence between principal trees,

---

†Thus parsing can be regarded as the process of recognizing and delimiting sublists (or, as noted in the preceding section, substrings that can be homomorphically contracted). The leftmost sublist to be recognized is commonly called a *handle*. Problems that may then be raised in formal language theory are: What restrictions on the recognition conventions, or grammar, are sufficient to guarantee that recognition and delimiting can be accomplished: (1) with a left-to-right scanning process, (2) with only a local examination around the sublist in question, (3) without false starts or mistaken identification, and (4) without ambiguity?

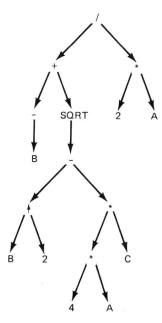

Figure 8-11 An expression tree (identical to that of Fig. 5-14).

list structures, and lists represented in a prefix (or postfix) notation is apparent, and so easily established, that it is customary to treat them as virtually synonymous.

In addition to providing insight into the connection between parsing procedures and a class of data structures, the preceding discussion has an important application in the practical use of computer data structures. Virtually all input and output devices (e.g., card readers or printers) are sequential, as are many low-cost peripheral storage devices (e.g., magnetic tape). A procedure that permits us to convert from principal trees, or list structures, to linear representations and back again (just as format procedures permit us to convert binary or hexadecimal representations of numeric data to BCD or display codes) is of real value. It would be clearly desirable if more general data structures could be converted to an equivalent linear representation by some similar process. The topological sort procedure developed in Sec. 6-1 represents a step in this direction. But because the correspondence is not unique, it is not by itself sufficient. There do exist techniques for converting various classes of more complex structures to equivalent sequential representations, viz., the K-formulae of Berztiss (1975), but the conversion algorithms tend to be expensive and/or fail to establish a unique correspondence.

So there is a kind of "natural" correspondence between principal trees and the nonrecursive list structure concept. Let us now consider a few of the shortcomings of this identification. If the list is recursive, then application of the correspondence displayed in (8-4) will clearly yield a cyclic representation

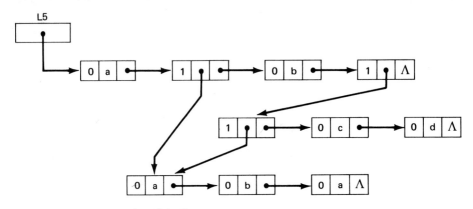

Figure 8-12 A representation of the list
(a, (a, b, a),b, ((a, b, a), c, d))
in which the common sublists (a, b, a) share storage.

that is not a tree. Even if the list structure is nonrecursive, we may still encounter practical problems. Consider the list structure

$$L5:(a, L6, b, L7)$$
$$\text{where} \qquad L6:(a, b, a) \qquad\qquad (8\text{-}5)$$
$$L7:(L6, c, d)$$

Written out as a simple parenthesized list, it would be

$$L5:(a, (a, b, a), b, ((a, b, a), c, d))$$

Since the "same" sublist L6:(a, b, a) appears twice in this list structure, it is
reasonable, given our customary concern for storage efficiency, to consider a
computer representation such as shown in Fig. 8-12. In this representation
only one copy of this sublist has been created and stored, but it is referenced,
or named, twice. If there are many duplicate sublists in the list structure then
a representation as shown in Fig. 8-12 can yield considerable savings in terms
of storage. Notice also that the procedure PRINTLIST, or any other traversal
process which employs auxiliary stacks, will work as well on this representation as on the tree-structured list of Fig. 8-5. On the other hand, neither the
ring structure shown in Fig. 8-6 nor the back-linked representation of Fig. 8-7
can be used. In these representations, *each reference to a sublist must have a
distinct representation.*

When considering lists such as L5 with duplicate sublist structures it
seems fairly natural to regard their abstract structure as acyclic graphs, as
shown in Fig. 8-13, rather than inflexibly linking the theory of list structures
to a theory of principal trees, as has been suggested in preceding paragraphs.
It is also worth nothing that the representation of L5 shown above is precisely
the representation of Fig. 8-13 under the Knuth transform as discussed in
Sec. 6-4. Any of the other techniques employed in that chapter for the representation of acyclic structures could be employed here.

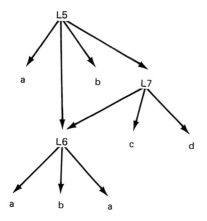

Figure 8-13 The list (a, (a, b, a), b, ((a, b, a),c, d)) regarded as an acyclic graph.

EXERCISES FOR SECTION 8-2

8-6 The generalized definition of a list is recursive since a list is "a linear structure, each of whose elements may themselves be lists." A structure consisting of a singleton element (whether atomic or not) is clearly linear. Consider the three lists named L1, L2, and L3 that are defined as follows:

$$L1:(L2)$$
$$L2:(L3)$$
$$L3:(L1)$$

Each is a list composed of a single element which is a list. One might graphically represent these lists as shown in the accompanying figure.

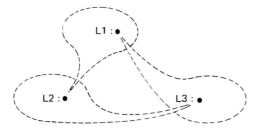

Ex. 8-6

Alternatively, consider the list defined as follows:

$$L1:(L2, L4)$$
$$L2:(L3, L1)$$
$$L3:(L1, L4)$$
$$L4:(L2, L3)$$

(*a*) "Sketch" the structure of this list.

(*b*) Would you want to call such structures lists? Why, or why not?

(*c*) Try to give a definition of a list that defines all, and only, nonrecursive lists.

A possible objection to the recursive definition of lists can be voiced by using an analogy from the theory of sets. The nature of the elements of a set are unspecified, and a set may contain other sets, or itself, as a member. For instance, the set of all sets must be an element of itself. It is known that such recursive inclusion can lead to logical contradictions, as in Russell's Paradox. In naïve set theory one retains the general definition, but tacitly refrains from employing recursive examples, much as we have limited ourselves to nonrecursive lists.

8-7 In these list structures, all cells have been tagged to indicate whether they are atomic or name cells. This is the prevalent practice. But an alternative is possible. One could assume that all (nonheader) cells of the list *reference* either some individual item of data or some data structure. The "referenced" structure could be tagged, perhaps in a header cell, to indicate its nature rather than tagging the referencing cell.

(*a*) Draw such a list structure representing the list L1 of (8-2). There are both advantages and disadvantages to such a representational convention.

(*b*) Discuss its ramifications if:

(1) the structures have relatively few atomic elements,

(2) the lists are linear structures over a set of graphs, not singleton values or characters (e.g., assigned values $f(x_i) = G$),

(3) the values assigned to atomic elements are real numbers.

* **8-8** Write and code an input procedure RDLIST, given a fully parenthesized list structure as illustrated in Fig. 8-5.

* **8-9** When a list structure has several common sublists, as in (8-6), it was suggested that a representation such as Fig. 8-12 might be more appropriate.

(*a*) Can the procedure RDLIST of the preceding exercise be modified to create this kind of representational structure, assuming only parenthesized list input such as (8-2) and (8-6)? How much "work" would be involved in discovering common sublists?

(*b*) Suppose that the input consists of named sublists, as in (8-3) and (8-5). How would you now implement RDLIST?

(*c*) The implementation of (*b*) will require maintenance of a run-time symbol table to keep the correspondence between a sublist's symbolic name and the location of its representation. What data structures would you use to build and keep the symbol table?

***8-10** (*a*) Code a version of PRINTLIST. (Use the stack procedures developed in Sec. 3-2.)

(*b*) Test it using one of the input procedures RDLIST from the preceding exercises.

8-11 Write a procedure CONCATENATE(L1, L2) which, given two lists L1 and L2, forms the list L:(L1, L2).

(*a*) What should it return as its functional value?

(*b*) Can the list L1 of (8-2) be constructed by strictly *pairwise* concatenation?

(*c*) Code this procedure so that it is compatible with RDLIST and PRINTLIST. Test it.

8-12 Add to your growing collection of list procedures a procedure HEAD(LIST, REST) that returns the first element of the specified list and a pointer (or name) to the remainder. Both may be empty. A procedure TAIL(LIST, REST) may be similarly included, as may a boolean procedure ATOMIC, which returns **true** if a specified element is atomic. Code a traversal routine, such as PRINTLIST, solely in terms of HEAD and ATOMIC.

8-13 (*a*) Define an "empty" list, which will be denoted by ( ).

(*b*) Is the list (( )) an empty list?

(*c*) How would you represent the empty list? Consider as a specific example the list

$$\text{L1:}((()\ ()\ (()\ ()))\ ()\ (()\ ()\ (())))$$

(*d*) Represent L1 as an acyclic graph in the manner of Fig. 8-13.

8-14 (*a*) Write a traversal process (without stacks) to print out a list represented as a ring structure, in which the last element of every list has a special tag.

(*b*) If header cells were included in the list representations, would it be preferable to have them "precede" or "follow" the list cells?

(*c*) Should the representation of Fig. 8-7 be considered a ring structure?

8-15 Compare the representations S_R given in Fig. 5-29 of a tree and Fig. 8-6 of a list structure. Are they in any sense similar, in any sense equivalent? Construct an example in which the abstract tree and list are equivalent (as given in this section), then compare the representations.

8-16 Is the procedure PRINTLIST given in this section equivalent to the following recursive procedure?

```
procedure printlist (list);
pointer  list;
begin
    pointer   cell;
    field     f,next,sublist;
    print "(";
    cell ←list;
    while cell ≠ null do
        if tag(cell) = 0
            then  Display assigned value of atomic cell.
                  print f(cell)
            else  Name cell, display sublist.
                  call printlist (sublist(cell));
        cell ←next(cell);
    print ")";
    exit;
    end
```

What criteria does one use to demonstrate program equivalence, or nonequivalence?

8-17 While we have concentrated almost entirely on nonrecursive lists and list structures, it is not hard to construct recursive examples. Shown in the accompanying figure is a representation of a recursive list structure. The design of a traversal process that examines every cell of the list structure without getting "trapped" in an infinite recursive loop is not hard *if* one uses an auxiliary stack, and *if* before pushing a name cell address down on the stack and following the SUBLIST link, that name cell is compared with all the other name cells referenced in the stack. (Of course, the stack is no longer a "stack" in the formal sense, but it remains one in an operational sense.)

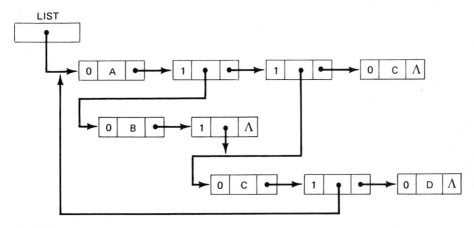

Ex. 8-17

(*a*) Code such a traversal algorithm. (Be careful. There are several possible pitfalls in the actual coding of this algorithm that are hidden by the deliberately vague description above.) Test your algorithm on the illustrated recursive list.

(*b*) Given a traversal procedure as above, one can write a process to print the list structure as a simple linear list, similar to PRINTLIST. But there is some question as to just what would constitute an appropriate linear listing of the structure. If the procedure follows the recursive loop, an infinite linear string will be produced. This is clearly undesirable. Yet the presence of recursion should be indicated some way. How? Give what you would consider to be an appropriate linear listing of the list structure above, and an algorithm to produce it.

(c) Will the recursive PRINTLIST procedure of Exercise 8-16 work on this structure? Can it be modified so that it will? How?

(d) The list structure above can be described by a grammar (actually many) that would generate it. Give such a grammar.

8-3 TWO APPLICATIONS OF LIST STRUCTURES

So far our discussion of list structures has been entirely within the context of formal languages and grammars. While this connection is of great theoretical interest to a computer scientist, there are other applications of more practical importance. In this section we develop two such applications.

The sublist concept is essentially one instance of the containment relation. Each sublist is contained in, or a constituent of, its "superlist." The same sort of containment relation is associated with mechanical devices that are built up out of constituent parts.

Consider, as a concrete example, the Acme Bicycle Company, which manufactures a line of superior bicycles, and assume it receives an order for seventy-five 10-speed racing bicycles (item number AZ3376-B). Before assembly can proceed, the various components of these bicycles must be manufactured, withdrawn from inventory, or ordered from subcontractors. Not only must all the various components be identified, but the quantities of each component item that will be needed must be determined as well. Again, for concreteness, let us assume that the following is a decomposition of a single 10-speed racing bicycle.

10-speed racer (item #AZ3376-B)
  1. Frame assembly
    1.1 Handlebar assembly
      1.1.1 Handlebar, chrome
      1.1.2 Hand grips, rubber (2)
      1.1.3 Handbrake assembly (2)
    1.2 Front fork
    1.3 Main frame, 26 in, men's
    1.4 Seat assembly
  2. Front-wheel assembly
    2.1 Wheel-rim assembly
      2.1.1 Wheel rim, 26 in
      2.1.2 Spokes (36)
      2.1.3 Tire, 26 × 1.24

    2.2 Hub, idle
    2.3 Ballbearing set (2)
  3. Rear-wheel assembly
    3.1 Wheel-rim assembly
      3.1.1 Wheel rim, 26 in
      3.1.2 Spokes (36)
      3.1.3 Tire, 26 × 1.24
    3.2 Hub, 10-speed
    3.3 Ballbearing set (1)
    3.4 Roller-bearing set (1)
    3.5 Drive-sprocket assembly
  4. Gearshift assembly
    4.1 Shift cable
    4.2 Shift lever assembly, 10-speed
    4.3 Rear-wheel shift assembly
  5. Foot-pedal assembly, 10-speed

Thus a single bicycle consists of five component parts, or elements. Each of these component assemblies in turn consists of component elements, and so forth. (For pedogogical simplicity, many further decompositions which might be expected in practice have been omitted.)

If the management of Acme were to computerize their production, it would be natural to represent each type of bicycle that they produce as a list structure in which each cell denotes one of the items that they handle, either as a finished product, intermediate component, or basic part. If the item is a composite assembly, then it becomes a name cell pointing to the sublist of its component elements. If the item is regarded as being primitive,† then it is treated as an atomic cell. Figure 8-14 illustrates a portion of a list structure that might be constructed to represent item AZ3376-B (10-speed racer) as described above.

In this organization, cells have been tagged with a 1 if they are composite items and zero if they are primitive items. In addition to the normal NEXT link and SUBLIST link fields, we have added a field to denote the quantity needed. Other assignment-function fields might also be appropriate, such as item number codes, location on plant floor where composite assemblies are to be assembled, locations in a warehouse where inventoried subitems can be found, cost, inventory value, number on hand, etc.

It is clear that, given a computer representation as in Fig. 8-14, the procedure PRINTLIST can, with minor modification, produce a hierarchical

---

†The quality of being "primitive" lies in the eye of the beholder. Readily, such "indivisible" items as nuts and bolts or spokes may be regarded as primitive or atomic, but so may such complex items as a 10-speed shift lever assembly, *if* the user, in this case the Acme Company, is unconcerned with their decomposition and treats them in their operation as single units (e.g., it subcontracts out the construction of these items and simply attaches them as simple components).

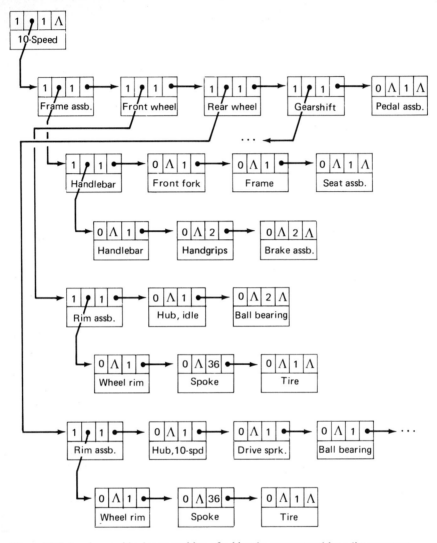

Figure 8-14 A subassembly decomposition of a bicycle, represented by a list structure.

description identical to that given above. The same traversal may indeed do much more, such as issuing inventory withdrawal orders, purchase orders, and job descriptions for various work stations.

If we examine Fig. 8-14, we see that we have a representation of a tree structure similar to Fig. 8-10. There are several duplicate cells that denote identical items, as is necessary in a circuit-free tree. In this case the duplication is not serious since the majority of those duplicated items are atomic. But one component assembly is also duplicated, the wheel-rim assembly; consequently, its entire representational substructure must be duplicated as well. It is evident that there is the potential for an excessive waste of storage, especially since it is

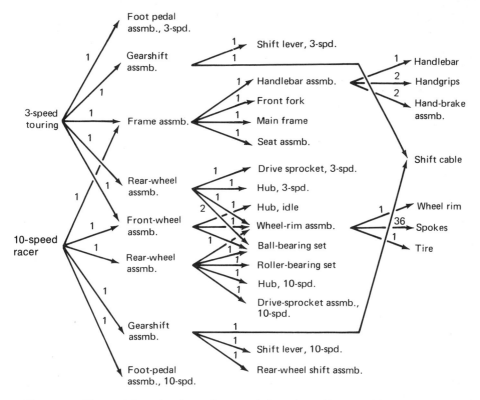

Figure 8-15 The partially ordered containment relation of two bicycles with shared component assemblies.

reasonable to expect the Acme management to insist on a duplication of subassemblies as much as possible. Given a line of several bicycle models, we would expect them to use standardized interchangeable parts whenever possible.

It pays here to step back a moment and examine an abstract model S_M of the component (or containment) relation that we are representing. In Fig. 8-15 we illustrate the component structure of two items in the Acme product line, the 10-speed racer and a 3-speed touring bicycle, in which many parts are shared. An edge assignment function (indicated by numbers on each edge) denotes the number of components needed in each assembly. It becomes apparent that containment is not really a tree-structured relation, but rather a more general acyclic relation. It would seem natural to devise a representation that is similar to Fig. 8-12, since our goals at that time were to avoid redundancy and conserve computer storage.

Figure 8-16 shows a portion of such a representation. Examination of Fig. 8-16 reveals a rather surprising fact. Cells which denote common atomic elements, for example, ballbearing sets, are still duplicated in the representation unless they have been homomorphically identified as a subassembly, as in the

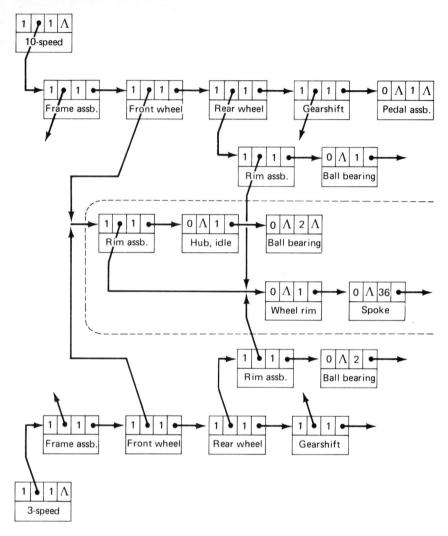

Figure 8-16 A portion of a list structure representing the components of two different bicycles. Assemblies enclosed in dashed lines are shared in common.

case of the wheel-rim assembly.† On reinspection we see that there are also many duplications of atomic cells in the representation of Fig. 8-12—even though our goal was to avoid just such redundant duplication.

†While it is obvious that atomic elements are different from sublist elements in a list, there are often other subtle differences that are easily overlooked, yet should be considered in the design of a structure. A key question seems to be: Does the cell represent an entity itself, or reference a representation stored elsewhere? Reconsider Exercise 8-7.

It should be evident that this figure is virtually identical to the preceding one, *except* that those cells encircled by the dashed line are now shared by two distinct list structures. Further, any process written to operate on the first representation will work equally well on the second representation, so we have gained a measure of storage efficiency with no loss of computational efficiency.

However, even though the representation of Fig. 8-16 is satisfactory in many respects, it would probably not be acceptable as a solution in the context of a practical problem. It has two significant drawbacks. Earlier in this section we indicated that there might very well be additional data (assignment functions) associated with items in this information structure other than just the quantity used in a particular assembly. Item number codes, location of assembly on plant floor, location in warehouse, cost, inventory value, and number on hand were suggested as possible examples. In fact, it is clear that in a realistic application the management would indeed want to have most, if not all, of this information readily available about all the items it handles—and possibly a good bit more, for instance, the names of its suppliers. There are two reasonable alternatives to the design of a computer system that will handle this additional information.

First, we could simply associate all this additional data with each cell in the data structure by adding extra fields to each cell. Naturally each cell must then be rather large. And consequently the duplication of even atomic cells would represent a fairly large storage overhead cost. Even more serious is the additional processing overhead. When an order is received—say, for example, for seventy-five 10-speed racers—the portion of the data structure associated with racing bicycles must be traversed to find which, and how many, component parts will be necessary. Required will be 225 ballbearing assemblies (2 for each front wheel, 1 for each rear wheel). These requirements would be checked against the NUMBER ON HAND field to see if the existing inventory is sufficient to cover this order. And this quantity would be deducted from the NUMBER ON HAND quantity. But then the *entire* data structure must be traversed to deduct this quantity from every "ballbearing" cell within the structure. Similarly, every time a shipment of ballbearings is received into inventory, the entire structure must be traversed again to update the information in this field. Clearly this processing overhead is intolerable.

A second, more practical, alternative is to create two separate data structures. The first structure would be a large sequential or random-access file containing one cell for each identifiable item handled by the company. Each cell in this file should contain that information particular to that item, such as its description, number on hand, supplier, etc. (In this context, it is more common to call the cells *records*. In business data processing this terminology is standard. But as noted in Chap. 1 they are really conceptually the same; both "cell" and "record" denote a block of consecutive storage locations that may be subdivided into fields.) Such a file structure is reasonably easy to update, in either a sequential or random-processing mode, as changes to information associated with individual items occur. The second data structure would represent only

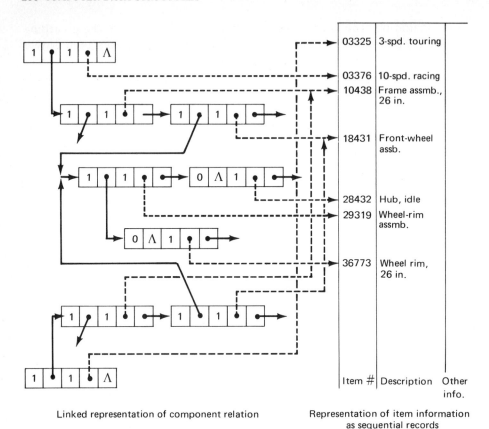

Item #	Description	Other info.
03325	3-spd. touring	
03376	10-spd. racing	
10438	Frame assmb., 26 in.	
18431	Front-wheel assb.	
28432	Hub, idle	
29319	Wheel-rim assmb.	
36773	Wheel rim, 26 in.	

Linked representation of component relation   Representation of item information as sequential records

Figure 8-17 A representation of a component assembly structure using two distinct data structures. The dashed lines indicate pointers from the linked relational structure into a file of sequential records.

the component containment relation that ties together all the individual items. It would most likely be a linked representation with additional pointers into the file structure. Figure 8-17 shows a portion of such a representation. This example is fairly typical of a *mixed data structure* in which a linked relational structure serves as an entry mechanism to a much larger body of information whose elements are essentially unstructured.† The nature of those pointers that link cells in the relational structure to records in the inventory file has been left undefined. If this kind of data structure were to be implemented as a classroom

---

†Many large files, of which an inventory file is one example, are essentially unstructured sets. Each element, or record, is a packet of information that is unrelated to the other records of the set. But although there may be no relationship that is inherent in the data itself, such files are typically organized in some fashion to facilitate processing. Most often they are sequentially organized, say on ascending order of the item number, to simplify sequential modification of the file.

exercise using incore storage and a programming language such as Fortran, then it would be natural to implement the inventory file by means of a sequential array. In this case the link might be the array index of the corresponding entry. In practice one would be reluctant to use an array of size sufficient to represent a typical corporation's inventory. Instead we would expect a separate inventory file in peripheral storage organized so that it can be accessed either sequentially or randomly. Then the pointer might be either the element's *actual address* in the peripheral device, or a *symbolic key* (see Chap. 9) by which it can be retrieved. A common choice for symbolic key would be the assigned item number.

Whatever detailed implementation is used, the reader should be able to code a process which, upon receipt of an order for a quantity of items, traverses the relational structure, tries to fill the order from inventory supplies, and if impossible issues instructions to assemble or order from subcontractors those items in excess of current inventory. Figure 8-18 shows the output from such a program.

Figure 8-18 Sample output from a program that updates an inventory file to reflect orders for composite items.

```
PROCESS AN ORDER FOR 130 OF ITEM   3325 3-SPEED TOURING BICYCLE

COMPONENT PARTS BREAK-DOWN OF A SINGLE ITEM
   3325 ( 1)-3-SPEED TOURING BICYCLE
      10438 ( 1)-FRAME ASSEMBLY, MENS, 26 INCH
         21109 ( 1)-HANDLE BAR ASSMB.
            33744 ( 1)-HANDLE BAR, CHROME
            33745 ( 2)-HANDLE BAR GRIP, RUBBER
            33746 ( 2)-HAND BRAKE ASSMB.
         23314 ( 1)-FRONT FORK, 26 INCH
         20866 ( 1)-FRAME, MENS, 26 IN., STEEL
         26310 ( 1)-SEAT ASSMB.
      18431 ( 1)-FRONT WHEEL ASSEMBLY
         29319 ( 1)-WHEEL RIM ASSEMBLY
            36773 ( 1)-26 INCH WHEEL RIM
            36774 (36)-WHEEL SPOKE, 26 IN. WHEEL
            36775 ( 1)-TIRE, 26 X 1.24
         28432 ( 1)-WHEEL HUB, FRONT, IDLE
         21163 ( 2)-BALL BEARING SET, 2-1/4 IN.
      18179 ( 1)-REAR WHEEL ASSMB.,3-SPD,26 IN.
         29319 ( 1)-WHEEL RIM ASSEMBLY
            36773 ( 1)-26 INCH WHEEL RIM
            36774 (36)-WHEEL SPOKE, 26 IN. WHEEL
            36775 ( 1)-TIRE, 26 X 1.24
         28997 ( 1)-WHEEL HUB, REAR, 3-SPEED
         22128 ( 1)-DRIVE SPROCKET, REAR,20 TEETH
         21163 ( 2)-BALL BEARING SET, 2-1/4 IN.
         21165 ( 1)-ROLLER BEARING SET, 2-1/4 IN.
      17364 ( 1)-GEAR SHIFT ASSMB, 3-SPEED
         21434 ( 1)-SHIFT LEVER, 3-SPEED
         26112 ( 1)-SHIFT CABLE, 36 INCHES.
      17307 ( 1)-FOOT PEDAL ASSMB., 3-SPD
```

ITEM OR ASSEMBLY	TOTAL QUANTITY NEEDED	ONHAND	WITHDRAW	BALANCE	NUMBER TO BE ASSEMBLED	PARTS TO BE ORDERED
3325 3-SPEED TOURING BICYCLE	130	43	43	0	87	
10438 FRAME ASSEMBLY, MENS, 26 INCH	87	131	87	44		
17307 FOOT PEDAL ASSMB., 3-SPD	87	210	87	123		
17364 GEAR SHIFT ASSMB, 3-SPEED	87	14	14	0	73	
18179 REAR WHEEL ASSMB.,3-SPD,26 IN.	87	18	18	0	69	
18431 FRONT WHEEL ASSEMBLY	87	106	87	19		
21163 BALL BEARING SET, 2-1/4 IN.	138	1740	138	1602		
21165 ROLLER BEARING SET, 2-1/4 IN.	69	835	69	766		
21434 SHIFT LEVER, 3-SPEED	73	320	73	247		
22128 DRIVE SPROCKET, REAR,20 TEETH	69	450	69	381		
26112 SHIFT CABLE, 36 INCHES.	73	62	62	0		11
28997 WHEEL HUB, REAR, 3-SPEED	69	475	69	406		
29319 WHEEL RIM ASSEMBLY	69	80	69	11		

```
PROCESS AN ORDER FOR  75 OF ITEM   3376 10-SPEED RACING BICYCLE

COMPONENT PARTS BREAK-DOWN OF A SINGLE ITEM
   3376 ( 1)-10-SPEED RACING BICYCLE
      10438 ( 1)-FRAME ASSEMBLY, MENS, 26 INCH
         21109 ( 1)-HANDLE BAR ASSMB.
            33744 ( 1)-HANDLE BAR, CHROME
            33745 ( 2)-HANDLE BAR GRIP, RUBBER
            33746 ( 2)-HAND BRAKE ASSMB.
         23314 ( 1)-FRONT FORK, 26 INCH
         20866 ( 1)-FRAME, MENS, 26 IN., STEEL
         26310 ( 1)-SEAT ASSMB.
      18431 ( 1)-FRONT WHEEL ASSEMBLY
         29319 ( 1)-WHEEL RIM ASSEMBLY
            36773 ( 1)-26 INCH WHEEL RIM
            36774 (36)-WHEEL SPOKE, 26 IN. WHEEL
            36775 ( 1)-TIRE, 26 X 1.24
         28432 ( 1)-WHEEL HUB, FRONT, IDLE
         21163 ( 2)-BALL BEARING SET, 2-1/4 IN.
      17734 ( 1)-REAR WHEEL ASSMB. 10-SPD,26IN
         29319 ( 1)-WHEEL RIM ASSEMBLY
            36773 ( 1)-26 INCH WHEEL RIM
            36774 (36)-WHEEL SPOKE, 26 IN. WHEEL
            36775 ( 1)-TIRE, 26 X 1.24
         22178 ( 1)-WHEEL HUB, 10-SPD, REAR
         22123 ( 1)-DRIVE SPROCKET SET, REAR
         21163 ( 1)-BALL BEARING SET, 2-1/4 IN.
         21165 ( 1)-ROLLER BEARING SET, 2-1/4 IN.
      16315 ( 1)-GEAR SHIFT ASSMB., 10-SPD
         26112 ( 1)-SHIFT CABLE, 36 INCHES.
         26303 ( 1)-SHIFT LEVER ASSMB., 10-SPEED
         26914 ( 1)-10-SPD SHIFT ASSMB.,REAR WHEEL
      17306 ( 1)-FOOT PEDAL ASSMB., 10 SPEED
```

ITEM OR ASSEMBLY	TOTAL QUANTITY NEEDED	INVENTORY			NUMBER TO BE ASSEMBLED	PARTS TO BE ORDERED
		ONHAND	WITHDRAW	BALANCE		
3376 10-SPEED RACING BICYCLE	75	10	10	0	65	
10438 FRAME ASSEMBLY, MENS, 26 INCH	65	44	44	0	21	
16315 GEAR SHIFT ASSMB., 10-SPD	65	76	65	11		
17306 FOOT PEDAL ASSMB., 10 SPEED	65	80	65	15		
17734 REAR WHEEL ASSMB. 10-SPD,26IN	65	25	25	0	40	
18431 FRONT WHEEL ASSEMBLY	65	19	19	0	46	
20866 FRAME, MENS, 26 IN., STEEL	21	103	21	82		
21109 HANDLE BAR ASSMB.	21	207	21	186		
21163 BALL BEARING SET, 2-1/4 IN.	132	1602	132	1470		
21165 ROLLER BEARING SET, 2-1/4 IN.	40	766	40	726		
22178 WHEEL HUB, 10-SPD, REAR	40	85	40	45		
22123 DRIVE SPROCKET SET, REAR	40	34	34	0		6
23314 FRONT FORK, 26 INCH	21	53	21	32		
26310 SEAT ASSMB.	21	706	21	685		
28432 WHEEL HUB, FRONT, IDLE	46	965	46	919		
29319 WHEEL RIM ASSEMBLY	86	11	11	0	75	
36773 26 INCH WHEEL RIM	75	355	75	280		
36774 WHEEL SPOKE, 26 IN. WHEEL	2700	2225	2225	0		475
36775 TIRE, 26 X 1.24	75	375	75	300		

The preceding list structure, as it has evolved, is an appropriate design for its intended practical application. But it has limitations. The most serious is best presented by means of an example. The two kinds of bicycle have been designed so that they share many components in common. For instance, the basic frame assembly is assumed to be identical for both. But is this reasonable? It seems much more likely that the basic frame assemblies might be *virtually* identical, but that some aspects, such as the kind of seat or kind of hand grip, might be somewhat different. One would like to be able to model and then represent a kind of *conditional relation* where the component relation holds in one case, but not in another. There are a number of ad hoc ways of introducing this kind of minor variability into a data structure without going to the expense of duplicating large chunks of it, but the author knows of no formal way of modeling the concept that is completely satisfactory. (See, however, Exercise 8-28.)

The two remaining potential deficiencies in this data structure should be noted. First, there are no links to, or way of accessing, the relational structure from the inventory file. For example, given an item number, say 003376, there is no way of locating a corresponding cell. Second, the relational structure is not back-linked. Suppose that the Acme Company were to redesign some component part. The design engineers might very well want to know *all* the assemblies of which the part is a component so as to discover possible incompatibilities in the new design. As it now stands, this information can be generated only by a procedure that exhaustively examines the entire relational structure and tests for the containment relation. The data structure may be modified so that these deficiencies disappear. The reader is encouraged (Exercise 8-26) to redesign the structure and to evaluate the additional cost in terms of both storage and processing overhead.

Many of the early advances in data structures arose in context of interactive graphic display; for example, ring structures were introduced as a means of effectively representing objects that were to be graphically manipulated and displayed (Williams, 1971). The fundamental conditions that compel the design of sophisticated structures are abundantly present in this application—fairly complex objects must be represented by small components, light spots, or pen strokes, all of which stand in predefined geometrical relationships to each other. Further, the constraint of interaction requires that the representing structures be dynamic and that manipulating procedures operated in nearly "real time."

But these very constraints which make the design of graphic structures so rich and interesting also make a systematic presentation difficult. There are too many variables, of both hardware and software, that must be considered. The characteristics of the instruction set of a display generator may make an otherwise ideal data structure unusable in one system. The method of generating interrupts may determine the feasibility in another system. Consequently we will have to be content with a presentation that captures the main themes and assume that readers will use a specialized text (such as Newman and Sproul, 1973) to acquire the details, and will then modify these structures to suit their particular needs.

To work from a concrete example let us assume that our display hardware has vector- (or line-) generating capacity. Given two parameters, an angle and a length, it draws a line of that length and in that direction from its current position (x, y) on the display surface to some new position (x_1, y_1). A third parameter, 0 or 1, indicates whether the moving spot (or pen) is to be illuminated (raised or lowered). A command

$$move\ (angle,\ length,\ 0)$$

simply moves the spot (or pen) from (x, y) to (x_1, y_1) where $x_1 = x + length \cdot \cos\ (angle)$ and $y_1 = y + length \cdot \sin\ (angle)$. The command

$$move\ (angle,\ length,\ 1)$$

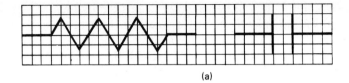

(a)

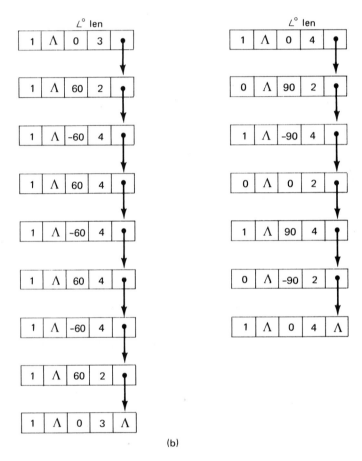

(b)

Figure 8-19 (*a*) Graphic representation of a resistor and a capacitor, and (*b*) their corresponding definition by means of a list of atomic strokes.

actually draws a line from (x, y) to (x₁, y₁). For pedagogical simplicity we will express angles in terms of degrees (although radians would be more common) and lengths in terms of arbitrary grid units.

Now suppose that we are creating drawings of electrical networks built up out of resistors and capacitors, as shown in Fig. 8-19(a). The graphical description of these objects in terms of basic strokes is shown in Fig. 8-19(b) as a list structure. Each cell has five fields, a TYPE field (which for atomic cells of type $= 0$, 1 also doubles as an off/on or up/down parameter), a COMPONENT field (which is unused in this figure), ANGLE and LENGTH fields, and NEXT cell field.

One kind of network that can be constructed from resistors and capacitors is shown in Fig. 8-20(a); it is called a pi network because of its general resemblence to the Greek letter π. Two or more pi networks can be combined in series to construct various kinds of filters as shown in Fig. 8-20(b). Figure 8-20(c) illustrates one representation of the graphical description of a two-stage filter using a list structure that is very similar to those already considered in this section. In this representation, name cells that reference a complete nonatomic object are of TYPE $= 2$. In the referencing name cells, the ANGLE field now denotes an angle of *rotation* while the LENGTH field becomes a factor of *magnification,* both of which are applied to the graphic description of the entire referenced object.

While the structure of Fig. 8-20(c) may be regarded as a description of the graphic properties of a filter, it is not in itself a graphic display of the object. A procedure, say DISPLAY, must be invoked that traverses the description and issues commands to draw each of the atomic vectors (or line segments) that comprise its graphic representation. A version of such a display process that is appropriate for the descriptive structure of Fig. 8-20(c) is given below.

```
procedure   display (component, alpha, magnify);
pointer     component;
real        alpha, magnify;
```

This procedure displays the "component" (defined by a simply linked list structure). The position of the object in the display field is determined by the current position (x, y) *of the spot, or pen. The figure is rotated through the angle "alpha" and magnified by the factor "magnify."*

```
begin
    pointer   cell;
    real      beta, size;
    field     angle, comp, length, next, type;
    cell ←component;
```

Traverse the list that defines this component.

```
    while cell ≠ null do
        beta ←alpha +angle(cell);
```

```
        size ←magnify * length(cell);
    if type(cell) = 2
        then  Name cell, display referenced component.
              call display (comp(cell), beta, size);
        else  Atomic cell, move spot or pen.
              call move (beta, size, type(cell));
        cell ←next(cell);
    exit;
    end
```

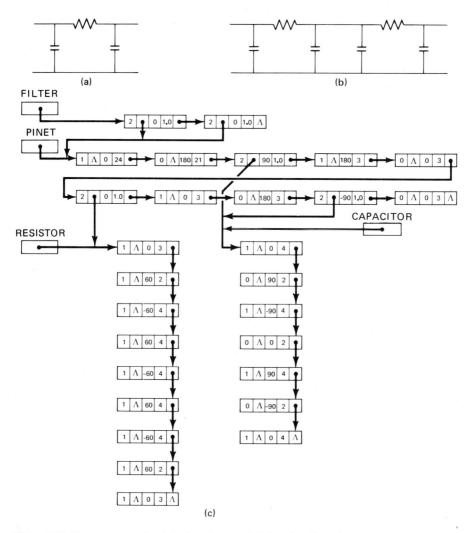

(c)

Figure 8-20 The representation (c) of a pi network (a) and a filter (b) in terms of component resistors and capacitors.

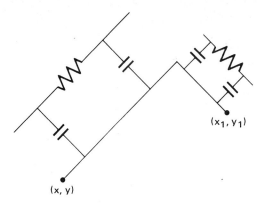

(x₁, y₁)

(x, y)

Figure 8-21 Two pi networks combined to create an "ill-formed" network.

It is clear that this procedure is virtually identical to the procedure PRINTLIST of the preceding section, save only that (1) the values assigned to atomic cells are drawn instead of printed, and (2) recursive calls to the procedure itself are used to traverse sublists rather than an explicit stack. Convince yourself that the sequence

call setxy (x, y);
call display (filter, 0.0, 1.0);

will generate Fig. 8-20(*b*), where the procedure SETXY initially positions the spot, or pen, at some desired position (x, y). Similarly, the sequence

call setxy (x, y);
call display (pinet, 45.0, 1.0);
call display (pinet, −45.0, 0.5);

will generate Fig. 8-21 and exit with the spot at (x_1, y_1).

We have tacitly assumed that the procedure MOVE issues an instruction to the display hardware to move the display spot LENGTH units in the direction ANGLE. A single command of this form is sufficient if the generated display is a "permanent" one, as on a pen-and-ink plotter or storage tube display. But many display devices employ a cathode-ray tube whose image quickly fades. The entire image must be *refreshed,* or redisplayed, on the order of every 30 milliseconds.† One solution in this case might be to call the procedure DISPLAY repeatedly. But such an approach has two significant drawbacks. First, execution of recursive procedure calls involves considerable computational overhead. Even if an explicit stack is used, the overhead of stack manipulation is nonnegligible. Also, a rotation and magnification must be computed for

---

†This figure varies widely according to the persistence of the particular phosphor used in the display-tube face. Thirty milliseconds denotes a refresh rate necessary to maintain an image without objectional "flicker" using a phosphor with "medium" persistence.

each cell in the structure. Thus the requirement that the entire description structure be traversed within the refresh cycle time severely limits the complexity of the figure that can be displayed—especially if the computer is also expected to interactively manipulate and modify the display. Second, and more important, the computer in which the descriptive structure resides must be dedicated, a luxury that not many of us can afford.†

The most common solution to the refresh problem is to associate with the display hardware a small amount of memory and a small processor with a limited instruction set, and to let this relatively inexpensive processor handle refreshing of the display. For the sake of this discussion let us assume a processor with the following instruction set.

Op† code	Other parameters	Meaning
0	A, L	Move spot L units at angle A from current (x, y) position.‡
1	A, L	Draw vector of length L at angle A.‡
2	address	Push jump to "address"
3	X, Y	Set spot at position (x, y)
4	address	Unconditional jump to "address"
7	—	Return to location following stacked push jump

†Clearly, the operation codes have been chosen to conform to the "types" of cells in the descriptive structure. Note that there are no arithmetic operators or conditional test operators.

‡Often the parameters of these instructions will be absolute X, Y values or X, Y increments. We retain the ANGLE, LENGTH parameters solely for pedagogical consistency. In practice they can be easily converted.

The procedure DISPLAY should now generate the structure shown in Fig. 8-22, or, if you prefer, *compile* the *program* shown in the figure. The display processor will keep the display refreshed by repeatedly executing this infinitely looping program.

If we regard the structure of Fig. 8-22 simply as a data structure, forgetting for the moment its nature as a program instruction sequence, it should become apparent that it is really a ring structure. The ordinary transfer of control to the next sequential instruction corresponds to the NEXT link of the list representation. The push-jump instruction corresponds to a name cell that refers to a new list (instruction sequence) while the return instruction functions as a header cell following the list which circularly points back to the referencing push-jump cell.

---

† Many of the early graphic data structures were designed for the large TX-2 computer at Lincoln Labs running in a dedicated environment.

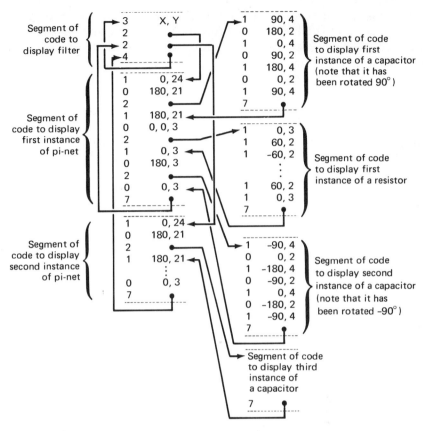

Figure 8-22 A display file which is repeatedly executed by the display processor to generate Fig. 8-20(*b*).

Our development of the DISPLAY procedure has been chosen so as to emphasize the fact that in most interactive display implementations there are actually two distinct data structures: a *display file* (as shown in Fig. 8-22) that resides in the storage of the display processor, and a *graphic data structure* [as shown in Fig. 8-20(*c*)] that is associated with a general-purpose processor. It is a common mistake to blur this distinction and refer to any structure which contains display information as a *display structure*. One may regard the DISPLAY procedure either as a kind of compiler or, as we prefer, a process that converts a graphic description that is compactly represented in terms of basic patterns into an expanded ring structure in which each *instance* of a pattern has a separate representation.

A dual representation of objects with graphical, or spatial, properties has several advantages. It is reasonable to assume that those objects which are represented in the data structure might have assigned properties other than just graphic properties. In our case we would expect the objects of the network to have electrical properties, such as resistance, impedance, etc., whose assigned values would be associated with the representing cells. One may invoke processes that operate on this representation—say, to calculate the resistance of the entire network or cost of building the network—which completely ignore its graphic properties. One can afford to assign many properties to these objects because they are defined but once as a *pattern*. Instances of the object are represented by a single referencing name cell to which only transformation values associated with that instance need be assigned.

Conversely, in the display file the structure has been stripped of all but its graphic display properties, so its cells are small. All the transformations associated with the display of any instance have been calculated and explicitly represented, so no arithmetic computation is needed.† Consequently, the display file can be rapidly traversed (or executed). Of course, the repeated representation of every instance (so that the structure is effectively a tree) wastes storage. This is the reason why we eschewed such representations in earlier applications. But in graphic display the constraint on the size and complexity of the image that can be displayed is seldom governed by the amount of storage available at the display processor. Rather it is constrained by the amount that can be traversed within the refresh cycle. This representational design minimizes the effect of that constraint.

The use of a display structure that is separate from the data structure that defines and generates it also introduces a number of problems. We can only sketch the nature of these problems. Much of the literature in this field describes specific solutions in terms of particular representational structures. The interested reader may turn to this literature for details. (See Williams, 1971, for a good survey and entry point.)

Since the system is interactive, we must expect to dynamically change both data structures. If the definition of a component in the graphic data structure is altered (say by a procedure REDEFINE(COMPONENT, LIST) which replaces the current description of the component with the indicated list), then every instance of its occurrence in the display file must be similarly changed. Conversely, if in an interactive operation a change is indicated by a light-pen interrupt associated with a portion of the graphic image, then that change must be reflected back in the defining list structure. One of the keys to this kind of interactive capability is the configuration of the display file. By using the push-jump instruction and effectively giving it a ring structure, those portions of code that display a single object instance are separated into isolated segments. It is properly called a *structured,* or *segmented,* display file. Entire segments (corresponding to component instances) can be altered, deleted, or added without recompiling

---

†These transformations would also include *clipping* those images that only partially lie within the display bounds of the viewing surface and totally eliminating all object instances that lie outside these display bounds. (The latter may significantly reduce the number of cells that must be traversed.) In more sophisticated displays, perspective transformation and "hidden line" elimination may be performed (Sutherland, 1974).

(displaying) the entire image.† This is the reason for having DISPLAY create such a hierarchical structure rather than a more simple linear structure (or linear sequence of instructions), as has been generated by all of our preceding traversal procedures.

But creation of a segmented display file is only part of the solution. In addition, various portions of both files must be carefully linked to one another. The list definitions of each component (pattern for the component) must be linked to each instance (name cell) of its use in the graphic data structure, and these in turn must be linked to their corresponding segments in the display file. In this way, after changing the definition of the component all instances of the component in the displayed image can be located and simultaneously modified. Conversely, each segment of the display file must be back-linked to the name cell of the data structure which generated it.

The reader will find it a challenging, but nevertheless reasonable, exercise to work out the details by which the various pieces of these two structures can be linked to one another. This exercise is essential if one is to develop an effective structure for interactive graphics applications, but it is also of more general interest. We are entering a period when data structures are increasingly being shared by separate computing processors which are linked in a distributed network. More accurately, each computer is operating on its own private, and often partial, representation of a common abstract data structure. The problems of establishing and maintaining a correspondence between these distinct representations are similar to those faced in interactive graphics, and many useful techniques may be found in this area. For this reason alone it is an application that is worth studying in detail, even if one ignores its purely graphic aspects.

EXERCISES FOR SECTION 8-3

8-18 It is not difficult to modify the traversal procedure PRINTLIST of Sec. 8-2 to produce a hierarchical listing of the component structure as given in Fig. 8-18. Instead of a linear listing of elements, each new element is printed on a new line; instead of parentheses to delimit the nesting of sublists, indention from the left margin is used. While coding such a procedure is primarily an exercise in the clear display of information and a demonstration of output formatting prowess, it is nevertheless interesting and worthwhile.

8-19 Verify that the preceding procedure, if a stack-controlled traversal is employed, would work equally well with the representations of Figs. 8-14, 8-16, and 8-17.

8-20 It can be shown that the points of a tree can be labeled or identified by a string of digits whose initial segments effectively *describe the path to it from the principal point*. Notice that in the component breakdown given in this section, the numbers 1.1.3, etc., are precisely this kind of tree iden-

---

†If segments are to be added and deleted from the display file, then the display processor will have to be provided with a small, dynamic, storage-management system. Normally an adaptation of one of those methods considered in Sec. 10-2 is employed.

tifier. (Recall also Exercise 5-23.) A portion of the tree they describe is shown in the accompanying figure.

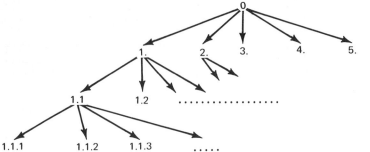

Ex. 8-20

(*a*) Complete this tree.

(*b*) Write a modified procedure, similar to PRINTLIST, which will traverse the list structure and produce a component parts breakdown with tree identifiers as shown in this section.

8-21 The breakdown of a bicycle's constituent components given in this section is admittedly abbreviated. If you are a cyclist you may wish to creat a more realistic decomposition. How do you decide which parts are atomic? How many distinct components have you identified? How much computer storage would be required to represent your decomposition?

*8-22 Implement a procedure that will process orders for the Acme Bicycle Co. and selectively modify an inventory file to produce output similar to Fig. 8-18. Can it be modified to maintain a minimum inventory level on those parts which must be ordered from outside suppliers? Can it anticipate future demand?

*8-23 The list structure devised for the Acme Co. represents the constituent element relation associated with bicycle manufacture. As in the preceding exercise, it can be used to supervise a large segment of their inventory control process, and a smaller segment of the job scheduling process. But the actual assembly process assumes an additional precedence relation in which certain components must be assembled before others. Is the given structure sufficient to represent the precedence relation as well? If not, what additional relational structure must be added?

8-24 It was stated in this section that only the duplication of those items that are homomorphically identified as subassemblies can be avoided, that duplicated atomic elements must still have separate representations. All the illustrated representations had this property, but it is not strictly necessary. If the *last* element of two component sublists is atomic, then that cell may be shared by both, as shown in the accompanying figure. In fact, this may be extended to read "if the terminal segments of two component lists are identical, then they may share a common representation." Why? In particular, why must they be terminal segments? Since the order of enumerating components is really irrelevant, we have the immediate question: How can one rearrange the order of elements in sublists so as to optimize common representation?

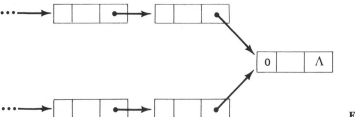

Ex. 8-24

*8-25 The tag field which indicates whether a cell is atomic in the list structures of Figs. 8-16 and 8-17 is totally unnecessary. Why?

*8-26 The simply linked list structure representing the decomposition of bicycles into their constituent assemblies was designed so that a traversal procedure, such as PRINTLIST, can easily access and enumerate the component parts of any given assembly. (In effect, it displays $\bar{R}(y)$, in the expanded form of a tree, where y denotes the assembly.) But to enumerate all the assemblies to which a given component part belongs (i.e., $L(y)$ or the inverse relation) requires an exhaustive search of the entire structure which is not trivial.

(*a*) Write a procedure CONTAINED (ITEMNO, LIST) that creates a list (sequential or linked) giving the item-number identifiers of every item immediately *containing* the specified item, or $L(y)$. How would the procedure be modified to find *all* components $\bar{L}(y)$ to which the item belonged, not just those immediately containing it? (Every element in the structure must be examined at least once to see if it contains the item, but you will want to avoid repeated examination of an element or duplication in the list. Assume, if you wish, an available tag field in every cell, but remember that all tags must be erased on exit.)

(*b*) Is this comparable to the path finding procedures of Chap. 6? In what ways?

8-27 Design a back-linked data structure that will explicitly represent the "contained in" relation, and thereby simplify the implementation of the procedure CONTAINED described above.

8-28 Instead of a single containment relation $\subseteq$ associated with the n different bicycles in the Acme product line, we may consider n different containment relations $\subseteq_i$, each denoting the component structure of a different bicycle. But relations are themselves merely sets (of ordered pairs) so we may form the intersection or union of relations. Now if item x is a component of assembly y in bicycle model i, then $(x, y) \in \subseteq_i$. If, further, it is a component in bicycle model j, then we also have $(x, y) \in \subseteq_j$, or more precisely, $(x, y) \in \subseteq_i \cap \subseteq_j$. Hence from the initial set of n distinct relations $\{\subseteq_i\}$ we may wish to consider the power set of all 2^n possible unions and intersection of these original relations.

(*a*) Design a data structure that will represent such an extended version of the containment relation. (*Hint:* In Fig. 8-15 an assignment function defined on the edges indicates the number of items involved in the containment relation. A second assignment value, such as $E_2 \cap E_4 \cap E_5$ to denote those relations of which this edge is a member, can also be employed and represented.)

(*b*) In this case is it necessary to consider all possible unions of the base relations, or will only intersections suffice?

8-29 A natural way of interpreting the distinction between name cells and atomic cells in a list representation is to regard the sublist referenced by a name cell as the *definition* of that object denoted by the cell. There may be several instances of the object in the structure, all of which have the same definition (whose representing name cells reference the same sublist). An element is atomic if "it is its own definition." This interpretation is of value in the graphic display application. Another example might be the distinction between variable and literal identifiers. If a string of characters is a variable identifier, then it references a value whose definition is provided by some other mechanism (usually an assignment statement); but if it is a literal identifier, then the characters of the string itself define the value that it references. There are a number of objections to viewing Fig. 8-16 or 8-17 within this "interpretation." What are they? How might the two file structures of Fig. 8-17 be reorganized so that the sequential file becomes a "file of atomic definitions" with cells in the relational structure constituting only instances of their use. (Note: the preceding question is really a philosophical question, and it is doubtful if a definitive answer can be given. Nevertheless it is an important one in computer science.)

8-30 Shown in the accompanying figure is a network known as a *Wheatstone bridge*. Draw its representing data structure.

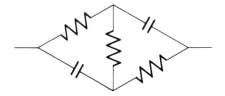

Ex. 8-30

* 8-31 Let a component in a graphic data structure be defined by a list of atomic strokes. When displayed, the spot or pen will start at some position (x, y) and end at some new position (x', y'). Thus the entire component may be regarded as a single stroke with ANGLE = arctan (y' − y/x' − x) and LENGTH = $((y' − y)^2 + (x' − x)^2)^{1/2}$. These overall graphic properties may be assigned to a header cell associated with the defining list. (Header cells have been conspicuously absent in our development.) Show the header cells that would be appropriate for the (*a*) resistor, (*b*) capacitor, (*c*) pi network, and (*d*) filter components of Figs. 8-19 and 8-20. Inclusion of such header cells in the representation will greatly simplify the solution of the following exercises.

8-32 Write a procedure REPLACE (cell, component) that replaces the component referenced by the specified name cell in a list structure with the new component. Note that (*a*) this procedure operates on only the defining data structure, not the display file, and (*b*) only one pointer need be changed, but (*c*) the new component may have to be rotated, expanded, or shrunk so as to fit in the "hole" left by the replaced component.

8-33 One would expect a graphic description, hence a representing list structure, to be built up by incrementally adding pieces until the entire component is complete.

   (*a*) Write a procedure APPEND (component1, component2, angle, length) that adds component$_2$ to the description of component$_1$.

   (*b*) Give the sequence of calls that would generate the structures of (1) the pi network, and (2) the Wheatstone bridge of Exercise 8-30.

   (*c*) Would it be helpful to have a component called LINE that consists of a single horizontal vector of unit length?

8-34 Good experience can be gained in many aspects of graphic display (especially the building and traversing of data structures) if one simplifies the output problems by using a static pen plotter.

   (*a*) Code the procedure DISPLAY to operate using your local plotter.

   (*b*) Devise a simple command language which when read from some input file will build a graphic data structure by issuing calls to APPEND and draw figures by invoking DISPLAY. (This is harder than it appears on the surface, and will emphasize many important details.)

   (*c*) Test this package by creating and displaying the figures of this section.

8-35 Use the routines of the preceding exercise to define components and figures in some other class of images, say architectural floor plans composed of walls, doors, windows, etc. Can you write a process that will use the data structure to calculate the square footage of a constructed room?

8-36 A graphic image consists of individual pieces, or components, which must fit together in a spatial sense. If each component has only two well-defined endpoints, or terminals, at which it can be attached to other components (for example, the resistor, capacitor, and Wheatstone bridge components), then there is little trouble in joining them in a coherent fashion. But if the spatial join must occur at several points, then it is easy to create *ill-formed* figures. Figure 8-21 is deliberately ill-formed to illustrate this kind of problem. Specification of these additional spatial constraints and their implementation constitutes a lovely puzzle for the ambitious reader.

8-37 The data structure given in this section is adequate for simple, planar, linelike drawings, such as electrical circuits, but suppose instead one were displaying scenes based on a model in three dimensions. Then we would need to represent an extra coordinate in each component of the graphic data structure (but not in the display file) and make provision for perspective and hidden lines in the display of these components. What additional fields would be provided in the (1) atomic cells, (2) name cells, and (3) header cells of the structure?

8-4 THE REPRESENTATION OF CONDENSATION GRAPHS

Let G = (P, E) be any graph (it may be the abstract model of any relational structure). Construct a new graph G* = (P*, E*) as follows: Let the points h_i of P* be the strongly connected components H_i of G. [Recall that a subgraph H is strongly connected if for any points x, y ∈ H, there exist paths $\rho_H(x, y)$ and $\rho_H(y,$

x). Since, if $x = y$ we have $\rho\,(x,\,y)$ by definition, every singleton point is a strongly connected subgraph. It is a component only if it is a maximal such subgraph.] Let $(h_i,\,h_j) \in E^*$ if and only if there exist points $x_i \in H_i$ and $y_j \in H_j$ such that $(x_i,\,y_j) \in E$. The graph G^* so constructed from G is called its *condensation graph*.

It should be evident that this construction, in fact, defines a homomorphism $\varphi\colon G \rightarrow G^*$, and that the points h_i of G^* abstractly "name" the strongly connected components H_i of G that they denote. We can therefore give a nonconstructive definition in terms of a homomorphism $\varphi\colon G \rightarrow G^*$. We will call G^* the *condensation graph* of G, if the preimage partition $\mathscr{P}_\varphi$ of P induced by φ is a partition of G into its strongly connected components. Figure 8-23 illustrates two typical graphs, together with their corresponding condensation graphs.

Since a correspondence has been established between homomorphism concepts and list structures, it would appear that we might employ some of the techniques of representing list structures developed in the preceding section in the construction of representations of arbitrary graphs G. Further, it is apparent that G_1^* and G_2^* (of Fig. 8-23) are simpler graphs: they have fewer points and they must be acyclic (Exercise 8-42). It seems reasonable to assume that one can devise cleaner computer representations of the condensation graph G^* than is possible with the original relational structure E. Since each of the points y_i^* in G^* denotes a subgraph in G, we can use name cells c_i in the representation

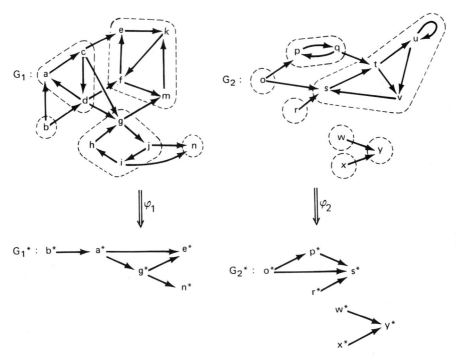

Figure 8-23 Two graphs G_1 and G_2, together with their condensation graphs G_1^* and G_2^*.

of G* to represent these points, and then let each name cell c_i point to a representation of the subgraph H_i in G which is its preimage under φ.

Figure 8-24 schematically shows such a representation of the graph G_1 of Fig. 8-23. With each point in G_1^* is associated its preimage subgraph in G_1. (The individual graphs G_1^*, H_1, H_2, H_3, H_4, and H_5 may be assumed to be represented by any of the techniques developed so far.)

Before we consider its computer representation in detail, we should first consider what may have been gained by such a homomorphic decomposition of the structure—and what may have been lost. Let us first assume that we are representing relations sequentially by means of adjacency matrices (as in Sec. 6-3). Since P_1 consists of 13 points, its straightforward representation by an adjacency matrix must involve 169 elements. There are, however, six smaller graphs in the decomposed representation of Fig. 8-24, consisting of 5, 1, 3, 4, 4, and 1 point each. To represent all of these by adjacency matrices requires $25 + 1 + 9 + 16 + 16 + 1 = 68$ elements. The storage requirements have been reduced by nearly $\frac{2}{3}$! The reduction in storage requirements will be nowhere as dramatic in the case of most linked representations; in fact, there may be no savings. Five additional points must be represented, but there are nine fewer edges in the decomposed structure. If edges are represented by distinct edge cells (as in Sec. 6-1), there are normally some slight savings; if edges are represented by field links, there are none.

Representational effectiveness cannot be measured in terms of storage efficiency alone. The issue of computational efficiency is of at least equal impor-

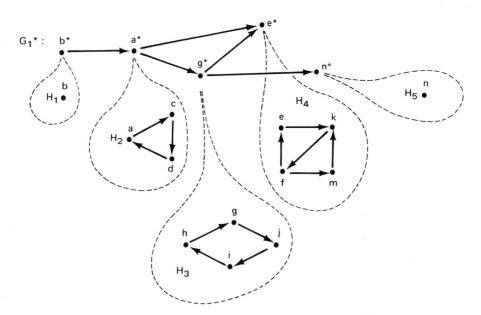

Figure 8-24 A homomorphic representation of the condensation graph G_1^*.

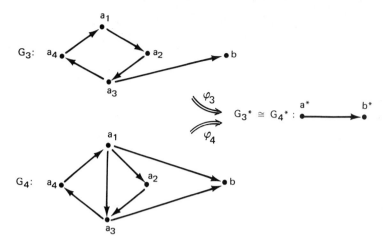

Figure 8-25 Two nonisomorphic graphs G_3 and G_4 with the same condensation graph.

tance. Suppose that the determination of path existence (accessibility or retrievability) is an important, and frequently used, procedure in the applications for which this data structure is designed. In Sec. 6-3 it was seen that path finding is a time-consuming process whose computational complexity is typically of at least order n^2, where $n = |P|$. But it is not hard to show the following:

Theorem 8-6 Let G^* be the condensation graph of G. ρ_G (x, z) if and only if ρ_G^* (x*, z*).

Consequently, to discover the existence of paths in G, only G^* need be searched, with a reduction of process complexity of $|P^*|/|P|$. If there are relatively few strongly connected components, as in our example, the resultant computational savings can be most significant.

Representation of a data structure G = (P,E) by its condensation graph G^* may result in more effective storage and path-finding procedures, but at a price. Although the theorem shows that the path relation ρ is preserved, the initial relation E on P is lost. Figure 8-25 illustrates two nonisomorphic graphs G_3 and G_4 with the same condensation graph G^*. If the relational information conveyed by E is crucial, then this method of representation is unacceptable.

Finally, Fig. 8-26 illustrates one possible linked computer representation S_R. In this case we have represented G^* after having first applied the Knuth transformation (as in Sec. 6-4). Each cell in this structure functions as do name cells of a list structure; it denotes a collection of atomic points of the representation. Each strongly connected subgraph H_i (the preimage of h_i^* under φ) is simply represented as a linked set of atomic points. No effort has been made in this case to represent the edge structure of these subgraphs, since it is known that a path exists from any member of the set to any other member. Associated with each of these atomic cells are two link fields; one indicates the next cell in

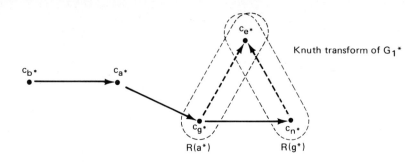

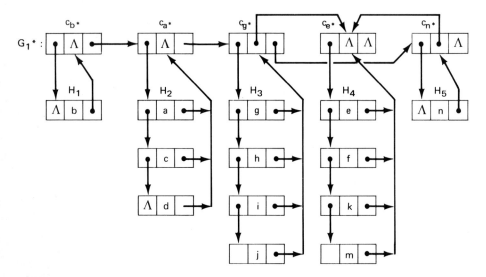

Figure 8-26 One computer representation S_R of the condensation graph G_1^* of Fig. 8-24, where G_1^* itself is represented using the Knuth transform and the subgraphs $H_i = \varphi^{-1}(x_i^*)$ are represented as linked lists.

the set, while the other points to its corresponding name cell in G^* (to its image under φ). The reader can conjure up many variations of this particular representation S_R, and is encouraged to do so.

EXERCISES FOR SECTION 8-4

*8-38 Draw the condensation graphs of the two graphs in the accompanying figure. How would you represent G_2^*?

8-39 Give an alternative definition that defines the condensation graph in terms of the path relation without explicit reference to the preimage partition:

    (a) Show that the two definitions are equivalent;

    (b) Which is easier to use in proving the assertions of the following exercises?

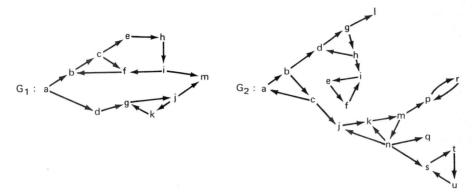

Ex. 8-38

8-40 We have been using the expression "*the* condensation graph of G." In fact, the condensation graph of any graph G is unique, but this assertion should be carefully stated in the form of a theorem and then proven. Do so. (*Hint:* You will have to show that two homomorphic images are the same, that is, isomorphic.)

8-41 Prove Theorem 8-6.

8-42 Formally state the following two assertions as theorems, then prove them.
   (*a*) The condensation graph of any graph must be acyclic.
   (*b*) Only acyclic graphs are their own condensation graphs.

8-43 Redesign the representation of Fig. 8-24 so that cells in the representation of G* may be either atomic cells denoting singleton points in G or name cells denoting nontrivial subgraphs of G.

8-44 Any partition of a point set P into equivalence classes with known properties—e.g., into connected components—can be exploited in the representation of the relation. Devise representations of the structure in the accompanying figure using:
   (*a*) adjacency matrices, and
   (*b*) linked data structures.

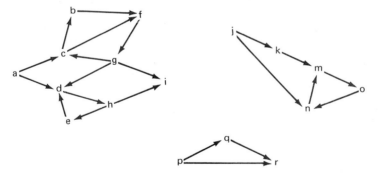

Ex. 8-44

8-5   GRAPH STRUCTURES

This chapter was begun with a definition and discussion of homomorphism concepts. It was followed by an assertion that the list concept in which an entire list of elements may be replaced by a single element referencing it is really nothing more than the computer representation of a homomorphism operator. But in Sec. 8-3, which exemplified a number of practical list structures, the term *homomorphism* was not even mentioned. The reader is likely to have emerged with the feeling that, in fact, the development of list structures is little more than the application of some reasonably straightforward rules of common sense. In part, this would be correct. In practice, many data structures are constructed on this basis. But in this section we hope to show that an awareness of formal generalized homomorphism properties can enable us to extend the list concept to other forms of data structure, and to analyze their behavior.

If the representation of linearly ordered lists as list structures, in which an entire sublist may be regarded as a single element, is so useful, it seems natural to generalize this approach to the representation of more general kinds of graphs or relations. Thus one would be led to define a *graph structure* as a relation on a set of elements, each of which may be either a point or itself a directed graph. In effect, given some original finite graph G, we would be identifying arbitrary subgraphs H of G and treating them as single subgraph elements in the graph structure G'. The condensation graphs of the preceding section illustrate just such a representation. The points of G' denote, or represent, subgraphs of G (its strongly connected components).

Unfortunately this appealing idea simply doesn't work in general. Given a sublist in a list structure, we know how to "reinsert" it into its higher-level list, so that by a simple traversal of the list structure we can reconstruct the original list of atomic points. Thus the homomorphic identification of certain sublists did not result in loss of any relational information that was present in the original simple list. Given a condensation graph, such as G* in Fig. 8-26, we cannot in general reconstruct all the edges that were present in the original relation E; but we can recapture the path relation ρ. Given any pair of points x, z $\in$ G, we know a path ρ (x, z) exists if and only if a path ρ' (x', z') exists in G'. Thus in this case the homomorphism φ abstracted away some of the detailed edge structure but preserved the more global path structure. But even though all homomorphisms are *path-preserving* (Theorem 8-3), they need not preserve the path structure. Consider, for example, Fig. 8-27, in which a homomorphic image G$'_1$ (from Fig. 8-1) is shown together with the preimage subgraph associated with each point. It is impossible to infer from G$'_1$ alone that (1) both the edges (a$_1$, b) and (a$_2$, b) exist in G, although we know at least one must, or (2) there is no path from b to d$_2$ in G.† We have lost the very valuable property of reconstructibility that was present in list structures.

However, by suitably restricting the kinds of graph G to be considered, and by restricting the kinds of subgraph H to be homomorphically identified as subgraph elements (in the condensation graph they were restricted to be

---

†In classical mathematical terminology, homomorphisms φ are single-valued maps—that is, given any graph G and any partition of G defining the homomorphism, the image G' under φ is unique. But inverse φ^{-1} mapping need not be single-valued. There may be a large set of graphs G$_i$ with the same partition Σ such that $\varphi_\Sigma : G_i \to G'$.

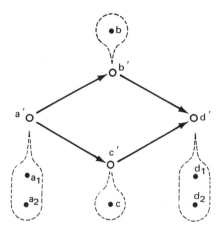

Figure 8-27 A homomorphic image of the graph of Fig. 8-1, together with the preimage subgraphs which map onto each point.

strongly connected components), a workable and useful concept of *graph structure* can be developed that is directly analogous to that of a list structure.

We will begin to develop this concept by first examining a concrete example. Consider the graph G on 10 points shown in Fig. 8-28. Five simple homomorphic contractions $\varphi_{[c,d]}$, $\varphi_{[b,c',f]}$, $\varphi_{[h,i]}$, $\varphi_{[b'',e,g,h'']}$, and $\varphi_{[a,b^{iv},j]}$ have been defined that reduce G down to a single point. Recall that a virtue of decomposing a homomorphism into simple homomorphisms is the notational convenience by which the subscript H in φ_H completely characterizes the mapping. This is clearly illustrated in the example. In Fig. 8-29 this contraction process has been redrawn in the form of a treelike assemblage in which the preimage of any element under the contractive process is denoted by a subgraph, or point, enclosed within dashed lines. Such a structure we will call a *graph structure* representing G, and denoted by $\mathscr{S}_G$. It is important that the reader examine both figures and convince himself that $\mathscr{S}_G$ really does, in some sense, correspond to G and the contractions defined on it. (We will establish this correspondence with more rigor, but for now the intuitive understanding is important.) Note that (1) end points of this tree are atomic points of G, and interior points are subgraphs, (2) edges in the tree denote images under one of the homomorphic maps, and (3) this figure is quite similar to Fig. 8-3.

Having derived such a treelike representation, the reader may well ask, "What good is it?" In Sec. 6-3 we considered algorithms to determine the existence of paths between specified points of a network. It was not in general an easy computational task. Given a graph structure representation, the problem of path finding is greatly simplified. One merely begins at those end points in the tree which correspond to the points in question, then work back up through the tree to that interior point corresponding to the smallest subgraph containing both. There is a path in G if and only if there is a path between the corresponding elements of this subgraph. For example, we see that there is no path from c to d because there is no path in the common subgraph covering them. There is a path from b to j because there is a path in that subgraph element

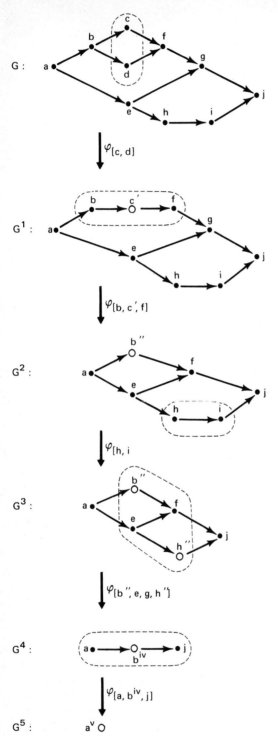

Figure 8-28 Reduction of the graph G by a sequence of simple homomorphisms.

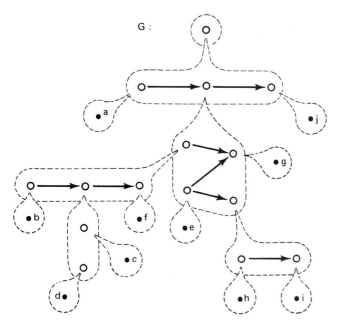

Figure 8-29 A treelike graph structure $\mathscr{S}_G$, whose elements (enclosed by dashed lines) are themselves graphs on one or more points.

covering them. (For a few additional random pairs of points, try to determine the existence of a path from the graph structure of Fig. 8-29 alone, and then verify your conclusions by refering to G in Fig. 8-28.)

Three fundamental questions remain to be answered. We must show that graph structures so constructed in fact preserve the path structure as they appear to. The subgraphs H_i, which serve as the kernels of the simple homomorphisms φ_i, were evidently chosen with care. We must characterize those subgraphs H that can be used in the construction of contractions with the desired path-structure-preserving property. And finally we must provide an effective procedure to construct a computer representation of the graph structure, given only the initial relation or graph G.

We first observe that for none of these kernel subgraphs H is there a path $\rho(x, z)$ between points of H which traverses points "outside" the subgraph. This is somewhat analogous to straight line paths that must lie inside convex geometrical figures. Consequently we make the suggestive definition that a subgraph H of G be called *convex* if any path $\rho_G(x, z)$, where $x, z \in H$, is completely contained within H. That is, if $y_i \in \rho_G(x, z)$, then $y_i \in H$. The set of convex subgraphs of a graph has many nice mathematical properties. The reader is encouraged to discover some of these by enumerating *all* the convex subgraphs of a small graph of four or five points, and then partially ordering this set by inclusion. It is particularly worth noting that if E is a linear relation—that is, G is a string or a list—then its set of convex subgraphs is precisely its set of

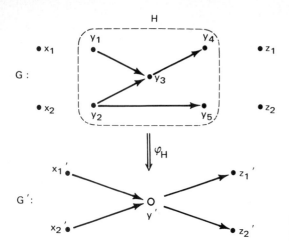

Figure 8-30 G is a partially completed preimage of G' under φ_H.

substrings or sublists. It is now not hard to show the following:

Theorem 8-7 H is the kernel of a simple homomorphism φ_H:G $\rightarrow$ G' whose image G' is acyclic if and only if H is convex.

Now consider the graph G' in Fig. 8-30 which is the image of some graph G under a simple contraction φ_H. Assuming that we know the kernel subgraph $H = \varphi^{-1}(y')$, we can begin to reconstruct its preimage G. At issue is: What edges exist between the various subgraphs that constitute the preimage partition of G? Since φ is a homomorphism we know by its definition that there must exist at least one edge of the form $(x_1, y_k) \in E$, where $y_k \in H$. If we further assume that φ preserves the path structure, we know that since y_1 is a minimal element of H, the edge (x_1, y_1) *must* belong to E. Otherwise we would have, in contradiction to the hypothesis that φ preserves the path structure, $\rho_{G'}(\varphi(x_1), \varphi(y_1)) = \rho(x_1', y')$ but not $\rho_G(x_1, y_1)$. The same argument shows that the edges (x_1, y_2), (x_2, y_1), and (x_2, y_2) must also belong to E. A similar proof involving the maximal elements of H, y_4, and y_5 shows that (y_4, z_1), (y_4, z_2), (y_5, z_1), and $(y_5, z_2) \in E$. Consequently the preimage G of G' under φ_H must contain Fig. 8-31 as a partial subgraph. It is possible that other edges, such as (x_1, y_4), may be present in G, but their presence or absence in no way affects the path structure. If in addition the preimage is known to be basic, then it is intuitively evident that the graph G of Fig. 8-31 is the *unique* possible preimage of G' under a simple homomorphism φ_H.

This construction has provided an informal proof that φ_H preserves the path structure of G only if for all $x \in L(H)$ and all $y \in min(H)$, $(x,y) \in E$, and similarly, for all $y \in max(H)$ and all $z \in R(H)$, $(y, z) \in E$. If one looks at the subgraphs [L(H);min(H)] and [max(H);R(H)], we note a striking regularity. A graph G = (P, E) is said to be *bipartite* if its point set P can be partitioned into

L(H)   R(H)

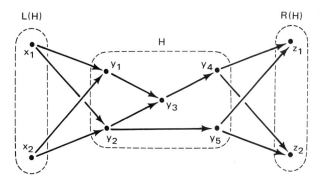

Figure 8-31 A preimage of G' (of Fig. 8-30) such that the homomorphism φ_H preserves the path structure.

two sets P_1 and P_2 with the property that for all edges $(x, y) \in E$, $x \in P_1$ and $y \in P_2$. It is further called *complete* if for *all* $x \in P_1$ and *all* $y \in P_2$, $(x, y) \in E$. The subgraphs [L(H);min(H)] and [max(H);R(H)] are both complete bipartite subgraphs, and we can rephrase our characterization of contractible kernels to read as follows:

Theorem 8-8 If G is basic, then the simple homomorphism $\varphi_H : G \to G'$, where G' is acyclic, preserves the path structure of G if and only if
  (*a*) H is convex, and
  (*b*) the subgraphs [L(H);min(H)] and [max(H);R(H)] are complete bipartite graphs.

For brevity we will call such kernel subgraphs m-M *subgraphs*.
     This result completely answers the first two of our fundamental questions concerning graph structures, *provided* we are willing to limit our attention to basic acyclic data structures. In any computer application, such as the representation of transitive implications in a semantic model, accessibility in a directory structure or task dependence in a PERT network, where it is only the path structure that is crucial, this is an eminently reasonable constraint since a nonbasic representation merely adds redundant information. But it in no way answers the problem of efficiently constructing the graph structure $\mathscr{S}_G$, given the original relation G = (P, E). It is patently impractical to examine all possible subgraphs H ⊆ G to determine whether they are m-M subgraphs.
     While it is unreasonable to examine all subgraphs H of a given graph G, it might be practical to examine all the subgraphs on only two points to see if they are m-M subgraphs. In an acyclic graph there are only two distinct subgraphs on two points; either $E_H = \emptyset$ or E_H consists of a single edge (x, y). Since in the first case the edge set is trivial, let us call it a τ subgraph, and since the latter edge relation is linear let us call it a λ subgraph. In fact, let us extend this terminology to any sized subgraph, and call one in which $E_H = \emptyset$, or E_H is linear, a τ or λ subgraph respectively. Similarly we can call a *contraction* (or simple

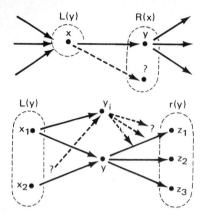

Figure 8-32 x and y_i are possible points that might be combined with the point y to form an m-M λ or τ subgraph.

homomorphism whose image is acyclic) with kernel H—that is, a τ subgraph—a τ contraction and denote it by τ_H. Analogously we have λ contractions λ_H.

By considering only τ and λ contractions, both the search for m-M subgraphs to serve as kernels and the representation of the contracting homomorphism themselves are considerably simplified. For each point y in the graph G it is sufficient merely to look at its set of left neighbors L(y). If L(y) is a singleton point $\{x\}$, then the subgraph H = [x, y] can be the kernel of a λ contraction if and only if R(x) is the singleton $\{y\}$. On the other hand, y may be an element in a τ subgraph H = [y, y_j]. If so, the possible candidates for y_j (assuming G is connected) are those points $y_j \in R(x_i)$ where $x_i \in L(y)$. [y, y_j] will be a τ-subgraph if and only if L(y) = L(y_j) and R(y) = R(y_j). Figure 8-32 illustrates these two possible cases. Consequently, if G is connected (as normally the case), even though every point y $\in$ P must be examined, the search is still local in that only points which are in some sense "near" y in the relation need be considered as possible two-point kernels for contraction. (If G is not connected, a global search must be conducted for isolated points.) The following procedure REDUCE illustrates such a search procedure that finds two-point m-M kernels and then represents the corresponding τ or λ contractions.

The representation of τ or λ contractions that must be generated by REDUCE is simplified because only the *set* of points constituting the kernel H of the contraction need be represented, say as a simple list, together with a tag indicating whether they constitute a τ or a λ subgraph. Figure 8-33 shows one such representation. The edges of the subgraph can be ignored since their presence, or absence, is indicated by the tag.

procedure reduce (g);
pointer g;

This procedure applies successive contractions to the graph G to form a graph struc-

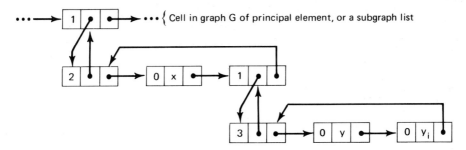

Figure 8-33 The representation of a two-point λ subgraph by a circular list whose header has tag 2. One of its elements is a two-point τ subgraph whose header cell has tag 3.

ture $\mathscr{S}_G$ corresponding to G. *On exit* g *points to the image graph which constitutes the principal point of the tree structure.*

begin
    pointer x, y, y1, z;
    set   h,ptset;
search:
    ptset ←points (g);
    for all y **in** ptset **do**
        begin set left, right;

        Try to find a contractible subgraph containing y.

        left ←lnbhr (y);
        right ←rnbhr (y);
        if left $\neq \emptyset$
            then   L(y) *is nonempty. If* L(y) = {x} *then it*
                    may be part of a λ *subgraph.*
               if size(left) = 1 **then**
                   x ←nxtelm(left);
                   if rnbhr(x) = 1 **then**
                       H = {x, y} *is an* m-M *subgraph.*
                       h ←setof (x, y);
                       call contract (g, h, λ);
                       go to search;

        y *may be part of a* τ *subgraph. Look for a point* y_1 *such that* L(y) = L(y_1) *and* R(y) = R(y_1).

        for all x **in** left **do**
            begin set possible;

            Consider all possible elements in R(x) *as possible candidates for* y_1.

            possible ← rnbhr (x);
            for all y1 **in** possible, y1 $\neq$ y, **do**
                if lnbhr (yl) = left **and** rnbhr (yl) = right

```
                        then   H={y, y1} is a τ subgraph.
                              h ←setof(y, y1);
                              call contract (g, h, τ);
                              go to search;
                  end
        else   L(y) is empty, so y is a minimal point.
              if right ≠ ∅
                  then   y is not an isolated point. Check only for inclusion in a τ
                        subgraph.
                        for all z in right do
                              begin set possible;
                              possible ←lnbhr(z);
                              for all yl in possible, yl ≠ y, do
                                  if lnbhr (y1)=∅ and rnbhr (y1)=right
                                      then   H = {y,yl} is a τ subgraph.
                                            h ←setof(y, yl);
                                            call contract (g, h, τ);
                                            go to search;
                              end;
                  else   y is an isolated point. If there are any others, they form a
                        τ subgraph.
                        for all x in ptset, x ≠ y, do
                              if lnbhr (x)=rnbhr(x)=∅ then
                                  h ←setof(x, y);
                                  call contract (g, h, τ);
                                  go to search;
    end;
    exit;
    end
```

The implementation of the set-valued functions LNBHR, RNBHR, SETOF, and POINTS depends on the method chosen to represent the graph G, and to represent sets of elements. Any of the techniques suggested in Chap. 6 may be used, but the dynamic nature of the reduction process makes a linked representation desirable. In this case the subprocess CONTRACT need only link the cells that had denoted x and y in G, as a set similar to Fig. 8-33, and replace them in the representation of G with a single name cell denoting their image point $\varphi(H)$.

The preceding process searches for, and contracts, only two-point m-M subgraphs. In consequence it may create an unnecessarily large graph structure, as shown in Fig. 8-34, to represent a λ(or τ) subgraph on more than two points. It is not hard to show the following:

Theorem 8-9 Any λ (or τ) contraction λ_H may be decomposed into a sequence of two-point λ (or τ) contractions so that $\lambda_H = \lambda_{H_1} \circ \lambda_{H_2} \circ \ldots \circ \lambda_{H_n}$.

This result ensures that the procedure REDUCE will in fact find and contract all

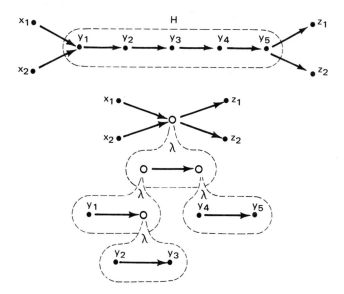

Figure 8-34 A redundant decomposition of a λ subgraph H.

possible λ and τ subgraphs. It also justifies the following procedure SIMPLIFY, which combines composed contractions of the same type into a single contraction.

procedure simplify (g);
pointer g;

This procedure simplifies a graph structure g by combining instances where a λ (or τ) subgraph is an element of a λ (or τ) subgraph. Note that every element of the graph structure $\mathscr{S}_G$ is examined by means of a preorder traversal; but that particular care must be taken since the representation is being changed in the midst of the traversal process.

begin
      pointer cell, header, last, nextcell, prev, stack1, stack2, x;
      field   f, next, tag;
      set   ptset;
      integer type;

      Form a set consisting of each of the elements of the graph g which is the principal point of the tree structure. Each element may serve as a name cell referencing a list structure "below" it.

      ptset ←points (g);
      for all x **in** ptset, tag (x) = 1 **do**

          Cell$_x$ of g denotes a subgraph element. Traverse its list structure combining similar subgraphs wherever possible.

```
            cell ←x;
            stack1 ←stack2 ←null;
traverse:
```

Begin traversing this subgraph list.

```
            header ←f(cell);
            type ←tag(header);
            prev ←header;
            cell ←next(header);
continuetraversal:
            while tag(cell) ≤ 1 do
                if tag(cell) = 1 then
```

This cell is a subgraph element. If it is of the same type as the current list, insert its list into the current one and continue; otherwise begin traversing it.

```
                    header ←f(cell);
                    if tag(header) = type
                        then   Same type. Insert this sublist into the current list.
                            next(prev) ←last ←next(header);
                            Find the last cell of this list.
                            nextcell ←next(last);
                            while tag(nextcell) ≥ 1 do
                                last ←nextcell;
                                nextcell ←next(last);
                            next(last) ←next(cell);
                            call takeit(cell, celsiz);
                            cell ←next(prev);
                        else   Different type. Stack type and
                            location in current list and
                            begin traversing this sublist.
                            call pushdown (stack1,prev);
                            call pushdown (stack2,type);
                            go to traverse;
```

This sublist has been traversed and all its sublists either traversed or combined with it. Back up to the higher level sublist (if any) and continue its traversal.

```
            if stack1 ≠ null then
                prev poptop(stack1);
                cell ← next(prev);
                type ←poptop(stack2);
                go to continuetraversal;
        exit;
        end
```

Reduction of the graph G of Fig. 8-28 by the process REDUCE, followed

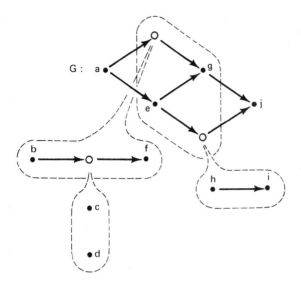

Figure 8-35 The graph structure $\mathscr{S}_G$ of the graph G of Fig. 8-28.

by its simplification, will yield a graph structure as pictured in Fig. 8-35. Note that there are significant differences. First, atomic elements denoting points of the original graph G have not been constrained to be only end points of the tree; they have been intermixed with subgraph elements in the representation. More importantly, the graph has not been completely reduced. The four-point subgraph enclosed by a dotted line, which is an m-M subgraph, was not discovered by the reduction process because it contains no m-M λ or τ subgraphs. By homomorphically contracting only λ and τ subgraphs we are able to (1) devise a reasonably efficient process that reduces a graph G and constructs $\mathscr{S}_G$, and (2) regard all subgraph elements simply as sets (represented as lists) with no need to represent their subgraph structure. But as shown, the price one pays for these advantages is that many m-M subgraphs, which are in theory contractible, may *not* be discovered and reduced.

As noted earlier, the representation of an abstract relation G_M by a graph structure $\mathscr{S}_G$ will often facilitate the determination and retrieval of paths. The reader is encouraged to write a procedure PATH(X, Z, Y) that operates on a graph structure representation and compare it to the procedures of Sec. 6-3. The advantage of a graph structure representation varies with the nature of the original relation G, but in no case is the path-finding process less efficient. Storage efficiency also varies with the particular relation G being represented (see Exercise 8-45). On one hand, additional cells must be included to represent subgraph elements; but on the other hand, when reduction occurs all the edges of a complete bipartite subgraph—e.g.,[L(H), min(H)]—are represented by a single link. An inconclusive investigation suggests that there is a slight reduction in the storage required to represent a "typical" graph.

The graph structure concept illustrates one way in which homomorphic transformations may be used to develop new representational techniques *with provable mathematical properties.* However, the particular development presented here is intended to be illustrative, not definitive. Exercises 8-50 and 8-52 suggest extensions and alternatives to this approach. For example, Haralick (1974) has also observed the role of complete bipartite graphs in the economical representation of graphs. But he creates a "covering" of such subgraphs and thereby derives a very different kind of representation.

Homomorphic reduction may also be used to analyze, and not necessarily represent, structures of interest. For instance, Hecht and Ullman (1974) use similar techniques to characterize *reducible flow graphs.* (In our terminology these are just directed graphs with a least point.) These graphs may be used as models of computing processes, and their homomorphic reduction brings out looping properties of the flow of control.

Hardware technology has reached the point where storage of structures containing millions of elements is both technically and economically practical. But we have little software that is capable of coping with structures of this magnitude. It appears that homomorphisms, which replace sets of data with just a single element and which were used to reduce the magnitude of understanding and compiling programming languages, will become an important tool in the use of very large relational data bases.

EXERCISES FOR SECTION 8-5

*8-45 Construct the graph structure representation of the two basic acyclic graphs G_1 and G_2 in the accompanying figure, and compare the number of cells needed in these cases with that of any other reasonable linked representation. These examples illustrate typical extremes of storage efficiency.

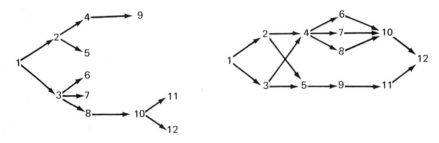

Ex. 8-45

8-46 Having developed a representational technique based on homomorphic contractions that need only preserve the path relation ρ, it is somewhat surprising to discover that any *basic* edge relation E is preserved as well. Write a procedure RNBHR which, given the cell address of any atomic element y, returns the set of atomic elements that constitute R(y) in the original abstract graph G_M.

*8-47 (*a*) Write a logical procedure PATH(X, Z) which determines the existence (or nonexistence) of a path $\rho_G(x, z)$, given a graph structure representation.

(*b*) Modify it to return a list, or array, of atomic points y_i which comprise the path.

8-48 Draw the smallest graph that contains no m-M λ or τ subgraphs. Does it look familiar?

8-49 In this section we eschewed the sequential representation of graphs, for instance, by their adjacency matrix A_G, because they are difficult to manipulate in a reduction process which constructs a graph structure from the original given relation.

(*a*) What problems are encountered when one tries to replace two elements (rows and columns of the representation) with a single element?

But they *could* be used to represent a known graph structure.

(*b*) Sketch a representation of Fig. 8-29 using adjacency matrices to represent subgraph elements.

(*c*) Are there storage savings over the representation of G by a single 10×10 adjacency matrix?

8-50 Sketch a version of a graph structure representation for which

(*a*) all points of G(atomic elements) are represented in a sequential file, while

(*b*) all cells in $\mathscr{S}_G$ are name (or subgraph reference) cells.

This representation, which should be very similar to Fig. 8-17, will more accurately embody the spirit of Fig. 8-29. How would this change affect the procedures REDUCE, SIMPLIFY, RNBHR, and PATH?

8-51 Suppose that the abstract relation G_M, which is being represented by a graph structure $\mathscr{S}_{G'}$ is a dynamic relation. As edges (x,y) are added or deleted, form G, $\mathscr{S}_g$ must be altered to reflect the change. Write procedures ADD (X, Y) and DELETE(X, Y) to dynamically alter a graph structure representation. (These routines are not easy.) Would it pay to record such changes as a "list of exceptions," and only periodically update $\mathscr{S}_G$ as this list became too long?

* 8-52 If the kernel H of a homomorphism φ_H is strongly connected, then φ_H preserves the path structure whether or not H is an m-M subgraph (Theorem 8-6). Let us call such homomorphisms σ (for strong) contractions. Furthermore, the strongly connected σ subgraph which serves as the kernel H can be simply represented as a list (as were λ and τ subgraphs) since we know that there is a path between any pair of points. Extend the graph structure concept to include σ contractions. Illustrate the extension by constructing the graph structure representations of the graphs of Exercise 8-38.

Will the edge structure be preserved? Can one implement the procedure RNBHR?

8-53 The reader may have perceived that the procedure REDUCE may be regarded as a parsing algorithm. It locates small portions of the input structure and "renames" them. Conventional parsing procedures operated only on linear structures (or strings), and the criterion for reducibility (or renamability) is the values assigned to consecutive elements; whereas this process uses the local structure of the relation itself as the reducibility criterion.

(*a*) Develop this theme further. (One might observe that all parsing algorithms contract only convex substructures, that a "program" is simply a representation of an abstract process which a compiler transforms into a different (machine-language) representation of the same abstract process, etc.)

Rules which govern a parsing operation are often described by means of a set of rewrite rules, or productions, which are expressed in the form of a grammar. By applying the rewrite rules in reverse one can generate structures rather than reduce them. Grammars which generate (or describe) nonlinear structures have been called *web grammars*.

(*b*) Formulate a generative web grammar with two rewrite rules that are analogues of λ and τ contraction.

Note that application of a rewrite rule will be more involved than in the case of conventional "string" grammars. Why?

(*c*) Use your grammar to generate some representative examples. Can you characterize the "language" or set of structures that are generated by the grammar?

NINE

DATA ACCESS

The entire content of this chapter is summed up by the question: How does a process identify and access some item of information to be used in a decision or a computation? Until now we have been largely able to ignore this issue because we have been using an intuitively evident accessing mechanism. Desired cells have been identified by pointer variables, say CELL, whose value is the actual storage location of the cell. Information associated with the cell, say NEXT (CELL), is then retrieved from predefined fields by an accessing and retrieval function. We have been using FETCH(CELL, NEXT), which has been designed so that its actual mechanism is largely invisible to the user. In short, a cell address and a field identifier have been regarded as sufficient to access the associated information.†

Now we must question this unspoken assumption, and in so doing begin to explore the question of how one references information. The philosophical implications of this question are held by some to be *the* central issue of computer science—of even more importance than "What is a computational process?" We will confine ourselves to a sampling of some of the more practical aspects of this question. But even so, we will encounter a surprisingly rich variety of topics which range from hardware addressing schemes, to symbol table maintenance, to language design, and to information retrieval in very large data bases. Although we can explore only a few of these ideas in any depth, it is hoped that they will serve as entry points for the interested reader.

---

†A different method of identifying cells and accessing information was briefly considered in the discussion of array representations in Chap. 7.

9-1 SYMBOL TABLES AND SEARCH TREES

A classic problem in computing is: Given some value, how can one obtain a functionally related value f(x)?† If the functional relation can be expressed by an algebraic expression, then f(x) can be simply computed. But frequently the functional relation is such that this is impossible. As a simple example, let x be the name of a city and let f(x) be its population. There is no way to compute the population of a city from its name. Instead the functional correspondence may be expressed by a table consisting of two indexed arrays as shown in Fig. 9-1. The argument array is searched for the given argument, say BOSTON, and the corresponding entry in the second array is returned as the functional value. This process is called function evaluation by *table lookup*. Coding a procedure to perform table lookup is readily a trivial exercise. But implementation of a fast procedure is not trivial (some computers have even been provided with hardware instructions to automatically perform table lookup). See for instance Price (1971).

In this section we want to devise and analyze methods of evaluating arbitrary functions which are explicitly defined by means of a functional table —although the table may bear little resemblance to that of Fig. 9-1. Throughout we will assume two rather special conditions. First, the arguments of the function—that is, its domain—will normally be strings of symbolic characters. For this reason the table of functional correspondences may be called a *symbol table*.‡ Second, the functional relationship will not be a static one. In particular, its domain can change; elements will be both added and deleted

---

†Function evaluation may be regarded as a special case of the more general problems of information retrieval—that is, given an argument x, how does one retrieve an associated value f(x)?

‡This terminology comes from the area of compiler design. The scanner, which actually reads a programmer's source code, must quickly recognize a variety of user-generated symbols such as variable identifiers, statement labels, and literal symbols; determine associated properties that have been declared for the symbol; and pass both to the parser module for syntactic analysis. It does this by building a "symbol table" into which properties are entered as declared and by looking up these entries on subsequent occurrences of the symbol. Since the speed of this operation can be critical to the overall speed of the compiler, a number of techniques, some of which we present in this section, have been developed. The reader may wish to look at Gries (1971) and Lee (1967) for details of various refinements.

City [i]	Pop [i]
Albany	129700
Boston	697200
Chicago	3550400
Detroit	1670100
.	.
.	.
.	.

Figure 9-1 The functional correspondence of cities and their populations expressed as a table.

dynamically during execution. Finally, the functional values, or range, will for the most part be integer storage locations.

Symbol table maintenance and evaluation will be implemented by three separate procedures. The function LOOKUP (argument) will search the symbol table for an entry corresponding to the argument and, if found, return the associated functional value. If no entry is found (i.e., the function is undefined on this argument), a null value will be returned. It is common in computer science to call the argument of a symbol table lookup a *key*.† We shall follow this practice. So a symbol table can be abstractly viewed as‡

$$\text{TABLE} = \{(\text{key, value}) \mid \text{key} \in \{\text{symbolic strings}\} \text{ and}$$
$$\text{value} \in \text{any set } V\}$$

while

$$\text{LOOKUP(key)} = \begin{cases} \text{value, if (key, value)} \in \text{TABLE} \\ \Lambda, \text{ otherwise} \end{cases}$$

The procedures ENTER(key, value) and DELETE(key, value) will add and delete, respectively, entries of the table. If several tables exist, these three routines may include the additional parameter TABLE.

If the table is represented by two sequential arrays as shown in Fig. 9-1, the procedures LOOKUP, ENTER, and DELETE are easily written and are left to the reader. We will complete only the analysis begun in Sec. 5-2 regarding the expected cost of maintaining and searching the symbol table.

Let $\mathscr{L}_1$, $\mathscr{L}_2$, $\mathscr{E}$, and $\mathscr{D}$ denote the expected cost of executing a "successful" lookup which finds the value in the table, an "unsuccessful" lookup which returns the nullvalue, the routine ENTER, and the routine DELETE, respectively. For simplicity we shall approximate the actual cost of executing these procedures by the number of comparisons or storage accesses. Consequently we will actually be letting $\mathscr{L}_1$, $\mathscr{L}_2$, $\mathscr{E}$, and $\mathscr{D}$ denote the expected number of storage accesses expressed as a function of the symbol table size. If we assume that the array of keys is unordered, then, as shown in Sec. 5-2, we have $\mathscr{L}_1 = n/2$ and $\mathscr{L}_2 = n$. In this case a new entry is made by simply adding another element to the end of each variable length array so $\mathscr{E} = 1$, independent of table size. So is deletion, since at worst the "last" entry need only be moved to replace the deleted entry, and $\mathscr{D} = 2$.

If we let λ_1, λ_2, ϵ, and δ denote the number of times, respectively, that each

---

†There is no real reason for using the term *key* rather than the standard mathematical expression *argument* except that this may be regarded as an instance of information retrieval where one commonly talks about search keys and retrieval keys. We use it solely because of this suggestive connotation.

‡As pointed out in Sec. 1-5, a function is just a special kind of relation, or if you will a graph. A table is just one more way of representing the elements, or edges, of the relation. And LOOKUP is just another implementation of the right neighbor operator. But because the relation is a function, LOOKUP is at most single-valued, not set-valued.

of these processes is executed in the course of a job, then the total cost of maintaining and searching the symbol table can be expressed by

$$\text{Cost(unordered table)} = \lambda_1 \cdot \mathcal{L}_1 + \lambda_2 \cdot \mathcal{L}_2 + \epsilon \cdot \mathcal{E} + \delta \cdot \mathcal{D}$$
$$= (n/2)\lambda_1 + n\lambda_2 + \epsilon + 2\delta \qquad (9\text{-}1)$$

$\mathcal{L}_2$ equals n because the entire table must be searched to discover that the key is not there. If the array of keys is ordered, say lexicographically, then on the average only half the table need be examined to discover that a key is missing. Hence, if we maintain an ordered search table, $\mathcal{L}_2 = n/2$. But there is a cost to keeping the table in an ordered sequence. With each entry and deletion an average of half the entries will need to be shifted so that $\mathcal{E} = \mathcal{D} = n/2$. Consequently,

$$\text{Cost(ordered table)} = (n/2) \cdot (\lambda_1 + \lambda_2 + \epsilon + \delta) \qquad (9\text{-}2)$$

Very commonly, if a key is not found in the table, it is immediately entered into it. Under these circumstances $\epsilon = \lambda_2$; and we discover the somewhat surprising inequality

$$\text{Cost(ordered table)} = (n/2)\lambda_1 + n\lambda_2 + (n/2)\delta$$
$$> (n/2)\lambda_1 + (n+1)\lambda_2 + 2\delta \qquad (9\text{-}3)$$
$$= \text{cost(unordered table)}$$

assuming that δ is not negligible. In the most general case, use of an ordered table lookup is actually less efficient than an unordered table. And Exercise 9-2 suggests that the magnitude of this inequality may be greater than it appears.

Actually comparison of these two sequential symbol tables is somewhat of an academic exercise. Essentially the cost of either is a linear function of n, the symbol table size. That is, each operation involving the symbol table is directly proportional to the size of the symbol table. For some problems, including the implementation of many special-purpose compilers, n is reasonably small and this is quite acceptable. But we will find that in the applications of interest to us, n will be very large. The lookup process would be just too expensive.

Sequential search procedures were rejected for much the same reason in Sec. 5-2 where instead binary search techniques were developed. A quick review will show that the procedure BSEARCH$_1$ implemented the function LOOKUP using a sequential representation. The procedure BSEARCH$_2$ combines both the processes LOOKUP and ENTER as a single process. They could have been easily separated. The latter binary search procedure employs a linked representation of the symbol table in tree form. Because we are assuming a dynamic environment, it is the only representation we will consider here. The issue of deleting elements from a linked representation of a tree was considered in Sec. 5-4.

There is little value to once again presenting detailed versions of the procedures LOOKUP, ENTER, or DELETE using a binary tree representation of the symbol table. Writing these is left to the reader. But as a prelude to a more

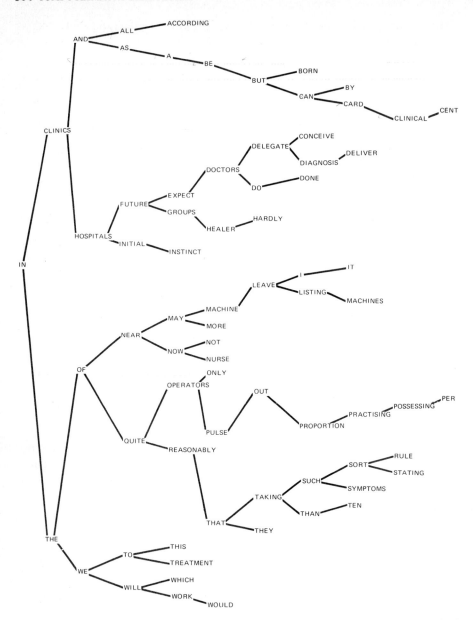

Fig 9-2 The binary retrieval tree whose structure has been determined by the order of words in the source text. Blanks follow all alphabetic characters in the collating sequence of the computer that generated this tree.

detailed analysis of their behavior it might be well to review the process by illustrating a typical tree-structured symbol table that has been dynamically grown from a sample input of natural text.

In the clinics and hospitals of the near future we may quite reasonably expect that doctors will delegate all the initial work of diagnosis to machine operators as they now leave the taking of a pulse to a nurse. Such machine work may be only listing of symptoms, but I can conceive machines which would sort out groups of symptoms and deliver a card stating the diagnosis and treatment according to rule. It would not do the work done by the clinical instinct of the born healer, but the proportion of practising doctors possessing this instinct can hardly be more than ten per cent.†

The unbalanced tree of Fig. 9-2 has 72 points. The length of the longest path is 10, and a bit of calculation will show that the average path, from the principal point to all points y, is 5.375. Such path lengths, which are often called the *depth* of the point y in the tree and denoted $d(y)$, are important because each search for an element of the table must follow one of them. To find the element y requires $d(y) + 1$ storage accesses and comparisons. Consequently the expected number of points that must be examined to lookup an entry in *this* symbol table is 6.375. This is much better than an expected cost of $72/2 = 36$ storage accesses that would be expected given a straight sequential search. But is it typical?

It is evident that the average path length will be minimal, and hence the expected lookup times $\mathcal{L}_1$ and $\mathcal{L}_2$ will be optimal, in a complete balanced binary tree as shown in Fig. 9-3. A tree is *complete* if y not maximal implies that $|R(y)| = 2$. It is *balanced* if for all points y with $R(y) = \{z_1, z_2\}$, $||R(z_1)| - |R(z_2)|| \leq 1$. Besides being optimal, the case of complete balanced search trees is much easier to analyze. First we need a few easily shown basic results.

†George Bernard Shaw, 1918, from the cover of *Computing Reviews*, April 1975.

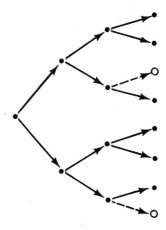

Figure 9-3 A complete balanced tree. Inclusion of two more points and edges (dashed) would yield a full tree of depth 3.

Theorem 9-1 Let $T = (P, E)$ be a complete binary tree with principal point t and $|P| = n$; then

    (a) the number of maximal (end) points is $2 \cdot |\max(T)| = n + 1$

    (b) the number of points at any depth k which is full is $N(k) = 2^k$

If further T is balanced, and d denotes the maximal length path, or depth then:

    (c) $2^d - 1 < n \le 2^{d+1} - 1$,

    (d) $d = \lfloor \log_2(n + 1) \rfloor - 1$.

The *expected*, or average, *path length* in a graph on n points which we denote $E(\rho, n)$ is readily obtained by summing the lengths of all paths $\rho(t, y)$ and dividing by the number of such paths. Since in a principal tree these paths are unique there are precisely n such paths and also we can sum over the various depths. Thus†

$$E(\rho, n) = \left(\sum_{y \in P} |\rho(t, y)| \right) / \text{number of paths}$$

$$= \left[\sum_{k=0}^{d} k \cdot N(k) \right] / n$$

$$= \left(\sum_{k=0}^{d} k \cdot 2^k \right) / \left(2^{d+1} - 1 \right) \qquad \text{if the tree is "full."}$$

Using these equations, it is not hard to calculate the expected path lengths for a few small "full" trees as shown in Table 9-1. From this table it is apparent that $E(\rho, n)$ approaches $d - 1$ as n becomes large. Based on this observation one may proceed to prove analytically that:

$$E(\rho, n) \to d - 1 = \lfloor \log_2(n + 1) \rfloor - 2 \qquad \text{as } n \to \infty$$

Since we are measuring the lookup costs $\mathscr{L}_1$ and $\mathscr{L}_2$ in terms of storage accesses, and since it requires $k + 1$ storage accesses to traverse a path of length

†The numerator of this expression is called the *total path length*.

Table 9-1 Expected path lengths in full trees of depth d on n points.

d	n	$E(\rho, n)$
0	1	0.00
1	3	0.66
2	7	1.43
3	15	2.21
4	31	3.16
5	63	4.06
6	127	5.05
7	255	6.03

k, we may conclude that the expected lookup times given a complete, balanced, binary tree-structured symbol table are $\mathcal{L}_1 = E(\rho, n) + 1 = [\log_2(n + 1)] - 1$ and $\mathcal{L}_2 = E(\rho, n) + 2 = \lfloor \log_2(n + 1) \rfloor$, respectively. (We assume an extra storage access in $\mathcal{L}_2$ to discover that no element exists at the expected point of the search tree.) The expected entry and deletion costs $\mathcal{E}$ and $\mathcal{D}$ are much more difficult to estimate. The cost of simply adding another element to a binary tree is negligible and removal is only slightly more complex. But the addition or deletion may cause a balanced tree to become unbalanced.† Balancing procedures exist (one of which we consider at the end of this section), but they are reasonably involved. Depending on the application, the cost of keeping a dynamic search tree in balance may effectively offset the advantage of optimal lookup, just as the cost of maintaining a lexicographically ordered sequential table exceeded its value in general [expression (9-3)].

This suggests that for many symbol-table applications, unbalanced binary trees may be appropriate. We return to the question: What is the value of $\mathcal{L}_1$ and $\mathcal{L}_2$ in this case? Or more precisely, what is $E(\rho, n)$? To determine $E(\rho,n)$ we must sum the lengths of all possible paths in *all possible binary trees* on n points. It is not easy to construct all possible binary trees on n points. Even more important, it is not completely clear what we mean by all such trees. Let us illustrate the problem by considering the case where n = 4, which is small enough to analyze exhaustively. There are only three nonisomorphic abstract binary trees on four points as shown in Fig. 9-4(*a*). One can count path lengths

---

†The extra point will also destroy "completeness" since a complete tree must have an odd number of points [Theorem 9-1(*a*)]. There is no way to prevent this.

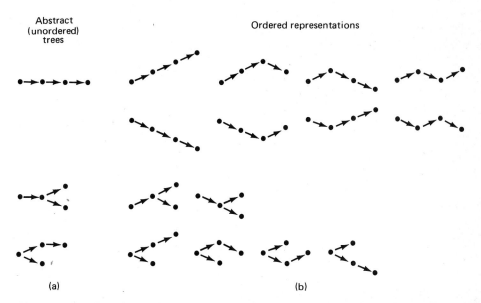

Abstract (unordered) trees	Ordered representations
(a)	(b)

Figure 9-4 Set of (*a*) abstract (or unordered) and (*b*) ordered binary trees on four points.

and show that the expected path length is $15/12 = 1.25$. Call this $E_1(\rho, n)$. However, there are 14 different representations of these three trees which arise from the ordering implied by the use of the R_1 and R_2 links. The expected path length, call it $E_2(\rho, n)$, over this set is 1.3214. Perhaps this is the correct figure, since the lookup procedure will actually operate on these representations and that is the cost we seek to measure. On the other hand, every representation is generated by a sequence of four entries, $\langle v_1, v_2, v_3, v_4 \rangle$. Its particular ordered structure depends on the order in which these values are entered. There are $24 = 4!$ different permutations of the order in which these values can be entered. Some representations can be generated by only one of the permutation sequences; others can arise as a result of two or more of the permuted input sequences (since there are only 14 representations). Assuming that the symbol table will be created from the input of a randomly ordered set of values, an expected path length that accounts for the probability a given representation will be generated,† which we will denote by $E_3(\rho, n)$, seems more reasonable. It appears that $E_3(\rho, n)$ is the best measure of expected path length in an unbalanced binary search tree. Table 9-2 summarizes some results for small binary trees. The last column presents values of observed mean path lengths that were obtained by generating (using ENTER) a sample of 20 binary trees from a randomly generated sequence of n integers. Although clearly not exact, these values appear to be good estimators for $E_3(\rho, n)$. See also Exercise 9-10. Although not ideal when compared with the expected path length in a complete balanced tree on n points, this table shows that use of unbalanced trees as symbol tables is not too bad—especially when one considers that the expected costs $\mathscr{E}$ and $\mathscr{D}$ of entering and deleting elements is little more than the cost of locating the element. That is, $\mathscr{E} \approx \mathscr{L}_2$ and $\mathscr{D} \approx \mathscr{L}_1$.

†This effect becomes very striking in binary trees with large n. For example, it can be shown that there are 2^{n-1} different ordered representations of the *linear* tree. But each is generated by only one permutation of the possible input sequences, and the probability of generating any becomes vanishingly small. On the other hand, representations of other trees appear with increasing frequency.

Table 9-2 Expected path length in binary trees.†

n	$E_1(\rho, n)$ abstract	$E_2(\rho, n)$ ordered	$E_3(\rho, n)$ generated	$\hat{E}_3(\rho, n)$ observed
2	0.5000	0.5000	0.5000	0.5000
3	0.8333	0.8333	0.8888	0.9444
4	1.2500	1.3214	1.2083	1.2000
5	1.5333	1.6762	1.4800	1.4857
6	1.8636	2.0051	1.7166	1.6750
10				2.7733
20				3.6666
50				5.1847

†$\hat{E}_3$ denotes average path length over a sample of 20 randomly generated trees for each n.

If the keys of the elements to be entered into the binary tree are known to arrive in a reasonably random order, then the preceding analyses show that a randomly grown binary tree may yield an attractive retrieval structure. But this may not be the case. The keys of the elements to be entered may show a pronounced order; they may even be totally ordered, say lexicographically. In this case some extra effort must be expended to construct a balanced tree. The effort to dynamically maintain a completely balanced tree (in the sense that for all y, $||T_{z_2}| - |T_{z_1}|| \le 1$, where T_{z_1} and T_{z_2} are the R_1 and R_2 subtrees of y) is normally prohibitive. Instead one often turns in compromise to _nearly balanced trees, called AVL trees_ (after their discoverers, Adelson-Velskii and Landis). These are also called _height-balanced_ trees.

By the height of a subtree T_{z_i}, with principal point z_i, we mean the length of the longest path in the subtree. We will denote its height by $h(T_{z_i})$. A tree is said to be _height-balanced_, or an _AVL tree_, if for all y, $|h(T_{z_2}) - h(T_{z_1})| \le 1$. Let us call the value $h(T_{z_2}) - h(T_{z_1})$ the _balance_ at the point y and denote it by bal(y). Readily, in an AVL tree it can only take on the values -1, 0, or $+1$. Points at which bal(y) exceeds these values are said to be unbalanced, and are called _critical_. Figure 9-5 shows a typical balanced AVL tree, together with two unbal-

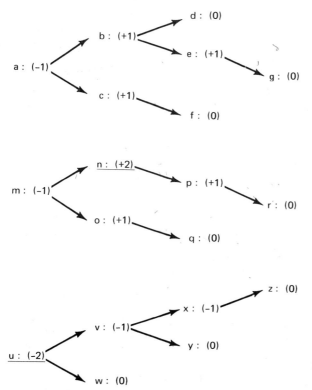

Figure 9-5 (a) A typical AVL tree. (b, c) Unbalanced AVL trees with critical points n and u.

anced trees. The balance assigned to each point is shown. The underlined points n and u are critical.

Lookup in AVL trees is identical to that of any binary tree. Based on a comparison of the search key with the value assigned to the points, R_1 or R_2 links are followed until either the desired element is found or a null link is encountered indicating that the element is not in the tree. If appropriate, a new element is entered at that point, just as it would be entered into any binary tree. But now the entry procedure must back up along the search path, reassigning balance values and looking for points that may have become critical. If such occur, then the local structure of the tree at that point must be reconfigured. A little consideration will show that only four possible cases can occur. Two of these cases, in which the critical point y has been assigned a new balance of $+2$, are shown in Fig. 9-6. The associated reconfigurations are commonly called *single* and *double rotations,* respectively. (The remaining two cases are simply mirror reflections in which the critical point y has balance -2.)

Two important features of this configuration, or rebalancing, process account for the popularity of AVL trees. First, the reconfiguration is a local one. It can be seen that at most three or four edges, respectively, need be altered. Second, at most one reconfiguration is ever necessary to rebalance the entire tree, since in all four cases the balance at the new principal point will be zero. Indeed the search back along the access path reassigning new balances can be terminated whenever a point is assigned a new balance of zero, since this implies that the new point was added to the "shorter" subtree. It cannot affect the balance at any other points.

Although AVL trees need not be perfectly balanced [see exercise 9-13(*a*)], we have called them nearly balanced. It may be more correct to say that they cannot be "too badly" imbalanced. The following theorem provides bounds on the possible imbalance.

Theorem 9-2 If $T = (P, E)$ is an AVL tree with $|P| = n$, then the maximal possible path length is bounded by

$$\lfloor \log_2(n + 1) \rfloor - 1 \le \max(\rho, n) \le 1.44 \cdot \log_2(n + 1) - 1.33$$

Further, the expected path length $E(\rho, n)$ has been empirically found to be approximately $\log_2(n + 1) + 0.25$. It is worth comparing the AVL tree of Fig. 9-7 with that of Fig. 9-2. Note that in this tree the longest path length is 7, while the expected path length is 4.525. Even though it is not completely balanced, it is clearly superior to the former.

We have tacitly assumed that retrieval of any of the elements in the binary tree is equally likely, that the distribution of requested search keys is uniform. This is seldom true in practice. Normally some keys are requested with a significantly higher frequency than others. In the text that generated Figs. 9-2 and 9-7, for instance, the words "the" and "of" are referenced 10 and 9 times, respectively, while most other keys are referenced only 1 or 2 times. We may "weight" the elements of a tree by values w_y denoting the frequency of refer-

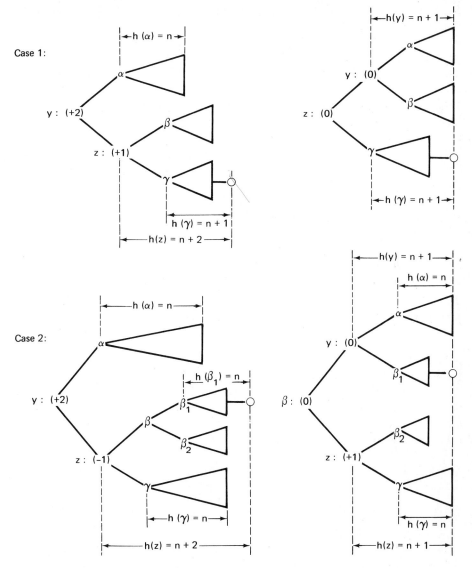

Figure 9-6 Two cases of unbalanced trees, together with their corresponding reconfigurations. In each, y is critical and ○ denotes the newly entered element.

ence. Then the *total weighted path length* is defined

$$T(\rho) = \sum_{y \in P} |\rho(t, y)| \cdot w_y$$

The *expected* weighted path length (obtained by dividing the total weighted path length by the number of retrievals) is 4.702 and 3.846, respectively, for

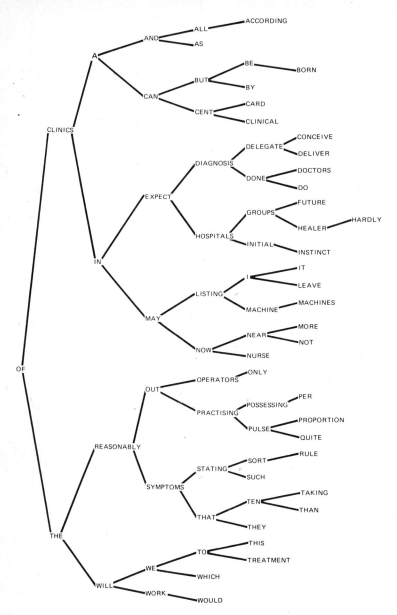

Figure 9-7 An AVL tree generated by the same portion of text as the binary tree of Fig. 9-2 (32 rebalancings were required.)

these two trees. In these situations it might make sense to alter the structure of the tree so that the more heavily weighted elements are closer to the principal point, thereby minimizing the total weighted path length. Several heuristic procedures for constructing such trees are discussed by Nievergelt (1974). Unfortunately the distribution of request frequencies is seldom known a priori, and the construction techniques are sufficiently expensive that these procedures are reasonable only with static files.

EXERCISES FOR SECTION 9-1

9-1 Implement the routines LOOKUP, ENTER, and DELETE that will operate on
   (*a*) an unordered sequentially represented symbol table,
   (*b*) a lexicographically ordered sequential symbol table. Experimentally verify the values of $\mathscr{L}_1$, $\mathscr{L}_2$, $\mathscr{E}$, and $\mathscr{D}$. Are they valid? Can a more accurate expression of these costs be based on a detailed analysis of the implementing code? Would it significantly alter the general conclusions of this section?

* 9-2 It is asserted in the text that with the unordered sequential symbol table, $\mathscr{L}_1 = n/2$. But there is reason to doubt whether any part of this statement is true! First, the symbol table is not really unordered; given the most likely implementation ENTER, the elements will be ordered by the time of occurrence. In addition, the following two heurisms appear to be valid. In natural text processing, the more common keys are likely to be encountered first and hence be at the beginning of the search sequence. If scanning block-structured computer programs, just the reverse is true; the most likely keys are those most recently declared. (Here one would search the array in reverse order.)
   (*a*) Test out these conjectures using
      (1) a body of natural text,
      (2) a Fortran source program, and
      (3) a block structured program, such as Algol or PL/1.
   (*b*) How will deletion occur in the case of a symbol table for a block-structured program?
   (*c*) Should the sequential symbol table arrays be implemented as stacks? Why?

9-3 The parameters λ_1, λ_2, ϵ, and δ are of evident importance for evaluating the relative effectiveness of various symbol table schemes. Yet they are dependent on the particular application and can be obtained only by experimental observation.
   (*a*) Building a lexicon (actually a symbol table) as in Exercise 5-10 never involves deletion, but λ_1 and λ_2 can be derived from the counts of that exercise. Determine λ_1 and λ_2. Note that $\epsilon = \lambda_2$.
   (*b*) Would it be preferable to express λ_1, λ_2, ϵ, and δ as frequencies rather than absolute counts? Why?
   (*c*) Describe an application in which $\delta \neq 0$.

* 9-4 Draw the unbalanced binary tree that would be generated by repeated calls to ENTER assuming a sequence of 27 keys input in the following order: LIVE, COMPUTER, VERY, BREAD, PIZZA, SOME, SMART, ALL, WOMAN, HOT, IS, THE, MATHEMATICS, SEE, A, TEACH, LARGE, BINARY, EAT, HOUSE, OF, UNIVERSITY, NEAR, RED, BEFORE, STUDY, MAN. What is the average path length in this tree? (Note that this input sequence was determined by a random number generator. Does this imply that the generated tree is a "random" tree?)

9-5 Prove that if a tree is balanced, then for all maximal points z_i and z_j,

$$\Big| |\rho(t, z_i)| - |\rho(t, z_j)| \Big| \leq 1$$

9-6 Restate Theorem 9-1, but for ternary trees, and then for n-ary trees.

9-7 The expressions for $\mathscr{L}_1$, $\mathscr{L}_2$, $\mathscr{E}$, and $\mathscr{D}$, which are functions of n based solely on the number of storage accesses involved in following a search path, ignore many other operations involved in symbol-table maintenance and lookup, for instance, extracting and setting links, allocation and deallocation of cells, etc. Can you obtain more accurate expressions for these expected costs? Should they be functions of more than just the size n of the symbol table?

* **9-8** Write and implement the procedures LOOKUP, ENTER, and DELETE which operate on a binary tree-structured symbol table.

9-9 Use the procedures of the preceding exercise in a number of simulation runs to test the validity of the expressions for $\mathscr{L}_1$, $\mathscr{L}_2$, $\mathscr{E}$, and $\mathscr{D}$ in the text, as derived in Exercise 9-7. Will you gain more information about these processes by simply recording observed execution times, or by adding instrumentation (whose overhead will invalidate observed execution times) that counts the occurrences of various steps in the procedure?

9-10 In addition to, or in lieu of, Table 9-2 one would very much like some expressions that approximate or bound $E_1(\rho, n)$, $E_2(\rho, n)$, and $E_3(\rho, n)$ as n becomes large.

  (a) Knuth shows that $E_2(\rho, n) \rightarrow n(\alpha\sqrt{n} - 3)$ for large n, where $\alpha = \sqrt{\pi} = 1.7724$.

  (b) The following table, derived from Table 9-2, suggests that $\hat{E}(\rho, n) \approx E_3(\rho, n) \rightarrow \beta\sqrt{n}$, for some β.

n	$\hat{E}(\rho, n)$	$\sqrt{n}/\hat{E}(\rho, n)$
2	0.5000	2.8284
3	0.9444	1.8339
4	1.2000	1.6666
5	1.4857	1.5050
6	1.6750	1.4623
10	2.7733	1.1402
20	3.6666	1.2196
50	5.1847	1.3638

  (c) It appears that $E_3(\rho, n) < E_1(\rho, n) < E_2(\rho, n)$ for large n. Can you prove, or else give evidence in support of, any of these contentions? (Note that none will be easy to establish.)

* **9-11** Implement a procedure which enters new elements into an AVL tree and reconfigures it as necessary to keep it height-balanced. (You may wish to simply modify the procedures already coded for Exercise 5-10.) A short two-bit field BALANCE must be associated with each cell. In addition, you may wish to add a second two-bit field DIR, which records the direction taken by the search path through the point. This extra information simplifies the task of reassigning new balances and reconfiguring the structure about critical points.

  Record the number of times that the tree is rebalanced, and calculate the average number of rebalancings per newly entered item.

9-12 Foster (1973) has shown that the notion of AVL trees can be generalized by permitting imbalances exceeding one. The procedures are essentially the same, except that instead of assigning the balance with a point, one uses a somewhat larger field and assigns the height of the subtree. Although the resulting tree is less well balanced, fewer rebalancings are required to maintain it. Generalize the procedures of the preceding exercise in this manner, and verify a few of the empirical results asserted in this article.

9-13 (a) Construct an AVL tree of height 5 with fewest points. (Note that this can be constructed by making the R_1 subtree of the principal point an AVL tree of height 4 with minimal points, and making the R_2 subtree a minimal subtree of height 3.)

(*b*) Using the recurrence relation suggested by this inductive construction, derive a general expression for the minimal number of points possible in an AVL tree of height n. It will be related to the Fibonacci numbers (Stone, 1972).

(*c*) Prove Theorem 9-2.

9-14 Given x, the functional value sin(x) may be retrieved by evaluating the polynomial (Taylor series expansion)

$$\sin(x) = x - \frac{x^3}{3!} + \frac{x^5}{5!} - \frac{x^7}{7!} + \cdots$$

It may also be evaluated by looking up the value in a table of values for $0 \le x \le \pi/4$ using linear interpolation and some basic trigonometric identities. Show that by carefully choosing the entries to the table, one can write a table lookup procedure that guarantees four-place accuracy, which is faster than the corresponding polynomial evaluation. (Note that this is primarily an exercise in coding skill, but it makes an important point. Table lookup was widely used to evaluate basic functions in early systems. Current systems approximate these functions by Chebyshev polynomials, which are much faster.)

9-15 Function evaluation and information retrieval are in reality identical problems; given an argument or search key x, one wants to retrieve some associated value f(x). Yet very different methodologies are associated with each. The characteristic difference appears to be that in one the retrieval process actually generates the desired item of information f(x) by means of computational operations, whereas in the other the item f(x) already exists and has been stored somewhere; the retrieval process only finds it. The distinction between implicitly and explicitly represented information is a recurrent theme in data structures. It partially explains why the set of all real numbers and the set of all binary trees, both of which are classes of data structures, are treated so differently. List other instances in this text where a distinction is made between implicit and explicit representation of information, and discuss its implications.

After recognizing the differences, it may be profitable to combine the two methodologies as illustrated by the preceding exercise. Some information retrieval systems store information "implicitly" by storing a procedure which could generate the information if required. Give an example in which an integer assignment function f associated with elements x of a tree can be represented by a field that contains a procedure entry point, not the integer value f(x) itself.

9-2 HASH CODING

Given a retrieval key k, the lookup procedures of the preceding section find the associated value f(k) by searching through either a linear or a binary tree structure to find the cell representing the element (k, f(k)). And as the set of keys (domain of f) gets larger, the cost of search time must inevitably increase—even though we may adopt various techniques to minimize its rate of increase. Retrieval by hash coding seeks, ideally, to eliminate all search time. The idea behind hash coding is quite simple. Even though the keys may represent symbolic strings or some other set of values, in reality all keys are represented in a computer by an integer value, by a sequence of bits. Temporarily regarding them as integer values, we may define an arbitrary function h(k) on the set S of keys called a *hash function* which maps S into the interval of integers $[L_1, L_r]$. Note that h may· be any sort of strange function subject only to the constraint that $h:S \rightarrow [L_1, L_r]$. For example, if $L_1 = 0$ and $L_r = 255 = 2^8 - 1$, then h(k) might be simply the function which returns the first seven bits of the representation of k.

When an element (k, f(k)) is entered into the symbol table or retrieval system it must be represented by a cell taken from the allocatable block of storage locations $[L_1, L_r]$. Why not use the cell whose address is h(k), $L_1 \leq h(k) \leq L_r$? Then on subsequent retrieval, given the key k, the lookup procedure need only reevaluate the function h(k) to obtain the address of a cell which is either empty [in which case $f(k) = \Lambda$] or represents the desired element (k, f(k)). No searching at all is involved.

There is one evident flaw in this method. It is quite possible that two different keys k_1 and k_2 in S may hash to the same address, that is, $h(k_1) = h(k_2)$.† But the cell with this address cannot be used to represent both the elements $(k_1, f(k_1))$ and $(k_2, f(k_2))$. Such a situation is called a *collision*. A well-chosen hashing function h can minimize the probability of collision, but not eliminate it altogether. All hash-coding systems must also include some mechanism for resolving collisions. Let us consider in turn each of these two subproblems—the choice of hashing function and the resolution of collisions.

It seems clear that a hashing function which uniformly "scatters" its function values h(k) throughout the range $[L_1, L_r]$ will tend to minimize the probability of collision. Even though the keys $k_1, k_2, \ldots, k_n$ may have very similar values when regarded as integers, their hash values $h(k_1), h(k_2), \ldots, h(k_n)$ should not "bunch up" with similar or identical values in $[L_1, L_r]$. For this reason this method of locating storage is sometimes known as *scatter storage*. One way of obtaining this scattering effect is to hash the key value k_1 (apply some apparently random and meaningless transformation to it) in such a way that even minor variations in the keys become grossly magnified in their hashed values, from whence comes the term *hash coding*. In effect, h should be the very antithesis of a continuous function. There has been considerable investigation of the properties of various hashing functions, such as in Maurer and Lewis (1975) and Knuth (1973); we give below only four of the more commonly used methods. For the purposes of example we will assume that all keys are decimal integer values.

An easy way to ensure that $L_1 \leq h(k) \leq L_r$ is to use simple *extraction*. In this, all but the last m digits (or bits) of the key are masked out to obtain an address relative to L_1. Thus

$$h(k) = \text{loworderdigits}(k) + L_1$$

---

† If h is a 1-1 function, then $k_1 \neq k_2$ must imply that $h(k_1) \neq h(k_2)$. In theory, given the domain S and range $[L_1, L_r]$, one should be able to construct a 1-1 function h which completely eliminates collisions. But in practice this is impossible, especially since one seldom knows a priori precisely what the domain S will be.

If all but the last three digits are masked and $[L_1, L_r] = [000, 999]$ then

$$h(400083) = 083$$

while

$$h(410073) = 073$$

Extraction, which only involves masking out the low-order digits, is normally very fast. As a variant one can extract the high-order or middle-order digits (or bits) from the key. If the set of keys are really numeric, then the low-order digits are of least significance and tend in general to be the most random. If the set of keys are really integer codes representing a set of symbolic data, then the low-order digits often tend to be identical—the internal code for the blank symbol in a left-justified representation. Extraction of the high-order digits, representing the first character or so of the symbol string, is slightly better, but still quite poor since many keys will begin with the same letter or pair of letters. Extraction by itself is generally an unsatisfactory hashing function. In combination with one of the following techniques it can be quite useful. Note that with extraction the size of the range must be a power of the base (which is 2 in most computer systems, but 10 in our examples).

Extraction of the m low-order digits is equivalent to remaindering modulo (base m). A superior result can be obtained by simple *division.* Let $r = L_r - L_1 + 1$ denote the size of the range; it need not be a power of the base. We may then define

$$h(k) = \text{remainder } \frac{k}{r} + L_1$$

Experience has shown that a better choice for the divisor is the greatest prime number less than r. Thus, if r = 1000 we might use 997 as the divisor, thus giving the hash function

$$h(k) = \text{remainder } \left(\frac{k}{997}\right) \quad \text{assuming } L_1 = 000 \text{ as before}†$$

This choice leaves three unused locations in the range, but the resultant improvement in the random scatter seems to be worth it. Since $400083/997 = 401$ remainder 286,

$$h(400083) = 286$$

Similarly, $h(410073) = 306$, while the key 405083—which using either extraction or division by 1000 would hash to the same value as 400083—now has hash value $h(405083) = 301$.

A goal of a good hashing function is to reflect any variability appearing anywhere within the digits of the key in its hash value $h(k)$. Division by a prime, in contrast to a composite number—or worse, a power of the base—tends to emphasize this property. Another method which exaggerates variability

---

†Note that this is just remaindering modulo (997). For most applications the standard MOD function, available with most systems, will be satisfactory. But for crucial high-density usage the user will often want to hand-code an optimized version.

throughout the string of digits comprising the key is called _radix transforma-tion._ Briefly, each digit of the key is evaluated as if with respect to the base (base + 1), that is, a base one higher than the normal base. It is then reinterpreted with respect to the original base. This rather opaque explanation can be made clearer by means of an example. We have been expressing our keys as integers to the base 10. We will want to evaluate the key as if the digits were in a base 11 number system. Thus

$$h(400083_{10}) = 400083_{11}$$
$$= 4 \cdot 11^5 + 8 \cdot 11^1 + 3 \cdot 11^0$$
$$= 644295_{10}$$
$$= \quad 295 \quad \text{after extraction}$$

Notice that after the radix transformation, extraction was used to ensure that h(k) would lie within the range. It is a final procedure whose operation is reminiscent of the bed of Procrustes. In practical implementation the binary key would be evaluated to base 3—or more likely, to save multiplications, groups of bits forming octal or hexadecimal digits would be interpreted to base 9 or base 17, respectively.

The three preceding hashing operations all implicitly assumed that the key was a one-word value. But symbolic keys with which hashing is most often as-sociated are often represented by two or more computer words. In _folding,_ the key is subdivided into two or more parts which are then numerically added. Normally the result is then hashed using either extraction or division. If the original symbolic key is represented by two (or more) words, then these would be folded by adding them together to get a one-word result which could then be hashed. Even if the original key is represented by a single word, it may be sub-divided into fields which are then added to one another in a folding operation. For example, the six digit keys of our running example might be folded into two 3-digit pieces. Then

$$h(400083) = 400 + 083 = 483$$

Folding clearly introduces variability throughout the input string into the hashed result. For instance,

$$h(405083) = 405 + 083 = 488$$

but on the other hand, variability in one part of the key may be balanced by that in another part, as in the example

$$h(410073) = 410 + 073 = 483$$

Folding followed by remaindering modulo a prime (division) appears to be a reliable general-purpose hashing function. However, if the set of keys has dis-tinctive properties, the reader may find it profitable to conduct experiments with that set and tailor a hashing function to the specific application.

A good hashing function tends to spread the hashing values h(k) uniformly throughout the range $[L_1, L_r]$. But inevitably some collisions occur where

$h(k_1) = h(k_2)$. If the system is hashing directly into cell storage, then the first element $(k_1, f(k_1))$ is entered into the cell with address $h(k_1)$. When the element $(k_2, f(k_2))$ is encountered and entered, its "proper" location $h(k_2)$ is found to be in use. Some other available cell with address $h'(k_2)$ (possibly the next sequential cell) must be found. On subsequent lookup the hashed location $h(k_2)$ will be calculated, but comparison of the stored key k_1 with the retrieval key k_2 will show that the correct element has not been accessed. Then the same procedure which obtained the available cell $h'(k_2)$ must be duplicated to find the stored entry $(k_2, f(k_2))$. The discovery of available auxiliary cells when collision occurs and rediscovery on retrieval is called *probing*. Probing which just involves looking at the next sequential cell is called *linear probing*. It is the least effective. Various probing methods have been proposed. The better ones can become quite involved, especially in a dynamic situation where elements are deleted as well as entered.

The following procedure handles collisions (or more properly ignores them) by hashing the keys into a set of pointers, not directly into the addresses of the representing cells themselves. The cells of all elements $(k_i, f(k_i))$ with a common hash value $h(k_i)$ are linked as a simple linear list for which the pointer with address, or index, $h(k_i)$ serves as a header. The list of cells is called a *bucket* and the procedure is sometimes called *hashing into buckets,* since all elements whose keys hash to the same value are collected together in a single "bucket." Figure 9-8 shows the configuration of such a hashed symbol table. In this figure, elements $(k_i, f(k_i))$ are represented by cells containing the key k_i itself and a single associated value $f(k_i)$. In practice there are commonly several values, or items of information, associated with an element that is accessed by a single key.

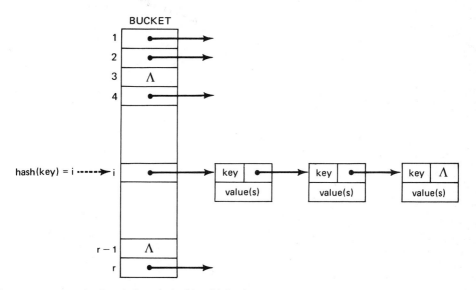

Figure 9-8 A hash-coded symbol table with buckets.

Hashing into buckets is slightly less efficient than hashing directly into the cell storage; however, it has two important advantages. First, it is extremely easy to implement, as illustrated by the procedures below. More importantly, it completely separates the distinct problems of access to stored representations from those of cell allocation for the representations (Chap. 10). With this method one may use keys to access elements that are represented by cells of different sizes, or that are located in widely separated blocks of storage.

procedure enter (k, cell);
integer   k;
pointer   cell;

This procedure enters an element (k, f(k)) into a symbol table that is hashed-coded into buckets. Note that it assumes that storage for the representation of the element has already been allocated, and that its address is given by the parameter "cell." A single field "nxtinb" (for next in bucket) is reserved in each representing cell for the exclusive use of this accessing mechanism.

```
begin
      integer            i, r;
      pointer array      bucket[1:r];
      field              nxtinb;
      common /buckets/   r, bucket;
      i ←hash(k) +1;
      nxtinb(cell) ←bucket[i];
      bucket[i] ←cell;
      exit;
      end
```

integer procedure hash (k);
integer   k;

This procedure hashes the one word key k which is regarded as an integer. It first folds the value of k in half, using two integer functions "high" and "low" which simply return the high order half and the low order half of the word right-justified. It then takes the remainder modulo r, where r denotes the number of buckets and is presumed to be a prime number.

```
begin
      integer            kfold, r
      common /buckets/   r, bucket[1:r];
      kfold ←high(k) +low(k);
      hash ←mod(kfold, r);
      exit;
      end
```

pointer procedure lookup (k);
integer   k;

This procedure returns the address of the cell representing an element identified by the one word key k, *which need not in fact be an integer value. If no such element exists the null value is returned. Access is by hashing into buckets.*

```
begin
      integer              i, r;
      pointer              cell;
      pointer array        bucket[1:r];
      field                key, nxtinb;
      common /buckets/     r, bucket;
      i ←hash(k) + 1;
      cell ←bucket[i];
      while cell ≠ null do
```

Search linked list for a cell identified by this key.

```
      if key(cell) = k
           then lookup ←cell;
                  exit
           else cell ←nxtinb(cell);
      lookup ←null;
      exit;
      end
```

Writing a procedure to delete elements from the system is left to the reader as Exercise 9-22. While a particular hashing function has been given for illustrative purposes, any other hashing function can be substituted for it. Perhaps the most striking characteristic of these procedures is how few executable statements are really needed to implement the entire hash-coding module. It is a method of access whose use in ordinary applications programs should be far more widespread.

The efficiency of hash-code techniques, which we will measure in terms of the expected number of cells that must be examined in order to retrieve a desired element, is a function of three basic parameters:

1. the distribution of search keys,
2. characteristics of the hashing function h, and
3. density of the hash values h(k) in the potential range $[L_1, L_n]$.

A programmer normally has little control over the first parameter. The essential characteristic of the hashing function is that it scatters the hash values h(k) in a fairly uniform fashion over the range. This is usually possible with the hashing techniques discussed earlier. However, better programmers may run a few simulations to test the uniformity by which their chosen hash function distributes its values given a sample of the expected keys. Fortunately the third parameter is the most critical in determining the efficiency of the technique, and it is the one over which the programmer has the most control. Unlike the lookup procedures of the preceding section, whose expected times $\mathscr{L}_1$, $\mathscr{L}_2$, $\mathscr{E}$,

α	L_1
0.1	1.05
0.5	1.25
0.75	1.38
0.9	1.45

Figure 9-9 The expected number L_1 of probes per lookup for various densities $\alpha = n/r < 1.0$.

and $\mathcal{D}$ are purely functions of the number n of elements in the system,† with hash coding the programmer can alter the expected lookup times by increasing or decreasing the amount of storage used by the system.

Let r denote the number of possible values in the range of the hash function h. It may be either the total number of cells available in the free store or the total number of buckets. As before, let n denote the number of elements, each with a distinct key, that will be entered into the system and stored. By the density we mean the ratio $\alpha = n/r$. Now, given any particular key k, there will be a sequence of one or more elements all of which have the same hash value h(k). To look up and retrieve the element (k, f(k)) at least one storage access, or probe, must be made. If there is a sequence of m elements with that hash value, then an expected $(m - 1)/2$ more probes must be made to retrieve it from the sequence. It can be shown, assuming a perfectly uniform distribution h, that the expected number of probes or memory accesses is

$$\mathcal{L}_1 \approx 1 + \frac{\alpha}{2}$$

Suppose that we are hashing directly into cell storage. Then of necessity, $r \geq n$ and $\alpha \leq 1.0$. Some typical values of $\mathcal{L}_1$ as a function of α are given in Fig. 9-9.‡ When hashing into buckets it is normal to have $r < n$. Hence expected values of $\mathcal{L}_1$ greater than 2.0 are common.

We have said that the expected lookup times $\mathcal{L}_1$ of hash-coded retrieval are largely a function of the density $\alpha = r/n$. But other factors also affect its efficiency, such as (1) the actual distribution of keys, (2) the extent to which the hashing function really approximates a uniform distribution of hash values, (3) the particular sequence by which elements are entered and then subsequently retrieved, and even (4) whether new elements are added to the front or the rear of the linked list comprising the bucket. Table 9-3 tabulates the results of minor variations in the hashing system that were generated by a class of students who

---

†Different methods have different expected cost functions, and a system designer can choose a method whose expected cost function appears to be minimal for the task at hand. But once chosen, the expected cost (in terms of time) is inexorably tied to the number of elements in the data structure.

‡This approximation of $\mathcal{L}_1$ is valid only if all elements in the sequence of elements that must be probed have the same hash value. In the case of hashing into buckets this is always true. Of those methods which hash directly to cell storage, only Maurer's method of "direct chaining" satisfies this condition. In both linear and random probing the sequence to be searched may contain elements with different hash values, a phenomenon known as *secondary collisions*. This changes $\mathcal{L}_1$. For example, given linear probing in a store with $\alpha = 0.9$, $\mathcal{L}_1 \approx 5.50$.

Table 9-3

Hashing method	Position of new entries in bucket	Max. no. of elements per bucket	Avg. no. of elements per bucket†	No. of empty buckets	Avg. no. of probes per look-up‡
Linear search (1 bucket)	front	78	—	—	31.56
First character of key (mod 47)	rear	10	3.71	29	3.16
Division (remaindering) of entire key					
mod 47	front	19	2.60	20	3.59
mod 47	rear	19	2.60	20	4.25
mod 49	front	18	2.16	14	3.36
mod 49	rear	18	2.16	14	3.93
Folding of key followed by division					
mod 47	front	5	2.11	13	1.71
mod 47	rear	5	2.11	13	1.61
mod 49	rear	5	2.06	12	1.75

†Average over nonempty buckets only.
‡Averaged over total life of system.
Note: 78 distinct keys, sample size, 138 lookups and/or entries. Theoretical value of $L_1 \approx 1.78$

were all assigned the same problem, but attacked it in different ways. The input sequence given on page 000 consists of 138 English words, comprising 78 distinct keys. Each key in the input sequence was first looked up, and if not present in the table it was added to its correct bucket (at either the front or the rear of the list). It should be noted that the expected number of storage accesses, or probes, per key is

$$\mathscr{L}_1 \approx 1 + \frac{\alpha}{2} = 1 + \frac{1}{2} \cdot \frac{78}{50} = 1.78$$

(since up to 50 buckets were available). Note also that the values in the column "average probes/lookup" are somewhat low since they were tabulated over the entire life of the system, including its early stages when there were few entries.

The preceding table is admittedly just anecdotal evidence. But it serves to illustrate some of the variances from the theoretical behavior than one can encounter in practice.

EXERCISES FOR SECTION 9-2

9-16 In the description of the hashing functions—extraction, division, radix transformation, and folding—there was an implicit assumption that the range $[L_1, L_r]$ denoted the addresses of one-word cells. This is acceptable if one is hashing into a range of buckets headed by one-word pointers. It is normally unreasonable if one is hashing directly into cell storage, since cells seldom consist of but a single addressable location. Write a more general procedure HASH(key, L_1, L_r, celsiz) which uses division to hash to cells of fixed size "celsiz" in the block of storage [L_1, L_r].

9-17 Most symbolic keys consist of $\leq$ 10 characters, but nevertheless, few can be assured of fitting in a single word. Write a hash function HASH(addr, j) which returns a hash value based on the contents of the j words (or bytes) beginning with the specified location "addr."

*9-18 A measure of the extent to which a given hashing function h uniformly scatters n different keys within a range of r possible hash values is given by (1) the maximum number of keys which map to a single hash value h(k), (2) the number of hash values which have no key that maps onto them, and (3) the average number of keys which map to each nonvoid hash value. A histogram of the number of keys which map to each hash value is also valuable for visualizing the uniformity of the distribution.

 (*a*) Implement several different hashing functions.

 (*b*) Compare them by running a test program which gathers the statistics above for the given identical sets (or domains) of keys.

 [The easiest way of getting a set of keys is to generate n random integers. But the results of the test are likely to be misleading. Even extraction will be almost perfectly uniform (assuming the random number generator is). Much more realistic results are obtained by reading a "typical" set of keys that might be expected in some application.]

9-19 Based on the evidence of Table 9-3, which basic method of hashing appears to yield the most uniform distribution of hash values?

*9-20 Implement the procedures ENTER, HASH, and LOOKUP, given in this section as general-purpose routines, for your own private use. Test them and gather statistics about their performance similar to Table 9-3.

9-21 The version of ENTER given in this section adds new entries to the front of the linked list representing a bucket. To add it to the rear of the list, must the entire list be traversed? Remember that in most situations LOOKUP will have first been called to determine that the key is not in the table.

9-22 Deletion of an element from a hash-code bucket involves no more than deletion of an element from any list; the cell to be deleted must be located, as must the "previous" cell in the list, since it is singly linked. Note, however, that there are two possible ways of identifying the element to be deleted: by its cell address or by its key. Thus either DELETE (CELL) or DELETE (KEY) might be used to call it.

 (*a*) If the former usage is adopted, how will the procedure access the previous cell in the bucket?

 (*b*) Should DELETE actually return the cell to the free store by calling TAKEIT, or should it just remove it from the bucket? Why?

 (*c*) Write a procedure DELETE.

9-23 In an unordered linear symbol table the expected number of storage accesses per retrieval is $\mathscr{L}_1 = n/2$. Consequently, in Table 9-3, $\mathscr{L}_1$ should be $78/2 = 39$, but in fact it was only 31.56.

 (*a*) What is the most likely explanation for this discrepancy?

 (*b*) Does it tend to confirm or discredit the other values of that table?

9-24 Most of the discussion has centered on the expected value of $\mathscr{L}_1$. Determine approximate expressions for $\mathscr{L}_2$, $\mathscr{E}$, and $\mathscr{D}$.

9-25 Suppose that the symbol table of a compiler for a block-structured language is implemented by hash coding into buckets. Then two distinct variables with separate entries in the symbol table may be identified by the same key, say the symbol X. Why?

 (*a*) Which entry should be returned by the LOOKUP procedure?

 (*b*) Should the procedure ENTER (invoked only when scanning declarations) add new entries to the front or the rear of the list comprising the bucket?

 On exit from a block, all variable symbols declared locally within that block should be deleted from the symbol table.

 (*c*) Devise a method for quickly deleting such symbols. (*Hint:* Consider multilinking the elements of the buckets so that all symbols declared at lexical level k are simply linked as LIST[K].)

9-3 EXTERNAL AND INTERNAL NAMES

The most fundamental way of accessing or referencing information is by means of an identifier or name. A lecturing professor who wishes to identify some particular element in a structure drawn on a blackboard may point to it and refer to it as *this* point. But neither the pointing finger nor the demonstrative pronoun "this" makes a good identifier when removed from the process of face-to-face communication. In this text, *symbolic identifiers* or *labels* have been used to reference specific elements of abstract structures. Thus we may speak of the point y, the edge e_3, or the graph G. More formally we will say that a set S *names* the elements of a set V if there exists a function (possibly into) id:S $\rightarrow$ V. That is, the elements of S name, label, or identify† the corresponding elements in P. The functional relation id is called the *naming convention*. If the elements of S are strings of symbolic characters, they are said to be *symbolic names* or identifiers. Note that the function id need not be a one-to-one function. An element v ϵ V may well have several names. If the function id is only well defined on a subset S' $\subseteq$ S—that is, it is a partial function—then it may be extended to all of S by appending a special element Λ to V and assigning id(s) = Λ for all s ϵ S $\sim$ S'.

A particularly useful set of names is a set of storage addresses, say 0000 through 9999. We may adopt the naming convention that the integer addresses name a fixed portion of the storage hardware and thus indirectly the current contents of that storage. Primative machine languages employ this convention for identifying items of information in storage. But humans are far more accustomed to using symbolic names when referring to items of information; we find the use of integer identifiers unwieldy. An essential step in the specification of computer processes has been the design of "programmer" languages. These allow the programmer to use symbolic names to reference information by establishing a functional correspondence between each symbolic name and a corresponding integer location. In assemblers and compilers this correspondence is represented by means of symbol tables. Every symbolic string, including variable and literal identifiers, labels, and procedure names, appearing in the source program is associated with a storage location.

In higher-level compiler languages the naming convention id, which associates symbolic names with corresponding data values, is really a composite function id = $id_1 \circ id_2$. The first component id_1 maps symbolic names into the set of relocatable addresses at compile time which are later converted to actual locations through loader and linking conventions. The second component id_2, which assigns actual data values to storage locations, is effectively established only at run time during execution. Because the second component of the identification function is dynamic, we have the concept of a *variable identifier*. The

---

†Neither the term *name* nor *label* is completely satisfactory here, since both have many other connotations. In many respects the term *identifier* is preferable, but we prefer to reserve this for a somewhat more general concept. By using *name* we seek to emphasize that s ϵ S identifies a *unique* element v ϵ V.

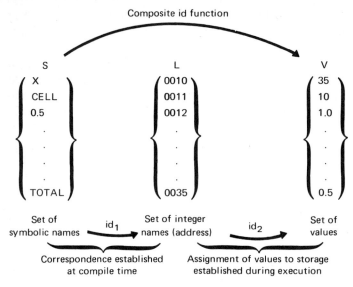

Figure 9-10 A schematic view of the correspondence between symbolic names and values.

symbolic identifier X always names the same storage location, but execution of an assignment operation changes the value that it names or identifies by changing the contents of that location. An assignment statement quite literally redefines the function id by varying the item of information ($v \in V$) identified by the symbolic name.

One of the essential features of higher-level compiler languages is that the composite nature of the naming function, which is schematically illustrated in Fig. 9-10, is deliberately hidden from the user. Only the overall composite function which associates data values to symbolic names is made apparent. The programmer is not supposed to be aware of storage locations and is never expected to use them.

This somewhat superficial introduction to the way that typical compilers establish a functional correspondence between symbolic names and their associated values has been presented for two reasons. The first is that throughout this text we have found it necessary to violate the standard conventions if we were to be able to manipulate general data structures by means of standard programming languages. Cells can only be referenced in terms of their storage addresses. And pointers (variables whose associated values or contents must be interpreted as storage locations) form the only means by which a process can gain access to a representational structure whose elements cannot be individually identified. A pointer variable in a process functions very much like the professor's finger at the blackboard. The variable identifier does not name an item of data; it only names the "pointing finger" to be followed.

Pointers are essential as a link between processes and a data structure on which they are operating. But there are many instances when we want to be able to identify the elements of the data structure itself. Both the "creation" and "transfer" (in the sense of input/output) of data structures require such naming capability. Thus a second, more compelling, reason to consider these aspects of compiler design is as follows: *If they are ever to use general data structures in a significant way, programmers must be able to build and maintain at run time those symbol tables to which they are accustomed to letting a compiler provide.* To justify this bald assertion let us consider the creation of a representation from an abstract model.

It is not hard to write procedures to construct a particular data structure or representation of a particular directed graph. A sequence of calls to subprocedures that create the necessary points and edges [such as POINT(Y)and EDGE(X, Y) described in Exercise 6-5] will suffice. It is evident that an instruction sequence of the form

pointer   g, w, x, y, z;
$$\vdots$$
w ←point(g);
x ←point(g);
call edge (w, x);
y ←point(g);   (9-4)
call edge (w, y);
call edge (y, x);
z ←point(g);
call edge (x, z);
call edge (y, z);

will create a representation of the graph shown in Fig. 9-11. But it creates only that structure. It is unreasonable to write a special-purpose procedure to create each of the many different structures one might wish to represent.

Conspicuously missing from Chap. 6 and all its exercises were any effective input procedures, yet it is surely preferable to replace the preceding nine statements with a general-purpose input process. That is, we want a procedure which will create the computer representation of an abstract structure *in accordance with a description,* or representation, *contained in some external file.* It should be able to construct a representation of this graph, together with many

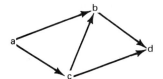

Figure 9-11 A simple graph on four points.

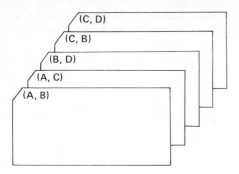

Figure 9-12 A punched-card description of the graph of Fig. 9-11

other graphs, based solely on a description of them. Figure 9-12 illustrates one such external representation in which the elements of the relation (i.e., edges) have been punched in fixed format, one edge per card.† Notice that in this punched-card representation, points of the graph are identified by the Hollerith characters {A, B, C, D}. The key step in the input process will be to establish a correspondence between the set of symbolic names {A, B, C, D} used in the punched-card representation and a set of integer storage locations used to name the cells of the computer representation. Establishment of this correspondence is precisely analogous to the naming function id_1, shown in Figure 9-10, save that it is done at run time.

Before presenting an input procedure, let us informally describe the way it might handle the first two records of the card file shown in Fig. 9-12. First, two new cells must be created, say with cell addresses 0015, and 0050, to represent the points known in the punched-card file by A and B, respectively. The correspondence must be recorded. Then the edge between these points (cells) is represented. The second card is processed differently. There is no need to create a new point to represent A. The routine need only look up the address of the corresponding cell. But no representation of the point C currently exists. It must be created. Then a representation of the edge (A, C) is created by passing these two cell addresses to the procedure EDGE. Thus the input process must build and interrogate a symbol table using procedures such as LOOKUP and ENTER of the preceding sections. Given these, it is not hard to implement the following input routine.

procedure input (g, file);
pointer   g;

This procedure inputs a structure g from the named file. That is, it creates a representation of the structure in accordance to its description on the file.

---

†This is by no means a preferred way of representing data structures in punched-card files; it is only illustrative. See Exercise 9-31.

```
begin
    pointer  p1, pw, x1, x2
    while not endof file do
        read p1, p2;
        format (1X, A1, 1X, A1);
        x1 ←lookup(p1);
        if x1 =nullvalue
            then   Create a new point corresponding to p1.
                   x1 ←point(g);
                   call enter (p1, x1);
        x2 ←lookup(p2);
        if x2 =nullvalue
            then   Create a new point corresponding to p2.
                   x2 ←point(g);
                   call enter (p2, x2);

        Represent the edge (p1, p2) by an edge (x1, x2).
        call edge (x1, x2);

    All records read.

    exit;
    end
```

Using this procedure as a model we can distinguish between the concepts of internal and external names. Elements of abstract data structures are identified by *external names* which are usually symbolic strings. Elements of representations are identified by *internal names* which are commonly integer addresses. The suggestive synonyms *symbolic key* and *actual key* are widely used in commercial applications.

A process is said to have *access* to a representation if it contains a pointer referencing at least one of its cells. Actually this is only a necessary condition of access. Effective access may require in addition an accessing mechanism together with various "access privileges," such as passwords.

In the sample process INPUT the variable names p1, p2, x1, and x2 are neither internal nor external names. They merely serve to identify four different pointer variables within the procedure itself. It is the value (or contents) of these pointer variables that is the name. This may appear to be an unnecessarily fine distinction. There seems little harm in referring to p1 as the external name of an element and x1 as its internal name, since it is clear from the context of the procedure that their values will always be external and internal names, respectively.† Moreover, Cobol would use the phrase "P1 IS SYMBOLIC-

---

†As we have noted before, the policy of ascribing properties of the contents of a variable to the variable itself is characteristic of higher-level languages. By declaring a variable to be **real** we are really asserting that its value will always be a real number (or more precisely, should be interpreted as a real value).

KEY" to declare that the value of that data item is an external name. But there are times when perception of the difference is important. See Exercise 9-26, for example.

Elements of representational structures may be identified by internal names which are used by referencing pointers within a process. How may entire structures themselves be named? If the structure has a *least* point, then one may tacitly assume that the name of the least point is the name of the entire structure, since a process which has access to the least point (e.g., a pointer to it) thereby gains access to the entire structure. Lists, stacks, queues, and principal trees are all characterized by the fact that they have a least point. Throughout we have been using variable pointers called LIST, STACK, or TREE. Although they actually referenced only a single cell in the structure we treated them as if they named the entire structure, since *by convention* they referenced the least points of the structures. (This is a major reason for calling the function id a *naming convention*.) This simplified naming ability has been the basis of several data manipulation languages which have restricted themselves to just this class of structures with least points (Shneiderman and Scheurerman, 1974). It probably accounts for the fact that these are the most useful and most studied computer data structures.

How can more general data structures without least points be named? Although pointers, such as g in the procedure INPUT, have been used to reference entire structures, we have been somewhat sketchy about their actual significance. The author prefers to allocate a separate cell in the representation to serve as a kind of header cell and denote the entire structure. Then it is easy to associate the address of this cell as an internal name corresponding to the external name by which the entire structure S_M is referenced. Fields within this cell may then be used (1) to begin a separate linear thread linking all the point cells of the structure, (2) to link to explicit representations of the sets of points and/or edges of the structure, (3) to link to only the minimal and maximal points of the structure, (4) to link to other cells denoting subsets or substructures, or any combination of these functions. Figure 9-13 shows a possible format of

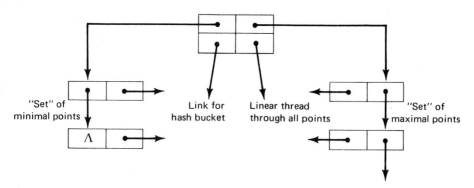

Figure 9-13 One of many possible formats of a graph header cell.

such a *graph cell*. In GRAAL (Sec. 6-2), one element x_i of the universe X of objects was used to denote the entire structure and appropriate cells were entered into its property ring. Neither of these methods is in any sense standard. Both impose additional overhead to any process which manipulates or alters the structure. The best way to name or reference entire data structures is still an open question, including the subquestion as to whether in certain kinds of applications one needs to name the entire structure at all.

The elements v of some set V may be identified by naming them with elements of some other set. But there are other ways of identifying and locating objects of interest. Objects may be identified by means of a characteristic property. The string "the first president of the United States" identifies precisely the same individual as does the string "George Washington." A variable may be identified by a symbolic name X or it may be identified by the string "a variable whose current value is 5.0." This latter string may identify the variable X, but it may also identify a number of other variables whose value is 5.0 at the time of utterance. This illustrates the fact that identifiers need not always denote unique elements; they often denote sets of elements. We will say that the elements of a set S *identify* elements in the set V, if there exists a function mapping S into the power set of V; that is, id:$S \rightarrow 2^V$. If the image id(s) is always a singleton set (or an empty set), then the elements of S *name* the elements of V.

A function of this form, in which the image id(s) of $s \in S$ may be a set $\{v_1, v_2, \ldots, v_k\}$, is just a relation from the set S to the set V with $R(s) = \{v_1, v_2, \ldots, v_k\}$. If identification is nothing more than a general relation, the reader may well ask what is the value of making a definition such as this. In a sense it has no value. The concept of identification is a very general one. It is as general as the theory of relations. Yet people tend to regard identification as a rather special process. By giving such a general definition we emphasize the fact that an identification process works only when some certain constraints are placed on the identifying relation (such as naming conventions) and that such conditions should be explicitly stated.

By *information retrieval* one usually means a process which returns the name, or names, of items of information that have been identified in this more general sense. These items may be identified by a single property ("an article about data structures") or a list of properties ("an article about linear structures, written after 1975, appearing in either the *Journal* or the *Communications* of the ACM"). Once the retrieval process returns a set of names (they may be internal or external names) the referenced items may be directly accessed. A major concern in the field of information retrieval is the specification of identifying properties in such a manner that the set of returned names is small. If given an identifying property s, it is known that $|\{id(s)\}| \leq 1$, then the identifying property s becomes a name. This is normally unreasonable to expect. But one might seek to place an upper bound, say $|\{id(s)\}| < m$, on the retrieval process.

Search procedures are fundamental tools in information retrieval. Given a large structured data base, one may initiate a search process to find a point x such that "$f_i(x) \geq 17.39$," "$f_j(x)$ is minimal," or "$f_k(x)$ denotes a winning configuration in a game-playing situation." Search in a structured data base is equivalent to path finding. It is this application which largely justifies the extensive treatment of path finding in Sec. 6-3. Formal properties of the data base affect the nature of search processes. It is frequently assumed that the structure is *connected* so that the search may be exhaustive if necessary. Search procedures frequently begin at one element and then "sweep" across the structure. Of key importance, therefore, are the *minimal* elements of the structure, since they may be used as entry points to search procedures. Similarly, properties of acyclicity and basicness, if known, may be used to optimize retrieval processes based on search techniques. The tree-structured symbol tables of Sec. 9-1 illustrate this latter point. The LOOKUP procedure is essentially a path-finding process. Yet by carefully organizing the structure to reflect a total ordering on the key values k_i, neither of the time-consuming depth-first or breadth-first search algorithms was necessary. The desired element was found (or shown not to exist) without constructing trial paths and without backtracking. The example of symbol-table lookup illustrates another common feature of information retrieval by search techniques.

We have been treating individual variable pointers as the basic mechanism by which processes access, or gain entry, to data structures. Instead one may regard an entire data structure as a pointer, or structured collection of pointers, to some other data structure. The representation of the bicycle-component relation shown in Fig. 8-17 is one example. A *directory* of file names maintained by an operating system is another. Frequently the actual search is conducted in this auxiliary structure before actual access is made to some larger data base to obtain the desired item(s) of information.

Instead of retrieving information by executing search *processes,* one may instead try to represent the identifying relation id as a *data structure.* A classic example of this approach is the concept of *inverted file structures,* which will be considered in Chap. 11. They attempt to directly model the identifying relationship.

The conventional way of identifying items of information in computer storage is by assigning addresses which effectively name the hardware locations which contain the items. Thus an element's internal name is purely an artifact of its particular assignment to hardware. It is in no sense intrinsic to the item itself. Given the address or name, a process can access and use the information. But much of the latter discussion suggests that many items of information are more naturally identified by their contents. Is there any way by which the items could be literally "addressed" by their contents? Alternatively, is there any way by which addresses could be permanently assigned independent of the particular hardware location to which it is assigned? The answer to both questions is yes, and these approaches to data naming and access are discussed in detail in the next section.

The concept of external and internal names was introduced from the context of the reasonably familiar problem of the input of data structures into core storage from an external file. This is really just a particular instance of a much larger problem in the management of data structures. With very large data structures, say with more than 10,000 elements, one must assume that the representation exists on some mass storage device with relatively slow access times,† not core storage. Procedures must be developed so that processes can identify and access relevant elements of this externally represented structure. If in addition one is operating in the context of a distributed network with multiple processors, then the structure may have to be transferred from one device to another, from one computing system to another. The transfers constitute input/output operations of massive proportions. While there is a paucity of effective solutions in this newly developing technology of very large data bases, the techniques developed in this chapter and in Chap. 11 often function as key components.

EXERCISES FOR SECTION 9-3

9-26 It would appear that the variable names w, x, y, and z in the sequence of statements (9-4) identify the points of the representation the sequence creates. Show that this is largely an illusion by recoding the sequence so that only three of these variable identifiers are used. Can it be done with only two pointer variables?

9-27 Procedures given in earlier sections did create data structures from input sequences; the tree-structured symbol table of Sec. 9-1 created by repeated calls to ENTER is a notable example. In a sense, the sequence of keys defined an abstract tree which was then represented. Would you want to regard this as an input operation? Justify your answer.

9-28 Lists can be input from an external file without involving external and internal names (see RDLIST in Exercise 8-9), and thus, by Theorem 8-5, so can principal trees. Can any other sort of relational structure be so input?

9-29 The input and output of lists can be performed without establishing an explicit correspondence based on internal and external names. Yet a correspondence must still be made between elements of the external file and elements (variables) of the program. How is this correspondence accomplished?

*9-30 Implement the procedure INPUT. Use it to test other procedures, such as path finding and topological sorting, that have been written for previous exercises. (Use any version of the subprocedures LOOKUP and ENTRY.)

*9-31 Implementation of INPUT raises many questions concerning its general utility. Revise it so that it can input:

 (*a*) graphs with edge assignment functions (test it by reading flow graphs or PERT networks as in Figs. 6-1 and 6-2),

 (*b*) graphs with isolated points, and

 (*c*) graphs with point assignment functions.

9-32 In standard Fortran, PL/1, or Cobol input/output operations a correspondence between elements of the external file and elements internal to the process must be made. A description of the external structure is given which governs the input/output operation.

---

†Such low-speed mass storage is commonly called *secondary storage* in contrast to high-speed random-access memories, which are called *primary storage*. Disk files are an example of the former; core storage is a prototype of the latter.

(*a*) How is the correspondence established?

(*b*) How is the external structure described? Give examples of differences in the I/O process that arise from different descriptions.

Technically input/output, or transfer of data, should be described in terms of three distinct processes: a process which accesses and gets an item from the external (internal) structure, a process which changes its representation (if necessary), and a process which accesses and places it in its proper position in the internal (external) structure. The proposed I/O specifications for Algol-60 were an attempt to specify the syntax of input/output operations within this logical framework.

(*c*) Read Knuth (1964). Does it provide more flexible I/O facilities for data structure transmission?

9-33 Input using the *namelist* concept (Fortran and PL/1 programming languages) employs external names. Explain.

9-34 It is stated that "cells can only be referenced in terms of their storage address." But in a typical scientific program, in say Fortran or PL/1, all items of information used by the process—that is variables, arrays, etc.—are given symbolic names by the programmer. Why can't all the cells of a general data structure be declared and given symbolic names by the programmer?

*9-35 External and internal names have been defined as those names referencing elements of abstract data structures S_M and their computer representations S_R, respectively. An alternative and in many ways more appealing definition is that they reference elements of data structures whose representation is external to the process or is internal to the process. Both definitions are difficult to make precise, as shown by the following questions.

(*a*) Can one refer to elements of an "abstract" structure, or must one always refer to some sort of representation? Remember that a drawing of a graph is a representation.

(*b*) What do the phrases "external to the process" and "internal to the process" mean? Is an array defined and created in one procedure but whose name is passed as a parameter to a subprocedure external to the subprocedure?

(*c*) Should one equate "external representation" with "permanent representation" and "internal representation" with "temporary representation"?

(*d*) Is the actual address of an element in a disk file an external or an internal name?

(*e*) Try to rigorously define the concepts of external and internal names.

9-36 Variable subscripting is a way of altering an array identifier during execution. Explain.

*9-37 Much of this section has been concerned with identifying elements of data structures which *exist independently* of any particular process using them. The techniques developed have been different from the way that scalar variables or arrays are referenced in "normal" programs.

(*a*) Can an array (or other variable) declared in a procedure have an independent existence "outside" the procedure? How? Do you consider such variables as data structures?

(*b*) Can a pointer exist without being embodied in a pointing process?

9-38 The problem of output was not even considered in this section. Assume that we have some representation of a data structure which we want to display on the line printer. Write a procedure PRINTG to do this. You will find that you must first solve two subproblems. First, you must devise a way of converting internal names to external names. [*Hint:* Consider appending a field to each representing cell which either explicitly contains the external name or else points to the entry (key, addr).] More importantly, you must decide what constitutes an adequate description of the structure, i.e., what should actually be displayed on the line printer. (This latter is a nontrivial problem of judgment, and the author knows of no completely satisfactory answer.)

*9-39 The elements of a set of identifying names can be manipulated just as any other set of values. Expressions such as "cell + 1" have been used when the names are integer addresses. In Snobol (Griswold, 1968) the data items of interest are strings which may be named and referenced by strings (e.g., id:S $\rightarrow$ S). Given a command to perform some operation, say to concatenate S with R, are the operands to be regarded as the identifiers themselves which would yield a new identifier SR, or the strings that they reference?

(*a*) How does Snobol resolve this ambiguity?

(*b*) What conventions has this text adopted? If "cell" is a pointer variable, does "cont(cell)" denote the contents of the variable itself or the contents of the referenced location?

(*c*) Explain the role of indirect addressing here.

(*d*) Suppose the operation is defined on the identifying names themselves. Need the result be a name? Is "cell + 1" a name? Is SR?

9-40 In his list language L⁶, Knowlton (1966) devised a unique naming convention in which item names literally described a process for retrieving them. Briefly, cell fields were named by letters such as {A, B, C, D, ...} while pointer variables were also restricted to single letters {..., X, Y, Z}. The string XAB then references the contents of the B field of the cell named by the A field of the cell named by the pointer X.

(*a*) Look up and read Knowlton's provocative paper.

(*b*) Give a necessary condition for any identifying string to be well formed. Can a sufficient condition be given?

(*c*) What are the strengths and deficiencies of this naming convention?

(*d*) How have we been naming fields?

9-41 In a mathematical expression such as

$$f(x, y) = x^2 + 3xy$$

there has always been ambiguity as to whether the string "f(x, y)" identifies the expression "$x^2 + 3xy$" or the value of that expression given values for x and y. In mathematics the question is largely academic since the correct interpretation is invariably clear from the context. In the design of programming languages which symbolically manipulate arithmetic expressions (in contrast to the numerical manipulation of standard algebraic languages) the issue becomes more critical. Design and code a small package of routines which will interpretatively implement a simple symbolic manipulation language. containing commands such as

$$f \leftarrow x**2 + 3*x*y;$$
$$g \leftarrow x + 3;$$
$$x \leftarrow 2;$$
$$h \leftarrow f + g;$$
$$\text{print } f(x);$$
$$\text{print } f(g);$$

If one ignores the very difficult problem of the simplification of expressions (Bobrow, 1968), then implementation of a simple system is not technically hard. Expressions can be represented by either lists or trees. But the reader will quickly come face to face with the issues: What do symbols mean? and What do identifiers denote? in a very concrete way. For example, does x denote an expression or a value? A more ambitious project will add symbolic differentiation (follow a postorder traversal in a tree representation) to implement commands such as

$$f(d, x) \leftarrow \text{diff}(f, x);$$

where the expression on the left should be regarded as similar to an array identifier f modified by formal subscripts d and x.

9-42 In automatic theorem proving and symbolic logic in general, "identifier" and "function" are regarded as *synonyms* [cf. Nilsson (1971), Robinson (1965)]. This is true in the syntax of Algol as well (Naur, 1963). Thus a functional expression such as SIN(0.5) is regarded not as a command to perform some computational process, but rather as simply a reference to the named value, in this case 0.4795. (Of course, accessing the named value may involve some computational work, but this may be equally true in accessing the value of the constant 0.4795 or the variable identifier X.) A variable expression such as SIN(X) still names a value, but in this case the particular value named depends on the current value of X. (Conversely, one may regard all symbolic names, e.g., the variable name X, as merely special parameterless functions which access the named item of information.) Symbolic names can be more complex strings. For example, the string "2 + 2" identifies an integer value which is more commonly known by the name "4." Similarly, all arithmetic expression simply name values.

What we have done here is to sketch some preliminary justifications for the thesis that *all computer programs involve little more than the manipulation of identifiers and the access of corresponding items in storage*. Either systematically extend this thesis or critically refute it.

9-4 ASSOCIATIVE AND VIRTUAL MEMORIES

Storage in which items of information are referenced by their contents (or value) rather than an independent set of integer addresses is called *content-addressable memory* or *associative memory*. It is an appealing idea because it is conjectured that much of human memory works in this fashion. It is doubtful if we establish separate "names" for all the various items of information that we store away in our memories. Consider a question such as "Does the road to Burnley Station turn left or right off Route 29?" It appears that the phrase "road to Burnley Station" serves as a pattern† which is simultaneously compared with all the many "packets" of geographical information we have squirreled away in our minds. That packet, or packets, which matches the pattern is brought to our attention together with all the other items of information that have been associated in that packet—such as how one gets to the road from the highway. The concept of access based on only a part of a packet's contents such that *all* associated information that has been stored in that item is retrieved is the source of the term *associative memory*.

A computer associative memory consists of a collection of r words of storage each n bits in length. n should be quite large since each word must be able to contain two or more fields if the associating property is to work. Supplementing this basic collection of storage are (1) a *pattern and mask register* in which the pattern, or key, on which to retrieve and its position, or field, within the words is indicated; and (2) one or more *response registers*. Figure 9-14 illustrates a configuration of an associative memory. The bit pattern 1011001 is set in the pattern and mask register with all other bits masked out. All r locations of the associative store are compared simultaneously (or in parallel) against the pattern register, and if there is a match, a corresponding bit is set in one of the response registers (which must be r bits in length). In the figure, at least three items were found with partial contents equal to 1011001.

Use of the response registers is the key to using an associative memory. As shown above, bits (or flags) are set in a specified register, say r1, in response to matches that are found in a pattern search. Suppose that the response to a different search is set in the register r2. By just performing boolean operations on these registers one can implement compound retrieval patterns. A statement of

---

†While linguistic phrases such as "road to Burnley Station" may be used as patterns in certain kinds of human information retrieval, it is likely that visual, aural, and even olfactory patterns are of more importance. It is fascinating to speculate on the mechanisms by which information in the human mind is represented, structured, and retrieved in contrast to computer representations.

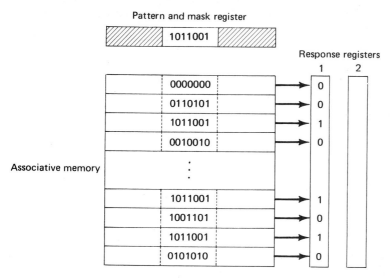

Figure 9-14 Configuration of an associative memory.

the form

r1 ←r1 V r2;

would flag in register 1 just those elements of the associative store which matched either pattern1 *or* pattern2. Similarly, all those elements matching pattern1 *but not* pattern2 could be flagged, and so on. The response registers are used to retrieve information from the memory. They are also used to enter it. Reversing the operation, a pattern in the pattern and mask register can be set to rewrite that portion of all items that have been flagged in a specified register.

The response registers r1 and r2 interact naturally with the associative memory in both data entry and retrieval. Their interaction with a conventional sequential process is somewhat more involved. Each response register identifies a set of information, so there must be a mechanism by which the set denoted by the register can be converted into a representation, perhaps a linked representation in which individual elements of the set can be identified, addressed, and used as operands in the process. Remember that, in theory at least, the items of the associative memory cannot be individually addressed. Such a transformation might occur by executing a statement of the form

seta ←r1;

But what should be the elements of seta? Should they be copies of the entire associative items flagged by register r1? Or should they be copies of only those portions of the associated items which are of interest? Both this problem and the value of associative memory can be better illustrated by two concrete applications.

In both applications we will be working with a collection of unspecified "objects"; they may be strings, numerical values, sets, functions, or what have you. Each object is assumed to be denoted by an internal name of fixed length such as a hardware address or index. In describing the applications we will always use symbolic names such as a, b, k, 1, f(k), etc. It is understood that they denote the corresponding internal name. Further, we will divide the words of the associative memory into fixed fields or components which will be denoted by comp1, comp2, comp3.

A symbol table can be implemented using an associative memory with two-component words. An element of the table (k, f(k)) will be denoted by setting comp1 and comp2 of some available word in the store to k and f(k), respectively. The procedure lookup can be implemented by the simple two-statement sequence

r1 ← find (k,*);
lookup ← comp2 (r1);

In this sequence the parameters k and * define the search pattern; * is used to denote the "don't care" condition in the second component. Consequently, the response register r1 flags the element of the table with field matching the search key k. The expression comp2(r1) creates a set whose elements are the objects of the second field of those associative items flagged by r1. The value of **lookup** is thus a pointer to this set of elements (presumably at most 1 if the keys are all distinct, or possibly empty).

Sequences to enter new elements to the table:

r1 ← find(Λ, Λ);
if empty(r1) **then** "overflow";
any (r1) ← newitem(k, f(k));

and to delete entries:

r1 ← find(k, f(k));
r1 ← newitem(Λ, Λ);

are nearly as easy to implement. Notice the use of the response register in statements storing new elements into the store. In the first instance, *any* of the words flagged by r1, but only one, will be set to the new value. In the second case all words flagged by r1 will be set to the specified value. More importantly notice that the expected lookup, entry, and deletion times, that is $\mathscr{L}_1, \mathscr{L}_2, \mathscr{E}$, and $\mathscr{D}$, are constant. Since the search process FIND is conducted by hardware which examines all items in the associative memory in parallel, this crucial step requires but two CPU cycles *regardless of the number of items entered into the symbol table.* Hardware associative memories permit extremely fast table-lookup operations.

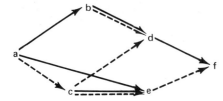

Figure 9-15 Two trees, E_1 (denoted by solid edges) and E_2 (denoted by dashed edges), defined on a common set of points.

For a second application, let us use an associative memory whose items are subdivided into three fields to represent abstract graphs, or relations. Figure 9-15 shows a set of six points, or objects, on which two tree-structured relations have been defined. The points are objects which have been denoted by a, b, . . . , f. The sets $E_1 = \{(a, b), (a, e), (b, d), (c, e), (d, f)\}$, and $E_2 = \{(a, c), (b, c), (c, d), (c, e), (e, f)\}$ are also objects which will be denoted by 1 and 2, respectively. The relations will be represented in the associative memory by a set of *triples* of the form $\{(1, a, b), (1, a, e), . . . , (1, d, f), (2, a, c), . . . , (2, c, e)\}$. Given this kind of representation, it should be apparent that the following sequence

r1 ← find(1, a, *);
rnbhr ← comp3(r1);

is an implementation of the right neighbor operator which generates the set $R_{E_1}(a) = \{b, e\}$. The set of all objects which are left neighbors of d with respect to E_2 but are not left neighbors with respect to E_1 is given by

r1 ← find(2, *, d);
r2 ← find(1, *, d);
set ← comp2(r1 ~ r2);

Compare the expected cost of this right neighbor procedure with those considered in Sec. 6-1. Is the cost of this associative implementation of rnbhr a constant independent of either $|P|$ or $|R(y)|$ as was the previous symbol-table lookup process?

Given the very fast and elegant implementation of procedures using an associative memory, it seems surprising that they have not been widely used in the representation of data structures. There are two reasons for this. The first and primary reason is cost. A single register of associative storage costs roughly as much as a single arithmetic operation register. But the cost of a module of r associative registers is not r times the cost of a single register. Because the parallel search capability must be wired in, the cost of a module is a *nonlinear* function of its size. Modules of 256 registers represent the current economic upper limit on associative memory size. To justify their expense, associative memories must be used in high-density, high-payoff applications. Representation of a page table in virtual memory implementations will be one such application.

Although large associative memories for the representation of large data structures are prohibitively expensive, they may be simulated. Equivalents may be simulated using either linked-list (Findler, 1972) or hash-coding methods. We will explore the latter much more thoroughly in the next section.

The second problem inhibiting widespread use of associative techniques concerns the linguistic specification of general procedures. Earlier we remarked on the central position of the response register and the ambiguity surrounding it. Each response register represents a set. In lieu of any other specification it represents a set of associative items, and in the latter example execution of the statement

seta ← r1;

should generate a set of triples. But in practice one seldom wants the triples themselves. The sequence which generated the set rnbhr, of right neighbors of a, created a set of simple objects consisting of only one field of those triples denoted by r1. The response to the search statement

r2 ← find(1, *, *)

which returns all of the edges in E_1 should be a set of pairs of objects. What conventions should be adopted to indicate the nature of the set returned by a retrieval operation? One would be tempted to assume that kind of set returned by a retrieval operation can be determined by the number of "blanks" or "stars" in the search pattern. But consider a retrieval statement such as

r1 ← find(*, c, *);

Clearly its intent is to find all right neighbors of the object c with respect to any relation defined on the system. This should be the set of simple objects or points {d, e}, not the set of pairs {(2, d), (1, e), (2, e)}.† Consequently a general-purpose associative language must have a syntax sufficiently rich that it can explicitly specify and use a much wider variety of sets than we have heretofore considered. This is not insurmountable, but the resulting complexities have inhibited its acceptance.

The concept of a virtual memory is very different. The prototype of an internal name has been a cell address, or the address of some location in random-access core storage. It is easiest to build linked data structures in core storage; it is easiest to write processes which access their data in core storage. But core storage is limited and it is expensive. As our data structures become large, its expense and its limited size force us to carefully weigh issues of economical representation and of possible free-pool overflow. Suppose instead that unlimited core storage were available; then there would be no upper bound on the

---

†Notice that these two sets have different cardinalities.

number or size of cells that could be used, and no upper bound on the internal names or addresses by which they would be referenced. Many of these representational problems now vanish. Perhaps the desire for unlimited core storage is a pipe dream, but surprisingly we can just *pretend* that storage is unlimited. Such storage is called *virtual memory*. To the programmer it appears that unlimited storage is available for the representation of data structures. Consequently many problems do in fact disappear. Naturally, aspects of the same problems reappear, but in different guise. In the remainder of this section we give a brief introduction to virtual memory concepts so that the nature of representational problems in this environment can be discussed. A more comprehensive discussion can be found in Denning (1970), whose terminology we use, and its implementation from an operating systems point of view in texts such as Freeman (1975). We will consider only implementation by means of paging methods.

The set of all internal names is called a *name space* or *address space*. This space will be subdivided into fixed-size *pages* of 1000 addresses (locations, words, or bytes) each.† Thus a virtual address of 10,295 would denote the relative location 295 on page 10. Consequently, virtual addresses may be regarded as consisting of two parts or fields, a *page number* and a relative *offset* within the page.

While we may pretend that data structures are represented in this unlimited virtual memory,‡ each page must in fact be physically represented in some form of hardware storage. At any given time, some pages may be represented in disk storage and others may be represented in core storage. But all exist somewhere, and they must be accessible. The set of all physical storage locations is called the *memory space*. It too is subdivided into chunks of 1000 addresses called blocks or page frames. A *block address* is the machine address of the first word or byte of the block. If it is a block of core storage, then the block address is a core address, say L_1, as we have been normally using. If the block is in disk or drum storage, then the block address is that used by the device. Disk addresses are typically of the form (d, c, h, s) where d is a drive or spindle number, c is a cylinder number, h is a read/write head number, and s is a sector number. All virtual pages are assigned to physical blocks.§

Let us assume for the moment that all virtual pages of interest have been assigned to in-core blocks, as shown in Fig. 9-16. Notice that pages which are

---

†Pages may be of any size. 1000, or more precisely 1024, is a common length, although some authors claim larger pages are preferable while others claim smaller pages lead to optimal use of storage. If the name space is subdivided into variably sized pieces, it is said to be a *segmented virtual memory*, and somewhat different implementation techniques are appropriate.

‡Even virtual memory is not really unlimited. It is bounded by the number of bits allocated to address fields of machine instructions. But this is generally large enough to give an illusion of unbounded storage.

§For pedagogic simplicity we will assume that all secondary storage is disk storage. In practice one might expect to see both disks and a high-speed paging drum as secondary storage hardware.

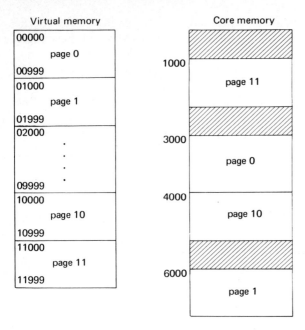

Figure 9-16 An assignment of virtual pages to blocks of core memory.

contiguous in the virtual memory need not be represented in contiguous blocks, although locations within a single block are contiguous. The shaded blocks do not represent pages of *this* virtual memory—perhaps they are being used to represent pages of some other user's virtual memory.

Every virtual address, such as 10295, as it is encountered in an instruction stream must first be converted into its corresponding memory address by means of a table lookup in a page table, as illustrated in Fig. 9-17. Here we are implementing yet another functional correspondence which maps one set of identifying names into another set of names in much the same way that symbolic external names were mapped into integer internal names. Any table lookup procedure will suffice. But since all links and pointers and all processes are given in terms of virtual addresses, the operand of nearly every machine instruction will have to be decoded. This density of use justifies the expense of hardware associative-memory modules for table lookup, and it is in just this special application that they are most often found.

Suppose that a virtual address references a page that has not been assigned to a block of core memory. Then the lookup in the page table will return a nullvalue indicating that the entry (page number, block address) has not been found. This is called a *page fault.* The page has been assigned to secondary storage. The process which maps virtual addresses into memory addresses must now search a second table which represents the mapping of pages into secondary storage; find the location of the missing page, and exchange it for one of the pages now assigned to a block in core memory. Page swapping is ex-

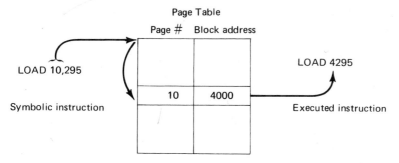

Figure 9-17 Conversion of a virtual address to a memory address by lookup in a page table.

pensive. Memory access to a virtual location already assigned to core takes about 1 microsecond. Access to a location on a page that must be swapped typically takes at least 10 milliseconds, an increase on the order of 10^4. Repeated page faults followed by their consequent page swapping lead to a condition in which the central processor spends an inordinate percentage of its time in the overhead of exchanging pages rather than computation. It is the price that an unwary programmer may have to pay for obtaining virtually unbounded storage.

The occurrence of page faults can be minimized if on the occurrence of a page fault, that page which is swapped out, or replaced, is the page which is least likely to be referenced in the near future. Various replacement strategies have been proposed. A reasonable choice is that page which has been least recently referenced, called the LRU strategy. (See Exercise 6-22 for an analogous problem.) Most analysis of replacement strategies has been based on a theory of *locality of reference*. This concept seeks to describe the pattern of memory references based on the structure of a process or program. For example, a tight loop would be considered a "locality" with a distinctive pattern of repeated memory references. It is assumed that for the pattern of storage references associated with each locality there is an optimal configuration of pages assigned to core. The goal is to minimize and possibly eliminate page swapping save when program control crosses the boundary from the locality into another.

We are less concerned with program structure than with data structure. The author is unaware of any formal theory of locality with respect to the assignment of data structures to pages, but it is an obvious problem. The literature abounds with descriptions of steps taken by systems designers to avoid representations which needlessly cross page boundaries. Let us consider three of the more evident steps. If at all possible, an entire array should be stored on a single page. (Most decent compilers will automatically assure this.) If the array is too large for a single page, say it is a $30 \times 30 \times 30$ array $[a_{ijk}]$, and if i and k are the indices of the innermost loops of the process, then the array should be decomposed in such a manner that cells representing the i-k planes are stored in a single block. Unfortunately, this is seldom an option open to the system designer, since the decomposition of arrays into sequential storage is bound to the associated accessing convention assumed by the language (see Sec. 7-1). The only alternative options are to restructure the process itself so that its looping structure reflects the storage policies of the implementing compiler, or if that is impossible, to implement one's own accessing conventions as described in Sec. 7-1. On occasion this latter option has paid large dividends in the reduction of paging overhead.

In linked representations it is clear that complete lists should be stored in a single page. If implementing a hashing function into buckets, then the array of pointers and the linked cells of its buckets should be confined to a single page.†
These two observations place an unusual constraint on cell allocation procedures such as GIVEME. Normally these procedures (see Secs. 3-3 and 10-1) simply allocate the next available cell in the free pool of cells. An optimal allocation routine in a paged environment would return a cell whose position in the virtual memory is dependent on the location of those cells it is to be linked to.

If a large linked data structure is to be represented over a number of pages, then it should be partitioned into page-sized neighborhoods so that the links between neighborhoods are minimized. Procedures to partition graphs have been widely studied and appear in diverse sources. In operations research they are called *line-balancing* problems, and in electrical engineering they appear as *network-partitioning* procedures whose goal is to position components of an electrical network on chips so as to minimize interconnections. The latter is a direct analog of the placement of cells in pages. Unfortunately, all these partitioning procedures assume an existing representation of the structure. Only in the case of very large structures with a relatively long and static expected lifetime would it pay to create an optimally partitioned copy using one of these procedures. A procedure, which must almost certainly be a heuristic strategy, to partition dynamic structures as they evolve constitutes a fascinating area of research.

The preceding strategies which seek to place coherent collections, or neighborhoods, of memory references on a single page create a different problem, called *internal fragmentation*. Consider the example of the $30 \times 30 \times 30$ array $[a_{ijk}]$. If to minimize page faults each of its 30×30 j-k cells is put in separate 1000-word pages, then in each page there will be 100 unused locations, or in the 30 pages needed to represent the entire array, 3000 unused locations. In a paged virtual memory, if any location of a page is used, the entire page must be reserved.‡ Arrays, data structures, and program segments seldom exactly fill pages. The unused wastage is the internal fragmentation. This waste can be minimized by using more, but smaller, pages. Denning (1970) shows that, based on empirical studies of expected program and array

---

†Or h(k) could hash into page numbers whose first location could be a pointer to the cells of that bucket, all of which are represented on that page.

‡In segmented virtual memory, segments of the exact size needed are reserved. There is no internal fragmentation. But see Sec. 10-2.

lengths, the optimal page size is ≤ 45 words. Smaller page sizes mean larger paging tables, which become too long for associative lookup techniques. Thus one begins to trade memory access time for storage. The issue of optimal page size has not yet been settled.

Internal fragmentation can arise from another source. In systems that manipulate dynamic data structures it is often desirable to eliminate the overhead of returning unused cells to the free store. Instead they are just discarded. New cells are allocated from the seemingly inexhaustible virtual memory. In time, early pages become quite sparse as more and more of their locations are discarded. Such sparse pages both waste storage and increase the probability of page faults. This form of internal fragmentation can be eliminated by a process called *compactification,* whose details are better left to Sec. 10-3.

EXERCISES FOR SECTION 9-4

9-43 Does a hash-coded symbol table using processes **enter, lookup,** etc., simulate a symbol table implemented by associative hardware? Justify your response.

*9-44 Three different ways (search tree, hash coding, and associative retrieval) have been presented for finding the functional value f(k) of an element k, given an explicit representation of the function f. The inverse problem of finding the set $\{k_i\} = f^{-1}(v)$, given some value v in the range, has been ignored.

(*a*) Write a short sequence of statements using an associative representation which returns the set $f^{-1}(v)$.

(*b*) Sketch what would be involved in finding $f^{-1}(v)$ in either of the hash-coded or search-tree representations.

(*c*) Exercise 9-38, which requires conversion from internal names back to external names, touches on this issue. But does it constitute a general solution to the problem of finding $f^{-1}(v)$?

9-45 An effective telephone directory can be represented by associative triples whose three objects denote the name of a telephone subscriber, the location (address) of the telephone, and its number. Consider the following set of associative items:

Name	Address	Telephone No.
(Black W.,	103 Cameron St.,	977-4663)
(Black W.,	17 E. Main St.,	977-4663)
(Jones H.,	1400 West Road,	295-6700)
(Jones R.,	1400 West Road,	295-0481)
(Jones R.,	1400 West Road,	295-0482)
(Peter T.,	855 Field Road,	973-5524)
(Smith A.,	200 High Street,	977-4303)
(Smith A.,	12 Windermere Rd.,	295-1196)
(Smith J.,	12 Windermere Rd.,	295-1196)
(White P.,	17 E. Main St.,	977-8448)

Give sequences of appropriate statements that would answer the following retrieval requests (and visually provide actual answers using the information above).

(*a*) What is a named individual's (e.g., R. Jones) telephone number?

(*b*) Who lives, or works, at a given address (e.g., 17 E. Main St., 1400 West Road)?

(*c*) At what address is a telephone to be found, and who is the listed subscriber (e.g., 295-1196, 977-4663)?

9-46 Consider the following associative items in a school data base, and the following queries.

Name	Subject	Grade
Black W.	Biology	D
	Mathematics	A
	Physics	B
Jones H.	Computer Science	A
	English	C
	Physics	B
Peter T.	Biology	D
	English	F
	Mathematics	C
Smith A.	Computer Science	D
	English	A
	Physics	A
White P.	Biology	F
	Computer Science	D
	Mathematics	C

(*a*) Who has taken computer science?

(*b*) Who received the most A's?

(*c*) Which subject gave the most D's?

(*d*) How many students failed at least one subject?

Given an associative representation of the data, can these questions be answered? Can they be answered by processes expressed in only the kinds of associative statements introduced so far? What linguistic constructs did you use to describe these retrieval processes?

9-47 The following sequence, which purports to find all objects which constitute a neighborhood of the object y [that is, all "adjacent" objects, $N(y) = L(y) \cup R(y)$], illustrates one of the limitations to performing all boolean operations directly on the response registers.

$$r1 \leftarrow find(1, *, y);$$
$$r2 \leftarrow find(1, y, *);$$
$$nbhrs \leftarrow comp2(r1 \vee r2);$$

(*a*) What is wrong with this sequence?

(*b*) What set does r1 $\vee$ r2 really denote?

9-48 A page of storage locations is in many respects identical to a linear sequential array. The page number functions as the array identifier, the block address functions as its base address (registers which hold block addresses are often called base registers), and the offset functions as the subscript or index. Assume that the $30 \times 30 \times 30$ array a_{ijk} has been represented so that each 30×30 j-k plane is allocated to a separate 1000-word page, as described in the text. Write an accessing function that will return the virtual address of the element a_{ijk}. Note that the representation is no longer purely sequential. Why? What serves as the base address $\check{L}_i$ of the j-k plane whose i index is fixed?

9-49 (*a*) Take one of your existing programs that performs matrix operations and determine the internal fragmentation arising from array placement alone. (Assume either 1000-word, or 1000-byte, pages or the size used at your installation. Two or more arrays may be packed into the same page, provided that all will fit.)

(*b*) Repeat the above exercise, but assuming pages of length 500 (or half the value used above).

(c) Normally only a limited number of pages may reside in blocks of core at any given time. These must contain both the program itself and its data. Suppose that only two pages of array data may be in core simultaneously. With the same program as in (a), determine how many times page faults occur from array references to pages not currently in core. (Note that this part is uninteresting unless three or more pages must be used to represent the arrays of the process.)

*9-50 Information about the behavior of processes using linked data structures in a paged environment can be obtained whether your own system is paged or not. Fields of cells are manipulated by the low-level primitive routines FETCH and STORE (Sec. 1-4).

These routines can be easily modified to gather paging statistics, as illustrated here in the case of FETCH.

> **integer procedure** fetch (cell, field);
> **pointer**   cell;
> **descriptor**   field;
>
> *This procedure retrieves the specified field of the cell in a simulated page environment. It counts the number of page faults.*
>
> **begin**
>   **boolean array**   page [1:n];
>   **integer**   fault, i;
>   **common**/pages/   fault, n, page;
>   i ← f(cell);
>   **if not** page [i] **then**
>   *page*[i] *continuing "cell" is not in core.*
>   **call** swap (i);
>   fault ← fault + 1;
>   fetch ← fetch'(cell,field);
>   **exit**;
>   **end**

Readily, this just serves as a statistics-gathering "front end" to the field-fetching process, which is called by the different name FETCH'. The function f simulates the assignment of the virtual address "cell" to page i. Any assignment schema, any page size, and any number of pages may be simulated. The array PAGE just records the current status of the page; it may be used to record other information about the pages. The routine SWAP just sets PAGE [i] to **true** and some other page to **false.** Any replacement strategy can be simulated. STORE is similarly modified.

(a) Run some of your existing programs using these modified versions of FETCH and STORE using different (1) page sizes and (2) replacement strategies.

(b) Other information that might be gathered includes: total number of references to each page, total simulated time each page was "in core," total faults per page, the ratios of faults/references and time-incore/references-for-each-page, etc. Collect this information as well.

(c) The results will not be completely accurate since references to cells that are made by process pointers are not intercepted. Does this contribute a significant error?

(d) How could one discover which substructures (either program or data) give rise to the most page faults? (It is easy to find which pages occasion the most faults, but this is much more difficult.)

9-51 (a) Partition the acyclic graph shown in the accompanying figure into three sets of seven points each so as to minimize the number of edges (connections) between the sets.

(b) Can you *prove* that your partition is optimal?

(c) Are the sets of the partition convex subgraphs?

(d) Can you formulate the strategy followed as a systematic procedure?

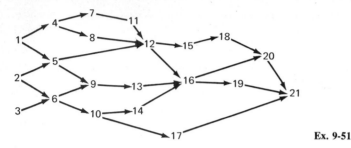

Ex. 9-51

9-52 Many graph-partitioning procedures generate only *convex partitions* in which all subsets are convex. While this is normally a good heuristic, show that the following assertion is false. *In an optimal partition* $\mathcal{P}$ *which minimizes the number of edges between sets, all sets must be convex.* Use the accompanying figure to derive a counterexample.

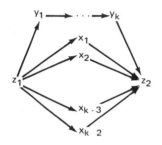

Ex. 9-52

9-5 LEAP

LEAP, an associative structure language developed by J. Feldman and P. Rovner (1969) is important for several reasons. First, it reflects a conception of abstract data structures that is somewhat different from the graph theoretic one that has been generally presented. Second, it has been implemented and used successfully to manage some relatively large scale data structures, especially in conjunction with the SPIRES project at Stanford. Its success has been largely due to its efficient simulation of associative retrieval by hash-coding techniques. In this section we examine certain portions of the LEAP system in considerable detail (as we did the GRAAL system in Sec. 6-2) in order to counterpoint the prevailing approach of this text with significant variations.

In the abstract model on which LEAP is based, one begins with a collection $O = \{o_i\}$ of unspecified objects.† They may be points, values, relations, etc. Within the system all objects are identified by internal names which will be cell

---

†Note that we will describe LEAP using the terminology and concepts that have been developed so far in this text. The reader will discover that the description found in this article seems very different because different words are used. Moreover, that article is primarily concerned with describing an Algol-like language used to manipulate LEAP structures rather than describing the structures themselves. Occasionally we shall try to indicate the correspondence between their terminology and our own by means of footnotes.

addresses. These cells may be used to represent various properties of the individual object, but for the moment this is of little concern. For the purposes of exposition we will use symbolic identifiers, viz., a, b, ..., y, z, to name objects. Fundamental to the LEAP concept is a collection A of *associative items.* Each associative item—or more simply, just item—is a triple of objects; that is, $a_j = (o_1, o_2, o_3)$. These two collections constitute an abstract data structure, or

$$S_M = (O, A)$$

Compare this with the definition of an abstract structure as a directed graph with assignment functions $(P, E, f_1, \ldots, f_m, g_1, \ldots, g_n)$ given in Sec. 6-1. In theory, the objects $\{o_i\}$ can enter into any kind of association with each other depending on their placement in an item. In practice, one can more effectively use the structure if it is interpreted with respect to certain conventions. The first component of every associative item is assumed to be an object that denotes either a relation or a function. Thus, as shown in the preceding section, a collection of triples (e, x, y), all of which have the same first component may be interpreted as a graph $G = (P, e)$. In an associative LEAP-like system, new relations can be defined on a collection of objects and existing ones changed at will. There is no need to reconfigure cell formats or change a series of links or pointers. One simply adds, or removes, triples from the collection A. Similarly, one can just as easily define relations between relations. For example, an assertion such as $E_1 \subseteq E_2$ would be represented in LEAP storage by a single triple $(\subseteq, e1, e2)$. Assignment functions need be treated no differently from relations. They are represented by triples of the form (f, x, y), where this is interpreted to mean that $f(x) = y$. The object x corresponds to a point in the graph, while the object (or more frequently the value) y corresponds to an element in some other data structure, say the set of real numbers.†

Given an associative representation of several relations and assignment functions (or attributes) on a set of objects, there are eight possible retrieval requests, interrogations, or questions that can be posed to the system. Both the form and corresponding semantic meaning of these questions are listed below:

1. (e, x, y): Is (x, y) ϵ e (or equivalently, is y ϵ $R_e(x)$, is e(x) = y)?
2. (e, x, *): Return $R_e(x)$ [or all values e(x)].
3. (e, *, y): Return $L_e(y)$ (or all objects whose e value is y).
4. (*, x, y): Return all relations containing (x, y) (or all functions f such that $f(x) = y$).
5. (e, *, *): Return the set of elements in the relation e.
6. (*, x, *): } Dubious meaning.
7. (*, *, y): }
8. (*, *, *): Return the entire associative structure.

---

†In the LEAP language this latter form is treated as canonical. The first component is called the *attribute,* the second component called the *object,* and the third called the *value.* Associative triples are denoted by the form (a ∘ o ≡ v) where the symbols ∘ and ≡ serve as suggestive delimiters.

Except for query 1, which is essentially a boolean predicate whose response is either true or false, all these retrievals return sets (possibly empty) of associative items. Interpretations can be given to queries 6 and 7, but their significance in practical application may be dubious. One real problem is to find a way of implementing a process to satisfy queries 1, 2, and 3 as efficiently as possible, since they constitute the bulk of the retrieval requests that occur in normal applications.

Recall from Sec. 9-2 that hash-coding techniques were used to simulate content-addressable storage. Retrieval of an item (k, f(k)) was controlled by the contents k of its "key field." Further, even though it is impossible to attain access and retrieval times on the order of two memory cycles that would be expected with true associative hardware, the expected number of lookup accesses,

$$\mathscr{L}_1 = 1 + \frac{\alpha}{2} = 1 + \frac{1}{2}\left(\frac{\text{no. of items}}{\text{no. of buckets}}\right)$$

appears to be reasonable, especially since the critical value α can be controlled by increasing the number of buckets. But previously, the hash-coded associative lookup had been based on the contents of a single field. It must be modified so that it is controlled by the contents of several fields where it is unknown in advance which of the fields, or components of the associative triple, are to be used. In the method of hashing into buckets, the hash value h(k) was treated as an index to a singly subscripted array of pointers, each of which referenced the simply linked list of elements constituting the bucket. To implement LEAP we will use a triply subscripted array of pointers. The cell representing the associative item (e, x, y) will be stored in the linked list whose referencing pointer is bucket[i, j, k], where i = h(e), j = h(x), and k = h(y). To retrieve any item say (e', x', y'), the system need only search the list bucket [h(e'), h(x'), h(y')]. If only two of the components of the desired item(s) are known, say (e', x', *), then the several lists beginning with bucket [h(e'), h(x'), k], where k = 1 through s, must all be searched. But even though the cells of several lists must be examined to see if their components match those of the specified search pattern, many more potential associative cells have been eliminated from the search procedure. The following procedure FIND illustrates in detail the retrieval mechanism. Note that it returns a set of associative items where this set is represented as a linked list of pointers ordered on ascending items addressed in the manner of Sec. 4-3. This is the representation of sets that is used in the LEAP implementation of Feldman and Rovner (1969). Note also the conditional for loop statements α, β, and γ. This is nonstandard Algol, but its meaning should be clear.

set procedure find (object);
pointer array object [1:3];

This procedure returns the set of all associative items (triples) whose components *match the specified nonnull objects. (If the pointer "object$_n$" is null, then it is treated as an * and the nth component is ignored in the search procedure.*

```
begin
    integer   i, j, k, n, q, r, s;
    pointer array   bucket[1:q, 1:r, 1:s];
    common/buckets/   q, r, s, bucket;
    find ← ∅;
```

Hash the three internal names (pointers) into bucket indices.

```
    for n = 1 thru 3 do
        if object [n] ≠ nullvalue
            then index [n] ← hash(object [n])
            else index [n] ← nullvalue;
```

Search for a match item in the linked list of associative items with header "bucket$_{ijk}$" where i=index 1, etc. If any of these indices, say k=index 3, is null, then all the lists, bucket$_{ij1}$ thru bucket$_{ijs}$ must be searched.

```
α:      if index [1] ≠ nullvalue
            then for i = index [1]    do
            else for i = 1 thru q
β:              if index [2] ≠ nullvalue
                    then for j = index [2]   do
                    else for j = 1 thru r
γ:                      if index [3] ≠ nullvalue
                            then for k = index [3]   do
                            else for k = 1 thru s
```

Search bucket$_{ijk}$ for matching items

```
                        cell ← bucket [i, j, k];
                        while cell ≠ nullvalue do
```

Do all nonnull components match?

```
                            for n = 1 thru 3 do
                                if object [n] ≠ nullvalue
                                    and object [n] ≠ field (n, cell)
                                    then go to nomatch;
```

Yes, add item to the set "find".

```
                            find ← find ∪ {cell};
nomatch:                    cell ← next(cell);
    exit;
    end
```

A procedure to enter new items into the associative store would employ a similar accessing mechanism. Its implementation is left to the reader; so also is a procedure $COMP_i$ which creates a set of simple objects which occur as the ith components of a set of associative items. See Exercises 9-65 and 9-66.

The behavior of this process and the structure of an associatively

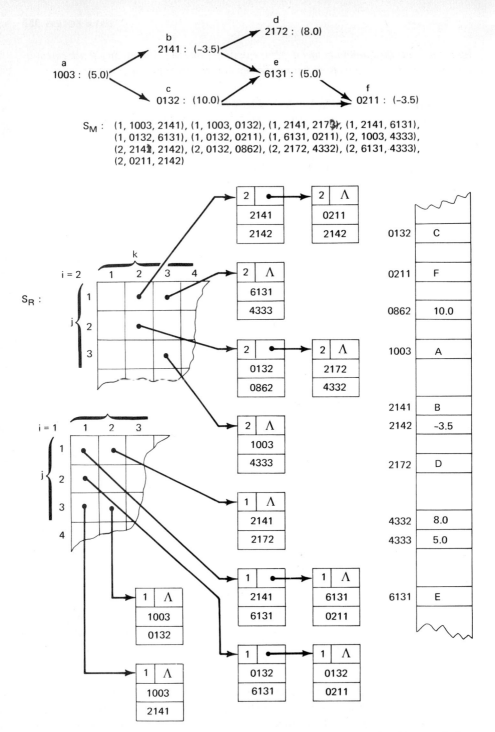

Figure 9-18 The representation of an abstract relation E and assignment function F by associative items.

implemented data base may become clearer if we look at a sample representation, as shown in Fig. 9-18. A small abstract relation together with a single assignment function f on six points (or objects) is first shown in the form of a directed graph. Its abstract representation in terms of associated triples is also shown, where in each triple internal names have been substituted for external names of objects. Finally, a representation involving an array of bucket pointers, linked lists of associative item cells, and cells representing each object in storage is given. This latter representation assumes the trivial hashing function h, which simply sets h(internalname) equal to the last digit of the internal name. (One would seldom use such a hashing function save for pedagogical reasons.) Desk check the behavior of both the procedures FIND and NEWITEM given this representation.

While the procedures FIND and NEWITEM constitute the heart of an associative-based system such as LEAP, there are a number of less important details which nevertheless may ultimately determine the utility and efficiency of the overall system. We will consider just two of these "small" details in the remainder of this section.

The upper bounds q, r, and s of the array of pointers bucket have not been specified. They need not be equal. Since normally there are relatively few objects (relations, functions, or attributes) that will serve as the first component of an associative item, the upper bound q can be quite small. In the example of Fig. 9-18 a bound of q = 2 would have been sufficient. On the other hand, a large number of items will have the same initial component. Efficiency will suffer if two or more relations hash to the same index.† q should be large enough to ensure that each relation, function, or attribute hashes to a different index if at all possible. We would also be willing to fool around with the hashing function or with the choice of internal names to guarantee this one-to-one hashing property.

Once the upper bound q is determined, we know that the array bucket will consist of q separate j-k planes of r · s cells each. Almost all retrievals in the system will arise from queries of the form (1), (2), or (3), in which the first component is given so that this decomposition of the array bucket seems natural. If implemented in a paged environment, it becomes essential. With either of the common queries of type (2) or (3), an entire row (j = 1 to r) or column (k = 1 to s) of bucket pointers must be followed. To avoid unnecessary page faults the entire j-k plane (with first index i fixed) should be contained on a single page.‡ Thus we also find that the upper bounds r and s should satisfy the constraint that r · s ≤ page size. Should r = s? It is not hard to show that if requests of

---

†This is much more serious than if two or more objects that may serve as the second or third component of an item hash to the same index value. Why?

‡Ideally all cells denoting associative items in one of the lists *bucket*[i, *, *] should also be confined to a single page. It may be the same page if r · s is small, or it may be another associated page. This provides good locality of reference, since at most two pages are involved in the search mechanism of most common retrievals.

type (2), (e, x, *), are significantly more frequent than those of type (3), (e, *, y), then it is best if r > s. Otherwise r < s is preferable.

The preceding discussion illustrates one more important situation where programmers may want to design their own array representation and accessing conventions, as described in Chap. 7.

When does an object have a value, and when is a value the object itself? This seemingly curious question has profound implications on both the representation of an associative system and the design of a programming language that will use it. We have tacitly assumed that the internal names of objects have been the addresses of cells representing that object. But examination of the representation of Fig. 9-18 will show that this is not true. There are no cells representing the objects (relations) E or F. Their associated internal names 1 and 2, respectively, are just integers with no particular significance. However, the internal names of those objects (points and real values) which may be the second and/or third component of an item do denote cell addresses in this representation. But need they? Those cells representing "points" contain only the external symbolic name of the point. They convey no other information about the object. In many applications one need never use such a symbolic identifier, and these cells can be eliminated. Then the integer internal names of "point" objects (that is, 0132, 0211, 1003, 2141, 2172, and 6131) become merely tokens denoting some object in much the same way that the internal names 1 and 2 were tokens for the objects E and F. And if any tokens can be used, why not choose the external names a, b, c, d, e, and f as tokens for these objects? Why convert them to internal names?

The handling of real assignment values in this representation by storing them in one-word cells seems correct. But again we may pause and raise questions. To print out the value associated with object 2141 (point b), a process would first have to invoke the query FIND(2, 2141, *). This will return the set consisting of the singleton object {2142}. 2142 is not the value to be printed; it is an object. To print the value -3.5, the process must access the value associated with this object. But note that the "association" is different. The object 2142 *is* the real number -3.5 in this representation. To indicate the difference we might add to the programming language a function

datum(object)

which returns the value stored in the cell addressed by *object*.† With this convention one can now write a program statement of the form

write datum(comp(find(2, 2141, *)));

which will print the real value -3.5.

---

†The LEAP language includes a function **datum**. It is similar to the concept of an atom, which was encountered in the list structures of Chap. 8; that is, an element that is to be treated as a primitive value, not as a mechanism to reference other elements.

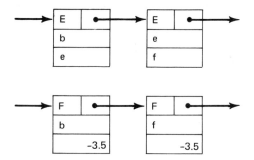

Figure 9-19 Typical cells in a representation in which objects are represented by their "own values," not storage addresses.

Instead of introducing a datum construct into the language and into the representation, it is possible simply to store the value in the component of the associative triple so that the value itself becomes the object. Typical associative items of this representation are shown in Fig. 9-19. Note that there is now no need to convert from external names to internal names since all names are external. Note also that there are no cells representing objects themselves; there are only cells representing associative items. This latter representation, in which objects are represented by their "own value," has considerable merit. It returns to the spirit of familiar compiler languages which have eliminated the concept of storage locations by treating variable symbols as if they denoted their own values. It simplifies the design of many procedures. While it is fine for certain kinds of applications, it also has drawbacks. Suppose that some of the values associated with objects are strings which cannot be stored in a single component of the associative item. They must be stored elsewhere, and a pointer to its representation must be reintroduced into the structure. Furthermore, the representation of objects by separate addressable cells permits the construction of "mixed" data structures. The representing cell may have several link and information fields. The object it represents may be part of several structures, some of which may be more effectively represented by linked or sequential techniques, some of which may be more effectively represented by associative techniques.

Data structures and data bases are whole entities. There may be several abstract structures, each of which may be represented by different techniques. They interact with procedures that use them and with programming languages that describe such processes. It is pedagogically, and practically, useful to separate out individual aspects—data access, set representation, dynamic cell allocation, representation of relations and of functions, etc.—and analyze each as an isolated phenomenon. Still, in overall design all must be considered together in a somewhat simultaneous fashion. The goal of the foregoing discussion has been to emphasize this interdependent nature.

EXERCISES FOR SECTION 9-5

9-53 Implement the procedure FIND using any suitable hash function. Gather statistics describing the distribution of associative items (triples) in the buckets.

9-54 Write and implement a procedure NEWITEM (o_1, o_2, o_3) which adds the indicated triple to the associative store.

9-55 Implement a procedure compi which creates and returns a pointer to the set of objects denoted by a linked set of triples.

(a) Need the resulting set of "simple objects" have the same cardinality as the argument set of items?

(b) Should the set of cells denoting the set of associative items be returned to the pool of free cells after executing this procedure?

(c) Estimate the expected cost of this procedure as a function of the size of the argument set.

9-56 If a retrieval request of the form

$$set \leftarrow comp3(find(e, x, *))$$

is implemented (as suggested in the exercise above) by first using FIND to create a set of associative triples, and then using COMP3 to create a second set of objects, computational efficiency suffers. Two sets must be created and each must be sorted in ascending order of internal names (or cell addresses). The creation and sorting of the first set of triples can be avoided by combining COMP3 and FIND as a single process which just creates the set of simple objects.

(a) Write such a process.

(b) What are its advantages?

(c) What are its disadvantages?

*9-57 Some feeling for the interaction between the representation of data structures and the programming languages which describe processes can be obtained by implementing a simplified version of LEAP using interpretive commands. Basic commands, or statements in the language, are read from the input file, interpreted, and then executed by calling appropriate procedures. The interpretive language should at least contain the statements such as

```
newitem(e, a, c);
newitem(f2, c, 5.0);
set1 ← find(e, *, x);
set2 ← comp2(set1);
list set3;
set2 ← intersect(set1, set3);
```

You may very well discover that additional commands are desirable. Add them. Of course, such a language will be nowhere near as powerful as LEAP itself, which as a compiled extension of Algol includes arithmetic and control statements. Nevertheless, the language should be suitable for a variety of simple data base creation and interrogation applications. (Note that if you use independent representation of objects by cells whose addresses serve as internal names, then you also build symbol tables that permit the conversion of external to internal names for input, and vice versa for output.)

9-58 Build a representation of the structure of Fig. 9-18 using this interpretive system. Query it.

*9-59 Because we have interpreted the first object of a LEAP item to be a relation, function, or attribute name does not mean it must always be so interpreted. The three objects of an associative item can be any objects at all, as shown in Exercises 9-45 and 9-46. Use the interpretive system of Exercise 9-57 to represent both data bases given in these exercises. It should be straightforward to answer the kinds of retrieval queries posed in Exercise 9-45. Can you extend the interpretive system to respond to the kinds of queries given in Exercise 9-46? What are the difficulties involved?

9-60 Shown in the accompanying figure is a tree.

    (*a*) Give the set of LEAP triples which define this tree. Let t1 denote the tree relation.

    (*b*) Give the augmented set of triples which represents a threaded tree as might be generated by THREAD. Is this the only possible thread? Why?

    (*c*) Give the set of triples which would represent T_1 as an ordered tree (with ordering on R(y) from top to bottom).

    (*d*) Compare this representation to a linked representation, as given in Sec. 5-4

    (*e*) Write a procedure to generate a thread through an ordered tree. Compare it to a process operating on a linked representation.

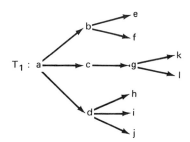

Ex. 9-60

9-61 Assuming an associative programming language which includes the processes NEWITEM, FIND, and $COMP_i$, and set capabilities, write procedures to:

    (*a*) Find the transitive closure of a relation using procedure (6-6) of Sec. 6-2.

    (*b*) Find the shortest paths using Floyd's algorithm (6-12 of Sec. 6-2).

    (*c*) Find the minimal (or maximal) objects of a relation.

    (*d*) Determine whether a given relation is a principal tree.

    (*e*) Thread a principal tree with respect to preorder, or postorder, traversal. (See also the following exercise.)

    (*f*) Critically evaluate the advantages of associative representations versus linked representations.

    (*g*) Recommend desirable features for an associative processing language.

9-62 Show that if requests (e, x, ∗) occur more frequently then (e, ∗, y), then it is preferable to set the upper bounds $r > s$. (*Hint:* Try an argument based on the numbers of associative items that are excluded from the search.)

*9-63 Consider a table of elements (k, f(k)) with a lookup procedure, such as that described in Sec. 9-2, which hashes only the key k into a linear array of bucket pointers. To find those keys k_i for which $f(k_i)$ equals some specified value, all elements must be examined. For instance, if the keys are a set of English words as shown in Fig. 9-2, and the values f(k) are a count of their occurrence in the input text, then it is impossible to quickly discover which words (if any) occurred exactly five times in the text (see Exercise 9-44). Characteristics of the straightforward implementation by hashing into 50 buckets were described by Table 9-3. An inverted retrieval capacity can be implemented by hashing instead into a doubly subscripted 7 × 7 array of bucket pointers where bucket [i, j] references the list of elements (k, f(k)) such that i = h(k) and j = h(f(k)).

    (*a*) Implement such a hashed storage and retrieval system.

    (*b*) Compare its observed performance with the results of Table 9-3.

    (*c*) Show that the expected number of accesses per entry and lookup, when both components are given, is still $1 + \alpha/2$; but that if only the key k or value f(k) is specified, $\mathscr{L}_1 = 7(1 + \alpha/2)$.

Assuming that the majority of retrievals are based on the key k, would it be preferable to:

(d) Hash into an 11×5 array of buckets,

(e) Hash into a 13×4 array of buckets?

In all cases there are approximately 50 buckets.

(f) Can you derive an expression relating the expected lookup accesses $\mathscr{L}_1(k)$, given k, with the expected lookup accesses $\mathscr{L}_1(f(k))$, given $f(k)$, as a function of the dimension of the array of buckets?

(g) How does one discover the optimal dimension, assuming a known distribution of retrieval requests?

DYNAMIC ALLOCATION OF STORAGE

A computing system which manipulates structures of any form must sooner or later come to grips with the problem of dynamically allocating, and deallocating, blocks of contiguous storage. Operating systems which manipulate program structures, and sophisticated applications programmers who manipulate their own data structures within the context of an existing operating system, face similar problems that normally differ only in size. In this chapter we will approach dynamic allocation from the point of view of typical applications programmers who are manipulating data structures of their own making in a known context. But many of the techniques will be equally applicable to an operating system viewed as the allocator of the system resource—storage. Throughout, we will refer to *users* which denote any procedures that invoke the dynamic allocation process.

By a *block* we mean a collection of contiguous storage locations with consecutive addresses.† When blocks have been of a fixed size we have been calling them *cells*. When the blocks are physically located in peripheral storage they are normally called *records*. *Block, cell,* and *record* will be synonyms for the same concept but used in different contexts.

---

†A block of storage in random-access core, disk, or drum storage need not be physically contiguous, provided the addresses of its locations are logically consecutive. A block of nonaddressable storage—e.g., magnetic tape—must be physically contiguous. In either case, one has a sense of "uninterrupted" storage.

We can simplify the problem of dynamic allocation somewhat by initially subdividing it into two relatively distinct subproblems, that of:

1. allocating blocks, or cells, of a few fixed sizes, and
2. allocating blocks of widely varying size or length.

10-1 ALLOCATION OF CELLS OF FIXED SIZES

We assume that there is an initial block of storage locations, with addresses L_1 through L_n consecutively, that is available to the allocation routines. In an applications program this initial block may be created by either an array declaration within a program or by issuing a run-time request to the system allocator. In the case of the operating system itself, this block will comprise all addressable storage, save possibly for some locations which are permanently reserved for communications purposes. In either case we assume that the addresses L_1 and L_n are known to the allocation routine.

If all requests to the storage allocator will be for cells of a single fixed size, say **celsiz,** then dynamic allocation is not hard to implement. One simply subdivides the initial block $[L_1, L_n]$ into cells of the specified size, then links them to form a *list of available storage* (LAVS) or pool of free cells. When a request is issued to the allocator it removes one cell from the list and returns its address to the requesting process. If the list is empty the request cannot be satisfied, storage *overflow* has occurred, and normally the allocation routine will terminate the job. When a cell is returned, or deallocated, it is simply added to the list. The routines SETUP, GIVEME, and TAKEIT, which were developed in Sec. 3-3 and then used in many subsequent procedures, employ just this simple straightforward approach. Readers may wish to quickly review this section to refresh their memory of this easy solution.

But in practice one seldom wants only cells of a single fixed size. In Chap. 5, trees built of cells with two or more words were traversed by stack-driven procedures that used cells of size 1. In the linked representations of more general graphs of Chap. 6, point cells are often of different size from edge cells. Both may be of different size from the cells of auxiliary stacks, or of graph cells used to denote the graph as a whole. In list structures, header cells, reference cells, and atomic cells need not be of identical size. In these earlier chapters there was a kind of tacit assumption that the free pool would be set up so that GIVEME always returned a cell of the largest size; if a smaller cell was required, only a portion of the cell would actually be used. The parameter CELSIZ in the routines GIVEME and TAKEIT was only a dummy parameter. This simple-minded approach is satisfactory in a strictly learning context, but becomes intolerable in any kind of practical application.

Three alternative solutions suggest themselves. First, if several different-sized cells will be required, say five, then five separate free pools of available cells could be created identical to that of Sec. 3-3. The obvious drawback to this approach is that if overflow occurs because of a request to just one of the free pools, then the entire run must be terminated. Since one can seldom predict accurately in advance the quantities or even proportions of the different-sized cells that will be required, the danger of premature overflow is very real. This approach, while easy, is seldom used and is not recommended.

If we want to minimize the danger of premature overflow, then, following the analysis of Sec. 4-1, we should initially allocate a single large block of storage for *all* cells. Each cell, as it is requested, should be "carved out" of this large block. Then the amount of storage given to cells of one size will be determined by actual usage, not predicted usage. Further, as unneeded cells are returned, those which are contiguous to each other or to the remaining unallocated block should be recombined. At all times one wants large blocks of undivided contiguous storage so that the allocation routines can dynamically adapt to the current patterns of usage. Carving cells out of an undivided block of storage is not difficult, but recombining returned cells is both tricky and time-consuming. We should like to avoid such overhead if possible. (It is not always possible, and the next two sections will explore methods of handling such allocation, together with its associated problems.)

The third alternative solution is a compromise. It seeks to combine the programming ease and execution speed of the first solution with some of the dynamic adaptability of the second. It has proven itself to be a very effective allocation routine, *provided:*

1. a relatively small number, say ≤ 10, different sized cells are requested,
2. the largest size cell is small relative to the total amount of storage available, say < 1 percent, and
3. the process does not create and return a large number of cells of one particular size which are not again used.

One need not know in advance the actual sizes nor the number of cells of any size that will be requested. The approach is quite easy. An initial block of n storage locations [L_1, L_n] is allocated. Unlike our previous version of SETUP, this block is not subdivided into a list of available cells—it is left undivided. A pointer FIRST indicates the first location of the undivided block, and a pointer LAST indicates the last location. Lists are kept which contain *only cells which have been allocated and returned at some previous time*. A separate list is maintained for each different-size cell. When a request for a cell of size i is received, that available list is first examined. If the list is not empty, then a cell is removed from the list and its address returned. If the list is empty, the first i locations in the undivided block are combined to form a cell (by incrementing the pointer FIRST), and its address is returned. All returned cells are simply added to their respective available lists. Once a block of i consecutive locations are designated as an i cell, they will always remain an i cell.

Figure 10-1 illustrates a configuration of the free pool at one time in a dynamic allocation process. Cells of size 1, 2, and 6 have been previously

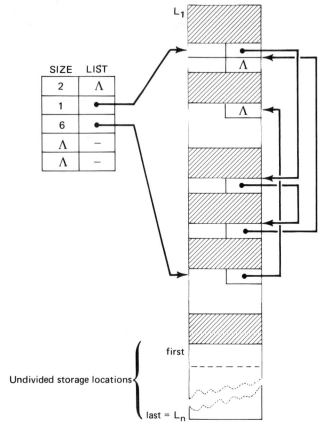

Figure 10-1 Configuration of a free pool allocating cells of size 1, 2, and 6. (Shaded portion denotes cells which have been allocated and are still being used by other processes.)

requested. Cells of size 1 and 6 have been returned and have been linked as lists. A request for a cell of size 1 or 6 will be satisfied by returning one of these cells. A request for a cell of size 2 will be satisfied by returning the first two locations of the undivided block (as indicated). A request for a cell of size 5 would be satisfied by first making an entry into the SIZE and LIST tables, then carving off five locations from the undivided block.

The following procedures SETUP$_2$, GIVEME$_2$, and TAKEIT$_2$, which the reader will notice bear striking resemblance to their counterparts in Sec. 3-3, present the details of this allocation mechanism.

```
procedure setup₂ (array, dim);
integer array   array [1:dim];
integer         dim;
```

This procedure makes an initial allocation of a block of "dim" consecutive storage locations which will be later carved up into a number of lists of available cells—each list containing only cells of a single fixed size. Note that the cell sizes are not specified in advance, but will depend on usage. Normally nsizes *will be* ≤ 10.

begin
    integer array   list [1:nsizes], size [1:nsizes];
    integer   first, i, last, nsizes;
    common /frpool/   nsizes, list, size, first, last;

    Initialize free pool parameters.

    first $\leftarrow$ loc(array [1]);
    last $\leftarrow$ loc(array [dim]);
    for i = 1 **thru** nsizes **do**
        size [i] $\leftarrow$ null;
    exit;
    end

pointer function giveme$_2$(celsiz);
integer celsiz;

This function locates a cell of the requested size in the free pool and returns the address of its first word (byte or location) as pointer value.

begin
    integer array   list [1:nsizes];size [1:nsizes];
    integer   first, i, last, nsizes;
    field   next;
    common /frpool/   nsizes, list, size, first, last;

    Find which list contains cells of this size.

    for i = 1 **thru** nsizes **do**
        if celsiz = size [i] **then go to** checklist;
        if size [i] = null **then go to** newcellsize;
    print "error message"; **stop** execution;
newcellsize:

    This is the first request for a cell of this size; enter it into the list of cell sizes.

    size [i] $\leftarrow$ celsiz;
    list [i] $\leftarrow$ null;
checklist:

    First see if there is a cell of this size on its available cell list.

    if list [i] $\neq$ null
        then *A cell of this size has been made available by a previous deallocation.*
            Remove it from the list and return its address.
            giveme $\leftarrow$ list [i];
            list [i] $\leftarrow$ next(list [i]);
            next(giveme) $\leftarrow$ null;
            exit

        else   *No free cells of this size currently exist. Try to carve one from the remaining undivided storage locations.*

           if first $+$ (celsiz $-$ 1) $>$ last

               then *Storage overflow.*

                    print ("error message");

                    stop execution

             else

                  giveme $\leftarrow$ first;

                  first $\leftarrow$ first $+$ celsiz;

                  exit

      end

procedure takeit$_2$(cell, celsiz);
pointer   cell;
integer   celsiz;

This procedure returns the specified cell to the list of available cells of the same size.

begin

integer array	list [1:nsizes], size [1:nsizes];
integer	i, nsizes;
field	next;
common /frpool/	nsizes, list, size, first, last;

    Find the corresponding available list pointer.

    for i $=$ 1 **thru** nsizes **do**

       if celsiz $=$ size [i] **then go to** insert;

    print ("error message"); **stop** execution;

insert:

    next(cell) $\leftarrow$ list [i];

    list [i] $\leftarrow$ cell;

    cell $\leftarrow$ null;

    exit;

    end

With this semiadaptive allocation scheme, overflow can occur with a request for a cell of size i (its list is empty and the undivided block is exhausted) even though many cells of size j are available. One can imagine a number of programming tricks to cope with this problem. If i $<$ j then a cell of size j can be returned, under the pretense that it is a smaller cell. If i $>$ j then the list of available j cells can be searched to see if two or more are contiguous and can be "combined" to form an i cell. Or we can seek to prolong the life of the undivided block by testing every returned cell for adjacency to the first undivided location. While the coding of such touches may be rather elegant, experience has indicated that they are worth neither the time to write them nor the execution time to perform the testing involved. In applications for which this allocation approach is appropriate, all lists tend to overflow at nearly the same time. Borrowing cells from another list normally prolongs execution for but a few more cycles. If there are in fact many cells in the j cell list, then this is an indication that the entire allocation scheme is inappropriate for the application and one of the techniques described in the following sections should be considered.

EXERCISES FOR SECTION 10-1

10-1 Give reasons for *not* representing the list of available storage (LAVS) as a sequential list. Give situations where such a sequential representation might be advantageous.

*10-2 Implement versions of SETUP$_2$, GIVEME$_2$, and TAKEIT$_2$ using your local programming language. Test them. If you have implemented various processes which used the previous version of these allocation routines, will there be any compatibility problems involved in substituting these revised versions?

10-3 As presented in this section, each list of available cells LIST [i] is a stack with cells taken from and returned to the top of the stack. What changes are required to make these queues?

10-4 The dynamic allocation routines SETUP$_2$, GIVEME$_2$, and TAKEIT$_2$ are not "user-proof." There are a number of ways in which a user process can inadvertently destroy the integrity of the free pool. Mechanisms can be devised which protect against some problems and reduce the danger of others, but which leave still others untouched. A partial list of problems follows:

(*a*) A cell that has been returned to one of the available lists may nevertheless be referenced and manipulated by a using process.

(*b*) A segment of the undivided free-pool storage may be referenced by a user process.

(*c*) A process returning an unused cell of size i by means of TAKEIT may claim it is of size j.

How would you try to guard against such errors? What is the cost, in terms of either execution or storage overhead, of your protective mechanisms? The statements in GIVEME and TAKEIT which null, respectively, the next field of the allocated cell and the actual pointer parameter CELL are simple, and almost automatic, protective mechanisms. To which problem are they a partial solution?

10-5 The life of the undivided block of the free pool can be extended by combining any returned cell which is adjacent to the first location into the undivided block and not adding it to its available list. Code the test that would discover this condition and the statement that would effect the recombination. To get some measure of the value of such additional code, try to estimate the expected number of times such recombination will be possible. Clearly this expected probability will depend on the nature of the processes which use the allocation system. How will the probability be affected if the processes build and manipulate many queues? Stacks?

10-2 ALLOCATION OF VARIABLE SIZED BLOCKS

The allocation scheme of the preceding section is based on the assumption that only requests for cells of relatively few different sizes would ever be handled. It is characterized by the fact that once a block of i consecutive locations is designated as an i cell, it remains an i cell for the remainder of the executing job. It is semiadaptive to the particular job only in that the designation of a block as an i cell or a j cell is deferred until it is absolutely required. This underlying assumption is reasonable in the case of many applications involving linked data structures, but for many other applications it is not; consequently the allocation approach becomes unacceptable.

Consider a situation in which the dynamic allocation process receives requests for blocks of widely differing lengths or sizes. We can assume that the requested lengths λ occur in some interval

$$\lambda \in [a, b]$$

where a denotes the smallest block that will be requested and b denotes the largest allocatable block. As examples one might consider the dynamic alloca-tor of an operating system which must find and allocate storage for a succession of jobs or programs of very different lengths; an input-output processor which allocates disk storage for a file of variable-length records; or a display process which must allocate storage for the segments of a display file, as described in Sec. 8-3. In these circumstances an individual storage location must be used, and used again, in blocks of different size.

There are several pieces to this allocation problem that can best be consid-ered one at a time. Let us begin by assuming that some allocation process, call it A, has been dynamically allocating blocks of storage from an initial block $[L_1, L_n]$ for a period of time. Other processes have been requesting blocks, using them for a while, then releasing them in an apparently random and unpredictable fashion. Figure 10-2 illustrates the overall configuration of storage at the current time. Shaded blocks have been allocated and are reserved for the exclusive use of individual requesting processes; unshaded blocks are available (they may have been allocated and subsequently returned) and may be used to satisfy future requests. Such an illustration is called a *memory map*. Looking at the memory map of Fig. 10-2, one can see that while more than half of the total storage locations are available, they are distributed among 14 avail-able blocks, none of which is particularly large. This phenomenon is called storage *fragmentation*. If the next request is for a fairly large block, it may, because of fragmentation, be unsatisfiable and a premature overflow condition will be indicated even though a large amount of storage is actually free. On the other hand, if the next request is for a fairly small block, then the allocating process has the option of carving it from anywhere within the 14 available blocks. Given such a choice, it would seem reasonable to allocate locations for the requested block in such a way as to minimize fragmentation. The procedure by which this decision is made is called an *allocation strategy*. Even though every allocation strategy can be frustrated by some particular sequence of

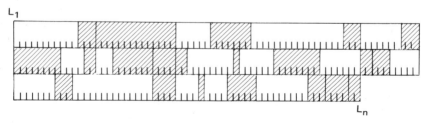

Figure 10-2 "Memory map" of fragmented storage. (Shaded blocks have been allocated, other blocks are available.)

requests and returns (see Exercise 10-6), we shall be interested in heuristic strategies which appear to minimize the expected fragmentation.

Before concerning ourselves with the problem of allocation strategies, let us dispose of some more or less routine subproblems. Any allocation process must maintain some bookkeeping which keeps track of the location and size of its available blocks. One solution is to store this information in the available blocks themselves. They can be linked as a list of available blocks using the first location. A second field indicates the length of that block. (Alternatively, it could be a pointer to the last location in the block.) Figure 10-3 shows the configuration of such a list of available blocks.

When a block, say $B = [L_{b_1}, L_{b_n}]$, is released by a user process, perhaps by executing the statement

$$\textbf{call } \text{takeit } (L_{b_1}, \text{length}) \qquad \text{where length} = L_{b_n} - L_{b_1} + 1$$

it must be returned to the available list. It could be added to the front of the list. But it is quite possible this block is contiguous with an available block $A = [L_{a_1}, L_{a_n}]$ in "front" of it (that is, $L_{a_n} = L_{b_1} - 1$), or with a free block $C = [L_{c_1}, L_{c_n}]$ "behind" it, or both. These blocks can be merged into a single longer block. The deallocation procedure TAKEIT should therefore search the

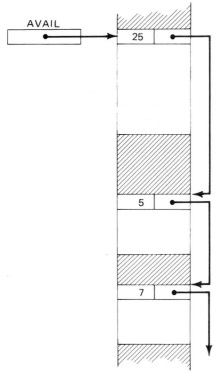

Figure 10-3 The configuration of a list of available blocks.

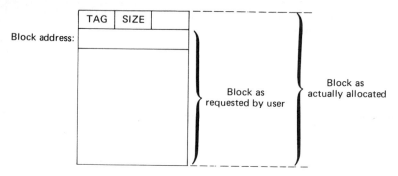

Figure 10-4 Possible format of an allocated block.

entire list of available blocks for possible contiguous blocks. The expected magnitude of this search can be halved if the list of available blocks is linked *in order of ascending storage address,* as shown in Fig. 10-3. (See also Exercise 10-1.) Consequently we will require that all processes operating on the list of available blocks maintain this order.

Before giving an example of TAKEIT as described above, let us ask if its usage seems reasonable. The second parameter gives the size of the released block and is supplied by the releasing process. This item of data—the size of available blocks—will be essential to the allocation process; yet we are insisting that every user process keep track of the size of every allocated block and supply that information on deallocation. Is this realistic? Is it safe?

It is better to label every allocated block of storage with its own size, so that on subsequent release it can be added to the available list with assurance. To do this the allocation process may precede each allocated block with one extra word of which the requesting process is, hopefully, unaware. This word contains the size of the block actually allocated and a distinctive tag which simplifies the generation of memory maps and which can provide a measure of protection, as suggested by Exercise 10-8. Figure 10-4 illustrates the configuration of blocks as actually allocated.

With these representation details settled, one can now write a deallocation procedure TAKEIT$_3$, as follows:

procedure   takeit$_3$ (block);
pointer   block;

This procedure deallocates a block that has been released by a user process and returns it to the list of available blocks. If adjacent to contiguous free blocks, it is combined to form as large an available block as possible. (Note that "block" actually points to the second, not first, location of the released block.)

begin
    pointer   avail, nxtblk, prev;
    field   next, size;
    common /frpool/ avail;

Find its position in the available list.

    prev ←loc(avail);
    nxtblk ←avail;
α: **while** nxtblk ≠ null **and** nxtblk < block **do**
        prev ←nxtblk;
        nxtblk ←next(nxtblk);

This block belongs between "prev" and "nxtblk".

    if prev =loc(avail)
        then avail ←block − 1;
            go to checkfollowingblock;

Is this block contiguous to the preceding block?

    if prev + size(prev) + 2 = block ⟵ — 2 reserved words per block
        then *Yes, combine them.*
            size(prev) ←size(prev) + size(block − 1);
            block ←prev + 1;
        else *No, link them.*
            next(prev) ←block − 1;
checkfollowingblock:
    if nextblk =null
        then next(block − 1) ←null;
            exit;

Is this block contiguous to the following block?

    if block + size(block − 1) =nxtblk
        then *Yes, combine them.*
            size(block − 1) ←size(block − 1) + size(nxtblk);
            next(block − 1) ←next(nxtblk);
        else *No, link them.*
            next(block − 1) ←nxtblk;
    exit;
    end

At the time a block is requested, suppose there exist two blocks in the available list—both of which are large enough to satisfy the request—where one is nearly the size of the requested block while the other is considerably larger. It seems intuitively evident that the larger should not be subdivided, since this leaves two relatively small available blocks and increases the probability that there may be no blocks large enough to satisfy some subsequent request. It tends to fragment available storage. Instead, the request should be satisfied with a portion of the smaller block. In general we expect to minimize memory fragmentation by allocating the requested storage in the smallest possible available block. This allocation process, called the *best-fit strategy,* is shown in the following procedure.

pointer procedure giveme$_3$(asksiz);
integer   asksiz;

This procedure allocates a variable length block of storage of "asksiz" locations. Actually a block of asksiz + 1 *locations are reserved, with the first location serving as block label. The routine is exited with "giveme" pointing to the second word of the block. The choice of which available block to subdivide is based on the best fit strategy.*

```
begin
        pointer          avail, bstblk, bstprev, block, prev;
        integer          actsiz, diff;
        field            next, size;
        common /frpool/  avail;
        actsiz ← asksiz + 1;
```

Find that block in the list of available blocks which is most nearly the requested size.

```
        diff ← 10¹⁰;
        bstprev ← prev ← loc(avail);
        bstblk ← null;
        block ← avail;
        while block ≠ null do
            if size(block) > actsiz and siz(block) − actsize < diff
                then bstprev ← prev;
                     bstblk ← block;
                     diff ← size(block) − actsiz;
            prev ← block;
            block ← next(block);
        if bstblk = null then "overflow";
```

"bstblk" now points to the best available block. Allocate the last "actsiz" locations.

```
β:      if diff = 0
            then
                    giveme ← bstblk + 1;
                    next(bstprev) ← next(bstblk);
                    next(bstblk) ← null;
            else
                    size(bstblk) ← diff;
                    giveme ← bstblk + diff + 1
                    size(giveme-1) ← actsiz;
        exit;
        end
```

If the best block is of the exact same size as the request (statement β above), then the entire block is allocated and is removed from the list of available blocks. Otherwise the remainder is kept in the available list. But often these remaining pieces of available locations are so small (remember that the goal of the procedure is to minimize DIFF) that there is little likelihood of their ever being used to satisfy a request. Instead they just clutter up the list of available blocks and add to overhead costs. It is customary when implementing this algorithm to set some threshold **small,** such that whenever the size of the remaining block would be less than **small,** the entire available block is given to the requesting process.

Neither TAKEIT$_3$ nor GIVEME$_3$ as presented set or examine tag fields in the reserved or available blocks. This and the preceding modification are easily made.

A striking feature of these allocation routines is that both must repeatedly walk through the list of available blocks. GIVEME$_3$ must examine all n blocks in the list for each allocation, while TAKEIT$_3$ examines an expected n/2 blocks with each release. If the list is at all long, then this tedious approach is computationally expensive. Several ways of minimizing this search time are suggested in Exercises 10-12 and 10-13. In view of this overhead problem it is a common policy to adopt a different allocation strategy in GIVEME. Instead of searching the entire list of available blocks for the best fit, the search is conducted only until the first available block large enough to satisfy the request is encountered. The requested locations are allocated from this block regardless of its size. This approach is called a *first-fit* strategy. Writing a first-fit allocation procedure is not difficult and is left to the reader (Exercise 10-10). The increase in execution speed, resulting from the nonexhaustive search of the list of available blocks, is primarily dependent on the length of this list. Empirical evidence based on simulation indicates that first-fit allocation is on the order of 10 to 20 times faster than best-fit allocation.

But the increase in speed of allocation is presumably purchased at the price of increased fragmentation, since the available blocks are being subdivided with less care. And increased fragmentation increases the probability of a premature overflow condition which may halt a job even though adequate storage exists to satisfy the request were it only in larger blocks.

Is the price too high?

We have been repeatedly using the term *fragmentation,* but save for a single illustrative example have given no sort of definition. Intuitively available storage is fragmented when it is distributed in (or "chopped up into") little pieces. But how "little" must these pieces be? One would like to be able to define a *measure of fragmentation* (see Exercise 10-16). Ideally this measure would be a number f associated with any particular configuration of available storage. With it, the size of available storage, and the average request size one would like to be able to predict the probability that the next request will be satisfiable. No such ideal measure has been discovered. We turn instead to direct empirical evidence based on computer simulations of the allocation process.

Simulation of the dynamic allocation process is not hard, and the reader will find it an interesting challenge.† Two simple lists AVAIL and RESRVD are maintained representing blocks of available and reserved storage. Each cell of a list contains the first and last location of the block. In addition a field of cells in the reserved lists denotes the (simulated) time the block will be released, while the corresponding field in the available list denotes the size of the block. Figure

---

†Discussion of more sophisticated simulation techniques can be found in MacDougall (1970).

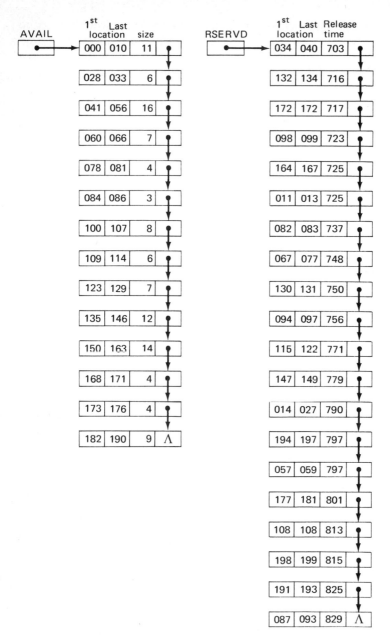

Figure 10-5 Two lists representing a simulated memory allocation (as shown in Fig. 10-2). List AVAIL is ordered by block location. List RESRVD is ordered by time of release.

10-5 shows the representation of a simulated memory of 200 locations [000, 199] distributed as shown in the memory map of Fig. 10-2 at a simulated clock time T = 700. The simulation process simply makes requests to the allocation routines for blocks whose length is randomly chosen from the interval L = [a, b] and whose duration is chosen from some distribution. A cell denoting the allocated block, together with its indicated release time, is added to the reserved list. Blocks are released from reserved status (cells removed from the reserved list) when the simulated clock reaches their release time. Statistics and possibly memory map snapshots are printed periodically. Figure 10-6 illustrates sample output from one such simulation run.

Even a single simulation such as this can be revealing (although you will gain much more insight into the allocation process by executing your own simulations which produce more detailed output). A dynamic allocation system is said to be in *equilibrium,* or to be *stable,* if blocks are being released at the same rate that they are being reserved. It is also assumed that the distribution of allocation requests is stable so that (1) the average size of a requested block is equal to the average size of a released block, and consequently (2) the fraction of the total storage that is free and reserved is constant. From Fig. 10-6 it can be seen that on this simulation run, the allocation system did not attain equilibrium until approximately time $T \geq 1400$.

It has been widely noted in various simulations of dynamic allocation processes that when equilibrium was attained there are roughly half as many available blocks as reserved blocks. Is this true in the case of Fig. 10-6? These repeated observations led to the conjectured *50 percent rule,* which was expressed as the following theorem and subsequently proven to be a valid generalization. Let A denote the number of available blocks and let R denote the number of reserved blocks.

Theorem 10-1. As a dynamic allocation system which coalesces released blocks attains equilibrium,

$$A \rightarrow \frac{1}{2} \cdot R$$

The preceding theorem is an assertion only about the numbers of available and reserved blocks. It says nothing about the percentage of storage that is reserved, the average size of reserved or available blocks, or the probability of storage overflow. But it can be used to derive the following result.

Let $\hat{R}$ denote the average size of a reserved block and $\hat{A}$ denote the average size of an available block. Let F_A denote the fraction of total storage that is free, or available, for allocation. Then we can state the following *unused memory rule.*

Theorem 10-2 If a dynamic allocation system, which coalesces adjacent released blocks, attains equilibrium with F_A of total storage free $(1 - F_A$ reserved), then $\hat{A} \geq k \cdot \hat{R}$ *implies* $F_A \geq k/(k + 2)$.

What is the value of k in the simulation of Fig. 10-6? Is the theorem true in this case? Note that a condition of both theorems is that the allocation system coalesce, or merge, adjacent blocks when they are released, as does the procedure

FIRST-FIT METHOD OF MEMORY ALLOCATION

MEMORY SIZE IS 10000 WORDS
STORAGE REQUESTS ARE POISSON DISTRIBUTED WITH MEAN ARRIVAL RATE = .250000 REQUESTS/UNIT TIME
        REQUEST SIZES ARE UNIFORMLY DISTRIBUTED IN < 20, 80>
        REQUEST DURATIONS ARE UNIFORMLY DISTRIBUTED IN < 1,1400>
SYSTEM STATISTICS ARE GATHERED EVERY 100 TIME UNITS
DURATION OF SIMULATION (UNLESS TERMINATED BY OVERFLOW) IS 3000 TIME UNITS.

| | NUMBER OF REQUEST,RELEAS THIS INTERVL | | WORDS RESERVED | BLKS | AVG R-SIZE | WORDS AVAILABLE | BLKS | AVG A-SIZE | PERCENT FULL | DISTRIBUTION OF AVAILABLE BLOCK SIZES | | | | | | | | | | |
TIME										<10	<20	<30	<40	<50	<60	<70	<80	<90	<100	>100
100	26	26	1200	25	48.00	8800	2	******	12.00	1	0	0	0	0	0	0	0	0	0	1
200	26	0	2560	51	50.20	7440	2	******	25.60	1	0	0	0	0	0	0	0	0	0	1
300	23	4	3312	70	47.31	6688	6	******	33.12	2	3	0	0	0	0	0	0	0	0	1
400	25	6	4236	89	47.60	5764	9	640.44	42.36	4	2	0	2	0	0	0	0	0	0	1
500	15	5	4814	99	48.63	5186	11	471.45	48.14	4	3	3	0	0	0	0	0	0	0	1
600	22	7	5502	114	48.26	4498	15	299.87	55.02	4	6	2	2	0	1	0	0	0	0	1
700	16	10	5804	120	48.37	4196	23	182.43	58.04	5	9	4	2	1	1	0	0	0	0	1
800	21	8	6448	133	48.48	3552	30	118.40	64.48	10	10	5	1	2	0	1	0	0	0	1
900	21	17	6566	137	47.93	3434	38	90.37	65.66	13	14	5	0	0	3	1	0	0	0	1
1000	28	17	7205	148	48.68	2795	47	59.47	72.05	18	17	4	2	0	2	1	0	0	0	1
1100	27	12	7905	163	48.50	2095	52	40.29	79.05	19	22	5	1	2	3	1	0	0	0	1
1200	24	22	8111	165	49.16	1889	62	30.47	81.11	19	21	10	3	1	3	1	1	2	0	3
1300	20	29	7731	156	49.56	2269	66	34.38	77.31	15	20	9	3	4	4	1	2	0	0	3
1400	24	15	8135	165	49.30	1865	66	28.26	81.35	19	22	5	7	6	4	2	2	2	1	1
1500	22	21	8206	166	49.43	1794	70	25.63	82.06	21	22	4	6	5	6	5	2	0	1	1
1600	17	27	7736	156	49.59	2264	71	31.89	77.36	14	18	8	9	8	6	3	3	2	0	2
1700	25	26	7745	155	49.97	2255	71	31.76	77.45	16	17	10	7	9	3	2	1	2	0	4
1800	22	18	7945	159	49.97	2055	72	28.54	79.45	21	19	9	5	7	3	0	3	1	0	4
1900	17	29	7324	147	49.82	2676	70	38.23	73.24	17	10	9	6	8	9	4	1	1	0	4
2000	26	20	7559	153	49.41	2441	72	33.90	75.59	21	11	7	9	7	5	4	0	5	1	3
2100	26	17	8015	162	49.48	1985	73	27.19	80.15	22	9	10	13	9	4	3	2	1	2	0
2200	25	25	7865	162	48.55	2135	73	29.25	78.65	28	11	9	8	6	3	4	1	1	2	3
2300	18	15	8024	165	48.63	1976	74	26.70	80.24	28	14	6	7	6	4	3	3	3	0	2
2400	16	36	7120	145	49.10	2880	72	40.00	71.20	20	11	8	7	5	5	3	1	2	0	5
2500	16	26	6603	135	48.91	3397	67	50.70	66.03	13	10	11	4	6	9	3	3	3	0	9
2600	22	20	6912	137	50.45	3088	60	51.47	69.12	11	9	15	0	4	5	0	2	2	1	11
2700	24	22	7180	139	51.65	2820	61	46.23	71.80	12	8	14	1	8	4	3	3	2	1	7
2800	23	19	7461	143	52.17	2539	63	40.30	74.61	12	12	11	3	5	8	5	3	2	1	6
2900	28	19	7943	152	52.26	2057	63	32.63	79.43	10	15	13	6	6	5	3	2	1	0	6
3000	17	22	7682	147	52.26	2318	64	36.22	76.82	12	13	11	5	6	4	6	3	0	1	3

NORMAL TERMINATION

Figure 10-6 Typical output from a simulation of a dynamic allocation process.

TAKEIT$_3$. Not all allocation systems do this (for example, the allocation techniques of Sec. 10-4). These assertions will not be true in the case of these systems.

Suppose we sought to design an allocation system which would always be able to fulfill allocation requests with a probability close to 1; that is, almost never suffered from premature overflow. Such assurance would seem reasonable if the average available block size Â were equal to the expected request size R̂. In the latter theorem $k = 1$, so that if we were to seek this condition with any diligence we would require an allocation system that never used more than $\frac{2}{3}$ of the potentially available storage. If we wish to make effective use of the total storage, say 80 to 90 percent, then this theorem shows that we must be content with blocks of available storage whose *average* size is very much smaller than the expected request size. This seems to be contradictory until we realize that it is the presence of only a few "large" blocks that is essential to the prevention of premature overflow. Empirical evidence suggests that it is not the average block size, but the *variance* of both available and requested block size that is crucial in determining the probability of overflow. The author is aware of no firm results regarding the effect of variance.

We initiated this analysis of allocation routines with the question: How does the use of the faster first-fit strategy affect memory fragmentation and the probability of premature overflow? We have not been able to answer this question. But by comparing the simulated performance of the best-fit and first-fit strategies for identical request streams, we can get empirical evidence concerning their suitability. Figure 10-7 summarizes the results of a large number of simulation runs by plotting the percentage of memory full at time of overflow (simulation parameters were chosen to ensure eventual overflow) against the average requested block size for the two strategies. It can be seen that best-fit is

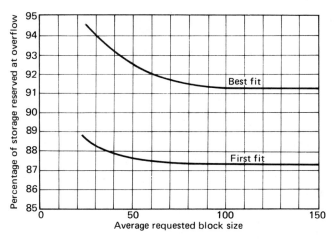

Figure 10-7 Percentage of storage utilization as a function of average-request block size. (Points obtained by averaging several simulations over a range of variances for a fixed-mean requested block size.)

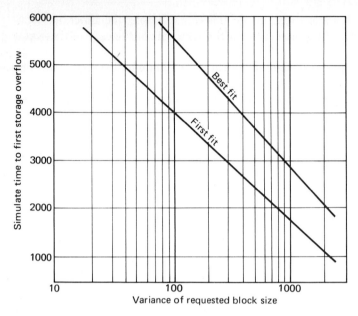

Figure 10-8 Time to first overflow as a function of the variance of requested block size. (Results based on simulated request streams with a fixed-mean requested block size and duration—chosen to ensure eventual storage overflow.)

consistently superior since it effectively utilizes from 4 to 6 percent more of the total storage. The preceding paragraph suggests that the variance of the request sizes is an important factor. Figure 10-8 shows the results of a series of simulations in which the average request size was held fixed, but the variance of the request distribution was changed. Again parameters were loaded to ensure eventual overflow and the time to overflow for each method recorded. It can be seen that the best-fit strategy is capable of handling a wider distribution of request sizes.†

The preceding simulations and analysis of allocation methods are of interest, and illustrate important techniques in investigating the suitability of computational techniques. But a note of caution should be sounded. The reader is likely to conclude that the best-fit allocation strategy is superior to the first-fit method because, even though it is computationally more costly, it will handle a wider variety of request streams and is less likely to fail. But we are comparing behavior in the rather special situation where storage utilization is in the range of 85 to 95 percent. With storage utilization of ≤ 85 percent, the probability of either method failing is essentially nil; with storage utilizations ≥ 95 percent, both invariably failed. So we are comparing the methods near the boundary of their domain of applicability; and we have shown that the useful domain of the best-fit algorithm is somewhat larger than the domain of the first-fit algorithm.

† Shore (1975) presents a more detailed analysis of similar simulations. It is an example of first-rate empirical research in computer science. It comes to somewhat different conclusions.

But in practice, one normally just alters these domains by opening up a few more thousands of storage locations to the allocation process and uses the much faster first-fit method. Only if one is operating within strict storage bounds, say representing data structures on a minicomputer or display processor, should one try to force a process to the limits of its effective operation. There is a serious danger in judging processes on the basis of only "worst-case" comparisons.

EXERCISES FOR SECTION 10-2

10-6 Assume that there are two available blocks of size 1000 and 900, respectively, and assume that there are requests for blocks of size 150, 800, and 900. Put these requests in a sequence:

(a) such that the best-fit method will satisfy the requests but the first-fit method will not;

(b) such that the first-fit method will satisfy the requests but the best-fit method will not.

10-7 In this section we added one extra location to each allocated block and each block was labeled with its own size because we claimed it was dangerous for the deallocation procedure TAKEIT$_3$ to rely on a user-supplied parameter SIZE. Yet in earlier versions of TAKEIT we had no apparent qualms about letting the calling procedure provide this vital parameter. Can you give reasons to justify this apparent contradiction in policy?

10-8 The label location preceding every allocated block records the size of the reserved block. But it may be inadvertently overwritten by a using process. By providing a distinctive tag the allocation system can hope to discover such alteration.

(a) What would be a "good" distinctive tag in your system? (Note that both 0 and 7_8 or G_{16} are poor tag choices on hardware that employs complement arithmetic. Why?)

(b) Modify the procedure TAKEIT$_3$ to test the tag for possible alteration of this word.

If the allocation routines have been privately written for a single user, then one can abort the job on discovery that the label location has been altered. But if this is a system allocation package shared by many users, then it must try to recover.

(c) Modify the procedure TAKEIT$_3$ so that on discovery of label alteration it nevertheless tries to recover the block using information in the available list and other reserved block labels. Were you forced to make some assumptions about the error? Would you like additional information in the label location?

10-9 Write a process, say MEMMAP (L_1, L_n), that will generate a memory map showing the distribution of reserved and free blocks of storage.

*10-10 Write an allocation procedure GIVEME$_4$ which employs the first-fit strategy. Note that if one employs a straightforward search step which always begins examining available blocks at the beginning of the LAVS, then the smaller block "remnants" will tend to accumulate at the beginning of the list while the larger unsubdivided blocks will accumulate at the rear of the list. Before long the search step will find itself repeatedly wading through a collection of the small remnants before it reaches available blocks of reasonable length, thereby nullifying much of the value of the first-fit strategy. A simple remedy is to begin each new search from that point in the LAVS where the previous one left off. It requires only one additional reference pointer, say BEGIN. Will it help to circularly link the list of available storage?

10-11 No version of SETUP has been given to create the initial configuration of available storage. Write one and implement a dynamic storage allocation system for your own private use.

10-12 By ordering the list of available blocks in ascending order of the block address, TAKEIT$_3$ need search, on the average, only half the available list to find the proper place for the released block and its possibly adjacent neighbors. One can reduce the expected number of searches to a fourth by simply keeping a pointer to the "middle" of the list together with the storage address of the referenced "middle" block. Now on return TAKEIT$_3$ compares the released block address with the "middle" block address to decide whether to begin search at the beginning or middle of the available list. What code is necessary to implement such a modification? Each of the list halves could again be halved. Following such an approach would soon result in maintenance of the available list as a *threaded binary search tree*. At what point does the cost of maintaining the binary search mechanism outweight the benefits of faster release times?

10-13 The preceding exercise discusses methods of decreasing search time in the release of deallocated blocks. The final design of GIVEME$_3$ and TAKEIT$_3$ included an extra word of storage preceding each reserved block. If one is willing to add a second word of extra storage to the end of each reserved block then there is no need to search the list of available blocks *at all* when releasing deallocated storage. The accompanying figure shows one format for these two additional bookkeeping labels, which are also called *boundary markers;* both available and reserved blocks are delimited by them. Basically on the release of a block TAKEIT simply examines the boundary markers of the two adjacent blocks to determine if they are free; if so, the blocks are merged, and if not, the block is simply inserted into the available block list.

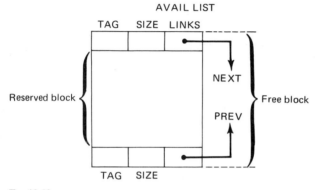

Ex. 10-13

(*a*) Rewrite versions of GIVEME and TAKEIT which include this improved representation.

Provision has been made for doubly linking the list of available blocks in order to simplify the insertion of the block into the list. But this is not really necessary.

(*b*) Show that there is no need to keep the list of free blocks in order of ascending storage location.

10-14 Best-fit allocation—and to a lesser extent, first-fit allocation—are slow because GIVEME must examine blocks which are too small to satisfy the request. Suppose instead that the LAVS were to be linked in *descending* order of block size (possible by Exercise 10-13). Would this modification pay off? Why?

10-15 Suppose that yourself, the author, or someone else were to propose a "measure of fragmentation"; call it f. What properties or characteristics should this measure have? That is, by what standards would you say that the proposed measure is a "good" measure or a "poor" measure? Make a short list of these criteria.

10-16 A common measure of fragmentation is average available block size $\hat{A}$. A second possible measure f might be:

$$f = \frac{\sum\limits_{b \in A} \text{size}(b)^2}{\left(\sum\limits_{b \in A} \text{size}(b)\right)^2} = \frac{\sum\limits_{b \in A} \text{size}(b)^2}{\left(\text{avail words}\right)^2}$$

(*a*) How well do these two measures of fragmentation satisfy the criteria for a good measure as established in the preceding exercise?

Surely one desirable characteristic is the ability to predict the probability of overflow. Consider the following case: The length of requested blocks is *uniformly* distributed over the interval [1, 20]. There are 20 available words divided into two blocks. Configuration C_1 consists of two 10-word blocks. Configuration C_2 consists of a 1-word and a 19-word block. The average available block size $\hat{A}(C_i)$ of both configurations is 10. $f(C_1) = 200/400 = 0.5$ while $f(C_2) = 362/400 = 0.9$.

(*b*) Show by considering all possible two-request sequences that:

prob(overflow by $T+2|C_1) = 300/400 = 0.75$
prob(overflow by $T+2|C_2) = 229/400 = 0.56$

Which is the better predictor? Why?

(*c*) Can you show that in all cases f is a better predictor of possible overflow than $\hat{A}$?

The best possible predictor of possible overflow *on the next request* is the size of the largest block.

(*d*) What criterion of a good measure does "size of the largest block" fail utterly?

10-17 A number of parameters may be used to describe a dynamic allocation environment. A partial list is:

M $=$ total memory size
λ $=$ requests/time $=$ prob. of request per time unit
μ $=$ average duration of reserved block (so that $1/\mu =$ probability that an individual block is released per time unit)
$\hat{R}$ $=$ average request size $\hat{R}$ ϵ [a, b],
R $=$ number of reserved blocks
$\hat{A}$ $=$ average available block size
A $=$ number of available blocks
F_A $=$ fraction of total memory available
$F_R = 1 - F_A =$ fraction of memory reserved or used

The first four parameters, M, λ, μ, and $\hat{R}$, are normally treated as independent and set at the beginning of a simulation run. The remainders are dependent variables, and a purpose of the simulation is to determine the nature of the dependence.

(*a*) Intuitively establish the following simple relationships:
(1) $R/\mu =$ release rate $=$ prob. of a release per time unit.
(2) At equilibrium, $R = \lambda \cdot \mu$
(3) $F_R = (R \cdot \hat{R})/M$
Note that (2) can be proven rigorously if request arrivals are Poisson distributed and request durations are uniformly distributed.

(*b*) For fixed M and R, say 5000 and 25, respectively, plot the relationship between λ and μ which ensures that at equilibrium, $F_R = 0.85$.

(*c*) Prove the more involved dependencies expressed in Theorems 10-1 and 10-2.

*10-18 Implement a driver program which simulates the request and release of variably sized blocks of storage. Use it to

(*a*) test the routines coded for Exercise 10-10, and

(*b*) describe the behavior of these routines. (For this latter you may wish to add sections to GIVEME and TAKEIT which collect statistical information, e.g., number of blocks examined before finding a suitable one.)

(*c*) describe how the inclusion of "small" remnants as additions to requested blocks affects the behavior of the system.

10-3 RETURN OF STRUCTURES

In all the dynamic allocation routines we have examined, deallocation has been caused by executing a routine TAKEIT which releases a single cell or block of storage. Since TAKEIT is called by a user process, it presumably is invoked by the process when it discovers that the data structure, or portion of a structure, to which the cell belongs is no longer of use. But how does the process "know" when a cell is no longer needed? In the case of dynamic stacks and queues it is quite evident that as elements are removed from the end of the list their representing cells should be released to the pool of available storage. But if the reader will reflect, except for this single case, we have been almost totally preoccupied in this text with the *creation* of data structures, not their destruction. It turns out that the release of structures, and particularly the release of substructures, constitutes one of the thornier aspects of this subject.

There are two distinctly different approaches to the release of data structures. The first is *user-initiated return,* in which the decision to return a structure is made by a user process; in its actual release TAKEIT functions strictly as a worker routine. It is the approach we have consistently followed. In the second method, called *garbage collection,* release is initiated and entirely controlled by routines of the dynamic allocation system itself. Let us first consider user-initiated return, since that is more familiar. The paramount issue here will be the *problem of responsibility*.

The problem of responsibility can be summed up by the questions: When is a data structure or a part of a structure no longer needed? and, When can a process assume the responsibility for making this decision and issue a destructive call to TAKEIT? One answer to the first question might be that a representation is unnecessary if no future reference will be made to the cells of that representation. It is a bit difficult to anticipate what will happen in the future, so it is wise to alter the condition of uselessness to read "... if no future reference *can* be made to the representation."† Cells of a representation can be referenced in two ways: by link fields of other cells in the representation or by pointer variables in processes. Again let us temporarily confine our attention to the former case.

Suppose that a process which has been using a list structure is through with it; it will no longer make any references to the list, and so it executes the statement

call erase (list);

to return the cells of its representation to the pool of available storage. If the list

---

†This is the criterion used in the dynamic allocation of storage in a block-structured language, such as Algol or PL/1. On exit from a block all local variables literally cease to exist. Consequently the representations of these variables can no longer be referenced, and their storage may be released.

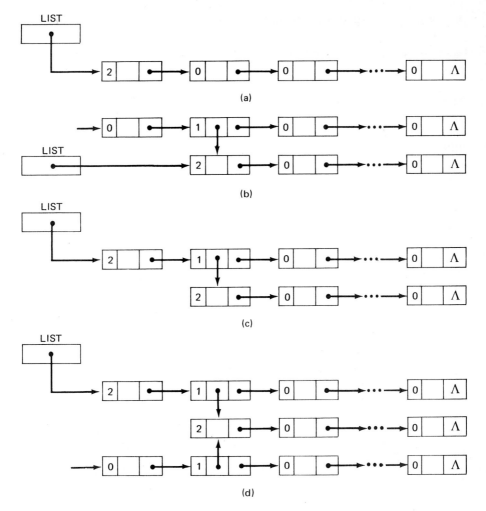

Figure 10-9 Four configurations of lists and list structures with header cells.

is a simple list, as shown in Fig. 10-9(*a*), the procedure ERASE should just "walk down" the list, returning its cells one at a time by repeatedly calling TAKEIT. But if the list is a sublist, as shown in Fig. 10-9(*b*), then it is evident that ERASE should not actually return any of its cells to storage since the list *can be referenced by another cell in the data structure*. If the list to be erased contains a sublist as shown in Fig. 10-9(*c*), then ERASE should return not only all the cells of LIST, but all the cells of its sublist as well. If not, those cells of the sublist, which can never again be referenced once LIST is erased, will never be returned to the pool of available cells for reassignment. They will be effectively "lost." However, if the sublist is shared by several lists, as shown in Fig. 10-9(*d*), then ERASE should return all the cells representing LIST, but none of the cells representing the sublist. Thus the procedure ERASE is expected to perform one of four very different operations, depending on the particular configuration of the data structure. By what criteria is it to assume the responsibility of actually returning a cell to the free pool by invoking TAKEIT?

First we might observe that the procedure name ERASE is probably a misnomer. We prefer to call the procedure RELEASE, since the user process merely "releases" the structure by announcing, in effect, that it has no further use for it. The decision whether to actually erase any part of, or all of, the representation is left up to the subprocedure. We will henceforth call this deciding procedure RELEASE. Now the decision to physically erase the cells of a released structure can be made on the following basis: the representation is to be erased if there are no name cells in some other data structure referencing it. The set of referencing name cells could be established by keeping and updating a set of "back pointers," but this is costly, unwieldy, and unnecessary. It is sufficient just to keep a *count* of the number of cells that reference the structure—possibly in an unused field of the header cell. Header cells were included in the list structures of Fig. 10-9 for just this reason. The field is commonly called the *reference counter,* or just RFCNTR. We will agree that the reference counter of any header cell RFCNTR(HEADER) will denote just the count of name cells in the data structure which reference that cell. Convince yourself that for all "superlists" in Fig. 10-9, RFCNTR(HEADER) should equal zero, while the value of the reference counter for each of the sublists in (*b*), (*c*), and (*d*) will be 1, 1, and 2, respectively.

We can now write a procedure RELEASE which checks the reference counter of each list or sublist to be erased and decrements the counters of those sublists referenced within the list. An example is the following stack-driven procedure.

procedure release$_1$ (list);
pointer   list;

This procedure releases the list structure referenced by the argument pointer. The list and any of its sublists are actually erased and returned to available storage if their reference counters are equal to zero.

begin
    pointer   cell, header1, header2, nxtcel;
    field   next, rfcntr, sublist, tag;

Stack all references to lists that may possibly be erased.

    call pushdown (stack, list);
    list ←null;
    while stack ≠ null **do**

        See if the list referenced by the top of the stack can be erased.

        header1 ←poptop(stack);

```
        if rfcntr(header1) ≤ 0
            then   Traverse this list and erase its cells.
                cell ←header1;
                while cell ≠ null do
                    if tag(cell) = 1
                        then  The list this name cell references may be erasable.
                              Decrease its reference counter by 1 and put a pointer
                              to it in the stack.
                              header2 ←sublist(cell);
                              rfcntr(header2) ←rfcntr(header2) − 1;
                              call pushdown (stack,header2);
                    nxtcel ←next(cell)
                    call takeit (cell, celsiz);
                    cell ←nxtcel;
exit;
end
```

The reader should verify that given the list structure of Fig. 10-10, execution of the statement

call release (list);

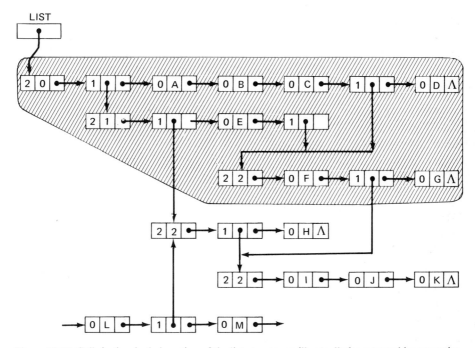

Figure 10-10 Cells in the shaded portion of the list structure will actually be returned by executing RELEASE(LIST).

will cause those cells in the shaded portion to be actually returned to available storage.

Traversal of large portions of the structure at the time of release is time-consuming, but it appears to be necessary if all the sublists are to have their reference counters decremented and if possible be erased. It turns out to be necessary only if all cells are to be erased at the time of their release. In implementing his SLIP system, Weizenbaum (1963) employed a neat trick which actually erases most cells just prior to their subsequent reallocation. In this approach an erasable list is simply added to the free pool by RELEASE; none of its sublists are even examined. Sublists are released by the allocation procedure GIVEME just before the referencing name cell is about to be reallocated. The interaction of these two procedures is shown below in detail.

procedure release$_2$ (list);
pointer   list;

This procedure checks the reference counter of the indicated list and returns its cells if possible.

begin
    pointer   cell, nxtcel;
    field   next, rfcntr;
    if rfcntr(list) > 0 **then exit;**
    cell $\leftarrow$ list;
    while cell $\neq$ null **do**
        nxtcel $\leftarrow$ ncxt(cell);
        call takeit (cell, celsiz);
        cell $\leftarrow$ nxtcel;
    list $\leftarrow$ null;
    exit:
    end

With certain list representations, this loop can be replaced with two or three statements to return the entire list.

pointer procedure giveme$_4$ (celsiz);
integer   celsiz;

This procedure returns the address of a cell at the front of the list of available cells, organized as a queue. If the cell was a name cell (tag $= 1$), then the sublist that it previously referenced is first released.

begin
    pointer   bottom, cell, header, nxtcel, top;
    field   next, rfcntr, sublist, tag;
    common /frpool/ top, bottom;
    cell $\leftarrow$ top
    if cell $=$ null **then** "overflow";
    if tag(cell) $= 1$
      then *Release the sublist referenced by this cell.*
        header $\leftarrow$ sublist(cell);
        rfcntr(header) $\leftarrow$ rfcntr(header) $- 1$;
        call release (header);

```
    nxtcel ←next(cell);
    if nxtcel = null then bottom ←loc(bottom);
    top ←nxtcel;
    next(cell) ←null;
    giveme ←cell;
    exit;
    end
```

Compare this procedure with GIVEME, as shown in Sec. 3-3, and with RELEASE$_1$. Note that the traversal stack has vanished. Where did it go? Besides eliminating the overhead of stack maintenance, the preceding technique of cell return tends to defer the actual work of returning cells and resetting links and pointers until cells are actually demanded from the free pool. In many applications large structures are released shortly before terminating the job. Since the referencing cells in the main list are added to the rear of the queue,† it is likely that the job will terminate normally before incurring the overhead of returning any of the sublists.

The inclusion of a reference counter field in the header cell of list representations‡ yields a mechanism that provides adequate information to resolve the "issue of responsibility," *provided* (1) sublist inclusion is a partial order relation, (2) all processes which create, or destroy, sublist dependency preserve the integrity of the convention and increment, or decrement, the counter appropriately, and (3) at most one pointer variable ever references any list. The first condition prohibits the use of recursive structures. The second condition implies that in any "public" system all operations that modify the representation must be performed by "system" procedures which are called by the user. The user must be locked out from any low-level interface with the representation. Neither of these conditions or their implications is unrealistic. But the last condition is. It implies that one cannot have pointer assignment statements of the form

$$\text{list}1 \leftarrow \text{list}2; \tag{10-1}$$

Complete protection against irresponsible erasure requires that a count be kept of all references made by either cells in the other structures or by pointer variables in procedures. The latter is possible only if all procedures are written in a common language whose compiler may be altered. On encountering a pointer assignment statement such as (10-1) the compiler must generate not only runtime machine code to replace the contents of the pointer variable list1

---

†This is the major reason for organizing the list of available cells as a queue rather than as a stack.

‡While phrased in terms of lists and sublists, this concept can be extended to any other representational unit, such as graphs and subgraphs, arrays and subarrays, etc., which are referenced by pointing to a single header element.

with the current contents of list2; it must also generate code to decrement the reference counter of the list currently referenced by list1, if nonnull, and increment the counter associated with the list referenced by list2, since on completion of the assignment statement list1 will also reference it. Such protection mechanisms may be incorporated into language design (see Exercise 10-27), but in practice seem to be little used. If, as this text has suggested, most procedures will be coded in an existing programming language, then there is no way to systematically count the number of times a representation is referenced within a set of procedures. It makes user-initiated return of structures a vulnerable process.

The most serious flaw in user-initiated return is the possibility that an unnecessary structure may simply never be released. This may arise because of programmer oversight, or because structures may become so complex that no process can really decide when a portion of it becomes unnecessary. The next method of returning data structures, called *garbage collection,* completely solves this problem.

Garbage collection, which has been used by many structure-manipulating systems and most notably LISP, is based on the assumption that the release of unreferenceable portions of data structures, called "garbage," will be initiated by the dynamic allocation routine GIVEME when it discovers that its list of available space is exhausted. The garbage-collecting procedure does this by (1) traversing every data structure referenced by any pointer variable in any process, (2) marking in a special field all cells encountered in the traversal process, and (3) on a second sweep through the block $[L_1, L_n]$ of storage, returning all *unmarked,* and therefore unreferenceable, cells to the list of available storage. This is an elegant approach, yet it has problems. One is that structures are most easily traversed with the aid of a stack mechanism. All traversal procedures of this text have employed either an explicit or an implicit stack. Yet the garbage collector is called precisely when the list of available cells has been exhausted and there remain no cells with which to build a traversal stack! In the following solutions we assume for simplicity that all structures are list structures and that all cells are of the same size.

There exist ways to traverse a list structure without a stack and to mark all cells that can be reached, or referenced, from a given set of pointer variables. One way is to initially mark all cells directly referenced by a procedure pointer variable. Then the marking process "sweeps" through the block $[L_1, L_n]$ of cell storage examining each cell. If it is marked, then those cells linked through the NEXT and/or SUBLIST fields may be marked (if they have not already been marked). Such sweeps are repeated until on one pass through the storage no new cells are marked. Since there exist worst-case examples where if m cells are marked, m repeated sweeps will be required, this is patently a rather unattractive marking algorithm. An improved version can be written by including a variable MINLOC, which points to that cell with minimal address which was just marked in the course of a sweep through $[L_1, L_n]$. The next sweep can begin at that location. This version, which is clearly superior to blind iterated marking, is still too slow. Nevertheless, we can make use of it in the following composite marking procedure.

Since traversal and marking are so much faster if an auxiliary stack is available it is reasonable to reserve a fixed, but small, amount of storage for the exclusive use of this important process, say k cells. As much of the traversal and marking process as possible will make use of this stack, but if overflow occurs the procedure must be able to fall back on the method of sequential sweeps through the block of cell storage. Hence it is a composite marking process. The following procedure, which implements the finite stack by a sequential array, illustrates the details.

procedure markcells

This procedure assumes a list structure similar to those of Sec. 8-3. Each cell has tag *and* next *fields, and name cells (tag = 1) have a "sublist" field as well, which links to the referenced sublist. In addition every cell is presumed to have a boolean "mark" field = (0 or 1), which is initially false (or 0) for every cell. On exit all cells that are "reachable" from a set of reference pointers will be marked as true.*

begin
```
        pointer array    stack[1:s], x[1:nrefptrs];
        pointer          cell, loc1, locn, minloc, refcel;
        integer          i, nrefptrs, s, top;
        field            mark, next, sublist, tag;
        common /system/  loc1, locn, nrefptrs, x;
        minloc ← locn + 1;
```

Initially mark all directly referenced cells and stack as many as possible. For the remainder set the pointer "minloc" so that minloc ≤ refptr[i], for i > m.

```
    for i = 1 thru nrefptrs do
        mark(x[i]) ← true;
        if i ≤ s
            then top ← i;
                 stack[top] ← x[i];
            else minloc ← min(x[i], minloc);
    go to popstack;
followlinks:
```

This cell is marked; mark any unmarked cells accessible from it.

```
    if tag(cell) = 1 then
        refcel ← sublist(cell)
        if not mark(refcel) then
```

> *Mark the first cell of this referenced list, but do not traverse it now. Instead push it down on the stack, or if the stack is full, set the pointer minloc so that it must be examined at least one more time.*

```
            mark(refcel) ← true;
```

```
            if top < s
                then  top ←top + 1;
                      stack[top] ←refcel;
                else  minloc ←min(refcel, minloc);
```

Follow the next link (if any) of this cell.

```
    if next(cell) ≠ nullvalue and not mark(next(cell)) then
        cell ←next(cell);
        mark(cell) ←true;
        go to followlinks;
popstack:
```

This list has been completely traversed and marked. Traverse any stacked sublists.

```
    if top ≥ 1 then
        cell ←stack[top];
        top ←top − 1;
        go to followlinks;
```

There are no stacked sublists to follow. Beginning with the cell minloc, *sweep through all of storage to see if there exist remaining untraversed structures.*

```
sweep:
    while minloc ≤ locn do
        begin
        cell ←minloc;
        minloc ←cell +celsiz;
        if mark(cell) then
```

This cell has been marked. Has the next cell in its list been marked? (Note that if it's a name cell, then the cell it references must have been marked.)

```
            if next(cell) ≠ nullvalue and not mark(next(cell)) then
```

Mark it, and begin following this sublist.

```
                cell ←next(cell);
                mark(cell) ←true;
                go to followlinks;
        end
    exit;
    end
```

Given this marking procedure, it is now straightforward to write a garbage-collecting procedure which first marks all accessible cells and then sweeps through the block $[L_1, L_n]$ of cell storage, and if a cell is unmarked, returns it to the list of available cells, or if the cell is marked, erases the mark.

Garbage collection gives rise to several interesting questions, many of which have no definitive answer. First, one wonders how much storage s should be reserved for the finite stack. Clearly this depends on how deeply nested the sublist structure will be. Between 50 and 100 locations does not seem unreasonable for this important process, but experiments with actual data may lead the user to revise this estimate. What is the expected cost of garbage collection? It is difficult to analyze the cost of that portion which sweeps through the entire storage since it is highly dependent on the order in which cells are sequentially distributed into this block of storage. We can, however, make a reasonable approximation based on the assumption that the marking traversal is essentially stack-controlled and that the subprocess that sweeps through the cells is infrequently, if ever, invoked. Let m and r denote the total number of cells encountered in the traversal (and hence marked) and the number of reference (or name) cells encountered. Let α denote the cost of accessing (following a link) and marking a cell, and let β denote the cost of pushing a name cell down on the stack and later popping it. Then since every cell encountered is accessed and marked and in addition every name cell encountered is stacked at least once, the following approximation holds.

$$\text{cost(marking)} \approx \alpha m + \beta r \leq (\alpha + \beta)m \qquad (10\text{-}2)$$

since $r \leq m$. Then letting n denote the total number of cells in storage (both reserved and free), one can estimate the cost per free cell obtained as

$$\text{Cost(marking/free cell)} \approx \frac{(\alpha + \beta)m}{n - m}$$

$$= (\alpha + \beta) \left[\frac{1}{(n/m) - 1} \right] \qquad (10\text{-}3)$$

We see from expressions (10-2) and (10-3) that as allocatable storage becomes full the cost of garbage collection increases porportionally, since there are more reserved cells to mark. But the cost per free cell obtained by the process increases much more rapidly since procedures are working harder to obtain fewer cells. For this reason many systems that employ garbage collection set a threshold that terminates a job with an overflow condition before actual overflow occurs, using the very reasonable heuristic that "a job which approaches the full use of dynamic storage is likely to overflow in the near future" and that continuation of the job under these conditions is not worth the cost.

A somewhat different situation arises when an allocation system is implemented in virtual memory. Garbage collection presupposes at least one sweep through a block $[L_1, L_n]$ of sequentially stored cells—to collect unmarked cells and remove the marks in marked cells—even if it is unnecessary in the marking procedure itself. In virtual memory systems the cells may be widely scattered in physical storage; they may be in various blocks of core and secondary storage. They may also be scattered through the virtual address space. As requests are made to GIVEME, new cells can be created in any unused portion of the virtual memory. In fact it would appear that the entire concept of overflow, which is based on the exhaustion of a finite block of

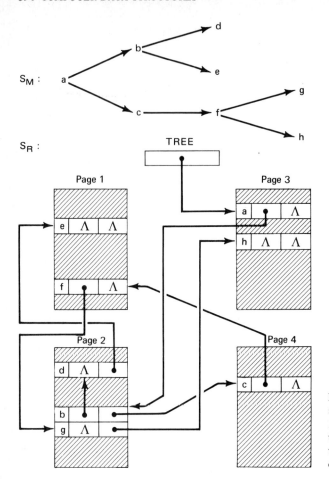

Figure 10-11 "Sparse" representation of a tree (using the Knuth transform) in paged virtual memory. (Shaded portions denote inactive dormant cells.)

storage locations, has vanished and that there is no need to return unused cells by either garbage collection or by user-initiated return. Technically this is correct. But instead a different condition, which is in some respects analogous to overflow and which we will perversely continue to call overflow, can occur. Consider a dynamic system implemented in virtual memory. Cells are allocated from pages of the virtual memory as needed. Unused cells that can no longer be referenced are not returned to the allocator but become inactive or dormant. Given a dynamic process executing over an extended period of time, one might find that 50 to 80 percent of the cells of a page have become dormant. More recently created portions of a structure which have been constructed with newly allocated cells will be compactly represented on a few pages, but older portions which have been extensively modified will be sparsely represented over a number of pages, as shown in Fig. 10-11. Eventually processes that reference these older portions, say in search algorithms, traversals, etc., will generate an increasingly disproportionate number of page faults. Overflow is said to occur when the frequency of page faults becomes "intolerable."†

The solution to this problem is not the collection and return of inactive dormant cells, but rather the compaction of currently active cells onto as few pages as possible.‡ This can be done by traversing the active cells of the structure, as in garbage collection, but instead of marking all encountered cells as active and returning the unmarked dormant cells, the entire structure is simply moved, or copied, into a new compact representation. In effect, all the old cells become dormant. If *all* the cells on a page are dormant, then the page itself is dormant, and it can never cause a page fault since it will never again be referenced.

It is not difficult to write a procedure to copy an existing data structure which traverses the old structure, say with the aid of a stack, while simultaneously building and referencing a symbol table which keeps track of the correspondence between old cells and their new duplicates. But the cost of creating and maintaining either a stack or a symbol table is to be avoided if possible.§ The following procedure recreates list structures, as found in Chap. 8; in newly allocated storage, both the stack and the table of corresponding cell addresses are built with the cells of the old structure. The NEXT link field of copied cells is set to point to the corresponding new cell. In name cells the SUBLIST field is used to link these copied cells into a stack.

procedure move (list);
pointer   list;

This procedure moves the entire structure accessible from the pointer list *to a new block of storage (currently being allocated by "giveme"). Old cells that have been copied are distinctively tagged (with 3) and the next link field is set to point to the corresponding new cell. The old structure is destroyed by this process.*

begin
       pointer   namecell, newcell, nextcell, nextnew, oldcell, refcell, top;
       field   next, sublist, tag;
       if list = null **then exit;**
       top ←null;
       oldcell ←list;
       newcell ←giveme(celsiz);

---

†There is no established criterion for what should be considered intolerable. Readily it should be based on the expected cost of compacting the existing structure versus the expected cost of unnecessary overhead generated by excessive page faults in anticipated future processes that will use the existing structure.

‡Nevertheless this operation is commonly called garbage collection (Fenichel and Yochelson, 1969).

§Moreover, requesting and releasing cells for a dynamic stack from the same storage that will be used to represent the newly copied data structure will work against the basic goal of compactification. Why?

copylist:

> *Copy the remainder of this list, beginning with* oldcell.

> tag(newcell) ←tag(oldcell);
> sublist(newcell) ←sublist(oldcell);
> **if** tag(oldcell) = 1 **then**
> > **if** tag(sublist(oldcell)) ≠ 3
> > > **then** *This name cell references an uncopied list. Stack the name cell using the sublist link. (Note: its contents have already been copied.)*
> > > > sublist(oldcell) ←top;
> > > > top ←oldcell;
> > > **else** *This name cell references a copied list. Simply reset link in corresponding "newcell" and ignore it.*
> > > > sublist(newcell) ←next(sublist(oldcell));
> nextcell ←next(oldcell);
> next(oldcell) ←newcell;
> tag(oldcell) ←3;
> **if** nextcell = null **then**

> > *End of list; fix up last duplicate cell.*

> > next(newcell) ←null;
> > **go to** poptop;
> **if** tag(nextcell) = 3 **then**

> > *Remainder of this list has already been copied, just link this "newcell" to the new copy.*

> > next(newcell) ←next(nextcell);
> > **go to** poptop;

> *Setup to copy the next cell in this list.*

> nextnew ←giveme(celsiz);
> next(newcell) ←nextnew;
> oldcell ←nextcell;
> newcell ←nextnew;
> **go to** copylist;

poptop:

> *Finish moving this list. Pick off top name cell in the stack. If the sublist (or cell) it references is still uncopied, begin copying it. If it has been copied, just change the sublist link of the corresponding newcell.*

> **if** top = null **then exit;**
> namecell ←top;
> top ←sublist(namecell);
> refcell ←sublist(next(namecell));
> **if** tag(refcell) = 3
> > **then** sublist(next(namecell)) ←next(refcell);
> > > **go to** poptop;
> > **else** oldcell ←refcell;

```
        newcell ←giveme(celsiz);
        sublist(next(namecell)) ←newcell;
        go to copylist
end
```

To understand this procedure the reader should apply it to several list structures and look at its various intermediate configurations. It is important that the process anticipate and be able to recognize portions of the structure that have already been copied (distinctively marked, in this case, by a tag of 3). The garbage collector, or cell compactor, must apply MOVE to every structure referenced by every pointer in every process and exit with that pointer referencing the corresponding cell in the new representation. Many pointers may reference the same structure, and some may reference cells within the structure that are not header cells.

Several compactification algorithms have appeared [e.g., Cheney (1970), Hansen (1969)] which compact LISP-like lists. Of even more interest are those procedures which literally copy, in the sense of duplication, without destruction of the original (Fisher, 1975). Efficient procedures of this type are much more difficult to devise and may require that structures to be copied have certain characteristics and be well formed.† They may be used for list compaction or as models of nondestructive input-output processes.

Comparison of user-initiated and garbage-collection methods of returning unused cells for reuse reveals strengths and weaknesses that are largely complementary. In user-initiated return systems there is no foolproof method of enforcing responsibility. Structures may be released by one process that can still be referenced by some other process, or unusable structures may not be released at all. The latter problem can be minimized by automatic system-initiated return, say of locally declared structures on exit from a block. But with garbage collection this is no problem at all. Also, one may waste the overhead of returning cells, which in short jobs may never need to be reused. On the other hand, the overhead of garbage collection (or list compaction) occurs in unpredictable spasms, which makes it undesirable for various real-time applications such as graphic display. More serious is the restriction it places on the use of pointer variables. So that they may be accessible by the collector process, *all* variable pointers must be either declared globally (in Algol-like languages), declared in COMMON (in Fortran-like languages), or else embodied in a special language, e.g., LISP, which has its own compiler or interpreter. All normally preclude the use of separately compiled subroutines and procedures. Finally, it

---

†It is dangerous for any garbage-collection scheme to assume that the list structure is well formed. A process may have temporarily deleted various links, say preparatory to adding a new cell whose request initiated the garbage collection. On the other hand, it is reasonable to assume that only well-formed structures will be duplicated.

is difficult to imagine the use of garbage-collection techniques with dynamic structures that are shared by several separate jobs, as in an extended computer network.

EXERCISES FOR SECTION 10-3

*10-19 Give examples to show that a simple mechanism of protection with reference counters can fail if there exist several pointer variables, possibly in different processes, that reference the same structure.

*10-20 Why is reference counter protection incompatible with recursive list structures? Give an example of the problem and a convincing argument that it has no effective solution. Can garbage collection handle recursive list structures? Why?

10-21 Weizenbaum suggestively calls pointer variables which reference a list, an *alias* of the structure. A structure may have only one *name*—the address of its header cell—but it may have several aliases. Moreover, they may be changed. Give examples to show that in a simple system of user-initiated return, execution of the statement

list1 ← list2;

which reassigns the alias list1 can
    (*a*) result in release of a list that may still be referenced, or
    (*b*) cause a list to be "lost" so that it can never be released.

10-22 The order in which reference counters are decremented and tested is quite crucial. RELEASE$_1$ decrements the counter (except for initially referenced list) before pushing a reference pointer down on the stack, and tests for zero after popping the reference off the stack. Suppose instead of decrementing the reference counter, the procedure tests for "one." What changes would be needed in the code?

10-23 The use of the stack routines PUSHDOWN and POPTOP in RELEASE$_1$ involve a needless bit of overhead, fetching and returning stack cells to the free pool. Nothing need be stacked unless there will actually be cells erased. Why? It is not difficult to rewrite this procedure so that the stack is built in these cells *before* they are actually returned to the free store. Do so. (Be careful of boundary conditions and the handling of reference counters.)

10-24 Suppose that different-sized cells are used in constructing the list structure; for example, the header cells may be different from either the name cells or the atomic cells. What changes are necessary to RELEASE$_1$? Can the procedures RELEASE$_2$ and GIVEME$_2$ (Sec. 10-1) be altered to provide for the release of sublists, built of variable-sized cells, at the time of reallocation? What is the problem?

*10-25 The reference counter mechanism for responsible return of representations effectively subdivides a representation into *protected units*. In this section "lists" were chosen to be the smallest protected unit, but one could choose to protect individual cells by including a reference counter in each.
    (*a*) Redraw Fig. 10-10 and modify the procedure RELEASE$_1$, assuming that each cell is individually protected.
    (*b*) List advantages and disadvantages to protecting individual cells with a reference counter.
    (*c*) Under what conditions would such protection seem most desirable?
    (*d*) How would one release circularly linked lists?

10-26 Let S_R be any representation of a directed graph in which a cell c_y is linked only to those cells $\{c_z\}$ representing the right neighbors of y. Define the integer point assignment function f where $f(y) = |L(y)|$.
    (*a*) Show that f so defined is a reference counter.

(b) Write a topological sort algorithm which repeatedly examines the cells of S_R and:
   (1) adds any point y, such that $f(y) = 0$, to the sort sequence, and
   (2) if y is added to the sequence, decrements $f(z_i)$ for all $z_i \in R(y)$.
(c) Show that the algorithm actually is a topological sort (Sec. 6-3).
(d) Use these observations to justify the assertion that responsible return of data structures, which is enforced by reference counters, demands that the protected units be nonrecursive.

*10-27 Consider the design of a programming language which includes the ability to keep count of references to data structures within processes.
   (a) We have frequently seen statements of the form

cell ← list1;

where both cell and list1 have been declared to be of type pointer. What generated machine code should be associated with this statement? In this language should there be several different types of pointer variables; say of type **list**, of type **set**, and of type **element**? Why?
   (b) Modify the sequence of code above so that after decrementing the reference counter of cell it is tested for zero. Will this solve the problem of "lost" structures in user- (or process-) initiated return?
   (c) Suppose that a pointer variable is passed as a parameter to a subprocedure; should a reference counter be changed? In what way?
   (d) What code associated with locally declared pointer variables should be generated on exit from a block or procedure?

10-28 Write a garbage-collection procedure using MARKCELLS.

*10-29 Implement a simple garbage-collecting allocation system. The interface with the user can be via the routines GIVEME and TAKEIT as before, but in this system TAKEIT should be a no-operation which merely sets the argument to null, and GIVEME should call the garbage collector when apparent overflow occurs. (Thus all your existing programs can be run with the only change being to put all pointer variables in all programs into some sort of COMMON storage so that they will be available to the garbage collector.)
   (a) Test the system with some old programs.
   (b) Compare the overall cost of programs run with garbage collection against those run with user-initiated return. [Note: This will not be a fair comparison because (1) a procedure written for a garbage-collecting system would not have the overhead of calling TAKEIT nor of those tests which decide if a cell can be returned, and (2) on the other hand, your jobs are unlikely to be long enough to make much use, if any, of the garbage collector.]
   (c) Estimate α and β for your implementation.

10-30 The procedure MARKCELLS which marks the accessible cells for the garbage collector assumes that all cells are of the same size. Rewrite a version of both this procedure and the preceding garbage collector which will handle variably sized cells. You may assume that either (1) all cells are preceded by an extra "boundary label" giving its size, or (2) the existence of a table which gives the size of each type of cell (denoted by its tag).

10-31 We have been treating the cost of garbage collection as if it were just the cost of marking reserved cells, as in expressions (10-2) and (10-3). Show that this is justified by deriving an expression for the cost of the entire garbage-collection operation. Are the other factors constant? Do they dominate the expression?

10-32 Derive a more accurate expression for the cost of marking reserved cells than that given in (10-2). In particular, note that a name cell is *not* stacked if the cell (list) that it references has already been marked. How can this be accounted for?

10-33 Plot the cost per free cell obtained using: (1) expression (10-3), (2) your best estimate of α and β for your system (or obtained from Exercise 10-29), and (3) $n = 1000, 5000$, or $10,000$ against m = number marked, $0 \leq m \leq n$. Can you make a valid plot of "cost versus percent full"?

10-34 It was claimed that the traversal process in garbage collecting effectively requires a stack, yet the method of RELEASE$_2$ effectively traverses a released substructure without requiring an explicit stack mechanism. Could a similar approach be employed in garbage collection? (Note that in one case the purpose of the traversal is to discover all substructures that *are referenced* by the release structure, while in the other case it is to discover all substructures that *cannot be referenced*.)

10-35 Will the procedure MOVE as written recopy

    (*a*) ring structures, say that given in Fig. 8-6?

    (*b*) recursive list structures?

    (*c*) the structure of Fig. 8-7?

    If so, give a convincing argument that it will. If not, modify the procedure so that it will.

10-36 A linked data structure need not have the form of those given in Chap. 8 (as we have assumed), but it can be assumed that each cell has at least two link fields, say LLINK and RLINK, and possibly more. An essential problem is to be able to tell when the field is actually a link to another cell of the data structure and when it is atomic.

    (*a*) What mechanism is used to indicate atomic fields in MOVE? Is it general?

    (*b*) Suppose the process could determine whether the contents of a field is a valid machine (or virtual) address. Is this test by itself sufficient to determine if a field is atomic? Can a field which contains a storage address be atomic? (Consider Fig. 8-17.)

    (*c*) Generalize the procedure MOVE so that it can handle a variety of data structures.

10-37 Write a procedure COPY(PTR) that will actually "copy" in the sense of creating a nondestructive duplicate of the structure referenced by the pointer

    (*a*) using a separate stack and symbol table, and

    (*b*) using no additional storage.

For the latter you may wish to restrict the kinds of structure to be copied, say to nonrecursive trees.

10-38 Assume the existence of one or more data structures which exist permanently as files on some secondary storage device. Assume that one or more processes have the authority (possibly enforced through a password file protection system) to modify and/or release portions of the structure.

    (*a*) Is the process of modification synonymous with that of release? Explain.

    (*b*) Give examples of situations where irresponsible release of portions of the structure can have disastrous effects on other processes which reference the structure and on other data structures which reference the structure.

    (*c*) Design a mechanism which tends to enforce responsible release (as opposed to just authorizing release).

    (*d*) What are the problems associated with a simple reference counter mechanism?

    (*e*) What are the problems associated with a garbage-collection approach?

10-4 THE BUDDY SYSTEM

The procedures of Sec. 10-3 which allocate blocks of variable size all maintain a list of available blocks. This approach to storage management is conceptually simple, and probably provides the best mechanism for avoiding excessive external fragmentation; but it is relatively time-consuming. The list of free blocks must be searched on allocation, and often on deallocation, of every block. Links and fields denoting block sizes must be maintained. In certain situations such as interactive operating systems and real-time applications one may be willing to sacrifice some potential fragmentation for speed. To be effective such an allocation system must be able to find and release free blocks *without searching*. The buddy system, which has been used by Univac in its Exec-8 operating system and by Knowlton (1966) in his L^6 system, is an interesting allocation approach which uses implicit addressing conventions to avoid many explicit links.

The buddy approach is based on four essential conventions. First, only blocks whose size is a power of 2 will ever be allocated. Thus blocks consisting of $2^0 = 1$ location, $2^1 = 2$ locations, $2^2 = 4$ locations, up to 2^m locations (where 2^m denotes the total size of available storage) may be allocated. If a process requests a block of size x, then it will be allocated a block of size 2^k where $2^{k-1} < x \leq 2^k$. Note that the allocation of the excess $2^k - x$ locations is called *internal* fragmentation, just as when pages in excess of actual requirements are allocated, and that in practice one often sets a lower bound, say $2^3 = 8$, on the size of blocks that will be allocated. The second convention requires that at least one bit of every block be reserved for exclusive use of the system. This may be the high-order bit of the first location in the block, or possibly the entire first location. Third, all free blocks of size 2^k will be chained in a common list. Hence there will be $m + 1$ reference pointers list[0], list[1], ..., list[m]. Finally, we assume that the initial configuration consists of a single free block of size 2^m; that is, $[L_1, L_n]$. For pedagogic clarity we will assume that the address of L_1 is 0000 and that the address of L_n is $2^m - 1$.

The basic allocation procedure is simply (1) determine the size of block 2^k which will satisfy the request (see Exercise 10-39), and (2) return the first block in list k. There is no searching. But suppose that list k is empty; in this case the allocator obtains a block of size 2^{k+1} from list $k + 1$, divides it to form two blocks of size 2^k, allocates the first of these blocks to satisfy the request, and inserts the other, called its "buddy", in list k.

Now we note two important facts about the addresses of these blocks. Since all blocks are stored in locations 0000 through $2^m - 1$, the address of any block of length 2^k is a multiple of 2^k. That is, its address will have the form

$$\text{blockaddress} = \text{XXX...XXX}\underbrace{000...000}_{k \text{ zeros}}$$

where X denotes bits that may be either 0 or 1. Moreover, if XXX...XXX000...000 is the address of a block size 2^k, then the address of its buddy will be

$$\text{buddyaddress} = \text{XXX...XX}\overline{\text{X}}000...000$$

where $\overline{\text{X}}$ denotes the complement of bit X. Hence the address of the buddy of any block of size 2^k can be found by just complementing bit $k + 1$.†

---

†If the base address L_1 of the storage area is not 000...000, one just subtracts L_1 from the given address, complements bit $k + 1$, and then re-adds L_1 to get the buddyaddress. It would appear that since L_1 is first subtracted and then added, these operations could be omitted and bit $k + 1$ complemented directly. Convince yourself that this is not so with an example where $L_1 = 0010$.

When a block of length 2^k is deallocated, TAKEIT uses the observation above to immediately access the buddy and check whether it is free. (The single bit in every block is reserved for just this purpose. It is set to 1 if the block is reserved, and 0 if free.) If the buddy is not free, the returned block is inserted into $list_k$. There is no need, and no effort is made, to keep the elements of this list in any order. If the buddy is free, then it is recombined to form a block of size 2^{k+1} which is returned to list $_{k+1}$.

The resultant procedures, both of which have been written recursively, are given below.

pointer procedure giveme$_5$ (celsiz);
integer celsiz;

This procedure allocates a block of size 2^k locations which will be sufficient to satisfy the request. It employs the buddy method.

begin
    pointer   block, buddy;
    pointer array   list[0:m];
    integer   k, m
    field   inuse;
    common /frpool/m, list;
    k ←whatk(celsiz);
    if k > m **then** "overflow";
    if list k ≠ null
        then *Allocate the first block in $list_k$.*
                giveme ←list[k];
                call remove (giveme, k);
        else *Fetch a block of size 2^{k+1} and subdivide it.*

                k ←k + 1;
                block ←giveme(2^k);
                buddy ←compl(block, k + 1);
                call insert (buddy, k);
                giveme ←block;
    inuse(giveme) ← 1;
    exit;
    end

procedure takeit$_4$ (block, celsiz);
pointer   block;
integer   celsiz;

This procedure returns a block to the free pool. If its buddy is free, they will be recombined to form a block of size 2^{k+1}.

begin
    pointer   buddy;
    pointer array   list[0:m];
    integer   k;
    field   inuse;

```
common /frpool/   m,list;
k ←whatk(celsiz);
inuse(block) ←0;
buddy ←compl(block, k + 1)
if inuse(buddy) = 1
     then  buddy is reserved.
          call insert (block, k);
     else  buddy is also free. Combine these blocks.
          call remove (buddy, k);
          if buddy < block then block ←buddy;
          k ←k + 1;
          call takeit (block, 2ᵏ);
exit;
end
```

Figure 10-12 presents a typical memory map generated by the buddy allocation method. Note that adjacent free blocks are not combined unless they are buddies. Consequently, Theorems 10-1 and 10-2 will not be valid in this method. List $_k$ is never searched to find the buddy of a returned block, but if the buddy is free then it must be deleted from the list. For this reason it is wise to doubly link these lists of available blocks of size 2^k. Finally, if the entire first

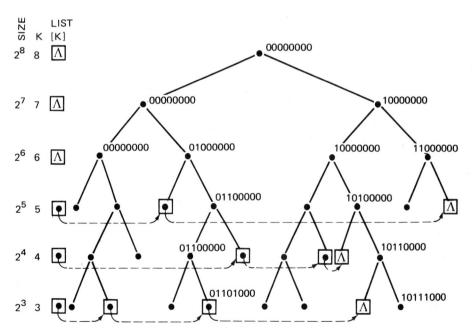

Figure 10-12 Memory map of reserved (solid circles) and free (open squares) blocks generate by a "buddy" allocation system.

word of each block is reserved for system use, then it can be subdivided into fields which denote the block size and give an explicit link to its buddy, thus saving some calculation on return.

The buddy method of dynamic allocation appears to be quite effective; in particular, it is fast. Its speed is achieved at a cost of increased fragmentation. That external fragmentation caused by the failure to recombine adjacent blocks which are not buddies seems to be quite tolerable. More criticism has been leveled at the internal fragmentation caused by allocating blocks only of size 2^k. One way of increasing the variety of allocatable block sizes is to subdivide blocks in accordance with a Fibonacci sequence. That is, if $\ldots f_{n-2}, f_{n-1}, f_n, \ldots$ are Fibonacci numbers and B is a block of size f_n, then it would be divided into two blocks of size f_{n-2} and f_{n-1}. (See Exercise 10-44.)

EXERCISES FOR SECTION 10-4

*10-39 Write optimized code that will implement the following two subprocedures used in buddy allocation:

(a) COMPL(BLOCK, K) complements the kth bit in the address BLOCK.

(b) WHATK(CELSIZ) finds that exponent k such that $2^{k-1} < \text{CELSIZ} \leq 2^k$. (*Hint:* Consider the binary representation of the integer CELSIZ.)

Also code standard list routines INSERT and REMOVE which add or delete the specified cell to that list whose index K is given.

10-40 If the entire first word of an allocated block is reserved for the system, then the definition of WHATK must be changed.

(a) Give the new definition and recode WHATK appropriately.

(b) What address should be returned by GIVEME?

(c) What are the advantages to reserving the entire word? To reserving but a single bit? Under what circumstances would you choose the latter?

*10-41 Code and implement a buddy system. GIVEME and TAKEIT have been presented as recursive procedures, but it is virtually trivial to convert the recursion into an iteration. How should SETUP function? Test these routines in some of your previous programming projects.

10-42 Use a simulation routine such as that of Exercise 10-18 to empirically measure the internal fragmentation characteristics of buddy allocation.

10-43 Empirically determine the expected internal fragmentation, assuming a *uniform distribution* of requested block sizes, by generating a random sequence of integer blocksizes $1 \leq \text{block-size} \leq 1000$ (or 1024), calculating k using WHATK, and recording blocksize $-$ k. Give a formula for the expected internal fragmentation as a function of the upper bound on the requested block size.

10-44 A sequence of numbers $\langle a_1, a_2, \ldots, a_k, \ldots \rangle$ is said to be a Fibonacci sequence if

$$a_k = a_{k-2} + a_{k-1}$$

The first two numbers a_1 and a_2, called the *generators* of the sequence, uniquely determine the remaining terms in the sequence. For example, if $a_1 = 1$ and $a_2 = 2$, then we have the sequence:

$$\langle 1, 2, 3, 5, 8, 13, 21, 34, 55, 89, \ldots \rangle$$

A buddy system based on a Fibonacci sequence would first determine that k such that $a_{k-1} < \text{cel-siz} < a_k$. If no block of size a_k in list k is available, then either a block of size a_{k+1} can be subdivided into blocks of size a_k and a_{k-1} or else a block of size a_{k+2} can be subdivided into blocks of size a_k and a_{k+1}.

(*a*) Empirically determine the expected internal fragmentation as in Exercise 10-43. Does choice of a different set of generators, say $a_1 = 5$ and $a_2 = 13$, change the expected fragmentation?

(*b*) On return of a block of size a_k, how will its buddy be located? How will you know whether its buddy is of size a_{k+1} or a_{k-1}?

(*c*) Implement a buddy system based on the Fibonacci sequence. See Cranston and Thomas (1975).

ELEVEN

FILE STRUCTURES

Computer scientists, programmers, and systems designers usually make a distinction between in-core data structures (with which we have been largely concerned) and file structures (which are typically represented in peripheral storage). In theory perhaps there should be no distinction. In all cases one is just concerned with a representation of an abstract structure; those theoretical properties of the abstract structure which are captured in one representation should be realizable in another representation independent of the physical storage device. In many respects this kind of a unified view can be a valuable one, but at some point one must begin to treat them differently. The source of the difference is simply that of magnitude. The term *in-core data structure* conveys the image of a structure involving a collection of hundreds, or possibly thousands, of individual elements.† By *file structure* we suggest collections of elements on the order of tens of thousands, hundreds of thousands, or occasionally more. It was stated in the preface that identical structures or systems which differ by one or two orders of magnitude are no longer "identical" and are possibly no longer even "similar." Processes and representational techniques which are appropriate in one case may no longer be reasonable. Such basic concepts as access and identification of elements change radically.

In this chapter we will explore some of the differences that arise when data structures become large.

---

†By an individual element we mean an individually accessible unit such as a cell or a record. Each element may be comprised of many fields, assignment values, or data items.

11-1 FILE ORGANIZATION

By way of a preliminary introduction let us develop a few fundamental concepts and terminology about files and the physical devices they can be represented on. Much of this material can be found in any introduction text on Cobol, which was designed primarily as a file-handling language—provided it has not been obscured by an excessive preoccupation with the details of the arithmetic statements, control statements, and various idiosyncrasies of the language itself. Rather than attempt to explain even the rudiments of the Cobol language, all terminology will be defined in terms of the concepts already developed in preceding chapters. To those readers already familiar with Cobol, or PL/1, the next few paragraphs should be largely review.

A *file* is a namable collection of elements. The elements of a file are called *records*.† A record, which is analogous to the concept of a cell in previous discussions, is the smallest unit of accessible information in the file. It is accessed by a READ operation which moves a copy of the record in the file to a known block of in-core storage, which is identified by a pointer or *record name*. A variable pointer usually references many different cells in the course of a process. So, too, a record name does not identify any particular record; instead it identifies or points to that record of current interest. The major difference in the implementation of this pointer concept is that the cell referenced by a pointer variable is reassigned by changing its value (an internal name or cell address) so that it denotes a new storage location. A record name always refers to the same storage location, but the record occupying that location is bodily changed. The records of a file need not be of identical format, any more than all the cells of a data structure need be of the same format. But customarily the records of a file are of one, or a limited number of, distinct types.

A record can be subdivided into *fields,* just as we subdivided cells into fields. Fields, which may also be called *data items,* are the smallest units of usable information.‡ A field is composed of *characters.* The number of characters comprising a field is its *length,* and the length of a record is the sum of its field lengths. Fields are identified by *item names.* This symbolic name implicitly conveys the location of the field within the record and its length, just as we have been using field names to identify portions within a cell.§ Figure 11-1 provides a kind of graphic summary of these basic definitions.

---

†In Cobol, files are immediately broken down into records. In many other file systems, files may be first subdivided into a hierarchy of intermediate units which are variously called *segments, subfiles,* or *file elements.*

‡In both Cobol and PL/1, records may be decomposed into a hierarchy of fields; fields may be further decomposed into subfields. Or alternatively, two or more contiguous fields may be identified for some purposes as a single field. Such hierarchical decomposition is sometimes called a data structure—usage of the term with which the author violently disagrees.

§We have always used field names in conjunction with, or qualified by, a cell pointer. In the same spirit, item names must always be associated with a record name. These languages allow explicit qualification of an item name with a record name, but more often the association is implicitly expressed by the manner in which item names are declared in the Data Division.

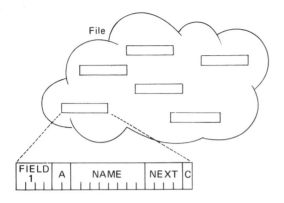

Figure 11-1 An individual record of length 19 comprised of five fields of length 4, 2, 8, 4, and 1, respectively, from a set of such records comprising a file.

Heretofore we have regarded the contents of a field to be a sequence of binary bits which were to be treated as an integer number. Treating a field as a string of symbolic characters assumed a special interpretation of the presumed integer value. The primitive building blocks of file structures are instead invariably *characters*. Treatment of these fields as numeric values now requires special interpretation. However, we will ignore the distinction between numeric and nonnumeric characters; it is largely an issue of appropriate field description and specification in the processing language. Similarly we will ignore description of the particular bit strings used to code each character, such as the ASCII, BCD, and EBCDIC codes together with a variety of system internal codes.† We will simply regard a field as a sequence of characters which the accessing process can interpret correctly.

A sequential representation is one in which the relationship between individual records is determined by their actual sequential position within physical storage. This may also be given as a canonical definition of a *sequential file*. The prototypes of sequential files are those which are physically represented as a file of punched cards (which may be regarded as prototypes of "records") or on magnetic tape. The "next" record is that which physically follows the one which has been most recently accessed. Abstractly one can view an externally represented sequential file as shown in Fig. 11-2. The *file name* references the file by identifying the first record in the file. Execution of a READ statement effectively identifies a record in the file, that one which was accessed by the READ statement. Execution of another READ statement will "advance" this

---

†This approach is in keeping with the spirit of earlier sections of this text. We did not discuss the coding of numeric data in any of its many possible forms—as binary, octal, hexadecimal, decimal, or floating point. We spoke of *address-sized* fields, independent of how addresses were really represented or interpreted. We chose to ignore these details, not because ignorance is desirable nor because they are unimportant. Quite to the contrary, such issues are often crucial to the specific layout of cells and records, to the transfer of externally represented data structures, and to their access. But this level of detail is not necessary for an understanding of data *structure,* and its inclusion quite often obscures the underlying principles.

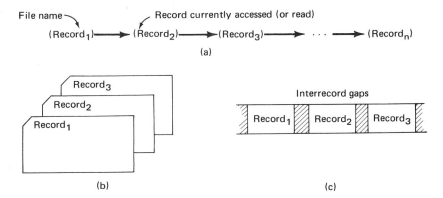

File name⌐

Record currently accessed (or read)

(Record₁)———→ (Record₂)———→(Record₃)———→ ··· ———→(Recordₙ)

(a)

Record₃

Record₂

Record₁

Interrecord gaps

Record₁ Record₂ Record₃

(b)

(c)

Figure 11-2 Sequential file representations as (*a*) an abstract linear relation, (*b*) punched cards, and (*c*) magnetic tape records.

virtual pointer to the next record. (It is worth comparing this figure with that of a simple linked list, such as shown in Fig. 3-18). It is evident that such sequential files are well suited for the representation of sets of data elements which are either unordered (regarded simply as a collection) or linearly ordered. It was in Chap. 4 that sequential representations were most heavily used in the representation of linear structures.

In our brief treatment we will want to focus on two essential aspects of file design: the utilization of storage, and the cost of accessing (reading or writing) a single record in the file.

Even though magnetic tape is no longer the important file storage medium that it once was, it is still widely used, and a number of important file concepts were developed in this context. Each record is recorded on magnetic tape as a continuous sequence of digital characters which are read (or written) as the tape physically passes under a read/write head at a fixed speed, typically on the order of 75 inches per second. A file, as shown in Fig. 11-2(*c*), is a sequence of records separated by *interrecord gaps*. Tape movement comes to a complete stop after reading (or writing) each record. The gaps are required to provide room to accelerate and deaccelerate the tape. It is not hard to see that the percentage of storage utilization is simply the ratio of record length divided by record length *plus* interrecord gap length. If we let g denote the length of the interrecord gaps and cpi denote the recording density (in characters per inch†), then storage utilization can be expressed as a function of record length k (char-

---

†Tape-recording densities are normally expressed in terms of *bits per inch*, or bpi. In the standard interchange codes, BCD and ASCII, each character is represented by a single "bit" (actually a frame of six bits of seven-track tape or eight bits on nine-track tape, which is just one bit wide measured along the tape), so bpi and cpi are equivalent. Other coding schemes may use frames that are two or more bits in length, in which case cpi must be calculated from bpi. It is easier if we express all functions in terms of characters.

acters per record), as follows:

$$\text{Storage utilization} = U(k) = \frac{(k/cpi)}{(k/cpi) + g} \qquad (11\text{-}1)$$

Transfer rate is the rate, measured in characters per second, at which information can be read (or written) from the external recording medium and passed to a central processor. Unless otherwise constrained by channel capacity, it is simply the product of the recording density times the tape transport speed; we will denote it by tr. If we let α denote the time required to bring a tape up to transport speed and then stop it, and let r denote the number of records in a file, one can calculate the total time to read (or write) a file of r records, each of length k, as:

$$T(r,k) = [\alpha + (k/tr)]r \qquad (11\text{-}2)$$

Expressions (11-1) and (11-2) become more meaningful if we replace the constant factors with typical values found in practice. Again, while these values are typical in the sense that they are actual values for a particular configuration of hardware and processor, they may not be those associated with your own system. Still, they convey a sense of the magnitudes involved. Assume that the length of the interrecord gap g is 0.5 inch, that $cpi = 800$, that $\alpha = 15$ milliseconds, and that the transfer rate tr is 60,000 characters per second. Then

$$U(k) = \frac{k/800}{k/800 + 0.5} = \frac{k}{k + 400}$$

and

$$T(r, k) = (15 + 0.016k)r \text{ milliseconds}$$

From these it is not hard to see that storage utilization of better than 50 percent will be attained only with records of length greater than 400 characters, and that the time to read a file of records is almost totally a function of the time α to bring the tape up to speed times the number of records. It is nearly independent of the transfer rate, except for very large k. Tape is most effectively used when the records are exceptionally long. In most applications the associated items of data cannot be logically subdivided into units (records) of sufficient length to fully exploit the characteristics of tape storage. But the same result can be obtained by grouping a collection of records, called *blocking,* as shown in Fig. 11-3. The number of records b per block is called the *blocking factor.* By blocking the file of records it is no longer necessary to separate every record with a gap of unrecorded tape nor to stop and start the tape with every transfer operation. Consequently, expressions (11-1) and (11-2) can be rewritten as

$$U(k, b) = \frac{bk/cpi}{bk/cpi + g} = \frac{bk}{bk + cpi \cdot g} \qquad (11\text{-}3)$$

$$T(r, k, b) = (\alpha/b + k/tr)r \qquad (11\text{-}4)$$

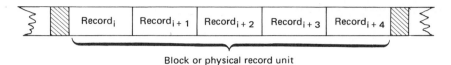

Block or physical record unit

Figure 11-3 A blocked file of records with blocking factor $b = 5$.

We had previously said that *cell, block,* and *record* are synonyms which all denote a contiguous piece of storage. It is clear, in this context at least, that *block* and *record* are not being used as synonyms even though they still refer to continuous chunks of storage. Here a record refers to those chunks of data into which a file of information has been logically subdivided and *which are actually delivered to* (or received from) *a process in an input/output operation.* A *block* is that chunk of data which is physically stored in the recording medium. Sometimes the terms *logical record* and *physical record* are used to differentiate these two meanings.

Sequential files that are represented by either punched cards or magnetic tape fall heir to various characteristics of these physical devices. It is impossible to read the nth record without first reading the preceding $n - 1$ records (at least in the sense of passing these preceding records through the reading mechanism). It is impossible to alter (repunch or rewrite) a record in the middle of a file. (The impossibility of repunching a card is evident. While one can imagine backspacing and rewriting a tape record, in practice it is at best very risky, since errors in positioning the read/write head and stretching of the dimensionally unstable tape itself make it unlikely that the new record will exactly overwrite the old record.) Consequently it is customary in business data processing to define a *sequential file* as a linearly ordered set of records, where

1. to access any record, all records preceding it in the linear order must first be accessed,
2. to alter any record, the entire file must be recopied, and
3. new records may be added only at the end of the file (i.e., they cannot be inserted into the order without recopying the file, as in 2).

Unfortunately this customary usage of sequential file tends to be confusing since linearly ordered files need not be stored in a physically sequential fashion. With different recording mediums, such as magnetic disk, they may be stored in either linked or partially linked representations. Nevertheless, in most systems, if a file is declared to be sequential, then the constraints (1), (2), and (3) above must be observed whether or not the characteristics of the actual storage device require them.

Magnetic disk is a prototype of a variety of storage devices which are generally called *random-access,* or *direct-access* storage devices (DASD). Unlike punched-card or tape files, records are stored in fixed locations that are individ-

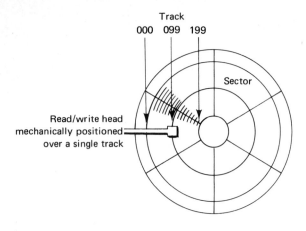

Track
000 099 199

Sector

Read/write head
mechanically positioned
over a single track

Figure 11-4 The tracks of a single recording surface subdivided into sectors.

ually addressable. Data is recorded on the surface of a magnetic disk in 200 concentric *tracks*†, as shown in Fig. 11-4. Each track, which typically consists of 15,000 characters, is subdivided into six or more *sectors* of fixed length. Data is read from (written on) the track by means of a read/write head which is mechanically positioned over the correct track. A disk *drive*, or *spindle*, consists of a stack of six or more disk plates which, save for the outermost, are recorded on both sides. A comb of read/write heads fits between the surfaces to access information in the tracks above and below the head, as illustrated in Fig. 11-5. All read/write heads of the comb are positioned over tracks with the same track number, although only one head can be active at any time. The collection of all tracks with the same track number is called a *cylinder*. (The concept of a cylinder is important because all records stored on a common cylinder can be accessed without physically moving the read/write heads.) A disk unit may consist of one or more disk drives or spindles. Locations in disk storage can be referenced by means of a four-part address consisting of drive number, cylinder number, read/write head number, and sector number. These addresses are commonly called *actual keys* to distinguish them from core addresses.‡ By using these actual keys, or disk addresses, a process has the capability of directly accessing any sector within the file—whence the name for this kind of storage device.

Before considering the direct- or random-access features of disk storage, it will be valuable to quickly consider the storage of sequential files on disk

---

†In practice, most disks have 203 tracks per surface, but only 200 of them, numbered 000 through 199, are addressable. The remaining three tracks are used as spares in the event of recording imperfections.

‡The format of actual keys, or disk addresses, varies considerably from system to system. While we will sketch their general use, readers will find it necessary to obtain many additional details pertinent to their own particular installation. Sometimes the read/write head number is called a track number, in the sense of being the first, second, etc., track of the cylinder instead of the first or second track of the surface.

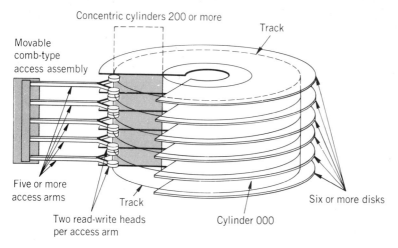

Concentric cylinders 200 or more

Track

Movable
comb-type
access assembly

Five or more
access arms

Track

Two read-write heads
per access arm

Cylinder 000

Six or more disks

Figure 11-5 A cylinder of 10 tracks on 10 recording surfaces, all with the same track address. (Reprinted from Sanders, *Computers in Business*, McGraw-Hill, 1975.)

devices and to rederive timing expressions similar to (11-2) and (11-4). Disk input/output times are dominated by three characteristic quantities: (1) average *head-positioning time* π denotes the expected time to physically move the comb of read/write heads from its current position to a new cylinder; (2) *rotational delay* ρ is the expected delay from the time that a head is positioned until the desired sector rotates under the head; and (3) *transfer rate* tr is, as before, the rate in characters per second at which data is transmitted to the central memory. The following timing expressions will be more meaningful if again we supply typical values for these constants. For the sake of this discussion we assume that π and ρ are 30 and 8.3 milliseconds, respectively, and tr is 1,130,000 characters per second.

Unlike punched-card or tape files, disk storage is seldom dedicated to a single job or user. Space in the disk must be allocated to many different files by the executive or operating system. (Some of the allocation techniques considered in Chap. 10 are appropriate for this purpose.) Although allocation of external storage is often out of the hands of an application programmer, it is neverless important to understand the method employed. It can drastically affect the performance of one's processes.

A sequential file may be stored using a linked representation, with a field appended to each record that points to the next record in the linear order. Let us assume first that storage for each record is randomly allocated throughout the disk wherever an available block can be found. Consequently the comb of read/write heads will, in general, have to be repositioned for each record access, and the timing expression will be given by:

$$T_1(r, k) = (\pi + \rho)r + (k \cdot r/tr)$$
$$= (30 + 8.3)r + .000885kr \qquad (11\text{-}5)$$
$$\approx 38.3r \text{ milliseconds.}$$

Notice that the expected head-positioning time so dominates this expression that it is effectively a function of the number of records r alone.

As in the magnetic tape case, the effect of head positioning can be minimized by blocking the file with several records per block. Now let the blocking factor b denote the number of characters per block, for example, 15,360. (Block lengths are commonly predetermined as a fixed number of sectors. Logical records may, or may not, be allowed to span two physical blocks.) This is a partially linked representation in that records are consecutively stored within a block, while blocks are linked with an appended pointer to the next block in the linear sequence. Under the assumption that blocks are randomly distributed throughout available storage, we have:

$$T_2(r, k, b) = \lceil kr/b \rceil \, (\pi + \rho) + k \, (r/tr)$$

$$\approx \left(\frac{\pi + \rho}{b} + \frac{1}{tr}\right) k \cdot r \tag{11-6}$$

$$= 0.0033 \, kr \text{ milliseconds}$$

Readily this is a marked improvement over the access time T_1 given in expression (11-5). But we can hope to obtain even better access time. Suppose that the executive system tries to allocate entire cylinders to a single file. Then even for unblocked files we would expect at worst a rotational delay to access each record yielding the apparently optimal expression

$$T_3(r, k) = \lceil kr/c \rceil \, \pi + \rho \cdot r + k \cdot (r/tr)$$

$$\approx \left(\frac{\pi}{c} + \frac{\rho}{k} + \frac{1}{tr}\right) k \cdot r \tag{11-7}$$

$$= (0.0009 + (8.3/k))kr \text{ milliseconds}$$

where c denotes the number of characters per cylinder, here taken to be 300,000.

Table 11-1†

Number of records	T_1 random dist., no blocking	T_2 random dist., w/blocking	T_3 allocation by cylinders	
			no blocking	w/blocking
r = 100	3.852	0.101	0.859	0.029
300	11.579	0.304	2.578	0.088
500	19.263	0.506	4.298	0.147
1000	38.526	1.013	8.596	0.295
3000	115.579	3.040	25.788	0.887
5000	192.632	5.067	42.981	1.479
10000	385.265	10.134	85.962	2.958

†Times (in seconds) to sequentially read or write r records assuming different disk allocation procedures. (Record size k = 300. In blocked files, a physical record length of 15,360 (entire disk track) is assumed so b = 5100.)

Table 11-1 provides a comparative summary of access times using these three ways of organizing disk storage. It is evident that the random placement of records in storage, as in the case of T_1, is nearly intolerable. It is not hard to verify the general accuracy of these expressions by timing a process which simply reads a specified number of records of given length. Figure 11-6 shows the results obtained in one series of tests by a Cobol program running under an operating system which allocated storage in randomly distributed blocks of 15,360 characters, as in the second expression. (One interesting sidelight to this test was the discovery that records declared to be of length 150 characters or less were allocated storage in blocks of only 5,120 characters. Consequently, in this system it was more costly to access records of length 100 than a comparable number of records of length 300!)

With direct-access storage devices, such as disk, a process may directly access any record of a file (or more properly, a physical block containing that record) by means of its actual key, or disk address. This is of special value when maintenance of a large data structure or file involves the periodic updating of only a relatively few records (see Exercise 11-7). Let us consider how direct access can be effectively utilized by a process.

It would be unusual to identify or name the records of any application by their disk address or actual key. One would expect the records to be identified

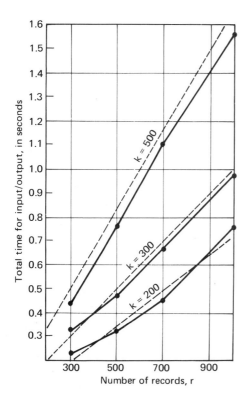

Figure 11-6 Theoretical (dashed) sequential access times T_2 versus observed (solid) access times for files of various length records. (Physical block size is 15,630 characters.)

by some symbolic key such as part number, employee name, social security number, or the like. The process must convert the symbolic key to its corresponding actual key in order to directly access and retrieve the record from storage. Chapter 9 discussed a number of techniques for performing such a conversion. The method of hash coding considered in Sec. 9-2 is one of the most commonly used in file applications. The hashing function h(key) maps the set of symbolic keys into a block of consecutive locations $[L_1, L_n]$. It would be difficult, if not impossible, to devise a hashing function which maps the set of keys into a set of record locations which have been randomly distributed throughout disk storage. Instead we must allocate a contiguous block, say an entire cylinder, to the file and let the hashing function scatter individual records of the file throughout this cylinder. Since all records will be on the same cylinder, both the drive-number and cylinder-number portions of the actual key will be constants for the file; only the read/write head number and sector number need be determined. It is possible to have the hashing function calculate both the head number and sector number. But it is easier, and more common, to have the hashing function determine just the read/write head number alone. All records whose keys hash to a common number are then stored in that track as a sequentially represented bucket of finite length. On retrieval all records of the track (or bucket) are read sequentially to obtain the desired one.

Figure 11-7 schematically illustrates the direct storage of a file by hash-coding techniques. In this case, remaindering after division by the prime number 19 has been used as a hashing function. The last track, which is never referenced by the hashing function, is reserved as an overflow track to store any record whose proper track, or bucket, has overflowed. Were we to use the

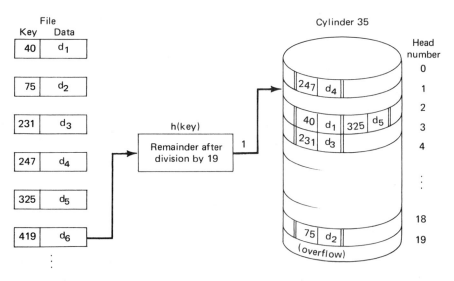

Figure 11-7 Schematic view of direct disk access by scatter storage (hash coding).

prime number 17 as divisor there would be three available overflow tracks. Notice that the records have been scattered all over the cylinder and that it is impossible to read the file sequentially *in ascending order of the identifying keys*.

Since all records are stored on a common cylinder, it appears that there should be no read/write head movement between record accesses so that $T_3(r, k)$ of expression (11-7) should nearly describe the time to access r records in a file of indefinite length. In reality this expression seldom describes the behavior of either direct or sequential [see Exercise 11-5(c)] access. Most jobs are executed in a time-sharing environment where it is customary to have control of the processor interrupted after any read/write request that requires access to external storage. Since at least one of the next set of jobs or the operating system itself is likely to issue its own external storage request, there is considerable probability that the comb of read/write heads will have to be repositioned for the next access to the file. Consequently there is often little value to having all records on the same cylinder, and $T_1(r)$ of expression (11-5) effectively describes the cost in time of all direct- or random-access requests for r records.

Direct access to individual records of a file is most often implemented by hash-coding techniques. It is both simple to implement and reasonably efficient. The nature of the method itself demands that a large block of contiguous disk storage be reserved for the file. Unfortunately the presence of such a large block does not yield the operational efficiencies (in terms of head movement) that one might expect. Yet, as we saw in Chap. 10, the allocation of large blocks (1) requires a relatively sophisticated, and slow, system allocation process, (2) increases the probability of storage overflow, and (3) decreases the effective utilization of the total storage available. Further space in excess of the *entire* file must be reserved *before* any of its records are entered. Under these circumstances one might be interested in direct-access methods which may themselves be marginally slower, but which would permit a less sophisticated allocation procedure to incrementally reserve smaller blocks for the file that may be distributed throughout available storage. We consider one such method in the next section.

Finally, it should be noted that all linked data structures considered in preceding chapters can be represented in external storage by just substituting disk addresses for core addresses in all link fields. But now the cost of following links is expressed by the function T_1. Unless (1) the number of links followed is very low or (2) the structure can be carefully blocked into coherent segments or pages, the cost is simply prohibitive. Most external structures are sequentially represented, or at least partially sequential.

EXERCISES FOR SECTION 11-1

11-1 For your own system:
    (a) Dig out from reference manuals and specifications the values of cpi, tr, and g.
    (b) Discover the value of α (the author has never found this stated in any specifications, but it

can be empirically measured by timing a program which does nothing but read a file of records of known length).

(c) For fixed k, say k = 100, evaluate and plot U as a function of b, and T as a function of r and b.

11-2 A standard magnetic tape is 2400 feet in length. Assuming records of length k = 100, what is the total number of characters that can be stored, given blocking factors b of 1, 10, and 20? (Assume cpi = 800, or that appropriate for your local installation.)

11-3 When a process requests a record in a blocked file, all the records of the block must be read and transferred to the central memory (or possibly a peripheral controller). But only the desired "logical" record is delivered to the process. Consequently the block of records must first be read into a buffer area, from which individual records can be delivered. Buffered input/output was examined in Sec. 3-3. Rewrite the procedures of that section with the assumption that each buffer now contains a block of b logical records.

11-4 How many characters of information can be stored in a disk-storage device consisting of 8 drives, or spindles; 200 cylinders per drive; 20 tracks (or read/write heads) per cylinder; and 15,360 characters per track? (Alternatively base your calculations on figures describing the disk devices of your installation.)

11-5 (a) Find the values of π, ρ, tr, b, and c that are appropriate for your own installation.

(b) Substitute these values in expressions (11-5), (11-6), and (11-7) and calculate a new table similar to that of 11-1.

(c) Empirically verify your expressions by timing a program which only reads a file of sequential records. Which expression describes the performance of your system? (If yours is an operating system, typically IBM, which allocates storage by cylinders, do you nevertheless find that $T_2(r, k, b)$ for some appropriate blocking factor is a more accurate predictor than T_3?)

11-6 Modify expression (11-7) to obtain a form $T_3(r, k, b)$ which yields the expected time to access records which have been stored in blocked form on a common cylinder.

*11-7 The time required to update a few records of a sequential file is a function of the total records in the file, essentially independent of the number of records that must be altered, since the entire file must be read and recopied. Direct access, although more costly, is only a function of the number of records that must be changed. Assuming that r = 5000, k = 100, and that $T_2(r, k, b)$ and $T_1(r, k)$ describe the expected times for sequential and direct access, respectively, plot the total times needed to update 10, 50, 100, 250, 500, and 1000 records, respectively. What percentage of the total records of the file must be changed to make sequential access the more attractive of the two?

11-8 Derive more accurate expressions T(r) for the time to directly access r records using hash-coding methods, assuming all records in a common cylinder and (a) no head movement between accesses, and (b) head movement between every access. Note that k in this case is effectively the total number of characters in the track, since in general the entire track will be read and rewritten on entry. A superior expression will take into account the possibility of additional accesses to the overflow track(s). The probability of this occurring is the probability that any given bucket of finite length will overflow, which is in turn a function of k, the individual record length, the length of the track, and statistics related to the distribution of the keys and the particular hashing function. The latter may be empirically determined by simulations such as Exercise 9-18.

11-9 Implement a hash-coded direct-access system assuming that your installation permits disk allocation requests and manipulation of disk addresses. (Alternatively, you may write a program in Cobol using the actual key feature.) Duplicate Exercise 9-20 and compare measured times.

11-10 A *drum* is a direct-access storage with characteristics similar to disk storage except that every track has a fixed read/write head. There is no head-movement cost π, although there is still rotational delay ρ in accessing operations. Develop a timing expression for random access to drum storage. (Use local value for ρ, or assume $\rho = 3.2$ milliseconds.) High-speed drums normally have less capacity (e.g., 400 addressable tracks of 15,000 characters each) and are reserved for high-density use such as files of the operating system itself or pages of executing jobs.

11-2 N-ARY RETRIEVAL TREES

In Sec. 5-2, ordered binary trees were introduced as a dynamic lookup and retrieval mechanism. In Sec. 9-1, where they were once again considered as an accessing mechanism, we took a much closer look at their retrieval properties. In particular, it was shown that the expected number of memory accesses per retrieval (or path length) in a complete balanced tree of m entries is $E(\rho, m) = \lfloor \log_2(m + 1) \rfloor - 1$; and it was conjectured (in Exercise 9-10) that in a "random" ordered binary tree $E(\rho, m) = \beta\sqrt{m}$, for some $\beta \approx 1.2$. If instead of a binary retrieval tree one were to use an n-ary tree with up to an n-way branch at each point in the retrieval path, one would naturally expect much shorter paths. Indeed, it is not hard to show that in a complete balanced n-ary tree $E(\rho, m) = \lfloor \log_n(m + 1) \rfloor$,† and to establish the conjecture that in a randomly grown n-ary tree $E(\rho, m) = \beta\sqrt[n]{m}$. Both of these are substantially smaller values. If this is true, why were not n-ary retrieval trees introduced much earlier? Why are they not used more extensively for in-core retrieval applications?

There are two answers to these questions. First, it is much easier to code and implement binary search algorithms. This is of pedagogical and practical importance. More importantly, in Sec. 5-4 it was shown that an excessive amount of storage would be wasted, and that exactly $(n - 1)m + 1$ of all link fields will be null. Core storage is of considerable value—there never seems to be quite enough—while cost of random memory access is relatively small. In contrast, external storage on peripheral devices is cheap, while access, especially random access, is dearly purchased. The nature of data structures represented on external files demands a different approach to data access.

We will use n-ary retrieval trees, but we will want to impose some formal constraints so as to avoid certain potential dangers. In particular we would want no points, other than end points, with only a few "out" edges; a tree that is reasonably well "balanced"; and one that can be dynamically altered. Surprisingly, the concept of a B-tree introduced by Beyer and McCreight satisfies all these desirable properties.

A B-*tree of order* n is an n-ary tree (P, E) with principal point t, such that:

1. $|R(t)| \geq 2$
2. for all $y \in P$, such that $y \neq t$ and y is not maximal, $|R(y)| \geq n/2$
3. for all maximal points $z_i, z_j, |\rho(t, z_i)| = |\rho(t, z_j)|$ (That is, all end points are at the same depth.)

Since the principal point has at least two right neighbors, and every other

---

†This expression is slightly different from the preceding one. It is not, in general, practical to store actual data items at internal points of n-ary trees (as we did with binary trees). Instead, all retrievable data elements are associated only with end points. It is not hard to show that the expected path length from the principal point to only maximal end points is just one greater than the expected length of all paths.

nonmaximal point y has at least n/2 right neighbors, it is not hard to show the following theorem.

Theorem 11-1 The expected path length to any maximal point z in a B tree of order n is given by

$$E(\rho, |\max(T)|) \leq \log_{n/2}\left(\frac{|\max(T)| + 1}{2}\right)$$

where $|\max(T)|$ denotes the total number of maximal points (or keys) in T.

Note that equality will occur in the "worst" case where $|R(y)|$ is exactly n/2. It can also occur in the "best" case as well where $|R(y)|$ is n. (See Exercise 11-14.) In effect we find that access time via B-trees is a relatively stable function of $|P|$ that is nearly independent of its particular structure.

Points in an n-ary B-tree can be represented by cells which contain n link fields, separated by n − 1 key values against which comparisons for n-way branching decision can be made. If for some given search key, subkey [i-1] ≤ key < subkey [i], then the desired data item with that key can be accessed (if it exists in storage) by following the link pointer[i]. Figure 11-8 illustrates the representation of such a point, which we will call a *node,* with a few typical comparison subkey values. Note that an additional redundant subkey field had been appended which is always *null.* Though unnecessary, it simplifies the search procedure somewhat and will prove of value when implementing a procedure to enter new items. Figure 11-9 shows a typical B-tree of order 5 which provides access to 45 distinct data items whose keys have been chosen to be the first 45 prime numbers. Notice that the maximal points, or nodes, of this tree are all at the same depth and that they consist of the data item itself. These nodes would naturally be represented by records of a different format—there need be no pointer or subkey fields; instead, they would consist of just the identifying key itself together with the associated information

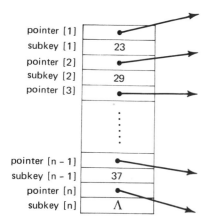

pointer [1]	
subkey [1]	23
pointer [2]	
subkey [2]	29
pointer [3]	
	⋮
pointer [n − 1]	
subkey [n − 1]	37
pointer [n]	
subkey [n]	Λ

Figure 11-8 Format of a cell in the representation of an n-ary B-tree.

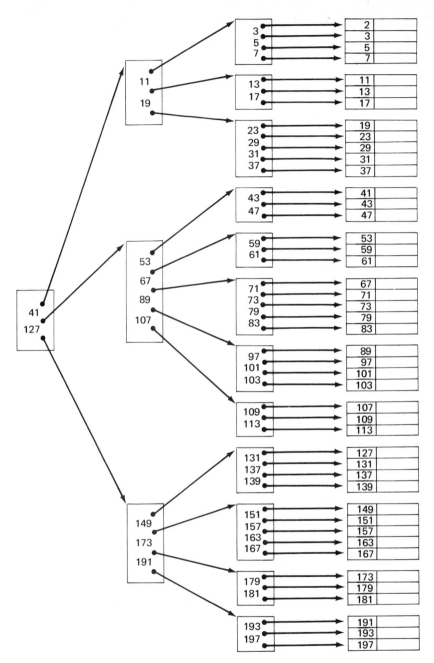

Figure 11-9 A 5-ary B-tree on the first 45 prime numbers.

of that item. A small tag field, say type, might be used to distinguish the two kinds of nodes and their corresponding formats.

Given this representation, it is now easy to write a search procedure which looks up and locates items with a desired key. Such a process LOCATE follows. Notice that (1) all data items and the B-tree itself are represented in external storage; consequently, all pointer variables contain disk (or other device) addresses, not core addresses, and are so declared. Also, given the external address of a node, it must first be read into a corresponding in-core workspace or cell of the processor before it can be used. Further, note that (2) this procedure does not actually return the desired item. Instead it returns the location in external storage where the desired record will be found, if it exists. The calling procedure must actually access the item and test its key to verify that it is correct. This search procedure never, in fact, accesses any end point of the B-tree on the assumption that the representation of those nodes, their length and format, will vary from application to application.

external pointer procedure locate (key);
integer   key;

This procedure locates an item identified by the search "key" in external storage and returns its address. Actually it returns an address where the item will be found if it exists. The record must still be accessed and its associated key tested for equality.

begin

integer	i, n, type;
integer array	subkey[1:n];
external pointer	node, tree
external pointer array	pointer[1:n];
common /system/	n, tree;

    node ← tree;
    type ← 0;
    while type ≠ 1 **do**

Access the record at location "node" and bring it into core storage.

    read node **into** type, (pointer [i], i = 1, n);

Find the correct edge from this point (or node) to the next level of the B-tree.

    i ← 1;
    while subkey [i] ≠ null **and** subkey [i] < key **do**
        i ← i + 1;
    node ← pointer [i];

Rightmost level examined, the pointer references a stored data item, possibly the desired one.

    locate ← node;
    exit;
    end

Items may be entered into a B-tree dynamically, but the growth pattern is rather different from that of binary trees. As new elements are entered into binary trees, they are added to the right of existing points (most often an end point) so that retrieval paths grow independently of one another. In a B-tree most new entries have no effect whatever on the expected path length. Consider the addition of a new data item with key = 15 to the B-tree of Fig. 11-9. Since the node to the left of it is only a three-way branch, a new subkey (with value = 15) and corresponding pointer is simply inserted into the node in its proper sequence, yielding a four-way branch as shown in Fig. 11-10(a). Only a single record (representing this enlarged node) need be rewritten in external storage. If instead we enter a new data item with key = 21, we find that the node to its left is already a five-way branch ($|R(y)| = 5$). There is no room to enter a new subkey and pointer. In this case the node y is "split" into two nodes y and y' with each becoming a three-way branch, as shown in Fig. 11-10(b). This splitting, of course, must affect the node x ϵ L(y). In this case it is simply "absorbed" by adding a new subkev and pointer, since it is only a three-way

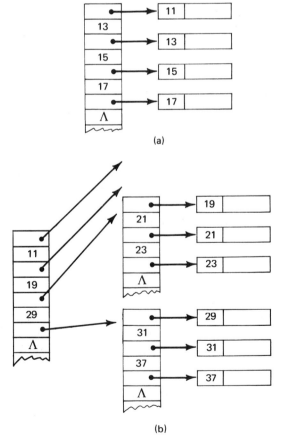

Figure 11-10 Changes to the configuration of the B-tree of Fig. 11-10 as a result of entering new data items with keys of (a) 15, and (b) 21.

branch. Notice that $|R(y)| = |R(y')| = 3 > 5/2$ so that the essential property of the B-tree is maintained; and that only two records, x and y, need be rewritten in external storage, and one new record y' created and written.

Readers should verify for themselves that entry of a new data item with key = 75 will force the splitting of two nodes and will result in a new subkey and pointer in the principal node. If the principal node must be split, then a new principal node x with $|R(x)| = 2$ is created. Only in this case is the accessing path length increased, and then the accessing path to every item is increased by one. The following procedure ENTER presents the details of this splitting process. The reader should desk-check it with several examples to ensure that all aspects are completely understood.

```
procedure enter (key, item);
integer            key;
external pointer   item;
```

This procedure assumes that a record, identified by "key," has been stored at location "item." An appropriate pointer to the record is entered into the n-ary B-tree.

```
begin
      integer                    i, k, n, newtype, type;
      integer array              subkey[1:n], newsubkey[1:n];
      pointer                    stack;
      external pointer           newnode, node, tempptr, tree;
      external pointer array     pointer[1:n], newpointer[1:n];
      common/system/            n, tree;
```

Find the last (rightmost) node in the access tree that would be expected to reference this item if it had already been entered. (Note that this duplicates that code in "locate" except that it also stacks the address of each record examined.

```
      node ← tree;
      type ← 0;
      while type ≠ 1 do
            read node into type, (pointer[i], subkey[i], i = 1, n);
            call pushdown (stack, node);
            i ← 1;
            while subkey [i] ≠ null and subkey [i] < key do
                  i ← i + 1;
            node ← pointer[i];
```

On exit from this **while** *loop, key* ≤ *subkey* [i] *and pointer* [i] *"should" point to the item, but presumably does not. One might add code at this point to discover if this key duplicates an existing key.*

```
      node ← poptop(stack)
addpointer:
```

Pretend that the node can contain $n + 1$ *pointers (by appending a temporary pointer) and insert the new pointer and key in their proper sequence.*

```
tempptr ←pointer[n];
for k = n thru i + 1 do
    pointer[k] ←pointer[k − 1];
    subkey[k] ←subkey[k − 1];
pointer[i] ←item;
subkey[i] ←key;
```

Was there in fact room for this additional key and pointer? If so, update the record and exit.

```
if subkey[n] = null then
    write type, (pointer [i], subkey [i], i = 1, n) outto node;
    call release(stack);
    exit:
```

No. Subdivide these n + 1 *keys and pointers into two nodes by creating a new node consisting of the* $\lfloor n + 1/2 \rfloor$ *high-order entries.*

```
newtype ←type;
last1 ← ⌊(n + 1)/2⌋;
k ← 1;
while last1 + k ⩽ n do
    newpointer[k] ← pointer[last1 + k];
    newsubkey[k] ←subkey[last1 + k];
    k ←k + 1;
newpointer[k] ←tempptr;
while k ⩽ n do
    newsubkey[k] ←null;
    k ←k + 1;
```

Request storage and store this new record.

```
newnode ←giveme(recordsize);
write newtype, (newpointer[i], newsubkey[i], i = 1, n) outto newnode;
```

Null copied entries in original node and write it back out to storage.

```
key ←subkey[last1];
for k = last1 thru n do
    subkey[k] ←null;
write type, (pointer[i], subkey[i], i = 1, n) outto node;
```

Now an entry using key (= subkey[last1]) and item (= newnode) must be inserted into the preceding node.

```
item ←newnode;
tempptr ←node;
node ←poptop(stack);
if node ≠ null then go to addpointer;
```

The principal node has just been split. Create a new principal node of only two entries.

```
newtype ←0;
```

```
    newpointer[1] ←oldnode;
    newsubkey[1] ←key;
    newpointer[2] ←newnode;
    for k=2 thru n do
        newsubkey[k] ←null;
    newnode ←giveme(recordsize);
    write newtype,(newpointer[i], newsubkey[i], i=1, n) outto newnode;
    tree ←newnode;
    exit;
    end
```

If a key and pointer to the newly entered item can be just inserted into a partially filled node by shifting the existing keys and pointers within the node, then the entry procedure is both simple and fast. Only if a full node requires splitting does the procedure become involved in requesting space for a new node, and only then does it access and rewrite its left neighbor. So it is reasonable to ask: How often do we expect a node must be split? Let r denote the total number of keys, records entered, or end points of the tree. Let i denote the total number of interior points, nonendpoints, or branching nodes. It is not hard to show (Exercise 11-11) that $r \geq 1 + (\lceil n/2 \rceil - 1) (i - 1)$. Since every interior node, save one, was created by a splitting operation, precisely $i - 1$ splits have occurred over the total life of the tree during which r entries have been made. The following theorem is a result.

Theorem 11-2 In a B-tree of order n, the expected number of splitting operations per entry E is given by

$$E = (i - 1)/r \leq 1/[(n/2) - 1].$$

As a corollary of this theorem we find that not only is lookup in a B-tree efficient, but its maintenance is as well—a factor that has contributed to its general acceptance.

We have found that the B-tree organization provides for effective random access by key. But suppose that we also want to be able to *sequentially* process the file *in ascending order of their keys.* This is a common expectation, especially in business applications, where files whose primary use is for individual record retrieval by key may also have to be listed in alphabetical order, or by ascending part number or by employee number, etc., to provide periodic reports. Such dual use is implicit in the organization of the widely used indexed sequential files. But no matter how effective B-trees may be for keyed retrieval, it is evident that 45 successive accesses by means of the B-tree structure is a poor way of sequentially accessing the file.

Looking again at the file of 45 records which are accessed by the B-tree of Fig. 11-9, we notice that the actual data items (end points of the tree) have *in the drawing* been grouped together in consecutive blocks. There are four

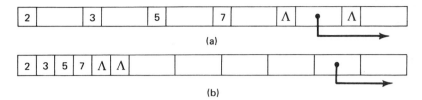

Figure 11-11 Two equivalent formats for the data blocks in an indexed sequential file organization, with (*a*) keys preceding individual records in the block, and (*b*) all keys preceding all records of the block.

records in the first "block," three records in the second "block," and so on. There is nothing in the procedure ENTER which suggests that the actual data records are consecutively grouped by blocks; they need not be. But they were drawn this way in the figure in order to suggest a useful modification of the pure B-tree concept. We can use two different kinds of records, or blocks, to represent the B-tree. Interior points will be represented by records, call them *index blocks*, with the same format as those shown in Fig. 11-8. The end points of the tree will be represented by blocks of a different length, called *data blocks,* which will contain both the keys and the records they identify. Figure 11-11 illustrates two possible formats for these new data blocks. Notice that in each data block there is one additional key field, which is always null, to serve as a flag in the search process. Further, an additional data field has been included, a portion of which can be used to point to the next sequential data block according to the linear ordering on the keys. The resulting data structure is shown in Fig. 11-12. It should be compared with that of Fig. 11-9. Notice that this B-tree contains one less level than the preceding example, and that sequential access is gained by means of the external pointer variable FILE, which names the file by giving the location of the first block.

There are three distinct disadvantages to this kind of file organization in contrast to either a straight sequential representation or the preceding B-tree representation. First, there is a considerable waste of storage. Both the index blocks and data blocks must be fixed-length blocks to provide room for insertion, although not all fields will normally be used. In index blocks composed of short subkey and pointer fields the cost of unused fields is relatively unimportant. But in data blocks, one would expect the length of data fields, or records, to be on the order of hundreds of characters. The presence of unused fields in these blocks can no longer be considered negligible, even though these blocks are represented in low-cost mass storage. A second disadvantage—in contrast to the preceding representation—is that many actual data records must be shifted in storage, both when new items are inserted into data blocks and when data blocks are split. Finally, we can no longer write standard entry and retrieval processes which are independent of the data records which are stored. Both LOCATE and ENTER must be rewritten with parameters which specify the length of the associated data records.

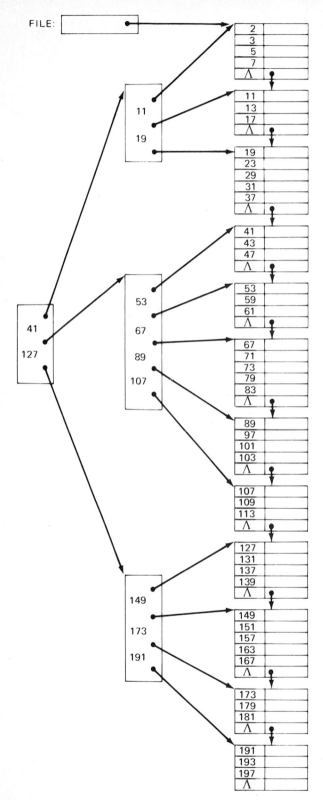

Figure 11-12 An indexed sequential file organization in which a B-tree accesses records sequentially stored in blocks.

But in spite of these drawbacks, the potential benefit of being able to both sequentially and randomly access the records of a file in different situations seems to make this kind of representation a valuable one. This kind of B-tree organization (or variants of it) is used in several successful file-handling systems. In these actual systems it is customary to build B-trees of order n, where $50 \leq n \leq 100$, and in which each index block might be an entire page. Review some of the properties of B-trees assuming n of this order or larger.

EXERCISES FOR SECTION 11-2

11-11 Let $T = (p, E)$ be a complete n-ary tree (i.e., $|R(y)| = n$ for all y where y is not maximal). Let r denote the number of maximal points, i.e., $r = |M_T|$. Let $i = |P| - r$ denote the number of interior points. Show that

$$r = 1 + (n - 1)i$$

Use this to establish the assertion that in a B-tree

$$r = 1 + (\lceil n/2 \rceil - 1)(i - 1)$$

11-12 Prove Theorem 11-2.

11-13 The threshold of $r = 1,000,000$ seems to be significant with most files in business applications containing fewer records (hundreds of thousands), and those data bases which are larger containing very many more. Assuming $r = 10^6$, what will be the expected depth of a B-tree if $n = 50, 100, 500$? What will be the worst case situations?

*11-14 What is the *minimal* number of new data items whose entry into the B-tree of Fig. 11-9 will force splitting the principal node, and hence increase its depth? Give the sequence of keys whose entry will force this. What is the maximal number of new items that can be entered without splitting the principal node or increasing its depth?

*11-15 An unbalanced B-tree has a great many points with $|R(y)| \neq n/2$. (It is unbalanced in the sense that it is decidedly not optimal.)

(*a*) Draw the B-tree that would be "grown" by entering items whose keys are the first 45 prime numbers in ascending order on these keys. Compare it to Fig. 11-9.

(*b*) Draw the optimal B-tree in which for all possible points $|R(y)| = 5$, using this same set of data.

(*c*) Is there any difference? Reconsider these cases adding the next 9 or 10 prime numbers.

(*d*) There exist a number of "balancing" techniques which will coalesce three adjacent nodes each with approximately n/2 pointers into two nodes with approximately 3n/4 pointers each. A formal approach can be found in Knuth (1973); there also exist a number of ad hoc procedures which, while they fail in special cases, still work well in practice.

*11-16 Code and implement the B-tree routines LOCATE and ENTER. Test these routines with the same sets of input data that were used to test the retrieval procedures of Chap. 9. Compare the results. (Coding this problem can be simplified somewhat by treating the block of core storage from which GIVEME allocates blocks *as if it were* external storage. This simplified simulation, in which all addresses are core addresses and no read or write commands are needed, can be used to measure the performance of many aspects of the organization. A somewhat more realistic simulation can be made by replacing the read/write commands with in-core block transfers. To really make use of external storage and test its behavior with larger data bases assumes an ability to make storage requests from the operating system. This may be difficult with some languages and/or systems.)

11-17 If repeated indexed access via the B-tree will be made, it makes sense to permanently keep the principal node, and possibly a few of its right neighbors, in a buffer area in core storage. How must LOCATE and ENTER be changed to provide for this?

11-18 Assuming a B-tree grown from a random sequence of keys, develop an expression to

predict the expected amount of unused storage. Use the programs of Exercise 11-16 to empirically verify your expression.

11-19 Using the results of this section, present expressions for the expected cost L_1 of looking up
an entry in a B-tree and the expected cost E of entering a new item into the tree. You should be able
at least to give upper bounds to these expected costs. (Note that the expected cost L_2 of looking up
an item which is not present is equal to L_1. Why?) Using the routines of Exercise 11-15, collect
counts which will give empirical support to your expressions.

11-20 No procedure has been given for deleting items from a B-tree. If the occurrence of deletion
is relatively rare, then readily one would just delete the subkey and pointer (and possibly modifying
other subkeys) with the minor risk of having some nodes with fewer than $\lceil n/2 \rceil$ branches. But if the
tree is really active, this simple approach becomes uneconomic. A deletion routine in which nodes
may be coalesced, instead of split, must be implemented. Devise such a procedure.

11-21 Justify the statement: The B-tree of Fig. 11-9 is the Knuth transform of an n-ary tree.

11-22 Notice that we use different criteria to evaluate the efficiency of binary retrieval trees in
Chap. 9 than that used for B-trees in this section. The former we judged on the basis of core memory accesses (effectively the count of key comparisons), while these latter we evaluate in terms of in-
put/output time.

    (*a*) Why? Is the use of different criteria justified?

    (*b*) Suppose the B-tree were represented in core. What is the expected number of key com-
parisons required to access an element?

11-23 Rewrite LOCATE and ENTER to operate on the representation using different-sized index
blocks and data blocks.

11-24 We have been tacitly assuming that the function id, which maps keys into elements of the file,
is one to one.

    (*a*) Suppose instead that several records may be identified by the same key. Sketch how this
would affect the representation of the file. Rewrite LOCATE so that it will, on successive calls, return the location of each record with the specified key and terminate this sequence by returning the
null value.

    (*b*) Many implementations of indexed-sequential files permit retrieval on the basis of just the
first k characters in the symbolic key (k > 0). Use part (*a*) to show how LOCATE can be modified
to handle this.

    (*c*) Suppose that the naming function id is not one-to-one, and that the different symbolic
keys could identify the same record. Could you use B-trees to access such multiply named
records in a random organization? In an indexed sequential organization?

11-25 Justify or dispute the following statement: A file is said to be sequential if it is organized so
that access conforms to a linear relation defined on some other set of elements which are called the
"keys" to the file.

11-26 Consider a straight sequential file with blocked representation. One of its major disadvantages is the inability to insert new records into the middle of the file without recopying at least the
remaining records of the file. Suppose instead that one or more empty records were adjoined to
each block as "padding." Then so long as padding remained in the block a record could be added by
merely shifting records within the block and rewriting just that block.

    (*a*) Flesh out such a system and incorporate a method of splitting blocks to add records to
blocks with no remaining padding.

    (*b*) Since we would normally want these blocks to be nearly full, refine the splitting process so
that on overflow of a single block, attempts would first be made to shift some of its records into adjacent blocks. Only if two adjacent blocks were full would they be split into *three* blocks.

    (*c*) Show that the refinement of part (*b*) will guarantee that all blocks can be assured to be at
least two-thirds full. Can it be generalized so that n full blocks are split into n + 1 blocks? Would
such a process pay off?

    Note that these refinements can also be made to B-trees.

11-3 INVERTED FILES

The preceding methods of direct access have assumed that each record of the file, or element of a data structure, is uniquely identified by a symbolic key. In Chap. 9 we emphasized the uniqueness of this identification function by calling it a naming function. The problem has been simply to implement the naming function which maps symbolic keys (external names) to actual keys (storage locations) in the most efficient manner. Suppose now, however, that we wish to access elements of a file that are denoted by some set of identifiers which need not be names, for which the map id:S → V need not be one to one. For concreteness consider a file of student information in which each record contains a variety of data about an individual student. Each record might be named by either the student's name, or a student number, or both. But in many instances we may be looking for a student (or group of students) whose name is unknown, but who is identified in some other manner, say by a set of characteristics. We may wish to retrieve information about the student(s) who is "a sophomore," "20 years old," and "resides in Monroe dormitory."

These characteristics are normally called *secondary keys*. They are properties or attributes of the records of the file. In a sense we seek to implement in mass storage a kind of associative retrieval similar to that of Sec. 9-4. In a *primary file* attribute values, properties, or data is associated with each record. In a file of secondary keys the relationship is inverted; a set of records (storage addresses) is associated with each value. Hence they may be called *inverted files*.

Figure 11-13 illustrates a very straightforward approach to the implementation of an inverted file structure. Corresponding to a given secondary key, say the value 20, is a set of records with that property. This set has been represented as a simple linked list of pointers. The pointer variable "20" names the set of all elements with this property; "sophomore" names the set of sophomores, and "Monroe" identifies the set of individuals in that dormitory. To retrieve information about the "20-year-old sophomore student(s) of Monroe dormitory" we need only create the intersection of these three sets—say by calling the procedure MEET twice. The information associated with the intersection set is that desired. Of course, this set need not consist of a single individual. It may contain many elements or it may be empty. (In the case of the illustrated example the set is not empty; it contains at least that element with external name "Mahursky.") The reader should note the similarity between this figure and Fig. 8-17. Both represent linked structures that are used to gain entry into a sequential structure.

The primary file of Fig. 11-13 is large, as are all data structures considered in this chapter. For a reasonably sized university we might expect $10,000 \le r \le 30,000$, with several hundred characters of information per record (student). Since each student has some age, a corresponding element must appear in one of the lists . . . "20," "21," . . . Similarly each student belongs to

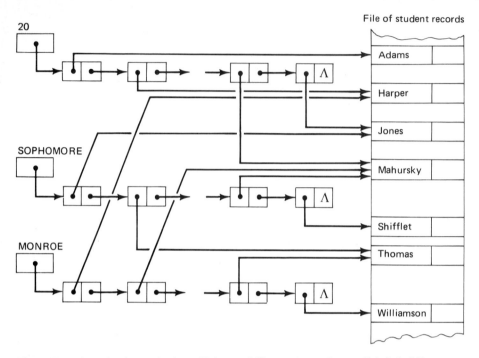

Figure 11-13 A retrieval organization with inverted files represented as explicit linked lists.

some class and lives in some residence† so there exist at least 3r cells in the structure of inverted lists. Even though each cell may be very much shorter (of sufficient length to represent only a NEXT link and an external pointer), it is unlikely that one could afford, or want, to keep this entire accessing structure in core memory. Normally the inverted lists are also stored as external files. A collection of several separate inverted files as shown in Fig. 11-14 seems to be more appropriate in general. For the reasons given in Sec. 11-1, these linearly ordered files should be sequentially represented with many individual records, or cells, per block. It becomes an interesting exercise to then implement the set-manipulation routines UNION, MEET, RCOMP, NXTELM, etc., using blocked sequential, rather than linked, representations. (See Exercise 11-28).

A retrieval structure in which each inverted list on a secondary retrieval key is a separate file is not normally sufficient by itself. It suffices only if the user knows precisely which files, and their names, are available for retrieval purposes. But consider a new user of the system, who is likely to ask: On what properties or characteristics can I base my retrieval search? What values exist

---

†While in this case each element of the primary file is on precisely one inverted list for each kind of attribute, this need not be the case in general. An attribute may be irrelevant and undefined for some elements of the file, or several values of the same attribute may be associated with a single element.

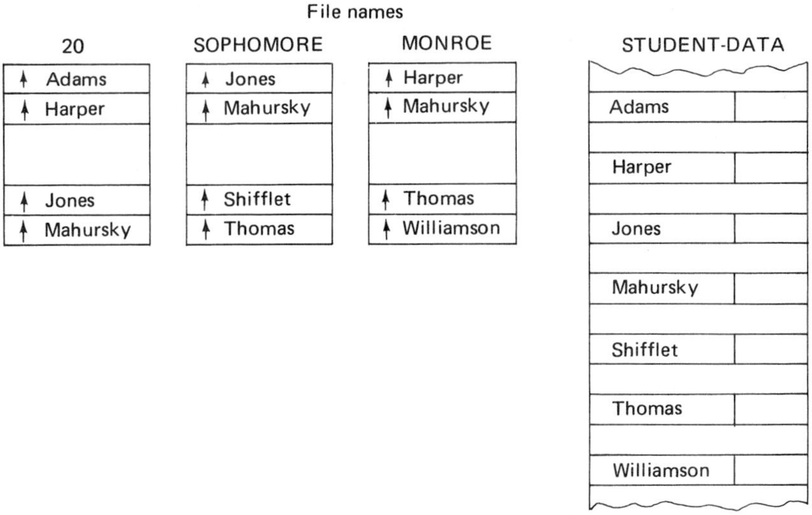

File names

| 20 | SOPHOMORE | MONROE | STUDENT-DATA |

Figure 11-14 A structure with each inverted file represented as a sequential file of records. [*Note:* ↑ Adams denotes a pointer to (or address of) Adam's record in the STUDENT file.]

in the range of any one of these characteristics? (For example, if "year in school" is one of the characteristics, are entering students identified as "freshmen," "first-year students," "plebes," or "first-semester students"?) In Figure 11-15 a linked tree structure has been added to describe the set of attribute types and the range of possible values of each type. Given an inverted retrieval structure of this nature, it is not hard for a user process, referencing only the pointer variable DESCRIPTORS, to discover under what attribute types records are classified, what values exist in the range of each attribute type, and (possibly interactively) respond to queries for elements of the primary file possessing various combinations of characteristics. Retrieval structure of this type, or variants of it, are frequently called *hierarchical systems*. The levels, or hierarchies, of the tree may be considerably deeper. Notice that in this case, the linked tree structure (which might permanently reside in core) serves as an entry mechanism to a second structure—the inverted files—which in turn serve as entry mechanisms to a primary data structure of real interest.

Inverted files, whether represented by linked lists or sequential files, are just ways of representing sets of objects. There are other ways of representing sets. And since the representation and manipulation of sets represented by linear structures are relatively expensive, one may want to consider alternatives. If there are not too many attribute values, then these sets (of elements with given characteristics) may be represented by tag bits, as in Sec. 6-2. Figure 11-16 shows a secondary key file organized in this fashion. In this rather brute-force approach there are as many records in the secondary file as in the primary file. But they are very much smaller records, so that an exhaustive sequential search of this file using bit-mask templates to look for complex combinations of

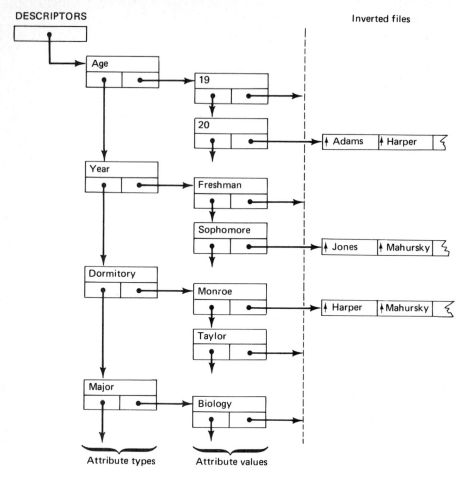

Figure 11-15 Inverted files of secondary keys based on hierarchically structure attributes.

	18	19	20	21	22	23	>23	Freshman	Sophomore	Junior	Senior	Other	Monroe	Taylor	
↟ Adams	0	0	1	0	0	0	0	0	0	1	0	0	0	1	...
↟ Harper	0	0	1	0	0	0	0	0	0	0	1	0	1	0	...
↟															

Figure 11-16 Representation of sets of secondary keys by tag bits.

retrieval conditions may be orders of magnitude faster than retrieval in the primary file itself. Variants of this general approach (Knuth, 1973) use the bit strings in the right of each cell as keys which hash-code directly to areas of primary storage, or replace them with multibit strings that can encode a longer number of secondary key values in ways that have fewer zeros in each string.

Instead of creating inverted file structures, direct secondary key retrieval can sometimes be implemented by structuring the primary file appropriately. To develop this approach let us change our terminology somewhat. A secondary key or attribute is often called a *retrieval index*. These retrieval indices may be numbered instead of named, so that, for example, "age" is called the first index, "year in school" might be called the second index, and "dormitory" may be considered the third index. Then a retrieval request for those "20-year-old sophomore students in Monroe dorm" might be coded as a triple (20, 2, Monroe). An alert reader may feel that this triple looks suspiciously like the subscript list (which are also called indices) of a three-dimensional array element, which is true. Referencing elements in an array can be regarded as a special case of retrieval by integer-valued secondary keys. Conversely, general secondary key retrieval can be regarded as the location of elements, or sets of elements, in an n-dimensional attribute space. Figure 7-11 was drawn to suggest just this sort of generalized extension. Consequently, in certain well-constrained applications, techniques of array representation—especially the partially linked methods of Sec. 7-2—can be effectively used in the context of file retrieval.

What is an attribute? Is it a type of characteristic or the value of some characteristic? We have used it both ways in this section. What is an index? Is it an attribute, a position in a subscript string, or a value in a subscript string? Are array referencing and file access by secondary keys really equivalent concepts? None of these terms have been carefully defined, and given the multiplicity of customary meanings it is easy to introduce needless complexity and confusion. It will pay us to step back and make use of the perspective obtained from an abstract approach to the problem couched in terms of formal definitions.

A file or data structure is simply a collection P of elements. (The convention of calling these elements *points* is particularly appropriate since by themselves they have no meaning, or no "body.") Information is associated with an element $x \in P$ by means of one or more assignment functions $f_i : P \to V_i$, which map elements of P into elements of the sets V_i. Then an *attribute* is just the name or identifier f_i of the assignment function, and an *attribute value* is that element $f_i(x) \in V_i$. The elements of the set P are said to be *named* by the elements of a set S if there exists an onto function id $: S \to P$. This yields a very simple abstract model which can be illustrated as in Fig. 11-17.

From this abstract view, it can be seen that an inverted file is just one way of implementing the inverse of the assignment function f_i, which is, in general, a relation f_i^{-1} from V_i to P; whereas access by primary (symbolic) keys is just the implementation of the function id $: S \to P$, which is again only a special kind of

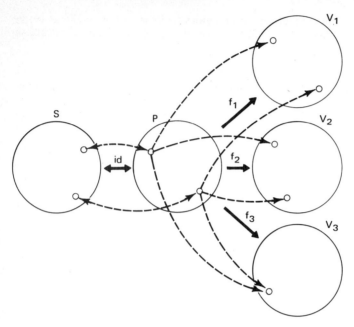

Figure 11-17 An abstract model of a data structure, or file P, which is named by element of S and which has assignment values in the sets V_1, V_2, and V_3.

relation. Since computer representation of relations has been the central theme of this text (although we have largely emphasized relations on a single set), we have in effect come full circle. One could once again return to Chap. 1 and begin to ask many of the same questions, but in a context where the points of the abstract structures S_M are themselves entire data structures. We would seek effective ways of representing relations between distinct data structures, ways of accessing information by following paths whose edges (or links) come from such relations, and notational ways of formally describing the kinds of processes that are being implemented.

EXERCISES FOR SECTION 11-3

11-27 The elements of the inverted lists of Fig. 11-13 are linearly ordered by ascending storage locations. Why is this advantageous?

11-28 Let $file_1$ and $file_2$ be two sequential inverted files which denote those elements of a primary file which exhibit properties p_1 and p_2, respectively. Write a procedure which creates the intersection of these two files—that is, a file which denotes those elements which have both property p_1 and property p_2. (Assume that both files are ordered on ascending storage locations, and that both are blocked with b records per block.) What is the cost of creating the intersection?

11-29 Consider the student data file which has served as the running example of this section. Suppose that each record is uniquely identified (named) by two different sets of symbolic keys—say by given name and by student number. Is it possible to implement direct access using *either* of the two keys.

(*a*) by means of two separate B-trees (such as shown in Fig. 11-9);

(*b*) by means of two separate hashing functions, or

(*c*) in such a manner that indexed-sequential retrieval is possible (e.g., with a B-tree such as shown in Fig. 11-12)?

In each case, either sketch how such retrieval would be implemented or demonstrate the impossibility of such retrieval.

(*d*) Is an indexed-sequential organization compatible with retrieval based on a set of secondary keys? Why?

*11-30 Consider a primary file, say a student data file, which is sequentially represented together with its associated inverted files. Let access to the inverted files be through a hierarchical linked structure as shown in Fig. 11-15. Presumably such a file will be dynamic. Write procedures to

(*a*) insert new elements into the primary file,

(*b*) add new attribute values as needed, and

(*c*) add new attribute types (corresponding to existing fields in the records of the primary file on which retrieval had not previously been implemented).

What is the expected cost of these update operations? (*Note:* You may want to use methods developed in Exercise 11-26.)

11-31 A fairly common, and important, application is *document retrieval*. Each record in the file represents a single document, article, or book, and contains such information as author, title, journal (if an article), publisher, date, call number (or location in library), etc., and possibly a brief abstract about its contents. We might reasonably expect retrieval, given (1) title, (2) author, or (3) a set of characteristics. These latter attributes are commonly a predetermined set of "descriptors," called *terms,* such as "data structures," "list processing," "programming language," etc., which approximately describe the contents of the document. (Descriptive terms may be assigned by the author or by some independent reviewer, and may be expressed in terms of coded categories, as in the ACM or AMS classifications schemes.)

(*a*) Give a fairly detailed sketch of an efficient document retrieval system. This system design problem is a rather lengthy one, and probably impossible if one attempts to handle all documents about all subjects. Instead, confine yourself to one which retrieves only documents about computer science or possibly some restricted area of computer science. In the course of the design you should answer the following questions:

(*b*) Which retrieval keys can be handled as unique identifiers (names) and which should be regarded as secondary keys?

(*c*) What will constitute an adequate set of descriptive terms? How will they be chosen? Will the set be expandable as new subjects are introduced into the area?

(*d*) How large will the file be? (If you have a computer science library, try estimating the current number of separate documents that would be individually represented.)

(*e*) How fast will the file grow? What is the expected rate of entering new elements?

(*f*) What is the format of an individual record? How many characters? Deciding the field structure layout(s) will introduce subsidary questions such as: Multiple authors? Titles of articles within books with titles? Continued articles? Revisions of books? Reviews of the document (e.g., computer reviews or math reviews)? Fixed-length or variable-length records? Number of descriptive terms? And so on.

(*g*) What is expected retrieval activity? Expected cost per retrieval? Cost of incremental entries?

Careful design of such a system is much harder than its actual implementation once the design is complete. Assuming that you have done a good job, you may want to implement a small system, say for a private collection, and measure its performance. (The next hardest chore will be actual data collection and entry, but this gets beyond the purview of this text.)

BIBLIOGRAPHY

Aho, A., and S. Johnson, LR Parsing, *Comp. Surveys,* **6**(2): 99–124 (1974).

Bellman, R., and S. Dreyfus, "Applied Dynamic Programming," Princeton Univ. Press, Princeton, N. J. (1972).

Berge, C., "Theory of Graphs and its Applications," Methuen Press (1962).

Berztiss, A., "Data Structures, Theory and Practice," 2d ed., Academic Press, New York (1975).

Bobrow, D. (ed.), "Symbol Manipulation Languages and Techniques," North-Holland Publ. (1968).

Cheney, C., A Nonrecursive List Compacting Algorithm, *C. ACM,* **13**(11): 677–678 (1970).

Corneil, D., and C. Gotlieb, An Efficient Algorithm for Graph Isomorphism, *J. ACM,* **17**(1): 51–64 (1970).

Cranston, B., and R. Thomas, A Simplified Recombination Scheme for the Fibonacci Buddy System, *C. ACM,* **18**(6): 330–332 (1975).

Crespi-Reghizzi, S., and R. Morpurgo, A Language for Treating Graphs, *C. ACM,* **13**(5): 319–323 (1970).

Davis, J., and M. McCullagh, "Display and Analysis of Spatial Data," Wiley, New York (1975).

Denning, P., Virtual Memory, *Comp. Surveys,* **2**(3): 153–189 (1970).

Dijkstra, E., "Notes on Structered Programming," Structered Programming (Dahl, Dijkstra, & Hoare), Academic Press, New York (1972).

Dodd, G., Elements of Data Management Systems, *Comp. Surveys,* **1**(2): 115–135 (1969).

Donovan, J., "Systems Programming," McGraw-Hill, New York (1972).

Earley, J., Towards an Understanding of Data Structures, *C. ACM,* **14**(10): 617–627 (1971).

Feldman, J., and D. Gries, Translator Writing Systems, *C. ACM,* **11**(2): 77–113 (1968).

Feldman, J., and P. Rovner, An Algol-based Associative Language, *C. ACM,* **12**(8): 439–449 (1969).

Fenichel, R., and J. Yochelson, A LISP Garbage-collector for Virtual Memory Computer Systems, *C. ACM,* **12**(11): 611–612 (1969).

Findler, N., et al., "Four High-Level Extensions of Fortran IV," Spartan Press (1972).

Fisher, D., "Copying Cyclic List Structures in Linear Time using Bounded Workspace," *C. ACM,* **18**(5): 251–252 (1975).

Floyd, R., Algorithm 97, Shortest Path, *C. ACM,* **5**(6): 345 (1962).

Foster, C., A Generalization of AVL Trees, *C. ACM,* **16**(8): (1973).

Freeman, P., "Software Systems Principles—A Survey," Science Research Assoc., Palo Alto (1975).

Gries, D., "Compiler Construction for Digital Computers," Wiley, New York (1971).

Griswold, R., et al., "The Snobol 4 Programming Language," Prentice-Hall, Englewood Cliffs, N.J. (1968).

Hansen, W., Compact List Representation: Definition, Garbage Collection, and System Implementation, *C. ACM,* **12**(9): 449–507 (1969).

Haralick, R., The Diclique Representation and Decomposition of Binary Relations, *J. ACM,* **21**(3): 356–366 (1974).

Harary, F., "Graph Theory," Addison-Wesley, Boston (1969).

Hecht, M., and J. Ullman, Characterizations of Reducible Flow Graphs, *J. ACM,* **21**(3): 367–375 (1974).

Hinds, J., An Algorithm for Locating Adjacent Storage Blocks in the Buddy System, *C. ACM,* **18**(4): 221–222 (1975).

Hoare, C., Notes on Data Structuring, "Structured Programming" (Dahl, Dijkstra, & Hoare) Academic Press, New York (1972).

Hopcroft, J., and J. Ullman, "Formal Languages and their Relations to Automata," Addison-Wesley, Boston (1969).

Knowlton, K., A Programmer's Description of L^6, *C. ACM,* **9**(8): 616–625 (1966).

Knuth, D., et al., A Proposal for Input-Output conventions in Algol-60, *C. ACM,* **7**(5): 273–283 (1964).

Knuth, D., *The Art of Computer Programming,* vol. 1, "Fundamental Algorithms," Addison-Wesley, Boston (1968).

Knuth, D., *The Art of Computer Programming,* vol. 3, "Searching and Sorting," Addison-Wesley, Boston (1973).

Lee, J., "The Anatomy of a Compiler," Van Nostrand Reinhold, New York (1967).

Liu, C., "Introduction to Combinatorial Mathematics," McGraw-Hill, New York (1968).

MacDougall, M., Computer System Simulation; An Introduction, *Comp. Surveys,* **2**(3): 191–210 (1970).

Martin, W. Sorting, *Comp. Surveys,* **3**(4): 147–174 (1971).

Maurer, W., and T. Lewis, Hash Table Methods, *Comp. Surveys,* **7**(1): 5–20 (1975).

Mealy, G., Another Look at Data, *Proc. FJCC,* 525–534 1967.

Mesztenyi, C., FGRAAL—Technical Documentation, *Univ. of Md. CSC Tech. Rpt. TR-200* (Oct. 1972).

Minicka, E., On Computing Sets of Shortest Paths in a Graph, *C. ACM,* **17**(6): 351–353 (1974).

Moyles, D., and G. Thompson, An Algorithm for Finding a Minimal Equivalent Graph of a Digraph, *J. ACM,* **16**(3): 455–460 (1969).

Naur, P. (ed.), Revised Report on the Algorithmic Language Algol 60, *C. ACM,* **6**(1): 1–17 (1963).

Newman, W., and R. Sproull, "Principals of Interactive Graphics," McGraw-Hill, New York (1973).

Nievergelt, J., Binary Search Trees and File Organization, *Comp. Surveys,* **6**(3): 195–207 (1974).

Nilsson, N., "Problem-Solving Methods in Artificial Intelligence," McGraw-Hill, New York (1971).

Ore, O., *Theory of Graphs,* Amer. Math. Soc., **38**(1962).

Pfaltz, J., Graph Structures, *J. ACM,* **19**(3): 411–422 (1972).

Pfaltz, J., Representing Graphs by Knuth Trees, *J. ACM,* **22**(3): 361–366 (1975).

Pooch, U., and A. Nieder, A Survey of Indexing Techniques for Sparse Matrices, *Comp. Surveys,* **5**(2): 109–133 (1973).

Price, C., Table Lookup Techniques, *Comp. Surveys,* **3**(2): 49–66 (1971).

Rheinboldt, W., et al., On a Programming Language for Graph Algorithms, *Univ. of Md. CSC Tech. Rpt. TR-158* (June 1971).

Riordan, J., "An Introduction to Combinatorial Analysis," Wiley, New York (1958).

Robinson, J., A Machine-oriented Logic Based on the Resolution Principle, *J. ACM,* **12**(1): 23–41 (1965).

Rosenfeld, A., "Picture Processing by Computer," Academic Press, New York (1969).

Shneiderman, B., and P. Scheurermann, Structured Data Structures, *C. ACM,* **17**(10): 566–574 (1974).

Shore, J., On the External Storage Fragmentation Produced by First-Fit and Best-Fit Allocation Strategies, *C. ACM,* **18**(8): 433–440 (1975).

Stone, H., "Introduction to Computer Organization and Data Structures," McGraw-Hill, New York (1972).

Sutherland, I., A Characterization of Ten Hidden Surface Algorithms, *Comp. Surveys,* **6**(1): 1–56 (1974).

Tiernan, J., An Efficient Search Algorithm to Find the Elementary Circuits of a Graph, *C. ACM,* **13**(2): 722–726 (1970).

Tutte, W., "The Connectivity of Graphs," Toronto Univ. Press, Toronto (1967).

Unger, S., GIT—A Heuristic Program for Testing Pairs of Directed Line Graphs for Isomorphism, *C. ACM,* **7**(1): 26–34 (1964).

Warshall, S., A Theorem on Boolean Matrices, *J. ACM,* **9**(1): 11–12 (1962).

Weinblatt, H., A New Search Algorithm for Finding the Simple Cycles of a Finite Directed Graph, *J. ACM,* **19**(1): 43–56 (1972).

Weissman, C., "LISP 1.5 Primer," Dickenson Publ. (1967).

Weizenbaum, J., Symmetric List Processor, *C. ACM,* **6**(10): 524–536 (1963).

Weizenbaum, J., ELIZA—A Computer Program for the Study of Natural Language Communication Between Man and Machine, *C. ACM,* **9**(1): 36–95 (1966).

Williams, R., A Survey of Data Structures for Computer Graphics Systems, *Comp. Surveys,* **3**(1): 1–21 (1971).

Zadeh, L., et al., "Fuzzy Sets and their Applications to Cognitive and Decision Processes," Academic Press, New York (1975).

INDEX

INDEX